LITERARY THEMES
for Students

LITERARY THEMES
for Students

Examining Diverse Literature to Understand and Compare Universal Themes

RACE AND PREJUDICE
VOLUME 1

Anne Marie Hacht, Editor

Foreword by Margaret Brantley

GALE
CENGAGE Learning

Detroit • New York • San Francisco • New Haven, Conn • Waterville, Maine • London

Literary Themes for Students: Race and Prejudice

Project Editor
Anne Marie Hacht

Editorial
Sara Constantakis, Ira Mark Milne

Rights Acquisition and Management
Lisa Kincade, Ronald Montgomery, and Jessica Sitt

Manufacturing
Rita Wimberley

Imaging
Leitha Eheridge-Sims, Lezlie Light, and Mike Logusz

Product Design
Pamela A. E. Galbreath

Vendor Administration
Civie Green

Product Manager
Meggin Condino

LIBRARY OF CONGRESS CATALOGING-IN-PUBLICATION DATA

Literary themes for students – race and prejudice : examining diverse literature to understand and compare universal themes / Anne Marie Hacht, project editor.
    p. cm. – (Literary themes for students)
  Includes bibliographical references and index.
  ISBN-13: 978-1-4144-0275-9 (set)
  ISBN-10: 1-4144-0275-9 (set)
  ISBN-13: 978-1-4144-0274-1 (vol. 1)
  ISBN-10: 1-4144-0274-0 (vol. 1)
  [etc.]
  1. Race in literature. 2. Prejudices in literature. I. Hacht, Anne Marie. II. Series.
PN56.R16L58 2006
809'.933355 – dc22   2006017454

ISBN-13:
978-1-4144-0275-9 (set)
978-1-4144-0274-1 (vol. 1)
978-1-4144-0284-0 (vol. 2)

ISBN-10:
1-4144-0275-9 (set)
1-4144-0274-0 (vol. 1)
1-4144-0284-8 (vol. 2)

This title is also available as an e-book.
ISBN-13: 978-1-4144-1887-2 (set)
ISBN-10: 1-4144-1887-6 (set)
Contact your Gale sales representative for ordering information.

Printed in the United States of America
3 4 5 6 7 8 14 13 12 11 10 09 08

Table of Contents

Foreword

SPEAKING UP: THE LITERATURE OF RACE AND PREJUDICE

Each volume of *Literary Themes for Students* brings together dozens of renowned works of literature that share a specific theme. The theme for this set of *Literary Themes for Students* is race and prejudice.

Examples of fear, ignorance, and misunderstanding dominate written human history until just a few hundred years ago. Written declarations of human rights date to the sixth century B.C. and Persia's Cyrus Cylinder. More than two millennia later, literature that gives voice to the voiceless began to flourish. With the Industrial Revolution came a boom in publishing, which was accompanied by a rise in literacy. The eighteenth century was also the Age of Enlightenment, which spawned the American and French Revolutions. At that time, people with inferior positions in society—namely women and slaves—began to tell their stories and make the case for equal rights.

The literature of race and prejudice serves a twofold purpose: to advance freedom and to protect it. Concentration camp survivor Martin Niemöller, vividly captures the power of testimony with this statement, which is engraved on the New England Holocaust Memorial:

They came first for the Communists,

and I didn't speak up because I wasn't a Communist.

Then they came for the Jews,
and I didn't speak up because I wasn't a Jew.
Then they came for the trade unionists,
and I didn't speak up because I wasn't a trade unionist.
Then they came for the Catholics,
and I didn't speak up because I was a Protestant.
Then they came for me,
and by that time no one was left to speak up.

*(New England Holocaust Memorial,
www.nehm.com/contents/niemoller.html
(April 30, 2006).)*

Some of the selections in *Literary Themes for Students: Race and Prejudice* represent the capacity of literature to change history. Abraham Lincoln famously called Harriet Beecher Stowe "the little lady who started the big war" after her novel *Uncle Tom's Cabin* brought the horrors of slavery to life in the American imagination and rallied support to the cause of abolition. A century later, Martin Luther King Jr.'s celebrated speech "I Have a Dream" became the icon of the Civil Rights movement in the United States. Both masterpieces are as potent today as when they were written.

Literature can also change the way history is understood. For instance, Dee Brown's *Bury My Heart at Wounded Knee* explodes the myth of civilization's victory over savagery in the settlement of the American West, describing episode after episode of ethnic cleansing. Anne Frank's *Diary of a Young Girl* (1947) gave a shocking look inside the Holocaust and helped a still-reeling world comprehend the terror of the war and the basic humanity of its victims. Both these books, along with many others that inform the modern view of the past, are included in this exploration of race and prejudice.

Literary Themes for Students: Race and Prejudice represents many perspectives on the struggle for equal rights. Mary Wollstonecraft acts as a passionate, reasoned advocate in her essay "A Vindication of the Rights of Woman" (1792). Mark Twain's protagonist in *Adventures of Huckleberry Finn* (1884) observes, records, and reacts to the injustice of slavery, even as he accepts it as a given. The nameless protagonist of Ralph Ellison's "King of the Bingo Game" (1944) is a victim of societal racism, while the narrator of Ernest Gaines's *Autobiography of Miss Jane Pittman* (1971) is a survivor. Selections that are studied include memoirs, polemics, novels, dramas, poetry, and histories—all bearing important contributions to the theme.

The works included in *Literary Themes for Students* represent a wide range of circumstances in which individuals experience prejudice. The discussion goes well beyond race, religion, and gender into ethnicity, social status, mental and physical health, and personal beliefs and behaviors. Among the titles presented are *Nisei Daughter*, which recalls the internment of Japanese Americans and *Angels in America*, which dramatizes the early years of the AIDS epidemic. Several essays examine dominant and recurring subthemes in the literature of prejudice. Each entry further explores the component themes particular to that specific work, such as education, sexuality, and violence.

Literary Themes for Students cannot take the place of experiencing firsthand the books it presents. This overview of the topics, historical contexts, and critical interpretations presented in these entries can guide readers who want to discover more. It gives learners a platform from which to launch their own exploration of race, prejudice, history, and literature. It celebrates how far human rights have come in a relatively short time and underscores how much further there is yet to go. It pays tribute to those who have spoken up, because they speak for all humanity.

Margaret Brantley
Brantley is a literature critic and a literary reference editor.

Introduction

PURPOSE OF THE BOOK

The purpose of *Literary Themes for Students* is to provide readers with an overview of literary works that explore a specific theme. The volumes analyze poetry, plays, short stories, novels, and works of nonfiction that address the theme in some capacity, and the reader discovers how that theme has been treated in literature at different times in history and across diverse cultures. *Literary Themes for Students: Race and Prejudice* (LTSRP) includes "classic" human rights literature often used in the classroom curriculum, as well as more contemporary accounts of race and prejudice and works by minority, international, and female writers.

These volumes begin with three overview essays that introduce the theme of race and prejudice in literature, dividing it by geography and culture into American literature, British literature, and world literature. There are also nine sub-essays, which break these themes down further into subthemes that correspond to recurring ideas in the literature of race and prejudice. Sub-essays examine particular titles that exemplify the subthemes and show how that subtheme has developed over time.

Each work is discussed in a separate entry. These entries include: an introduction to the work and the work's author; a plot summary, to help readers understand the action and story

of the work; an analysis of themes that relate to the subjects of race and prejudice, to provide readers with a multifaceted look at the complexity of human rights literature; and a section on important historical and cultural events that shaped the author and the work, as well as events in the real world (from the time of the author or another time in history) that affect the plot or characters in the work.

Additionally, readers are presented with a critical overview discussing how the work was initially received by critics and how the work is presently viewed. Accompanying the critical overview is an excerpt from a previously published critical essay discussing the work's relation to the theme of race and prejudice. For further analysis and enjoyment, an extended list of media adaptations is also included, as well as a list of poems, short stories, novels, plays, and works of nonfiction that further address the theme of race and prejudice, and thus students are encouraged to continue their study of this theme.

SELECTION CRITERIA

The titles of each volume of *LTSRP* were selected by surveying numerous sources on teaching literature and analyzing course curricula for a number of school districts. Our advisory board provided input, as did educators in various areas.

HOW EACH ENTRY IS ORGANIZED

Each chapter focuses on the ways in which an entry relates to the theme of race and prejudice. Each entry heading includes the author's name, the title of the work being discussed, and the year it was published. The following sections are included in the discussion of each entry:

Introduction: a brief overview of the work being discussed. It provides information about the work's first appearance, any controversies surrounding its publication, its literary reputation, and general details about the work's connection to the theme of race and prejudice.

Plot Summary: a description of the events that occur in the work. For poems, some additional insight into the context and interpretation of the poem—and discussion of symbols and elements—is provided. The plot summary is broken down by subheadings, usually organized by chapter, section, or stanza.

Themes: a discussion of how the work approaches the issues of race and prejudice through various themes. Each theme is addressed under a separate subheading. Several of the major recurring themes are discussed at more length in individual sub-essays.

Historical and Cultural Context: a discussion of the historical and cultural events that appear in the work or that affected the writer while the work was being written. This can include large-scale events such as wars, social movements, and political decisions, as well as smaller-scale events such as cultural trends and literary movements. If the work is set during a different time period from that in which the author wrote it, historical and cultural events from both periods are included.

Critical Overview: a discussion of the work's general critical reputation, including how it was initially received by reviewers, critics, and the general public. Any controversy surrounding the work is treated in this section. For older works, this section also includes information on the ways that views of the work have changed over time.

Criticism: a previously published critical essay discussing how the work addresses the issues of race and/or prejudice. When no appropriate criticism could be found, commissioned essays were written to deal specifically with the work.

Sources: an alphabetical list of sources used in compiling the entry, including bibliographic information.

In addition, each entry includes the following sidebars, set apart from the rest of the text:

Author Biography Sidebar: a brief biography of the author, including how he or she was affected by or led to write about race and prejudice.

Media Adaptations: a list of film, television, and/or stage adaptations, audio versions, and other forms of media related to the work. Source information is included.

OTHER FEATURES

LTSRP includes "Speaking Up: The Literature of Race and Prejudice," by Mo Brantley, a writer and editor of language arts reference books. This is a foreword about how the literature of race and prejudice can help contemporary readers appreciate how far human rights have come in a relatively short time and how far there is yet to go.

Each entry may have several illustrations, including photos of the author, depictions of key elements of the plot, stills from film adaptations, and/or historical photos of the people, places, or events discussed in the entry.

Nine sub-essays discuss various subthemes of race and prejudice literature: ethnicity; gender; religion; sexual orientation; social class and caste; disability, illness, and social stigma; ethnic cleansing, genocide, and exile; slavery; and segregation. Each sub-essay addresses approximately ten works that deal directly with the subtheme, and discusses how treatment of that theme has changed over time.

A Media Adaptation list compiles nearly seventy films, plays, television series, and other media that deal with the subjects of race and prejudice. The adaptations are organized by subtheme for easy access.

The *What Do I Read Next?* section provides over ninety plays, short stories, poems, novels, and nonfiction works on the subject of race and prejudice. These works are also organized by subtheme.

An overview essay about prejudice in British literature analyzes how the depiction of prejudice and the quest for equality have changed since Shakespeare's time. Poems, plays, short stories, novels, and nonfiction works that exemplify Britain's attitude toward race and prejudice are examined and provide students with an overview of British literature about human differences since the country's days as a colonial superpower.

An overview essay on the themes of race and prejudice in American literature analyzes how the history of the nation is tied to its "melting pot" identity and the ways in which its literature reflects America's attitude toward race and its relationship with peace. Discussion of key poems, plays, short stories, novels, and nonfiction works reflect the evolving place of race and prejudice in the literature and culture of the United States.

An overview essay on the themes of race and prejudice in world literature analyzes how such issues have been viewed in differing cultures and time periods around the world. Discovery, interaction, fear, and the quest for understanding have left their imprint on world literature throughout history, and this essay provides students with a brief survey of how that literature reflects the values and attitudes of the cultures that produced it.

CITING

When writing papers, students who quote directly from any volume of *Literary Themes for Students: Race and Prejudice* may use the following general formats. These examples are based on MLA style. Teachers may request that students adhere to a different style, so the following examples should be adapted as needed.

When citing text from *LTSRP* that is not attributed to a particular author (i.e., from the Themes or Historical Context sections), the following format should be used in the bibliography section:

"The Awakening." Literary Themes for Students: Race and Prejudice. Ed. TK. Vol. TK. Detroit: Thomson Gale, 2006. TK–TK.

When quoting a journal or newspaper essay that is reprinted in a volume of *LTfS*, the following format may be used:

Khan, Shahnaz, "Reconfiguring the Native Informant: Positionality in the Global Age," in *Signs: Journal of Women and Culture and Society*, Vol. 30, No. 4, 2005, pp. 2022–2023; excerpted and reprinted in *Literary Themes for Students: Race and Prejudice*, Vol. TK, ed. TK (Detroit: Thomson Gale, 2006), pp. TK–TK.

When quoting material reprinted from a book that appears in a volume of *LTSRP*, the following form may be used:

Sinsheimer, Hermann, *Shylock: The History of a Character*, Benjamin Blom, 1963, p. 17; excerpted and reprinted in *Literary Themes for Students: Race and Prejudice*, Vol. TK, ed. TK (Detroit: Thomson Gale, 2006), pp. TK–TK.

WE WELCOME YOUR SUGGESTIONS

The editorial staff of *LTSRP* welcomes your comments, ideas, and suggestions. Readers who wish to suggest themes and works for future volumes, or who have any other suggestions, are cordially invited to contact the editor. You may do so via email at ForStudentsEditors@gale.cengage.com or via mail at:

Editor, *Literary Themes for Students*
Gale
27500 Drake Road
Farmington Hills, MI 48331-3535

Acknowledgments

The editors wish to thank the copyright holders of the excerpted criticism included in this volume and the permissions managers of many book and magazine publishing companies for assisting us in securing reproduction rights. We are also grateful to the staffs of the Detroit Public Library, the Library of Congress, the University of Detroit Mercy Library, Wayne State University Purdy/Kresge Library Complex, and the University of Michigan Libraries for making their resources available to us. Following is a list of the copyright holders who have granted us permission to reproduce material in this volume of *Literary Themes for Students: Race and Prejudice (LTSRP)*. Every effort has been made to trace copyright, but if omissions have been made, please let us know.

COPYRIGHTED MATERIALS IN *LITNM*, VOLUME 2, WERE REPRO DUCED FROM THE FOLLOWING PERIODICALS:

African American Review, v. 29, spring, 1995 for "Race and Domesticity in 'The Color Purple'" by Linda Selzer. Reproduced by permission of the author./ v. 35, spring, 2001 for "Invented by Horror: The Gothic and African American Literary Ideology in 'Native Son'" by James Smethurst. © 2001 James Smethurst. Both reproduced by permission of the respective authors.—*The American Enterprise,* v. 14, September 3, 2003. Copyright 2003 American Enterprise Institute for Public Policy Research. Reproduced with permission of *The American Enterprise,* a national magazine of Politics, Business, and Culture (TAEmag.com).—*The American Indian Quarterly,* v. 21, summer, 1998. Copyright © 1998 by the University of Nebraska Press. All rights reserved. Reproduced by permission of the University of Nebraska Press.—*Black American Literature Forum,* v. 24, summer, 1990 for "Singing the Black Mother: Maya Angelou and Autobiographical Continuity" by Mary Jane Lupton. Reproduced by permission of the author.—*College Literature,* v. 19, October-February, 1992. Copyright © 1992 by West Chester University. Reproduced by permission.—*Criticism,* v. 28, summer, 1976. Copyright © 1976 Wayne State University Press. Reproduced with permission of the Wayne State University Press.—*Critique: Studies in Contemporary Fiction,* v. 33, winter, 1992. Copyright © 1992 by Helen Dwight Reid Educational Foundation. Reproduced with permission of the Helen Dwight Reid Educational Foundation, published by Heldref Publications, 1319 18th Street, NW, Washington, DC 20036-1802.—*ELH,* v. 70, summer, 2003. Copyright © 2003 The Johns Hopkins University Press. Reproduced by permission.—*Explicator,* v. 58, summer, 2000; v. 60, summer, 2002. Copyright © 2000, 2002 by Helen Dwight Reid Educational Foundation. Both reproduced with permission of the Helen Dwight Reid Educational Foundation, published by Heldref Publications, 1319 18th

Street, NW, Washington, DC 20036-1802.—*Frontiers: A Journal of Women's Studies,* v. 26, June 5, 2005. Copyright © 2005 by the Frontiers Editorial Collective. All rights reserved. Reproduced by permission of the University of Nebraska Press.—*Journal of American & Comparative Cultures,* v. 24, spring, 2001. Copyright © 2001 Basil Blackwell Ltd. www.blackwell-synergy.com. Reproduced by permission of Blackwell Publishers.—*Journal of American Culture,* v. 22, winter, 1999. Copyright © 1999 Basil Blackwell Ltd. www.blackwell-synergy.com. Reproduced by permission of Blackwell Publishers.—*Journal of the West,* v. 39, January, 2000. Copyright © 2000 by Journal of the West, Inc. Reproduced by permission.—*Judaism: A Quarterly Journal of Jewish Life and Thought,* v. 48, winter, 1999. Copyright 1999 American Jewish Congress. Reproduced by permission.—*Melus,* v. 19, winter, 1994; v. 22, summer, 1997. Copyright *MELUS: The Society for the Study of Multi-Ethnic Literature of the United States,* 1994, 1997. Both reproduced by permission.—*The Midwest Quarterly,* v. 43, spring, 2002. Copyright © 2002 by *The Midwest Quarterly,* Pittsburgh State University. Reproduced by permission.—*Modern Drama,* spring, 1999. Copyright © 1999 by the University of Toronto, Graduate Centre for Study of Drama. Reproduced by permission.—*New Statesman & Society,* v. 6, February 12, 1993. Copyright © 1993 New Statesman, Ltd. Reproduced by permission.—*Partisan Review,* v. 70, winter, 2003 for "Anne Frank: The Redemptive Myth" by Judith Goldstein. Reproduced by permission of the author.—*Perspectives on Political Science,* v. 31, fall, 2002. Copyright © 2002 by Helen Dwight Reid Educational Foundation. Reproduced with permission of the Helen Dwight Reid Educational Foundation, published by Heldref Publications, 1319 18th Street, NW, Washington, DC 20036-1802.—*South Atlantic Review,* January, 1993. Copyright © 1993 by the South Atlantic Modern Language Association. Reproduced by permission.—*Southern Cultures,* v. 6, summer, 2000. Reproduced by permission.—*Studies in American Fiction,* v. 24, spring, 1996. Copyright © 1996 Northeastern University. Reproduced by permission.—*Texas Studies in Literature and Language,* v. 36, 1994 for "Freedom, Uncertainty, and Diversity: 'A Passage to India' as a Critique of Imperialist Law" by Kieran Dolin. Copyright © 1994 by the University of Texas Press.

Reproduced by permission of the publisher and the author.—*U.S. News and World Report* v. 115, August 30, 1993. Copyright 1993 U.S. News and World Report, L.P. Reprinted with permission.—*USA Today,* December 12, 2001 for "Like the Taliban, Some U.S. Parents Fear Free Minds" by Mark Mathabane. © 2001 by Mark Mathabane. Reproduced by permission of the author.—*Western Folklore,* v. 51, 1992. © 1992 by the California Folklore Society. Reproduced by permission.—*The World and I Online,* v. 13, June, 1998. Copyright 1998 News World Communications, Inc. Reproduced by permission.

COPYRIGHTED MATERIALS IN LITERARY THEMES FOR STUDENTS: RACE AND PREJUDICE, WERE REPRODUCED FROM THE FOLLOWING BOOKS:

Achebe, Chinua. From *Hopes and Impediments: Selected Essays.* Copyright © 1988 by Chinua Achebe. Used by permission of Doubleday, a division of Random House, Inc., and in Canada and the UK by Emma Sweeney Agency on behalf of the author.—Bosmajian, Hamida. From *Children's Literature.* Yale University Press, 1996. Copyright © 1996 by Hollins College. All rights reserved. Reproduced by permission.—Cassedy, Patrice. From *Understanding 'Flowers for Algernon.'* Lucent Books, 2001. Copyright 2001 by Lucent Books, Inc. Reproduced by permission of Thomson Gale.—Kruger, Steven F.. From "Identity and Conversion in 'Angels in America'," in *Approaching the Millennium: Essays on 'Angels in America'.* Edited by Deborah R. Geis and Steven F. Kruger. The University of Michigan Press, 1997. Copyright © 1997 by the University of Michigan. All rights reserved. Reproduced by permission.—Powers, Jessica, "'Kaffir Boy': An Analysis," *www.Suite101.com,* October 17, 2001. Reproduced by permission of the author.—Tompkins, Jane. From *Sensational Designs: The Cultural Work of American Fiction 1790-1860.* Oxford University Press, 1985. Copyright © 1985 by Oxford University Press, Inc. Used by permission of Oxford University Press, Inc.—Yamamoto, Traise. From *Masking Selves, Making Subjects: Japanese American Women, Identity, and the Body.* University of California Press, 1999. Copyright © 1999 by The Regents of the University of California. Reproduced by permission of the publisher and the author.

National Advisory Board

Contributors

Sylvia M. DeSantis: DeSantis holds a master's degree in English and is an instructional designer and instructor for the Pennsylvania State University libraries. "Disabilities, Illness, and Social Stigma" essay.

Carrie Evans: Evans is a writer and editor with a bachelor's degree in journalism and a master's degree in social work from The University of Texas at Austin. Major work on *The House on Mango Street* and *Roll of Thunder, Hear My Cry*.

Koryn Fisher: Fisher holds a master's degree in English education and is a freelance writer and editor. Major Work on "King of the Bingo Game" and "Sexual Orientation" essay.

William F. Gillard: Gillard holds a master's degree in English and teaches at Fairleigh Dickinson University. Major work on *Ceremony*

Joyce E. Haines: Haines holds a Ph.D. in educational policy and administration, and teaches at the University of Kansas Division of Continuing Education, Kansas City Kansas Community College, and online courses for Community College of Southern Nevada. Major Work on *Farewell to Manzanar*.

Jonathan Lampley: Lampley is a doctoral candidate in English at Middle Tennessee State University and is a freelance writer. "Gender" essay.

David Layton: Layton holds a Ph.D. in English literature and teaches at Santa Monica College, University of Phoenix, and American Intercontinental University. Major Work on *Kaffir Boy*.

Cambria Lovelady: Lovelady holds an M.A. in creative writing from the University of Memphis and is a writer and editor for educational materials. Major work on *A Room of One's Own, Angels in America, The Awakening,* "Everything that Rises Must Converge," "I Have a Dream," and "Slavery" essay.

Natasha Marin: Marin is a freelance writer and poet. Major work on *A Raisin in the Sun, Blacks, The Color Purple,* and "What You Pawn, I Will Redeem." Critical essay on "What You Pawn, I Will Redeem."

W. Todd Martin: Martin holds a Ph.D. in English and teaches at Huntington College. "Ethnicity" essay.

Kate McCafferty: McCafferty holds a Ph.D. in American literature and teaches ESL abroad. Major Work on *Native Son* and *Vindication of the Rights of Woman*.

David L. McLean: McLean holds a master's degree in English and is a freelance writer. Major Work on *The Merchant of Venice* and *A Passage to India*.

Ray Mescallado: Mescallado holds a master's degree in English and is a freelance writer. Major Work on "A Good Day."

Annette Petrusso: Petrusso is a freelance writer and editor with a B.A. in history from the University of Michigan and an M.A. in screenwriting from The University of Texas at Austin. Major work on *The Autobiography of Miss Jane Pittman* and *Flowers for Algernon.*

Tom Pearson: Pearson is a freelance writer and editor. Major work on *The Autobiography of Malcolm X.*

Laura Baker Shearer: Shearer holds a Ph.D. in American literature and works as an English professor and freelance writer. Major work on *The Souls of Black Folk* and *Uncle Tom's Cabin.*

Paula R. Stiles: Stiles holds a Ph.D. in medieval history and works as an English tutor. "Ethnic Cleansing, Genocide, and Exile" essay.

Melanie Ulrich: Ulrich holds a Ph.D. in English literature from The University of Texas at Austin and is a freelance writer. Major work on *To Kill a Mockingbird.*

Frederic Will: Will holds a Ph.D. in comparative literature and teaches at Mellen University. Major essays on Race and Prejudice in World Literature, Race and Prejudice in British Literature, and Race and Prejudice in American Literature.

Greg Wilson: Wilson is a freelance literature and popular culture writer. Major work on *Bury My Heart at Wounded Knee, Anne Frank: The Diary of a Young Girl, Heart of Darkness, The Adventures of Huckleberry Finn, I Know Why the Caged Bird Sings, Nisei Daughter,* and "The Negro Speaks of Rivers." Critical essays on "The Negro Speaks of Rivers" and *Nisei Daughter.* "Religion," "Class and Caste," and "Segregation" essays.

Literary Chronology

1564: William Shakespeare was born on or about April 23 in Stratford-upon-Avon, Warwickshire, England.

1596: William Shakespeare's *The Merchant of Venice* is published.

1616: Shakespeare died on April 23 in Stratford-upon-Avon, Warwickshire, England.

1759: Mary Wollstonecraft was born on April 27 in Hoxton, England.

1792: Mary Wollstonecraft's *A Vindication of the Rights of Woman* is published.

1797: Wollstonecraft died on September 10 of complications from childbirth.

1811: Harriet Beecher was born on June 14 in Litchfield, Connecticut.

1835: Mark Twain was born Samuel Langhorne Clemens in 1835 in Missouri.

1850: Katherine O'Flaherty Chopin was born on February 8 in St. Louis, Missouri.

1852: Harriet Beecher Stowe's *Uncle Tom's Cabin* is published.

1857: Joseph Conrad was born Jozef Teodor Konrad Korzeniowski on December 3 in Berdiczew, Podolia, Russia (now Ukraine).

1868: William Edward Burghardt Du Bois was born on February 23 in Great Barrington, Massachusetts.

1879: Edward Morgan Forster was born on January 1 in London, England.

1882: Adeline Virginia Stephen was born January 25 in London, England.

1884: Mark Twain's *The Adventures of Huckleberry Finn* is published.

1896: Stowe died on July 1 in Hartford, Connecticut.

1899: Kate Chopin's *The Awakening* is published.

1902: James Mercer Langston Hughes was born on February 1 in Joplin, Missouri.

1902: Joseph Conrad's *Heart of Darkness* is published.

1903: Alan Paton was born on January 11 in Pietermaritzburg, Natal, South Africa.

1903: W. E. B. Du Bois's *The Souls of Black Folk* is published.

1904: Chopin died on August 20 of a brain hemorrhage in St. Louis, Missouri.

1908: Dorris (Dee) Alexander Brown was born on February 28 near Alberta, Louisiana.

1908: Richard Wright was born on September 4 in Roxie, Mississippi.

1910: Twain died of heart disease on April 21 in Redding, Connecticut.

1914: Ralph Waldo Ellison was born on March 1 in Oklahoma City.

1917: Gwendolyn Brooks was born June 7 in Topeka, Kansas.

1919: Primo Michele Levi was born on July 31 in Turin, Italy.

1919: Monica Sone was born Kazuko Monica Itoi in Seattle, Washington.

1921: Langston Hughes's "The Negro Speaks of Rivers" is published.

1921: Alex Haley was born on August 11 in Ithaca, New York.

1924: E. M. Forster's *A Passage to India* is published.

1924: Conrad died on August 3 of a heart attack in Bishopsbourne, Kent, England.

1925: Mary Flannery O'Connor was born March 25 in Savannah, Georgia.

1925: Malcolm Little was born on May 19, 1925, in Omaha, Nebraska.

1926: Nelle Harper Lee was born on April 28 in Monroeville, Alabama.

1927: Daniel Keyes was born August 9 in Brooklyn, New York.

1929: Martin Luther King Jr. was born on January 15 in Atlanta, Georgia.

1929: Virginia Woolf's *A Room of One's Own* is published.

1929: Anne Frank was born on June 12 in Frankfurt, Germany.

1930: Lorraine Hansberry was born on May 19 in Chicago, Illinois.

1933: Ernest James Gaines was born in 1933 on a plantation in Louisiana.

1934: Jeanne Wakatsuki Houston was born on September 26 in California.

1940: Richard Wright's *Native Son* is published.

1941: Woolf committed suicide by drowning on March 28 in Lewes, Sussex, England.

1943: Mildred Delois Taylor was born on September 13 in Jackson, Mississippi.

1944: Ralph Ellison's "King of the Bingo Game" is published.

1944: Alice Walker was born February 9 in Eatonton, Georgia.

1945: Frank died in March at the Bergen-Belsen concentration camp.

1947: Primo Levi's "A Good Day" is published.

1947: Anne Frank's *The Diary of a Young Girl* is published.

1948: Leslie Marmon Silko was born on March 5 in Albuquerque, New Mexico.

1948: Alan Paton's *Cry, the Beloved Country* is published.

1953: Monica Sone's *Nisei Daughter* is published.

1954: Sandra Cisneros was born December 20 in Chicago, Illinois.

1959: Lorraine Hansberry's *A Raisin in the Sun* is published.

1960: Wright died on November 28 of a heart attack in Paris, France.

1960: Harper Lee's *To Kill a Mockingbird* is published.

1961: Flannery O'Connor's "Everything that Rises Must Converge" is published.

1963: Martin Luther King Jr.'s "I Have a Dream" is published.

1963: Du Bois died on August 27 in Accra, Ghana.

1964: O'Connor died on August 3 of lupus in Milledgeville, Georgia.

1965: Hansberry died of lung cancer on January 12 in New York, New York.

1965: Malcolm X was assassinated on February 21 in New York, New York.

1965: Malcolm X's *The Autobiography of Malcolm X* is published.

1966: Daniel Keyes's *Flowers for Algernon* is published.

1967: Hughes died on August 22 of a cerebral hemorrhage in St. Louis, Missouri.

1968: King was assassinated on April 4 in Memphis, Tennessee.

1970: Forster died on June 7 in Coventry, England.

1970: Dee Brown's *Bury My Heart at Wounded Knee: An Indian History of the American West* is published.

1971: Ernest J. Gaines's *The Autobiography of Miss Jane Pittman* is published.

1973: Jeanne Wakatsuki Houston's *Farewell to Manzanar: A True Story of Japanese American Experience during and after the World War II Internment* is published.

1976: Mildred D. Taylor's *Roll of Thunder, Hear My Cry* is published.

1977: Leslie Marmon Silko's *Ceremony* is published.

1982: Alice Walker's *The Color Purple* is published.

1984: Sandra Cisneros's *The House on Mango Street* is published.

1987: Levi died of an alleged suicide on April 11.

1987: Gwendolyn Brooks's *Blacks* is published.

1988: Alan Paton died of throat cancer on April 12 in Botha's Hill, Natal, South Africa.

1992: Alex Haley died of cardiac arrest on February 10 in Seattle, Washington.

1994: Ellison died on April 16 of cancer in New York, New York.

2000: Gwendolyn Brooks died on December 3 of cancer in Chicago, Illinois.

2002: Brown died on December 12 in Little Rock, Arkansas.

Overview
Essays

RACE AND PREJUDICE IN AMERICAN LITERATURE

RACE AND PREJUDICE IN BRITISH LITERATURE

RACE AND PREJUDICE IN WORLD LITERATURE

Race and Prejudice in American Literature

Introduction

Is literature a mirror held up to nature, which can render the fullness of life, in all its goodness and evil? Or is literature a lamp that shines out to illuminate all it touches, rather than a mirror that merely reflects? Reading literature is simply a way of opening our eyes to the new, of seeing more, and so we should embrace both of these perspectives, the mirror and the lamp.

The mirror metaphor helps the reader see why the world reflected in literature is full of both ugliness and beauty; literature spares nothing in its hunger to reveal life just as it is. The lamp metaphor takes readers to the same place, shining a light on various aspects of human experience. Throughout the history of the United States, many of the most painful issues of the day—prejudice, discrimination, violence, exclusion—have found their way into the stories and accounts of American literature. In examining texts dealing with race and prejudice throughout the course of American history, readers can see what has changed, and sadly, what has not. Discrimination based on differences—skin color, religion, gender, and the like—continue to plague this country even today. If the mirror of literature reveals actions and perceptions, the lamp of literature shows the effects of these actions and perceptions, and thus it implicitly suggests what might be done to change them.

Ethnicity

From the Greek root *ethnos* (tribe, social group, community), ethnicity refers to one's primary cultural setting: for instance, black, Asian, white, Hispanic, or Jewish. American authors bring a wide range of ethnic backgrounds to the reader's consideration. Ignorance is often a major factor in promoting racial prejudice, but knowledge and understanding are powerful forces toward overcoming such surface differences based on the color of one's skin or the country of one's origin. Literature shows readers the world through someone else's eyes, and thus can broaden the experience and tolerance of strangers for strangers.

Writer Laurence Yep has experienced the effects of mainstream American prejudice toward Asian cultures. Yep attended school in Chinatown but lived in an African American neighborhood of San Francisco. This diverse exposure made him sensitive to racial difference in general, and to his own particular difference from mainstream America. His young-adult novel *The Star Fisher* (1991) deals with prejudice toward Chinese Americans in 1927 Clarksburg, West Virginia. Yep's historical perspective allows readers to see how racial prejudices have changed between the time in which the story is set, and the contemporary time in which it was written.

At the start of the novel, Joan Lee and her family have moved to Clarksburg, where her father sets up a laundry business. There are no other Chinese in the town, and the Lees feel isolated and lonely. Though the three children of the family acclimate fairly rapidly, the parents—as is so often the case among immigrants—remain torn between two cultures. As the intermediaries between two cultures, the children experience strife from both sides. It is only toward the end of the novel, during a pie social, that the family begins to gain some acceptance. That seemingly trivial social event proves to be the catalyst for a new racial sensitivity in the community, and afterward, the Lees' Chinese heritage no longer seems an impediment to living a happy life in Clarksburg.

A powerful firsthand account of a childhood awash in discrimination before World War II and during its early years is Maya Angelou's memoir *I Know Why the Caged Bird Sings* (1969). Angelou is a highly influential author, historian, playwright, and civil rights activist.

Her first full-length literary work, *I Know Why the Caged Bird Sings* tells the story of her early life through the end of high school. She and her brother are shuttled between the stability and security of life with their grandmother in the impoverished, segregated, and potentially violent South in the 1930s, to the material comfort but psychological and physical danger of life with their mother in St. Louis, to the empowerment of life in the relatively integrated world of World War II–era San Francisco. After a tragic and traumatic episode in the young girl's life, she meets Bertha Flowers, whom she describes as "the lady who threw me my first life line." She recalls this lesson from Mrs. Flowers:

> Your grandmother says you read a lot. Every chance you get. That's good, but not enough. Words mean more than what is set down on paper. It takes the human voice to infuse them with the shades of deeper meaning.

Throughout her formative years, Maya (then known as Marguerite) relies on her intellect, determination, and family to build the strength and insight that will lead her to become a civil rights activist and United States Poet Laureate in later years.

Farewell to Manzanar (1973), by Jeanne Wakatsuki Houston and James D. Houston, continues the theme of struggle and triumph. Jeanne Houston describes her family's experience as Japanese Americans living in California in the wake of the bombing of Pearl Harbor. The consequences of that attack, for the Wakatsukis and many other Japanese American families, were dramatic and rapid. As suspicion and fear of Japanese increased, Executive Order 9066 required people of Japanese descent living on the West Coast to relocate to internment camps. The Wakatsukis were therefore transferred to the Manzanar internment camp in the California desert, where they lived confined for three years. *Farewell to Manzanar* traces the humiliation and psychological strain imposed by internment, told from the point of view of seven-year-old Jeanne, who witnessed firsthand how "[t]olerance had turned to distrust and irrational fear. The hundred-year-old tradition of anti-Orientalism on the west coast soon resurfaced, more vicious than ever." The memoir follows their return to their old life and the humiliation and confusion from the sanctioned racism that follow the author into adulthood.

David Guterson's *Snow Falling on Cedars* (1994) also takes the reader to the world of Japanese American culture, this time a decade after World War II. Guterson's novel is set on San Pedro Island, off the coast of Washington State, in 1954, at a time when the lingering influence of wartime hostilities are still keenly felt. When a murder occurs on the small island, the latent racism of the community rises to condemn a man based on his ethnicity.

The novel opens on the trial of a fisherman, Kabuo, a member of the Japanese community on the island. He is charged with the murder of a fellow fisherman. The racially tense climate casts suspicion onto the Japanese fisherman, but justice demands more than suspicion. In addition to the main plotline of the murder and accusation, several developments greatly enrich Guterson's story, and make this book an inquiry into ethnic consciousness. Readers are introduced to a local newspaper man who had a love affair with the woman who became Kabuo's wife before the incarceration of the Japanese community during the war. Readers also meet the German wife of the dead fisherman, and are introduced to an irony: no one feels suspicious of this bigoted German, who in all social respects contrasts poorly with her Japanese fellow community members.

Alice Walker, renowned author of *The Color Purple* (1982), was the first black woman to win the Pulitzer Prize in literature. In her story "Everyday Use," a mother and her younger daughter, Maggie, await the visit from Dee, the older daughter, who has grown away from the family and become part of a more mainstream Americanized generation of blacks. Walker's short story examines how concepts of racial identity vary from generation to generation. Dee has become involved in the Black Consciousness movement, and has changed her name to Wangero Leewanika Kemanjo, because, as she states, "I couldn't bear it any longer, being named after the people who oppress me." Her mother reminds her that she was named after her aunt Dicie, but Dee refuses to relent. She then begins to collect items from around the house—the butter churn, some quilts—items that the narrator and Maggie use every day, to use as display pieces: "I can use the churn top as a centerpiece for the alcove table . . . and I'll think of something artistic to do with the dasher." Dee's misguided attempt to identify

with her heritage turns her connection with her past into cold, unusable museum pieces. "Everyday Use" illustrates how older and younger African Americans can inhabit different worlds in a twentieth century that increasingly divides the pre–civil rights cultural world from the post–Martin Luther King world.

Like Houston and Walker, Chicana poet Lorna Dee Cervantes reveals her experiences of life through the filters of her ethnicity and the self-identity that arises from it. Though America has always been a melting pot, and at its best has absorbed multiple racial energies, there has unofficially always been an underclass based on ethnicity—black, Native American, and until recently, Hispanic. However, as Cervantes illustrates in her poem "Poem for the Young White Man Who Asked Me How I, an Intelligent Well-Read Person, Could Believe in the War between Races" (1981), intellect has nothing to do with it. She argues, "Racism is not intellectual," and people are often unwilling to admit to modern issues of discrimination in the home of the free:

> Every day I am deluged with reminders
> that this is not
> my land
> and this is my land.
> I do not believe in the war between races
> but in this country
> there is war.

Sherman Alexie, born in Spokane, Washington, and raised on the Spokane Indian Reservation in Wellpinit, Washington, has earned a place as one of the most distinguished Native American writers of the day. In his novel, *Indian Killer* (1996), he presents John Smith, a Native American of an unknown tribe living with his adoptive white parents. It is clearly with irony that Alexie names his protagonist John Smith, the same name as the English explorer associated with the first American settlement in Jamestown and the Indian princess Pocahontas. This man is a construction worker on a skyscraper, and at the same time, appropriately, a loner given to reflection on his heritage. In his mind, Smith imagines that by a single stroke of white murder, he might symbolically wipe out the whole history of oppression of Native Americans.

Having committed this symbolic murder, Smith goes on to systematic revenge against the white man, and the city of Seattle teems with racial tension and fear. In this thriller are diverse types who become drawn into the orbit of

Smith's action. An Indian student activist, a white anthropologist student of Native American culture, an ex-cop who fancies himself a spokesman for the Indians, and a right-wing talk show host: all these and more demonstrate the multifaceted communal response to the Indian killer's actions. Like Guterson in *Snow Falling on Cedars*, Alexie uses a thriller to bring intense issues of American culture to the fore.

William Bell's *Zack* (1999) is an original and thought-provoking work of young adult fiction about a young man living in Toronto, the son of a white Jewish father and a black southern mother. Zack has never taken interest in his mother's background until, one day, he is rummaging through a box in the family attic. He finds there an old musket ball and a piece of interlocking iron circles; vestiges, he discovers through his research for a high school paper, of the possessions of Richard Pierpont, a black slave who made his way to Canada in 1812. With this discovery, Zack grows curious about his mother's family in Mississippi, and the side of his heritage he has never been interested in before. This curiosity leads Zack to travel to Mississippi and meet his maternal grandfather, a gentle old man who harbors unreserved hatred of whites. This man's voice is only one of many bigoted voices, both black and white, that Zack encounters on his trip to the U.S. South. Essentially the novel consists of Zack's learning experience, and it tells the truth about the reality of racial discrimination, but at the same time it also asserts the individual's ability to grow and understand.

The Native American, the Asian, the Chicano, and the African American components of American culture comprise precious contributions to the unique voice of this country. Unlike European countries, the United States has never been homogeneous, and thrives on diversities and the unprogrammed contributions of these diverse ethnic groups. From Maya Angelou to William Bell, these texts cry out for the rights of the individual, regardless of his or her race.

Gender

When European settlers first arrived in America, they brought with them an established social and cultural gender bias that cast women as second-class citizens. This subjugation of women was at that time nothing new, and has existed in almost every culture on the globe. However, as the newly formed nation of America grew, the role of women was constantly reexamined. While women long remained persecuted and limited in choice, movements toward equality and recognition began to spread. Women in the twentieth century finally earned the right to vote, and the right to make their voices heard.

Nathaniel Hawthorne's *The Scarlet Letter* (1850) is set in colonial Boston of the mid-1600s, not long after the first arrival of the Puritans on the east coast of America. It is a story about the place of and expectations on women in a Puritan society, and the double standards that can ruin a woman and leave a man unscathed. The Puritan theocracy was in full sway at the time the novel was set, providing a claustrophobic religious atmosphere that lies behind the tragic events of the tale.

The story tells of a woman, Hester Prynne, who for understandable but "unacceptable" reasons has committed adultery with the local minister, Arthur Dimmesdale. As her punishment she must wear a scarlet "A" as an outward symbol of her adultery, publicly displayed across the bosom of her dress. Despite great pressure, Hester refuses to reveal her lover's identity. In fact, the town never seeks to condemn the man involved with Hester, and Dimmesdale never comes forward in her defense. She is left to bear the burden of the affair alone, with dignity and integrity intact despite her circumstances, as Dimmesdale lives silently with his guilt. Hawthorne masterfully illustrates the consequences of a soul-thwarting religious environment, in which hypocrisy, guilt, and jealousy consume people's lives. When Hester and Dimmesdale must part at the end of the novel, she asks him what he sees for their future. While she hopes that they might be together in the afterlife, as "surely, we have ransomed one another, with all this woe!", the scarlet letter Dimmesdale wears on his conscience prevents him from thinking such: "The law was broke!— the sin here so awfully revealed—let these alone be in thy thoughts!"

In 1873, Louisa May Alcott published *Work: A Story of Experience*, in which she explores the limitations of her culture as they impinged on women's work possibilities. Alcott, author of *Little Women*, records her unhappy experiences as a domestic servant. She is acutely sensitive to inequalities in labor practices toward women, actions that would considered sexual harassment today, and conflicting atmospheres between men and women that hinder the process of organized work. Like Edith Wharton in *The House of Mirth,* Alcott sees labor on all levels as essentially valuable and honorable, and insists on an appropriate setting for women in the workplace. *Work: A Story of Experience* was written in a time when, by and large, women did not work outside of the home, and if they did, it was in "feminine" occupations such as nursing and teaching. However, as the end of the nineteenth century neared and attitudes toward women in the workplace were shifting, Alcott became an important voice for increasing women's rights.

Just over twenty-five years later, Kate Chopin published *The Awakening* (1899), which combines elements found in both *The Scarlet Letter* and *Work: A Story of Experience* about the changing world of women with regard to sex, independence, and a life outside the home. The book caused profound shock across the country, with many readers and critics calling it vulgar and inappropriate, as the protagonist, Edna Pontellier, broke every social convention expected of polite, well-mannered women.

Over the course of a summer at Grand Isle, a retreat for the wealthy off the coast of Louisiana, Edna falls in love with Robert Lebrun and begins an "awakening" as to how she wants to live her life. As she allows herself to entertain forbidden thoughts—admitting that she is not a "mother-woman," that she does not really love her husband, and that she is entitled to a life of her own choosing—she feels a "certain light . . . beginning to dawn dimly within her," and she begins to "realize her position in the universe as a human being, and to recognize her relations as an individual to the world within and about her." Now fully awake to the world and its possibilities around her, she cannot return to her old life. Turn-of-the-century New Orleans, however, only allows for women to be mothers and wives, or lonely spinsters. Her society is not ready for a woman like Edna, and she is shunned and whispered about. In a final act of self-possession, proving that she does not belong to her children or her husband or even the limited society of New Orleans, Edna ventures into the ocean alone, to "wander in abysses of solitude."

Both Alcott and Chopin write of women and women's issues as they are embedded in an immediate social context, whereas Hawthorne, writing a half century earlier, deals with "the woman issue" of his day on a relatively abstract and moral level. The link between Hester Prynne in the seventeenth century and Edna Pontellier in the nineteenth century is interesting, however; though over two hundred years have passed between each woman's story, both are punished and ostracized for their sexuality and conduct because they are women. Neither of the men in these stories is subject to any such scrutiny.

Like *The Awakening*, Willa Cather's *O Pioneers!* (1913) is concerned with the issues of women's inner development. *O Pioneers!* introduces the Bergsons, a hardy family of American settlers who are faced with making a living on the austere plains of Nebraska, where even today one can find the occasional sod house that recalls the rough living conditions of yesteryear.

Many of the settler families move off the plains to easier living but less productive soil; however, Alexandra Bergson, who inherits her father's farm after his death, decides to remain there with her mother and three brothers. Through her hard work and determination, the farm eventually becomes a success. The novel focuses on Alexandra, as she gains peace of mind with the relative success of the farm, and is then beset by problems. The life of a female farm owner among male farmers is very difficult, and many doubt Alexandra's abilities to make decisions on her own. But the farm makes her happy, and she is determined, like Edna in *The Awakening,* to be fulfilled on her own terms, and like Alcott, she struggles against preconceived notions of what a woman can and cannot do. Cather writes, "The history of every country begins in the heart of a man or a woman."

The Feminine Mystique (1963), by Betty Friedan, was one of the seminal texts of the later twentieth-century feminist movement. By the time of this text, more than a half century has passed since the works of Chopin and Cather. Women had the right to vote since 1920, and two world wars had brought women into the workplace in droves. The new birth control pill enabled women to separate their sexual identities from their reproductive destinies. Though domesticity and traditional female social roles remain prized, in the 1960s a liberation movement took place and questioned those roles and expectations, changing the position of women in America forever.

A Japanese American family with their belongings waiting for internment National Archives and Records Administration

In *The Feminine Mystique*, Friedan sympathizes with women in roles that require them to be financially, intellectually, and emotionally dependent upon their husbands. Her careful analysis tracks this state of affairs in her own moment, to the cultural psychology of middle-class suburban America after World War II. Men returned from the war wanting mothering from their wives. Women, who had been a presence in the wartime workplace, returned home to the responsibilities of caretaking and home-making. At the same time, there was a revolution in technology that confused the older conceptions of women's housekeeping roles. Thanks to frozen dinners, pre-made mixes, washing machines, and dryers, housework was no longer the all-consuming chore it had been. Women were at last free to do something personal with

their lives. *The Feminine Mystique* examines the limited and stifling place that society has made for women, and how social conventions have long subjugated women in detrimental ways.

Toni Morrison, who won the Nobel Prize for Literature in 1993, is a dominant voice in examining the experience of African American women in a largely white culture. In her novel *Sula* (1973), Morrison devises a provocative and profound plot that seems to apply some of Friedan's concepts about society's influence on women. Two friends take different paths in life in their hometown of Medallion, Ohio. Nel remains at home, leading a conventional womanly life, while Sula takes off for the big city. She goes to college, spends time with men, and generally tests the bounds of her place in the world, as it was defined for her in 1920s America.

When Sula returns to Medallion, she and Nel have great trouble restoring their original closeness. This important detail clearly illustrates Morrison's subtle way of working through the issue of African American women's freedoms, both in relation to society as a whole and in relation to each other as women: "Because each had discovered years before that they were neither white nor male, and that all freedom and triumph was forbidden to them, they had set about creating something else to be." Like Alcott, Cather, and Chopin, Morrison is concerned with women and their human development; unlike the other three, however, Morrison sets the problem in the context of race, with its discriminatory aspects, a factor that greatly complicates the women's freedom issue.

Margaret Atwood's *The Handmaid's Tale* (1985) is a dystopian tale of a future nation where women's sole functions are reproduction and domestic labor. Due to the ravages of pesticides, nuclear radiation, and pollution, most of the women in Gilead have become infertile. The few women who are fertile are transferred to camps and trained to be handmaidens, and as such they give birth to the upper-class citizens. Infertile women from the lower classes are "Marthas," who serve as house help. Women are not allowed sexual freedom, as they are today; they are allowed to engage in sex only for the purpose of reproduction. The women in Atwood's novel are slaves who live in a world of limited freedoms much more reminiscent of Hawthorne's *The Scarlet Letter* than *The Awakening* or *The Feminine Mystique*.

The central figure of the novel is Offred, whose name means literally "of Fred"—women's identity only exists in terms of the males who own them. In a complex set of plot turns, Offred is assigned to a general and his wife to give them an heir. At first the general's wife is too jealous to permit the process, but ultimately she arranges for Offred to sleep with her chauffeur in order to become pregnant and give her a child. Satire, eroticism, and a lightning fast plot establish a complex portrait of the future, and about the place of women in it. In terms of the place of women in society, Atwood's imaginary future cautions about the possibility of a regressed society that considers women as possessions, not individuals.

From Hawthorne to Atwood, these books revolve around issues of gender, identity, and freedom. They show not only how American society has viewed women over the centuries, but also how women view themselves and each other. In the literature of race and prejudice, the topic of gender discrimination crosses all ethnic and cultural lines, as women of every background struggle to define, fulfill, and rejoice in their roles in life.

Religion

Prejudice can hinge on religion in many different ways. In some cases, religious beliefs can become a tool of intolerance and discrimination against other people's values. At the same time, religious followers themselves can become the victims of prejudice and shunned by mainstream society. Religious wars can pit one vast institution against another, and in a country like the United States, that prides itself on religious freedom and tolerance, religion can be a powerful tool for both uniting and dividing.

Cotton Mather's *Decennium Luctuosum* (*Gloomy Decade*) (1699) springs from a cultural context that is difficult for modern readers to understand. It is worthwhile to reach back into that world using literature as a lamp, for it challenges readers to rethink the contemporary world. Mather's essay is concerned with the Puritan settlers' war against the Indians, and he establishes a stern polarity between the two forces. The battle between Christian good (the settlers) and pagan evil (Native Americans) is at stake here, in a battle not only military, but a battle fought on the spiritual level as well. Mather's view sharply highlights the character of contemporary society, where is it often the case—as it was in Mather's time—that people of different beliefs are assumed to be evil, and therefore must be controlled.

Set during the same time is Arthur Miller's play *The Crucible* (1953), which focuses on the witchcraft trials of seventeenth-century Salem, Massachusetts. This play was written during the period of Senator Joseph McCarthy's hearings into anti-American and Communist activities. In fact, McCarthy's own inquiry methods resembled those of some of the Salem Puritans: innuendo, rumor, hearsay, false allegation, the stirring of public alarm.

The events Miller portrays in this play have their origins in late seventeenth-century Puritan texts, like those of Cotton Mather. Early in the play, an African slave from the Caribbean and several young girls are found dancing around a cauldron in the woods. Onlookers suspect them of a witchcraft rite; one of the young girls, Mary Warren, worries, "the whole country's talkin' witchcraft! They'll be callin' us witches." The rumor turns into a full-blown investigation, charges circulate, and a whole circle of rumor-accused "witches" is found guilty and hanged. This is the same world of irrational mass judgment that pinned the "A" on the bosom of Hester Prynne in Hawthorne's *The Scarlet Letter*. As Miller notes in act 1, the religious hysteria justified otherwise taboo actions, as the witch hunt was a "long overdue opportunity for everyone so inclined to express publicly his guilt and sins, under the cover of accusations against the victims."

Religious persecution did not end with the Puritans or even with the forming of the American democracy. It persists to this very day. In "David's Star" (1999), a short story for young adults by Jacqueline Dembar Greene, readers learn of the pride and distress that young Jewish people can experience in contemporary culture. The distress often lies in a painful dilemma: whether to announce one's Jewishness, and be open about it—and possibly vulnerable—or to hide it, and remain secure. In "David's Star," the protagonist chooses to keep her religious identity quiet, until her boss's blatant anti-Semitism forces her into action. The star referred to in the title of the story is the hexagram often used to symbolize Judaism, similar to the Christian cross. For the protagonist, religious expression wins out, for it is an intense facet of her personality. The central dilemma in the story, and in everyday life in general, is how to balance respect for one's own religious beliefs and respect for those that differ.

John Krakauer's *Under the Banner of Heaven: A Story of Violent Faith* (2003) examines the Mormon fundamentalism that leads to violence and murder in the real life case of the Lafferty brothers in 1984. Historically, Mormons have been largely shunned by mainstream America for their practice of polygamy (now abandoned), secretive rituals, and clannish tendencies. To radical Mormon Fundamentalists, the abandonment of polygamy one hundred years ago was indicative of the church's straying from its founding mandate. With this departure, discrimination arose within a church that was itself more or less

discriminated against by the mainstream: those who believed in following the original mandates of plural marriage against those who no longer practice it. Fundamentalist sects exist throughout North America, and live on the fringes of society; as Krakauer notes, "leaders of the mainstream church are extremely discomfited by these legions of polygamous brethren." It was within one of those sects that the Lafferty brothers, believing to hear God's voice, murdered their sister-in-law and her toddler child in 1984.

Crossing Over: One Woman's Exodus from Amish Life (2001) tells the tale of Ruth Irene Garrett, who was imprisoned within the strictures of the Amish environment as tightly as any ethnic, sexual, or dysfunctional fetters could hold her. In a traditional Old Order Amish family—there are some one hundred and fifty Old Order Amish communities scattered through North America—the father wields great dominance, the women are submissive, and the entire outside world is viewed with suspicion. In fact, the greatest sin in this culture is to abandon one's home setting. The penalty for such abandonment is that one is banned, or shunned, according to the dictate that henceforth such an exiled person is not to have communication with any Amish person. It is a wholly insular world, such as that depicted in Krauker's *Under the Banner of Heaven*.

This ban carries a painful consequence for Garrett. Her need for freedom and her natural passion lead her away from her Amish home. After marrying a non-Amish man, she is shunned, and pays a heavy price in broken relationships. Her father and the community are merciless, though her mother's natural love provides some space for communication and compromise. Religious doctrine clings like a tight noose around Garrett's neck. From the standpoint of the Amish head of a family, his religious belief system is not one arbitrary choice among many; it is the only right choice, with no room left for compromise.

Religious prejudice can lead people to oppress others as easily as it can lead them to be oppressed themselves. In a paradigm that readily casts believers as righteous and nonbelievers as heathens, antagonists in matters of religious difference may discount each other's very humanity. More than with other sources of prejudice, people may choose or reject a certain religion as their conscience demands. If literature casts light on the experiences of others, then tolerance and respect may emerge from the reading experience as valid choices, too.

Sexuality

The battle over sexual preference has been bitterly engaged during the twentieth century, and is very far from over. Literature on the topic tends to support sexual freedom, and yet such support is far from assured in America today.

Gertrude Stein's *Melanctha* (1905) begins late in the protagonist's life, as she cares for her friend Rose Johnson, whose baby has just died. Melanctha has had an unhappy childhood, contributing to a tight bond between Rose and Melanctha. In one flashback, readers witness a fight between Melanctha and her father, James Herbert. It is clear from that fight that Melanctha prevails over her father, and in that way gains a sense of her own power. She begins to take an interest in that power, and in order to learn more about it, she begins "wandering," a hard-to-define activity that continues throughout her life. "Wandering" tends to mean loitering in the parts of Bridgepoint where she meets and toys with male manual laborers. She flirts with these men, watches them at their work, and listens to them tell stories, all the while observing her effect on them. Sexual energy pervades the whole narrative. There is a bisexual mystery to Melanctha that draws her both to Rose and the male laborers.

The erotic suggestiveness of this tale caused difficulty for Stein, who was already under constant criticism. It is possible to see Melanctha herself as an early Stein, sexually hungry and diffuse, profoundly observing, and faithful to her friends, just as she remained faithful to her own lifelong companion, Alice B. Toklas.

James Baldwin's *Giovanni's Room* (1956) is a classic of gay consciousness literature. The story begins with David, an American who leaves his family to go to Paris. While he is there awaiting his girlfriend Hella, who is traveling in Spain, he becomes involved with an Italian bartender named Giovanni. David is led to question his sexual identity, but not to define himself as a homosexual. After Hella returns, David leaves Giovanni to return to her. In the meantime, however, Giovanni falls on desperately hard times. When a rich bar proprietor tries to demand sexual favors from Giovanni in return

for a job, Giovanni murders the proprietor, and is sentenced to die on the guillotine.

As a result, David experiences overwhelming guilt for having abandoned Giovanni. David starts having sexual encounters with sailors, and when Hella discovers this secret life, they break up. Baldwin's tale itself is well crafted and sensational but also self-probing. It raises the question of sexual identity as a part of the universal quest for self-understanding. Like Stein, Baldwin is primarily interested in personal liberation.

Alice Walker's *The Color Purple* (1982) is an intricate tale of rape, incest, love, and family ties. Protagonist Celie has borne two children, both the result of rape and both taken from her. To escape a similar fate, her sister Nettie leaves the country with a missionary family bound for Africa. Celie's life is dominated by harsh and violent men that affect her self-image; thus she comes to see herself as ugly and worthless. When Shug Avery, a soulful singer and lover to Celie's husband, enters her life, Celie falls in love with her, and in that relationship finds some peace and joy: "I look at Shug and I feel my heart begin to cramp." In her relationship with Shug, Celie feels tenderness and love for the first time, and finds the strength to leave her abusive husband and make her own life.

Zami, A New Spelling of My Name (1982), by Audrey Lorde, takes its origins from the Caribbean culture of Grenada. The book is what the author calls a "biomythography," an account of her life as a black gay woman growing up in New York City. The author's pride and panache ultimately allow her to keep her head above the tides of prejudice and social limitation. During the process of a Catholic schooling, her struggles in library school, and her emergence as a poet of distinction, the physical passion and buoying energy of the erotic keep the author conscious of her identity and pride. The title of the book is a key to her spirit: "Zami" is a Caribbean name for women who work together as lovers and fellow laborers. In both Walker's and Lorde's works, their sexuality provides the freedom they need to live their lives well.

Randall Kenan's *A Visitation of Spirits* (1989) is set in a small town in North Carolina. It concerns a young man, Horace Cross, who is raised in a deeply religious family, and who studies theology with the hope of becoming a pastor. He struggles to define his intellectual identity among the more traditional believers of his family. He must also come to terms with his sexuality; he is a homosexual in a community that has no tolerance for that lifestyle. The religious and the sexual identity themes come together as the plot progresses, and Horace seeks to reconcile those two facets of his life. He has always been drawn to the demonic-exorcist dimension of his religion, and he experiences his sexual preference in accordingly dramatic terms:

> I remember watching men, even as a little boy. I remember feeling strange and good and nasty. I remember doing it anyway, looking, and feeling that way. I remember not being able to stop and worrying and then stopping worrying.

In reading these works, from Stein to Kenan, one has a consistent sense of the pleasure that comes with expressing one's sexuality. Yet among these examples, only Lorde exults in that pleasure wholeheartedly, without a sense of guilt or furtive secrecy. For Baldwin and Walker, for example, the quest for sexual satisfaction is part of a complex dance of the mind. For Kenan, the homoerotic appears to be tinged with the unholy. Each generation of literature examining the struggles of being gay in a straight world creates a little more understanding among the reading public, and thus paves the way for readers and writers alike to express themselves more freely.

Social Class and Caste

More than ever, people's social standing is entwined with their net worth. Families of "genteel poverty" may once have had easier lives than the laboring classes, and families of "old money" may have looked down on the gaudy "nouveau riche," but those distinctions of heritage have all but given way to simple distinctions of numbers of dollars. In the United States, prejudice against the impoverished has supplanted the prejudice formerly generated by the class system. The disadvantages of poverty are visible with ever greater clarity—in housing, medical insurance, and access to education—as the gap between the "haves" and the "have nots" widens and never stops expanding.

Edith Wharton's *The House of Mirth* (1905) is an extensive novel of manners. Its protagonist, Lily Bart, is a socially prominent young Manhattan woman targeted by a variety of aspiring suitors, all of whom are attracted by her basically flirtatious nature, combined with her refusal to play the high social game.

Throughout the novel, Bart spars with social conventions. She is far from a maverick, yet she is impatient with what is required to be a social conformist. An ominous turn in Lily's fortunes occurs toward the end of the novel, and with this the story makes a groundbreaking statement. After becoming addicted to gambling in response to a sudden need for quick money, she is faced with poverty and dependence. She makes the decision (a radical one for someone in her class) to find a job and earn her living. She takes a job in the millinery business, sewing on the line and sharing the destiny of the ordinary worker. Lily's decision illustrates Wharton's argument that one can be trapped even in high comfort, and freed while in servitude, though her protagonist perceives just the opposite reality.

Upton Sinclair's *The Jungle* (1906) is a fictionalized account of the author's firsthand observations of raw industrial capitalism in nineteenth-century Chicago, when working conditions in factories were often unsanitary and unsafe, and management cared little for employees. Jurgis Rudkus, and his wife and baby, are Lithuanian immigrants who find themselves introduced into this cutthroat world: Jurgis gets a job in a meatpacking plant, and he and his small family take lodgings in a rat-infested apartment. The job is filthy and dangerous, work that only desperate immigrants are willing to take. The companies exploit their workers, knowing that the jobs are their only source of income and that they generally have no other options. While Jurgis is initially excited to be a part of the slaughterhouse—"to be given a place in it and a share in its wonderful activities was a blessing to be grateful for"—he quickly sees that the management of the company is corrupt, and that his fellow workers hate their demeaning, demanding jobs: "Jurgis . . . thought he was going to make himself useful, and rise and become a skilled man; but he would soon find out his error—for nobody rose in Packingtown by doing good work."

The immigrants are taken advantage of, swindled, and worked until they are ill and then cut off without pay while they recover, until they either die early or are forced into crime to survive. Their poverty and desperation makes them expendable nonhumans to the powerful industrialists. Intending to shed light on the class inequalities of capitalism, Sinclair instead focused world attention on the failures of the

U.S. meatpacking industry, sparking reform and leading to the Meat Inspection Act and federal inspectors in the industry.

Tillie Olsen's poem "I Want You Women Up North to Know" (1934) was triggered by a letter written by a Mexican American woman in Texas, harshly criticizing management in the San Antonio garment industry. The letter raised fundamental questions of workers' rights, and specifically charged indifference to the underclass workers in San Antonio. This letter coincided with a growing prominence of the Communist Party of America, the workers' labor movement, and unions; Olsen was involved in all of these. Like the undervalued workers in Sinclair's *The Jungle*, Olsen exposes the immigrant and lower-class labor used to make clothing for the upper class:

> i want you women up north to know
> how those dainty children's dresses you buy
> at macy's, wannamakers, gimbels, marshall
>   fields,
> are dyed in blood, are stitched in wasting flesh,
> down in San Antonio, "where sunshine spends
>   the winter."

John Steinbeck's *The Grapes of Wrath* (1939) deals with the epic struggles of the Joad family. They are Oklahoma farmers caught in the nightmare of the Dust Bowl, the drought and dust plague of the central United States plains during the 1930s that drove hundreds of thousands of displaced farmers west to California in search of work and new lives: "They streamed over the mountains, hungry and restless—restless as ants, scurrying to find work to do—to lift, to push, to pull, to pick, to cut—anything, any burden to bear, for food."

Steinbeck introduces readers to a powerful selection of victims, and conveys an overwhelming sense of the dignity of these people's struggle to survive. His fictional account assumes a historical quality as he records visions of the farmers moving west, for a chance to start over, hopeful that their futures will be prosperous. There are evils and con men along the way, but in their moments of rest, these migrants share their lives with one another and empower each other's determination: "The people in flight from the terror behind—strange things happen to them, some bitterly cruel and some so beautiful that the faith is refired forever." Like Upton Sinclair and Tillie Olsen, Steinbeck brings to light the harsh realities of the laboring-class—always vulnerable to the economic necessities of

the moment, and likely to be disregarded by government and industry.

The Outsiders (1967) by S. E. Hinton is the story of rivalry between two teenage gangs, the Greasers (poor kids) and the Socs (mainstream popular kids). Initially, young Ponyboy Curtis, a Greaser, sees the rivalry as a kind of game. But when one of his fellow Greasers, Johnny, kills a Soc during a fight, Ponyboy is forced to reconsider his lifestyle, which he never wholeheartedly embraced in the first place. He has a romantic temper and is sensitive to nature, two characteristics not often found—or expected—of lower-class gang members. By a complex series of chances, Ponyboy comes off unscathed and uncharged from several street fights, though he loses two of his best friends in one night. At the end of the tale he is back in school with an assignment to write a composition for English class. As he is fumbling for ideas, he opens a book in which there is an old letter written to him by Johnny, now dead. In that letter, Johnny urges Ponyboy to remain "gold," and to continue to enjoy sunsets. Ponyboy is deeply touched, and comes to a realization that gangs of any sort have a social function, in that they embrace people who are longing for some goodness they can only crudely express. Hinton's novel shows the Greasers, poor but not wretched, with every bit as much worth and humanity as their wealthier rivals.

Eric Schlosser's *Fast Food Nation* (2001) addresses the dark side of America's fast-food industry. Within that industry, Schlosser sees the origins of many contemporary ills: the leveling out of local difference and regional character; the promotion of mall culture; the epidemic of obesity; the growing split between rich and poor; the expansion of American cultural imperialism throughout the world; and the exploitation of a lower income, often immigrant, workforce. In many ways, Schlosser's book echoes Sinclair's *The Jungle,* as it exposes the degrading conditions and employment practices used in a popular and successful industry. Like turn-of-the-century meat packaging plants in Chicago, fast-food restaurants and modern slaughterhouses rely on cheap, unskilled, replaceable labor to keep costs down. As Schlosser points out, once fewer teenagers were seeking employment at fast-food chains, they "began to hire other marginalized workers: recent immigrants, the elderly, and the handicapped." He argues that the industry basically exploits its workers because they have no other options: the industry "now employs some of the most disadvantaged members of American society . . . people who can barely read, whose lives have been chaotic or shut off from the mainstream."

The literature of social class discrimination and oppression is often concerned with the harsh and sometimes dangerous conditions faced by the poor. A century ago, it was an eye-opening revelation for most Americans to learn both that money does not buy happiness and that poor workers are often exploited. Though social and legal changes have been tried to level the ground between "haves" and "have-nots," the same challenges and misconceptions between the classes still exist. For this reason, the literature of social class discrimination and oppression is still vital to our ethical evolution.

Disability, Illness, and Social Stigma

Prejudging, that is, making up one's mind in advance, is a fundamental part of human psychology. It speeds decision making and interactions, and often proves helpful, as when it lets us decide that people in uniform are responsible, smiling people are friendly, or people with body art are unconventional. A prejudgment is not necessarily correct, but neither is it discriminatory. Discrimination enters in when we assume that people with a certain trait—race, religion, ethnicity, economic status—are bad because of it. Disabilities and illnesses often provide such a trait, and harmful prejudice against their victims can be particularly insidious.

William Faulkner's "A Rose for Emily" (1930) is a short study of the personal price paid by victims of harsh social standards. The story is narrated in the first-person plural of "we," which extends to the reader the feeling that Emily is an outsider from the rest of the community. Emily is a member of a distinguished Southern family with significant sway in their small town. As she was growing up, her father never approved of any of her suitors and did not allow her to date. Upon the death of her father, Emily turns quickly to finally find a boyfriend. The man whom she chooses is quite naturally the kind of person her father would have rejected: a Yankee, and a laboring man.

Emily and the young man appear in public, and though the community may find this startling, they show signs of love. Over time, the

community learns that her suitor is "not a marrying man" who "liked men," but they believe that Emily will change him. The townspeople believe briefly that they have married, but the man disappears. She falls sick, and is hardly seen in public for decades, becoming the subject of speculation and gossip around town. When Emily finally dies, her relatives come to the house after the funeral. They enter a remote locked room, and there they find Emily's suitor reduced to his skeleton, lying in a bed. On the pillow beside him is the indentation of a head, and on it a strand of the aged Emily's iron gray hair. The stigma and embarrassment of unreciprocated love was too much for Emily to bear, and so she shut herself in her house with a body, which, silent and dead, could not judge her nor refuse her love.

John Steinbeck's *Of Mice and Men* (1937) is about two itinerant ranch workers, George and his friend Lennie, who is mildly mentally disabled. Lennie is a large powerful man with a weakness for soft furry animals, which he often pets so enthusiastically that he kills them. George tries to protect Lennie, but they get tangled up with a jealous husband and a flirtatious wife working on a ranch. The wife tries to comfort Lennie after he accidentally kills a puppy, letting him stroke her hair. She screams when he touches her too roughly, and he accidentally kills her as well. At the end George finds Lennie and consoles him, but shoots him rather than let the angry mob get their hands on him, apparently yielding to the only possible solution. This story is bleak and potent. Lennie is a gentle giant whose disability promotes occasional, and disastrous, loss of control. While he deserves the reader's pity, Steinbeck also makes it difficult to exercise that pity.

Just as Steinbeck's novel concludes with George deciding Lennie's fate, Jay Gould's essay "Carrie Buck's Daughter" (1984) concerns the actions of others with regard to disabled individuals. The essay discusses the famous 1927 case of *Buck v. Bell*, in which the Supreme Court of the United States supported Virginia's forced sterilization policy to prevent "defectives" from reproducing. Carrie Buck, a poor young lady with an illegitimate seven-month-old child, was judged to be "feebleminded," as was her infant daughter. The court argued that rather than perpetuate a cycle of mental disability, the best course of action was to sterilize Buck to prevent further "feebleminded" children who might someday give birth to future generations of "feebleminded" children. It later became clear that Carrie Buck was institutionalized not because of her "defective" intellect, but because of her pregnancy, which was most likely the result of a rape. Though her daughter, a student of average abilities, died in childhood, Carrie Buck lived into her seventies and proved a normal, productive person. The forced sterilizations in Virginia continued until 1972, and though they were a thing of the past at the time of Gould's essay, he writes so that their victims may be recognized, mourned, and honored.

Alice Hoffman's *At Risk* (1988) is a novel about an ordinary American family: Polly, a mother struggling to establish her career as a photographer; her husband Ivan, an astronomer; and two children: eleven-year-old Amanda, an aspiring gymnast, and Charlie, who is eight and attracted to the sciences. They are a happy and typical American family, fully normal until Amanda is diagnosed with HIV/AIDS, the consequence of a blood transfusion five years earlier. In 1988, HIV/AIDS was a heavily stigmatized disease that spelled certain death. The story traces the widespread fallout of this crushing diagnosis, taking the reader from one perspective to another as the community comes together in concern. *At Risk* is the story of how a global disease is a personal struggle for the victims and their loved ones, but also an opportunity to find strength and hope.

While most individuals would not choose to have a disability or illness, the Binewski family in Katherine Dunn's National Book Award–winning *Geek Love* (1983) purposely create "freaks" for their own traveling circus. For example, the narrator, an albino hunchback dwarf, recounts how her parents prepared for her birth, after the birth of her limbless older brother and conjoined twin sisters: "My mother had been liberally dosed with cocaine, amphetamines, and arsenic during her ovulation and throughout her pregnancy with me. It was a disappointment when I emerged with such commonplace deformities." In the Binewskis' world, deformity is normal, and even desirable. The realm in which this family lives is an ordinary world seen from a totally topsy-turvy inner perspective, with all norms overthrown and abandoned.

Don Trembath's young adult novel *Lefty Carmichael Has a Fit* (1999) addresses the disease epilepsy, a disability with a fallout that often exposes the sufferer to public attention and embarrassment. As people are usually fearful of things they cannot understand or control, many see Lefty's illness as something to be afraid of. Lefty, brought up in a working-class community, has great trouble dealing with his affliction, which causes difficulties with his classmates, problems with his romantic life, and expulsion from school. His identity becomes linked with his illness. Ultimately, good medical suggestions and advice from a girlfriend help get the situation under control, and Lefty is able to live peacefully with his illness, rather than let it control his life.

The illnesses, disabilities, and social stigmas discussed in these works all illustrate how people's lives can be affected not only by physical and mental ailments, but also by the reactions and reception of others. As readers sympathize with characters like these, they realize that, as difficult as diseases and disabilities are to endure, the reactions of other people may be the cruelest affliction to endure.

Ethnic Cleansing, Genocide, and Exile

Throughout the history of the New World, there has been conflict between indigenous populations and incoming settlers that usurp the land and resources. The conflict frequently leads to oppression or expulsion of the earlier landholders, and in some cases, the extermination of entire cultures. In North, South, and Central America, Europeans and their American descendants destroyed native populations and cultures.

The Spanish priest Juan Ginés de Sepúlveda, in *The Just Causes for War Among the Indians* (1550), presents what he sees as a justification for the Spanish wars of colonization in the New World. He argues that the native Indians are naturally inferior to the Spaniards, and therefore should serve as slaves and have no role in governing themselves. De Sepúlveda's rhetoric is echoed in Cotton Mather's *Decennium Luctuosum,* which was written one hundred and fifty years later. Although many of the native populations were technologically advanced with solid infrastructures and local governments, the Spaniards refused to see them as equals. By casting themselves as superior to the native Indians, the Spanish justified taking the land and resources that the Indians had. One of the most severe examples of this subjugation of native peoples is recounted in John Hemming's *The Conquest of the Incas* (1970), which examines the gradual destruction of the Incas' advanced civilization in present-day Peru. Inca culture was militarily, administratively, and architecturally developed when the Spanish entered their kingdom in the early sixteenth century. Spain itself was growing explosively and rapidly extending its overseas empire. Hemming provides the perspective of both the Spanish Conquistadores and the Incas, as a band of one hundred Spaniards, led by Francisco Pizzaro, began the series of spectacular conquests that within a century subdued a vast native empire.

Some three hundred years later, Native Americans in the United States faced the same oppression and displacement as the Incas. *The Trail of Tears* (1975), by Gloria Jahoda, details the removal of thousands of Native Americans to reservations in the western United States. The trigger to this mass exodus was the passage of the Indian Removal Act in Congress in 1830. By the terms of this act, available state lands west of the Mississippi River could, at the discretion of the President, be allocated for Indian tribal resettlement. This was the background to what, in Jahoda's telling, is a compassionate look at the Native American plight.

Joseph Bruchac's *The Journal of Jesse Smoke* (2001) presents a fictionalized young adult account of the Indian removals treated in *The Trail of Tears*. The Cherokee Nation is forced to relocate from their lands in the U.S. South more than one thousand miles to Oklahoma. More than one in five Cherokees die on the journey. Jesse Smoke is a teen among the thousands of Cherokee boys involved, and in his diary entries he tells of his daily miseries during the exile, the deaths along the way, the curses of the government militia, and the total uncertainty waiting at the other end. With such accounts of the cruel inhumanity of white men's earlier attitudes toward native peoples, readers are struck by how easily Europeans seeking freedom from oppression in the New World become oppressors themselves. These accounts help modern readers recognize that righteousness is not inherent in a people but is defined by their behavior.

Native Americans are not the only Americans to have experienced ethnic cleansing. In *Everything is Illuminated* (2003), Jonathan Safran Foer writes a novel about the search for answers and understanding of how the Holocaust continues to affect families around the world. In the summer after his junior year of college, the protagonist—also named Jonathan Safran Foer—travels to the Ukraine, looking for the woman who saved his grandfather from the Nazis. The novel gives an account of genocide, sixty years and a continent removed. The effects of World War II and the treatment and extermination of Jews in Europe continues to haunt the generations that came after the war. Jonathan searches for the woman who saved his grandfather, but is also deeply affected by the fates of those who were not able to escape Nazi extermination. While on the search, one of his elderly guides thinks back to his own experience with the Nazis, which fills him still with regret and shame remembering it over half a century later:

> the guards put him in the synagogue with the rest of the Jews and everyone else was remaining outside to hear the cryingofthebabies and the cryingoftheadults and to see the black spark when the first match was lit by a young-man who could not have been any older than I was . . . it illuminated those who were not in the synagogue those who were not going to die.

The modern-day histories and fictions about the Trail of Tears and the conquest of the Incas and other native cultures remind readers that genocide and ethnic cleansing leave a mark of great loss on history. However, Foer's book differs markedly from the studies of the subjugation and extermination of the Incas or Native Americans. His character's quest is more personal, to renew contact with a blessed force in his own history.

Slavery

The forced labor of millions of Africans and, in much smaller numbers, Native Americans is as old as the American Republic. By the eighteenth century, African slavery was the mainstay of the economy in the South. Overall, the treatment of slaves, beginning with their nightmarish transatlantic passage, was devastatingly harsh: labor conditions were unsparing and families became separated, with compensation almost nonexistent. It is therefore not surprising that the institution of slavery was a chief reason for the U.S. Civil War, or that the problems of racial tension remain acute in the United States today, even after the strides of the civil rights movement.

Lillian Gish and Lars Hanson in a scene from the 1926 film The Scarlet Letter *Springer / Corbis-Bettmann*

One of the best-selling books in the United States during the nineteenth century was Harriet Beecher Stowe's *Uncle Tom's Cabin* (1852). The book was hugely influential in arousing sympathy for black slaves in America, and raising awareness of the evils of the slave system. The story is involved but affecting, and in the end makes the reader weep with sympathy for Tom, who has been a faithful slave, aiding his masters, and spreading love around him. He does this so successfully, say detractors, that "Uncle Tom," has (ironically enough) become a derogatory epithet for a black person who has sold out to the white world.

Whether that "Uncle Tom" charge is true of Stowe's protagonist is debatable. What is certain is that *Uncle Tom's Cabin* was the first major American novel to address the harsh conditions of slavery in hopes of bringing about a change. Even one of Tom's first owners, Mrs. Shelby, calls slavery "a curse to the master and a curse to the slave!"

Margaret Mitchell, the author of *Gone with the Wind* (1936), writes about slavery from a different perspective, in terms of both time and geography. While Stowe wrote of conditions a decade before the Civil War from a Northern perspective, Mitchell writes seventy years after the war from a Southern point of view. Like many Southern writers of the time, Mitchell' depicts the antebellum (pre–Civil War) South, including slavery, in a romanticized way. Though her protagonist Scarlett O'Hara lives on a large, successful Georgia plantation, the plot of the story pays little attention to the slaves that keep the plantation running. Several of the slaves and house servants are secondary players in the story, but never once do they complain about their conditions, nor is the institution of slavery depicted as anything but pleasant and satisfying. The slaves in *Gone with the Wind* appear content, happy, and more than willing to continue in a life of servitude. If Stowe presents an unyieldingly harsh perspective on slavery and slave owners in *Uncle Tom's Cabin*, Mitchell certainly whitewashes the reality of slavery in her novel.

Alex Haley's *Roots* (1973) traces his own African American family's history back to Kunta Kinte, captured as a boy by West African slave traders and taken over the dreadful Middle Passage to the Americas. The tale advances through seven generations, from slave ship to plantation to the Reconstruction, to the present day of Haley's writing, in the form of his telling the historical story to his daughter, who will then pass it on to her children. Haley's vision of this history reached a large audience through a successful television miniseries. With all the suffering, cruelty, perseverance, and triumph of the greatest dramas of Western literature, Haley brings his own family's drama to life and inspired countless Americans to discover their own roots.

Slave ships like those that brought Kunta Kinte and millions of African slaves to the Americas traversed Atlantic and Caribbean waters for hundreds of years. David Pesci's *Amistad* (1997) recounts an episode of the slave ship *Amistad* (which ironically means "friendship" in Spanish). The ship was headed from one Cuban port to another when the slaves onboard rebelled and took control of the ship. They tried to steer it east toward Africa, but the Spanish navigator managed to bring the ship close to the coast of Connecticut. The Spanish filed suit against the slaves for mutiny and murder, but the U.S. Supreme Court found that the initial transport of slaves from Africa to the Americas was illegal, so they were not legally slaves and therefore free. The Africans returned home to Africa in 1842. The case may be considered an early victory for the Abolitionist cause, which was soon to prevail entirely, and to usher in the demise of slavery in the United States. Unlike Stowe's Uncle Tom or the slaves in *Gone with the Wind* that were depicted as content or resigned to their fates, the men described in *Amistad* and the characters in *Roots* embody resistance to the horrible existence of slaves, and provide a perspective that for many years went unnoticed.

Joyce Rockwood Hudson's book *Apalachee* (2000) deals with slavery of a different kind. The novel brings together Native American tribes living in the Eastern Panhandle of Florida, sandwiched between exploitative missionaries and English soldiers with their Indian allies. The friars have brought disease and a foreign religion, Christianity, which they attempt to impose on the native population. But all that changes when the English, coming in from the colony of Carolina, invade Spanish Florida with the help of the native Creek Indians. In the clash of colonial forces, the native peoples lose regardless of which side wins the actual physical battles.

This cultural conflict is presented through the eyes of a Native American shamaness, Hinachuba Lucia, who is caught up in the turbulent cultural conflict around her. After being driven from her homeland by the English, she is captured by Creek Indians and sold into slavery in Carolina. She becomes a house slave on a turpentine plantation near Charles Town. Through this novel, readers see a different side of American slavery than the one that comes most readily to mind.

Another lesser-known aspect of American slavery was that in some instances, black people could also be the enslavers. Edward Jones's *The Known World* (2004) enters the domain of black slave ownership, and probes through that set of relationships to a fresh understanding of the damaging ripple effects of slavery. With the help of his mentor, a white man of power in the county, Henry Townsend, a black farmer, bootmaker, and former slave, is enabled to set himself up with his own plantation and his own slaves. Townsend, as a black slave owner, is not an anomaly in the county, either: "In 1855 in Manchester County, Virginia, there were thirty-four free black families . . . and eight of those free families owned slaves." At his death his widow falls into despair and can no longer maintain the plantation, and the relative calm of the farm collapses: slaves start to escape and to fight among themselves as they had not done before. White speculators hang around the Townsend plantation, looking for escaping slaves they can capture and sell. At the same time, white slaveholders from other plantations begin to sense the discontent of their slaves, who realize their own economic value. Jones's novel offers a perspective on slavery that seems more alarming than previous ones in that freed slaves—once the property of others—opted to own slaves themselves.

One hundred and fifty years separate *Uncle Tom's Cabin* from *The Known World*. In that interval, African Americans have excelled in every area of American life, and the evil of slavery is more recognized around the world. Pesci, Hudson, and especially Haley help readers see that slavery was a complex and long-lasting institution with far-reaching consequences.

Segregation

In the years following the Civil War, African Americans made great progress on the social, economic, and political fronts. They owned farms and businesses, enjoyed the right to vote, and held public office. But in 1877, with the withdrawal of federal troops from the South and the end of Reconstruction, the period of progress ended. The U.S. Supreme Court case *Plessy v. Ferguson* (1896) determined that state-mandated segregation was permissible as long as the races had "separate but equal" facilities; they may have been separate, but they were rarely equal. That state of segregated affairs was maintained until *Brown v. Board of Education* (1954) abolished segregated schools, and the Civil Rights Act (1964) outlawed discrimination in schools, restaurants, and businesses. Even still, change was slow.

In his 1945 poem, "Will V-Day Be Me-Day Too?," Langston Hughes voices the thoughts of a black soldier at the end of World War II. After fighting for his country, seeing his friends die, and making a patriotic sacrifice, the soldier wonders if, after he returns to the United States, he will still receive inferior treatment because he is black. After years of fighting and having "dropped defeat / Into the Fascists' laps," and fighting against Hitler and his plan to exterminate a group of people based on ethnicity, he fears America will cling to "Jim Crow" laws that oppress and segregate black citizens: "When I take off my uniform, / Will I be safe from harm— / Or will you do me / As the Germans did the Jews?"

C. Van Woodward's *The Strange Career of Jim Crow* (1955) speaks to the concerns raised by Hughes's returning soldier. Woodward's book argues that the era of slavery in America after the brutal Middle Passage of the Atlantic (outlawed in 1807), was more human, even more humane, than the era that followed the Reconstruction. For Woodward, that "Jim Crow" era was consciously contrived within the Southern states as a way of legalizing the underclass status of blacks by institutionalizing it through supposed "separate but equal" statutes and laws that segregated blacks from the opportunities and resources of mainstream white culture.

As tyrannical as segregation was, Mildred D. Taylor's young adult novel *Roll of Thunder, Hear My Cry!* (1976) offers a view of one family's efforts to resist it. This novel is the story of a black family in the South in the 1930s whose fortunes are more prosperous than

its neighbors, and tries to use its influence to enable other black families to boycott a white-owned supply store they depend on but that takes advantage of them. The plot unfurls into increasing crisis—the children both experience and retaliate against racist incidents, the father is shot for trying to patronize a different store, one of the children's friends is duped into a robbery by white boys and is threatened with lynching, and the family's crop is destroyed. The only resolution in the end is the children's realization of the injustice of their situation in life and the dawning will to resist.

Charles Fuller's drama, *A Soldier's Play* (1981), contains two interwoven plotlines. The primary action takes place on a fictional army base in Louisiana after World War II. The environment is deeply segregated, and in that atmosphere a black sergeant is murdered on the base. The Army, anxious to give a cloak of legality to the proceedings that will follow, calls in a young black Army lawyer to investigate the murder. The Army expects and anticipates a whitewash, but gets the opposite. The captain finds the murderer, to no one's satisfaction. None of the cliché expectations is realized, either concerning the murderer's identity or the racist atmosphere surrounding the trial.

The second plotline of the play concerns flashbacks to the relationships between the murdered black officer and the black soldiers he commanded in the field. With this thematic complexity of the play, readers become aware of the intricate social interrelations that racial tension brings upon all who are involved. These intricacies are similar to the ones in Jones's *The Known World,* where the plaguing mysteries of racism are intensified between people of the same race. *A Soldier's Play* highlights the point that, while not all whites are racist, not all blacks are friends of liberty. The truth can be confusing as well as liberating.

Walter Dean Myers's *Now is Your Time!: The Afro-American Struggle for Freedom* (1991) is a study of the lives and historical contexts of a number of highly successful African Americans. He takes the reader into the lives of a freed slave, an investigative reporter, an artist, and an inventor, thus offering a broad palette of role models for young adult readers. As someone who grew up on the streets of New York and experienced Jim Crow racism and its devastating effects on millions of black men and women, Myers has made it his mission as a writer to provide encouraging stories of hope and triumph within the black community. By offering profiles of blacks in a variety of fields and professions, Myers continues to show a way beyond the limits and oppression of racism.

Rosa Parks and James Haskins wrote *Rosa Parks: My Story* (1992), a young adult biography of Rosa Parks, the woman whose refusal to give up her bus seat to a white man in 1955 fanned the flames of the civil rights movement. This was indeed an epoch-making refusal, leading to the Montgomery Bus Boycott headed by a young Dr. Martin Luther King Jr. Surrounding these history-making events a remarkable life of dignity and determination unfolds. She details her difficult search for educational opportunity, her loving and supportive husband, and her dawning awareness that women's contributions to the civil rights movement were undervalued by their male colleagues. More than anything else, Parks and Haskins's book reminds readers that individuals absolutely have the power to change the world and make it a better place.

Conclusion

What conclusions can be drawn by looking through the lens of literature onto the wide palette of American prejudices? Perhaps that, despite the imperfections of this society, it may benefit yet from a lively chorus of critical intelligences, of writers able and willing to look the facts of prejudgment in the eye, and to help readers understand some of the pains imposed upon the people in society. With all this reflection and illumination of prejudice, marginalization, discrimination, and transcendence, the literature serves both as a mirror and as a lamp. Literature is a powerful tool for recording those reflections, capturing the illumination, and in the end, perhaps, helping humankind inch toward incremental improvements in the world.

SOURCES

Angelou, Maya, *I Know Why the Caged Bird Sings,* Bantam Books, 1993, originally published in 1969, pp. 93, 98.

Cather, Willa, *O Pioneers!*, Signet Classic, 1989, p. 50, originally published in 1913.

Cervantes, Lorna Dee, "Poem for the Young White Man who Asked Me How I, An Intelligent, Well-Read Person Could Believe in the War Between Races," in Vol. 2 of *The Heath Anthology of American Literature,* 2d ed., edited by Paul Lauter, D. C. Heath, 1994, pp. 3101–103, originally published in 1991.

Chopin, Kate, *The Awakening,* in *Case Studies in Contemporary Criticism: Kate Chopin:* The Awakening, edited by Nancy A. Walker, Bedford Books of St. Martin's Press, 1993, pp. 31, 136, originally published in 1899.

Dunn, Katherine, *Geek Love,* Vintage Books, 1983, p. 8.

Foer, Jonathan Safran, *Everything is Illuminated,* Perennial, 2002, p. 251.

Hawthorne, Nathaniel, *The Scarlet Letter,* Bantam Books, 1989, p. 233, originally published in 1850.

Houston, Jeanne Wakatsuki, and James D. Houston, *Farewell to Manzanar,* Dell Laurel-Leaf, 1995, pp. 16–17, originally published in 1973.

Hughes, Langston, "Will V-Day Be Me-Too Day?", *The Academy of American Poets,* www.poets.org (January 4, 2006).

Jones, Edward P., *The Known World,* Amistad, 2003, p. 7.

Kenan, Randall, *A Visitation of Sprits,* Vintage Books, 1989, p. 248.

Krakauer, Jon, *Under the Banner of Heaven: A Story of Violent Faith,* Anchor Books, 2003, p. 5.

Lewis, Sinclair, *The Jungle,The Berkeley Digital Library,* sunsite.berkeley.edu/Literature/Sinclair/TheJungle (January 4, 2006), originally published in 1906.

Miller, Arthur, *The Crucible,* in Vol. 2 of *The Heath Anthology of American Literature,* 2d ed., edited by Paul Lauter, D. C. Heath, 1994, pp. 1983, 1989, originally published in 1953.

Morrison, Toni, *Sula,* Plume, 1982, p. 52, originally published in 1973.

Olsen, Tillie Lerner, "I Want You Women Up North to Know," in Vol. 2 of *The Heath Anthology of American Literature,* 2d ed., edited by Paul Lauter, D. C. Heath, 1994, pp. 1396–98, originally published in 1934.

Schlosser, Eric, *Fast Food Nation: The Dark Side of the All-American Meal,* Perennial, 2001, p. 71.

Steinbeck, John, *The Grapes of Wrath,* Viking, 1939, pp. 132, 256.

Stowe, Harriet Beecher, *Uncle Tom's Cabin,* Pocket Books Enriched Classic, 2004, p. 44, originally published in 1852.

Walker, Alice, *The Color Purple,* Pocket Books, 1982, p. 77.

———, "Everyday Use," in *The Norton Anthology of African American Literature,* edited by Henry Louis Gates Jr. and Nellie Y. McKay, W. W. Norton, 1997, pp. 2391, 2392, originally published in 1973.

Race and Prejudice in British Literature

Introduction

Literature is at least as old as the fifth millennium B.C., and has accompanied mankind's most daring efforts to carve a place for culture in the slippery surface of time. The first sustained writing records are of accounting and inventorying, but it was not long before writing became the record of preference for preserving past events and giving interpretations of the world. It is no wonder that literature has made itself a faithful chronicler of human woes, as well as of human joys.

British culture is a relatively old Western culture. To read *Beowulf*, dating from the eighth century, is to reach into the recesses of Norse and Anglo-Saxon experience, and into the outposts of the Roman Empire. With the Norman invasion of the eleventh century, the tapestry of British culture grows richer. The faint hues of something like a modern English nation, with all of its diversity, begin to appear. With two millennia of historical memory, British literature encompasses great cultural development. But beyond that, the British literary tradition also acknowledges the worst kinds of human experience: cultural repression, racial prejudice, slavery, marginalization of poor and disadvantaged minorities, and indifference to legitimate sexual and spiritual needs.

Ethnicity

People's ethnicity or skin color is among the most easily observable characteristics that can

mark them for prejudice or discrimination. Large immigrant and expatriate communities in England often insulate themselves in an attempt to maintain their cultural identity and protect themselves from what they see as the threat of the dominant culture. In general, the Anglo population also keeps its distance from immigrant communities, resulting in a division between the two groups. This issue became important long ago when Britain became a world naval power, from the sixteenth through the nineteenth century; Britain became an international society but it resisted becoming a melting pot.

In *The Merchant of Venice* (1598), William Shakespeare depicts a caricature of the Jew (a stock victim in Elizabethan English writing) in the moneylender Shylock. At the same time, this figure emerges on the stage a uniquely sympathetic human character.

Bassanio, a Christian merchant of Venice, is in love with a rich woman, Portia, and needs money to travel to her. Bassanio's friend Antonio offers to get the money for his friend's trip, and borrows it from Shylock, who imposes one condition on Antonio: if he cannot repay on time, Shylock will be entitled to take a pound of his flesh. (Shylock, it must be said, has a well-founded grudge against Antonio, who has defamed him and his religion.) When news comes that the ship carrying Antonio's assets has gone down and he will not have the money to pay Shylock, the moneylender demands his pound of flesh.

Here begins the complex morality of the play. Portia, now Bassanio's wife, appears in disguise to serve as judge at Antonio's trial. She passes judgment in favor of Shylock, but adds a condition: Shylock is to take only and exactly one pound of flesh—no blood. If he exceeds or varies that amount, he will be found guilty of trying to take the life of Antonio and will have to pay with his own life. Ultimately Shylock is accused of conspiring to murder Antonio and is forced to strike a deal, including becoming Christian, in return for his life.

It is a fact that anti-Semitism was an accepted attitude not only in Renaissance England but throughout the Middle Ages, when Jews were viewed chiefly as moneylenders and takers of interest—a practice harshly criticized in the Christian New Testament. While Shylock is characterized as rapacious, remorseless, and vengeful—all Jewish stereotypes—he is, at the same time, a sympathetic character. Shakespeare's depiction, then, was groundbreaking and controversial in its time. Shylock rightly laments the wrongs done to Jews, and insists on their humanity: "If you prick us, do we not bleed? If you tickle us, do we not laugh? If you poison us, do we not die?" Readers are left, consequently, with a character portrayal that is both vulgar and beautiful, and which takes its tone from the actor in every performance. One interpretation goes so far as to make Shylock the only fully human person in the play— yet he must swallow a pound of prejudice to gain that honor.

Three hundred years after Shakespeare's Jewish caricature, Rudyard Kipling's poem "The White Man's Burden" (1899) was intended as advice to the American government, which had involved itself as a colonial power in the Philippines. (The United States had recently won and bought the Philippines from Spain in the Spanish American War.) Kipling's dehumanizing sentiments about "new-caught sullen peoples, / Half devil and half child" are not far from Elizabethan England's attitude toward Jews. Kipling's advice—that America should take responsibility for civilizing the new colony— reflects his own experience growing up in British colonial India. He claims that white people have the responsibility to rule and develop native populations in colonial areas. The use of the word "burden" in the title indicates that he believes it is a heavy responsibility that the white "civilized" world is obligated to shoulder: "Take up the White Man's burden— / Ye dare not stoop to less."

The complicated and complex result of centuries of the "white man's burden" is illustrated by Nobel Prize–winning poet Derek Walcott in "A Far Cry from Africa" (1962). The grandchild of African slaves, Walcott is from St. Lucia in the British West Indies, where he received a British education. As he contemplates the African veldt (open, uncultivated land) before him, he finds himself torn between the two parts of his heritage. On the one hand there are the Kikuyu, the dominant ethnic group in Kenya. Walcott describes them as "quick as flies," and says, in reference to their bloody practices of assaulting the colonists, that they "Batten upon the bloodstreams of the veldt, / Corpses are scattered through a paradise." On the other hand, he has no sympathy for the colonists either, and sees colonial policy as an implementation of oppression and violence. His African heritage and colonial education in the British West Indies collide within him; he speaks of being "poisoned with the blood of both," as he is kindred to the oppressed and the oppressor. He feels the prejudices of both sides. In the end he asks how he is to choose between "this Africa and the English tongue I love?" He has no place, or one too many places, to call home.

The confluence of ethnicities and races is evident in modern-day London, a melting pot of immigrant communities and multiculturalism. Zadie Smith, in *White Teeth* (2000), writes about the potential for a new social and cultural world in Britain, one where the myriad of immigrants and ethnicities that reside in the country relate and interact. Her novel concerns two families, the Joneses and the Iqbals, who are brought together across time and racial barriers. It all began in the British Army, where Bengali Muslim Samad Iqbal fought side-by-side with Archibald Jones. Iqbal and his family later move to London, where the friendship between the Iqbals and the Joneses continues. In considering this kind of example, the reader envisions the unique potential of a formerly vast empire for bringing diverse cultures together. The two families, brought together fighting for the British Empire, form a lasting friendship that integrates many of their common hopes and disappointments. In a twist on Kipling's directive, each family helps to carry the other family's burden.

In the novel *Maps for Lost Lovers* (2004), Nadeem Aslam takes readers inside the life of a self-enclosed and isolated Pakistani community within London. It is a quite different depiction of the city from that offered by Smith, where families of different ethnicities live and socialize together. Aslam's novel represents the reality that the fusion of foreigners with British culture can be difficult, even tragic.

Two lovers, Jugnu and Chanda, have disappeared from a tightly knit Pakistani community, and no one has any clues where they have gone. The unmarried couple had been living together, a shocking decision within their small community. When their bodies are discovered five months after their disappearance, Chanda's brothers are arrested for their murders. Shockwaves reverberate in the community, and

one couple especially, Jugnu's brother and sister-in-law, must work through their emotions and shock over Jugnu and Chanda's fates. The sister-in-law, Kaukab, struggles to remain true to her Islamic principles, but begins to reevaluate certain aspects, and with them her entire value system. At the same time, the tense inner struggle of the Muslim Pakistani community in London becomes vivid. Readers gain insight into the dangerous generational conflict that can haunt a community of immigrants, and into the struggle of immigrants to maintain their ethnic identity in a new land.

The distance between Kipling's work and that of Smith and Aslam may seem immeasurably far, though it is only a century. During that century, the "new-caught sullen peoples" of Kipling's "White Man's Burden" have become fellow soldiers, citizens, next-door neighbors, and entire communities within Britain, struggling to apportion a place to their own traditions in a rapidly evolving new culture.

Gender

Although Britain's history has seen a number of powerful queens ruling the country and empire, women, by and large, did not enjoy positions of power or privilege in British society until the nineteenth and twentieth centuries. Long thought to be the "weaker" sex, British women lived domestic lives as wives and mothers, possessions of their fathers or husbands. Still, the British literary tradition has seen a fair share of strong and influential women, both as characters and as writers. It is interesting to compare and contrast the magnificence and intelligence of women on the page against the harsh, oppressive reality they lived in until recent centuries.

In a time when education, employment, and social freedoms were largely off-limits to women, Mary Wollstonecraft, in her essay *A Vindication of the Rights of Woman* (1792), argues for two crucial guarantees for women: the right to freedom of thought and the right to education. This text was one of the first extensive studies of the "woman question," and though it may seem tame today, it lies at the foundation of much of the early feminism of the nineteenth century.

As an educator, Wollstonecraft grew convinced that women were harmfully subjugated to men, and that their lives were unnecessarily limited. She likens the condition of women to that of African slaves: "Is one half of the human species, like the poor African slaves, to be subject to prejudices that brutalize them?" She argues forcefully for women's education, the social equality of men and women, and for marriage to be an equal partnership; in short, Wollstonecraft advocates allowing women to "participate [in] the inherent rights of mankind." However, she was far from challenging the importance of the family. The period of her work, the Revolutionary epoch in France, guaranteed that, as an Englishwoman, she would be cautious about any call to radical social change. Society was under many threats, and no Englishwoman was about to challenge the security of the family.

In *Jane Eyre* (1847), Charlotte Brontë describes the education and growth of a young English woman through the first nineteen years of her life and the ways in which she demands equal treatment and respect. Jane has the misfortune to end up living with a cruel aunt and attending a bitterly strict boarding school. Before long, though, she finds herself on her own, and seeks a post as a governess. She meets Mr. Rochester, the master of the house where she becomes employed. She begins to fall in love with Rochester, who eventually declares the feeling mutual. As the day for their marriage approaches, however, Rochester grows increasingly arrogant; at the marriage ceremony, there is an intrusion by two men who declare that Rochester has been previously married. Jane cannot go through with the wedding, and fears that living out of wedlock with Rochester would put her in a subordinate position to him, which she cannot tolerate. After several other romantic hardships, Jane reunites with Rochester, who is by now a physically broken man, but capable of profound love. They marry, and Jane reaches a stage of mature love and happiness. It has not been easy, especially because she demands an equal partnership, refusing to live as a mistress. She is a strong woman, one not easily fitted to the prejudices of her age. Brontë, along with her sisters Anne and Emily, were among England's first female novelists. The literary environment of the time was so hostile and dismissive of women authors that, for many years, the women published under male pseudonyms: Acton (Anne), Ellis (Elizabeth), and Currer (Charlotte) Bell.

Female writers were not alone in addressing women's issues in their texts. With the essay "The Subjection of Women" (1869), John Stuart Mill adds his voice to the British feminist tradition. In an era when women were legal possessions of men, Mill's stance is revolutionary and bold: "the principle which regulates the existing social relations between the two sexes—the legal subordination of one sex to the other—is wrong in itself, and now one of the chief hindrances to human improvement." Mill echoes Wollstonecraft's sentiment that both sexes would benefit from the liberation of women. He writes that both men and society at large will benefit from the infusion of women's abilities. Mill's main concern is liberty; he argues that where one person in society is free, all the others will profit from it, for from freedom comes ingenuity, exuberance, and good planning.

The strong British tradition of libertarianism, seen clearly in the works of Wollstonecraft and Mill, was forcefully expressed throughout the nineteenth century. *Middlemarch* (1871), by George Eliot (who, like the Brontës, used a male pseudonym; her real name was Mary Ann Evans), is one of the great milestones in this development. The novel, like *Jane Eyre*, traces the search for marital happiness by an idealistic young woman, Dorothea. Where initially Dorothea imagines that "[t]he really delightful marriage must be that where your husband was a sort of father," as she matures, she comes to see that marriage is a difficult institution: "Poor Dorothea . . . had not, as we know, enjoyed her husband's superior instruction so much as she had expected." Dorothea suffers in a marriage that is not an equal partnership, as do most of the other characters in this complex novel. For Eliot, the strictures and conventions surrounding marriage make it the most difficult adjustment for women to make.

Thomas Hardy's *Tess of the D'Urbervilles* (1891) is the fictional study of a woman's search for happiness, which, defined as it is by men and marriage, is never completely within her control. Like Jane Eyre and Eliot's Dorothea, Tess is, in part, a tragic victim. Tess's father believes they might be related to a local wealthy family, and arranges for her to become their maid. She is seduced (possibly raped) by Alec, the actual heir of the family fortune, and bears an illegitimate child. Women in Tess's position—single, unmarried mothers—in the nineteenth century were subjected to intense discrimination. Tess enters the snares of lust blended with Victorian moralities, falls victim to two more ill-fated romances, murders the lover who has twice debased her, and ends up hanged for her crime. This novel, like those of Eliot and Brontë, paints the most vivid possible picture of a woman's difficult social role in Victorian England. Prejudice dogs her until she is desperate, and she reacts violently.

Until the mid-nineteenth century, women authors were largely absent from British literature. In her essay *A Room of One's Own* (1929), Virginia Woolf argues that the reason for this is because they have not had the independent wealth and the private space to create work of art. Woolf admires the strength of character that it must have taken the Brontës and Jane Austen to write unapologetically as women, for they had no template to follow and no standards to work toward. However, Woolf argues, the barriers holding back female writers must be eradicated altogether. One step toward the "equalization" that Jane Eyre, Dorothea, and Tess sought, Woolf suggests, is for women and men to be more like one another. Writers should not think of themselves as either a female writer or a male writer, for "a great mind is androgynous." She further states that one should endeavor to be labeled merely as a writer without the qualification of gender: "one must be woman-manly or man-womanly." Woolf builds on Wollstonecraft's and Mill's fight for equal access, adding her views on what must be the next step in the process.

The removal of gender barriers fostered by androgyny was the subject of Woolf's 1928 novel, *Orlando*. The novel is a fantasy biography of a sixteenth-century Elizabethan nobleman, both resembling and indirectly addressed to Woolf's female lover, Vita Sackville-West. The story evolves as the nobleman, at times male and at times female, witnesses three centuries of European history. Coming to life in the sixteenth century, Orlando passes through imperial Muscovite times, the eighteenth century in England, and the twentieth century, having a myriad of experiences. Throughout, Woolf uses Orlando's fluid gender to comment on the issue of gender identity. Her approach remains playful, but her point is insistent: gender identity is mutable and shifting. *Orlando* maintains the theme of androgyny that Woolf proposes in *A Room of One's Own*, suggesting that an intersection of male and female virtues is both more real and more ideal when describing gender. The rich character of Orlando is intended to embody such an intersection.

All of the texts covered here stress a woman's need to be free of limiting social strictures. Only Woolf, however, is able to even conceive of a more flexible society and make positive proposals of what women need once those strictures have been loosened. The struggle for gender equality saw increasing progress throughout the twentieth century.

Religion

Throughout history, religion has often served as a vehicle through which prejudices are perpetuated. In some cases, religious beliefs engender intolerance of other people's beliefs. At the same time, religions themselves can become the victims of other people's disparagement. In British literature, religion has been depicted as both a weapon and a defense.

Jonathan Swift's *A Modest Proposal* (1729), originally published as a pamphlet, purports to be a solution to the famine and overpopulation that was crippling Ireland under eighteenth-century British rule. Ireland, Swift's homeland, was overflowing with crowds of Catholic children, and the burden on the country to feed and house them was too great. Swift's "modest" and satirical proposal is to use these children for food, leather, and fine ornaments, thereby reducing the density of the Catholic population and improving the country's economic health. It is clear long before the punch line that Swift intends to satirize the brutality of England's Protestant regime in a bitter religious assault. Animosity and even violence had long been a part of the relationship between Irish Catholics and English Protestants. It is an issue that has continued into the twentieth century, largely in Northern Ireland, which remains a part of the United Kingdom.

Like Swift, Maria Edgeworth in *Harrington* (1817) indirectly critiques existing religious institutions. While Swift uses satire, Edgeworth fictionalizes a rabid anti-Semitic character in order to condemn anti-Semitism. As in Shakespeare's day, anti-Semitism was not uncommon in England in the nineteenth century. In Edgeworth's anti-Semitic protagonist, she undermines her own point about resisting religious bigotry by making her prejudiced character a fascinating one. It is a difficult tightrope Edgeworth walks, akin to satire. She maintains her balance, thanks to the validity of her critique, but the rope wavers as does her objectivity. An interesting message one might take from the story is that even those with the best intentions sometimes fall into the same behaviors and attitudes they purport to deplore.

While texts on women's rights were proliferating in nineteenth-century England and were, on the whole, entering an open and progressive dialogue, texts on Christian/Jewish religious relations sailed much more troubled waters. Sir Walter Scott's *Ivanhoe* (1819) is a historical novel reaching far back into the conflict between the Saxons and Normans in England. The novel traces the destiny of Wilfred of Ivanhoe, a noble Saxon family serving the Norman King Richard I. At the outset of the novel, Wilfred is returning from the Crusades, military ventures sanctioned by the Vatican to "reclaim" the city of Jerusalem from the Muslims. Wounded in a tournament, Wilfred is nursed back to health by Rebecca, who is Jewish. Suspected of bewitching Christian men into loving her, Rebecca is tried for sorcery and is acquitted only after the Christian man who accused her dies from the stress of the ordeal. Ivanhoe defends Rebecca, but marries a Christian.

In the essay "Agnosticism and Christianity" (1889), Thomas Henry Huxley writes that it was "inevitable that a conflict should arise between Agnosticism and Theology." Agnostics believe that it is impossible to know for certain if there is a God. According to Huxley, at the time it was thought that anyone claiming to be agnostic was merely using that label "in order to escape the unpleasantness which attaches to their proper denomination" of "infidel" (unbeliever or rejecter of religion). There is a difference, Huxley argues, and therefore sets out to defend the rights of agnostics who, in a prevailing Christian society, experience prejudicial treatment because of their religious—or lack of religious—views. Huxley, for his part, ardently insists that his quarrels are not with theology (the inquiry into the existence and nature of God), but with sectarianism (sects of religion like Catholicism and Protestantism), which claims the truth of a particular religion's avenues to God over any others.

In his book *The Crusades* (2001), David Nicolle chronicles the origins, historical development, and outcome of these Church-sanctioned raids on the Holy Land in the later Middle Ages. In the First Crusade of the late eleventh century, European warriors and mercenary soldiers sought to defend the Byzantine Empire from encroaching Muslim forces, and seize Jerusalem from Muslim control. (Jerusalem is a holy city for Christianity, Judaism, and Islam.) The Crusaders conquered Jerusalem and set up several small Crusader states. One hundred years and two crusades later, Jerusalem was back under Muslim control. Without a doubt, massive religious prejudice, on the parts of both the Crusaders and the Muslims, was instrumental in fueling these huge religious adventures. But, as accounts like Nicolle's show, many other factors entered into the Crusades besides religion. The Holy Land itself was of commercial value as an important trading location to all involved. There were also various lucrative way stations throughout Europe at which the Crusaders systematically constructed fortifications and staged plundering raids. Military ardor, in the service of Western fiefdoms—present-day nations did not yet exist—was strong, and plunder reflected the self-interest of the commanders. In addition to economic factors, local Western rulers were eager to acquire new territory to rule. All these motives were manifested as religious prejudice to justify the Crusades.

Religion has been a sensitive subject throughout the history of Britain and the world. Where human passion combines with conviction of religious belief, the possibility for discrimination, hate, and even warfare becomes quite real, as the literature presented here has shown. The British are far from alone in their experience with religious persecution, but British literature offers views from every side of the issue as awareness of different "sides" has evolved over centuries.

Sexuality

The battle over sexuality and sexual preference was bitterly engaged in Britain during the twentieth century, and is very far from settled. From novels about women who are punished for pursuing the same sexual freedom that men are free to enjoy, to tales of homosexual love affairs that have long been taboo in British society, literature about sexuality is by its nature among the most intimate and personally revealing of all literature. Disapproval of unconventional sexuality remains a socially ingrained prejudice the world over, though more and more writers feel the freedom to openly address these issues.

In *The Picture of Dorian Gray* (1891), Oscar Wilde finds an indirect way to examine the effects of moral decadence on one's life. The key figure of the story is handsome young Dorian Gray, who has his portrait painted by Basil, an outstanding painter. Dorian is so impressed with his depiction in the painting that he decides he wants to be forever young; for the privilege, he will give his very soul. Instead of Dorian growing old, the painting will do so in his place. Dorian falls in love with an actress, but once they make plans to marry she loses her acting ability. He mistreats her and she commits suicide. When he looks at his portrait, he sees that cruelty has entered into its expression.

From that point on, Dorian plunges into a sensuous lifestyle with hetero- and homosexual love affairs, excesses at the banquet table, and various other indulgences. When he later decides to reform his life, after having killed Basil, he finds that the portrait has turned bitter and cynical. He throws himself at it, slashes it, and, in the process, kills himself. All at once the painting becomes youthful and beautiful, and Dorian is a shriveled mass of decay.

The tale is both sensual and moralistic, and suggests at the end that Dorian's vices, sexual and otherwise, have turned him into an ugly monster. The tale itself is more interesting considering that Wilde, a homosexual himself, was in court on charges of sodomy four years after the publication of the novel. He was well aware of the stakes for which he wrote. He served two years in prison for "gross indecency," a punishment that today seems draconian; however, in many cultures, homosexual activity is still considered a sin against society.

The novel *Maurice,* by E. M. Forster, was published in 1971, but was written at the beginning of World War I. Because of prevailing bias against homosexuality in the early nineteenth century, Forster delayed publishing the novel, fearing it might damage his literary reputation and create legal troubles (like Wilde's sodomy trials just fifteen years earlier). The work traces an identity quest, like that in Wilde's *The Picture of Dorian Gray.* At the novel's opening, Maurice is a fourteen-year-old, privileged member of Edwardian society. He and his two sisters have

been brought up by their widowed mother in unexceptional circumstances. Forster takes the reader through the protagonist's public school life, on to Cambridge as a student, and then to Maurice's father's stockbroking firm: a standard career path for one in Maurice's social setting.

His first homosexual love affair occurs while Maurice is a student at Cambridge, but it breaks up when his lover decides to marry. His conventional career pattern makes it easy for Maurice to conceal his homosexual inclinations, and he considers fighting his homosexuality. But when he falls for the gamekeeper on the country estate of his first lover, his resolve fails. It is a happy affair, as is the conclusion of the novel, a marked turn from the outcome of Wilde's character Dorian Gray, whose "vices"—which include homosexuality—lead to his death. By giving the novel a happy twist, which Forster himself declared he did not believe in, he meant to turn the screws on the repression of British society, intolerant as it largely was in regard to homosexual relationships.

In the play *Mrs. Warren's Profession* (1893), George Bernard Shaw, a socialist with strong opinions about the evil of money, brings a cool analytical eye to bear on the profession of prostitution, framing it in terms of economics. In so doing, he believes, he introduces a new humanity to the stage, one that brings the much-maligned profession of prostitution out of the shadows and introduces the individuals behind it. As Mrs. Warren tells her daughter Vivie, "It's not work that any woman would do for pleasure, goodness knows; though to hear the pious people talk you would suppose it was a bed of roses."

Previously unaware of this income source for her mother, Vivie is at first sympathetic. She buys into the notion that her mother had to rely on charm to support herself. But she also believes the work to be in her mother's past. The situation changes for Vivie when Sir George Crofts, a man twenty-five years her elder, sets his sights on her. When she learns that the money with which he proposes to support her derives from an international brothel operation that her mother runs, Vivie is appalled and disgusted. She quarrels bitterly with her mother, especially furious about her mother's "fashionable morality." Her mother, however, believes prostitution to be preferable to poverty, and suggests it is society's fault that, as a woman, those were her only two choices: "I always wanted to be a good woman. I tried honest work; and I was slave-driven until I cursed the day I ever heard of honest work." In the end, Vivie refuses her mother's money and severs their relationship.

Irish poet Seamus Heaney's poem "Punishment" (1975) connects the pre-Roman punishment for adultery with modern images of Irish women's punishment for consorting with British soldiers in Northern Ireland. In doing so, he illustrates that nearly two thousand years of time have done little to change the consequences of a woman's sexual activity. Heaney describes the body of a young girl dug up from an English bog where it was buried in the first century. The frailty of the skeleton is touching and lonely, and the probable fate that led to this burial increases the pathos of the scene. The body was weighted by "stone, / the floating rods and boughs." The girl's head has been shaved, and eyes blindfolded "to store / the memories of love." Heaney feels sympathy for the girl and her unfair fate, but knows he would not have saved her at the time, when prejudice and hate ruled her small community: "I almost love you / but would have cast, I know, / the stones of silence." He knows this about himself because at the time he is writing, the same thing is happening to Northern Irish women who are found in the company of British soldiers. The Irish Republic Army (IRA) shaves their heads and chains them to public posts to expose them to ridicule. Heaney thinks that these women would understand the bog girl's fate, "the exact / and tribal, intimate revenge."

Sexuality remains taboo in many parts of the world and in many religions, but still finds its way into literature where the imagination is free to speculate, reflect, and interact with ideas and values that society forbids. Wilde did so in *The Picture of Dorian Gray*, using the image of the painted portrait to address issues of morality, human change, and fear of death. He invites readers to consider and perhaps rethink their prejudices toward the sensual life. He does not insist on one single conclusion, but rather opens discussion, as does Forster's *Maurice*, which asks readers: are two men in love such a bad thing? Would you deny them happiness? Shaw puts a prostitute on stage and then allows her daughter to judge her. Undoubtedly the audience will be divided; some will side with Mrs. Warren, some with Vivie, and others will go home questioning, just as Heaney does after viewing the bog girl. More than anything, these works create a dialog with their audiences, freeing not just the writers, but the readers and observers, to consider new ideas about sexuality.

Social Class and Caste

Prejudice against the impoverished is a serious issue in the United Kingdom. There is a wide divide between the "haves" and "have nots," as in many societies, but there also remain strong signs of the class system. In a stratified society where rank and position have long been highly prized, the divisions between classes—monarchy, aristocracy, tradespeople, and working class—sharpen the economic divide.

Jane Austen's *Pride and Prejudice* (1813) is a novel of manners set in drawing rooms and other social spheres of the English countryside. Elizabeth Bennet is one of five daughters in an upper-class rural family, and her mother assumes responsibility for securing husbands for each of the girls. The suitor with the most potential for Elizabeth's hand is Mr. Darcy, a Londoner who is at first inclined to disregard country folk as being below his social station. However, Elizabeth's wit and charm convince Darcy otherwise. After the expected ups and downs in a novel of this nature, Darcy proposes to Elizabeth.

Social mechanisms and expectations fill the book, and accurately reflect nineteenth-century English society, where marrying outside of one's class is not only unthinkable, but akin to social suicide. Conversations in this society are full of innuendo, and prejudgments and prejudices are only natural in a society that is based on assumptions about people and class. One does not, in Austen's work, find the grosser prejudices of a culture, as they might link to race or religion, but the finely textured interplay of inviolable opinions. Though they may seem silly in a larger historical context, they are no less hurtful or damaging for those involved.

In *Oliver Twist* (1837–1839), Charles Dickens presents a very different slice of the class society than the one in Austen's novel. He looks at an England clumsily entering the Industrial Revolution, with its child labor and terribly long work days in the factory. During this time, local government officials were responsible for caring for pauper children—children without parents or support. As more and more families moved from rural farms into cities like London for job opportunities, many found they could not afford to support their children in the expensive city. Officials were required to find workhouse employment for these youngsters, who would then be apprenticed into some skilled occupation.

Young Oliver Twist is born in a workhouse and does not know who his parents are. He is taken advantage of by the other boys in the workhouse, who one day talk him into asking for a second helping of food—a breach of etiquette that gets Oliver sent off as an undertaker's apprentice. From there, harassed and mistreated by older boys, he runs away to London. There he is welcomed by a boy criminal, the Artful Dodger, and introduced to Fagin the Jew and his circle of bold master criminals. While doing what he must to survive on the streets, Oliver is lucky enough, in the ensuing wrangle of mishaps, to meet the compassionate Nancy and a savior in the form of Mr. Brownlow. Eventually Oliver discovers his lost family and acquires the inheritance due to him, and the criminal Fagin is hanged. The tale ends as a kind of melodrama, but not before scoring many points against human unkindness and indifference toward the defenseless poor in industrialized England.

To speak of prejudice against the poor, in the case of Oliver and his ilk in Dickens's novel, would be an understatement. The British government was unable to exercise anything like the required supervision of the welfare of the people. Playwright George Bernard Shaw exposed the same situation for prostitution sixty years later in *Mrs. Warren's Profession*, which was a little-governed but lucrative fringe product of the new society.

Shaw once again examines issues of class and stigma in his play *Pygmalion* (1913), which looks at several aspects of the class system. The springboard to this story is the ancient Greek myth of Pygmalion, a young man who tires of unfaithful women and turns his back on the entire sex. To replace living women, he creates a superb sculpture of a woman and adores it as though it were a real woman. One day Venus, the goddess of beauty, catches news of this adoration, and turns the sculpture into a living woman. That is what Professor Henry Higgins, a rather authoritarian linguist, proposes to do— create a whole new woman—with the essentially raw material of Eliza Doolittle, a Cockney flower girl.

The very premise indicates Higgins's class prejudice, as he supposes that Eliza needs or wants to change, or that she would have a better life in a higher class. Cockneys are working-class inhabitants of London's East End, known for a distinct dialect that was once considered "improper" and a marker of the working class. Higgins's associates are initially skeptical about his plans, as they are unsure that he can change Eliza's class by merely changing her clothes and style of talk: "you can't take a girl up like that as if you were picking up a pebble on the beach." Undaunted, the professor teaches her standard English, then goes on to change her clothes, her style of behavior, and her overall attitude. Ultimately, tired of being the professor's project, Eliza falls in love with a young aristocrat—a member of the social level she has now attained—and marries him.

Shaw was insistent that the play was no love story. Rather it is class commentary, as was *Mrs. Warren's Profession*. Shaw was a shrewd observer of class markers, and in the character of Eliza Doolittle, proves how learnable the class posture really is. The famous Oxford accent, still a highbrow cultural factor today, is learnable, as are styles of dress and manners. Shaw's devastating commentary on the pretenses of a class system comes down to this: the only inherent difference between people of different classes is money. The prejudice that sustains the upper class is paper thin.

A point of view similar to Shaw's comes through in D. H. Lawrence's poem "How Beastly the Bourgeois Is" (1929). Though Shaw punctures the pretenses of the elite in *Pygmalion* and Lawrence focuses his attention on the bourgeois or middle class, both attack the social inequality that has its roots in prejudice against other lifestyles and classes. The bourgeois may appear to live contented, controlled lives, but Lawrence argues that the façade evaporates in the face of even the smallest difficulty: "Watch him turn into a mess, either a fool or a bully. / Just watch the display of him, confronted with a new demand on his intelligence, / a new life-demand." The bourgeois, Lawrence says, lacks the flexibility to meet human challenges face-to-face; he is rattled by an existential situation and is spiritually dead: "Touch him, and you'll find he's all gone inside / . . . / under a smooth skin and an upright appearance."

The poem and the play both poke fun at social pretensions: Higgins's on the one hand, those of the bourgeois "mushroom" on the other. At the same time, both Shaw and Lawrence are themselves expressing prejudices against what they see as excess or lifestyle error. Prejudices, in other words, are everywhere. The lesson, then, is surely not that people should claim to be entirely free of prejudices, but that they should see them for what they are, and try to correct them in light of values like sympathy, honesty, and tolerance.

The Road to Wigan Pier (1937), by George Orwell, takes a harsh look at industrial life in northern England, which, in the century following the ugly industrialization shown in Dickens's *Oliver Twist*, has seen few improvements. Yorkshire and Lancashire were, in Orwell's time, centers of the coal industry, complete with the inevitable dirt, low wages, and unsafe working conditions. In Part One of the book, Orwell details life in the industrial North. He introduces a family who runs a small shop and a cheap lodging place, along with some of their boarders, who are old and poor. Orwell ventures down into a coal mine to look at the deplorable nutrition, clothing, and wages of the workers. It is a sobering glimpse of the British underclass of the time, and is reminiscent of Upton Sinclair's similar exposé of the U.S. meatpacking industry in *The Jungle* (1906). In the second part of the book, Orwell examines the prospects for socialism in Britain and expounds his own view, which is similar to that of Shaw in *Mrs. Warren's Profession*. Orwell criticizes the middle-class ownership of the Socialist Party in Britain, given that the middle class—think of Lawrence's poem on the bourgeois—have no sense of how the underclass lives.

In *Angela's Ashes* (1996), Irish writer Frank McCourt writes of the grimness of his upbringing in a lower-class Irish neighborhood where poverty, violence, and sorrow are commonplace:

> [N]othing can compare with the Irish version [of childhood woes]: the poverty; the shiftless loquacious alcoholic father; the pious defeated mother moaning by the fire; pompous priests; bullying schoolmasters; the English and the terrible things they did to us for eight hundred long years.

Born in Brooklyn during the Great Depression, McCourt and his family moved back to his parents' homeland, Ireland, when McCourt was a young boy. While his father works and drinks and his mother tends to the smaller children, McCourt is left to fend for himself. He must lie, cheat, and occasionally steal to help his family survive, much in the way Oliver Twist is forced to scrounge for his survival. Eventually, McCourt manages to save a little money and return to America, an isolated immigrant in the country where he was born. But this is only after he has survived his youth, living regularly on the verge of starvation, surrounded by typhoid and pneumonia, and on edge with his shiftless father and hopeless mother.

The one hundred and fifty years between Oliver Twist's struggle to survive and McCourt's account of his childhood saw little improvement in the lives of the poor. Both stories depict equally pinched childhoods, surrounded by unkindness and social indifference. D. H. Lawrence, who was the fourth child of a struggling, alcoholic coal miner, had an upbringing similar to McCourt's. Such writers show that writing can prove a recourse to the pain of memory, and the power of survival cannot be underestimated, but victims of the class system, from Oliver Twist and Eliza Doolittle to Frank McCourt, are in some part of themselves deeply harmed.

Disability, Illness, and Social Stigma

It is not just the color of a person's skin, their gender, or their religion that can be subject to prejudice and discrimination. Any major differences from the status quo, including physical and mental conditions that cannot be easily explained, are potential fodder for fear. And from there prejudice is merely a step away.

Thomas de Quincey, author of *Confessions of an English Opium-Eater* (1821), was a distinguished man of letters, friend to the great Romantic poets, and a consumer of opium for over fifty years. His first and most famous book is a testimony to this extended experience. In it he explains his poverty, his writing career, his dreams, and the opium addiction that serves as a kind of vehicle for his memoir. The fact that he was able to publicly reveal and write about his addiction indicates a level of acceptance unknown to many other marginalized groups. This generosity of spirit extends to de Quincey himself, who writes unapologetically of consorting with prostitutes: "at no time of my life have I been a person to hold myself polluted by the touch or approach of any creature that wore a human shape."

The potential for de Quincey to be stigmatized was based on his drug addiction, which is often considered a disease. There are many examples in literature of illness and disease making a person an outcast, as in the poem "In the Children's Hospital" (1935) by Hugh MacDiarmid. Readers witness a scene in which war wounds and disabilities are given a patriotic whitewash. Tommy, a young soldier who has returned from World War I without legs, is put on display for visiting royalty. Though his nurse insists that he is not ready to walk on his prosthetic legs, the princess bids him to do so anyway. War veterans must frequently face the attitude that their losses are readily outweighed by the nation's gain. Another common reaction to wounded veterans is one of timidity and avoidance, as people are unsure how to acknowledge veterans' injuries and losses.

In another poem, "The Hunchback in the Park" (1941), Dylan Thomas examines children's cruelty to a person who is physically different. Unlike the opium addict or the war veteran, the hunchback of the poem's title has been born with an affliction that renders him the target of ridicule and, as a result, he is isolated. This "solitary mister" has become an oddity in the park, "Drinking water from that chained cup / That the children filled with gravel." The children mock his hunchback, and chase him around the park. The hunchback returns to his hiding place in the evening, his "kennel," but even there he is not secure. Given the nature of childhood, and its reliance on the familiar and expected, it is unlikely that children will ever overcome their suspicion of those who are different. It can only be hoped that as children grow and mature, their willingness to accept and tolerate all people grows as well.

Unlike works in which disability, illness, and social stigma are factors that serve to marginalize the individual, *Under the Eye of the Clock: The Life Story of Christopher Nolan* (1987) is a memoir that celebrates—rather than pities or hides—the life of a young man with cerebral palsy. Restrictions such as a wheelchair and dependence on others for all his daily needs have built in Nolan a huge appetite for freedom. He writes of experiences at school where the other children tease him, mock him, and ask him every sort of impertinent question about his life. He gets by with the help of the occasional sympathizer, his family, a local priest, and his

powerful will to surmount the difficulties of his disability. Eventually, new medicines help him control his spastic movements, and he is able to type. Writing and literature provide Nolan a path to freedom unlike any he has previously known. Memoirs such as Nolan's remind readers of the drive someone can have to experience the simplest pleasures in life and to be accepted by society, even when achieving those things means surmounting significant obstacles.

In *Year of Wonders: A Novel of the Plague* (2001), Geraldine Brooks writes a stark tale of the Black Plague, which has besieged a tiny and isolated British lead mining and farming village in the late seventeenth century. As the stranglehold of the disease grows, the townspeople fall ever deeper into superstition and terror. As in the story, when the plague struck it was unstoppable, killing tens of thousands in England alone. Those infected with it were quarantined, separated from their families and community, and left to their fate. In the grip of such desperate terror, people often require a scapegoat, someone or something to blame for their affliction. In Brooks's novel, witches are found to satisfy the communal bias that evil forces are responsible for the village's calamity.

The plague victims in *Year of Wonders* are treated differently because of their physical illnesses, and *Under the Eye of the Clock* illustrates how individuals with physical handicaps are often subject to prejudices. Mark Haddon's novel *The Curious Incident of the Dog in the Night-Time* (2003) shows how individuals with neurological disorders—invisible to the naked eye—can meet with misunderstandings and discrimination. Haddon places readers in the mind of an autistic narrator to create a world unfamiliar to most. At once readers recognize the difficulty society has dealing with this person. The crux of the difficulty, in the present case, is that the mind of Christopher John Francis Boone does not experience its own emotion, and therefore cannot understand the emotions of others. This inability to relate emotionally to others places Christopher on the outside of interactions with schoolmates, neighbors, and his own parents.

As is often the case with autistic children, Christopher is highly intelligent. He is mathematically skilled, memorizes things easily, and relates well to animals, but he does not understand people—he will barely permit them to touch him. Yet this difficult situation is endurable until an event changes the status quo, and the novel becomes a mystery with Christopher at the center of it. Incorrectly accused of murdering his neighbor's dog, Christopher turns to cold logic—his forte—in his effort to defend himself, but only betrays the fact that he cannot understand the way others' minds work. His dilemma is heightened when his pursuit of the mystery leads him to discover the unraveling of his own parents' marriage. At this point, readers feel all the intensity and pain of a mind misplaced in the messy human world.

Accounts of prejudices based on handicaps and illnesses have been present in British literature for hundreds of years. As in the cases of other common prejudices, such as those centering on ethnicity, class, and gender, writers have sought to give a voice to the unheard, those in society who are marginalized because of their differences. By doing so, writers erase some of the fear of the unknown associated with illness, disability, and addiction, and perhaps even inspire tolerance and acceptance.

Slavery

The forced labor of other human beings has been utilized to the advantage of conquering nations since the beginning of recorded history. England was a major player in the transatlantic slave trade, and its own citizens were subjects of slavery as well.

Aphra Behn's *Oroonoko, or The Royal Slave* (1688) is a short novel about an African prince who is captured and sold into slavery. Before his capture, Oroonoko is deeply in love with the lovely Imoinda, who is sold as a slave and taken to Suriname in South America, which was then a British possession. Oroonoko himself is tricked into going aboard a slave trader ship offshore of his native African country, where he is taken prisoner and shipped off with other slaves. He is bought by Trefry, a British gentleman who likes him perhaps because he seems so unlike what the man's prejudices led him to expect from Africans. Trefry installs Oroonoko on the same Suriname plantation where Imoinda is settled, and the two reunite, marry, and have a child. Though Oroonoko's slave experience appears almost positive in the beginning, by the middle of the story he has come to see the harsh reality of a slave's life: "They suffered not like men, who might find a glory and fortitude in

oppression, but like dogs that loved the whip and bell." Oroonoko knows that he does not want his child to be brought up in slavery. Therefore, he kills his wife and child, and leads an unsuccessful slave rebellion. In the end, he is caught and put to death by his enemies. The ugliness of prejudice and oppression is vividly portrayed in Behn's novel, which is one of the first novels written by a woman in Britain.

As novels and accounts such as *Oroonoko* began to expose the inhumanity and brutality of slavery, the abolitionist movement gathered momentum in England. William Wordsworth's poem "To Thomas Clarkson. On the Final Passing of the Bill for the Abolition of the Slave Trade" (1807) is dedicated to Thomas Clarkson, one of Britain's most vocal opponents to slavery, whose work helped pass the Abolition of the Slave Trade Act in England in 1807. In the poem, Wordsworth praises Clarkson for being resolute in fighting for the bill, and for being a staunch enemy of the slave trade. Wordsworth assures the gentleman he can rest in peace, having struggled for humanity: "And thou henceforth wilt have a good man's calm, / A great man's happiness; thy zeal shall find / Repose at length, firm friend of human kind!" Though the law celebrated in Wordsworth's poem abolished the slave trade, it did not abolish the institution of slavery itself. Slaves in British colonies were not freed until 1833.

Though British slaves were freed more than one hundred and sixty years ago, slavery has not left the collective memory of literature. In *Westward to Laughter* (1969), Colin McInnes writes a historical novel probing the slave trade and the condition of slavery in the West Indies. The narrator is a young Scotsman who finds himself forced into slavery on the Caribbean island of Laughter. He attempts to free himself, and is thereby involved in a slave uprising. The consciousness of Caribbean slavery remains vivid in Britain, where a large community of Caribbean blacks keeps the history of their ancestors' oppression alive through remembrance and acknowledgement.

As *Westward to Laughter* illustrates, accounts of slavery in British literature and history do not only include African and Caribbean people. Slavery and indentured servitude of Irish and English citizens was not uncommon throughout Britain's past; in fact, the patron saint of Ireland was a slave for a short time.

Eileen Dunlop's *The Tales of St. Patrick* (1996) creates a vivid tapestry of details in the life of St. Patrick, who brought Christianity to Ireland. Born in fifth-century Roman England, Patrick was enslaved by Irish raiders and taken to Ireland as a youth. For six years he lived in harsh bondage and cared for his master's flocks, all the while focusing on prayer and his belief in God. Pope Celestine I later gave Patrick the mandate to bring the Irish people together as one under God and to convert them to Christianity. The old days of enslavement, in which Patrick tested himself and his faith, bore fruit in a life of holiness and imagination. Dunlop's *The Tales of Saint Patrick* provides a bright patch in a very dark subject matter that seldom ended so positively.

Kate McCafferty's *Testimony of an Irish Slave Girl* (2002) also deals with the theme of white slavery. In the mid-seventeenth century, tens of thousands of Irish men, women, and children were sold as indentured slaves by their families, who were facing crushing debt. Many of these Irish slaves were transported to the Caribbean, where they worked the plantations together with black slaves from Africa. Others of these Irish victims were kidnapped from Ireland by pirates or sold to pirates by the occupying British government. In most cases, these Irish indentured servants, theoretically bound only to a specific length of servitude, were never freed, and spent the rest of their lives in slavery.

McCafferty presents the fictional story of a slave girl, Cot Daley, abducted from her home in Galway in 1651. The style of the novel mimics the first-person frankness of slave narratives written in great numbers by African slaves in the eighteenth and nineteenth centuries. Cot is sold from one plantation to another in the Caribbean, working as a house servant and in the fields. She suffers the inevitable abuse from her British slave masters and is regularly whipped and beaten. She joins a mixed-race slave revolt, marries an African fellow slave, gives birth to their children, and is thrown in prison. The color of Cot's skin does not distinguish her for preferential treatment; like all slaves, she is treated not as a human being, but as merely a possession to be bought and sold.

McCafferty's novel adds to the reader's understanding of the slave trade, specifically how race was only one factor. Dark-skinned people were the primary victims of the Atlantic slave trade, yet white slaves also existed. This is no consolation to anyone, but points to the overwhelmingly commercial interests behind slave trading. Racism against blacks grew mightily after they had been transformed into an underclass in South America, the Caribbean, and North America. The roots of slavery run deep, and remain visible today, both in the literal sense—in certain African countries like Mauritania and Sudan—and more loosely in international industries like the sex trade, where young women are shipped like commodities to overseas markets.

Conclusion

The impulse to prejudge is deeply human, a way to evaluate the multitude of experiences that humans have. After all, without some systematic preferences in life—certain friends rather than others, certain kinds of ice cream rather than others—humans would be simply conscious recording machines, empty observers of the world. But the harm in prejudice occurs, and occurs on a massive scale, when one begins to generalize broadly and to act on generalizations, either through violence, exclusion, or attitudes of disdain. Education is an aid in reducing those tendencies to generalize and act out, and exploring the literature of centuries of British experiences and voices provides invaluable perspectives with which to advance humanity's understanding and reduce its prejudgments.

SOURCES

Behn, Aphra, *Oroonoko, or The Royal Slave*, in Vol. 1 of *The Norton Anthology of English Literature*, 2d ed., edited by M. H. Abrams, W. W. Norton, 1993, p. 1901, originally published in 1688.

De Quincey, Thomas, *Confessions of an English Opium-Eater*, in Vol. 2 of *The Norton Anthology of English Literature*, 2d ed., edited by M. H. Abrams, W. W. Norton, 1993, p. 447, originally published in 1821.

Eliot, George, *Middlemarch*, Penguin Books, 2003, pp. 6, 357, originally published in 1871.

Heaney, Seamus, "Punishment," in Vol. 2 of *The Norton Anthology of English Literature*, 2d ed., edited by M. H. Abrams, W. W. Norton, 1993, pp. 2424–25, originally published in 1975.

Huxley, Thomas Henry, "Agnosticism and Christianity," in Vol. 2 of *The Norton Anthology of English Literature*, 2d ed., edited by M. H. Abrams, W. W. Norton, 1993, p. 1450, originally published in 1889.

Kipling, Rudyard, "The White Man's Burden," *The Literary Network*, www.online-literature.com/kipling/922 (January 4, 2006), originally published in 1899.

Lawrence, D. H., "How Beastly the Bourgeois Is," in Vol. 2 of *The Norton Anthology of English Literature*, 2d ed., edited by M. H. Abrams, W. W. Norton, 1993, p. 2128, originally published in 1929.

McCourt, Frank, *Angela's Ashes*, Scribner, 1996, p. 11.

Mill, John Stewart, "The Subjection of Women," in Vol. 2 of *The Norton Anthology of English Literature*, 2d ed., edited by M. H. Abrams, W. W. Norton, 1993, p. 1012, originally published in 1869.

Shakespeare, William, *The Merchant of Venice*, in *The Complete Works of Shakespeare*, The Wordsworth Poetic Library, 1994, p. 401, originally published in 1598.

Shaw, George Bernard, *Mrs. Warren's Profession*, in Vol. 2 of *The Norton Anthology of English Literature*, 2d ed., edited by M. H. Abrams, W. W. Norton, 1993, p. 1734, originally published in 1893.

———, *Pygmalion*, *Project Gutenberg*, www.gutenberg.org/dirs/etext03/pygm110.txt (January 5, 2006), originally published in 1913.

Thomas, Dylan, "The Hunchback in the Park," in Vol. 2 of *The Norton Anthology of English Literature*, 2d ed., edited by M. H. Abrams, W. W. Norton, 1993, pp. 2282–83, originally published in 1941.

Walcott, Derek, "A Far Cry from Africa," in Vol. 2 of *The Norton Anthology of English Literature*, 2d ed., edited by M. H. Abrams, W. W. Norton, 1993, pp. 2358–59, originally published in 1962.

Woolf, Virginia, *A Room of One's Own*, Harcourt Brace, 1981, pp. 98, 104, originally published in 1929.

Wollstonecraft, Mary, *A Vindication of the Rights of Woman*, in *A Vindication of the Rights of Men, A Vindication of the Rights of Woman, An Historical and Moral View of the French Revolution*, Oxford University Press, 1999, pp. 225, 261, originally published in 1792.

Wordsworth, William, "To Thomas Clarkson. On the Final Passing of the Bill for the Abolition of the Slave Trade," *EveryPoet.com*, www.everypoet.com/archive/poetry/William_Wordsworth (January 5, 2006), originally published in 1807.

Race and Prejudice in World Literature

Introduction

Suffering and loss pervade world literature, reflecting that there is no guarantee of happiness, safety, or peace for humanity. Literature opens readers' eyes to events and lifestyles they would perhaps not otherwise experience, and with those experiences they come to understand the dark things that one human being will do to another out of fear, hate, greed, and ignorance. There is a difference, however, between the darkness that is an essential part of life, and the imposed darkness that results from prejudice and discrimination.

Essential darkness includes the inescapable problems of life, and not—for these are not essential—the cruelties individuals impose on one another. Cruelty is not part of the natural course of life, but is rather the product of distorted will. Prejudice and hate are imposed darkness: the misuse of intelligence and willpower, the damage individuals do each other by racial prejudice, deprecation, and oppression of others—on the individual and the national levels. World literature reflects this kind of willful distortion in issues of ethnicity, gender, religion, sexuality, social class, disability and illness, genocide and exile, slavery, and segregation. Prejudices, as is illustrated in texts from the around the world, are evils that do not *have* to exist.

Ethnicity

The diversity found on the planet Earth is truly astounding and comprises a vast array of unique

traditions, languages, customs, and beliefs. While this diversity can be an endless opportunity for learning and tolerance, it is often the seed of mistrust, discrimination, and hatred. Ignorance frequently plays a major part in promoting racial prejudice, but the antidote to this ignorance is readily available: knowledge and understanding can go a long way toward overcoming differences based solely on the circumstances of one's birth.

Polish author Jerzy Kosinski's *The Painted Bird* (1965) is a novel about a young boy in World War II Poland separated from his parents and left to survive as well as he can on his own. He is constantly on the move from one village to another, trying not to let people know that he is Jewish, for this would be a death sentence for him. The novel illustrates the inhumanity of a war situation in which one's heritage becomes a death warrant, even for a defenseless child. The narrator begins to see himself as the Germans do. He starts to think his life is worthless, and that he deserves to die because he is nothing more than an insignificant Jew to them, not a human being. In the face of a sharply dressed German officer, he feels "like a squashed caterpillar oozing in the dust, a creature that could not harm anyone yet aroused loathing and disgust. . . . I had nothing against his killing me."

The horror of World War II's institutionalized prejudice did not teach humanity any lasting lessons. Shortly after the war, South Africa's government enacted apartheid, a harsh policy of racial segregation. A white writer who had grown up under and opposed to apartheid, J. M. Coetzee wrote *Waiting for the Barbarians* (1982), which deals with black/white relations from the context of the antiapartheid movement. The figure at the center of the novel is a magistrate, a white official working on the margins of the Empire. The Central Government begins to fear that the barbarians (read: blacks) on the far side of the Empire are planning to invade. All diligence must be taken to keep the barbarians at bay; the Magistrate is therefore asked to keep a close eye out for dissent. Government investigators arrive to interrogate two "barbarian" prisoners in the city where the Magistrate works. The Magistrate begins to realize that his heart is with the barbarians (the blacks), who are feared due largely to reputation and misunderstanding. A tragic and instructive story unfolds from that point, and with it the reader gains a fresh sense of the devastating consequences of racial stereotyping. At the time of Coetzee's writing, many whites in South Africa feared an uprising of the majority black population. Like the government in the novel, they were "waiting" for what they considered an inevitable race war. Their reaction to such a possibility illustrates how tenuous the minority ruling class felt its hold over the majority truly was.

Blacks and Jews are far from the only groups to have been victimized by racial politics and discrimination. Like the Native Americans in North, Central, and South America, native New Zealanders known as the Maori have long been victims of social neglect and scorn. Just as the Native Americans were driven from their ancestral lands and relocated, Maori were forced out of tribal lands by the colonial British in the 1860s. Without their land on which to hunt and fish, many Maori moved to urban areas where they experienced racism and marginalization.

Alan Duff's novel *Once Were Warriors* (1990) presents the Hekes, a Maori family living in a public housing slum in Auckland, New Zealand. The Heke family exemplifies the struggle of modern-day Maori, who are torn between their native culture and the Pakeha (white) world in which they are forced to live. The Hekes are denied both a cultural identity and a way of life, and as a result, the father is a violent, unemployed alcoholic, one son turns to gangs and another is in reform school, while their eldest daughter hopes to leave the Maori world behind and assimilate fully into the white world. As the title of the novel indicates, the Maori were once powerful, independent warriors, but the effects of racism have left many broken, lost, and without an identity. Their frustration and hopelessness makes them self-destructive as they move further from their sources of ancestral pride, but no closer to a new foundation. They must reclaim their heritage and self-esteem before the downward spiral can stop.

The Maori family in *Once Were Warriors* has lost its cultural identity, straddling the line between a lost way of life and a racist majority culture. Like the Maori, the Hmong people of Cambodia have long been victims of racial contempt; both groups were embedded in larger, dominant cultures. Dia Cha addresses the Hmong destiny in her memoir, *Dia's Story Cloth* (1996).

Hmong culture has long been devoted to fine needlework, and stitchers have recorded national history in their cloths. The maintenance of national history—and by extension, cultural identity—is especially important to the Hmong, as they were displaced first from China, then from Laos-Cambodia, by the effects of the Vietnam War. Needlework provides a venue for historical awareness among the Hmong in a shaky world of displacements. In her cloth, which is a series of literary quilting pieces evoking Hmong history, Cha weaves a thread of identity for a people tossed on the waters of history. Her family is equally storm-tossed: her father was killed in the escape from Laos to Thailand, and her family faced the inevitable hard times of first-generation immigration into the United States. Like the Jewish child in *The Painted Bird* and the Hekes in *Once Were Warriors*, Cha's family struggles to maintain ties to their culture once they are removed from their native land. Through her family's story cloth, Cha is determined to preserve her people from the kind of cultural memory loss inflicted on the Maori.

Indian author Jhumpa Lahiri's *The Namesake* (2003) traces the passage of the Gangulis, a Bengali couple in an arranged marriage who immigrate to the United States. After arriving in Cambridge, Massachusetts, Ashoke goes to work, while his wife, Ashima, remains restlessly nostalgic for home. A key challenge in their Americanization effort is the naming of their first child, born in the United States. The cultural clash over the occasion illustrates the Gangulis' tenuous position as new Americans who hold to Indian cultural traditions. In India, it is traditional for parents to wait, sometimes for years, to name their children: "In India parents take their time. It wasn't unusual for years to pass before the right name, the best possible name, was determined." In the meantime, the infants receive pet names, until their true names are decided upon. In America, as Ashima learns, babies are named immediately: "they learn that in America, a baby cannot be released from the hospital without a birth certificate. And that birth certificate needs a name." The baby ends up with a compromised name—Gogol—which becomes history, strength, and misunderstanding between the immigrant parents and their first-generation American child. Growing up an immigrant, a stranger in a strange land, Gogol is forever falling through

trapdoors into a past he does not share with his parents.

Prejudice can be supple. It intrudes into cultures and lives in a myriad of forms and affects both the oppressors and the oppressed in many different ways. Kosinski and Cha write from direct experience of racial annihilation, while Coetzee and Duff show the cultural damage wrought by institutionalized racism. Lahiri is concerned with the quieter transition from one culture into another, a transition greatly complicated by the racial issue. Cultural identity links people to their past, and maintaining and preserving that identity is often a key to their future.

Gender

The history of second-class citizenship for women is ancient, stemming from concepts like "property," "parentage," and "inheritance," dating back to the earliest societies. Women existed legally at the mercy of stronger, richer, more powerful men, a situation that changed little throughout the world until the twentieth century. World literature contains many depictions of women who refused this arrangement with varying degrees of discrimination, isolation, and success.

Russian author Leo Tolstoy's *Anna Karenina* (1877) presents a powerful female character who flouts societal conventions, and the backlash ultimately leads to her ruin. In the beginning, Anna is depicted as a virtuous woman, sedately married to the upper-class Alexei. The marriage is paper thin and passionless, and soon Anna falls for a dashing courtier, Vronsky. As in Flaubert's novel *Madame Bovary*, Anna falls for a man more glamorous than her stodgy husband. Anna gives birth to Vronsky's child, but her husband forgives her. Anna begs for a divorce, which Alexei refuses. She and Vronsky leave for Europe together, and they are shunned by society because they are traveling together unmarried. As revenge for embarrassing him with her conduct, Alexei refuses yet again to grant her a divorce. She begins a downward spiral of despair. Vronsky loves her, but she feels that he cannot truly love her since she cannot be his. In the end, she throws herself in front of a train and ends her life.

Anna Karenina is about the human condition and the complex, often tragic things that can occur, especially for the less powerful. Anna is too passionate not to create havoc around her as she follows her heart, and yet she is also a victim of the stereotyped roles to which she is expected to conform. Unable to conform to those roles, she takes her life rather than survive in misery. A similar fate awaits Edna, the unconventional protagonist in American Kate Chopin's *The Awakening* (1899), who cannot return to her traditional roles as wife and mother after she is "awakened" to the freedom of life on her own terms.

Henrik Ibsen's play *A Doll's House* (1879) presents another unconventional heroine, Nora. Like Anna and Edna, Nora is stifled by marital conformity. As the title of the play suggests, Nora is treated by her husband as a pretty thing, just a doll for display. However, she refuses to continue living that way, and decides to make a life on her own: "I have to stand completely alone, if I'm ever going to discover myself and the world out there." Her husband, Torvald, begs her to stay, but she refuses: "it would take the greatest miracle of all. . . . You and I both would have to transform ourselves to the point that—Oh, Torvald, I've stopped believing in miracles." Unlike Anna and Edna, Nora actually leaves and lives. However, public outcry over Nora's behavior demanded an alternate ending to the play, one in which Nora returns to her family, feeling that her children need her more than she needs her freedom. Ibsen wrote this ending, which he called a "barbaric outrage," for use if the audience demanded it.

A different analysis of women's self determination and empowerment is presented by Doris Lessing in *The Golden Notebook* (1962). The novel's protagonist, Anna, attempts to live as freely as a man, taking up the torch that Nora has lit at the end of *A Doll's House*. She has written one successful novel, and is now keeping four notebooks as part of her growing literary career. One of these notebooks carries a black cover, and in it she reflects on the African experiences of her earlier life. In a red-covered notebook she writes of her political life, especially of her disillusionment with communism, the reigning alternative ideology of her time. In her yellow notebook she writes a novel with herself as heroine. And in her blue notebook she writes a personal day-by-day diary. In the end, having fallen in love with an American writer and

feeling her own sanity teetering, she decides to bring the strands of her four notebooks together in one tale, in the golden notebook.

In the end, Anna likewise reintegrates the compartments of her life. She accepts her growing disillusionment with communism, an ideology on which Western culture wasted many hopes. She also comes to accept her emotional weaknesses and the fact that she has been sexually betrayed. She tries to relieve the tensions in her family and friendships. In short, she works to make her writing the catalyst to becoming the whole woman she wants to be.

Chi-tsai Feng, in *The Three-Inch Golden Lotus: A Novel on Foot Binding* (1985) takes readers into a world where women are evaluated (in part) by the smallness of their feet. The smaller a woman's feet, the more beautiful and valuable she is considered; thus the women in this society have the same ornamental function Nora sees for herself in *A Doll's House*. Feng's story takes place in China in the late 1800s and early 1900s. When Fragrant Lotus's grandmother decides to bind her feet, a tradition reaching back thousands of years, it opens the door to Fragrant Lotus's own rapid upward mobility, with possibilities normally unknown to a person of lower class like herself. Aristocrats begin to seek her out. Her date book is crowded. However, the Maoist era is on the horizon, a period when foot binding seems only a contemptible reminder of the dynastic past with no place in the present. Fragrant Lotus continues to uphold the virtues of the dainty foot, but finds her world no longer shares her point of view. Feng's novel catches the moment when a new type of woman is emerging, banishing the old-fashioned traditions and practices like foot binding that now seem archaic and even cruel. What was once considered beautiful is now considered a deformity.

Bharati Mukherjee addresses the theme of women in a foreign culture in her novel *Wife* (1992). This novel reflects one kind of debilitating experience of immigration, a harsher transition than that depicted by Lahiri in *The Namesake*. Dimple, a young Indian woman, and her husband move from Bengal, India, to New York City. The transition is a rough one, and Dimple grows increasingly withdrawn as she realizes how different she is from the new culture in which she finds herself. Unable to comprehend a way to survive in his alien and inhospitable environment, Dimple kills her husband and herself. *Wife* is a testament to the fact that the feelings of exclusion and hopelessness present in Ibsen's *A Doll's House* and Flaubert's *Madame Bovary* from over a century earlier remain a part of some modern Western women's lives in the twentieth century.

In many contemporary cultures, women remain the property of their husbands or fathers with no legal rights. Souad, the Palestinian author of *Burned Alive: A Victim of the Laws of Men* (2003), recounts her disfiguring and near-fatal experience in such a society. As a member of a small Palestinian community, Souad broke a cultural taboo by engaging in premarital sex, a grave dishonor to one's family that is punishable by death. Her brother-in-law, with the support of her parents, poured gasoline over her and set her on fire. Souad escaped alive but with burns over ninety percent of her body. In contrast, her male lover was not punished. Though in permanent exile today, Souad wrote of her experiences with the hope of helping to change Palestinian tradition. It is hard to imagine a more dreadful path to testimony, and yet news of similar "honor killings" continue to attract the world's attention.

It is true that women have come a long way in the last century, and yet it is only partially true. All over the world, women are still marginalized and lack the power to shape their own destinies. In many places they have gained equal legal rights, but continue to bear most of the childrearing responsibility without the same pay scales as men. In more repressive male-dominated societies, women's access to education, health care, and even free movement is dictated by the men in their lives. Control over their own bodies, voices, and lives is still a hazy dream. Works by the writers who have lived and survived, or perhaps escaped, bring the plight of women in such closed societies to the awareness of a broader world, where their struggles for progress gain support and momentum.

Religion

The history of the world is a story of conflict, and the seed of many of those conflicts has been religion. Nations have been built and battles fought to defend a belief or to spread a religion. World literature, therefore, is rich with examples of how religious prejudice and persecution has altered the world and affected its people.

Nicholas Cardinal Wiseman was the first Archbishop of Westminster, and one of the dominant leaders of Roman Catholicism in England in the nineteenth century. In that highly visible role he wrote *Fabiola, or the Church of the Catacombs* (1886), a collection of vignettes of life in the early days of the Church in ancient, pagan Rome. This was the city of the Coliseum, where Christians would sometimes be sent to fight wild animals, and where the crucifixions of early Christians were common events. The work takes the reader inside the worlds of heroes of the faith, like the young virgin Saint Agnes or the idealized soldier, Saint Sebastian, and invites the reader to experience the drama of those sacrifices that proved decisive in the survival of the Church. Cardinal Wiseman's book shows the strength and resolve necessary to stand in the face of persecution and prejudice, even when it might cost one's life.

European Jews in the 1930s and 1940s faced a similar vicious persecution, though on a larger scale. Religious prejudice and hate turned to genocide and mass murder in World War II, when six million Jews died in Nazi extermination camps. Anne Frank's *The Diary of a Young Girl* (1947) recounts the terror, monotony, and anxiety experienced by a Jewish family hiding from the Nazis during the German occupation of Amsterdam. The atmosphere of threat is appalling. Holed up like a ghost in the attic, Anne writes of her experience in a diary that went on to make her one of the most moving witnesses to the brutality of war. As news of what is happening to Jews across Europe reaches the attic, Anne reflects on the fate of her people: "I get frightened myself when I think of close friends who are now at the mercy of the cruelest monsters ever to stalk the earth. And all because they're Jews." The Franks themselves were ultimately discovered, and all but Anne's father died in concentration camps. What is perhaps most moving, knowing the outcome, is Anne's tenacious belief throughout her ordeal in hiding: "that people are truly good at heart." A victim of the most malevolent persecution of a religious group, Anne persists in upholding the highest ideals of her faith.

Religions, like nation-states, carry out their own imperial takeovers. Cardinal Wiseman depicted early Christianity when it was fighting for its survival. Over fifteen hundred years later, Christianity was no longer a threatened religion, and in fact was asserting itself across the globe. Nigerian novelist Chinua Achebe, in *Things Fall Apart* (1958), explores the breakup of traditional African culture and religion in the face of invading Christianity and its missionaries. The tensions emerging from within organized religion are central to this classic.

This brief, complex tale highlights a protagonist, Okonkwo, who is a figure of power in his Ibo village. Because of his eminence, he is chosen to be the guardian of a young boy, Ikemefuna, who is taken prisoner by the tribe. Okonkwo assumes this responsibility, but when the elders decree that the boy must die in order to satisfy local gods, Okonkwo insists on taking part in the murder. That act is the beginning of Okonkwo's downfall. He and his family are sent into exile for seven years. While he is away, Christian missionaries convert many members of the tribe—including Okonkwo's oldest son, Nwoye—and whites introduce a new kind of government into the village. When Okonkwo and some of his native loyalists prepare a rebellion to throw out the Christians and their institutions, he learns that the village as a whole no longer supports him. He blames Christianity for the divided village: "You do not know what it is to speak with one voice. And what is the result? An abominable religion has settled among you." It all ends badly for Okonkwo, who hangs himself, and the key to the collapse is the tension between religions, and the gentle mercilessness of Christianity toward the ancient ways. No religion can afford to lack a quiet weaponry, and it is no surprise that prejudice is among those weapons.

In *The Name of the Rose* (1983), Italian author Umberto Eco looks closely at the internal struggles for power and influence that were at the heart of the medieval Catholic Church. In Eco's account, prejudice and conflict are as rampant within the Church as without.

This historical novel opens in 1327 with a visit by William of Baskerville to an isolated Benedictine Monastery in northern Italy. William is on assignment to inspect the monastery, which has a library that is the richest in Christendom. The Abbot of the Monastery strictly controls access to the library holdings. During William's visit, conspiracies and murders take place within the monastery, indicating how precious, and incendiary, the materials contained in this priceless library are. The library itself is an object of interest throughout the learned world of the time. Many turbulent cultural currents cross throughout the tale, including the conflict of the Papacy with the Franciscan order over the issue of voluntary poverty and the struggle of the Papacy with the Holy Roman Emperor. Though one might expect the Church to be above internal prejudices and infighting, its history shows otherwise, for whoever holds the knowledge holds the power.

The novel *Shame* (1997), by Tasalina Nasarina, takes the reader outside the Judeo-Christian orbit of the West and explores the violent religious repercussions of an event that took place in India in 1992. After the Partition in 1948 which created the separate nations of India and Pakistan, large numbers of Hindus relocated to India. The relationship between majority Hindus and minority Muslims has long been tense and antagonistic. In 1992, Hindu extremists destroyed a sacred Muslim mosque in Ayodhya, India. The outcry this provoked was harsh, but the Muslim retaliation was equally— Nasarina would say much more—violent. *Shame* traces the effects of this Muslim retaliation on a Hindu family living in Bangladesh.

The novel's narrator is the young son of the Hindu family, cynical and hard to discipline. He tells of the brutalities of the Muslim counterattack, including the abduction and probable death of his sister, Maya. The heavy toll of religious revenge cycles that go back to ancient times plays itself out, and Nasarina's novel shows the individual impact of these sweeping cultural and religious clashes. It did not stop with the events recounted in the novel, for the Muslim authority pronounced a *fatwa* against Nasarina, making it a holy Muslim duty to kill this writer. The text illustrates the dreadful consequences of one religion battering another, both in print and in life.

When religions clash, both factions invariably believe that they are on the side of "right." Because each faction is convinced of their righteousness and moral superiority, these conflicts rarely end with any surrender, concession, or understanding. Whether the fight is within sects of the same faith, between new ways and old, or between ancient enemies, the repercussions are shattering. History is written by the victors, but in the case of conflict over religion, there is always another chapter still to be written.

Sexuality

Prejudice in matters of sexual choice takes very different forms worldwide. While the Western industrialized world is currently debating issues such as gay lifestyle and even gay marriage, these options are taboo for many more conservative parts of the world, such as Africa, the Middle East, and parts of Asia.

Thomas Mann's *Death in Venice* (1929) presents the issue of sexuality as an obsession taking control of its victim, in this case a distinguished German scholar and writer. Gustave von Aschenbach has reached a point in his self-disciplined scholarly life where he needs a break by the sea. He gravitates to Venice, a city he has always longed to revisit. He establishes himself in a seaside hotel, and from his window grows increasingly obsessed with a handsome, androgynous teenaged boy who passes regularly along the beach. For von Aschenbach, the boy is both an erotic image and the image of a beautiful Greek god. At this point news comes that Venice is under siege from cholera. Instead of escaping, von Aschenbach elects to remain in Venice, absorbed by the miasmic beauty of this stranger. He dies for his obsession, infected by the plague. Though today Mann's character von Aschenbach would be considered a pedophile preying on an innocent child, Mann's intent while writing the novella was neither predatory nor strictly sexual. He wished to create a story about a man's longing that could not be admitted or openly shared, and therefore taken to a grave hastened by its secrecy.

Japanese writer Yukio Mishima's *Confessions of a Mask* (1949) shares with Mann's story a fascination with homosexuality and a sensitivity to the surrounding presence of death. Both stories appeal for sensitivity to the gay consciousness, but in its most inward and private dimensions, Mishima's book is an autobiographical novel. As a young man he is preoccupied with his own body, and there is a strong death component in this self-desire. Mishima is drawn to images of such sufferers as Saint Sebastian, the slim Christian martyr perforated by arrows. At the same time, the young Mishima likes the idea of being attracted to the beauty of his best friend's sister, for heterosexual attraction is what society expects. The girl becomes a woman, then marries and returns again to the city where Mishima lives. The two meet, and when she asks if he has had sex yet, Mishima grows hugely aware of his impotence. He falls victim to the supposition that a man should be able to make love to a woman. Mishima's novel shows how social prejudice against homosexuals can affect their identity and self-worth. Young Mishima lives in a world of "should haves" that cripple his personal growth.

Argentine Manuel Puig's *Kiss of the Spider Woman* (1976) is also about homosexuality, but with a liberating, rather than a masochistic, twist. The setting of the novel, a prison cell, provides a perfect context for acting out the perils and potentials of a human relationship. The world outside is a harsh, judgmental police state, but the imagination has free range inside the four walls of the cell. The older prisoner, Molina, enjoys a mental game that allows for his inner freedom, retelling the plots of his favorite movies. Molina identifies with the female protagonists of the movies he recounts, and he begins by telling his cellmate, Valentin, of a film in which a woman turns into a panther whenever she kisses a man. Molina considers himself a dangerous homosexual lover, like the panther woman, and Valentin, an at-first dour political ideologist, falls for his fellow prisoner's mind. The homoerotic relationship that forms during this six-month incarceration is as liberating to the men as getting out of jail could be: "It's as if we're on some desert island. . . . Because, well, outside of this cell we may have our oppressors, yes, but not inside."

Social Class and Caste

Prejudice against (or indifference toward) the impoverished is rapidly becoming a global form of oppression. The disadvantages of global poverty can be seen with ever greater clarity—in housing, in medical care, in access to education, and frequently in issues of simple nutrition—as the gap between the rich and the utterly destitute widens throughout the world. There have always been richer and poorer, but since urbanization and industrialization became linchpins of the economy in the nineteenth century, writers have focused on the struggles of surviving in the modern world.

In his vast series of novels, *La Comédie Humaine* (*The Human Comedy*), the French author Honoré de Balzac depicts many aspects of the new middle-class industrial life of France in the period following the Napoleonic Wars. That life was marked by the development of unbridled capital acquisition, with laborers frequently reduced to pawn status. In perhaps the most famous of his novels, *Le Père Goriot* (*Father Goriot*) (1834), Balzac probes deeply into the issues of wealth and poverty. Much of the action of the novel emanates from a Parisian boardinghouse, at which Goriot, a formerly wealthy merchant who has spent all his money on his two ungrateful daughters, resides. A fellow boarder is Rastignac, a student from the country who is trying to make a life in Paris and ambitiously hoping to link up with a wealthy wife to make his fortune.

Rastignac insinuates himself into the good graces of Goriot's daughter, Delphine. At the end of the novel, after twists and turns in Paris society and underworld, Rastignac is Delphine's lover and the chief heir to Goriot's fortune. Rastignac is on the upward ladder that will lead him to an important post as Cabinet Minister. A brutal climate of early capitalism pervades this world, in which money and power are everything, and love is merely a means to an end.

In *The Communist Manifesto* (1848), Karl Marx and Friedrich Engels address the questions of rampant capitalist ambition seen in Balzac's novels, where the drive for money and power corrupts society. The *Manifesto* begins by tracing the sequence of man's historical development as successive stages of polar opposites: free man and slave, upper class and lower class, lord of the manor and serf, then capitalist oppressor and oppressed. For Marx and Engels, the wealth accumulated by the masters of capitalism has been essentially stolen from the workers, who produced that wealth. The inevitable course of history, the *Manifesto* suggests, will lead to the workers taking violent control of the means of production, regaining their own rightful profits, destroying the idea of the nation-state, and establishing something like a worker's paradise. Marx and Engels's social and economic thoughts in the *The Communist Manifesto* would go on to inspire revolutions worldwide, from Lenin in Russia to Mao Zedong in China to Che Guevara in South America.

Balzac, Marx, and Engels share an analytical eye for the structure of society and the conflicts that emerge from the focus on amassing and investing capital. The same withering look at a ruthless economic order is evident in Victor Hugo's novel, *Les Misérables* (1862). This melodramatic but deeply touching novel is set in France after the fall of Napoleon. The protagonist, Jean Valjean, spent his early adulthood jailed for stealing a loaf of bread for his family, which was "always on the verge of destitution." Upon finally being released from jail, he crosses paths with a cleric, who sets him on the straight and narrow.

Valjean becomes mayor of a small town, but is hounded by a police inspector, Javert, who is determined to arrest him. Valjean escapes the officer, and in the meantime finds himself the protector of an orphan girl, Cossette. He takes her in and raises her in Paris, where she falls in love with Marius, a young revolutionary. It is a time of great unrest in Paris, as the poor are preparing to revolt against the rich ruling class in the manner predicted in *The Communist Manifesto*. A poor woman points out the hypocrisy of their rulers:

> I'd like to strangle the lot of 'em, the rich, the so-called charitable rich, living in clover and going to Mass, and dishing out sops and pious sentiments. They think they're our lords and masters and they come and patronize us and bring us their cast-off clothes and a few scraps to eat.

The whole theme is perhaps overdrawn, but the novel is emotionally rich and full of insights into the kind of cutthroat social developments Balzac depicts in his work. Hugo has a warmer heart than Balzac and allows love some room in the shaping of human affairs. Both writers bring indifference to the poor into sharp relief, and help shape the public debate about their plight by using people's names, human faces, and moving stories to illustrate their societal dilemma.

Gustave Flaubert, author of *Madame Bovary* (1857), was sensitive to the social issues plaguing nineteenth-century France. In his story "A Simple Soul" (1877), Flaubert writes a simple tale of a quiet life in the French countryside, not in the vast economic battleground of Paris. This short story portrays Félicité a simple and quiet maid so "economical" that "when she ate she would gather up crumbs with the tip of her finger, so that nothing should be wasted of the loaf of bread." Félicité is not a victim of social prejudice as such, but of the quiet sad integrity of the little life, the life without interesting horizons because there is no money or time to achieve them.

The explicit injustice of a caste society could not be more sharply highlighted than in Mulk Raj Anand's *Untouchable* (1935). The Indian caste system has historically been a rigid social stratification in which it was nearly impossible to improve one's lot. Until recent decades there were five recognized castes, with several thousand informal subcastes. At the bottom level of the caste system (which is much less enforced in contemporary times) are the untouchables. In this novel, one of India's most respected novelists illustrates the plight of the untouchables. The protagonist, Bakha, is fixed in an inherited occupation, latrine cleaner, from which he can only escape in his mind. This handsome, gifted untouchable—locked into his position in caste society—becomes Anand's vehicle for assessing many tempting formulas of reform. Civil disobedience, Marxist, and Muslim ideologies all offer themselves as imagined escapes, and Bakha's thoughts travel down all of those paths. Anand has, however, been criticized for the very dilemma he sets before the reader: for Bakha to be a convincing and realistic untouchable, he can hardly be the philosopher Anand makes him, as he would have had no education. Yet, without that philosophical dimension, the character of Bakha is simply a *thing* engaged in eternal base toil rather than a human. Prejudice is much too gentle a term for the vise that pins the character of Bakha in place.

In *A Bend in the River* (1979), V. S. Naipaul moves the social class critique to Africa, early in postcolonial times in Zaire. Naipaul's principal character, Salim, is a trader whose post is situated at a bend in the vast river, around which lays the still-untamed African jungle. It is his business to sell assorted supplies such as household wares and school materials to natives from the interior who travel by river to trade. He is a Muslim Indian, part of the trader community of long standing in eastern Africa. His ethnicity makes him an outsider in Africa, where Indian and Asian traders are subject to animosity and even violence as they grow successful. East Africa is itself a poor region that was abandoned by Europeans when colonialism collapsed. Naipaul is liberal with his criticisms, both of the Africans for having let their country deteriorate after the departure of the Europeans, and for the Europeans, who left things in shambles. In a partly abandoned village on the lake, the clash of cultures, mistrust, and anxiety are evident signs of Africa's colonial past:

> The Africans who had abandoned the town and gone back to their villages were better off; they at least had gone back to their traditional life and were more or less self-sufficient. But for the rest of us in the town . . . it was a stripped, Robinson Crusoe kind of existence. . . . if we had worn skins and lived in thatched huts it wouldn't have been too inappropriate.

What in Balzac is commentary on the first boisterous exuberance of modern wealth making is by Naipaul's time part of the winding down of late capitalism and the negligence of colonialism. All these writers, though, provide a means through which those not usually faced with the dilemma social rank can be made to consider the issue and see its sufferers as fellow human beings. It is comforting to believe that status is earned, particularly among those who enjoy some status; the literature of social prejudice helps the "haves" see the "have nots" less as architects of their own fates and more as victims of circumstance.

Disability, Illness, and Social Stigma

World literature is full of characters that are "misfits" to society, either in their actions, appearance, health, or mental states. For one reason or another, either from fear, ignorance, or indifference, characters of this sort have often been subject to ridicule and prejudice in the real world. In literature, though, they are given a chance to prove themselves as individuals worthy of compassion and love. With this literary understanding comes the opportunity for real-world understanding, as well as greater tolerance.

Victor Hugo's *The Hunchback of Notre Dame* (1831) transports the reader into the French social critique of the new middle class and capitalist culture of the nineteenth century. In it, Hugo reaches back to fifteenth-century Paris for the setting in which to make his nineteenth-century social points. The central figure of this novel is Quasimodo, the bell ringer of the great cathedral of Notre Dame, in the center of medieval Paris. Because he is born with a physical deformity, his parents abandon him, but he is taken in by the archdeacon of Notre Dame. The archdeacon gives him the job of ringing the church's bells, which deafens him. Quasimodo has a sweet, gentle nature, but is routinely ridiculed and ostracized because of his appearance. When Esmeralda, a beautiful young street woman, is condemned as a witch, Quasimodo hides her in the bell tower of the cathedral to protect her from the vigilantes in the city. For a moment at least, Quasimodo and Esmeralda are connected by their shared experience of being treated as unacceptable outsiders by the harsh Paris crowds. Supposing that Quasimodo's deformity indicates a foulness of soul, the crowd assumes that he is assaulting Esmeralda, rather than protecting her. In an effort to free (and capture) the woman, the attacking citizens bring on tragic results for both Quasimodo and Esmeralda. Quasimodo's unusually reflective and sensitive soul is a poignant feature of the text, showing the dignity of a person that society might discriminate against in any century. Hugo's novel gives a clear image of the way prejudice deforms its objects.

Like *The Hunchback of Notre Dame*, Fyodor Dostoevsky's *The Idiot* (1868) deals with the paradox of a beautiful soul who is unrecognized as such because he is somehow disabled. Prince Myshkin is a pure soul, distinctive for his simple honesty, and therefore suspect in a society that runs according to subtly embedded rules and can stand only a limited amount of directness. From the beginning, when he returns from the sanatorium where he has been sent for treatment of his epilepsy, readers know that Myshkin is going to capsize in the sea of social conflicts awaiting him:

> The readiness of the fair-haired young man in the cloak to answer all his opposite neighbour's questions was surprising. He seemed to have no suspicion of any impertinence or inappropriateness in the fact of such questions being put to him.

Myshkin is an outcast who becomes the subject of scorn because he embraces the truth. As he idealistically plans toward marriage, he discovers that he is embroiled with a scheming circle of competing contenders. Myshkin is indifferent to social norms, and because of that, society takes him for an idiot. With this novel, Dostoevsky holds a mirror to a society that had made truth a social blunder, and the honest men victims of discrimination.

Another innocent is scrutinized by society in Colombian author Gabriel García Márquez's short story, "A Very Old Man with Enormous Wings" (1968). The story illustrates how people who are different can automatically be subject to suspicion and curiosity. As in *The Hunchback of Notre Dame*, the reader wonders at humanity's

lack of compassion, and its willingness to so quickly reject what is not understood.

One rainy season, Pelayo finds an old man with weather-beaten wings mired in the mud on the beach. Pelayo brings the man back to his house and places him in the chicken coop in his yard. The villagers gather to see this curiosity, formulating many theories about him: he could be an angel, a supernatural being, or a castaway sailor. Though they cannot agree on what he is, there is a mutual agreement that he is definitely not like them. Pelayo and his wife begin to charge people for the opportunity to look at the old man, as he if he were a creature in the zoo. So many people come to stare at the old man that "they had to call in troops with fixed bayonets to disperse the mob that was about to knock the house down." Before long, Pelayo and his family have enough money to build a mansion and their child regains his health after a long illness. The novelty of the old man begins to wear off, and people stop coming to see him when it appears that he is not an angel after all, but merely a human with wings. People lose interest in the man, and he becomes deliriously ill. Rather than have compassion or sympathy for the man's condition, Pelayo and his wife come to regard him as a nuisance: "it [is] awful living in that hell full of angels," his wife shouts. The old man eventually recovers his health, grows new wings, and flies away. The story is a parable about people's readiness to strip the humanity from those who are different, and how, in doing so, they miss out on those people's magic.

Korney Chukovsky's works demonstrate the power of disparaged minorities and individuals to proudly rise up and find themselves. In Chukovsky's memoir, *The Silver Crest: My Russian Boyhood* (1976), he recounts how he was able to overcome the social stigma of his childhood and family in order to control his own future. Chukovsky was born to an unwed mother, a serious social taboo in the Stalinist Soviet Union of the 1940s and 1950s. As an illegitimate child, he is subjected to scorn and dismissed from school; no longer able to wear the silver school crest on his cap, he loses his identity and friends. Whereas once he had belonged, the loss of his silver crest means he is a social outsider with limited opportunities open to him. As an adult he becomes a painter, and is again scorned by society, since he is homeless at the time, so people assume that he lacks respectability. As he matures, however, he gradually establishes himself as a distinguished man of letters. He refuses to be kept down or limited because of a social more that robs people of their dignity and denies them all opportunity. Chukovsky's account of self-determinism is a welcome contrast to Quasimodo's bell tower or the old man's chicken coop, limited spaces that stigmatized people are forced to inhabit because society's prejudices force them into confinement.

While the social stigma associated with birth is abating in many countries, the stigma surrounding HIV and AIDS continues to be strong and deadly in some areas of the world. In some cultures, the disease is associated with immorality and sin, and infected persons sometimes keep the disease a secret for fear of the social repercussions. Chu T'ien-wen's novel, *Notes of a Desolate Man* (1999), is a sophisticated reflection on gay love and gay survival in the face of the AIDS crisis in China. As the story opens, the narrator, Xiao Shao, has lost a childhood friend to AIDS. Depressed over his friend's demise while simultaneously shocked that he is still disease-free himself, Xiao thinks back on his lovers and friends. He reflects on mortality and risk, and on the chances his friend Ah Yao had been taking—not only in his sexual life but as a political radical as well. From the plateau of these reflections, and in the course of an urbane and scholarly narration, Xiao goes on to think of the nature of romantic love, of writing, and of a younger generation preoccupied with video games while Taiwan teeters on the brink of extinction. The life in the narrator's mind provides him with a brilliant if shaky haven from the part of the world that kills directly. A striking parallel to Xiao's feeling of isolation in the face of AIDS is the setting of Taiwan, an island off the coast of China that has long fought to be independent of Chinese rule. The Chinese government, however, refuses to allow Taiwan to break away and become an independent nation. Just as Taiwan is caught between two opposing forces, T'ien-wen depicts a character straddling a similar divide in his own life.

Alan Brennert's *Moloka'i* (2003) pursues the theme of personal marginalization by society, and of the social prejudice that makes that marginalization particularly painful. Throughout history, the disease of leprosy has made outcasts of its sufferers. Leprosy is an infectious, disfiguring skin disease, and for centuries, sufferers were quarantined to leper colonies and kept apart from the rest of society. In this respect, leprosy has long been a disease that causes social nonexistence before physical death. In the late nineteenth century, a leper colony existed on the remote Hawaiian island of Moloka'i. Brennert's novel follows the pain and isolation of a young girl sent to Moloka'i by her family. She must leave everything familiar and beloved behind her, and reach inside herself for the courage that brings human beings through to hard-won triumph despite being pushed outside of society.

Victims of prejudice suffer from the discrimination they face, whether it is because of physical, mental, or social conditions. Writing from around the world presents characters who face these prejudices and show readers just how damaging they can be. Literature shows those who remain misunderstood, such as the old man with wings and Quasimodo; those who refuse to bow to it, like Myshkin in *The Idiot*; and those who rise above it, like Chukovsky and the leper girl in *Moloka'i*.

Ethnic Cleansing, Genocide, and Exile

When prejudice and discrimination are extended to national and international levels, or where entire races, cultures, or ethnicities are involved, there looms the threat of ethnic cleansing and genocide. These horrific conditions can lead to forced exile or relocation, and the loss of a people's homeland and identity. The twentieth century has seen its share of such large-scale exile and genocide—Armenia, Nazi Germany, Bosnia, Cambodia, Rwanda—but the practice of exterminating whole ethnic or religious groups is centuries old.

The book of *Exodus* (fourteenth century B.C.) in the Bible recounts the departure of the Jews from Egypt, where they had been living for four hundred years. As the Jewish population rises in Egypt, the Pharaoh decides to enslave them in order to preserve his balance of power: "the Israelites have become much too numerous for us. Come, we must deal shrewdly with them or they will become even more numerous" (New International Version). The Pharaoh fears the rising population because "if war breaks out, [the Jews] will join our enemies, fight against us and leave the country." From that point on, by the Pharaoh's decree, the Jews are systematically harassed and singled out for murder and slave labor by the Egyptians. The plan does not work, however, and the Jewish population continues to grow. In response, the Pharaoh institutes an attempt at genocide: all male Jewish babies are to be thrown into the Nile River to prevent future generations from reproducing. However, one man, Moses, manages to escape the fate of male Jews, and rises up to become the chosen leader of the Israelites.

After enduring many excruciating hardships, the Jews are led by Moses out of the land of bondage into the desert of Israel. Many miracles herald this flight out of Egypt, in the course of which, for instance, the Red Sea is parted to let the Jews cross. Water and food are miraculously provided in the desert. Moses is met by God on Mount Sinai, and receives the Ten Commandments. A noble future lies ahead for these emigrants, who eventually settle in the land God promised to them in Israel. There is no minimizing their sufferings, however, which were prototypes of those sufferings nature and oppression inflict on refugees to this day.

Franz Werfel's novel *The Forty Days of Musa Dagh* (1934) is set during the genocide of the Armenians by the Turks in 1915. The massacre in question was eclipsed by World War I, which diverted the world's attention from the Turkish government's systematic move to extirpate their neighbors and bitter ethnic rivals. In the novel, Gabriel Bagradian, an Armenian by birth and an officer in the Turkish army, leads five thousand Armenian villagers to the top of "the mountain of Moses," Musa Dagh, to fend off the attacking Turkish army. The resistance effort is far too small to repel the vastly superior numbers of the Turks, but the courage of their stand makes these Armenians models of inspiration to their people. Werfel's book was one of the first published accounts of the Armenian genocide and forced exile in Turkey, and though it is fictionalized, it is considered an important piece of history. The book was banned by the Nazis as a threat to the people of Germany. Through his novel, Werfel hoped to ensure that the systematic destruction of a group of people never goes unnoticed or unacted upon again. As the twentieth century unfolded, however, Werfel's vision went woefully unfulfilled.

Less than a decade after Werfel's account of the Armenian genocide, one of the worst genocides in human history was underway in Europe. Elie Wiesel's memoir *Night* (1960) opens in 1941, in Wiesel's village of Sighet, in Transylvania.

Elie is a happy and studious young man who, along with his family, is unaware of the impending perils that they, and all European Jews, will face. It is not until 1944, when the German army occupies Sighet and the first Jewish deportations begin, that the brutal truth becomes plain to everybody. The villagers are transported to Auschwitz, the most notorious of the Nazi concentration camps. Wiesel, his sister, and his parents are placed in a crowded cattle car and transported to Auschwitz, where Wiesel's mother and sister are separated from him. He never sees them again.

When he and his father arrive at the camp, they are faced with scenes from hell—babies being burned to death; starving, emaciated men; and the stink of human flesh being incinerated. The men in the camp are under no illusion about their fate: "Don't let yourself be fooled with illusions," a fellow prisoner tells Wiesel, "Hitler has made it very clear that he will annihilate all the Jews before the clock strikes twelve, before they can hear the last stroke." By the time the Russians liberate the camp, in April 1945, Wiesel is one of the few survivors of the original group from Sighet. After being released, he wakes, looks in a mirror, and sees a living corpse stare back at him. Wiesel's memoir is often credited with bringing to the world's attention the holocaust that killed six million Jews. Like Werfel's novel, however, Wiesel's account of genocidal horror was not the last such event that would wind up chronicled in print.

In *The Rape of Nanking* (1997), Iris Chang shines the spotlight on another relatively ignored episode of genocide. The Second Sino-Japanese War (1937–1945) was a binational struggle for power between the Chinese and the Japanese. The Chinese Nationalist government, under Chiang-kai Shek, seemed a threat to Japanese interests on the Chinese mainland, and the two sides fought heavily for dominance. The event chronicled by Chang in *The Rape of Nanking* refers to the atrocities carried out by invading Japanese forces, in December 1937, in the revered ancient Chinese city of Nanking.

In a two-month period, some three hundred fifty thousand Chinese soldiers and civilians were slaughtered with the permission (and Chang suggests, encouragement) of the Japanese government. This book gives a chilling account of the kind of smaller-scale brutality triggered by ethnic cleansing impulses, throughout history and around the globe. Chang sees this terrible episode in a large context, as part of man's inhumanity to man, a manifestation of the damage human beings voluntarily impose on one another. Like Werfel and Wiesel, Chang uses literature as a mode of remembrance, in hopes that history will not repeat itself with future bloody genocides.

It is not yet to be, however, for in nearby India and Sri Lanka, centuries of religious, social, and cultural violence continue their cycle even today. That there is no easy end to the pockets of local violence in the world is evident from the civil war in Sri Lanka between the Tamils and the Sinhala, the two ethnic groups left to battle over the local power that became available when the British withdrew from their colonialist enterprise. This civil war, which pits racially opposed groups against one another—like the Biafran War in Nigeria or the Hutu/Tutsi massacre in Rwanda—began in 1983, and is still ongoing. This struggle is at the heart of Sri Lankan–born Michael Ondaatje's novel *Anil's Ghost* (2000).

The main character, Anil Tissera, is a Sri Lankan who leaves her country when she is eighteen. She becomes a forensic anthropologist, and works in the killing fields of Guatemala exhuming victims of that country's civil war. She returns to Sri Lanka fifteen years later and teams up with a Sri Lankan archeologist. Together, they let their minds and imaginations flow freely into the histories they find in the bones, familiar names, and memories, evoking all the poetry and horror of the death that is spilled around them on all sides. As the body count rises from Sri Lanka's civil war, Anil and the archeologist are able to find answers and evidence hidden in the remains of the victims of this violence. Anil finds herself involved in the struggle in ways she never imagined. Like Wiesel's *Night*, *Anil's Ghost* portrays the impact of ethnic cleansing and genocide on the individuals who must live with their realities. Accounts such as these depict abstract and remote historical events and bring them to the reader in a highly personal manner.

Before the civil war in Sri Lanka that led to ethnic cleansing between two tribes, a genocidal and political massacre took place in Cambodia from 1975 to 1979. In Loung Ung's memoir, *First They Killed My Father: A Daughter of Cambodia Remembers* (2000), Ung reminds readers that the communist faction the Khmer Rouge killed some two million people, almost one-fourth of the Cambodian population, during the second half of the 1970s. Under the reign of the Khmer Rouge, intellectuals, professionals, ethnic Vietnamese, Christians, Muslims, Buddhist monks, and anyone with connections to the former government were killed. It is considered one of the bloodiest political reigns of the twentieth century, on a par with Stalinist Russia and Nazi Germany.

In 1975, when Cambodian cities were about to be emptied to make way for an imagined agrarian communist utopia, five-year-old Ung is living in the capitol Phnom Penh. She is one of several children of a well-placed government official, a child of privilege and of a thousand small pleasures around the city. Under the brutal regime of Pol Pot and the Khmer Rouge, she is separated from her family, driven out into the countryside, and forced to labor as a child soldier in a camp for orphans. Ung writes about how it is essential to her survival to keep her privileged background hidden, and how she is forced to endure the dispersal and murder of her family members. After the war, and in the writing of the book, Ung reassembles her understanding of what happened to her under Khmer Rouge, and of the immense calamity that befell Cambodia. By the power of her book she makes an effort to rescue history from its nightmare.

Two decades later, in 1994, hundreds of thousands of Tutsis were murdered in the span of one hundred days by Hutus in Rwanda. Gil Courtemanche's novel *A Sunday at the Pool in Kigali* (2003) is set at the start of the genocide. The protagonist is Bernard Valcourt, a Canadian filmmaker who has been sent to Kigali, in Rwanda, to set up a television station. The story takes place in the early 1990s, and though the genocidal struggle between Hutus and Tutsis has not yet started, the disaster is already in the air. During the colonial era in Rwanda, the whites arbitrarily created the ethnic distinctions based solely on their physical appearance, and had favored the taller, lighter-skinned Tutsis. Hutus were getting ready to revolt against decades of marginalization.

Valcourt regularly finds himself poolside at his hotel with other members of the local elite and the expatriate community. There Gentille, a lovely waitress who, though Hutu, looks like a Tutsi, captures his eye and his heart. Valcourt comes to know the threatened Tutsi community, then the entire Rwandan culture, shadowed as it is with impending massacre, not to mention the endless scourges of AIDS and poverty. Through a love affair—which becomes a love affair with a culture as well as an individual—Courtemanche pulls the reader deep into the individual experience of genocide.

Novels and memoirs can be some of literature's most powerful forms, as they memorialize and interpret what sometimes seems to lack meaning. In a world that has known, survived, and repeated so many instances of genocide, forced exile, and ethnic cleansing, literature serves as a memorial to the fallen who can no longer speak for themselves, and as a warning to those who survive or follow.

Slavery

The forced labor of members of certain ethnicities, minorities, or religions has occurred to some extent on every inhabited continent in the world. Slavery reduces humans to the level of possessions and units of labor, but literature about slavery tries to reintroduce the humanity of the victims of this institution, and remind readers that slaves, too, are individuals with the same feelings, fears, hopes, and dreams as any member of the human race.

An early firsthand account of modern slavery is *The Interesting Narrative of the Life of Olaudah Equiano: or, Gustavus Vassa, the African* (1794). Equiano was born in present-day Nigeria and sold into slavery as a child. He was taken to England, where he at first found himself a slave to a captain in the Royal Navy, and then a slave to a Quaker merchant. As Equiano explains in his narrative, he was able to buy his freedom by saving money and trading commodities, a rare occurrence in the eighteenth century. He went on to become a sailor, sailing the Mediterranean, Atlantic, and Caribbean. He also sailed to the Arctic as part of an expedition hoping to reach the North Pole. Upon returning to England, he became instrumental in the movement to abolish the slave trade, which provided the impetus for Equiano's writing this autobiography. Not only did his book become a bestseller, but it made its author wealthy. Equiano used his own experiences with the inhumanity of slavery to campaign against the entire institution. His is a story of suffering, oppression, and ultimately, victory and hope.

Slavery was finally abolished throughout the British Empire in 1833.

Another slave who was able to escape the horror of the system was Mary Prince, whose *The History of Mary Prince, a West Indian Slave* (1831) recounts her life as a slave in the Caribbean. Like Equiano, Prince writes about the degradation and suffering imposed by slavery from personal experience. She escaped in 1828 and made her way to London. Her *History* became an overnight bestseller, and was praised by abolitionists for its frank depiction of the life of a slave. Personal narratives such as Prince's and Equiano's were extremely influential in the antislavery movement in Britain. These accounts had the power to transform a remote practice that happened to "other people" in a far-off place into personal stories, putting a face on the brutal practice of slavery.

Though legally abolished by the twentieth century in most countries, the practice of slavery continued. In the 1930s, the political fervor sweeping the world in the wake of *The Communist Manifesto* (1848) and World War I led many to see industrialization and capitalism as a new form of slavery. Scottish writer James Mitchell, a Marxist critic and novelist, published *Spartacus* (1933) in tribute to the Roman gladiator who led a slave revolt in 73 B.C. against his tyrant Roman masters. This sustained rebellion, which claimed one hundred and thirty thousand slave adherents, was a genuine threat to the Roman Republic for a while, and required repeated campaigns to defeat it. For Mitchell, as for fellow Spartacus admirer Karl Marx, this slave uprising exemplified perfectly the power of the underclass to strike back. The historical Spartacus was far from an ideologist and had no interest in overthrowing the Roman state. He simply wanted freedom for himself and his followers. In the politically charged 1930s, it was impossible to believe that personal freedom was enough, and Spartacus had come to be seen as an inspirational figure well ahead of his time.

Russian author and Nobel laureate Alexander Solzhenitsyn, like Equiano and Prince, was himself a slave. Though he was not bought or sold, he was nevertheless forced into a hard labor camp where he was a slave of the Soviet government. In 1945, Solzhenitsyn was sent to the Gulag, or prison internment camp, for ten years. His crime had been making derogatory comments about Soviet dictator Joseph

Stalin in a letter to a friend. In the novel *One Day in the Life of Ivan Denisovich* (1962), Solzhenitsyn shares his firsthand experience about the steady stream of small indignities that make up daily life in a prison camp. It is an existence where every day is mind-numbingly monotonous:

> In all the time he spent in camps and prisons, Ivan Denisovich had gotten out of the habit of worrying about the next day, or the year. . . . Winter after winter, summer after summer—he still had a long time to go.

Control over even the smallest of things becomes a victory in such a repressive situation. One day he finds that he has managed, unintentionally, to pocket a spoon from the dining hall, and that he has gotten away with it. It is the triumph of the slave who has nothing more to expect. Where Equiano, Prince, and Mitchell show some degree of triumph over the institution of slavery, Solzhenitsyn's *One Day in the Life of Ivan Denisovich* offers no such hope. It is the story of the average slave, like the multitude of slaves the world over who have suffered anonymously.

Though centuries of literature have shown the brutality and inhumanity of slavery, the institution is not a thing of the past. Human trafficking is widespread even today, and supports a modern slave system that exploits women, children, ethnic and religious minorities, the poor, and the desperate. It is an underground economic force still strong in some parts of the world. Mende Nazer reminds contemporary readers about the ongoing reality in her memoir *Slave* (2003). In 1994, Nazer is kidnapped from her Nuba village in Sudan by Mujahedin raiders. Many of the villagers are raped or murdered, and several young girls, including Nazer, are kidnapped and sold as slaves. Without knowing of her family's survival after the attack, Nazer is brought to a home in Khartoum, the capital of Sudan, and forced to work as a domestic servant. The urban landscape of Khartoum is alien to Nazer, as she grew up without conveniences like electricity, eating utensils, or automobiles. The family she works for are cruel, and they beat her regularly. She is given no bed, no regular food, and no payment. After seven years, she manages to escape when she is sent to London to work for another family. Nazer's account has brought the issue of slavery back into the world's view, and human rights groups are investigating Sudan and other African nations believed to be involved in his modern slavery. Like Equiano's narrative, Nazer's is making it hard for those who never encounter slavery to ignore what happens to foreign people in far away places.

In the National Book Award–winning novel *All Souls' Rising* (1995), Madison Smartt Bell presents a historical story that rivals that of Spartacus for spontaneous violence in the service of freedom. Here the subject is the Haitian slave rebellion of 1791, in the first months of which twelve thousand people lost their lives. The fighting took place in part between black slaves and white slave owners, but the situation was made more complex by the shifting alliances among slaves, French royalists, French revolutionaries, and more than sixty-four different classifications of people of mixed race. The action focuses on the earliest months of the rebellion, which would last more than a decade. There are no clear instigators or victims. Full understanding and appreciation of this work is not a simple matter of distinguishing the good guys and the bad guys, or naming the winners and losers. History tells us that Haitian slaves won their freedom, but novels like Bell's show the complexities and ambiguities of conflicts with so much at stake for so many.

For those who do escape slavery, the legacy of having endured enslavement is a painful burden. This pain is a central fact in Nora Okja Keller's novel *Comfort Woman* (1997). The book deals with a Korean mother and a daughter, who are both deeply affected by the mother's slavery during World War II. The mother was kept as a sex slave during the Japanese occupation of Korea. She cannot shake her mind free from this terrible memory, which in some ways echoes the issues of Chan's *The Rape of Nanking*. The American-born daughter cannot penetrate the history her mother has endured, and can only understand her mother's burden in a limited way as her mother approaches the end of her life. Love unites the two women in the end, as the trauma of slavery is shown in Keller's novel to never fully subside.

Slavery is as old as civilization, but the power of literature to affect the institution is relatively new. The inhumanity of slavery becomes impossible to ignore when the slaves themselves tell of their experiences, showing that spirit and humanity not only exist, but can survive even in the harshest conditions. Literature has helped to stamp out slavery in many times and places, and will continue to force the free people of the world to confront the evil wherever it continues to exist, until it is no more.

Segregation

Many nations throughout the world have permitted or encouraged barriers between ethnicities, religious groups, genders, or between society and the pariahs it marginalizes. These barriers impose separation, or segregation. Beyond individual prejudices, legally designed and enforced segregation—or in the case of South Africa from the 1940s to the 1990s, apartheid—support state-sanctioned brutality and suffering. Institutionalized segregation continues in some areas of the world even today, despite literature's success in raising awareness and demolishing barriers. Divided communities are weakened as they relegate some members to second-class status; the literature about segregation and apartheid speaks for the strength of communities that are whole.

In a move not unlike what would follow in South Africa, in 1931 the Australian government issued an edict declaring that all aboriginal black girls were to be—willingly or not—integrated into mainstream white society, educated, and put into domestic (or other) service. To do this, aboriginal peoples were separated from their homelands and families and relocated to isolated "native settlement stations" that resembled the U.S. Japanese internment camps during World War II. In *Rabbit-Proof Fence: The True Story of One of the Greatest Escapes of All Time* (2002), Doris Pilkington describes how three adolescent sisters—Molly (the author's mother), Gracie, and Daisy—bravely defied this edict that separated them from everything they had ever known.

The girls are removed to a native settlement station twelve hundred miles from their home, and begin indoctrination into white culture. That means a ban on speaking their own language and on maintaining their cultural heritage, and heavy stress on learning white household skills. For these three independent and high-spirited girls, this exile is intolerable. After less than a month, they escape, making the two-month journey back to their home village by following the fence that runs nearly the whole north-south axis of Australia. The three girls' refusal to accept their desperate circumstances

and their drive to return home despite the dangers of the trip is a story of remarkable courage and unwavering faith in the rightness of their quest. These girls never internalize the indoctrination and barely hesitate when they see their chance to flee. A different kind of courage is needed to challenge the only status quo one has ever known.

In *Biko* (1979), Donald Woods writes about a man who came to represent the most tenacious and daring opposition to South Africa's apartheid. Biko was the leader of the nonviolent Black Consciousness Movement, which rejected the minority white version of "truth" in matters of race and identity. Woods was one of the few outspoken white supporters of Steve Biko, and in his writing he explores the circumstances of Biko's life, and especially of his suspicious death in police custody in 1977. Woods himself showed a particular brand of courage in publishing Biko's story while still under apartheid rule. The courage that Biko showed in fighting apartheid is echoed in Woods's book, which itself proved an important instrument in raising awareness about the gross injustices being carried out by the government of South Africa in the late twentieth century.

Throughout the 1970s and 1990s, racial tension in South Africa was extremely high. That tension and fear is captured in Nadine Gordimer's *July's People* (1982), in which the South African novelist looks into the mindset of South African whites who are not necessarily racists, yet are affected by the racial tension that surrounds them. The dilemma she highlights springs from a possible future (at the time, a future still to be imagined) in which a black revolution has overthrown apartheid society. The protagonists, a middle-class white family, are driven into hiding after the revolution, and must seek refuge in the home of their servant, July. The reactions of the former servant and his employers to their new role reversal highlight the tyranny of power as much as the abasement of powerlessness. It was an eye-opening polemic when it was published during apartheid's darkest days.

A nonfiction account of life under true South African apartheid is captured in Mark Mathabane's *Kaffir Boy: The True Story of a Black Youth's Coming of Age in Apartheid South Africa* (1987). Mathabane describes the rough living conditions of his youth in the

1960s and 1970s in the shantytown of Alexandra. There was no running water, electricity, or heat; police frequently raided homes and arrested citizens; corruption and abuse were rampant. The book is a crushing indictment of the pain of the segregated black underclass during apartheid, and Mathabane's purpose is to force whites to see these conditions: "The white man of South Africa certainly does not know me. He certainly does not know the conditions under which I was born and had to live for eighteen years." Fortunately there is a ray of promise at the end of the story. Mathabane receives a tennis scholarship to a college in the United States, where he is able to permanently escape the confines of apartheid. However, he cannot escape his past or his memories of oppression: "I knew that I could never really leave South Africa or Alexandra. I was Alexandra, I was South Africa, I was part of what Alan Paton [author of *Cry, the Beloved Country*] described as 'a tragically beautiful land.'" Mathabane's story, released before the end of apartheid, was another important step in the demise of the system a few years later.

Great courage is required of anyone, man or woman, rich or poor, white or black or brown, who is determined to realize a full life and reach out to his or her country and world. For many people, Nelson Mandela has become the contemporary symbol of this courage. In his autobiography, *Long Walk to Freedom: The Autobiography of Nelson Mandela* (1994), the Nobel Peace Prize–winner helps readers to understand how he survived twenty-seven years in prison on South Africa's Robben Island for fighting against apartheid. Steve Biko, Mark Mathabane, and the conflicted whites of Gordimer's *July's People* were all thrashing around in an effort to achieve an end to a segregated world while Mandela remained imprisoned. His story and experiences, however, end in a way that fulfills the hopes of all who fought against apartheid with him: four years after being released from prison, Mandela became South Africa's first black president. He not only survives his ordeal; he triumphs. His life is a testament to the power of perseverance, forgiveness, and unity, and his story is inspiring proof that one person can have an enormous impact on the world.

Segregation is also found in more historically ingrained incarnations. Many societies around the globe keep women at a lower status than men in terms of rights, legal protection, and freedom. Jean P. Sasson shows the extent to which segregation affects women, even royalty, in Muslim Saudi Arabia in *Princess: A True Story of Life Behind the Veil in Saudi Arabia* (1992). This book transports readers from the racially segregated world of Steve Biko and Mark Mathabane to the gender segregation of conservative Muslim society in Saudi Arabia. The external differences between the two settings could not be more extreme: from the squalor of a South African shantytown to wealth, comfort, and fine things inside a Saudi palace. Within the walls of the palace, however, the Saudi Princess is as segregated from the full human world as is the black township dweller: "Although I was only seven years old, . . . I first became aware that I was a female who was shackled by males unburdened with consciences." The unidentified Saudi princess who is the subject of this book yearns to break free from her life of confinement and enjoy the same liberties as the powerful men.

Segregation is the impulse to separate and subjugate a portion of the population that makes those in power uncomfortable. They do not worry about dehumanizing the targeted group, because they do not perceive them as fully human anyway. After the twentieth-century attempts, failures, and regrets about attempts at legalized racial separations, civilized people no longer accept segregation as a moral option. Literature has been instrumental in making the cruelty and injustice of segregation vivid in worldwide imaginations. Literature will continue to portray the humanity of other separated segments of humanity, and remind us that there is still much more progress to be made. To be kept apart is to be deprived of one's full humanity, and the literature of segregation illustrates that pain.

Conclusion

Literature shows that prejudice and are instances of imposed darkness that individuals willfully elect to live in and thus inflict on others. With the right human exercise of will, racism, gender discrimination, caste and underclass thinking, institutions like slavery, and segregation could be remedied. Humans working and thinking in concert could eliminate these evils. For them to do so, it is necessary for them to think it in their interest to do so. Literature about the reality, experience, and aftermath of the different manifestations of prejudice help give a human voice to the tragedies and bring home to the presumably "uninvolved" that it affects them, too. The books serve as testaments of these dire events and warnings about the need for vigilance to guard against recurrences of evils believed extinct. They serve as chronicles of ongoing wrongs humankind has yet to eradicate. Literature is our reality, our history, and our future, teaching us not to forget, not to repeat, and not to relent.

SOURCES

Achebe, Chinua, *Things Fall Apart*, Anchor Books, 1958, p. 167.

Dostoyevsky, Fyodor, *The Idiot*, *Online-Literature*, www.online-literature.com/dostoevksy/idiot/1/ (January 11, 2006), originally published in 1868.

The Book of *Exodus*, in *The Life Application Bible*, New International Version, Tyndale House Publishers, 1988, originally written in the fourteenth century B.C., p. 105.

Flaubert, Gustave, "A Simple Soul," *Literature Network*, www.online-literature.com/gustave-flaubert/simplesoul/1/ (April 18, 2006), originally published in 1877.

Frank, Anne, *The Diary of a Young Girl*, the definitive edition, edited by Otto H. Frank and Mirjam Pressler, translated by Susan Massotty, Bantam Books, 1995, originally published in 1947, p. 72

Hugo, Victor, *Les Misérables*, translated by Norman Denny, Penguin Classics, 1976, originally published in 1862, pp. 93, 647.

Ibsen, Henrik, *A Doll's House*, in Vol. 1 of *Ibsen: Four Major Plays*, revised edition, translated by Rolf Fjelde, Signet Classic, 1992, originally published in 1879, pp. 111, 114.

Kosinski, Jerzy, *The Painted Bird*, 2d ed., Grove Press, 1976, originally published in 1965, p. 114.

Lahiri, Jhumpa, *The Namesake*, Houghton Mifflin, 2003, pp. 25, 27.

Márquez, Gabriel García, "A Very Old Man with Enormous Wings," in *Collected Stories*, translated by Gregory Rabassa and J. S. Bernstein, Harper Perennial, 1984, pp. 220, 224.

Mathabane, Mark, *Kaffir Boy: The True Story of a Black Youth's Coming of Age in Apartheid South Africa*, Free Press, 1986, pp. 3, 348.

Naipaul, V. S., *A Bend in the River*, Vintage International, 1989, originally published in 1979, p. 25.

Puig, Manuel, *Kiss of the Spider Woman*, translated by Thomas Colchie, Vintage International, 1991, originally published in 1978, p. 203.

Sasson, Jean P., *Princess: A True Story of Life Behind the Veil in Saudi Arabia*, Windsor-Brooke Books, 2001, p. 26.

Solzhenitsyn, Alexander, *One Day in the Life of Ivan Denisovich*, translated by Ronald Hingley and Max Hayward, Bantam Books, 1963, p. 47.

Wiesel, Elie, *Night*, translated by Stella Rodway, Bantam Books, 1960, p. 76.

Major Works

THE ADVENTURES OF HUCKLEBERRY FINN

ANGELS IN AMERICA

THE AUTOBIOGRAPHY OF MISS JANE PITTMAN

THE AUTOBIOGRAPHY OF MALCOLM X

THE AWAKENING

BLACKS

BURY MY HEART AT WOUNDED KNEE: AN INDIAN
HISTORY OF THE AMERICAN WEST

CEREMONY

THE COLOR PURPLE

CRY, THE BELOVED COUNTRY

THE DIARY OF A YOUNG GIRL

"EVERYTHING THAT RISES MUST CONVERGE"

FAREWELL TO MANZANAR: A TRUE STORY OF
JAPANESE AMERICAN EXPERIENCE DURING AND
AFTER THE WORLD WAR II INTERNMENT

FLOWERS FOR ALGERNON

"A GOOD DAY"

HEART OF DARKNESS

THE HOUSE ON MANGO STREET

The Adventures of Huckleberry Finn

MARK TWAIN

1884

Mark Twain's classic *The Adventures of Huckleberry Finn* (1884) is told from the point of view of Huck Finn, a barely literate teen who fakes his own death to escape his abusive, drunken father. He encounters a runaway slave named Jim, and the two embark on a raft journey down the Mississippi River. Through satire, Twain skewers the somewhat unusual definitions of "right" and "wrong" in the antebellum (pre–Civil War) South, noting among other things that the "right" thing to do when a slave runs away is to turn him in, not help him escape. Twain also paints a rich portrait of a the slave Jim, a character unequaled in American literature: he is guileless, rebellious, genuine, superstitious, warmhearted, ignorant, and astute all at the same time.

The book is a sequel to another of the author's successful adventure novels, *The Adventures of Tom Sawyer*, originally published in 1876. Although *The Adventures of Tom Sawyer* is very much a "boys' novel"—humorous, suspenseful, and intended purely as entertainment—*The Adventures of Huckleberry Finn* also addresses weighty issues such as slavery, prejudice, hypocrisy, and morality.

After Twain finished writing the first half of the novel, he expressed doubts about the book's potential success. In a letter to his friend William Dean Howells in 1877 (quoted by biographer Ron Powers in *Mark Twain: A Life*), Twain confessed: "I like it only tolerably well, as far as

BIOGRAPHY

MARK TWAIN

Mark Twain was born Samuel Langhorne Clemens in 1835 in Missouri, one of seven children. He spent much of his childhood in the Missouri town of Hannibal, which served as the model for the fictional town of St. Petersburg in both *The Adventures of Tom Sawyer* and *The Adventures of Huckleberry Finn*. The year after his father died, twelve-year-old Clemens left school and apprenticed at a local newspaper printer, which helped establish his career course for the rest of his life. Clemens also spent several years working on a Mississippi riverboat as a teenager absorbing scenes and situations that would appear later in his writing. During this time he first heard the nautical term "mark twain," which would become his pen name.

Just as the Civil War got underway, Clemens headed out west and secured a position writing for a local newspaper in Virginia City, Nevada.

This was where he first became known as Mark Twain, and where his humorous works first caught the attention of the reading public. His greatest early successes were mostly travelogues, including his first book, *The Innocents Abroad*.

Twain went on to write several American classics, including *The Adventures of Tom Sawyer, The Adventures of Huckleberry Finn, Life on the Mississippi, The Prince and the Pauper,* and *A Connecticut Yankee in King Arthur's Court*. Even during his lifetime, Twain was considered by the reading public to be one of the greatest American writers.

Twain continued writing until his death in 1910 at the age of seventy-four. In addition to his acknowledged classics, he left behind a large body of unfinished and smaller works, many of which have been published posthumously.

I have got, & may possibly pigeonhole or burn the MS [manuscript] when it is done." Fortunately, Twain did not burn the manuscript; when it was published in England in 1884 (U.S. publication 1885), it quickly became the most successful book Twain had yet written.

Soon after it was published, the public library in Concord, Massachusetts, refused to carry *The Adventures of Huckleberry Finn* because of its perceived crudeness. This ban turned into a publicity coup for Twain and his book. In a letter published in the *Hartford Courant,* the author responds gratefully, noting that "one book in a public library prevents the sale of a sure ten and a possible hundred of its mates." Twain also notes that the library's newsworthy action

> will cause the purchasers of the book to read it, out of curiosity, instead of merely intending to do so ... and then they will discover, to my great advantage and their own indignant disappointment, that there is nothing objectionable in the book after all.

Despite Twain's assurances, the book continues to spark controversy over its subject

matter even today. Some modern critics argue that the book is inherently racist in its depiction of Jim and its frequent use of the term "nigger." Other critics, speaking in support of the book, point out that the terms used in the book are authentic to the story's setting; they also point out that Jim is by far the most heroic character in the novel, and is the only major character to demonstrate kindness and self-sacrifice without hesitation. The book has generated so much critical material that a special edition containing both the novel and several important essays was published by Bedford Books in 1995 under the title *Adventures of Huckleberry Finn: A Case Study in Critical Controversy,* edited by Gerald Graff and James Phelan.

Despite the controversy surrounding the book, *The Adventures of Huckleberry Finn* is widely recognized as Twain's masterpiece, and is often identified as "the Great American Novel." Respected writers such as William Faulkner and T. S. Eliot have written of the book's importance to American literature. And although critics have been divided on the book's

" IT WAS AWFUL THOUGHTS AND AWFUL WORDS,

BUT THEY WAS SAID. AND I LET THEM STAY SAID; AND

NEVER THOUGHT NO MORE ABOUT REFORMING.

I SHOVED THE WHOLE THING OUT OF MY HEAD, AND

SAID I WOULD TAKE UP WICKEDNESS AGAIN, WHICH WAS

IN MY LINE, BEING BRUNG UP TO IT, AND THE OTHER

WARN'T. AND FOR A STARTER I WOULD GO TO WORK AND

STEAL JIM OUT OF SLAVERY AGAIN; AND IF I COULD

THINK UP ANYTHING WORSE, I WOULD DO THAT, TOO."

Mark Twain AP Images

merits since its first publication, Pulitzer and Nobel Prize–winning author Ernest Hemingway, in *Green Hills of Africa*, offers *The Adventures of Huckleberry Finn* its most well-known and enduring compliment:

> All modern American literature comes from one book by Mark Twain called *Huckleberry Finn*.... All American writing comes from that. There was nothing before. There has been nothing as good since.

PLOT SUMMARY

The Adventures of Huckleberry Finn, which takes place along the Mississippi River sometime in the 1830s or 1840s, begins with two brief statements to the reader that appear before Chapter 1; both of these display Twain's trademark sense of humor. In the first, under the heading "Notice," Twain warns readers against attempting to find any sort of deep meaning in the book. He lists different punishments for readers who seek motive, moral, or plot within the narrative. The second, called "Explanatory," assures readers that the dialects used by different characters in the book are based on real regional dialects, and have been researched thoroughly. As Twain notes, "I make this explanation for the reason that without it many readers would suppose that all these characters were trying to talk alike and not succeeding."

Chapters 1–3
The Adventures of Huckleberry Finn is written as a first-person narrative from the point of view of

the title character, Huckleberry (or Huck) Finn. Huck addresses the reader directly throughout the work, and occasionally refers to events that occurred in one of Twain's previous works, *The Adventures of Tom Sawyer,* in which Huck was a supporting character. Of the previous book, Huck notes, "That book was made by Mr. Mark Twain, and he told the truth, mainly."

Huck picks up his story where it left off in *The Adventures of Tom Sawyer*: he and Tom, two boys who live on the Mississippi River in the Missouri town of St. Petersburg, found a large amount of gold left by robbers in a cave. The money—amounting to six thousand dollars each—has been put in the care of Judge Thatcher, who gives the boys interest earnings in the amount of one dollar each day. Huck has been unofficially adopted by the Widow Douglas (to the apparent dismay of her sister Miss Watson), who hopes to transform the rough-edged boy into a forthright young man. For Huck, such a life is too restrictive; as he puts it, "All I wanted was to go somewhere; all I wanted was a change."

One night Tom Sawyer shows up to take Huck to a secret meeting with some other boys;

as they sneak away from the house, one of Miss Watson's slaves—Jim—hears the boys, who carefully evade him. Tom takes the group of boys to a cave along the river. He plans to start a gang of highway robbers to terrorize the local roadways, killing and ransoming the men travelers and kidnapping the women—who, according to the plan, would eventually fall in love with them. The group discusses the logistics of such an operation, including what a "ransom" is and what happens when the robbers' cave becomes overfilled with kidnapped women and men waiting to be ransomed. Soon enough, Huck realizes that Tom's gang of robbers is only meant to engage in pretend robberies; this disappoints him, though he still plays along. Tom also tells Huck how to summon a genie from a tin lamp; Huck later tries this without success, and decides "all that stuff was only just one of Tom Sawyer's lies."

Chapters 4–6

Over the next several months, Huck becomes accustomed to his life with Widow Douglas and Miss Watson. He even starts growing fond of school. One morning, Huck finds tracks in the snow outside the widow's house; he is certain they belong to his father, called Pap, an abusive drunk whom Huck has not seen for over a year. Huck immediately visits Judge Thatcher and gives up his fortune to keep his father from getting hold of it, selling it to the judge for a single dollar.

Huck returns to his room one night to find Pap waiting for him. Pap threatens to beat Huck if he continues going to school. Pap tells him, "You've put on considerable many frills since I been away. I'll take you down a peg before I get done with you." Then Pap takes Huck's only dollar to buy whisky.

Pap visits Judge Thatcher in an attempt to get at Huck's money. Thatcher and Widow Douglas try to secure legal guardianship of Huck, but the judge who hears the case is not willing to "interfere" and officially break up Huck's "family." Later, the same judge takes Pap into his home in an attempt to help him straighten his life out. Pap promises to reform, but he continues to drink and gets kicked out of the judge's house.

Pap persists in his legal fight for Huck's money, and occasionally beats his son for continuing to attend school. As Huck states,

"I didn't want to go to school much, before, but I reckoned I'd go now to spite pap." Eventually, Pap snatches Huck and takes him to a secluded log cabin on the Illinois side of the Mississippi River, where he keeps the boy against his will. Kept away from the widow, Huck soon returns to his comfortable old ways, wearing rags for clothes, smoking, and swearing. Pap beats him regularly, however, and Huck waits for a chance to escape.

Chapters 7–9

One morning, while checking some fishing lines, Huck spots an empty canoe drifting down the river. He hides the canoe to help when he makes his escape. Later that day, Pap leaves for town, and Huck sees his chance. He stages the cabin so it appears that someone has broken in and killed him, and that his body is somewhere in the river. This, he believes, will keep Pap and Widow Douglas from trying to track him down. He takes the canoe, stocked with some food and tools, to a heavily wooded island in the middle of the river called Jackson's Island.

The next morning, Huck wakes to the sound of cannon fire; he sees smoke near the ferryboat upriver, and figures out what is happening. "You see, they was firing cannon over the water, trying to make my carcass come to the top." The ferry draws closer to the island, and Huck sees many people he knows aboard it, including Pap, Judge Thatcher, and Tom Sawyer. Once the ferry departs, Huck knows they will not return.

After a few days of camping and fishing, Huck finds evidence of others nearby. He leaves for a different part of the island, and is surprised when he sees Miss Watson's slave Jim camped alone in the woods. Huck approaches, but Jim—thinking Huck has died—is terrified by what he assumes to be Huck's ghost. Huck explains how he escaped from Pap's cabin, and asks why Jim is out in the woods. Jim tells Huck that he ran off when he heard Miss Watson was planning to sell him to a slave trader from New Orleans. Huck promises not to tell Jim's secret to anybody.

Huck and Jim find a large cavern in the center of the island, and decide it would make a suitable camp protected from the elements. One night, they see a frame house drifting down along the river; they row the canoe out to it and climb inside, where they find a dead man who has been shot in the back. Jim covers the dead man's face and tells Huck not to look at it.

The two also find some supplies in the house, including some knives, candles, and a hatchet, which they gather up and take with them.

Chapters 10–12

One evening, Huck finds a rattlesnake in the cave and kills it; as a prank, he leaves it in Jim's bed to find later that night. When Jim gets in bed, however, he finds not just the dead rattlesnake but also its live mate, which bites him. It takes four days for Jim to recover.

Huck, feeling anxious for excitement, decides to put on a dress and bonnet—found when they scavenged the drifting house—and go ashore, pretending to be a girl. He comes upon a shanty occupied by a woman he has never seen before, and knocks on the door.

Pretending to be a girl named Sarah Williams, Huck listens as the woman tells him about the latest news in town: Huck Finn has been killed, and Miss Watson's slave Jim is the main suspect since he disappeared the very night after Huck did. A three-hundred-dollar reward has been offered for the apprehension of Jim, and the woman's husband is part of a group of men preparing to search Jackson Island for the fugitive slave. During the course of the conversation, the woman realizes that "Sarah" is actually a boy, and confronts him. Huck invents a new lie, calling himself George Peters, and manages to earn the woman's sympathy as well as a snack for the road. Huck hurries back to the island and warns Jim about the coming search party.

Huck and Jim set off from the island and continue down the Mississippi River, passing St. Louis and other towns along the way. One stormy night, they spot a steamboat wrecked on some rocks. Huck convinces Jim to board it and see if they can find anything worth taking. Once on board, Huck clandestinely discovers three criminals are already on the wreck; two of them have the third tied up, with the intention of leaving him to die. Huck tells Jim they should set the criminals' boat adrift and escape themselves, but Jim informs him that their own raft has broken loose and drifted away.

Chapters 13–15

Huck and Jim search the perimeter of the wrecked steamer in search of the criminals' boat. They find it, and as soon as the opportunity presents itself they hop in and cut it loose. Afterward, Huck feels bad about leaving the criminals aboard the sinking wreck; not wanting to be responsible for anyone's death, even thieves and murderers, he decides to stop downriver and let someone know there are people trapped aboard the wrecked steamer. Huck and Jim catch up to their raft and reclaim it. Soon after, Huck spots a ferryboat and approaches the captain with a tale about a horse-ferry getting snagged on the wrecked steamboat. He tells the captain that his family is stuck on the sinking wreck. As the ferryboat heads off to help, Huck feels proud of this good deed:

> I wished the widow knowed about it. I judged she would be proud of me for helping these rapscallions, because rapscallions and dead beats is the kind the widow and good people takes the most interest in.

Soon after, Huck sees the wreck of the steamer floating downstream, with no sign of survivors. He feels bad for the gang of criminals, but quickly recovers. He and Jim sort through the plunder the criminals had stashed in their boat, finding cigars, books, blankets, and clothes, among other things. As they smoke the cigars, the two discuss the lives of kings, particularly King Solomon and the "dolphin" (Dauphin, the heir to the French throne), a boy who had been destined to become the king of France but either died or went into hiding after the French Revolution to avoid execution.

Huck and Jim continue down the river, trying to reach a town called Cairo, where the Ohio River flows into the Mississippi; there, they hope to proceed up the Ohio River on a steamboat to reach one of the "free states" where Jim would no longer be considered a slave. They get stuck in a fog bank and become separated, with Jim on the raft and Huck in a canoe. When Huck finally catches up with Jim—who has fallen asleep—he wakes Jim and plays a prank on him, convincing Jim that he must have dreamed up the whole separation. When Huck reveals his prank, Jim, who had been overjoyed to see Huck again, gets upset; he had considered Huck his friend and had been worried about him, but Huck's only interest was in making Jim look like a fool. After thinking it over, Huck apologizes to Jim.

Chapters 16–18

As they continue on their search for Cairo, Huck begins to question the morality of his own actions. He is, after all, helping a slave escape his owner—an action Huck sees as a betrayal to the owner. Still, when a group of men approaches Huck looking for runaway slaves,

Huck protects Jim by keeping the men away from the raft; he hints to the men that his father is on the raft, and that he has smallpox.

Huck and Jim soon realize that they have drifted far south of Cairo and the Ohio River. Since taking the raft against the current is impossible, they devise a plan to canoe back upriver during the night in search of Cairo; however, they find their canoe has disappeared. As they drift downriver looking for someone willing to sell them a canoe, their raft is struck by a steamboat headed upriver; the two are separated, and Huck struggles to shore.

Huck falls into the company of the Grangerford family, who take him in (Huck tells them his name is George Jackson). Huck soon discovers that the Grangerfords are in the midst of a feud with another local family, the Shepherdsons. Huck also discovers—through the family's slaves—that Jim is alive and well, and that their old raft is still seaworthy. Before Huck can leave the Grangerfords, though, the feud between the families explodes: daughter Sophia Grangerford runs away with Harney Sheperdson to get married, and neither family approves. This culminates in a gunfight between the two families, and Buck Grangerford—youngest of the clan, and Huck's closest friend in the family—is killed. Huck escapes the trouble, finds Jim, and they continue down the river.

Chapters 19–21

As Huck searches for berries near the shore one day, two men run toward him and beg Huck to help them reach safety, saying a search party of men and dogs is after them. Huck takes the two back to the raft, where they reveal their stories: the two are con men, each running a different racket, who happened across each other during their separate escapes from angry townspeople. The two men try to outdo each other with their stories. The younger man claims to be the rightful Duke of Bridgewater, while the older claims to be none other than the now-elderly Dauphin, the rightful heir to the throne of France. Each of the men asks for special, "royal" treatment from the other, and Huck and Jim end up acting as servants for both. Huck eventually admits to the reader that he knows the men are not really royalty (though he refers to them as "the duke" and "the king" throughout the rest of the book), but he plays along just to keep things peaceful.

Huck tells the two inquisitive con men that Jim is his family's slave, and that he and Jim are on their way to live with Huck's uncle south of New Orleans. The group reaches a small town, and finds the entire population away at a prayer meeting; the duke helps himself to the local printing office, earning some cash and printing flyers that advertise Jim as a runaway slave from a plantation near New Orleans. By showing the flyer, the group is free to travel the river during the day as well as night; if anyone inquires about Jim, they can say he is a runaway slave who has already been caught.

Chapters 22–24

The duke and the king continue to ply their trade as they move along the river, posing as distinguished actors and swindling locals out of the admission to their show; they always manage to stay one step ahead of the angry townspeople. Then the con men hear of an inheritance yet to be claimed by a local dead man's distant brothers, and decide to pose as the two brothers so they can get the inheritance.

The men show up at the village posing as Harvey and William Wilks, brothers to Peter Wilks, who is deceased. Harvey, played by the king, affects an English accent, while William—played by the duke—pretends to be a deaf-mute. Huck acts as their servant, while Jim stays at the raft.

Chapters 25–27

The two "Wilks brothers" are welcomed by the townspeople, including Peter Wilks's three nieces, Mary Jane, Susan, and Joanna. Mary Jane gives the king a letter revealing the location of Peter's hidden fortune, which amounts to nearly six thousand dollars that is to be left to the nieces. The girls entrust the fortune to their new uncles. Huck, who has grown fond of the girls, decides he will not let the con men steal their inheritance, and steals it back from the duke and the king. He is almost caught, and in a panic he drops the money into the deceased Peter's coffin.

The con men auction off the Wilks family's slaves, and then discover that the inheritance money is missing. Huck shrewdly suggests that the slaves stole the money, and were now beyond the reach of the con men. The duke and the king believe him.

Chapters 28–30

As the con men prepare to auction off the rest of Peter Wilks's property for cash, Huck realizes—much to his consternation—that the only way to help the girls is to tell Mary Jane the truth, even though telling the truth seems to him "so kind of strange and unregular." He tells her everything, including where he left the money.

Just as the duke and the king finish selling off the Wilks estate, two men arrive in town claiming to be the real Harvey and William Wilks. Unsure whom to believe, the townspeople grab Huck and the con men until the matter is sorted out. Peter's coffin is exhumed—part of a test to determine which set of Wilks brothers can identify a tattoo on Peter's chest—and the townspeople discover the money inside the coffin. In the excitement, Huck escapes from the crowd and makes his way back to the raft. As he and Jim start off down the river, the duke and king catch up and board the raft.

Chapters 31–33

The king and the duke, desperate for money, spend their time huddled in secret conversations. Meanwhile, Huck and Jim plan to leave the two con men behind as soon as the opportunity arises. At one stop, Huck slips free of the king and the duke in a town and runs back to the raft, hoping to escape with Jim. When he arrives, Jim is nowhere to be found. He discovers that the king and the duke have sold Jim off to locals as a runaway slave; by presenting the fake flyer the duke had printed—the one offering a two-hundred-dollar reward for Jim—they sell their "rights" to Jim for forty dollars in cash. In this way, the duke and the king manage to swindle the locals and betray Huck and Jim.

Huck debates what he should do; he knows that "the right thing and the clean thing" is to write a letter to Miss Watson, telling her the location of her runaway slave. However, when he thinks of what a great friend Jim has been, he decides to follow the path of "wickedness" and help Jim escape. As Huck surveys the Phelps farm, where Jim is being held, he is spotted by one of the family's slaves and is mistaken for a visiting nephew. Huck plays along, and soon discovers that the "nephew" he is impersonating is none other than Tom Sawyer. Tom's Aunt Sally and Uncle Silas welcome the boy into their home as their nephew.

Huck manages to intercept the real Tom Sawyer before he reaches the Phelps farm, and after convincing Tom that he is not a ghost, explains the whole situation to him. Tom is thrilled at the prospect of adventure; not only does Tom pretend to be Sid Sawyer (since the Phelpses have already met "Tom"), but he also agrees to help Huck free Jim.

Chapters 34–39

Tom and Huck come up with plans to set Jim free. Huck's plan is straightforward and simple, which is why Tom objects: "What's the good of a plan that ain't no more trouble than that? It's as mild as goose-milk." Instead, Tom devises an elaborate plan reminiscent of a classic adventure novel, deliberately avoiding any easy or obvious solutions. For example, instead of lifting up the leg of the bed to slip Jim's chain off, Tom insists they saw through the leg of the bed—and that only after Huck convinces him that sawing through Jim's leg is not a viable option. Instead of using the door to escape Jim's cabin prison, Tom decides they will tunnel their way out.

Tom and Huck fill Jim's cabin with snakes, rats, and spiders to make his prison more dire, and continue working on equally absurd things like a rope-ladder that will never be used and a "warning letter" to tell Uncle Silas of impending trouble. Aunt Sally notices that items such as shirts and spoons are disappearing from the household, but does not suspect that Tom and Huck are using them for any big escapade.

Chapter 40–42

On the night of the escape, Uncle Silas brings additional men to guard Jim's cabin, but Jim and the boys slip out through the tunnel and head for the woods. They are spotted, and some of the men open fire. Although they escape, Tom is shot in the calf and needs a doctor. Instead of running away to safety, Jim insists on staying with Tom while Huck gets a doctor. However, Huck gets trapped back at the Phelpses' before the doctor returns. Eventually the doctor, Tom—still ill from his wound—and Jim all show up at the farm. The doctor tells everyone that Jim "ain't a bad nigger," and that he helped the doctor treat Tom's wound even though he knew staying would cost him his freedom.

When Tom recovers the next morning, he tells Aunt Sally all about their plan to free Jim—not knowing that Jim has been recaptured. Tom objects, and reveals that Miss Watson, Jim's former owner, died two months before; in her will, she stipulated that Jim be set free. When asked why he would go through so much trouble to set a free man free, Tom says he "wanted the

An illustration of a Mississippi riverboat by Currier and Ives Corbis-Bettmann

adventure of it." At that moment, Tom's Aunt Polly appears at the Phelps farm and reveals the true identities of "Sid" and "Tom." She also confirms that Jim is a free man.

Huck makes two important discoveries. Tom tells him that Judge Thatcher is still holding Huck's money for him, all six thousand dollars and more. Then Jim confesses to Huck that the dead man he saw in the frame house floating down the river, so many weeks before, was actually Huck's father.

Tom suggests that he, Huck, and Jim head for the Indian Territories to have some adventures. Huck ends his story, saying:

> But I reckon I got to light out for the Territory ahead of the rest, because Aunt Sally she's going to adopt me and sivilize me and I can't stand it. I been there before.

THEMES

Slavery

Slavery is one of the key thematic elements in *The Adventures of Huckleberry Finn*. The novel takes place in Missouri in the 1830s or 1840s, at a time when Missouri was considered a slave state. Soon after Huck fakes his own death, he partners with Jim, a runaway slave from the household where Huck used to live. Although the book purports to be about Huck's "adventures," the story is driven by Jim's attempt to achieve freedom and safety for himself, and ultimately for his wife and children. Huck is, in a sense, just along for the journey; however, it is Huck's perspective on Jim's struggle that allows the author to address the topic of slavery in a unique and entertaining way.

By telling the story from the point of view of a young white man raised amid slavery, Twain looks at the issue from an entirely different viewpoint than previous writers: while Huck almost never fails to do the "right" thing in the eyes of the reader, because of his upbringing he cannot help but feel that his actions are actually wicked and immoral. When Huck first finds Jim, he promises not to reveal Jim's secret: "People would call me a low down Ablitionist and despise me for keeping mum—but that don't make no difference. I ain't agoing to tell."

As Jim believes he is close to achieving his own freedom, his thoughts turn toward saving his family from slavery. Huck is shocked by Jim's plans, which he relates to the reader:

> He was saying how the first thing he would do when he got to a free State he would go to saving up money and never spend a single cent, and when he got enough he would buy his wife, which was owned on a farm close to where Miss Watson lived; and then they would both work to buy the two children, and if their master wouldn't sell them, they'd get an Ab'litionist to go and steal them.

The issue of slavery plays a part in the most important events in the book: Jim runs away because he believes he will be sold to a slave trader and separated from his family; Huck lies to people he meets to hide the fact that Jim is a runaway slave; the king turns Jim in as a runaway slave—not knowing Jim actually *is* one—just to con some locals for cash; Tom and Huck help Jim escape his captors so he can again try for his freedom; Jim forfeits his freedom in order to help keep Tom alive; and finally, the pair realize that all their running and scheming was in vain because Jim is a free man after all.

Dehumanization

In *The Adventures of Huckleberry Finn*, blacks are subject to dehumanizing treatment from nearly every white character in the book. This is not inconsistent with a tale set in the pre–Civil War South, where blacks were routinely viewed as property above all else. Indeed, one of Huck's primary inner conflicts deals with his "wicked" impulses to treat Jim as more than just someone's property. Additionally, Jim's escape is prompted when Miss Watson considers selling him off to a slave trader despite the fact that Jim has served her well and she knows that such an action would separate Jim from his family.

One notable example of the white characters' disregard for black characters' humanity occurs in Chapter 32, when Huck shows up at the Phelps residence pretending to be Tom Sawyer. Huck, speaking to Aunt Sally, invents a mechanical problem that held up the boat he supposedly traveled on:

> "It warn't the grounding—that didn't keep us back but a little. We blowed a cylinder-head."
>
> "Good gracious! anybody hurt?"
>
> "No'm. Killed a nigger."
>
> "Well, it's lucky; because sometimes people do get hurt."

For many characters in the novel, the notion that blacks are indeed people simply seems beyond any consideration. In many scenes, Twain appears to be satirizing the callousness with which people at that time routinely dismissed the black people's personhood. The insensitivity is so pervasive that even Jim accepts the premise that he is "property," and is proud of how much he is worth; in Chapter 8, while pondering his freedom, Jim tells Huck, "I's rich now, come to look at it. I owns myself, en I's wuth eight hund'd dollars."

In the final chapters of the book, Tom Sawyer devises an elaborate plan to free Jim from the cabin where he is being held. Tom treats Jim as a sort of set-piece in his grand escape production, without any noticeable regard for Jim's comfort or needs; Tom asks Jim to perform nonsensical and in some cases impossible acts, and even fills Jim's bed with spiders and snakes. Ultimately, Huck is the only major character to treat Jim with the respect of an equal—and even when he does, he curses himself for doing what he believes is an immoral thing.

Prejudice

Throughout the novel, the white characters operate under the belief that Jim—because he is black—simply cannot comprehend certain concepts and explanations. Huck in particular comments on numerous occasions about Jim's inability to understand the way the world works. The recurring irony in *The Adventures of Huckleberry Finn* is that the white characters frequently have an inaccurate or even absurd view of how the world works themselves.

Twain uses this device to great comic effect by showing that Jim often has more common sense or cleverness than the other characters in the book, though prejudice prevents the other characters from seeing it. For example, when Huck tries to explain to Jim why it is natural for French people to speak a different language, Jim takes Huck's own flawed logic and turns it on its head, "proving" that it makes no sense at all for French people to speak a different language. Huck fails to even acknowledge that Jim has outwitted him, stating simply, "I see it warn't no use wasting words—you can't learn a nigger to argue."

Similarly, in Chapter 35, Tom ponders whether or not they should saw through Jim's leg for the planned escape—not because it is necessary, but because he has read of such things in adventure books. Eventually Tom decides,

"There ain't necessity enough in this case; and besides, Jim's a nigger and wouldn't understand the reasons for it, and how it's the custom in Europe; so we'll let it go."

Even when Jim is recognized for his commendable actions, as in Chapter 42, prejudice still taints the acknowledgment he receives. When Tom is shot during the attempt to free Jim, Jim decides he will not leave Tom until a doctor has treated him, even though such an act will probably cost Jim his freedom. When Jim says this, Huck tells the reader he knows Jim is actually "white inside"; the implication in Huck's words is that only a white person could show such kindness and consideration for another person. And though any white person who had been instrumental in helping to save Tom's life would have been hailed as a hero, the doctor's praise is limited to simply letting everyone know that Jim "ain't no bad nigger."

HISTORICAL OVERVIEW

The Missouri Compromise

The Missouri Compromise, also known as the Compromise of 1820, was an agreement reached between antislavery legislators from the North and pro-slavery legislators from the South. In this agreement, Missouri was allowed to enter the Union as a slave state, but all other territories north of Missouri's southern border were forbidden from practicing slavery.

By 1820, the issue of slavery was becoming an incendiary topic in the United States. Many people in the North felt that the practice violated the basic tenets of a free country. Many in the South, who relied heavily on slave labor to support industries critical to the country as a whole, disagreed. States began to establish their own laws regarding slavery, and quickly split into two groups: "free states," which comprised the northern half of the country, and "slave states," which made up the southern half.

In 1819, Alabama was officially admitted to the United States as a slave state; this made the total number of free and slave states equal. When Missouri sought statehood, some lawmakers from the North insisted that the Missouri state constitution include language forbidding the practice of slavery. Many lawmakers from the South felt that new states, like all previous states, should be free to decide—without federal intervention—whether or not to allow

slavery. When Maine was admitted as a free state in 1820, a compromise was proposed: Missouri would be admitted as a slave state, but all other territories north of Missouri's southern border would be forbidden from joining the country as slave states. (These territories included what would eventually become Kansas, Iowa, Wisconsin, Minnesota, and the Dakotas.)

The Missouri Compromise, like most effective compromises, was not popular with lawmakers on either side of the issue. Charles Richard Johnson, in *Africans in America: America's Journey through Slavery*, expresses a view common in the North: "The Missouri Compromise temporarily calmed the sectional rift but did nothing to resolve the problem of an immoral system in a society that stressed its morality." Former President Thomas Jefferson, however, supported the southern point of view that the compromise violated a state's ability to make its own laws; in a personal letter, currently archived at the Library of Congress, Jefferson expressed his doubts about what the Missouri Compromise would ultimately accomplish:

> A geographical line, coinciding with a marked principle, moral and political, once concieved [sic] and held up to the angry passions of men, will never be obliterated; and every new irritation will mark it deeper and deeper.

Although Jefferson's dire prediction eventually came true, the Missouri Compromise served as a crude yet effective way to address the divisive issue of slavery in the United States for nearly forty years. Indeed, it was not until the *Dred Scott* case in 1857—in which the Missouri Compromise was ruled unconstitutional—that the rift over slavery would finally split the country into two factions poised for war.

Slavery along the Mississippi River

In the early 1800s, the Mississippi River and its tributaries served as the primary trade route for the western portion of the United States. The river ran south from Canada through "free states" such as Iowa before flowing through the "slave states" of the South like Missouri, where *The Adventures of Huckleberry Finn* takes place. With the advent of the steam-powered riverboat, trade became possible not just from north to south—following the current of the river—but also against the current from south to north. New Orleans became an important port for supplying slaves to plantations and farms located on the fertile lands along the Mississippi River in states such as Arkansas, Mississippi, and Missouri.

In *Black Life on the Mississippi: Slaves, Free Blacks, and the Western Steamboat World,* Thomas C. Buchanan reveals that this era of two-way river traffic also meant that runaway slaves from the South could use the Mississippi River as a means of escaping north, where they would be considered free. As Buchanan puts it, "Riverboats connected city and country, North and South, slavery and freedom." Many slaves were used as workers on steamboats; according to Buchanan, "Imprecise steamboat schedules and the crowds at levee districts made slaves' off-the-boat freedoms possible. With boats circulating in and out of ports, slaves were able to elude masters and agents."

In *The Adventures of Huckleberry Finn,* escaped slave Jim hopes to raft down the Mississippi River to its junction with the Ohio River. From there, according to Huck, "We would sell the raft and get on a steamboat and go way up the Ohio amongst the free States, and then be out of trouble." (Illinois, just across the Mississippi River from Missouri, was also technically a free state, but the white population was often both sympathetic to their slave-holding neighbors and hostile to free blacks.) This type of journey was not uncommon for slaves hoping to reach freedom.

Race Relations in Missouri Before and During the Civil War

Though *The Adventures of Huckleberry Finn* takes place decades before the Civil War, Twain wrote the book in the mid-1880s. The intervening fifty years saw many changes in race relations in the state of Missouri, some of which had consequences that affected the entire country.

While Missouri was classified as a slave state in 1820, it was not a region with a long history of slavery. White settlement of Missouri was still fairly new at the time, and the slave-dependent "plantation way of life" of the Deep South was not well established there. Still, Missouri became home to a court case many believe directly led to the Civil War: *Dred Scott v. Sanford.*

In 1857, a slave named Dred Scott sued for his freedom after his original owner died. Scott had lived for many years in Illinois and the Wisconsin Territory, both of which were considered free regions without slavery; however, Scott had ultimately been brought back to the slave state of Missouri. After a lower Missouri court found in favor of Scott, the case was eventually appealed all

the way to the U.S. Supreme Court. In a landmark decision, the Supreme Court ruled against Scott, stating that he was property belonging to his former master's estate. The backlash from this ruling mobilized antislavery advocates throughout the northern United States, further polarizing North and South and leading indirectly to the secession of the Confederate South and the Civil War.

During the Civil War, Missouri was a "border state" that separated the antislavery Union from the pro-sovereignty Confederacy; though Missouri was considered a slave state prior to the war, its citizens voted to remain a part of the Union. In fact, the state was claimed as an ally by both sides during the war, and developed two governments: one favoring the Union, and one favoring the Confederacy. Although Missouri was very much a state divided, majority sentiment remained with the Union. As Eric Foner notes in his book *A Short History of Reconstruction,* Missouri was one of the border states that "underwent internal reconstructions that brought to power new classes anxious to overturn slavery and revolutionize state politics."

CRITICAL OVERVIEW

When *The Adventures of Huckleberry Finn* was published in 1884, Mark Twain was already a very successful writer. However, his popularity did not always translate to favorable reviews from critics who questioned the true literary merits of his "humorous" works.

Upon its publication, the book enjoyed the best initial sales of any of Twain's books; according to biographer Ron Powers, writing in *Mark Twain: A Life,* the first edition of the novel continued to be printed for six years. An unnamed reviewer for *Athenaeum* boldly agrees with the reading public, stating that "the book is Mark Twain at his best." Brander Matthews, writing for London's *Saturday Review,* notes, "Although it is a sequel, it is quite as worthy of wide popularity as *Tom Sawyer.*" Matthews also remarks that "the essential simplicity and kindliness and generosity of the Southern negro have never been better shown than here by Mark Twain."

Some reviewers noted the skill and inventiveness with which Twain presented the unique dialects of the region; an unnamed reviewer for the *San Francisco Chronicle* even calls Twain "the Edison of our literature," and calls the

An illustration of Huck Finn from The Adventures of Huckleberry Finn, *by Mark Twain, 1884* Public Domain

book "eminently readable." A reviewer for the *Hartford Courant* describes the story as "so full of life and dramatic force, that the reader will be carried along irresistibly." However, T. S. Perry, in a mostly positive review for the *Century Illustrated Monthly Magazine,* noted a flaw in the book that has been echoed by many modern critics: "It is possible to feel, however, that the fun in the long account of Tom Sawyer's artificial imitation of escapes from prison is somewhat forced." A reviewer for the *San Francisco Evening Bulletin* offers both praise and insult in the same breath: "It is an amusing story if such scrap-work can be called a story." The reviewer also notes that the story contains "very little of literary art," and is rather "a string of incidents ingeniously fastened together."

The book was subjected to numerous other criticisms as well. Just one month after its American publication, the public library of Concord, Massachusetts, chose not to offer the book to its patrons; the reason, according to

biographer Powers, was "because of its coarseness of language and questionable morals." Newspapers across the country ran articles about the Concord ban, and many reviewers concurred with the library's decision. An unsigned reviewer for the *San Francisco Daily Examiner* states that the book is "well described by the author, as being without a motive, a moral, or a plot." A reviewer for the *Boston Daily Advertiser* refers to the novel as "wearisome and labored," while an unnamed reviewer for the *Boston Evening Traveller* describes the book as "singularly flat, stale and unprofitable." This same reviewer also offers a particularly harsh insult contradicted by the book's steady sales: "It is doubtful if the edition could be disposed of to people of average intellect at anything short of the point of the bayonet."

In response to such harsh criticisms, an unsigned reviewer for the *Atlanta Constitution* fired back: "It is difficult to believe that the critics who have condemned the book as coarse, vulgar and inartistic can have read it." The reviewer notes that "the moral of the book, though it is not scrawled across every page, teaches the necessity of manliness and self-sacrifice." Indeed, in the decades after it was first published, literary scholars praised *The Adventures of Huckleberry Finn* as one of Twain's most morally complex works.

In more recent years, however, the novel has not received the attention or acclaim it once commanded from readers and critics. Although many critics point to the literary failings of the book's final chapters, the main source of complaint for modern readers is the racist attitude presented by many of the characters, especially Huck. Specifically, many modern readers have remarked on the fact that the word "nigger" appears so liberally and unapologetically in the book—even though the term is authentic to the antebellum Missouri diction Twain works hard to recreate. The American Library Association, which tracks the number of "challenges" leveled at controversial books in libraries nationwide, lists *The Adventures of Huckleberry Finn* as the fifth most-challenged book in libraries between 1990–2000.

Despite the controversies that surround it, *The Adventures of Huckleberry Finn* is still widely considered Twain's masterpiece; according to biographer Ron Powers, the book has sold in excess of twenty million copies worldwide.

MEDIA ADAPTATIONS

An abridged audio adaptation of the novel was released by Caedmon in 1998. This version is narrated by Ed Begley, and is currently available in audiocassette format.

An abridged audio adaptation was released in CD format by Naxos Audiobooks in 1995. This version features narration by Garrick Hagon.

An abridged audio adaptation narrated and adapted by Garrison Keillor was released by Highbridge Audio in 2003. This version is currently available in both audiocassette and CD format.

An unabridged audio adaptation, narrated by Dick Hill, was released in 2001 by Brilliance Audio. It is currently available in both CD and audiocassette format.

An abridged audio adaptation narrated by Wil Wheaton was released by Dove Audio in 1993; this version is currently available as a digital download through audible.com.

An electronic version of the book was released for Microsoft Reader by Amazon Press in 2000. This version features an introduction by John D. Seelye, and is available through amazon.com.

The first filmed adaptation of *The Adventures of Huckleberry Finn* was a black-and-white silent film released in 1920. The film was directed by William Desmond Taylor, and is not currently available.

Another filmed adaptation was released in 1931 by Paramount; this was the first "talking" version of the film, directed by Norman Taurog and starring Jackie Coogan—a child star most famous for his role as the title character in Charlie Chaplin's masterpiece *The Kid*—as Huckleberry Finn. This version is not currently available.

Yet another film based on the book was released in 1939 by MGM; this version was directed by Richard Thorpe and starred Mickey Rooney in the title role. It was released in VHS format by MGM in 1999.

A full-color film adaptation of the novel was released by MGM in 1960. The film was directed by Michael Curtiz, and starred Eddie Hodges as Huck and Tony Randall as the king; it is currently available on DVD through Warner Home Video.

A filmed musical adaptation of the novel was released by MGM in 1974, directed by J. Lee Thompson and featuring songs by Richard and Robert Sherman (famous for their work in movies such as *Mary Poppins* and *Chitty Chitty Bang Bang*). This version is currently available on DVD through MGM.

An adaptation of the novel was released by Disney in 1995; this version starred Elijah Wood as Huck Finn and Courtney B. Vance as Jim, and was directed by Stephen Sommers. Although every film adaptation has been criticized to some degree for not staying true to the book, this version in particular features a radically altered ending. This version is currently available on DVD from Walt Disney Video.

The novel has been adapted for television several times: first in 1955, then again in 1975 (with Ron Howard in the title role), yet again in 1981, and once more in 1985. The 1975 version was released on VHS by Twentieth Century Fox in 1996, and the 1985 version was released on VHS by MCA Home Video in 1992. None of these versions is currently available.

An animated television adaptation of *The Adventures of Huckleberry Finn* was created by Koch Vision in 1984. This version was released on DVD in 2006.

Big River: The Adventures of Huckleberry Finn, a stage musical version of the novel, began its run on Broadway in 1985 and remained there until 1987. This version featured music and lyrics by legendary country musician Roger Miller, with performances by John Goodman and René Auberjonois, among others; a soundtrack of the original cast recording was released by Decca U.S. in 1990, and is currently available in CD format.

CRITICISM

Gregory Fowler

In the following excerpt, Fowler discusses how Twain's Adventures of Huckleberry Finn *has contributed to America's discourse on race and racism.*

There are many instances in American society where we attempt to distance ourselves from our more shameful moments and embrace those that are more flattering to us. Nor are we the only ones to do so. Twain comments on the phenomena in *The Innocents Abroad* when he is passing through Versailles and sees that all the images being recalled are of victories, not of their defeats or embarrassments. The same is evident in America. It is impossible not to be moved by the Holocaust Museum on The Mall in Washington, D.C., and one of the underlying motifs of the Museum is how America acted as the Grand Savior in coming in and helping free the Jews from concentration camps. Still one cannot help being struck by the outcry on the other hand when a museum commemorating the Trail of Tears or the years of slavery are proposed. Americans would rather not recall that.

Such a failure to truly digest our history keeps many Americans in the cyclical racism which perpetuates itself. W. E. B. Dubois stated that the question of the American twentieth century would be race. Although the man was a genius, he didn't have to be to make that observation; the issues that caused the greatest difficulty at the Constitutional Convention in the eighteenth century had been race, the issue which had plagued the nation in the nineteenth century and caused it to enter into the most costly war during its existence had been race, and since much of the country at the turn of the twentieth century was seeking ways to continue the status of blacks as second-class citizens, it was quite evident that the Civil War was only another step in the process, and certainly not the last. Lynchings were prominent at the beginning of the twentieth century; in the middle, lynchings like that of Emmet Till would still be in the news; at the end, in 1998, they would continue to haunt the nation as James Byrd Jr., a black man in Texas, was dragged behind a truck until his head and other body parts were scattered over several miles.

Racism still exists and procreates; no one disputes that. But the process of social evolution has caused the form of racism to morph in some interesting ways.

While the issue seem to be growing, few if any have so epitomized the issue as Mark Twain, especially his book *Adventures of Huckleberry Finn*, considered to be the great American novel by quite a few scholars and the origin of American writing by even more. *Huck Finn* is one of those books that attracts attention not because critics assert that it is a badly-written book but because it is too well-written; that is, it refuses to avoid language and topics that some would rather not deal with. The timeliness of Twain's work is evident when records show that attempts to ban it somewhere in America have occurred every single year in the 1990s. No other book or established writer in the American canon ignites such hostile debates. Each school year some parent has raised the issue of banning the novel or rewriting it to soften the usage of words like "nigger" and Jim's broken English. This is counter productive. Avoiding the fact that such events happened either (1) convinces youth that it is a problem that should continue being avoided, or (2) suggests that it is a problem no longer significant or already solved.

This seems to be one of the two things Mark Twain proposes in his writings to help solve the race problem in America; it is what he meant in a letter he wrote as a recommendation for the gentleman who later became a mentor for Frederick Douglass—that to a certain extent whites owe them, not that it could be made up in reparations but in an acknowledgment that blacks are penalized because of their blackness and that the problems of white segregation and Jim Crow laws last even long afterwards. Mark Twain becomes the first American to truly ask whites to look in that mirror, and acknowledge some benefit from what was (and still is) going on with blacks. As with the Germans in Berlin, with the alcoholic or domestic abuser, the acknowledgment should not bring about unbearable guilt; rather it should begin the process of healing.

Malcolm X put it best: If someone has stabbed you in the back, and at some point they become "gracious" enough to pull the knife out of your back, they should at least acknowledge the fact that it is going to leave some type of scar. Much of African American literature and Twain's own writings deal with the frustration that blacks feel because no matter what they achieve, white society would never be able to simply look beyond the color of the skin they see before them; every action, good or bad, must be judged within the context of blackness. If a black succeeds or does something outstanding, he is looked at as the exception to his race—any black in this position can probably recall hearing white society say (not always directly) something along the lines of, "You're not like the rest of them!" Any negative black action must be read within the context of race as well. This is what Twain is examining in the character of Jim; no matter how noble he may act he will always be regarded as a nigger—Huck follows this principle throughout most of the novel. When he does begin to see things differently he notices this discrepancy in how the Phelpses treat Jim. He has been good and sacrificed himself to save Tom Sawyer, so the community resolves not to curse him anymore. Of course since he is a nigger they never think about removing some of the heavy chains around his neck. As Fishkin points out, this is exactly the same frustration Malcolm X voices years later when he cries, "Do you know what white racists call black Ph.D.'s?" and answered "Nigger!"

It is hard to forget the horrible scene in *Huck Finn* when Pap is ranting at Huck. His words, however, help us to later appreciate Huck's dilemma when trying to help Jim. If this is the only authority in Huck's life, can we blame him for his fears and deformed conscience?

Perhaps one of the most telling lines in Pap's ranting is his suggestion that allowing a nigger to vote had kept him from doing the one thing within his legal and moral power to do to change things in his favor, which was vote himself. What it reflects is a growing disillusionment with a government and a distancing of oneself from it. This is dangerous, for what option is then left to Pap? The only action we see him admit to taking after that sense of distancing is an assault upon the nigger himself—he shoves the nigger off the road when he wants to get by. Such disillusionment is evident even more so in modern society. While the percentage of people who are voting steadily falls, the percentage of people expressing anger or rejecting the government grows, and the only action left available to them outside of the voting booth is vigilante justice. Hence we have larger citizen militias and more beatings, murders, and incidents designed not so much to effect change but to express a distancing from the system. Pap is the first of the Angry White Males.

The second proposal or assertion that Mark Twain makes which would ease racial tension in America is to discard the concept of race as an absolute. This suggestion has gained popularity in the last decade, as popular and scientific works assert that what we believe to be race is largely a cultural construction. Twain examines this false color line explicitly in *The Tragedy of Puddn'head Wilson*. When Rowena, a very light skinned Negress, exchanges her own legally black child (by a white man) for the legally white one, no one knows the difference. Like a number of African American writers during this period, Twain is playing with the color line arguing against the validity of race construction. It is the same question argued genetically by a number of scholars. In 1991, papers like *The Washington Post* ran features asking the question, "Does Race Exist?" arguing that if we attempt to classify people based upon one characteristic, even skin color, the definition of race becomes meaningless. My students were shocked to know that there are some races considered white who are darker than black people and some races considered black who are lighter than many Caucasians.

The process of redefining or re-naming has long played a significant role in American life. It is evident with Mark Twain a.k.a. Mr. Brown a.k.a. Samuel Clemens. It is evident with other figures dealing with race, like Malcolm X, a.k.a. Detroit Red a.k.a. Malcolm Little a.k.a. El Hajj Malik El-Shabazz. It is not incidental that Twain's most famous work on race is centered around Huckleberry Finn who constantly changes names and takes on different identities from the little girl he pretends to be with the widow to ultimately claiming to be Tom Sawyer. The power of naming and redefining one's self outside of societal norms is what enables Huck (and the novel) to continue.

The problems which have been stereotypically assigned to groups of people based on race are evident in all aspects of society, further reducing the constructs of race, but the obstacles to overcoming racism are just as evident on all sides. Whites are not alone in their unwillingness to deal with the past as it really was. The vehemence with which some blacks attack Twain for what they (mistakenly) see as his racism is matched only by the antipathy many whites seem to have for Malcolm X, but no two stories are more American than these two. Instead of the vehement anger voiced by many, these two Americans—their lives and their writings—should be among the most inspirational. It is true that Twain's background is filled with events typical of any white youth growing up in Missouri during the pre-Civil War years; it is also true that Malcolm's writings, his anger, his gullibility are understandable given his background. What is important, however, is not where these two humans began, but where they were able to go from there, and how they did so. Any reader who cannot be moved by the courage of these men to accept responsibility for their futures, regardless of their pasts, misses the greatest examples of what it means to be American. For like these two, it is true that America has some skeletons which continue to haunt her—high among these are its racism and homophobia.

There is a passage in *Huckleberry Finn* which spells it out precisely. As they float down the great river Huck says, "What you want, above all things, on a raft, is for everybody to be satisfied, and feel right and kind towards the others." The race card in America has always been a potential threat to overturning our raft.

Like the book itself, the argument does not end with despair or closure, but with hope and possibility. Huck ventures off to new adventures. He is not, at that point, a perfect human being or completely reformed, but we know through his experiences that there is hope. He has already taken steps which leave us with the sense that as he grows older, he will grow wiser as well.

Time allows atrocities to occur in the short term—lynchings, slavery, relocation, concentration camps—but overriding them all, inevitable, unstoppable, progress marches on. Mark Twain himself is a wonderful example of this; as the son of a slave owner, it is not surprising that many of the views Twain espoused during his youth and early twenties were typically racist. Indeed, as Arthur Pettit notes, the height of Twain's racism seems to occur during the 1860s when he is out West. Much of his writing during this period profited from his use of the tradition of the black buffoon as scapegoat to entertain whites. He continues in this vein for a time after 1867, but once he becomes a member of the eastern establishment and the son-in-law of a man who had been a leading conductor of the Underground Railroad, Clemens begins a reevaluation of himself and the Negro, a turning point that within a year would lead him to launch a new career towards service to the black race. Like Huck Finn and his creator, Samuel Clemens, though we are not yet where we wish to be, there is hope that as we grow older, we too will grow wiser.

Source: Gregory Fowler, "'If I Warn't Too Drunk to Get There...': On Race," in *Journal of American & Comparative Cultures*, Spring 2001, pp. 49–58.

SOURCES

Buchanan, Thomas C., *Black Life on the Mississippi: Slaves, Free Blacks, and the Western Steamboat World*, University of North Carolina Press, 2004, pp. 20, 23.

Foner, Eric, *A Short History of Reconstruction*, Harper Perennial, 1990, p. 18.

Hemingway, Ernest, *Green Hills of Africa*, Scribner Classic/Collier, 1987, originally published in 1935, p. 22.

"Huckleberry Finn and His Critics," in the *Atlanta Constitution*, May 26, 1885, as quoted on the website Mark Twain in His Times, presented by the University of Virginia Department of English, etext.virginia.edu/railton/huckfinn/atlanta.html (April 14, 2006).

Jefferson, Thomas, "Transcript of Letter: Thomas Jefferson to John Holmes," on the Library of Congress website, Thomas Jefferson Exhibit, www.loc.gov/exhibits/jefferson/159.html (April 14, 2006).

Johnson, Richard Charles, with Patricia Smith and WGBH Series Research Team, *Africans in America: America's Journey through Slavery*, Harvest/HBJ Book, 1999, p. 306.

Matthews, Brander, Review of *The Adventures of Huckleberry Finn* by Mark Twain, in the *Saturday Review*, January 31, 1885, *Mark Twain in His Times*, University of Virginia Department of English, etext.virginia.edu/railton/huckfinn/satrev.html (April 14, 2006).

Perry, T. S., Review of *The Adventures of Huckleberry Finn* by Mark Twain, in *The Century Illustrated Monthly Magazine*, May 1885, *Mark Twain in His Times*, University of Virginia Department of English, etext.virginia.edu/railton/huckfinn/satrev.html (April 14, 2006).

Powers, Ron, *Mark Twain: A Life*, Free Press, 2005, p. 490.

Review of *The Adventures of Huckleberry Finn* by Mark Twain, in *Athenaeum*, December 27, 1884, *Mark Twain in His Times*, University of Virginia Department of English, etext.virginia.edu/railton/huckfinn/satrev.html (April 14, 2006).

Review of *The Adventures of Huckleberry Finn* by Mark Twain, in the *Boston Daily Advertiser*, March 12, 1885, *Mark Twain in His Times*, University of Virginia Department of English, etext.virginia.edu/railton/huckfinn/satrev.html (April 14, 2006).

Review of *The Adventures of Huckleberry Finn* by Mark Twain, in the *Boston Evening Traveller*, March 5, 1885, *Mark Twain in His Times*, University of Virginia Department of English, etext.virginia.edu/railton/huckfinn/satrev.html (April 14, 2006).

Review of *The Adventures of Huckleberry Finn* by Mark Twain, in the *Hartford Courant*, February 20, 1885, *Mark Twain in His Times*, University of Virginia Department of English, etext.virginia.edu/railton/huckfinn/satrev.html (April 14, 2006).

Review of *The Adventures of Huckleberry Finn* by Mark Twain, in the *San Francisco Chronicle*, February 20, 1885, *Mark Twain in His Times*, University of Virginia Department of English, etext.virginia.edu/railton/huckfinn/satrev.html (April 14, 2006).

Review of *The Adventures of Huckleberry Finn* by Mark Twain, in the *San Francisco Daily Examiner*, March 9, 1885, *Mark Twain in His Times*, University of Virginia Department of English, etext.virginia.edu/railton/huckfinn/satrev.html (April 14, 2006).

Review of *The Adventures of Huckleberry Finn* by Mark Twain, in the *San Francisco Evening Bulletin*, March 14, 1885 *Mark Twain in His Times*, University of Virginia Department of English, etext.virginia.edu/railton/huckfinn/satrev.html (April 14, 2006).

Smith, Henry Nash, and William M. Gibson, eds., *Mark Twain-Howells Letters: The Correspondence of Samuel L. Clemens and William Dean Howells,* Vol. 1, Harvard University Press, 1960, p. 144, as quoted in *Mark Twain: A Life*, by Ron Powers, Free Press, 2005, p. 388.

"The 100 Most Frequently Challenged Books of 1990–2000," American Library Association, www.ala.org/ala/oif/bannedbooksweek/bbwlinks/100mostfrequently.htm (April 15, 2006).

Twain, Mark, *Adventures of Huckleberry Finn: A Case Study in Critical Controversy,* edited by Gerald Graff and James Phelan, Bedford Books, 1995.

Twain, Mark, letter published in the *Hartford Courant,* April 4, 1885, *Mark Twain in His Times*, University of Virginia Department of English, etext.virginia.edu/railton/huckfinn/satrev.html (April 14, 2006).

Angels in America

TONY KUSHNER

1992

Tony Kushner's two-part play, *Angels in America* (1992), has been lauded by critics and audiences alike as one of the most important American plays of the twentieth century. Set during the dawn of the AIDS crisis in the 1980s, *Angels in America* freezes a period in American history when homosexuals were firmly outside of the mainstream, AIDS was a death sentence, and political leaders were preaching compassion without showing it. The play captures the fear, hate, ignorance, and prejudice that shrouded the AIDS epidemic in its early years, and shows the toll of the disease on individual health, social status, and identity, as well as on society as a whole.

The main plotline of *Angels in America* revolves around two couples living in New York City in the mid-1980s. Within those two pairs, each of the four individuals is struggling to come to terms with his or her identity. Louis and Prior are a gay couple living together until Prior falls ill with AIDS. Joe and Harper Pitt are a married Mormon couple; Harper is addicted to Valium, and Joe is a closeted homosexual. As the play progresses, the couples' lives become increasingly entwined as they search for ways to understand their places in the world. All of these characters are members of at least one group that leaves them marginalized or subjects them to prejudice and ridicule: Louis is Jewish, Prior has AIDS, Harper is a Mormon woman, and Joe is a gay Republican. In addition to these primary

characters, characters such as Roy Cohn, a public figure and closeted homosexual dying of AIDS; Belize, a black ex-drag-queen; and Hannah, a Mormon mother, also experience life on the fringe of society. They all live in a time and a nation that denies them the right to be who they truly are. Though the primary themes of *Angels in America* relate to identity, illness, and sexuality, issues of religion, race, gender, and political affiliation resonate just as loudly in the play.

During this time of upheaval and crisis for these characters, Prior is visited by the Angel, who declares Prior a prophet. The play captures a particular era in American history at a pivotal point: with so much death and disaster, humanity must make a decision to progress. Leaving things in their current state, or even regressing into past behaviors and lifestyles, is not an option. Harper sums up Kushner's ideal toward the end of the play: "In this world, there is a kind of painful progress. Longing for what we've left behind, and dreaming ahead."

One distinguishing aspect of the play is that only eight actors play the more than thirty roles within the play. Each actor plays at least two significant roles and various minor roles. For example, the actor playing the main role of Joe also plays Prior I, an Eskimo, the Mormon father in the Diorama Room of the Mormon Visitor's Center, and the Angel Europa. The significance of Kushner's casting direction is that it creates the literal impression that people are all the same. The audience sees that the actor playing Joe is the same person playing the Eskimo and the frontier Mormon settler, and establishes the idea that everyone—regardless of race, gender, religion, or sexual orientation—is essentially human, with hopes, fears, families, and lives that are important to them. Perhaps Kushner hopes that out of this realization should come compassion and empathy for all of humanity.

The two parts of *Angels in America*, *Millennium Approaches* and *Perestroika*, were initially published and performed separately. *Millennium Approaches*, for which Kushner won a Pulitzer Prize and a Tony Award for Best Play, was first presented by the Eureka Theatre Company in San Francisco in May 1991. It opened on stage in London in January of the following year. *Perestroika* opened in London in November 1993. The two parts of the play tell one cohesive story, though Part

> " THIS DISEASE WILL BE THE END OF MANY OF US, BUT NOT NEARLY ALL, AND THE DEAD WILL BE COMMEMORATED AND WILL STRUGGLE ON WITH THE LIVING, AND WE ARE NOT GOING AWAY. WE WON'T DIE SECRET DEATHS ANYMORE. THE WORLD ONLY SPINS FORWARD. WE WILL BE CITIZENS. THE TIME HAS COME."

One can also be considered a standalone play, and was initially reviewed as such. Together, the two parts of the play have a running time of just over six hours. The script is available in its entirety in book format from the Theatre Communications Group.

In addition to the Pulitzer Prize and Tony Awards, *Angels in America* has received numerous other awards and accolades, including the New York Drama Critics Circle Award, the London Drama Critics Circle Award, a Kennedy Center Award, and the Los Angeles Drama Critics Circle Award for Best New Play.

PLOT SUMMARY

Part One: Millennium Approaches

The play begins with the list of characters, some of which the author stipulates should be played by the same actor. For example, the actor playing Hannah also plays Henry the doctor and the ghost of Ethel Rosenberg. In Kushner's "Playwright's Notes," he gives instruction on staging and props, telling stage managers that "it's OK if the wires show, and maybe it's good that they do, but the magic should at the same time be thoroughly amazing."

Act One: Bad News

Act One takes place between October and November 1985, in New York City. Sarah Ironson's funeral is being presided over by Rabbi Isidor Chemelwitz, and though the rabbi did not know her personally, he says that because she came to America from the old country, "she carried the old world on her back across the ocean," and made it a part of her family's legacy. The rabbi says that such great voyages no longer exist in the modern world.

BIOGRAPHY

TONY KUSHNER

Tony Kushner was born in New York City on July 16, 1956. His parents were both classically trained musicians, and they moved the family to Lake Charles, Louisiana, when Kushner was a baby. He returned to New York in 1974 and attended New York University, where he received a bachelor's degree in English literature. In 1984, he received a master's degree in directing from NYU. Two years before he graduated, Kushner's first play, *The Age of Assassins* (1982) was staged in New York.

Since then, he has written and directed over two dozen plays that have been staged around the United States and abroad. From 1990 to 1992, he was the playwright-in-residence at the Julliard School of Drama, and he has been a guest artist at Yale University, Princeton University, and the NYU theater program. Besides plays, he has written books, movies, magazine articles, operas, and musicals. In 2005, he was nominated for an Academy Award for his screenplay of Steven Spielberg's movie *Munich*.

As a Jewish homosexual, Kushner's own personal experiences with racism, prejudice, and fear have become subjects that he explores in his writing. *Angels in America*, which won the Pulitzer Prize in 1993, examines all of these themes and the repercussions each of them have on life in America.

Scene 2 opens in lawyer Roy Cohn's office, where he is screaming into several telephone lines at once. Joe, a clerk for the Court of Appeals, stands waiting to talk to Roy. Roy's conversations make a show of his power and influence. Roy offers Joe a job working in Washington, D.C., for the Attorney General. Joe is unsure about the job, as he does not want to move his wife, Harper. Roy tells Joe to talk to her about it.

Harper is at home, listening to the radio and talking to herself. Her imaginary friend, Mr. Lies, appears, and Harper tells him that she feels history is on the verge of something big, since it is only fifteen years until the millennium. Joe comes home and asks if Harper would like to move to D.C.

Louis and Prior are outside the funeral of Louis's grandmother, Sarah Ironson. The men are a couple, and Louis remarks that he "always get[s] so closety at these family gatherings" and apologizes for not introducing his boyfriend to his family. Prior says he does not blame him for hiding it. Prior then shows Louis a lesion on his arm. Prior tries to joke about it, but Louis does not play along. Prior knows the lesion indicates AIDS and is a death sentence. Louis refuses to accept it. Prior tells Louis that he is afraid Louis will leave him when he starts to get really sick. Louis does not disagree.

In a split scene, Joe and Harper discuss moving to D.C., and Louis is at his grandmother's graveside service. Harper does not want to move. Joe asks how many pills she took that day, and Harper reluctantly answers, "None. One. Three. Only three." The scene shifts to Louis asking the rabbi about what the Holy Writ says about leaving someone in a time of need. When the rabbi asks why a person would do such a thing, he replies in the abstract, saying, "Maybe vomit . . . and sores and disease . . . really frighten him, maybe . . . he isn't so good with death." Back in Joe and Harper's apartment, Joe is trying to convince Harper that things are changing for the better in America under President Reagan's policies, and that he has a chance to be a part of it if they move to D.C. Harper tells him it seems that the world is not getting better, but Joe accuses her of having emotional problems that keep her from going outside. Harper confronts Joe about the walks he sometimes takes, and tells him that he never should have married her because he has "all these secrets and lies." Joe tries to reassure her. Harper tells Joe, "The world's coming to an end."

Scene 6 opens during the first week of November. Joe happens upon Louis crying in the men's room of the courthouse where they both work. Louis is crying over Prior's illness, and senses that Joe is gay. Joe denies it. The next scene is a dream sequence in which Prior and Harper appear in each other's dreams (Harper is having a drug-induced hallucination), though they have never met each other. When they meet in the dream/hallucination, Harper tells Prior, "In my church we don't believe in homosexuals," to which Prior responds, "In my church we don't believe in Mormons." Prior tells Harper that Joe is gay, confirming Harper's suspicions. After Harper vanishes from Prior's dream, he hears a booming voice commanding him to "Look up, look up, / prepare the way." He is confused, and feels ill.

When Joe comes home that evening, Harper demands to know where he has been. He tells her he has been walking—code for what Harper believes are homosexual trysts—and she insists that he tell her exactly where he has been. She asks him if he is gay, and he denies it. The scene switches to Prior and Louis in bed. Prior has two new lesions. Louis asks if Prior would hate him if he left him in his illness. Back in Joe and Harper's apartment, Harper wants to ask God if Joe is gay, and Joe tells her it does not matter one way or the other. He tells her he fought to suppress the "wrong, or ugly" part of himself, and that "my behavior is what I know it has to be." Prior and Louis talk about Prior's ancestors, who were shipwrecked in a small lifeboat after a storm at sea. Whenever someone on board got sick, they pitched them into the sea. Louis begs Prior not to get any sicker.

Scene 9 opens with Roy Cohn visiting his doctor, Henry. Henry tells Roy that he has AIDS, and Roy responds that that is a disease that strikes "homosexuals and drug addicts"; he denies being either, though it is clear to Henry that Roy is gay. Roy rejects the label of homosexual: "Homosexuals are men who know nobody and who nobody knows." As a powerbroker and political figure, he refuses to be classified in a group without power: "Because *what* I am is defined entirely by *who* I am. Roy Cohn is a heterosexual man, Henry, who f—s around with guys.... AIDS is what homosexuals have. I have liver cancer." Henry suggests that Roy use his power to get the experimental AIDS drug, AZT.

Act Two: In Vitro

Act two spans from December 1985 through January 1986. Prior is much sicker, and is lying on the floor in pain, calling for Louis. Louis wants to call an ambulance, but Prior does not want to go to the hospital. Prior loses control of his bowels, and there is blood. He tells Louis not to touch him or the blood. Louis quietly says to himself that he cannot handle this. Later, when Prior goes to the hospital, Louis prays for Prior to die if he is not going to fully recover.

Joe comes home to Harper sitting in the dark. She tells him she is going to leave; he begs her to stay because he has been praying about their marriage, and asking "God to crush me, break me up into little pieces and start all over again." He feels like the biblical Jacob wrestling the angel. In the next scene at a bar, Roy tells Joe to leave Harper if she will not go with him to D.C. Joe protests, telling Roy that he cannot leave her because she needs him. The scene shifts to Central Park, where Louis picks up a stranger and has sex with him. He tells the stranger, "Infect me. I don't care. I don't care." The man leaves. The scene shifts back to Joe and Roy at the bar. Roy continues to tell Joe not to let Harper stand in the way of his life: "Life is full of horror; nobody escapes, nobody; save yourself."

Prior's friend Belize, a former drag queen who is now a nurse, is visiting Prior in the hospital. Prior tells Belize about the voice he keeps hearing, and Belize tells him he is just imagining it. When Belize leaves, the voice returns, telling Prior to prepare to be part of "A marvelous work and a wonder . . . a great error [to] correct, with the rule, sword and the broom of Truth!" Prior is confused.

Joe and Roy are out at a fancy restaurant with Martin, a publicist for the Reagan Justice Department. They talk politics, and about Joe's possible move to D.C. Roy tells them that the New York State Bar Association is trying to disbar him. Roy postures and denies past unethical practices, declaring that he will continue to be a lawyer for as long as he lives. Later that afternoon, Joe and Louis encounter each other again on the steps of the Hall of Justice in Brooklyn. They discuss their situations at home, and feel a connection, though neither of them fully acknowledges it. That night, Joe calls his mother Hannah in Salt Lake City and tells her he is a homosexual. She tells him he is being ridiculous, and to go home to Harper. "We will just forget this phone call," she says.

Scene 9 is a split scene, in which Harper and Louis tell Joe and Prior, respectively, that they are leaving them. Both couples are splitting up. Prior is furious that Louis would leave him when he is sick and dying, and though heartbroken, tells him to get out for good. Harper tells Joe that he should go to D.C. without her. Harper leaves the scene with her imaginary friend Mr. Lies. After Louis leaves, Prior says, "I wish I was dead." Hannah puts her Salt Lake City house up for sale in order to move to New York City.

Act Three: Not-Yet-Conscious, Forward Dawning

It is January 1986, three days after the end of act 2. Prior is dreaming about two of his ancestors, both also named Prior Walter. Prior I died of the plague, "The spotty monster. Like you, alone." Prior II calls Prior "Prophet. Seer. Revelator," and Prior is confused.

In the next scene, Louis and Belize are in a coffee shop, discussing politics, AIDS, and racism. Louis argues, "there are no gods here, no ghosts and spirits in America, there are no angels in America, no spiritual past, no racial past, there's only the political." Their conversation then turns to Prior. Louis asks how he is doing, and Belize tells him that Prior is not doing well. Louis tells him he does not know what to do anymore, and that Prior's illness made him nervous and afraid. Louis wants some kind of comfort from Belize, but does not get it.

In a brief scene, Harper retreats to a snowy fantasy land with Mr. Lies. He convinces her that she is hallucinating, but she does not care. She says she wants to stay there and mend.

Hannah arrives in New York City. Joe does not pick her up at the airport, so she tries to make her way to Brooklyn, but gets lost and ends up in the Bronx. That same day, Joe is at Roy's apartment, where he tells Roy that he will not go to D.C. Roy thinks he is stupid for passing up such an opportunity. Roy tells Joe about his involvement in the 1951 Rosenberg Trial, in which Ethel Rosenberg was found guilty of being a communist spy and later executed. Roy claims he pressured the judge to impose the death sentence. Joe is horrified; he had looked up to Roy as a mentor. When Joe leaves, Roy is visited by the ghost of Ethel Rosenberg. He tells her, "I'M NOT AFRAID OF YOU OR DEATH OR HELL OR ANYTHING!" She tells him she will be seeing him soon. Roy suffers an attack of some sort, and Ethel calls for an ambulance. He tells her he is immortal, and will never die. She laughs and tells him, "History is about to crack wide open. Millennium approaches."

Scene 6 opens with Prior I watching Prior in his bed, telling him that tonight is the night that he will receive his revelation. Prior hears the beating of wings, and is terrified. He calls out for Louis. At the same time, Louis is sitting on a bench in the park when Joe approaches and asks Louis if he knows the story of Lazarus from the Bible, the man who was raised from the dead by

Jesus. Joe touches Louis's face, and the two of them leave together. Back in Prior's room, the sound of wings has become a deafening roar. There is a cracking noise from the ceiling, triumphal music, and a cascade of multicolored lights. Prior is frightened, then awestruck, whispering, "*Very* Steven Spielberg," at the entrance of the Angel. Ceiling plaster crashes to the floor, and the Angel descends and floats above Prior's bed: "Greetings, Prophet; / The Great Work begins: / The Messenger has arrived."

Part Two: Perestroika
Act One: Spooj

Part Two opens with Aleskii Antedilluvianovich Prelapsarianov, the world's oldest living Bolshevik. Bolshevism is traditionally associated with Russian socialists in the early twentieth century; the term is frequently associated with communism. Prelapolsarianov asks, "Can we Change? In Time? And we all desire that Change will come." While he believes that change is needed, he prefers to wait on theory before commencing to change. As Prelapsarianov finishes his speech, the Angel is hovering over Prior's bed. Prior tells it to leave.

At the same time, Harper imagines herself again in her imaginary winter-land with her imaginary friend Mr. Lies. Joe enters the scene, uncertain of where he is. Harper asks him to come back, but this time it is he who says he cannot stay. Joe's mother Hannah picks up the phone at Joe and Harper's apartment and hears that Harper has been found in a park in Brooklyn, chewing on a tree. She rushes to retrieve her daughter-in-law.

When Prior awakens, his bedroom ceiling is intact as if the Angel had never come. He calls Belize at the hospital and tells him that his eyes feel funny, and realizes that he is crying. He says that not only is he scared, but "also full of . . . Joy or something. Hope." Belize learns he will be taking care of Roy, and quickly calls Prior to tell him, calling Roy "New York's number one closeted queer." When Belize goes into Roy's room, Roy demands a white nurse instead, and the two of them trade insults and threats. After Belize leaves, Roy calls Martin Heller to get himself a private stash of the experimental medication AZT.

Louis and Joe are at Louis's new apartment. Louis begins to seduce Joe, who is at first hesitant to act on his homosexual feelings, but eventually gives in. Louis and Joe make love.

Act Two: The Epistle

Three weeks later, Belize and Prior attend the funeral of a friend. Prior is dressed in a long coat and a scarf draped like a hood. He remains in this costume throughout the rest of the play. Belize tells Prior he is dressed "like Morticia Addams," but Prior counters that he is dressed "Like the Wrath of God." He tells Belize he has been given a prophecy.

Scene 2 returns to the night that the Angel visited Prior in his bedroom as Prior tells Belize what happened. The Angel tells Prior that he must pull up his kitchen tiles in order to reveal the "Sacred Prophetic Implements." Prior refuses, then hears a noise in the kitchen. He goes out and returns with a dusty suitcase that had been hidden under the tiles. The suitcase contains a pair of glasses, and when Prior tries them on, he sees visions and instantly takes them off, terrified. Prior is sexually aroused by the Angel, who is androgynous (neither exclusively female or male), and they have sex. Afterward, the Angel explains that humanity's insistence on progress and exploration have caused a problem in Heaven. According to the Angel, God became bored after seeing all that humanity was doing and discovering, and left Heaven. God has not been seen since. Prior summarizes the Angel's position for Belize: "It's all gone too far, too much loss is what they think, we should stop somehow, go back." Prior tells the Angel to leave. The Angel tells him that he cannot outrun his responsibility as a prophet, and cannot escape that duty. Prior decides, "Maybe I am a prophet. Not just me, all of us who are dying now. Maybe we've caught the virus of prophecy. Be still. Toil no more."

Act Three: Borborygmi (The Squirming Facts Exceed the Squamous Mind)

Scene 1 is a split scene, in which Joe and Louis are in bed in Louis's apartment, and Hannah is caring for Harper in Joe and Harper's apartment. Louis sleeps while Joe can see Harper standing in her underwear while his mother tends to her. Harper then enters into Joe's bedroom, telling him, "Don't worry, I'm not really here. I have terrible powers. I see more than I want to see." Harper asks Joe why she is there, and he says he does not know; she tells him that he has summoned her. Harper tells Joe that he is turning into her, pathetic in love.

That same morning, Roy is feeling increasingly sick in his hospital room. He has a continuing conversation with Ethel; he denies that he is dying, and she waits patiently for the inevitable. Belize enters and sees Roy's stash of AZT, and tells him that his stash could help dozens of people. Roy does not care. Belize demands ten vials. They argue, throwing racist insults at one another. Belize ends up taking some of Roy's AZT. Ethel laughs at him.

That afternoon, Hannah and Harper are in the Diorama Room of the Mormon Visitor's Center, where Hannah works. The diorama portrays a family of early Mormon settlers. Hannah enters with Prior, giving him a tour. Prior and Harper discuss Mormonism, and then the lights dim and the diorama begins, telling the story of the Mormon exodus to Utah. Prior and Harper both see Joe and Louis in the diorama, kissing; it is a figment of their mutual imagination. Prior leaves, and Harper turns to the Mormon Mother in the diorama, asking for help. The Mormon Mother tells Harper to leave her heart behind, "Can't carry no extra weight." They leave the Visitor's Center together.

That afternoon, Joe and Louis are at the beach; it is cold as they sit on the dunes. Louis tells Joe that he wants to see Prior again. Joe begs him not to leave, offering to change everything about himself—"I'm flayed. No past now. I could give up anything"—in order to keep Louis. Louis leaves Joe on the beach.

Later that evening, Roy asks Belize what death is like. Belize tells him it is "[l]ike San Francisco" and full of beautiful black deities. Roy tells him it does not sound like Heaven.

Harper and the Mormon Mother are at the Brooklyn Heights Promenade. The Mormon Mother tells Harper that God changes people by splitting them open and making them walk around with their guts out. From the side of the stage, Louis dials Prior's number from a payphone, and tells him he wants to see him.

Act Four: John Brown's Body

Scene 1 is a split scene. Joe is visiting Roy in his hospital room; Louis is sitting alone on a bench. Roy has a somewhat paternal moment with Joe, giving him a deathbed blessing. Meanwhile, Prior enters the scene with Louis and sits on the other end of the bench. Louis tells Prior he wants to come back, but Prior does not believe the sentiment: "You cry, but you endanger nothing in yourself. It's like the idea of crying when you do it. Or the idea of love." Joe tells Roy that he has left Harper and has been spending time with another man. Roy tells him to end whatever he is doing with the other man and go back to his wife for the sake of his political reputation, and never discuss it again. On the park bench, Prior tells Louis not to come back until he is bruised on the outside as a show of his pain.

The next day, Joe is sitting in his office. Belize and Prior are outside the door; they have figured out that he is Louis's new lover. Prior goes into Joe's office on a pretense, saying that he knows Harper, then Belize goes into the office; Joe recognizes Belize as Roy's nurse. They improvise a cover-up reason for being there and leave. The next day, Belize and Louis meet at the Bethesda Fountain in Central Park. Belize makes the Roy-Joe connection for Louis. Louis feels sorry for himself, and cannot believe he has been sleeping with someone associated with Roy Cohn.

Meanwhile, Joe goes to the Mormon Visitor's Center and talks to Hannah. He tells Hannah that he is going to take Harper home with him, but his mother says that that is not the best idea. It appears that Harper has already run away, and Joe tells Hannah it was a mistake when he called her and told her he was gay. Joe leaves at the same time that Prior enters. Prior connects Joe, Harper, and Louis. Prior begins to feel faint, and collapses. He asks Hannah to call for an ambulance. That afternoon, Harper is still at the Promenade in Brooklyn. It is freezing cold, and she is dressed in a light dress and no shoes. Joe appears with an umbrella, and they both turn to look at the Manhattan skyline as they talk. Harper says it is "Judgment Day."

At the hospital, Prior tells Hannah about the Angel, and how he has been consumed with "this ice-cold, razor-blade terror that just shouts and shouts 'Keep moving! Run!' And I've run myself.... Into the ground." Hannah tells Prior about the angel that appeared to Joseph Smith and sparked the Mormon religion. Prior asks if there are any prophets in the Bible that have ever refused their calling, and Hannah says yes. Prior wants to know what God does to them, and Hannah responds, "He.... Well, he feeds them to whales." She then tells him not to be afraid: "An angel is just a belief, with wings and arms that can carry you. It's naught to be afraid of. If it lets you down, reject it. Seek for something new." Just then, Prior can sense the Angel's approach.

That same evening, Harper and Joe are back in their apartment. They have just had sex, and Harper asks if he imagines men when he is with her. He quickly dresses and tells her he is going back to Louis. When he leaves, she knows it is a final goodbye. Joe arrives at Louis's apartment as Louis is reading through a large stack of paperwork. He is reading cases that Roy Cohn has been involved with in the past, several of them anti-gay, and discovers that Joe was the ghostwriter: "This is an important bit of legal fag-bashing, isn't it? They trusted you to do it. And you didn't disappoint." Joe begs forgiveness and pleads that he is in love with Louis. When Louis tries to force Joe to leave, they get into a physical fight, with Joe beating Louis until he is bloody and bruised.

That night, Roy is visited by Ethel. He knows he is dying, and is happy to be dying a lawyer, even as the Bar Association was trying to have him disbarred. Ethel gleefully breaks the news that they disbarred him that afternoon, so he will, in fact, die without his prized title. He feigns death and she sings him a Yiddish song to comfort him. Ecstatic that he fooled her and made her sing, he finally dies.

Act Five: Heaven, I'm in Heaven

In Prior's hospital room, Prior and Hannah witness the return of the Angel. Following Hannah's advice, Prior tells the Angel that he rejects his role as prophet. Hannah tells him that he must wrestle the Angel, just as Jacob did in the Bible. In the midst of their wrestling match, a ladder to Heaven descends, and the Angel tells Prior to climb.

Everyone in Heaven is dressed as though it is a Hollywood film about ancient times, and Heaven itself looks like San Francisco after the big 1906 earthquake. Prior sees Harper, and begs her to stay with him in Heaven because "The world's too hard." Harper tells him that she cannot stay because she has never felt more alive, and she vanishes.

Belize has called Louis to come and take Roy's stash of AZT before it is confiscated. He asks Louis to say the Kaddish, the Jewish prayer for the dead, over Roy. Louis hesitates, but Belize tells him,

> He was a terrible person. He died a hard death. So maybe.... A queen can forgive her vanquished foe. It isn't easy, it doesn't count if it's easy, it's the hardest thing. Forgiveness. Which is maybe where love and justice finally meet. Peace, at least.

At two in the morning, Joe enters his apartment and sees Roy's ghost. Roy tells Joe that Louis deserved the beating Joe gave him; he tells Joe to show that same type of force in the world outside.

Back in heaven, Prior meets with the Continental Principalities, angels representing each continent. He tells them to stop waiting around for God because he is never coming back, and if he were to come back, they should sue him for abandonment. They let him rejoin the living, and he slips back into his hospital bed. The next morning, he tells Belize and Hannah about his experience. Louis comes in, visibly beaten up from his fight with Joe. Belize gives Prior the AZT from Roy's room, but Prior refuses it. Louis tells Prior that he wants to come back to him.

Harper and Joe are in their apartment, and she tells him that she wants a credit card, and that he can know where she is by the locations of the charges. He tells her to call occasionally, but she refuses: "No. Probably never again. That's how bad. Sometimes, maybe lost is best. Get lost. Joe. Go exploring." She gives him two Valium. The scene is split with Louis and Prior at the hospital, and Prior tells Louis that even though he loves him, Louis can never come back. Later that night, while Louis and Prior are still in Prior's room, and Joe is in his apartment alone, Harper is on an airplane bound for San Francisco, looking out the window and thinking about progress.

Epilogue: Bethesda

Prior, Louis, Hannah, and Belize are all at the Bethesda Fountain. Louis and Belize are talking politics, Hannah is reading the *New York Times*, and Prior is frail but well. Prior thinks about the angel statue they are sitting under, and says, "I like them best when they're statuary. They commemorate death but they suggest a world without dying." He says that the days of homosexual men dying of AIDS in secret are over, and the country will move forward and accept homosexuals into society. The play ends with a directive to the audience that includes them in this progress: "You are fabulous creatures, each and every one. / And I bless you: *More Life*. / The Great Work Begins."

THEMES

Sexuality

Sexuality is a major component of *Angels in America*, and plays a substantial role in the plot. In a review of two books about Kushner entitled "The Square Root of Queer," Walter Bilderback asserts that *"Angels in America*'s queerness is like the 'Russian-ness' of Chekhov's plays—it is its skin. Without queerness, *Angels* would be a shapeless blob. . . . [Q]ueerness gives *Angels* a concrete grounding." Set in the 1980s during the explosion of the AIDS epidemic in New York City, the play illustrates how closely AIDS and homosexuality became associated during this time period, as well as the position of homosexuals in society at the time. As Belize says, "We don't [count]; faggots; we're just a bad dream the real world is having." In the characters of Joe, Roy, and Prior, the reader sees three different men deal with their sexuality.

As the play opens, Joe is married to Harper, but she suspects that he is keeping secrets from her; she hints that she thinks he is gay. Joe denies this several times—to Harper and later to Louis—before he reluctantly admits his sexuality. As a Mormon, he sees his homosexuality as a failure: he calls his homosexual feelings "wrong" and "ugly," and tells Harper "I have fought, with everything I have, to kill it." He even ghostwrites anti-gay legislature while working with Roy. However, once he acts on his impulses with Louis, he can finally embrace his sexuality, coming out to his mother, Harper, and even Roy Cohn. He rejects his past and his religion, and tells Louis, "I can be anything I need to be." Although Joe undergoes the most dramatic sexual awakening in the play, in the end, his future is the least resolved of any of the characters.

Roy, unlike Joe, is vehemently opposed to revealing his true sexuality. In fact, when Joe tells Roy that he has been seeing a man, Roy tells him to end it immediately and go back to Harper: "Listen to me. Do what I say. Or you will regret it." Roy is a closeted homosexual who has crusaded against gays for the sake of staying in power. Roy accepts an image of a homosexual as someone who is weak and powerless, and refuses to let himself—or Joe—be categorized as such. When his doctor diagnoses him with AIDS, Roy tells him, "AIDS. Homosexual. Gay. Lesbian. You think these are names that tell you who someone sleeps with, but they don't tell you that." He says that they reveal a lack of power instead, a lack of influence and "zero clout." Roy refuses his diagnosis, and tells his doctor to diagnose him with liver cancer instead.

The character of Prior reveals the lonely, frightening path that many gay men faced in the 1980s as AIDS patients. Yet Prior, along with Belize, is one of the few characters who makes no apology for his sexuality, though he is aware of how others may perceive him. He tells Hannah, Joe's Mormon mother, "I'm a homosexual. With AIDS. I can just imagine what you [think]." Perhaps it is his refusal to deny his sexuality that makes him the perfect candidate for a prophet. In the end, he realizes his responsibility on behalf of the gay community suffering from AIDS: a spokesperson announces, "This disease will be the end of many of us, but not nearly all, . . . we are not going away."

Illness

The fear and reality of AIDS is never far from the action of *Angels in America*. During the 1980s, AIDS was thought to be highly contagious and an unavoidable death sentence. Because of this mentality, all of the characters are affected by their proximity to the disease. Roy, who tries desperately to conceal the true nature of his illness, acknowledges that having a disease like AIDS puts a person outside of the mainstream: "The worst thing about being sick in America . . . is that you are booted out of the parade. Americans have no use for sick." Louis takes Roy's sentiment a step further, telling Belize:

> What AIDS shows us is the limits of tolerance, that it's not enough to be tolerated, because when the sh— hits the fan you find out how much tolerance is worth. Nothing. And underneath all the tolerance is intense, passionate hatred.

Through the play, Prior grows increasingly ill with AIDS. From the time he shows his first lesion to Louis, Louis is uncomfortable with Prior's disease, and it changes their relationship. He cannot handle the idea of Prior becoming sicker, or even dying. Prior jokes, "Apartment too small for three? Louis and Prior comfy but not Louis and Prior and Prior's disease?" Though he tries to joke about his condition, he is scared and sad: "one so seldom gets what one wants, does one? No. One does not. One gets f—ed. Over. One . . . dies at thirty, robbed of . . . decades of majesty."

Despite his misery, Prior's illness becomes a way for him to transcend society's prejudice and discrimination against homosexuals and people with AIDS. His illness becomes a fundamental part of his identity and a new life mission as a prophet. He tells Louis, "This is my life, from now on, Louis. I'm not getting 'better.'" In Steven F. Kruger's "Identity and Conversion in *Angels in America*," he notes that "Closely wrapped up with the play's analysis of sexuality is a recognition of how AIDS . . . becomes not just a category of heath or illness but also of identity." Prior finds purpose and joy in his identity in a way that Roy never could; Roy accepts his death but refuses to be associated with AIDS: "AIDS is what homosexuals have. I have liver cancer."

Early in the play, Louis says, "there are no angels in America." By the end of the play, the audience comes to see, through Prior, that perhaps there are angels after all: those dying horrible deaths from AIDS on the fringe of society. Those dead, he says, "will be commemorated and will struggle on with the living."

HISTORICAL OVERVIEW

AIDS in the United States

The AIDS epidemic in the United States officially began in 1981 when the Center for Disease Control (CDC) documented a preliminary strain of the virus in five gay men in California. Almost from the beginning, the disease was thought of—and stigmatized—as a "gay" disease. Though time and science have proven that anyone engaging in the exchange of body fluids through actions such as unprotected sex or sharing needles is susceptible to the disease, the early years of the epidemic further segregated the gay community from mainstream society. At the time, it was thought that AIDS could be transmitted through touch, kissing, or even sharing a bathroom with someone with the disease. As Kushner tells Patrick Giles in "The Angels Have Landed," "I don't think there's ever been a community struggling as hard as the [gay community] was at the moment the epidemic first appeared, while also having to deal with devastation and grief on that scale."

Both HIV (the virus that causes AIDS) and the disease itself spread rapidly in the 1980s and affected a disproportionate number of gay men in the beginning. According to the CDC website, sex between men has been the most common form of exposure to the disease, followed by the sharing of drug needles, and heterosexual sex. Several hundred AIDS patients received the disease through blood transfusions in the 1980s and early 1990s.

Since the beginning of the epidemic, the CDC reports that 529,113 Americans had died of the disease by the end of 2004. Advances in testing and treatment—such as the AZT that Roy Cohn stockpiles in the play—have resulted in the largest number of people living with AIDS since the beginning of the epidemic. AIDS-awareness programs have also helped destigmatize the disease, and reports of new cases have dropped significantly since the 1990s thanks to increased education and a cultural shift, at least somewhat, away from high-risk activities. Unfortunately, the AIDS epidemic continues unabated in many areas of the world where the disease remains stigmatized.

The Rosenberg Trial

Roy Cohn flaunts his involvement in the Rosenberg Trial throughout the play, and because of it, he is haunted by Ethel Rosenberg as he nears death. Ethel and her husband Julius are historical figures (as is Roy Cohn) that were convicted and executed as Soviet spies in 1953, during the escalation of the cold war and the perceived communist threat to democracy.

Julius and Ethel were both born to Jewish families in New York in the 1910s. They met at a Young Communist League meeting, married, and had two children. Julius worked on radar equipment for the Army Signal Corps, and because of this expertise he was recruited by the KGB (Soviet secret police) for help with the Soviet development of atomic weaponry. Julius passed secret information and documents to the Soviets. With the help of this information, the USSR tested its first atomic bomb in 1950. One of the individuals who was caught giving this information away, Sgt. David Greenglass, implicated his sister Ethel and her husband Julius as fellow spies.

The Rosenberg trial, which began in 1951, was a media circus, with the country divided on whether or not the couple was guilty. Both Ethel and Julius invoked their Fifth Amendment right not to incriminate themselves while on trial, a move that was seen as an admission of guilt by the jury. Both were

sentenced to death as spies, though there was little actual evidence proving that Ethel was ever involved in the actual trading of secrets. Roy Cohn, the Assistant U.S. Attorney, prosecuted the case, and wrote famously that he influenced the judge's decision to give Ethel the death penalty as well. The extent of his involvement remains unknown. The Rosenbergs were executed in the electric chair on June 19, 1953. They were the only Americans to executed for espionage during the cold war.

CRITICAL OVERVIEW

Since their earliest stagings, the two parts of *Angels in America* have been critical darlings; many consider the work among the most important plays in twentieth-century American theater. Reviews and critical essays often applaud Tony Kushner's clever writing, the sensitive presentation of the subject matter, and the play's continuing resonance with audiences. As Robert Brustein's 1993 review of *Angels in America* in the *New Republic* notes, the play "received unanimous praise at every step in its journey," and is "the authoritative achievement of a radical dramatic artist with a fresh, clear voice." In "Angels in America: An Epic of the Early Years of AIDS is Making Many Americans Realise How Far They Have Come in the Fight for Healing and Tolerance, and How Far They Still Have to Go," Janice Hopkins Tanne writes, "You won't see many masterpieces in your lifetime. *Angels in America* is one." In "Ambivalence, Utopia, and a Queer Sort of Materialism: How *Angels in America* Reconstructs the Nation," David Savran comments that "Not within memory has a new American play been canonized by the press as rapidly as *Angels in America*." He quotes several glowing reviews, including John Lahr's review in the *New Yorker* calling *Perestroika* a "masterpiece," and John Kroll's review in *Newsweek* calling both parts of the play "the broadest, deepest, most searching American play of our time." Noted literary critic and theorist Harold Bloom included *Angels in America* in *The Western Canon* (1994), his list of the most important works of Western literature of all time.

Not all initial reviews of the play were positive, however. Andrew Sullivan's 1993 review in the *New Republic* does not share the glowing praise that overwhelmingly met *Angels in America*. Sullivan calls *Millennium Approaches* "a crushing disappointment" and "contrived," and argues that "gay life—and gay death—surely awaits something grander and subtler than this."

The play received renewed attention in 2003, when it was made into an HBO movie. Upon the release of the two-part feature, Brad Goldfarb and Patrick Giles interviewed Kushner, director Mike Nichols, and several of the actors in "The Angels Have Landed." Giles calls the play "nothing less than a cultural phenomenon." Director Mike Nichols tells Goldfarb that "Part of the beauty of *Angels in America* is the complexity of the relationships and the complexity of the ideas." In "Redemption When We Need It Most," a review of the HBO adaptation, Paul Buble calls Kushner "one of the great figures in the history of the American dramatic stage," and writes that *Angels in America* "is likely to remain Kushner's apex as a popular artist for a long time."

Many critics feel that Kushner's treatment of homosexual themes in the play is groundbreaking and significant. Savran quotes prominent sexual identity scholar John Clum, who proclaims that the play "marks a turning point in the history of gay drama, the history of American drama, and of American literary culture." In "The Revolution Has Been Televised," Lawrence Christon asserts that *Angels in America* played a major role in how gays were perceived in the 1990s by presenting multidimensional characters. Christon quotes market researcher Jeffery Garber, who notes that "Every minority is happy at first just to see itself portrayed in mainstream media. It's only after time that they get impatient with one-dimensional portrayals and start looking for more realistic depictions." *Angels in America* provides some of those important realistic characters. James Fisher links the depiction of homosexuality in Kushner's play to the tradition of Tennessee Williams in the 1950s and 1960s. In "'The Angels of Fructification': Tennessee Williams, Tony Kushner, and Images of Homosexuality on the American Stage," Fisher notes how both Williams and Kushner seek to create homosexual characters full of depth and humanity: "the emergence of Williams, and those dramatics like Kushner following in his footsteps, says much on a subject about which the stage has been silence for too long."

MEDIA ADAPTATIONS

In the Wings—Angels in American *on Broadway* (1993), part of the American Playhouse series, examines the unique staging and production of *Angels in America*. It is currently unavailable.

Angels in America was adapted for HBO in 2003 by Kushner, who wrote the screenplay. The cast includes Al Pacino as Roy, Emma Thomson as the Angel, and Meryl Streep as Hannah and Ethel Rosenberg. The miniseries won five Golden Globes and eleven Emmys, including Outstanding Writing for Kushner. It is available on DVD from HBO Home Video.

The score to the HBO adaptation, with music by Thomas Newman, is available on audio CD from Nonesuch.

Perhaps the greatest testament to the power of Kushner's play is that it continues to be relevant in today. Though AIDS treatments have made it possible to live a relatively healthy and long life with the disease, the play's chronicle of the initial epidemic still strikes a chord with audiences. In a review of the 2005 London staging of *Angels in America* titled "Taking Wing," Wenzel Jones calls the play "a cultural icon." In Terri Roberts's review of the same staging, Kushner's writing is lauded as being "by turns adventurous, lyrical, hilarious, and harsh, and ... always compelling." Roberts also notes that the play, set in the mid-1980s "still holds up."

CRITICISM

Steven F. Kruger

In the following excerpt, Kruger explores how characters' complex, overlapping identities in Angels in America *create contradictions and challenges for them.*

Constituting Identity

Written, as Kushner makes explicit, out of a "Left politics informed by liberation struggles ... and by socialist and psychoanalytic theory" (2:154), *Angels in America* is at least in part the product of gay identity politics, and central to its political argument is a consideration of sexual identity. The play explores Harper's troubled marriage to Joe, the ways in which this confines both her and him, and the ways in which Harper's fantasy life recapitulates but also enables a certain escape from the unsatisfactory heterosexual relation. The play depicts the closeted figures of Roy and Joe struggling to *dis*identify from gayness. And it displays complex, indeed contradictory, definitions of gayness as, for instance, both strength and weakness—in Roy's words: "Homosexuals are men who know nobody and who nobody knows. Who have zero clout" (1:45); in Prior's: "I can handle pressure, I am a gay man and I am used to pressure, to trouble, I am tough and strong" (1:117).

Closely wrapped up with the play's analysis of sexuality is a recognition of how AIDS—identified in the popular imagination with a gayness conceived of as always already diseased and weak—becomes not just a category of health or illness but also of identity. Roy's disavowal of gayness is simultaneously a disavowal of identity as a person with AIDS: "AIDS is what homosexuals have. I have liver cancer" (1:46). Prior, unlike Roy, claims despised identities, but his bitter assessment of the world's treatment of "faggots" and people with AIDS echoes Roy's: "We don't [count]; faggots; we're just a bad dream the real world is having" (2:42).

Race, ethnicity, and religion are similarly prominent, and similarly conflicted, categories of analysis in the play. Belize's and Louis's political positions are shown to differ particularly around the question of race, in ways clearly connected to their differing experiences of racial identity (1:89–96). Jewishness and Mormonism figure importantly in constituting a sense of identity for most of the play's characters—Louis and Roy, Hannah, Harper, and Joe. The marginality of each of these religious traditions is shown to contribute to the individual's sense of his or her place (or lack of place) in the structures of power. Even Roy, despite his self-confident assertions, feels Jewishness as an obstacle to maintaining political centrality: "The disbarment committee: genteel gentleman Brahmin lawyers, country-club men. I offend them, to these men ... I'm what, Martin, some sort of filthy little Jewish troll?" (1:66–67). Prior Walter's identity as "scion of an ancient line" (1:115) is bodied forth onstage in the figures of the prior Priors who serve as the Angel's heralds; the stability of the Walter family seems a crucial factor in shaping Prior's emerging identity as (reluctant) prophet for the Angel's deeply conservative political project—"YOU MUST STOP MOVING!;" (2.:52)—a project that Belize suggests is Prior's own fantasy: "This is just you, Prior, afraid of the future, afraid of time. Longing to go backwards so bad you made this angel up, a cosmic reactionary" (2:55).

While a gender analysis is less prominent in the play than the consideration of sexuality, AIDS, race, religion, and ethnicity, it nonetheless remains important for the depiction of Harper, who, especially in her engagement with the fantasy figure of the Mormon Mother, recognizes something about her own silencing and disempowerment: "His mute wife. I'm waiting for her to speak. Bet her story's not so jolly" (2:70). And gender is important in the politics of some of the men's self-identifications—particularly those of Belize and Prior as ex–(or ex–ex–) drag queens; thus, though Belize himself suggests that "All this girl-talk shit is politically incorrect... We should have dropped it back when we gave up drag" (1:61), he responds with anger to Louis's assessment of drag as "sexist." (1:94).

The play also importantly, if playfully, suggests that the very taking of political positions—Joe's being a Republican, for instance—may be an act of self-identification not unlike the claiming, or disclaiming, of a sexual identity, such as Joe's disavowal of gayness (see 1:29).

As this sketch at some of the play's identity concerns should suggest, *Angels in America* does not arise from or depict a politics that consists simply in embracing an identity position like gayness as the sufficient basis for a political movement. We might indeed see the play as in part a response to criticism, particularly from within feminism, of an identity politics that fails to recognize the multiple determinants of identity; in the words of Elizabeth Spelman, for instance:

> Dominant feminist theory locates a woman's true identity in a metaphysical space where gender is supposed to be able to roam free from race and class... [T]hough doing this appears to be necessary for feminism, it has the effect of making certain women rather than others paradigmatic examples of "woman"— namely, those women who seem to have a gender

identity untainted (I use the word advisedly) by racial or class identity, those women referred to in newspapers, magazines, and feminist journals simply as "women," without the qualifier "Black" or "Hispanic" or "Asian-American" or "poor."

Kushner's interrogation of gayness similarly recognizes the nonunitary nature of such a category, its differential constitution in relation to other determinants of identity. The play presents us with gay men who are white and black, Jewish and Mormon, conservative and liberal, butch and femme, and certainly not easily unified or unifiable under a single political banner. Thus recognizing the differences within identity categories, the play furthermore emphasizes that any individual's identity is potentially contested and riven: sexuality, gender, and race do not come together without conflict and contradiction. Harper must negotiate between being a thoughtfully articulate woman and being a Mormon woman of whom silence is expected. Joe must navigate the rift between homoerotic desire and political and religious beliefs that insist on the repudiation of that desire. Roy, committed to Republican, McCarthyite political positions and to the political "clout" these bring him, denies as strongly as possible the potentially marginalizing force of his Jewishness and homosexuality. And so forth.

The complexity of identity in *Angels in America* also arises from Kushner's conception of it as social and relational: one is not oneself in isolation but only in contrast to, in solidarity and negotiation with a variety of other selves. This is obviously true among the main characters of the play, in which, for instance, Prior's state of health reveals or even determines much about how Louis thinks of himself or in which Joe's and Harper's decisions are crucially related to their sense of the other's identity. The others who shape the self may also be internalized figures from the past—an Ethel Rosenberg who returns punishingly to urge Roy on to death. They may be powerful historical presences like the Priors of Prior's heritage or like Louis's grandmother. And they may, most "bewilderingly" (1:30), be a complex mixture of the "real" and the fantastic, as when Prior and Harper, who have never met, somehow appear in each other's dreams/hallucinations to reveal crucial information about each other that each has not, at least consciously, realized (1:33–34, 2:68, 2:121–22). In such scenes even a character's

fantasies and imaginations are conceived of as not solely his or hers. These gather their full meaning only in relation to, even interpenetration with, one another—just as, in Kushner's stagecraft, the "split scenes" suggest that discrete actions must, if we are to understand them fully, be read together: Harper and Joe's relationship defines Prior and Louis's, and vice versa, as both couples appear simultaneously onstage.

Identities so complexly defined entail certain *political* possibilities—cross-identifications like Harper's and Prior's and renegotiations of identity and difference that might make certain shifts in power relations possible, might, for instance, allow Joe to move from a simple disavowal of homosexuality to a reconsideration of it that also entails rethinking political and religious alignments. But the play also is careful not to depict identity simply as fluid and thus subject to easy, volitional change; nor does it attach a utopian political fantasy to the belief that identity might be renegotiated. Despite the presentation of identity as complex, as multiply determined, as relational, identity stubbornly remains identity, a marker of something unique to—given and intractable in—the person. Roy evokes "the immutable heart of what we are that bleeds through whatever we might become" (2:82), and, while Roy should by no means be taken as a reliable spokesman, the belief in such a "heart" is not his alone. A similar notion is at work when Harper reassures Prior that, despite his having AIDS, his "most inner part" is "free of disease" (1:34) or when Joe reassures Louis that, despite his having left Prior, he is "in [him]self a good, good man" (2:38) with "a good heart" (2:75). All of these assessments *may* be erroneous—they are each challenged elsewhere—but they nonetheless express a strong sense of the depth and stability of identity. The first speech of the play, Rabbi Isidor Chemelwitz's eulogy for Sarah Ironson, calls attention to a material heritage that is inescapable, "the clay of some Litvak shtetl" worked into her children's bones (1:10). The self may be always on a "voyage" and a "journey" (1:10–11), it may move somewhere new, but it also returns continually to a place of origin in a movement beyond the control of individual will, a function of constraints placed on the self by the history into which it is born.

If the self is not constituted by some simple, unconflicted claiming of identity, if, as well, it is not formed in isolation from others but, rather, responds to a whole variety of (political) pressures, it also is not so easily changed or reshaped. Indeed, having recognized, in Kushner's conception of identity, the potential for political change, we must also recognize that the *how* of that change is problematic. The "Great Question" with which *Perestroika* begins is "Are we doomed? ... Will the Past release us? ... Can we Change? In Time," Here, as stated by Prelapsarianov, the "World's Oldest Living Bolshevik," the question is explicitly political, and its "we" is the we of world history, not of identity politics or personal psychology (2:13). But in Kushner's play, with its insistence on the merging of the political and the personal, the question does not only resonate with the grand narratives of international politics. Indeed, the same Great Question reappears later in *Perestroika*, transposed into the language of the individual: Harper asks her fantasy figure, the Mormon Mother, "How do people change?" (2:79). Whether raised by Harper with personal urgency or by Prelapsarianov as he searches for the next "Beautiful Theory" to "reorder the world" (2:14), this is perhaps the play's central political question.

Source: Steven F. Kruger, "Identity and Conversion in *Angels in America*," in *Approaching the Millennium: Essays on "Angels in America,"* 1997, pp. 151–55.

SOURCES

"Basic Statistics / Statistics and Surveillance / Topics / CDC HIV/AIDS," *Center for Disease Control*, www.cdc.gov/hiv/topics/surveillance/basic.htm (March 27, 2006).

Bilderback, Walter, "The Square Root of Queer," in *American Theatre*, Vol. 15, No. 4, April 1998, pp. 45–47.

Brustein, Robert, Review of *Angels in America*, in *New Republic*, Vol. 208, No. 21, May 24, 1993, pp. 29–31.

Christon, Lawrence, "The Revolution Has Been Televised," in *Daily Variety*, Vol. 287, No. 19, April 28, 2005, pp. A4, A5, A10.

Fisher, James, " 'The Angels of Fructification': Tennessee Williams, Tony Kushner, and Images of Homosexuality on the American Stage," in *Mississippi Quarterly*, Vol. 49, No. 1, winter 1995–1996, pp. 12–32.

Goldfarb, Brad, and Patrick Giles, "The Angels Have Landed," in *Interview*, Vol. 33, No. 11, December 2003, pp. 170–74.

Jones, Wenzel, "Taking Wing," in *Backstage West*, Vol. 12, No. 9, February 4, 2005, p. 13.

Kushner, Tony, *Angels in America: A Gay Fantasia on National Themes*, Theatre Communications Group, 1995.

Roberts, Terri, Review of *Angels in America*, in *Backstage West*, Vol. 12, No. 10, March 3, 2005, p. 19.

Savran, David, "Ambivalence, Utopia, and a Queer Sort of Materialism: How *Angels in America* Reconstructs the Nation," in *Theatre Journal*, Vol. 47, No. 2, May 2005, pp. 207–27.

Sullivan, Andrew, Review of *Angels in America*, in *New Republic*, Vol. 36, No. 1, June 21, 1993, p. 46.

Tanne, Janice Hopkins, "Angels in America: An Epic of the Early Years of AIDS is Making Many Americans Realise How Far They Have Come in the Fight for Healing and Tolerance, and How Far They Still Have to Go," in the *British Medical Journal*, Vol. 327, No. 7428, December 12, 2003, p. 1412.

The Autobiography of Miss Jane Pittman

ERNEST J. GAINES

1971

The novel *The Autobiography of Miss Jane Pittman*, first published in 1971 by Dial Press, is arguably the best-known work by author Ernest J. Gaines. The text consists of a fictionalized autobiography of Jane Pittman, a woman born into slavery who lived to be nearly one hundred and ten years old. While Jane is still a child, the Civil War ends and the slaves are freed; she is forced to make her own way in the world. Though her first goal is to leave Louisiana for Ohio, the home of a Union soldier who showed her some kindness, Jane never manages to leave the state and spends the rest of her life working in Louisiana. Gaines uses Jane's experiences and her distinctive first-person voice to explore the effects of slavery, emancipation, racism, Reconstruction, and the civil rights movement on African Americans. To a lesser degree, he also considers the consequence of these events on whites, both poor and rich.

Gaines spent nearly three years writing *The Autobiography of Miss Jane Pittman*. For the first year, the novel was not an autobiography but a collected fictional biography that consisted of different people telling Jane's story as well as discussions of related historical topics. He soon found that Jane's own voice was more powerful and decided to make the book a fictional autobiography, an idea inspired by Gertrude Stein's *The Autobiography of Alice B. Toklas* (1933). Like his fictional creation, Gaines was also born and raised on a plantation, the River

"I HAVE A SCAR ON MY BACK I GOT WHEN I WAS A SLAVE. I'LL CARRY IT TO MY GRAVE. YOU GOT PEOPLE OUT THERE WITH THIS SCAR ON THEIR BRAINS, AND THEY WILL CARRY THAT SCAR TO THEIR GRAVE. THE MARK OF FEAR, JIMMY, IS NOT EASILY REMOVED. TALK WITH THEM, JIMMY. TALK AND TALK AND TALK. BUT DON'T BE MAD IF THEY DON'T LISTEN. SOME OF THEM WON'T EVER LISTEN. MANY WON'T EVEN HEAR YOU."

Lake Plantation, in Louisiana. Many stories he heard throughout his childhood about plantation life ended up in this novel.

While many of Gaines's other novels and short stories also reflect this culture, the character of Jane was influenced by a very important woman in his life: a maternal great-aunt named Augusteen Jefferson. She was Gaines's primary caregiver until the age of fifteen, and worked to ensure that he was fed and clothed. She was also determined and vigorous, and though handicapped, she did not feel sorry for herself. Gaines dedicated the novel to her. The fictional town of Bayonne that appears in the novel is also based on a community near his childhood home, New Roads. Like Jimmy in the last section of the novel, Gaines himself wrote letters for the older African American people who lived on the plantation and could not read or write themselves.

The Autobiography of Miss Jane Pittman is classified by some critics as a slave narrative, a personal story told by former slaves that describes their lives from enslavement to their escape or freedom. Slave narratives were usually shared orally, but were sometimes published, like Frederick Douglass's *Narrative of the Life of Frederick Douglass* (1845) and Harriet Jacobs's *Incidents in the Life of a Slave Girl* (1861). Gaines himself drew on similar slave narrative sources, such as those included in *Lay My Burden Down: A Folk History of Slavery* (1945), edited by B. A. Botkin, to create Jane's voice in the novel. This voice remains authentic in the text in Jane's pronunciation of certain words—using "beero" for "bureau," for

BIOGRAPHY

ERNEST J. GAINES

Ernest James Gaines was born in 1933 on a plantation in Louisiana. As a child, he spent much of his time at the plantation's former slave quarters, as had several generations of his family. The eldest of twelve children, Gaines was raised by a great-aunt, worked in the fields, and received his early education at small, part-time schools. His aunt was disabled, and many storytelling visitors stopped by to see her often. Gaines learned much about telling stories from such gatherings.

When Gaines was fifteen years old, he moved to California to live with his mother and stepfather. His relocation was prompted at least in part by a lack of high schools in his part of Louisiana open to black students. While in California, Gaines had access to a library that allowed black patrons; this was a first for him, and he subsequently became a voracious reader. He was particularly influenced by Russian writers like Ivan Turgenev, who wrote about rural people with a truth Gaines found inspiring.

Gaines soon decided on a writing career for himself. While attending San Francisco State University, he published his first work, a short story called "The Turtles." All of his novels and short stories, including *The Autobiography of Miss Jane Pittman*, are set in Louisiana and reflect the culture in which he was reared. As of 2006, he is Professor Emeritus of English at Louisiana University at Lafayette, where he continues to write.

example. Gaines also read African American folklore and related histories as background sources.

The Autobiography of Miss Jane Pittman was published in its first paperback edition by Bantam in 1972 and reissued in 1982. (In 1998, a hardcover edition titled *The Autobiography of Miss Jane Pittman: And Other Related Readings* was published by Houghton Mifflin School.) Gaines was awarded a fiction gold medal by the Commonwealth Club of California in 1972. The novel's popularity increased in 1974 when an acclaimed, though controversial, television movie based on the novel was made. The controversy arose as a result of the changes made to the story in the television adaptation, including Jane drinking from the water fountain in the courthouse and a white person interviewing Jane. The novel itself has been banned and censored in school districts across the country since its publication. Many parents and teachers object to the repeated use of the word "nigger," as well as other frank representations of racism found in the novel.

Regardless of the book's controversial nature, millions of readers continue to find inspiration in Jane's story. Her life story, stretching from slavery through the civil rights movement, offers a glimpse at a century of profound struggles and changes for African Americans.

PLOT SUMMARY

Introduction
A narrator's statement opens *The Autobiography of Miss Jane Pittman*. The narrator, a schoolteacher, informs readers that the story that follows is based on interviews held over nine months in 1962 with Jane Pittman and others who knew her. Miss Jane was already well over one hundred years old, a former slave who had spent the whole of her life in Louisiana. After assuring readers that Miss Jane's voice has been retained through her word choice and sentence structure, the narrator tells readers that she died about eight months after the interviews were completed.

Book I: The War Years
Jane's recollections begin during the Civil War. She is a slave about eleven or twelve years old who takes care of her master's children. Both Confederate and Union soldiers come by the plantation on their way to battle. While giving water to some Yankees, Jane tells one inquiring soldier that her name is Ticey and her master beats her with a cat-o'-nine-tails. The soldier, Corporal Brown, gives her another name: "Ticey is a slave name, and I don't like slavery. I'm go'n call you Jane." After the Union troops leave, Jane's master beats her because she insists

her name is Jane Brown and not Ticey; then she is forced to work in the fields.

A year or two after this incident, the master gathers his slaves and tells them that they are free. While the freed slaves are generally happy upon hearing the news, most are unsure what to do. Their former master offers them work at the plantation as sharecroppers. This means they would work his land, just as they did as slaves, but they would keep a small share of the harvested crops as payment. Many of the slaves are afraid to leave, in part because they might be killed by whites looking to harm former slaves. Jane and a few others decide to go north. She wants to go to Ohio, where Corporal Brown lives. She has no family; her mother was murdered when Jane was quite young, and she did not know her father, who lived on another plantation.

Jane and the others leave the plantation, with a woman called Big Laura taking charge of the group. Jane remembers that "we had heard about freedom, we had even talked about freedom, but we never thought we was go'n ever see that day." During the journey, some of the former slaves decide on new names. Many choose last names like Lincoln, Washington, and Douglass. Jane gets into a physical altercation with a "slow-wit fellow" who decides to take the name Brown. When he tries to drag her into the bushes, Big Laura hits him on the back until he releases Jane. When they stop for the night, Big Laura watches over Jane as she sleeps.

The next morning as Jane awakes, patrollers (poor whites who were former members of the Confederate Army, the Ku Klux Klan, and other such organizations) are amidst the group, looking to kill the now-free African Americans. Jane hides in the bushes with Big Laura's young son Ned. All except Jane and Ned are killed, including Big Laura and her infant daughter. Jane gathers up the food and some belongings, and takes Ned away from the scene. She is stunned by what she has just seen, but is unable to cry: "I had seen so much beating and suffering; I had heard about so much cruelty in those 'leven or twelve years of my life I hardly knowed how to cry."

While Jane and Ned keep walking toward Ohio, they meet many people, both black and white, who feed them and offer help. Though they receive invitations to stay at different places and even spend the night at a shelter for former

Martin Luther King, Jr. leads the March on Washington, DC, 1963 National Archives and Records Administration

slave children, Jane persists in her goal and takes Ned with her. Everywhere they go, they see the scars of war. One day, they come across a cabin in which an old white man lives. He informs Jane that to go to Ohio, one must go east, not north, and shows her a map to explain why. Jane does not understand and is not sure she should trust him. When she asks the old man why she should believe him, he says, "I might be a Secesh [Confederate soldier].... Then I might be a friend of your race. Or maybe just an old man who is nothing. Or maybe an old man who is very wise." She decides that instead of being stubborn as she has been, she will listen to others when they try to tell her she is wrong. The old man tells her how to get to Ohio and in which cities she might find Brown. After they leave the cabin, Jane and Ned walk on, hiding from people they see, until Ned grows tired one day. Jane asks a white man, whose name is Job, for a ride.

Job takes them to his dilapidated cabin. His wife is not pleased by the presence of Jane and Ned. After Jane and Ned spend the night, Job takes them away the next day to his friend Bone. Job drops them off near Bone's plantation with instructions on what to say. Bone hears Jane's story and offers her a job. Though he wants to pay her less than what he pays his other women field workers, she insists she can work just as hard as they can. Ned will go to school while she works outside. Bone gives them a small cabin to live in. Jane proves her worth by clearing as much land as the other women, and soon gets equal pay.

Book II: Reconstruction
For a while, Jane and Ned lead a decent life working for Bone, and Jane begins to feel maternal toward Ned: "I felt like I hadn't just kept Ned from getting killed, I felt like I had born him out of my own body." He calls her Ma, even though she is only ten years older than he is. Jane records listening to speeches by both Republicans and Democrats at an event in a town square, but violence breaks out and she takes Ned and hides under the platform. The secret groups, like the Ku Klux Klan, that cause violence there and elsewhere do not bother Bone nor his workers because he is a prominent Republican.

Bone soon gathers everyone and tells them he no longer owns the property because it is being returned to its former Southern owners. He also tells them that the North is very concerned with putting the country back together and funding a Southern revival. He pays them their wages, and many of the former slaves leave. Jane and Ned stay, as she decides, "I had no more faith in heading North than I had staying South." Jane goes to work for the new owner, an ex-Confederate soldier named Colonel Dye. She remains his employee for a number of years.

Later, a committee is formed by black Civil War veterans reporting on how blacks are being treated in the South. Ned, now in his late teens, joins the committee. Jane notes that Ned has grown quite serious by this time, and changed his name from Ned Brown to Ned Douglass, after Frederick Douglass. Many of the returning slave owners do not like the committee, and Dye tells Jane to make Ned withdraw. Because Ned will not quit, some men dressed in "their sheets" visit Jane and Ned's cabin and physically harm

her while Ned is working with the committee. When Ned returns home and finds out, he suggests that they move away. Jane refuses, but convinces him to leave.

After living by herself for a while, Jane moves in with Joe Pittman, a widower with two daughters, and becomes his wife. She recalls that she hesitated to start a relationship with him at first because she is not able to have children of her own. Her lack of fertility was probably caused by a beating when she was young. Jane and Joe do not marry in a church, but instead just live together. Joe soon wants to leave Dye's plantation and find more lucrative work with horses elsewhere. Jane does not want to move until she hears from Ned, and Joe agrees. For various reasons, it takes a year for Ned's letters to reach her. She discovers that Ned went to Kansas, then attended school and became a teacher. After that, he joined the army; he currently serves in Cuba. Jane also discovers that Ned has been sending her money.

Jane, Joe, and his daughters prepare to leave the Dye plantation and move to where Joe has found a job breaking horses. Colonel Dye does not want him to leave, and makes him come up with more than one hundred and fifty dollars to pay back an old debt. While Joe acknowledges that Dye had helped him when he was being troubled by the Ku Klux Klan, he did not know about the debt. Joe goes to extraordinary measures to raise the funds, and the family moves on to land owned by Mr. Clyde, some ten days' travel away.

Jane also gets a job at Mr. Clyde's working in the main house. She spends the next ten years in the Clydes' employ. Joe loves his job breaking horses, though Jane is afraid that he will die doing it. She often has dreams about the many ways he could die, especially when he goes on trips to gather up horses to break. She asks him to move and become a farmer or some other occupation, but Joe tells her "the way things is a colored man just can't get out there and start farming any time he want." Seven or eight years after they move to Clyde's, Joe returns with a wild black stallion that Jane is sure will be the death of him. She goes to a fortune teller to see if her bad feeling about the horse is right, and the fortune-teller confirms it. The night before the stallion is to be broken, Jane cannot sleep and lets the horse out of the corral.

Joe sees the horse leave and goes after it, with the hopes of roping it and bringing it back. When the rest of the men catch up with him, Joe is "tangled in the rope, already dead." Jane is heartbroken and does not have a relationship with another man in the same way again. A few years later, she becomes involved with a fisherman named Felton Burkes. With him, she moves to an area near the St. Charles River, where she spends most of the rest of her life. He only stays with her for three years before disappearing. She supports herself by taking in laundry.

Soon after Felton leaves, Ned returns with his family. The year is 1899. It has been twenty years since Jane last saw Ned. She tells readers that Ned will only live another year before he is shot in a contract killing by Albert Cluveau. Ned is now married to a woman named Vivian and has three children. He has come back to teach black children based on the beliefs of Frederick Douglass, who thought that the races should work together. Jane is scared by what he is proposing, and many people reject Ned's ideas because "they knowed what he was preaching was go'n get him killed." No one in the area will let him teach in their building, so he buys a home and teaches there while building his own school.

Jane has known Albert Cluveau, a white Cajun man, for some time. They fish in the same area in the river. He sometimes follows her home, eats her fried fish, and drinks her coffee. Cluveau does small chores for her as she needs it. He repeatedly tells her that he has had to kill at least twelve people of both races. She often tries to get him off the subject, but cannot. Cluveau tells her he might be told to kill Ned because of the school he wants to build. Jane tells Ned, but he remains determined to complete his plan: "I will build my school. I will teach till they kill me."

Two weeks before his death, Ned gives a speech to many African Americans, most of them young, gathered by the river. Jane and his family are also there. In the river nearby, many white people listen in boats passing by. Ned speaks out about the rights of black people and slavery, and he says that both black and white have earned the right be Americans: "America is for all of us. . . . don't run and do fight. Fight white and black for all of this place." After the speech, Ned tells Jane, "I'm go'n die, Mama," though she knows "he had no fear of death."

Soon after the speech, Cluveau disappears and does not come around Jane's house. Ned begins building his school and Jane fears for his life. While Ned is hauling lumber for the building one night with several of his young students, Cluveau meets them on the road. Ned instructs the boys to continue on with their learning, then begins to run toward Cluveau. Cluveau has been ordered to shoot Ned in the leg so that he would have to crawl before being killed. Cluveau shoots him there, but Ned just keeps coming until Cluveau shoots him a final time.

Others build the school Ned started, but Cluveau is never brought to justice. He goes out of his way to avoid Jane, but she knows she will see him someday so that she can say what she needs to say to him. When they finally meet on a road, Jane warns Cluveau that when he dies, he will die screaming: "when the Chariot of Hell come rattling for you, the people will hear you screaming all over this parish." Though Albert lives for another ten years, he is indeed screaming and fearful upon his death.

Book III: The Plantation

After Albert dies, Jane is ready to move again. A friend, Aunt Hattie Jordan, works on a nearby plantation owned by the Samson family. She convinces Jane to take a job there. Jane works in the fields. Soon after moving to the Samson plantation, Jane also joins the local Christian church. Though she has been around church-going people all her life, it is not until now that she finds religion because she has "nothing else in the world but the Lord," and is finally ready to fully commit herself to her beliefs.

Jane relates some situations she observes in the Samson family. Robert Samson is married to Amma Dean and is the father of Tee Bob. Samson also has an older son, Timmy, whose mother is one of the black women who lives on his property. Everyone knows that Timmy is Samson's son, as there is a strong resemblance between them, and Timmy is much more like his father than Tee Bob. The brothers are attached to each other and ride horses together. When they visit the fields, Tee Bob often helps Jane with her work. When Aunt Hattie dies, it is Tee Bob who convinces his parents to bring Jane, now in her sixties, to work in the house doing the cooking and other household chores.

Jane occasionally rides a horse down to the fields to visit her friends who still work there. One day, Tee Bob and Timmy play a trick on her, causing the horse she is on to run off wildly. Though the horse eventually stops at a gate, Amma Dean is unhappy with the situation and Timmy's attitude toward her. Timmy is forced to leave the plantation soon afterward because of a run-in with a white overseer, Tom Joe, who has long hated Timmy and the Samsons.

Jane tells of the death of Huey Long, governor of Louisiana. She believes he was a friend of the poor of both races, noting that he provided books for the schools. Jane also speculates on why he was assassinated, though she is not surprised by his fate: "Look like every man that pick up the cross for the poor must end that way." Around this time, the Samson plantation hires its own teacher to educate the black children that live there. Jane continues to work as a cook for the Samsons, and shares her quarters with some of the teachers. The first one, Miss Lilly, is enthusiastic in her belief in education, but leaves after a year.

Nearly two years after a male teacher, Joe Hardy, is run off the property for improprieties, Mary Agnes LeFabre, a Creole woman, is hired as the teacher. Tee Bob becomes infatuated with the light-skinned Mary Agnes. At the time, Tee Bob is a student at Louisiana State University, but makes every excuse to come home to see her. Mary Agnes shows no interest in him, other than the expected politeness, but Tee Bob falls in love. Tee Bob's family and friends grow concerned about his obsession with Mary Agnes. One Friday, Tee Bob confides in a college friend, Jimmy Caya, about his feelings. Jimmy tells him that Tee Bob can have a physical relationship with Mary Agnes ("she's there for that and nothing else"), but cannot make her his wife. Tee Bob punches him. Mary Agnes is already packing her suitcase to leave the Samsons. Tee Bob tries to convince her to run away with him, but she refuses.

Jane is unsure exactly what happened next, but Mary Agnes later reveals that Tee Bob swung her around and nearly knocked her out. Tee Bob then went into the house and killed himself in the library. Samson considers charging Mary Agnes with Tee Bob's death, if not killing her outright himself. No charges are filed nor action taken against her due to the intervention of the family minister, Jules

Raynard. Mary Agnes immediately goes to New Orleans. Jules tells Jane that everyone is at fault for Tee Bob's death, including himself and Jane, because "We tried to make him follow a set of rules our people gave us long ago. But these rules just ain't old enough."

Book IV: The Quarters

In the opening of the final section, which takes place in the 1930s, Jane begins talking about the child she and many others believe will be "the One," a young boy named Jimmy. The One will be a leader on the Samson Plantation, if not the whole parish. Lena, his great aunt and primary caregiver for some time, believes he is the One nearly from the moment he is born. By the 1940s, Jane has moved out of the relatively nice servants' housing near the main house into different, more primitive quarters on the property. She watches Jimmy grow, do well in school, and show his intelligence.

Jane has Jimmy read the sports section and comics of the newspaper to her. Jane is a particular fan of Jackie Robinson and the New York Dodgers, as well as boxer Joe Louis. Because Jane is always happier when she hears that Robinson did well in his games, Jimmy regularly lies to her about how well he played, even if he did not play at all. Jimmy also reads the Bible aloud and writes letters for her and the others who cannot not read or write.

Eventually Samson divides his land and sells pieces of it to those who had worked it as sharecroppers or laborers. Jane and some other African American laborers remain in their homes, the old quarters, and do not plan to leave until their deaths. They are still convinced that Jimmy will be a leader, and they make sure that he behaves appropriately. By the time he is twelve, Jane and others want him to embrace the Christian faith. He finally does so in August 1951 and is baptized. They want him to be a minister or deacon, but he is not interested. Eventually, Jimmy leaves to live with his mother in New Orleans and go to school. He returns to visit, but is no longer an enthusiastic churchgoer.

A few years after Jimmy leaves, the civil rights movement begins. Samson does not want any of the black people who live on his property participating in any demonstrations. He lets them live on his property for free, and believes it is his right to control them. When someone who lives on his property does participate in a demonstration, his whole family is forced to move out. Jimmy returns and speaks out about the movement at church: "Reverend King and the Freedom Riders was winning the battle in Alabama and Mi'sippi, but us here in Luzana hadn't even started the fight." Many of the church members balk at what he is proposing and refuse to support him, though Jane generally does. Jane later counsels him to talk to people more, instead of trying to push them to change immediately.

Jimmy and a friend plan a demonstration against the separate water fountains and bathrooms at the nearby courthouse. A black girl drinks from the white water fountain and is jailed. Jimmy tries to convince every black person around, including Jane, to show up in support. Though Jane and Lena agree to go, many of their peers say they are too afraid. On the morning of the demonstration, many more people from the Samson Plantation than Jane expected are ready to go. Samson drives up and reports that Jimmy was shot dead earlier in the morning. Though Samson tells them to go home, a few still plan to go to the demonstration, including Jane, who walks past Samson to go there.

Jackie Robinson Archive Photos, Inc. | Getty Images

THEMES

Slavery and the Slave Mentality

Throughout *The Autobiography of Miss Jane Pittman*, slavery and its effects color nearly every thought and every action of every character. The story takes place in Louisiana from the Civil War through the civil rights movement in the mid-twentieth century, nearly Jane's entire lifespan. In the first few pages of the novel, Jane and the other slaves are granted their freedom after the Union victory in the Civil War. Yet neither Jane and her fellow former slaves nor the white people who had possessed them can easily break out of the roles they lived with for so many years. The racism inherent in the slave system does not end with Emancipation.

After Emancipation, the aftereffects of slavery remains in control of these people's lives not just socially and psychologically, but also economically. When Jane and the other slaves are told they are free, some leave, but many stay. Their former master offers those who choose to remain a job working the plantation's property on shares. Instead of exploring other options,

many stay put. Though their former master says they can work as much as they want and worship as long as they want on Sundays, he still runs their lives through economics.

Those former slaves who try to leave and go north, as Jane originally intends to do, face many harsh realities. Because they often lack education, some, like Jane, do not even know where North is. They have no funds to get there and no sure job prospects. As a hunter tells Jane, freedom "ain't coming to meet you. And it might not be there when you get there, either." Even getting there is perilous, as Jane's own journey proves. Traveling with Big Laura, the group is attacked by white patrollers.

Years after slavery has ended, the plantation economic model remains viable as Jane describes it. When she is advanced in age, she works and lives on the Samson plantation as the cook and a household servant. Though she is paid, she lives in nearby servants' housing and is basically treated by her employers as a household slave. Jane is liked and respected, but kept in her place by her employers and by her own survival mentality.

Even at the end of the book, nearly one hundred years after slavery had been abolished, a slave mentality of fear keeps hold. Jimmy, anointed "the One" by many of the African Americans who watch him grow up, becomes involved in the civil rights movement. Many of the blacks who still live on the Samson property do so without charge for rent or water, and Samson tells them that they cannot join in any demonstrations unless they and their families want to be forced out. He believes that none of them will. While talking to a lawman one day in town about the recent destruction of a Freedom Riders bus, Jane overhears Samson tell the officer that his "niggers know better" than to get involved with the civil rights movement and, referring to Jane, says, "Over a hundred [years old].... She know what'll happen if they ever try it."

Jane refers to the slave mentality that rules the rural black community in Louisiana as a "black quilt" that each individual must decide to push off his or her back. When the blacks on Samson's former plantation resist Jimmy's pleas to join the civil rights movement, Jane identifies the reason for their resistance: "Black curtains hang at their windows, Jimmy: black quilts cover their body at night: a black veil cover their eyes." She pleads with him to understand that it will take more than a couple of days to change their way of thinking after decades of oppression and racism. Jane proves that she herself is not afraid to confront the slavery mentality that has scarred her both physically and mentally when she crosses Samson to join the demonstration Jimmy died organizing.

Social Rules

Racism can also be seen in the rules that govern social interaction between blacks and whites in *The Autobiography of Miss Jane Pittman*. Blacks are almost universally poor in the book, work as servants and laborers, and are at the bottom of the social ladder. A few, like Ned and Mary Agnes LeFabre, are teachers, but education affords them no real status in the eyes of the white people in the novel. In fact, their education makes them an even bigger target for hate and suspicion. While there are poorer white people who work for white landowners, these white people can take physical action against blacks and suffer no legal consequences. For example, Albert Culveau kills Ned under orders. Though two of Ned's students witness the crime, the sheriff who interviews them twists their words so that no charges are ever filed against Cluveau.

The most dramatic example of how racism and prejudice pervade social rules in *The Autobiography of Miss Jane Pittman* comes in Tee Bob's pursuit of Mary Agnes. The way Jane describes it, everyone knows that Tee Bob cannot marry nor have a legitimate relationship with Mary Agnes because she is of mixed race. Both blacks and whites are concerned about Tee Bob's interest in her because they know he is headed down an unacceptable path.

The situation comes to a head when Tee Bob confides his feelings to college friend Jimmy Caya. Jimmy tells him the truth as he knows it, explaining the social barriers between Tee Bob and Mary Agnes: "Don't you know who you are? Don't you know what she is? Don't you know these things yet?" Tee Bob punches Jimmy after Jimmy tells him that Tee Bob can have a physical relationship with Mary Agnes, but nothing else. The breaking of social rules leads to consequences. Though Tee Bob wants Mary Agnes to run away with him and get married, she refuses. Jules Raynard spells it out simply: "She was a nigger, he was white, and they couldn't have nothing together. He couldn't understand that, he thought love was much stronger than that one drop of African blood." Because of this, Tee Bob kills himself. Jane and others believe that Tee Bob has always been soft and would have come to some self-inflicted harm sooner or later, but the rules of a racially separate society contribute to his death.

Sacrifice

Tee Bob's death is not the only sacrifice to a culture dominated by race and prejudice. Throughout *The Autobiography of Miss Jane Pittman*, a number of characters lose their lives trying to challenge the racism of their society. In particular, Gaines depicts the deaths of Ned and Jimmy as conscious acts of martyrdom in a racist society. Both Ned and Jimmy know their actions are controversial before their ultimate demise, and yet continue on the path they believe is right. Ned even tells his crowd that death is possible as a consequence of their actions, but says, "if you must die, let me ask you this: wouldn't you rather die saying I'm a man than to die saying I'm a contented slave?"

Ned is warned in numerous ways that building a school for black children is not acceptable in his place and time. Though Cluveau warns Jane that he could be ordered to kill Ned, Ned is already aware that his actions could lead to his death. His wife, Vivian, tells Jane that Ned knew this before they moved to Louisiana. Despite Ned's murder, the school is built and used to educate students for years. He also becomes an example to many of the young people in the community.

Jimmy is involved in the civil rights movement and knows that getting African Americans in his region interested in the cause will be difficult. He is also aware of the potentially deadly consequences. Speaking in the church, Jimmy says,

> Some of us might be killed, some of us definitely going to jail, and some of us might be crippled the rest of our life. But death and jail don't scare us—and we feel that we crippled now, and been crippled a long time, and every day we put up with the white man insults they cripple us just a little bit more.

Though Jimmy is killed before the demonstration, it only makes certain African Americans, like Jane, more supportive of his cause.

HISTORICAL OVERVIEW

Slavery, Emancipation, and Reconstruction

Until the end of the Civil War, it was legal in certain states in the United States to own African Americans as slaves. In 1860, there were approximately four million black slaves in the South—about a third of the region's population. They were owned by only a quarter of the whites who lived there. While not all slaves were abused by their masters, they could not legally marry, many were not allowed to stay together as families, and most were denied education. In the novel, Jane says she does not know her father because he lived on another plantation, and it is implied that she received no education as an enslaved child. Southerners fought to continue slavery for many reasons, including the widespread belief that it was their right and the way of nature; it was also a certainty that the economy of the South would fall apart without it. While the Civil War was not fought specifically to end slavery, slaves were formally freed at the end of the war in 1865 with the Thirteenth Amendment to the Constitution.

Hundreds of years of forced dependency left many former slaves unsure what to do when slavery ended. Many left for other parts of the country. However, the economic model of the South remained relatively unchanged. Many African Americans continued to work on plantations as household and field servants, often for low pay. Most also had to pay for their own housing and food—basics that were provided during slavery. Federally mandated groups like the Freedman's Bureau worked to help African Americans with the transition during the Reconstruction (1865–1877). The Reconstruction was the period after the Civil War during which federal troops occupied and governed over the former Southern states. As a condition to rejoin the Union, the states were required to ratify the Thirteenth and Fifteenth Amendments (ending slavery and guaranteeing the right to vote for black men, respectively). Though there were some who came from the North to educate former slaves, there were also many people, especially Southern whites, who wanted to keep former slaves uneducated and dependent on whites. This situation persisted for many years after Emancipation, forcing people like Ned in the novel to move to find opportunities for education and work.

In addition to offering limited educational opportunities, the post–Civil War years in the South were full of violent attacks on former slaves. Though slaves often faced some ill treatment while being held in servitude, they also were property with value. After slaves were freed, whites who employed the newly emancipated people had no reason to protect them any longer since they were replaceable. White Southerners—former Confederate soldiers, members of secret groups like the Ku Klux Klan, and others—took their frustrations over losing the war as well as their continued racial hostility out on blacks. Jane and her group of fellow former slaves are victims of such an attack only a few days into their freedom; only Jane and Ned survive. Later on, they escape continued harassment because they work first for Bone and then for Colonel Dye. The white men's names and status offer them a certain amount of protection from the violence for which few white individuals ever faced punishment.

Federal laws were passed during Reconstruction to improve the life of African Americans. African American men were given the right to vote and hold public office. Blacks held office in Louisiana from 1867 to 1877 and passed laws against segregation. When Reconstruction ended in 1877 and federal troops left the South, Southern Democrats opposed to integration took office and soon erased these gains. Many Southern states found ways to undermine integrationist laws by using poll taxes and other means to prevent blacks from having a voice in government. Earlier, Black Codes were also passed by most state legislatures in the South to control blacks socially. Such codes prohibited blacks from marrying outside their race, from being on city streets during nighttime hours, and from assembling in large groups. In the 1890s, further social control of blacks came in the form of Jim Crow laws passed by state legislatures in the South. Under these laws, blacks and whites had to have separate public facilities, including schools, water fountains, hospitals, and cemeteries. Such laws were declared legal by the Supreme Court decision of *Plessy v. Ferguson* (1896). This case focused on a Louisiana law that called for separate accommodations for blacks and whites on railway cars.

The Civil Rights Movement

Changes were afoot in the 1930s and 1940s for blacks in America. Racial barriers began to fall in areas like professional sports. Jane's favorite baseball player, Jackie Robinson, began playing for the Brooklyn Dodgers in 1947. In the 1950s and 1960s, the civil rights movement in the United States worked to challenge the oppressive racial legislation in the South. As African Americans protested in many venues, both actively and through passive resistance, laws began changing to support the equality they sought. For example, in 1954, the U.S. Supreme Court declared the segregation of public schools illegal in the case of *Brown v. Board of Education*. Though the court case mandated desegregation, it would take many years for this to actually take place. In Louisiana, New Orleans fought integration until 1960, when violence and civil unrest accompanied its realization. Eventually, schools improved and integration spread throughout the whole state. A Civil Rights Act was passed in 1957 with a Civil Rights commission formed as a result. Seven years later, another Civil Rights Act was passed that also outlawed segregation in public buildings and racial discrimination in employment opportunities.

In the last section of the novel, Jimmy is an active member of the civil rights movement working to bring about such changes. He tells Jane that he has worked with civil rights leader Martin Luther King Jr. and he hopes to duplicate the success of the mid-1950s protest King helped organize around Rosa Parks, who refused to give up her seat on a Montgomery, Alabama, bus to a white person. Jimmy has a young girl drink out of a water fountain labeled for whites only in a community near the Samson plantation in order to spark a protest. Though this protest leads to Jimmy's death, it also empowers Jane to stand up to Robert Samson and go to a rally that Jimmy organized.

CRITICAL OVERVIEW

From its first publication in 1971, *The Autobiography of Miss Jane Pittman* has been highly regarded and praised by critics. It also helped establish the reputation of Gaines as an important American novelist. Nearly all of the initial reviews of the book were positive, with critics extolling its power and realism as the civil rights movement of the 1960s reached its end. In *Publishers Weekly*, the reviewer is laudatory, calling the book "a very human story" and noting that Gaines "writes movingly and honestly here of the generation that went before." L. W. Griffin, writing in the *Library Journal*, praises Gaines's depiction of Jane, noting, "Through it all shines the reality of Jane's courage, fortitude, intelligence, and nobility—the worth of a human being. It is a measure of Gaines's stature as a writer that Jane lives, with all her foibles and quirks." In the book *Ernest J. Gaines: A Critical Companion*, Karen Carmean praises Gaines's depiction of Jane as well, writing that she has "memorable fullness and depth, imbuing her with the flaws and virtues of a whole people." Though Carmean thinks the male characters in the novel "are more thinly drawn," she concedes that "they do carry a good deal of thematic weight."

Author Alice Walker, reviewing *The Autobiography of Miss Jane Pittman* in "Jane Didn't Stay in a Corner" for the *New York Times Book Review*, finds depth in Gaines's work. Walker calls *The Autobiography of Miss Jane Pittman* a "grand, robust, most valuable novel that is impossible to dismiss or to put down." In the review, Walker notes that Gaines is balanced in his portrayal of both blacks and whites, and creates a sense of humanity in them all. She concludes,

Like the beautifully vivid, sturdy and serviceable language of the black, white and Creole people of Louisiana, Gaines is mellow with historical reflection, supple with wit, relaxed and expansive because he does not equate his people with failure.

Gaines's novel has remained a critical favorite, and its reputation as a deep novel has remained intact. Critics and scholars have explored many aspects of *The Autobiography of Miss Jane Pittman* over the years, including the way Gaines uses symbolism and imagery, how the four men in Jane's life can be analyzed, and how spirituality is woven into the text. In " 'We Ain't Going Back There': The Idea of Progress in *The Autobiography of Miss Jane Pittman*," William L. Andrews offers an interpretation of the text primarily through Jane's spiritual and psychological evolution. Referring to Jane's final confrontation with Robert Samson, Andrews notes, "Her psychological development through the book has prepared her for this ultimate act of self-assertion, the unprecedented yoking of the faraway and evanescent ideal of socio-political progress with the accrued folk traditions of spiritual progress."

Some critics continue to see Jane as the embodiment of all African Americans who survived slavery. In "The Black Pseudo-Autobiographical Novel: Miss Jane Pittman and Houseboy," Bede M. Ssensalo analyzes the novel as a fictional autobiography. Ssensalo argues that readers come away feeling as though the novel is centered "not around a solitary heroine but around a people whose collective deeds border upon the heroic. . . . [T]he autobiography itself is that of a people." Carmean reiterates the importance of the novel in this respect:

> *The Autobiography of Miss Jane Pittman* helped to explain why African Americans demanded recognition. Other writers had treated the struggle, but not as memorably as Gaines, whose timing, moreover, seemed perfect for a nation attempting to compensate for widely recognized and legally sanctioned racism.

The novel is not without its detractors, however. As Clarence V. Reynolds points out in "Banned Somewhere in the U.S.A.: Many African American Classics are Consigned to Another Insidious 'Black List,'" *The Autobiography of Miss Jane Pittman* was pulled from the reading list of a middle-school classroom in Texas in 1995 "after complaints about racial slurs in the book." The book was later reinstated by

MEDIA ADAPTATIONS

The Autobiography of Miss Jane Pittman was adapted into a television movie for CBS in 1974. It starred Cicely Tyson in the title role and won nine Emmy Awards. The teleplay was written by Stacy Keach, Jr. and directed by John Korty. It is available on DVD through Sony Wonder.

The Autobiography of Miss Jane Pittman was released in an unabridged version on audiocassette by Recorded Books in 1994. It is narrated by Lynne Thigpen. It is currently out of production.

The Autobiography of Miss Jane Pittman was released in an unabridged version on audiocassette by Blackstone Audio Books in 1997. It is narrated by Tonya Jordan.

school officials. The novel appears on many banned or censored book lists across the country. Despite these controversies, *The Autobiography of Miss Jane Pittman* remains a classic of American literature.

CRITICISM

Marcia Gaudet
In the excerpt that follows, Gaudet examines the relationship between the written novel and an empowering oral story-telling tradition.

In listening to a story told orally, one listens to the *voice* of the person telling the story. In a written text based on oral tradition, the author creates the illusion of the spoken voice and must maintain it with consistency and authenticity. As John Callahan points out, "Speech is Gaines' gift, and he reoralizes the written word with the old immediacy of oral storytelling." In the literary tradition of Twain, Faulkner, and Welty, Gaines is able to capture the illusion of the spoken voice on the printed page. Eudora Welty says, "It takes art to make something read as though it were spoken—of a very high kind, I think." In addition to good literary reproduction of dialect, Gaines adapts the oral tradition of telling personal experience narratives and life stories to the literary medium. Callahan further notes, "In writing as well as speech, voice articulates the self and the self's capacity for form and eloquence." Like Gaines' aunt, Miss Jane is a recorder of her own life and the events surrounding it (though Miss Jane's experiences are not those of Gaines' aunt). The black history teacher comes to record Miss Jane's life story because she has not only lived a long life, but she is recognized by her own people as someone capable of narrating her own life. Though she is illiterate, her intelligence, verbal acuity, and folk wisdom are evident to her folk community. Keith Byerman says, "Gaines has used the folk form to present the black folk experience. *Jane Pittman* embodies the history of those who had no one to record their stories."

While *Miss Jane Pittman* as a whole uses the frame of the extended personal experience narrative of autobiography, many narratives are about others or about historical events. Throughout the novel, there are stories of the folk history, freeing of slaves, the major floods, the death of Huey Long, etc. But it is the personal anecdotes that Miss Jane tells about herself that create the illusion of Miss Jane as an oral narrator on an intimate basis with the reader, and this holds the entire narrative together. Miss Jane tells of life in slavery, love and marriage to a strong man and the effects of his death, and the hardship of finding a place for herself in the world. Callahan says, "She's mastered the representative anecdote and in her eloquence persuades us that what she leaves out is really there in her (and potentially our) imagination."

Miss Jane begins her narrative with a personal anecdote by saying, "It was a day something like today." She then tells how the Yankee soldier, Corporal Brown, re-named her Jane Brown, instead of Ticey, her slave name. As an adult over 100 years old, she calls back into memory her vulnerability as a child and shares this with the reader. She says, "I stood there grinning like a little fool. I rubbed my foot with my big toe and just stood there grinning. The other troops was grinning to me … It was the prettiest name I had ever heard."

In other personal anecdotes she tells about her attraction to a young school teacher, the pain of finding out she was "barren," her visit to a hoodoo lady to protect her husband, and the death of Joe Pittman—the most important person in her life—and her need to come to terms with the feeling that in trying to protect him, she had caused his death. Speaking of Joe Pittman's death, she says:

> When Joe Pittman was killed a part of me went with him to his grave. No man would ever take his place, and that's why I carry his name to this day. I have knowed two or three other men, but none took the place of Joe Pittman. I let them know that from the start.

In the anecdote about Black Harriet and the competition and conflict among women workers in the fields, Miss Jane acknowledges her own part in a situation that ends in tragedy. She says:

> I got to say it now, we was all for it. That's how it was in the field. You want that race. That made the day go. Work, work, you had to do something to make the day go. We all wanted it. We all knowed Katie couldn't beat Harriet, but we thought the race would be fun.

Later in the book, Miss Jane talks about the "high water" of 1927, and says the "old people, the Indians, used to worship the rivers." She says that they respected the rivers and found strength in them and explains that she has also experienced that with certain things:

> There's an old oak tree up the quarters where Aunt Lou Bolin and them used to stay. That tree has been here, I'm sure, since this place been here, and it has seen much much, and it knows much much. And I'm not ashamed to say I have talked to it, and I'm not crazy either. It's not necessary craziness when you talk to trees and rivers. But a different thing when you talk to ditches and bayous. A ditch ain't nothing, and a bayou ain't too much either. But rivers and trees—less, of course, it's a chinaball tree. Anybody caught talking to a chinaball tree or a thorn tree got to be crazy. But when you talk to an oak tree that's been here all these years, and knows more than you'll ever know, it's not craziness; it's just the nobility you respect.

Sandra Stahl has illustrated how the personal narrative serves to create a feeling of intimacy between the teller and the listener. She says, "Without apology, the personal narrative makes a gesture toward intimacy," and "The personal narrative recounts an event, but it also displays a personality." In addition, she says, "The personal narrative, through its typical abundance of esoteric allusions maintains the illusion, if not the reality, of intimacy between teller and listeners."

Stahl's analysis of the personal narrative as creator of intimacy between teller and listener applies also to the fictional narrator seeking to create a sense of intimacy with the reader. Gaines' novel tells much more than the story of Miss Jane, but it is Miss Jane's own personal experience stories that engage the reader with a sense of intimacy with her and tie the narrative together by establishing a believable and acceptable character with a clear narrative voice. Barry Beckham points out that Miss Jane takes the reader/listener into her confidence and addresses the listener directly. For example, she says, "I want to tell you a little story just to show you how these people look at things, and this story is true."

Jeff Titon says, "Personality is the main ingredient in the life story," even though "It is a fiction, just like the story." We come to know the *fictional* narrator of a life story also through the self-revelation and through the personality displayed. In addition, we come to know the subject in life histories, as Elliott Oring contends, through the creation of an authentic voice. In order to maintain the illusion of the oral form, the author must in some way create the voice and the sense of intimacy that an oral personal experience narrator has with his audience.

In his article on personal narratives and the novel, David Stanley discusses "the close relationship between the hearing of personal narratives and the reading of personal novels." Stanley points out that the personal novel "may be autobiography masked as fiction." This is not the case with Gaines' novel; in fact, it has been called "fiction masquerading as autobiography." The fictional dimension of "real" personal narrative and life stories is widely recognized. Jeff Titon says, "What appears to be a person telling a life story is usually an informant answering a series of questions. Then by a common ruse the interview comes to masquerade as a life story." Thus, Miss Jane's story would seem not unlike authentic life stories, except that the narrator is part of the fiction.

Stanley also discusses the role of the narrator in personal narrative and in the novel. He says:

> The personal narrative, in other words, is a selective construct which masquerades as truthful reenactment. The personal novel, on the other hand, is fiction in which the narrator is not present with the same immediacy as the performer of the personal narrative, and in which the narrator and the author are seemingly not closely related. . . .

> The personal novel thus adopts many of the conventions of the personal narrative but reverses that of the immediacy of the author, so that the reader is simultaneously tempted to conceive the work as personal narrative and to reject the same idea. The disappearance of the author, I think, leaves the reader with contradictory clues to the work. . . .

Contradictory clues, I think, are there only if the author does not succeed in maintaining the illusion of disappearing. The author *must* disappear in order to create the illusion—the narrative voice must take over and the reader must interact with and respond to the voice of the narrator. In *Miss Jane*, Gaines created the illusion of the immediacy of the narrator to the extent that he, the author, is forgotten. According to Gaines, this is as it should be if the author has created his character effectively and found an authentic voice. Gaines says:

> That thing is supposed to take over and you're not supposed to sense that writer ever again. . . . I'm disappearing if I am writing from that first-person point of view. I'm totally disappearing because I must put everything into that character.

> I must in some way—and that's how we come back to the voice thing—give her all this information and let her tell this the way she would tell it, as an illiterate black woman a 100 years old talking about these things. I must let her do it. . . . I have to give her that information as if she were just holding a regular conversation with her friends on the porch.

Gaines also says, "It's knowing the place, knowing the people, and then letting your imagination take over to a certain extent." He says that he was trying to produce a "folk autobiography," and the book has been often called that. He establishes Miss Jane on an intimate basis with the reader through her personal narratives and then keeps her in character by maintaining the narrative voice of a 100 year old illiterate black woman that he bases on the voices he heard in the folk community. Gaines' ideas about the importance of the single voice "speaking" to the reader in fiction seem similar to the concern of anthropologists with the person speaking. Barbara Kirshenblatt-Gimblett says that American anthropologists realized the advantages of an autobiographical account in achieving coherence and vividness and saw that it was not only an ethnographic device but also "a literary genre for capturing the vividness of the living speaker." She also says, "If the anthropologists could not experience a culture that had, in his view, all but disappeared, he could experience the person who remembered how things were. And the life history made it possible to convey a sense of that experience."

Source: Marcia Gaudet, "Miss Jane and Personal Experience Narrative: Ernest Gaines' *The Autobiography of Miss Jane Pittman*," in *Western Folklore*, Vol. 51, No. 1, Janurary 1992, pp. 25–30.

SOURCES

Andrews, William L., "'We Ain't Going Back There': The Idea of Progress in *The Autobiography of Miss Jane Pittman*," in *Black American Literature Forum*, Vol. 11, No. 4, Winter 1977, pp. 146–49.

Carmean, Karen, "*The Autobiography of Miss Jane Pittman*," in *Ernest J. Gaines: A Critical Companion*, Greenwood Press, 1998, pp. 59–78.

Gaines, Ernest J., *The Autobiography of Miss Jane Pittman*, Dial Press, 1971.

Griffin, L. W., Review of *The Autobiography of Miss Jane Pittman*, *Library Journal*, Vol. 96, No. 5, March 1, 1971, p. 860.

Review of *The Autobiography of Miss Jane Pittman*, *Publishers Weekly*, Vol. 199, No. 10, March 8, 1971, p. 64.

Reynolds, Clarence V., "Banned Somewhere in the U.S.A.: Many African American Classics are Consigned to Another Insidious 'Black List,'" in *Black Issues Book Review*, September–October 2003.

Ssensalo, Bede M., "The Black Pseudo-Autobiographical Novel: Miss Jane Pittman and Houseboy," in *African Literature Today: 14 Insiders and Outsiders*, edited by Eldred Durosimi Jones, Heinemann, 1984, pp. 93–110.

Walker, Alice, "Jane Didn't Stay in a Corner," in *New York Times Book Review*, May 23, 1971, pp. 6, 12.

The Autobiography of Malcolm X

ALEX HALEY
MALCOLM X

The Autobiography of Malcolm X (1965) ranks among the most important nonfiction books of the twentieth century and is a seminal work of the autobiography genre. Told in direct and affecting prose, the book follows Malcolm's life through its many phases: his life as a zoot-suited hustler on the streets of Harlem; his rise through the ranks of the Nation of Islam; and, finally, his pilgrimage to Mecca and rethinking of his stances on racism, politics, and spirituality.

Beginning with a frightening scene of the Ku Klux Klan driving his family away from Malcolm's birthplace in Omaha, Nebraska, the book's clear and concise style makes an excellent vehicle for Malcolm's depiction of his life and evolving philosophy. He describes the disintegration of his family in Depression-era Michigan as well as his high times as a dandy hustler on the streets of Boston and New York. The twin shadows of racism and prejudice are forever present. As a child, Malcolm experiences both racism's outright horror as well as its subtler, institutionalized incarnation. As a young adult, he straightens his hair and adopts the dress and culture of the white world, slowly but surely working his way toward prison through drugs and crime.

Self-transformation is an important theme in *The Autobiography of Malcolm X*. While in prison, he is introduced to the world of Elijah Muhammad and his Nation of Islam. After studying single-mindedly until he is paroled,

> SINCE I LEARNED THE *TRUTH* IN MECCA, MY
> DEAREST FRIENDS HAVE COME TO INCLUDE *ALL* KINDS—
> SOME CHRISTIANS, JEWS, BUDDHISTS, HINDUS,
> AGNOSTICS, AND EVEN ATHEISTS! I HAVE FRIENDS WHO
> ARE CALLED CAPITALISTS, SOCIALISTS, AND
> COMMUNISTS! SOME OF MY FRIENDS ARE MODERATES,
> CONSERVATIVES, EXTREMISTS—SOME ARE EVEN UNCLE
> TOMS! MY FRIENDS TODAY ARE BLACK, BROWN, RED,
> YELLOW, AND *WHITE!*"

Malcolm is released from prison and becomes one of the movement's leading ministers. Malcolm's final transformation comes after his split with the Nation of Islam as he makes the holy pilgrimage to Mecca. His encounters with Islam as practiced in the Middle East and his experiences with the vast array of pilgrims begin to alter his strongly held ideas about race and class. He returns to the United States with a new outlook on the country's racial issues and new ideas about organizing a movement to end the oppression of the nation's African Americans. Before Malcolm X can realize his new vision, he is assassinated during a speech at New York's Audubon Ballroom.

Writer Alex Haley had just retired from twenty years in the U.S. Coast Guard when he heard about the rise of the Nation of Islam, the provocative version of African American Islam spearheaded by Elijah Muhammad in Detroit. When Haley moved to New York, he pitched an article about the Nation of Islam to *Reader's Digest* and was put in touch with one of the Nation's fiery ministers, Malcolm X. This began a relationship that would culminate with two years' worth of interviews with Malcolm X. At first distrustful of Haley, Malcolm would arrive at Haley's Greenwich Village apartment after a busy day and regale the writer with Nation of Islam philosophy and praise for Elijah Muhammad. When Haley stumbled on the subject of Malcolm's mother, Malcolm began to talk more freely. What resulted from their time together is at once a fascinating, personal

biography and a document of the racial attitudes and tensions of twentieth-century America.

PLOT SUMMARY

Chapters 1–2

The Autobiography of Malcolm X begins with Louise Little, Malcolm's mother, pregnant with him at the time, facing the Ku Klux Klan, who had surrounded the family home in Omaha, Nebraska, and were demanding to see Earl Little, Malcolm's father. Malcolm describes his father as a Baptist minister and outspoken proponent of Marcus Garvey's black independence movement.

As soon as Malcolm is born, Earl Little uproots his family of six children and moves to Milwaukee, and then on to Lansing, Michigan. But the outspoken Earl soon draws the attention of the Black Legion, a white supremacist group who reviles the Littles for settling in the "white" part of Lansing. In 1929, Malcolm recalls his earliest vivid memory: the family waking up to a house on fire and a mad scramble to escape alive. After the fire and subsequent move to East Lansing, Malcolm remembers a permanent tension settling in between his parents. At this point, Malcolm becomes aware that his father spares him from the often vicious beatings he sometimes administers to the other Little children. Malcolm believes that even his father is affected by his much lighter skin tone, which he inherited from both his West Indian mother and his father. For Malcolm, this insight is one of his first in a series of realizations about how blacks and whites relate to one another in America.

In 1931, Earl Little storms out of the house after arguing with Louise and never returns. His body is later found almost cut in two near some local railroad tracks, his head smashed in on one side. Malcolm recalls the family unraveling after Earl's death. With eight children and no father, the Littles begin receiving visits from state welfare officials, and, while the state's money helps the family, it chips away at Louise's sense of pride. "The physical downhill wasn't as quick as the psychological. My mother was, above everything else, a proud woman, and it took its toll on her that she was accepting charity." When Louise is jilted by a suitor from Lansing, her grasp on reality begins to give way.

The welfare officials come more often, now with specific suggestions about the children

BIOGRAPHY

ALEX HALEY AND MALCOLM X

Malcolm Little was born on May 19, 1925, in Omaha, Nebraska. Although a talented student, Malcolm dropped out of school and turned to petty crime in New York and Boston. He discovered Islam while serving a prison sentence for a burglary, and emerged in 1952 a devoted follower of the Nation of Islam, soon adopting the name Malcolm X. With Malcolm's devotion and leadership, the movement ballooned from a few hundred members to tens of thousands in a decade. Disillusioned with the organization in early 1964, Malcolm made a pilgrimage to the holy city of Mecca, a pilgrimage all Muslims are required by their faith to make at least once in their lives, and started practicing orthodox Islam. He returned from Africa with a new vision of hope and unity for the future, but was assassinated on February 21, 1965, in New York.

Born in Ithaca, New York, on August 11, 1921, Alex Haley is best known for his *The Autobiography of Malcolm X* and *Roots: The Saga of an American Family*. Raised with extended family in Henning, Tennessee, Haley heard family histories from his grandmother who told stories of her ancestor, Toby, who had been brought from Africa as a slave. While Haley would not follow up on these stories until his genealogical epic *Roots: The Saga of an American Family*, they likely played a role in his racial consciousness and interest in writing.

In 1963, Haley interviewed Malcolm X for *Playboy* magazine. Malcolm asked Haley to work on an autobiography, and Haley spent the next two years writing what would become *The Autobiography of Malcolm X*. *Roots* was published in 1976, and tells the story of African Kunta Kinte, his enslavement, and the successive generations of his family in America. In 1977, the book won the Pulitzer Prize for Literature. In 1993, he published *Alex Haley's Queen: The Story of an American Family*, the fictionalized account of a different branch of his family. Haley was at work on another project based on his family when he suffered a heart attack and died in Seattle, Washington, on February 10, 1992.

being placed in different foster homes. Malcolm is upset at the thought of being separated from his siblings, but is placed with the family of his friend Big Boy, the Gohannases. In 1937, Louise is placed in the state mental hospital in Kalamazoo, Michigan, and all of her children become wards of the court. Malcolm's presentation of this part of his past reveals the depth of his feeling toward white people. "A white man in charge of a black man's children! Nothing but legal, modern slavery—however kindly intentioned."

With his increasingly rebellious attitude, Malcolm is expelled from school and placed in a detention home in Mason, Michigan. There, he comes into favor with the couple who run the facility, Mr. and Mrs. Swerlin. To his surprise, Malcolm likes the Swerlins, and his attitude improves, so much so that the Swerlins defer his transfer to reform school. He eats with the Swerlins, sweeps, and generally helps around their home. But as kind as the Swerlins are, Malcolm notes their inherent, and often grossly displayed, prejudice.

To his surprise, the Swerlins manage to get Malcolm into Mason Junior High School and find him a part-time job. Malcolm remembers the prestige that came from being a "novelty," one of the school's very few black students. This prestige and his charisma even make him class president of the seventh grade. During this time, his half sister from his father's first marriage comes to visit from Boston. Ella makes a big impression on the Little children. As Malcolm remembers, "She was plainly proud of her very dark skin." In 1940, Malcolm visits Ella in Boston, a pivotal event in forming his perspective on race and the world in general. The black world of Boston's Roxbury district amazes

Malcolm X Bettmann/Corbis

Malcolm—the throngs of black people, the music, the food, the churches—all of this is different from anything he had ever seen in Michigan, and it makes his world back home seem small, confining, and very white. As he remembers, "It was then that I began to change—inside." The very week he finishes eighth grade, Malcolm Little once more boards a bus for his sister's home in Boston, this time to stay.

Chapters 3–7

What Malcolm first encounters in Boston is the section of Roxbury known as "the Hill," a genteel neighborhood peopled by more "cultured" Negroes. But Malcolm finds himself more comfortable when he explores the downtown section of Roxbury, a "world of grocery stores, walk-up flats, cheap restaurants, poolrooms, bars, storefront churches, and pawnshops." Malcolm soon meets a fellow Michigander named Shorty, who gets him a job at the Roseland State Ballroom shining shoes and from time to time selling liquor and marijuana to the crowds that attend the venue's concerts and dances. The roaring nightlife of the Roseland introduces young Malcolm to many firsts: cigarettes, liquor,

marijuana, and gambling. In retrospect, Malcolm sees this as a descent into a degraded and self-hating existence. In one of the book's most vivid passages, he describes his first "conk," a painful process of straightening the hair necessary to achieve the smooth hairstyle popular with African American hipsters of the era. "This was my first really big step toward self-degradation: when I endured all of that pain, literally burning my flesh to have it look like a white man's hair."

Over the next several years, Malcolm descends deeper into the life of a hustler. This is a journey he sees in retrospect as a well-trodden path:

> Like hundreds of thousands of country-bred Negroes before who had come to the Northern black ghetto before me, and have come since, I'd also acquired all the other fashionable ghetto adornments—the zoot suits and conk that I have described, liquor, cigarettes, then reefers—all to erase my embarrassing background.

Chapters 8–9

Malcolm describes the fantastic personalities of Harlem, where he moves after World War II: the numbers runners, the pimps, the con men, the burglars, the prostitutes—all coming together to create the fabric of the neighborhood's underworld. Amid all this, Malcolm becomes "Detroit Red," a hustler in his own right with a bustling business delivering marijuana to traveling musicians. After running afoul of a local tough, Malcolm and Shorty return to Boston and form a robbery crew with two white sisters who help case prospective targets. Caught and convicted after a burglary, Malcom is sentenced to ten years in Charlestown State Prison.

Chapters 10–12

Malcolm recalls his first year at Charlestown as one of rebellion and sullenness. He curses the Bible and God. "Eventually, the men in the cellblock had a name for me: 'Satan.' Because of my antireligious attitude." However, he does meet an erudite con named Bimbi who regales his fellow inmates with learned speeches on a range of topics. Malcolm is impressed and begins to take correspondence courses in English and Latin. In 1948, Malcolm receives a letter from his brother Philbert who tells him about the Nation of Islam. He also hears from his brother Reginald, who tells Malcolm he is coming to visit to show him how to get out of prison. While

Malcolm thinks that his brother will tell him about some scheme of escape, Reginald tells Malcolm about Allah, Elijah Muhammad, the Nation of Islam, and the evils done to blacks by the "devil white man."

Through prolific correspondence with his family back in Detroit, Malcolm begins to learn about the message of Elijah Muhammad and Wallace D. Fard, the Nation of Islam's spiritual founder: of the white race's corruption of nonwhite people throughout the course of history, of enslavement, and of the ways that whites keep the black people of America oppressed, poor, and powerless. Soon, Malcolm begins writing letters to Elijah Muhammad every day. Malcolm is transferred to the Norfolk Prison Colony, which has an extensive library. He reads voraciously on a variety of subjects as his belief in Elijah Muhammad and his message grows. By the time of his parole in 1952, Malcolm is ready to dive headlong into the world of the Nation of Islam. He drops "the white slavemaster name of 'Little'" and becomes known as Malcolm X.

Chapters 13–15
Now that Malcolm is free from prison, his world revolves around the Nation of Islam and its charismatic leader. "Never in prison had I studied and absorbed so intensely as I did now under Mr. Muhammad's guidance." An activist by nature, Elijah Muhammad puts Malcolm to work opening more and more temples around the United States, culminating in his arrival in New York City to found Temple Seven. "For Mr. Muhammad's teachings really to resurrect American black people, Islam obviously had to grow, to grow very big. And nowhere in America was such a single temple potential available as in New York's five boroughs."

In New York, Malcolm presides over the bustling temple and marries one of its members, Betty X, a tall nursing student from Detroit. They would go on to have six daughters together, two being twins born after Malcolm's death. By 1959, the Nation of Islam, or "Black Muslims," as they are popularly known, is gaining national attention. Late that year, a television special about Black Muslims called "The Hate That Hate Produced" is broadcast. He recalls, "Every phrase was edited to increase the shock mood. As the producers intended, I think people sat just about limp when the program went off." Malcolm describes fielding a seemingly endless string of phone calls about the program and the purported hatred flowing from the Nation of Islam. A whirlwind of negative press about Malcolm and the Nation of Islam follows. He expects this from the white media, but is troubled by other critics, specifically his fellow African Americans: "Even so, my bitterness was less against the white press than it was against those Negro 'leaders' who kept attacking us." Eventually, with Elijah Muhammad's approval, Malcolm "began returning their fire."

Malcolm recalls developing his oratory style, a style that frequently gives credit to the Nation of Islam leader and his teachings. He explains how he would address a crowd at an all-black meeting:

> The Honorable Elijah Muhammad is the first black leader among us with the *courage* to tell us ... something which when you begin to think of it back in your home, you will realize we black people have been *living* with, we have been *seeing*, we have been *suffering*, all of our lives! Our *enemy* is the *white man!*

The Nation of Islam begins to hold huge rallies, all featuring passionate addresses promoting black independence and a distrust of the "white man." This brings national attention, not only from the press, but from government officials at all levels. Malcolm knows that the FBI and other agencies are watching them closely. He has now ascended to the elite ranks of the Nation of Islam and he is awed by his faith and his position. As a guest speaker at Harvard, he reflects on his rise from hoodlum to minister. He likens himself to Icarus, the boy of Greek myth with wings fixed with wax, who falls when he tries to fly too high. "Standing there by that Harvard window, I silently vowed to Allah that I never would forget that any wings I wore had been put on by the religion of Islam."

Chapter 16
In the early 1960s, Malcolm begins hearing rumors and negative remarks about his trajectory within the Nation of Islam. Ideas circulate that he is trying to take over the Nation or that he is making large sums of money. He brushes aside the rumors about himself. But in 1962, Malcolm begins to suspect that some other rumors about the Nation of Islam might be true, namely, that Elijah Muhammad has been involved in several romantic liaisons with secretaries in the organization. As the evidence of these improprieties builds, Malcolm suffers:

"I can't describe the torments I went though." Before confronting the leader himself, Malcolm visits several of the women who are involved. "From their own mouths, I heard their stories of who had fathered their children." When he confronts Muhammad, the leader explains to him that he is following in the footsteps of David, Noah, Lot, and other patriarchs of the past. Malcolm is shocked, but tries to think of all of the leader's good qualities as outweighing these transgressions. Malcolm tries to prepare some within the Nation for the media storm that is brewing, but instead, the Nation sees him as stoking the fire of controversy.

After President John F. Kennedy is assassinated in Dallas in 1963, Malcolm gives perhaps his most infamous interview with the press. "Without a second thought, I said what I honestly felt—that it was, as I saw it, a case of 'the chickens coming home to roost.' " This is a public relations disaster for the Nation of Islam, and Elijah Muhammad "silences" Malcolm, and forbids him to speak or perform services for ninety days. But this remark, together with his airing of Elijah Muhammad's illicit affairs, creates a chasm between Malcolm and the Nation of Islam that would be permanent. Malcolm begins to suspect that Elijah Muhammad is using him as a scapegoat, and that he has even ordered him killed. A former assistant skilled in explosives admits that he had been ordered to rig Malcolm's car with a bomb. "But this brother, it happened, had seen too much of my total loyalty to the Nation to carry out his order. Instead, he came to me. I thanked him for my life." Malcolm's split with the Nation of Islam and Elijah Muhammad is complete, and he turns his attention to building a new Islamic organization, Muslim Mosque, Inc.

What Malcolm has in mind is an organization that will accept African Americans of all faiths and put into action what the Nation of Islam has only discussed. It is to be a "working base for an action program designed to eliminate the political oppression, the economic exploitation, and the social degradation suffered daily by twenty-two million Afro-Americans." On a personal level, he feels he needs to take the trip that every Muslim tries to fulfill at least once in his lifetime, the pilgrimage to the holy city of Mecca.

Chapters 17–19

In some of the book's most moving prose, Malcolm describes his visit to the Ka'ba, the holiest place of Islam. In the Middle East, Malcolm is taken aback by the variety of Muslim pilgrims he encounters. Some with blue eyes, blond hair, and the whitest skin he has ever seen are crowded together with the darkest of Africans. The pilgrims eat together, often with their hands and from the same plates and bowls. They sleep together on the same mats, and, of course, they pray together. Malcolm begins to review and revise some of his ideas about race and about Islam:

> In America, 'white man' meant specific attitudes and actions toward the black man, and toward all other non-white men. But in the Muslim world, I had seen that men with white complexions were more genuinely brotherly than anyone else had even been.

After a revelatory visit to Africa, Malcolm returns to New York in May 1964 to begin building his organization. While his message has been changed by his pilgrimage and visit to Africa, he is still regarded as the angriest black man in America. Now, he is hounded by the press; he also suspects that he is marked for death by the Nation of Islam. In the penultimate chapter, Malcolm's narrative voice is prophetic and resolved. He feels that he will die a violent death and that, posthumously, he will be used by the white media and other factions:

> You watch. I will be labeled as, at best, an "irresponsible" black man. I have always felt about this accusation that the black "leader" whom white men consider to be "responsible" is invariably the black "leader" who never gets any results."

Epilogue

The final chapter takes place after Malcolm's assassination on February 21, 1965, at Harlem's Audubon Ballroom. Written by Alex Haley, the epilogue provides a behind-the-scenes look at how the book came to be. Haley and Malcolm spent hundreds of hours together—Haley dutifully tape recording and transcribing the conversations the two had in Haley's Greenwich Village apartment. Haley recounts his first contact with Malcolm and how the two came to trust each other and become friends. The chapter describes the events leading up to Malcolm's murder as well as the funeral and the events following. Wistfully, Haley reflects on his work bringing this book to fruition. "He was the most electric personality I have ever met, and I still can't quite conceive him dead. It still feels to me as if he has just gone into some next chapter, to be written by historians."

THEMES

Pan-Africanism

Early in *The Autobiography of Malcolm X*, Malcolm describes his father's devotion to black leader Marcus Garvey. Born in Jamaica in 1887, Garvey was one of the leading lights of Pan-Africanism, a movement to unify all people of African descent as part of a global community, throughout the early part of the twentieth century. In addition to building a membership of nearly one million in his United Negro Improvement Association, Garvey also founded the Black Star Line, a shipping line established to bring black people from all over the world back to "Mother Africa." Malcolm remembers his father's dedication to Garvey's philosophy. "He believed . . . that freedom, independence and self-respect could never be achieved by the Negro in America, and that therefore the Negro should . . . return to his African land of origin." The idea of an African diaspora (African people and their descendants living outside of Africa) and the notion that black people from around the globe should unite continues to surface in Malcolm's thinking. In his autobiography, he describes the powerful rhetoric of a Nigerian official: "South and Central and North America contain over *eighty million* people of African descent. . . . The world's course will change the day the African-heritage peoples come together as brothers!"

Religion

The Autobiography of Malcolm X deals extensively with religion. Throughout the course of the book, Malcolm analyzes Christianity as practiced in the United States, Judaism, and, of course, Islam. While he does examine the theology of Islam at some length, his examination of other religions is focused on culture, ethos, and morality. He sees Jews as controlling operators in the black ghettos, a view that is shared by his brother Reginald, who tells Malcolm that all whites are devils. When Malcolm suggests that his Jewish friend Hymie may be a good person, Reginald responds, "What is it if I let you make five hundred dollars to let me make ten thousand?" Malcolm sees Christianity as yet another tool of oppression wielded by the white man that "brainwashed this 'Negro' to always turn the other cheek, and grin, and scrape, and bow, and be humble, and to sing, and to pray, and to take whatever was dished out."

Although Malcolm leaves prison believing that Islam as presented by Elijah Muhammad and the Nation of Islam is the natural religion for the black American, his pilgrimage to Mecca transforms his approach to Islam, especially with respect to matters of race and equality:

> During the past eleven days here in the Muslim world, I have eaten from the same plate, drunk from the same glass, and slept in the same bed (or on the same rug)—while praying to the *same God*—with fellow Muslims, whose eyes were the bluest of blue, whose hair was the blondest of blond, and whose skin was the whitest of white.

Racism

Issues revolving around class are central to *The Autobiography of Malcolm X*. For Malcolm, the two distinct classes are the whites, who have political, social, and economic power, and African Americans, who are disenfranchised and oppressed. However, even as a child, he sees that issues of class can exist in subtler forms, even within the African American community. Upon moving to Boston after eighth grade, he explores "the Hill," a "snooty-black neighborhood" home to blacks "acting and living differently from any black people I'd ever dreamed of in my life. . . . [a]nd look[ing] down their noses at the Negroes of the black ghetto."

Malcolm is appalled at black people who try to become more "white" by adopting "white" forms of speech and dress. For Malcolm, this is symbolized by the "conk," a hairstyle that relaxes curly hair so that it straightens and lies flat. Getting his first conk elevates him from the "country Negro" class into the class of the hip blacks who live in the city. The painful conking process involves applying a burning lye-based mixture, and as Malcolm says, "This was my first really big step toward self-degradation: when I endured all of that pain, literally burning my flesh to have it look like a white man's hair."

Malcolm's pilgrimage to Mecca has a powerful effect on his concept of race. In the Middle East, he sees white, blond and blue-eyed pilgrims eating, sleeping, and praying with dark-skinned Africans. He also experiences the most brotherly hospitality from fair-skinned people, though, racially, they are far removed from the "devil white man" of America. He begins to gain a more subtle understanding of the complexities of race and class. "It was when I first began to perceive that 'white man,' as commonly

Denzel Washington, as Malcolm X, stands at a podium outside the Apollo Theater, in a scene from the 1992 film Malcolm X *The Kobal Collection. Reproduced by permission*

used, means complexion only secondarily; primarily it described attitudes and actions."

HISTORICAL OVERVIEW

The American Civil Rights Movement

While the speeches, marches, and sit-ins of the 1960s are the most powerful images of the American civil rights era, the seeds of this movement were planted in the nineteenth century, at the close of the Civil War. Freed slaves were not yet citizens of the United States, and many southern states enforced restrictions that kept ex-slaves at the level of second-class citizens. To protect the interests of black southerners, Congress passed the Civil Rights Act of 1866, which created and legally protected the civil rights of African Americans. While federal troops were still in the region during the years after the war—a period known as Reconstruction—the law provided

only scant protection from the discriminatory practices of many white southerners.

With the end of Reconstruction in the late 1870s, southern states began to enact "Jim Crow" laws that severely restricted access to public spaces, services, and opportunities for black people. These discriminatory practices were given legal sanction with the *Plessy v. Ferguson* case of 1896. One of the civil rights movement's landmark cases, *Plessy v. Ferguson* established the legality of "separate but equal" facilities for blacks and whites. In practice, however, these separate facilities were rarely equal, and the Jim Crow laws of the South were sanctioned by the highest court in the land. The case of *Brown v. Board of Education of Topeka* reversed Plessy. Initially brought before the U.S. District Court in Kansas, Brown went all the way to the Supreme Court where it ruled that "separate educational facilities are inherently unequal" in 1954. Brown marked the federal court's support of the burgeoning desegregation movement.

The Civil Rights Act of 1964 is the most sweeping legislation of the American civil rights movement. Proposed by President Kennedy in 1963, the bill was finally put through Congress by Lyndon Johnson despite an eighty-day filibuster mounted by Southern Democrats. Though designed primarily to protect African Americans, it also prohibited discrimination in employment, housing, schools, and all public accommodations based on race, color, religion, sex, or national origin.

The Nation of Islam

The Nation of Islam was founded by Wallace Fard in 1930 and aimed to overcome the social, economic, political, and spiritual barriers encountered by blacks in the United States. While adopting many of traditional Islam's teachings, Fard incorporated his own vision into his Detroit mosque. One of his earliest disciples was Elijah Poole, who later took the reins of the organization and changed his name to Elijah Muhammad. Fard disappeared in 1934, and, in his absence, Elijah Muhammad proposed that Fard was God incarnate.

Under Muhammad, the Nation of Islam grew by establishing mosques throughout the United States. In 1952, the Nation of Islam gained its most prominent and controversial minister, Malcolm X. Born Malcolm Little, Malcolm X had been introduced to Muhammad and the Nation of Islam while in prison. A fervent student and powerful speaker, Malcolm X became the movement's most recognizable face. Eventually, Malcolm X split with the Nation as he became disillusioned with Elijah Muhammad's personal behavior. Malcolm X was assassinated in 1965.

After Muhammad's death in 1975, the Nation of Islam split into two factions. Wallace Muhammad, Elijah's son, tried to bring the group's vision closer to mainstream Sunni Islam. Wallace Muhammad openly disagreed with his father's separatist views and renamed the organization the Muslim American Society. Opposing Wallace Muhammad was Louis Farrakhan, who became the leader of New York's mosque and spokesperson for the group that wanted to keep Elijah Muhammad's teachings intact. In 2000, Wallace Muhammad and Louis Farrakhan publicly reconciled and their two organizations began working together to host events and promote their message.

Two finalists stand on the podiums with their heads bowed and raised fists at the 1968 Mexico City Olympics Corbis/Bettmann

CRITICAL OVERVIEW

Well-received by critics upon its publication in 1965, *The Autobiography of Malcolm X* has become one of the classics of twentieth-century American literature. As critic Robert Bone wrote in the *New York Times* in 1966, "Malcolm's book, without a doubt, has had a major impact on the younger generation."

Within a few years, critics were recognizing the book's importance as literature beyond its power as a social catalyst. As Barrett John Mandel notes in 1972:

> *The Autobiography of Malcolm X* is a great work of didactic literature with a wide audience which its narrative and emotional appeal are doing their share to mold and direct. The impact of the work on most readers is intense, immediate, and enduring.

Critics also lauded Alex Haley's participation in the creation of the book. Haley's participation may serve to provide the reader with a more nuanced understanding of Malcolm. Critic David P. Demarest writes, "As it stands, *The Autobiography* may avoid the problems of both the autobiography's lack of objectivity and the biographer's limited knowledge."

The Autobiography has become standard reading on college campuses, and, as Marilyn Kern-Foxworth notes in a 1985 article, "It ... had popular appeal; it was not uncommon to find young black men on street corners, in subways, or walking along the street with copies of the book in their hands." Decades after his death, Malcolm X's story retains its power in the cultural canon, earning a place on several prestigious lists, including the Modern Library's "100 Best Nonfiction" books in English of the twentieth century and the New York Public Library's "Books of the Century."

CRITICISM

Paul John Eakin

In the following excerpt, Eakin argues that The Autobiography of Malcolm X *challenges traditional notions of the genre to which it ostensibly belongs.*

When a complex and controversial figure writes a book that has achieved the distinction and popularity of *The Autobiography of Malcolm X,* it is inevitable that efforts will be made to place him and his work in the perspective of a literary tradition. Barrett John Mandel, for example, has identified in Malcolm X's story the paradigm of the traditional conversion narrative. His reading of Malcolm X's autobiography, and it is a characteristic one, assumes that the narrative expresses a completed self. Further, Ross Miller has suggested that such an assumption is central to the expectations we bring to the reading of any autobiography: "The pose of the autobiographer as an experienced man is particularly effective because we expect to hear from someone who has a completed sense of his own life and is therefore in a position to tell what he has discovered." Even Warner Berthoff, who has admirably defined Malcolm X's "extraordinary power to change and be changed" as "the distinctive rule of his life," seems to have been drawn to this sense

MEDIA ADAPTATIONS

The Autobiography of Malcolm X was the inspiration for the documentary *Malcolm X: His Own Story as it Really Happened* in 1972. The film is narrated by Ossie Davis and James Earl Jones and is directed by Arnold Perl, who would go on to cowrite the screenplay for Spike Lee's film *Malcolm X* in 1992. It is available on VHS from Warner Home Video.

In 1992, *The Autobiography of Malcolm X* was adapted for the screen by American filmmaker Spike Lee. The film stars Denzel Washington as Malcolm, Al Freeman as Elijah Muhammad, and Angela Bassett as Betty Shabazz. Entitled *Malcolm X*, it is available on VHS and DVD from Warner Home Video.

of the completed self when he attempts to locate the *Autobiography* in a special and limited literary tradition, that of the political testament in which "some ruler or statesman sets down for the particular benefit of his people a summary of his own experience and wisdom." The rhetorical posture of Malcolm X in the last chapter would seem to confirm Berthoff's reading and to fulfill Miller's autobiographical expectations, for it is indeed that of the elder statesman summing up a completed life, a life that has, as it were, already ended:

> Anyway, now, each day I live as if I am already dead, and I tell you what I would like for you to do. When I *am* dead—I say it that way because from the things I *know*, I do not expect to live long enough to read this book in its finished form—I want you to just watch and see if I'm not right in what I say: that the white man, in his press, is going to identify me with "hate."

If Malcolm X's anticipation of his imminent death confers on this final phase of autobiographical retrospection a posthumous authority, it is nevertheless an authority that he exercises here to defend himself against the fiction of the completed self that his interpreters—both black and white, in the event—were to use against him. Each of his identities turned out to be provisional, and even this voice from the grave was the utterance not of an ultimate identity but merely of the last one in the series of roles that Malcolm X had variously assumed, lived out, and discarded.

Alex Haley's "Epilogue" to the *Autobiography* reveals the fictive nature of this final testamentary stance which Berthoff regards as definitive. Here Haley, Malcolm X's collaborator in the *Autobiography* reports that the apparent uncertainty and confusion of Malcolm X's views were widely discussed in Harlem during the last months of Malcolm X's life, while Malcolm X himself, four days before his death, said in an interview, "I'm man enough to tell you that I can't put my finger on exactly what my philosophy is now, but I'm flexible." Moreover, the account of the composition of the *Autobiography* given by Haley in the "Epilogue" makes it clear that the fiction of the autobiographer as a man with "a completed sense of his own life" is especially misleading in the case of Malcolm X, for even Haley and the book that was taking shape in his hands were out of phase with the reality of Malcolm X's life and identity. Thus Haley acknowledges that he "never dreamed" of Malcolm X's break with Elijah Muhammad "until the actual rift became public," although the break overturned the design that had guided Malcolm X's dictations of his life story to Haley up to that point. The disparity between the traditional autobiographical fiction of the completed self and the biographical fact of Malcolm X's ceaselessly evolving identity may lead us, as it did Malcolm X himself, to enlarge our understanding of the limits and the possibilities of autobiography.

. . .

What concerns us here, is not the much-studied features of conversion and the ease with which they may be translated into the formal elements of autobiographical narrative, but rather the natural and seemingly inevitable inference that the individual first discovers the shape of his life and then writes the life on the basis of this discovery. Some version of this temporal fiction, of course, lies behind most autobiography, and I would emphasize it as a corollary to Miller's definition of the completed self: the notion that living one's life precedes writing about it, that the life is in some sense complete and that the autobiographical process takes place afterward, somehow outside the realm of lapsing time in which the life proper necessarily unfolds. The evangelical bias of conversion narrative is especially interesting in this regard, for it supplies a predisposition for such an autobiographer to accept this supporting fiction as fact, since he believes that conversion works a definitive transition from shifting false beliefs to a fixed vision of the one truth. It is, accordingly, when a new discovery about the shape of one's life takes place during the writing of one's story that an autobiographer may be forced to recognize the presence and nature of the fictions on which his narrative is based. The experience of Malcolm X in his final period did foster such a recognition, and this knowledge and its consequences for autobiographical narrative may instruct us in the complex relation that necessarily obtains between living a life and writing about it. However, before we consider the *Autobiography* from the vantage point of the man who was becoming "El-Hajj Malik El-Shabazz" (Chapter 18), let us look at the *Autobiography* as it was originally conceived by the man whose first conversion in prison had transformed him from "Satan" (Chapter 10) to "Minister Malcolm X" (Chapter 13). This is, of course, the way we do look at the *Autobiography* when we begin to read it for the first time, especially if we are relatively unfamiliar with the life of Malcolm X.

Malcolm X describes the "first major turning point of my life" at the end of the second chapter, his realization that in white society he was not free "to become whatever *I* wanted to be." The shock to the eighth-grade boy was profound, for despite his traumatic childhood memories of the destruction of his family by white society, Malcolm X had embraced the white success ethic by the time he was in junior high school: "I was trying so hard . . . to be white." What follows, in Chapters 3 through 9, is Malcolm X's account of his life as a ghetto hustler, his first "career," just as his role as a Black Muslim minister was to be his second. If Allah preserved him from the fate of an Alger hero or a Booker T. Washington, from a career as a "successful" shoeshine boy or a self-serving member of the "black bourgeoisie," he was nevertheless destined to enact a kind of inverse parody of the white man's rise to success as he sank deeper and deeper into a life of crime. This is the portion of the *Autobiography* that has been singled out for its vividness by the commentators, with the result that the conversion experience and its aftermath in Chapters 10 through 15 have been somewhat eclipsed. It would be possible, of course, to see in the popularity of this section nothing more than the universal appeal of any evocation of low life and evil ways. In addition, this preference may reflect an instinctive attraction to a more personal mode of autobiography with plenty of concrete self-revelation instead of the more formal testimony of an exemplary life.

If the *Autobiography* had ended with the fourteenth or fifteenth chapter, what we would have, I suggest, is a narrative which could be defined as an extremely conventional example of autobiographical form distinguished chiefly by the immediacy and power of its imaginative recreation of the past. It is true that this much of the *Autobiography* would usefully illustrate the survival of the classic pattern of conversion narrative in the contemporary literature of spiritual autobiography, but this interest would necessarily be a limited one given Malcolm X's reticence about the drama of the experience of conversion itself. For Malcolm X the fact of conversion is decisive, life-shaping, identity-altering, but unlike the most celebrated spiritual autobiographers of the past he chooses not to dramatize the experience itself or to explore its psychological dynamics.

. . .

At the end, then, Malcolm X came to reject the traditional autobiographical fiction that the life comes first, and then the writing of the life; that the life is in some sense complete and that the autobiographical process simply records the final achieved shape. This fiction is based upon a suspension of time, as though the "life," the subject, could sit still long enough for the autobiographical "I," the photographer, to snap its picture. In fact, as Malcolm X was to learn, the "life" itself will not hold still; it changes, shifts position. And as for the autobiographical act, it requires much more than an instant of time to take the picture, to write the story. As the act of composition extends in time, so it enters the lifestream, and the fictive separation between life and life story, which is so convenient—even necessary—to the writing of autobiography, dissolves.

Malcolm X's final knowledge of the incompleteness of the self is what gives the last pages of the *Autobiography* together with the "Epilogue" their remarkable power: the vision of a man whose swiftly unfolding career has outstripped the possibilities of the traditional autobiography he had meant to write. It is not in the least surprising that Malcolm X's sobering insights into the limitations of autobiography are accompanied by an increasingly insistent desire to disengage himself from the ambitions of the autobiographical process. Thus he speaks of the *Autobiography* to Haley time and again as though, having disabused himself of any illusion that the narrative could keep pace with his life, he had consigned the book to its fate, casting it adrift as hopelessly obsolete. Paradoxically, nowhere does the book succeed, persuade, more than in its confession of failure as autobiography. This is the fascination of *The Education of Henry Adams*, and Malcolm X, like Adams, leaves behind him the husks of played-out autobiographical paradigms. The indomitable reality of the self transcends and exhausts the received shapes for a life that are transmitted by the culture, and yet the very process of discarding in itself works to structure an apparently shapeless experience. Despite—or because of—the intractability of life to form, the fiction of the completed self, which lies at the core of the autobiographical enterprise, cannot be readily dispatched. From its ashes, phoenix-like, it reconstitutes itself in a new guise. Malcolm X's work, and Adams' as well, generate a sense that the uncompromising commitment to the truth of one's own nature, which requires the elimination of false identities and careers one by one, will yield at the last the pure ore of a final and irreducible selfhood. This is the ultimate autobiographical dream.

Source: Paul John Eakin, "Malcolm X and the Limits of Autobiography," in *Criticism*, Vol. 28, No. 1–3, Summer 1976, pp. 230–42.

SOURCES

"100 Best Nonfiction," Modern Library, www.random house.com/modernlibrary/100bestnonfiction.html (April 13, 2006).

Bone, Robert, "A Black Man's Quarrel with the Christian God," in *New York Time Book Review*, September 11, 1966, pp. 3, 14.

"Books of the Century," New York Public Library, www. nypl.org/research/chss/events/booklist.html (April 13, 2006).

Demarest, David P., Jr., "The Autobiography of Malcolm X: Beyond Didacticism," in *CLA Journal*, Vol. 16, No. 2, December 1972, pp. 179–87.

Kern-Foxworth, Marilyn, "Malcolm X" in *Dictionary of Literary Biography*, Vol. 38: *Afro-American Writers After 1955: Dramatists and Prose Writers*, edited by Thadious M. Davis, Gale Research, 1985, pp. 115–19.

Mandel, Barrett John, "The Didactic Achievement of Malcolm X's Autobiography," in *Afro-American Studies*, Vol. 2, No. 4, March 1972, pp. 269–76.

"The Official Website of Malcolm X," The Estate of Malcolm X, www.cmgww.com/historic/malcolm/index.htm (April 13, 2006).

X, Malcolm, and Alex Haley, *The Autobiography of Malcolm X: As Told to Alex Haley*, Ballantine Books, 1965, reissue edition, 1987.

The Awakening

KATE CHOPIN

1899

When Kate Chopin's *The Awakening* (1899) was published, there were significantly fewer women writing fiction than there are today. Authors of the time did not generally address a woman's desires or concerns, except in the context of her duties as wife and mother. As a result, *The Awakening* was a bombshell in a society that embraced a rigid morality and a strict code of social behavior. Main character Edna Pontellier's disregard for social conventions and gender roles earned contempt from critics and readers alike, and the novel secured a persistent negative reputation for the author. At the same time, the novel gave voice to a new generation of women, making an important contribution to the burgeoning women's movement of the early twentieth century.

At a time when cultural norms indicated that a woman's place was in the home, any woman who resisted that role was subject to discrimination and ridicule. Popular nineteenth-century fiction emphasized a woman's duty, joy, and fulfillment in the domestic realm, but as the twentieth century approached, fiction began exploring the social changes on the horizon. *The Awakening* is the story of Edna Pontellier's journey from a sleepy, discontented life to one fully under her own control. The romantic attentions of Robert Lebrun and Alcée Arobin bring her to life, but her awakening is far more than physical: it is spiritual, social, and personal. She begins to take her art more seriously, takes a

lover, moves into her own apartment, rejects social conventions that do not suit her, and allows herself to admit that she is not a maternal woman.

Edna chooses to follow her natural inclinations rather than letting her culture's restrictive standards prevent her from living the life to which she has awakened. To learn who she truly is, she is willing to risk becoming a social outcast: "By all the codes which I am acquainted with, I am a devilishly wicked specimen of the sex. But some way I can't convince myself that I am." There is little she can do with her self-knowledge, however, especially in the insular Creole community of New Orleans.

The publication of *The Awakening* caused great alarm in a society still clinging to the rigid moral codes created during the Victorian era, the period in the 1800s when Queen Victoria ruled Great Britain. Chopin's book was never banned, but her literary reputation was seriously damaged by the critical and public outcry over its content, specifically over Edna's romantic relationships with two men outside of her marriage, her unwillingness to be a wife and mother, and her refusal to conform to society's expectations. Much like Edna, Chopin faced hostility for her decision to speak openly about female sexuality and a woman's private thoughts. In Chopin's male-dominated society, an independent and liberated woman was considered both threatening and unnatural. Some critics argue that Chopin knew this and that this knowledge was what motivated her to end the novel with Edna swimming out into the ocean. Others contend that the closing scene shows Edna rising above the limitations imposed on women in Victorian society and making the ultimate claim of self-possession.

> I don't want anything but my own way. This is wanting a good deal, of course, when you have to trample upon the lives, the hearts, the prejudices of others.

PLOT SUMMARY

Chapters I–III

Annoyed by a squawking parrot, Léonce Pontellier leaves the porch of the main house where he has been sitting and moves to a chair outside his own cottage. The cottages and house are part of a private resort on Grand Isle, a vacation spot popular with members of New

BIOGRAPHY

KATE CHOPIN

Katherine O'Flaherty Chopin was born on February 8, 1850, in St. Louis, Missouri. Her father died young, and her mother was left to raise four young children alone. She attended the Academy of the Sacred Heart, where she was taught domestic skills, as women then were not expected to do anything else with their lives. She married Oscar Chopin in 1870, and had six children. Shortly after their marriage, the Chopins settled in New Orleans, where Kate was exposed to Creole society as well as the politics of race and gender that were sweeping through the city and the entire nation in the late nineteenth century. When Oscar died in 1882, Chopin returned to St. Louis.

Chopin began to write poems and short stories for magazines and newspapers. When she failed to find a publisher for her first novel, *At Fault* (1890), she had it privately printed. Her first collection of short stories, *Bayou Folk* (1894), received national acclaim. However, as her topics became increasingly controversial—women who did not want to marry, were independent, or were unfulfilled as wives and mothers—she had difficulty selling her stories. Her last novel, *The Awakening* (1899), was roundly condemned by critics.

Chopin died in St. Louis on August 20, 1904, of a brain hemorrhage.

Orleans Creole society. He surveys the scene in front of him, including his two young sons and their nurse. His wife, Edna, and her swimming companion, Robert Lebrun, return from the beach. Léonce decides to go play billiards at a nearby hotel. Robert and Edna talk on the porch.

When Léonce returns later that night, he is drunk. He wakes Edna and tries to engage her in conversation, but she is too tired. Irritated, he checks on their sons and tells her the eldest,

Kate Chopin The Library of Congress

Raoul, has a fever and needs her attention. When she argues that Raoul is perfectly well, Léonce "reproach[es] his wife with her inattention, her habitual neglect of the children." Awake and furious, Edna goes outside and cries, filled with an "indescribable oppression." In the morning, Léonce prepares to return to New Orleans for the workweek. He gives Edna the money he had won the previous evening and says goodbye to the boys. Several days later, he sends a box of candies and treats. Edna shares them with the other women at the resort, who all sing Léonce's praises.

Chapters IV–VI
Edna is "not a mother-woman," meaning she does not have maternal interest in her children. Adèle Ratignolle, on the other hand, is a prime example of a mother-woman, a beautiful pregnant woman who spends her time knitting baby clothes and talking about her children. Listening to Adèle and Robert talk freely about taboo subjects in public, Edna blushes. They speak more freely about sex, emotions, and their bodies than Edna does. She feels like an outsider in Creole society, as she grew up in Kentucky and is not a Creole.

Every summer, Robert attaches himself to one of the women at Grand Isle. The previous summer it was Adèle, and this summer it is Edna. As Edna sketches a picture of him, Robert begins to make gestures and comments suggesting a familiarity that makes Edna uncomfortable. Nearby, Adèle puts away her knitting and complains of faintness. She faints, and Robert rushes to her side; Edna wonders if she fainted to get attention. Robert invites Edna to go bathing in the ocean. Initially she tells him no, but she changes her mind.

As she wonders why she agreed to go, "A certain light [is] beginning to dawn dimly within her,—the light which, showing the way, forbids it." She begins to realize her place as a human being and individual in the world. As she moves nearer the sea, she finds that it invites "the soul to wander for a spell in abysses of solitude."

Chapters VII–VIII
Edna and Adèle go to the beach together one morning without their children. As they sit on the beach, Edna recalls walking through a large field of tall grass as a child and says that she feels just as free and unguided this summer as she did as a child in the field. Adèle responds by saying, "*Pauvre chérie*" (poor darling), but Edna is confused by her reaction.

Edna thinks about the men to whom she was attracted growing up and the famous actor who appeals to her still. In contrast, her marriage to Léonce lacks passion, and she is only fond of her children in "an uneven, impulsive way." She tells much of this to Adèle, and feels flushed and liberated admitting it. Robert, with the women's children in tow, finds them. As they head back to the resort, Adèle tells him to leave Edna alone; she is concerned that Edna will take Robert's harmless affections seriously. They argue over whether he should be taken seriously or not, and Robert says there is no possibility of Edna misunderstanding his platonic intentions. Later, Robert and his mother, Madame Lebrun, discuss the trip to Mexico he is planning for the beginning of next month.

Chapters IX–XI
Several weeks after Adèle and Robert's talk, there is a party for the families at the resort. Robert entreats Mademoiselle Reisz, an unconventional older woman, to play the piano. The sound of Reisz's playing conjures feelings of

hope and solitude in Edna, and she is moved to tears. Reisz tells Edna she is the only one who truly appreciates her playing. Robert suggests a late-night swim, and the group heads to the beach. Edna, who has been struggling to learn to swim all summer, suddenly feels confident enough to try it on her own. She swims out too far and panics when she sees the distance she must cover to get back. Though she recovers herself and swims in, she tells no one what happened. Edna decides to walk back to the resort alone, but Robert catches up with her. At her cottage, she lies in a hammock and Robert stays with her a while. Though they do not talk, the silence is "pregnant with the first-felt throbbings of desire."

Léonce tells Edna to come inside when he arrives at the cottage, but she does not. He demands that she come inside. She is surprised that she ever let him talk to her like that before, or that she submitted. She refuses to come inside, so Léonce comes outside and sits silently with her. Near dawn, when Edna finally decides to go inside and sleep, she asks Léonce if he is coming. He tells her that he will when he is ready.

Chapters XII–XIV

Edna rises early the next morning and sends a servant to wake Robert so they can go to mass at a nearby island. On the boat over to the island, Robert flirts with Mariequita, a young Spanish girl. Edna is enjoying the boat ride, feeling unanchored herself. Robert quietly suggests they go alone together to Grand Terre the next day and go fishing the day after. They imagine several plans that involve the two of them being together.

Feeling unwell and restless inside the church, Edna leaves in the middle of the service, and Robert follows. He takes her to Madame Antoine's house where she can rest. Edna sleeps deeply for most of the afternoon, and she and Robert dawdle at Antoine's house. Returning to the resort, Edna learns that Léonce has gone to a nearby hotel and will be back that evening. She and Robert part, having spent the entire day together. Edna waits for Léonce to return, feeling that "she was seeing with different eyes and making the acquaintance of new conditions in herself that colored and changed her environment." She wishes that Robert would have stayed with her to wait for Léonce.

Chapter XV–XVII

At dinner, Edna learns from the other guests that Robert is leaving for Mexico that evening. She is bewildered and does not hide her emotions. He tells the group he made the decision that afternoon. After finishing her coffee, Edna returns to her cottage. Robert comes to see her. He starts to tell her that he is leaving because they are growing too close but stops himself. Edna "recognize[s] anew the symptoms of infatuation" in herself.

Days later at the beach, Reisz asks Edna if she misses Robert greatly. Since Robert's departure, Edna has been spending her time swimming and visiting with Madame Lebrun, seeking Robert in their conversation and in the family photo album. Edna reads a letter from Robert, but it does not mention her. She and Reisz discuss Robert, and Edna is "glad to be talking about Robert, no matter what [is] said." Reisz gives Edna her New Orleans address in hopes that Edna will visit.

Every Tuesday Edna receives visitors, society women who come to the Pontelliers' richly appointed home in the French Quarter. This has been her traditional receiving day for six years, but one Tuesday after returning from Grand Isle, Edna leaves the house instead of receiving guests. Léonce chides her for overlooking "*les convenances*" (social conventions) that secure their place in society. Unhappy with the taste of his dinner, Léonce leaves to eat at the club. Whereas Edna would once have tried to reprimand the cook or make amends with Léonce, she now lets Léonce go without a word. While pacing in her room, she drops her wedding ring, and "When she [sees] it lying there, she stamp[s] her heel upon it, striving to crush it." She then smashes a vase, which brings the maid. The maid hands Edna her wedding ring, which she slips back onto her finger.

Chapters XVIII–XXI

Feeling alienated from the world around her, Edna gathers several of her sketches and goes out to visit Adèle. On the way, she thinks longingly of Robert. She eats lunch with Adèle and Mr. Ratignolle and leaves feeling depressed over this scene of "domestic harmony" that seems to Edna to carry "an appalling and hopeless ennui" (boredom). Edna believes that Adèle's life has no place for strong emotions, either positive or negative, and offers no chance to experience "life's delirium."

To Léonce's displeasure, Edna abandons all pretense of being *"en bonne ménagère"* (a good housewife). He wonders if Edna is becoming mentally ill. She begins sketching regularly, using the maids and her children as models. She is often happy "without knowing why," but sometimes she finds herself filled with inexplicable sorrow.

Edna decides to visit Reisz to hear her play piano again. Having lost her address, she attempts to locate her but no one appears to know where she has moved. She goes to Madame Lebrun's house seeking information and meets with Victor, Lebrun's youngest son and Robert's brother. Victor flirts with her and she discovers that Robert has sent two letters, neither of which contains a message for her. She learns Reisz's address and leaves to pay her a visit.

Once at Reisz's tiny apartment, Edna is unsure if she even likes the older woman. Reisz has a letter from Robert that is all about Edna, which she eventually shares with her. Reisz then begins to play a Chopin impromptu, as Robert had requested she do. Edna sobs and asks if she may return and visit Reisz often, a request that the older woman welcomes.

Chapters XXII–XXV

Léonce visits the Pontelliers' family doctor, Dr. Mandelet, and tells him that something is wrong with Edna: "Her whole attitude—toward me and everybody and everything—has changed." The doctor suggests sending Edna to her family in Kentucky for her sister Janet's wedding, but Edna refuses to go. He then tells Léonce that "women are moody and whimsical" and that whatever has gotten into her will eventually pass. Léonce arranges for Mandelet to come over on Thursday evening and observe Edna. The doctor wonders if another man is causing these changes in Edna.

Edna's father, the Colonel, comes to New Orleans to buy a wedding gift and new clothes for Janet's wedding. Edna entertains him by sketching him and taking him to a gathering at the Ratignolles'. When Mandelet comes for dinner, he finds Edna radiant and full of life. She and her father recount their day at the race track, where she has met Alcée Arobin. The guests all exchange stories, and Edna tells a story about a pair of lovers that escape to an island to live together. Mandelet suspects that Edna is having an affair with Arobin.

The Colonel tries to convince Edna to attend Janet's wedding, but she refuses. Léonce is headed to New York for business, and he plans to stop in Kentucky for the wedding and to "endeavor by every means which money and love [can] devise to atone somewhat for Edna's incomprehensible action." Edna is left alone; her father and Léonce depart and her children go to Madame Pontellier's for an extended visit. Edna explores her empty house as if she had never been there before and enjoys the solitude of eating alone in her *peignoir* (nightgown).

Edna increasingly feels "as if life [is] passing her by, leaving its promise broken and unfulfilled." She frequents the race track and often sees Arobin and Mrs. Highcamp there. Arobin is drawn to Edna's knowledge of horses, which she acquired as a child in Kentucky. Arobin escorts Edna home after she dines with them. Edna finds herself agitated after he leaves, wanting "something to happen—something, anything; she [does] not know what." Several days later, Arobin takes Edna to the races, just the two of them. Arobin makes a guarded advance toward Edna, an act that both excites and repels her. She tells him to go away. She thinks about Arobin and wonders what Robert would think if he knew.

Chapters XXVI–XXVIII

Arobin sends Edna a note apologizing for his behavior. Fearing that she may have overreacted, Edna invites Arobin to call on her any time he is free. He begins to visit often, and Edna finds herself attracted to him. Edna visits Reisz and tells her that she is going to move into a small house by herself, seeking the "feeling of freedom and independence." Reisz asks for the true reason behind Edna's decision, and Edna realizes that she does not want to "belong to another than herself" anymore. Edna decides to throw a dinner party before she moves out. Reisz gives Edna another letter from Robert and tells Edna that Robert is in love with her. Edna discovers that Robert is coming back to New Orleans. For the first time, she admits that she loves him.

Arobin senses the improvement in Edna's mood when he visits that evening. He also tells Edna he can sense that she is preoccupied. They kiss: "It was the first kiss of her life to which her nature had really responded. It was a flaming torch that kindled desire." Edna is conflicted about the kiss but does she not feel remorseful or ashamed. Instead, she feels that she is seeing things clearly for the first time. She recognizes that she responded to Arobin largely because he was accessible and realizes with regret that it was not love that enlivened her this way.

Chapters XXIX–XXXI

Edna moves into a small apartment around the corner from her house. She takes along only the things she purchased herself, leaving behind everything Léonce has bought for her. Arobin arrives, but Edna refuses to be alone with him and makes sure her maid is always in the room. Edna tells Arobin to stay away until the dinner party she is throwing two days later to celebrate her move.

Ten guests come to Edna's party, at which Edna reveals that it is her twenty-ninth birthday. Though surrounded by friends, Edna once again finds herself depressed and filled with "a sense of the unattainable." Robert's brother Victor begins to sing a song that Robert once sang to Edna; his singing unnerves her and she begs him to stop. After the guests leave, Arobin remains. Edna closes up the house and leaves for her apartment with Arobin escorting her. Inside the house, Arobin makes advances toward Edna and they make love.

Chapters XXXII–XXXIV

Léonce disapproves of Edna's decision to move into the apartment, worrying that people will think financial difficulties are forcing the Pontelliers to take a smaller home. To save face, he arranges to have their house remodeled and announces that he and Edna are summering abroad, demonstrating that they have plenty of money. Edna feels as though she has lost social status but has gained spiritual understanding and individuality. Edna goes to see her children and is happy spending time with them.

Edna goes to Reisz's house. She lets herself in and meets with Adèle, who is late in her pregnancy. Adèle says Edna is acting like a child, "without a certain amount of reflection which is necessary in this life," and tells her that there are rumors about Arobin's visits to her home. Adèle leaves; while Edna waits for Reisz to return, Robert arrives. She did not know he was back, and their meeting is awkward. Edna asks him why he never wrote to her. Robert walks her home, and she invites him to stay for dinner. He is jealous when he discovers Arobin's picture, which Edna has been using to sketch from. After dinner, Edna and Robert begin to recover some of the intimacy they had known at Grand Isle. Robert leaves when Arobin stops by, and Edna tells Arobin not to stay. She feels that she and Robert have drifted apart, and she is jealous of the Mexican women he spent time with while he was gone.

Chapters XXXV–XXXVI

The next morning, Edna wakes with a feeling of hope and thinks about Robert. She receives three notes: one from her children, one from Léonce, and one from Arobin. She responds to the first two but tosses Arobin's in the stove. Robert does not come to visit her. She continues to see Arobin, who, detecting her "latent sensuality," has become enamored with her. She stops hoping for Robert's visits.

Edna discovers a secluded garden in the suburbs and begins spending time there. While eating a picnic lunch there one day, she sees Robert. She demands to know why he has been avoiding her. He tells her she is cruel for asking these questions because nothing can ever come of their relationship: "as if you would have me bare a wound for the pleasure of looking at it, without the intention or power of healing it." They return together to Edna's apartment, and Edna kisses him. They declare their love to each other. Edna leaves to go to Adèle, who is in labor, but makes Robert promise to stay and wait for her, no matter how late she returns.

Chapters XXXVII–XXXIX

Adèle is delirious with pain during her labor, and Edna wishes that she had not come. She perceives Adèle's delivery as a "scene of torture." As Edna is leaving, Adèle tells her to remember her own children before making any decisions. Mandelet walks Edna home, and she tells him that she will not be going abroad with Léonce this summer because he can no longer tell her what to do. The doctor appears to sympathize with her. Back at her apartment, she thinks about Robert and how she really should consider her children before making any decisions. She decides to think about them later. Robert is not there when she goes inside. She finds a note that reads, "I love you. Good-by—because I love you." She lies down on the sofa but does not sleep.

The next day at Grand Isle, Victor is making repairs to the main house, and Mariequita is keeping him company. Edna appears unexpectedly. She tells them she has come alone to rest and is going for a quick swim before dinner. On her walk down the beach, she recalls the depression she felt the night before. Robert is the only person she wants near her, but she realizes that her feelings for him will fade one day, "melt out of her existence, leaving her alone." She feels that she can never be happy because of her children. She knows she must consider them first, but this means that she can never live the life she wants. If she did so, people would disapprove of them as well as her, staining their reputations and limiting their future. They have thus "overpowered her and sought to drag her into the soul's slavery for the rest of her days." She stands naked on the empty beach, then enters the cold water and begins to swim. She grows tired as she swims out, but continues, thinking of Léonce, her children, Reisz, and Robert. Her strength gone, she thinks back to the endless grass field of her childhood.

THEMES

Sexuality

At the turn of the century, respectable women were generally seen only as wives and mothers. They were believed to lack sexual desire, even in the relatively down-to-earth Creole society of New Orleans. Female sexuality was solely a means to an end: motherhood. It was scandalous for a woman to desire a man who was not her husband, but it was even more outrageous for her to act on that desire. Polite society shunned such women, though men were not subject to the same scrutiny. For example, it is well known at Grand Isle that Robert attaches himself to a new woman every summer, but when one of them begins to return his affections—the married Edna Pontellier—she is the one judged to be irresponsible. Adèle pleads with Edna to "think of the children! Remember them!" as Edna pursues both Robert and Arobin, but neither of the men is asked to do the same. Robert's flirtations are generally considered harmless, but Adèle warns him not to mislead Edna: "She is not one of us; she is not like us. She might make the unfortunate blunder of taking you seriously." Edna's relationship with Arobin, however, is what truly begins to awaken her sexuality. For

the first time, she feels genuine desire and even love. As she explores these feelings and surrenders herself to a new-found sensuality, she begins to feel "a flaming torch that kindled desire." Her sexuality becomes a gateway that leads her to reconsider her life.

Class Distinctions

Edna's husband, Léonce, reveals the importance of class distinctions in the *The Awakening*. His concerns with outward signs of wealth and class, and with improving their social station, recur throughout the novel. He constantly worries about making a social error, lest it be held against him. He also fears being looked down on by the social elite, or—worse yet—excluded from New Orleans society. These fears motivate many of his actions. When Edna begins leaving the house at the time she normally receives visitors, Léonce is immediately concerned with how her behavior might affect their social standing: "we've got to observe *les convenances* if we ever expect to get on and keep up with the procession." Later, when he learns that Edna moved out of the house, he is not concerned about why she left. Instead, he focuses on how others will perceive her move, "and above all else, what people would say." He begins remodeling their house to justify Edna's relocation, and he announces in the newspaper that they will spend the summer abroad to ensure that everyone knows they are not in financial trouble or slipping in social standing: "Mr. Pontellier had saved appearances!"

As Léonce strains to keep up, Edna relishes the idea of escaping class expectations. She withdraws from her "fashionable acquaintances" and spends time with Mademoiselle Reisz, who is something of an outcast. Not being Creole herself, Edna always feels like an outsider in the tightly knit society. She draws strength and satisfaction from her decision to remain on the outside, instead of striving for inclusion.

Gender Roles

Edna openly acknowledges that she is not like the other women at Grand Isle or those in her social class. While they bask in the role of motherhood, Edna declares that she is "not a mother-woman." She tells Adèle—a paragon of femininity and matronly responsibility, a "faultless Madonna"—that she would "give up the unessential" for her children but would not give up herself. Edna feels that she should have more

Sunset over a lake Robert J. Huffman. Field Mark Publications. Reproduced by permission

typically motherly feelings toward her young sons, but those feelings arise only occasionally. For the most part, she feels relief when the boys are away from her. She compares witnessing Adèle's delivery to watching torture. Adèle admonishes Edna to remember her children when considering her affairs with Arobin and Robert, but Edna comes to resent her sons, feeling as though they possess her, "like antagonists who had overcome her."

Edna senses that she is different from typical women in other ways, as well. She has no interest in being a wife, feeling that Léonce keeps her as a possession. Their bond is a loveless one, and as she comes to know herself she sees that he will never understand her real needs and desires. When Robert confesses his love and tells her that he wants to marry her, she scoffs at the idea of belonging to any man, even a man she truly loves:

> I am no longer one of Mr. Pontellier's possessions to dispose of or not. I give myself where I choose. If he were to say, "Here, Robert, take her and be happy; she is yours," I should laugh at you both.

In *The Awakening*, respectable women of the nineteenth century have only two options: become a blameless wife and mother like Adèle Ratignolle, or a spinster like Mademoiselle Reisz. A woman could reject domesticity only at the risk of becoming a social outcast. Society offered no middle ground, and Edna is ultimately stuck in the middle, unable to be her true self. She recognized this feeling in herself as a young girl, seeing a "dual life—that outward existence which conforms, the inward life which questions."

Mademoiselle Reisz recognizes Edna's dual life as well, telling her "The bird that would soar above the level plain of tradition and prejudice must have strong wings." Edna is connected to or compared with birds several times in the novel, but the ultimate strength of Edna's wings is revealed when she returns to Grand Isle alone, and sees a bird with a broken wing "reeling, fluttering, circling disabled down, down to the water." Shortly thereafter she steps into the water a final time. The novel ultimately leaves the reader to decide whether Edna's suicide is an admission that she was wrong to defy social conventions or a defiant assertion of her right to freedom and self-determination.

Isolation

There are two types of isolation in *The Awakening*: that which is imposed on Edna by the upper-class Creole society, and that which Edna imposes on herself in her quest of self discovery. The first sort of isolation makes her feel uncomfortable, but the second kind is initially a comfort and later a burden. From the beginning, Edna feels "different from the crowd" because she is the only non-Creole among the vacationers at Grand Isle. She is not used to the way they act or their open conversations about subjects that are typically taboo. The others recognize her outsider status as well; as Adèle reminds Robert, "She is not one of us."

The isolation that she feels because she is not a Creole, a mother-woman, or a loving wife eventually leads to a self-imposed isolation in which Edna shuns society's dictates to follow her own heart. The ocean, which begins and ends Edna's awakening, invites her to "wander for a spell in abysses of solitude." Having chosen to do so, in both the water and her life, Edna seeks her own company and advice. In her introduction to *The Awakening*, Nancy A. Walker notes that the novel was originally to be called *A Solitary Soul*. Finding herself alone after her children, husband, and father eventually leave, "she breathed a big, genuine sigh of relief."

Though she revels in her solitude, what she truly desires is to be with Robert, on her own terms. She is attracted to Mademoiselle Reisz's freedom, but not her loneliness; Edna wants love to be part of her life. She explores the kind of woman she is becoming and contemplates the possibilities her new freedom holds, but those around her find her decisions perplexing and suspect. In "'A Language Which Nobody Understood': Emancipatory Strategies in *The Awakening*," Patricia S. Yaeger notes that in her solitude, "Edna finds herself speaking a language as impenetrable to others as the parrot's babble [at the beginning of the novel]." But when she finds she cannot control others after Robert leaves a second time, she realizes that her solitude is much deeper than she had imagined and no longer necessarily of her choosing. Solitude implies agency and choice, but Edna's solitude becomes isolation, in which she feels involuntarily separated from everything and everyone.

She returns to Grand Isle and strips naked when she realizes she is "absolutely alone" on the beach. Her aloneness here is both literal and figurative, as Edna has decided to end her life. The word "alone" recurs throughout the novel, underscoring Edna's desire to pursue her passions without interruption, but also reflecting the social and spiritual alienation she experiences.

HISTORICAL OVERVIEW

Victorian Values

The reign of Queen Victoria in England is known as the Victorian Era, which lasted from roughly 1837 through 1901. The Victorian culture was British, but its strict morality quickly spread to the United States. It was a time of increasing interest in scientific discoveries, marked by the publication of Darwin's *On the Origin of Species* (1859) as well as advances in medicine and industry. As science moved forward, religious beliefs were questioned. Developing technology and industry brought many farmers and their families into the city, shifting populations from rural communities to urban centers. Some urban areas became slums, full of those who were unable or unwilling to take advantage of the prosperity offered by urban living. This, in turn, led to the development of distinctive social classes in urban areas, with a small upper class, a middle class striving to better itself, and a large working class.

These changes in daily life created a desire to protect that which was human from the rising tide of science and industry. A strict moral code was thought to be part of the solution, one which clearly defined gender roles and expectations. Women's clothing covered their bodies completely, and discussions about body parts such as legs and arms were considered inappropriate. Any mention of sexuality was strictly off-limits, and kissing during courtships was considered indecent. The word "prudish" is often used to describe this time period. In such an atmosphere, it is easy to see why Edna was initially uncomfortable in the presence of free-speaking Creoles like Robert, Arobin, and Adèle. It is also clear why Edna's conduct with Arobin and Robert was scandalous and controversial, both to other characters and to readers of the novel.

The Women's Rights Movement

In early nineteenth-century America, women were often portrayed as fragile and dependent on men. Adèle Ratignolle exemplifies the traditional nineteenth-century woman who delights in being a wife and mother and who appears wholly focused on serving her husband and children. At this time, the law did not allow women to get a divorce, vote, or manage their own money. Women who worked outside the home—generally middle- and lower-class women forced to help support their families—had only a few job options, including factory worker, secretary, maid, teacher, and nurse. Women who were not married by twenty-five were generally considered spinsters.

As time passed, women's rights steadily increased. In her introduction to *The Awakening,* Nancy A. Walker writes that Fanny Fern, a popular *New York Ledger* columnist in the 1860s, "argued for political, economic, and even clothing reform for women." In 1890, Susan B. Anthony and fellow suffragists founded the National American Woman Suffrage Association (NAWSA) advocating equal pay, the right to vote, and the right to divorce. They campaigned vigorously for women's suffrage, and by the time *The Awakening* was published in 1899, Colorado, Utah, and Idaho had granted women the right to vote. Two decades later, national women's suffrage was granted with the ratification of the Nineteenth Amendment to the Constitution. Though Kate Chopin herself was not a suffragist or an active participant in social reform, many of her female protagonists act unconventionally, defying social standards to pursue individual freedom.

Creole Culture

Though the term "Creole" has evolved over centuries, when Chopin was writing it identified people with a mixed Spanish and French heritage living along Louisiana's gulf coast. Creoles were white and born in America; they were typically upper class and spoke both French and English. They used the term to distinguish themselves from Cajuns and foreigners moving to the gulf area. There was also a group known as Creoles of Color, which traced its roots back to the African and Caribbean influences in Louisiana culture and were either black or of mixed race. Until the Civil War, free Creoles of Color enjoyed many rights and freedoms that were virtually unknown to blacks and mixed-race people elsewhere in the South.

As Chopin's novel reflects, the Creoles in New Orleans lived principally in the French Quarter while non-Creoles lived on the other side of Canal Street in the "American" section of town. France's refusal to side with the Confederacy during the Civil War ruptured Creole New Orleans's connection to what it considered its mother country. Nonetheless, French influence remained strong in New Orleans throughout the nineteenth century.

The criteria that identify Louisiana Creoles have long been the subject of debate and continue to be disputed. For example, some reserve this label exclusively for white French-speakers, while others seek a more inclusive definition. In addition, there are other groups that describe themselves as Creole but which are unrelated to the Louisiana Creoles, such as the Creole populations of Portugal and Latin America.

CRITICAL OVERVIEW

Prior to Kate Chopin's publication of *The Awakening*, she was best known for stories of local culture and color. Her collection of short stories *Bayou Folk* (1894) received favorable reviews but was routinely dismissed as merely depicting the eccentricities and lifestyles of a specific region. In her introduction to *The Awakening*, Nancy A. Walker writes that "Reviewers emphasized the quaint foreignness of her Louisiana characters as though she had described exotic butterflies observed under a microscope, and the word most frequently applied to the stories in the collection was 'charming.'" Undeterred, Chopin continued writing short stories and was published in prestigious magazines such as *Vogue, Harper's*, and *Atlantic Monthly*. When Chopin's second collection, *A Night in Acadie* (1897), was published, it met with the same response as *Bayou Folk*, and was relegated to the categories of lightweight women's fiction and local color. Determined to prove herself more than a regional writer, Chopin published *The Awakening* in 1899.

Aside from two positive reviews—one from a writer who was also a reader for Chopin's publisher and the other from her hometown newspaper, the *St. Louis Republic*—response to the novel was overwhelmingly negative. Edna's behavior was criticized, but Chopin was blamed as well for the immorality she seemed to embrace. An unnamed reviewer for the *St. Louis Globe-Democrat* declared that *The Awakening* was "not a healthy book," saying that "it cannot be said that either of the principal characters claims admiration or sympathy." Many critics of the time took exception to Edna's sexual affair with Arobin. Emily Toth, one of Chopin's biographers, is quoted in Walker's introduction, pointing out that "reviewers of *The Awakening* virtually ignored a number of potential targets for their disapproval, concentrating instead on Edna's sexual liaison with Alcée Arobin." Though the novel was never officially banned, its negative reception may have contributed to its being largely ignored as literature until the mid-1950s.

Modern critics have been kinder. In her essay "Tradition and the Female Talent: *The Awakening* as a Solitary Book," critic Elaine Showalter calls the novel a "revolutionary book," but notes that critics in Chopin's time panned the book as "'morbid,' 'essentially vulgar,' and 'gilded dirt.'" In "'A Language Which Nobody Understood': Emanipatory Strategies in *The Awakening*," Patricia S. Yaeger calls the book "one of the great subversive novels." In a modern review of *The Awakening* for *Herizons* under the heading "Feminist Classics," Stacy Kauder writes that the novel "stands the test of time," providing modern readers with two positive role models: Edna Pontellier and Chopin herself, "who chose to write in opposition to conventional society."

CRITICISM

Cynthia Griffin Wolff

In the following excerpt, Wolff examines the social conditions that restricted Victorian-era women, and how Edna's choice to escape from these constraints was ultimately doomed.

Critics admire the "modernism" of Chopin's work, the strong spareness of the prose and the "minimalism" of a narrative whose absences are at least as important as its action and whose narrator maintains strict emotional and moral neutrality. What we may not fully appreciate is the relationship between these elements and

MEDIA ADAPTATIONS

Directed by Mary Lambert, *Grand Isle* (1991) is a film adaptation of *The Awakening*. It stars Kelly McGillis as Edna, Adrian Pasdar as Robert, and Julian Sands as Arobin. It is available on VHS from Turner Home Video.

An electronic version of the novel is available in both Microsoft Reader and Adobe Reader formats through Amazon.com.

An abridged audio version of *The Awakening* is available on CD from Naxos Audiobooks. It is read by Liza Ross.

An unabridged audio version of *The Awakening* is available on CD and in MP3 format from Tantor Media. It is read by Shelly Frasier.

Edna Pontellier's personal tragedy, a relationship whose terms are announced by the apparent disarray of the novel's brilliant beginning. This is a tale about not speaking, about disjunction—about denials, oversights, prohibitions, exclusions, and absences. Not merely about things that are never named, but most significantly about stories that cannot be told and things that can be neither thought nor spoken because they do not have a name.

After about 1849, the notion of a "woman's sexual awakening" became, by definition, an impossibility—a contradiction in terms—because the medical establishment in America began to promulgate the view that normal females possessed no erotic inclinations whatsoever (and one cannot awaken something that does not exist). William Acton, the acknowledged expert on the nature of women's sexuality and author of "one of the most widely quoted books on sexual problems and diseases in the English-speaking world," wrote:

> I have taken pains to obtain and compare abundant evidence on this subject, and the result of my inquiries I may briefly epitomize as follows:—I should say that the majority of women (happily for society) are not very much

troubled with sexual feeling of any kind. What men are habitually women are only exceptionally. It is too true, I admit, as the divorce courts show, that there are some few women who have sexual desires so strong that they surpass those of men, and shock public feeling by their consequences.

Acton's work elaborated a comprehensive system of women's "inequality" to men; and it was so universally respected that his sentiments can be taken to represent opinions that were held throughout much of America during the second half of the nineteenth century.

The official "scientific" and "medical" view can be stated quite simply: an average woman (a "decent" woman) possesses no sexual feelings whatsoever. Thus it is not enough to say that *The Awakening* is a novel about repression (that is, about a situation in which a woman possesses sexual feelings, but is prohibited from acting upon them). It is, instead, a novel about a woman whose shaping culture has, in general, refused her right to speak out freely; this is, moreover, a culture that construes a woman's self-expression as a violation of sexual "purity" and a culture that has denied the existence of women's libidinous potential altogether—has eliminated the very concept of sexual passion for "normal" women.

The consequences are emotionally mutilating (in the extreme case, some form of mental breakdown would result). In such a culture, if a "respectable" woman supposes herself to feel "something," some powerful ardor in her relationship with a man, she can draw only two possible inferences. Either her feelings are not sexual (and should not be enacted in a genital relationship), or she is in some (disgraceful) way "abnormal." Moreover, because there is presumed to be no such entity as sexual feelings in the typical woman, a typical (i.e. "normal") woman will literally have no words for her (nonexistent) feelings, will have access to no discourse within which these (nonexistent) passions can be examined or discussed, will be able to make no coherent connection between the (unintelligible) inner world of her affective life and the external, social world in which she must live. Finally, if she feels confusion and emotional pain, her culture's general prohibition against speaking out will make it difficult, perhaps impossible, to discuss or even reveal her discomfort.

Medical and psychological experts concluded that although women had no sexual drives per se, they often possessed a passionate desire to bear children: such ardor was both "normal" and (inevitably) sexual. On these terms, then, sexual activity—even moderate sexual "desire"—was appropriate in "normal" women. However, a profound displacement or confusion was introduced by this accommodation: the language of feminine sexuality became inextricably intertwined with discourse that had to do with child-bearing and motherhood.

Scholars have accepted almost as cliché the fact that in late Victorian America "motherhood" was exalted as an all-but-divine state. However, if we do not also understand the oblique (and contradictory) sexual implications of this cultural ideal, we may be unaware of the confusion and conflict it engendered.

Any woman would find this concatenation of denials and demands unbalancing; however, in Edna's case, the already vexed situation is heightened by a severe conflict of cultures. In a society where the actual experiences of women were diverse and the normative pronouncements were stringent, Chopin has constructed a novel where extremes converge to demonstrate the malignant potential of these normative attitudes, and she marks the summer at Grand Isle as the moment when crisis begins.

Creoles permit themselves an extraordinary freedom of sensual expression. Thus a lusty carnal appetite in men is taken for granted. However, the case of Creole women is different, for their sexuality may exist only as a component of "motherhood." Nevertheless, so long as they accept this model, women, too, may engage in a sumptuous sexual life. Mme Ratignolle, the "sensuous Madonna," embodies the essence of ardor and voluptuary appetite thus construed.

The Creole world is more densely erotic than any community Edna has encountered. It revels frankly and happily in the pleasures of the flesh—not merely enjoying these delights with undisguised zest, but discussing them in public with no shame at all.

This strange world, with its languorous climate and frankly sensuous habits, is a world where "normal," "respectable" women openly vaunt pleasures that are unfamiliar to Edna Pontellier. She is fascinated, stimulated, eventually profoundly aroused. And although she is bewildered by these new sensations, once having been touched by them, she becomes unwilling to pull away.

Edna's easiest option is "collusion," to become a "mother-woman"; however, she rejects this role violently because of the displacements and forfeitures that it would impose. If, like Adele, she were willing to disguise her erotic drives in the mantle of "motherhood," she might indulge the many delights of the body as Adele patently does. However, such a capitulation would not allow her really to possess her own feelings—nor even to talk about them directly or explicitly. It would maim the "self," not unify and affirm it: like Adele, Edna would be obliged to displace all of her sexual discourse into prattle about "the children" or her (pregnant) "condition," fettering her carnal desires to the production of babies; and part of what was really inside (that is, her sexual drive) would have been displaced on to something outside (society's construction of female appetite as essentially "maternal"). In the process, the authority and integrity of her identity would have been compromised, and instead of making contact with the outside world, she would be merged into and controlled by it. Edna loves her children and is happy to be a mother; however, she refuses to define her sexuality in terms of them.

In some primitive way, silence also is Edna's only appropriate reaction to society's way of defining female sexuality: for if women were imagined to have no sexual feelings, not to speak would (ironically) be the way to "communicate" this absence. Yet not to speak has an annihilating consequence: it is, in the end, not to be—not to have social reality. One can never affirm "self" merely through silence and fantasy—can never forge that vital connection between the "me" and the "not-me" that validates identity. (Even the "fantasy" of art is embedded in an act of communication between the "me" and the "not-me".) A "self" can mature only if one strives to articulate emotions; learning to name one's feelings is an integral component of learning the extent and nature of one's feelings, and what is undescribed may remain sways "indescribable"—even to oneself—"vague" and even "unfamiliar."

Indeed, the dispassionate tone of Chopin's novel may be related to the complexity of Edna's quest, for Edna cannot "solve" her problem without an extraordinary feat of creativity. She must discover not merely a new vernacular with which to name her feelings—not merely a new form of plot that is capable of containing them—but also an "audience" that both comprehends and esteems the story she might ultimately tell. Thus the true subject of *The Awakening* may be less the particular dilemma of Mrs. Pontellier than the larger problems of female narrative that it reflects; and if Edna's poignant fate is in part a reflection of her own habits, it is also, in equal part, a measure of society's failure to allow its women a language of their own.

When Leonce begins to discern the differences in Edna's manner and takes his concerns to Dr. Mandelet, their conversation is uncannily similar to these nineteenth-century discussions of woman's nature.

> "She's odd, she's not like herself. I can't make her out. . . . She's got some sort of notion in her head concerning the eternal rights of women." . . .

> "Woman, my dear friend," [the Doctor responds,] "is a very peculiar and delicate organism—a sensitive and highly organized woman, such as I know Mrs. Pontellier to be, is especially peculiar. . . . Most women are moody and whimsical."

Mlle Reisz and Alcee Arobin (characters in Edna's nascent narratives and audiences for them) both hold out the possibility that Edna might resolve her dilemma by usurping the prerogatives of men. Yet each offers a "solution" that would constrain Edna to relinquish some significant and valued portion of herself.

Mlle Reisz holds out the independence that men can achieve in a career. Yet Edna chooses not to follow this avenue; and Mlle Reisz's admonition that the artist "must possess the courageous soul" may have been less of a deterrent than a statement about the example of that lady's own life. Fulfillment through aesthetic creativity appears to offer authentic expression to only one portion of the self. Mlle Reisz "had quarreled with almost everyone, owing to a temper which was self-assertive and a disposition to trample upon the rights of others"; having no sensuous charm or aesthetic allure ("a homely woman with a small weazened face and body and eyes that glowed"), she presents a sad and sorry prospect of some future Edna-as-successful-artist. What woman seeking sexual fulfillment would willing follow the pathway to such a forfeiture of feminine sensuous pleasure as this?

Arobin offers the opposite. Something simpler, but equally wounding. Lust. Sex divorced from all other feelings. The expression of that raw libido that was presumed to be part of men's nature (as "virility"), but categorically denied as a component of the normal female. Yet Edna finds that limiting sexuality to this form of expression imposes a distortion fully as destructive as society's construction of "maternity."

Female sexuality had been falsified by the construct of "maternity" ; however, there was one barbarous component of femininity, one consequence of feminine sexuality, that even the mother-woman could never evade.

In the nineteenth century, with its still-primitive obstetrical practices and its high child-mortality rates, she was expected to face severe bodily pain, disease, and death—and still serve as the emotional support and strength of her family. As the eminent Philadelphia neurologist S. Weir Mitchell wrote in the 1880s, "We may be sure that our daughters will be more likely to have to face at some time the grim question of pain than the lads who grow up beside them. . . . To most women . . . there comes a time when pain is a grim presence in their lives."

She concludes with a narrative gesture of sorts—a concatenation of the parlance of "maternity." Perhaps it is a tale of the son, Icarus, defeated by overweening ambition: "A bird with a broken wing was beating the air above, reeling, fluttering, circling disabled down, down to the water." Perhaps a tale of babies: "Naked in the open air . . . she felt like some new-born creature, opening its eyes in a familiar world that it had never known." Most likely, it is a tragic inversion of the birth of Venus: "The touch of the sea is sensuous, enfolding the body in its soft, close embrace."

So Edna has failed. Or rather, being a woman with some weaknesses and no extraordinary strengths, Edna has chosen the only alternative she could imagine to the ravaging social arrangements of her day. However, we must not overlook the fact that if her heroine faltered, Kate Chopin fashioned a splendid success. *The Awakening* is the new narrative that Mrs. Pontellier was unable to create: not (it is true) a story of female affirmation, but rather an excruciatingly exact dissection of the ways in which society distorts a woman's true nature.

Source: Cynthia Griffin Wolff, "Un-Utterable Longing: The Discourse of Feminine Sexuality in *The Awakening*," in *Studies in American Fiction*, Vol. 24, No. 1, Spring 1996, pp. 3–23.

SOURCES

Chopin, Kate, *The Awakening*, in *Case Studies in Contemporary Criticism: Kate Chopin:* The Awakening, edited by Nancy A. Walker, Bedford Books of St. Martin's Press, 1993, originally published by Herbert S. Stone, 1899.

Kauder, Stacy, Review of *The Awakening*, in *Herizon*, Vol. 18, No. 3, Winter 2005, p. 44.

Review of *The Awakening*, St. Louis University, pages. slu.edu/student/mercurrm/doc8.html (November 10, 2005), originally published as "Mrs. Chopin's Surprise Novel," in the *St. Louis Globe-Democrat*, May 13, 1899.

Showalter, Elaine, "Tradition and the Female Talent: *The Awakening* as a Solitary Book," in *Case Studies in Contemporary Criticism: Kate Chopin:* The Awakening, edited by Nancy A. Walker, Bedford Books of St. Martin's Press, 1993, p. 170.

Yaeger, Patricia S., "'A Language Which Nobody Understood': Emancipatory Strategies in *The Awakening*," in *Case Studies in Contemporary Criticism: Kate Chopin:* The Awakening, edited by Nancy A. Walker, Bedford Books of St. Martin's Press, 1993, pp. 271, 291.

Walker, Nancy A., "Introduction: Biographical and Historical Contexts," in *Case Studies in Contemporary Criticism: Kate Chopin:* The Awakening, Bedford Books of St. Martin's Press, 1993, pp. 4, 10, 13, 16.

Blacks

GWENDOLYN BROOKS

1987

Blacks (1987) is a 512-page collection of Gwendolyn Brooks's poetry and prose, written between 1945 and 1986. Brooks is one of the most influential black writers in contemporary American literature. An accomplished and prolific writer of poetry, fiction, and nonfiction, Brooks has the distinction of being the first African American writer to win a Pulitzer Prize. Critics recognize her as writing in two distinct modes: her early work is formal, characterized by a strict use of rhyme scheme and established poetic forms, while her later work is less controlled and more vernacular, meaning it uses more common, everyday language. Both styles are represented in *Blacks*. The majority of her writing explores the experiences of blacks within her community, who encounter racism and poverty as part of their everyday lives. Brooks regularly turns to the South Side of Chicago, which she calls "Bronzeville" in many of her books, as a source of inspiration for her work.

Blacks encompasses many of the issues that affect the black diaspora (native Africans and their descendants living outside of Africa), using a variety of distinct perspectives. The book contains selections from eleven of Brooks's books of poetry and an autobiographical novel called *Maud Martha*. Brooks's approach varies in each section, ranging from the succinct portraits of *A Street in Bronzeville* to the more political "preachments" of *To the*

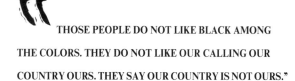

"THOSE PEOPLE DO NOT LIKE BLACK AMONG THE COLORS. THEY DO NOT LIKE OUR CALLING OUR COUNTRY OURS. THEY SAY OUR COUNTRY IS NOT OURS."

BIOGRAPHY

Diaspora. Her characters include children, preachers, soldiers, entertainers, the mentally ill, squirrels, and even ghosts. References to historical figures, such as writer Langston Hughes and Black Nationalist leader Malcolm X, interweave with more personal poems that recount the speaker's experiences with prejudice. Many of her poems capture an important moment in a character's life. Together, these voices reflect the black community's diversity as it continues to resist damaging racist stereotypes.

The detailed array of characters and experiences that Brooks captures helps to dismantle stereotypes and makes *Blacks* more than a mere literary concept piece. In a way it is a tribute, a far-reaching testimony to the variety of events, influences, and perspectives that occur in the black community. The poems in *Blacks* explore the abstract idea of blackness (as perceived in the larger social context), using concrete events and specific individuals. This approach affects the reader powerfully—*Blacks* becomes an archive, a definitive history, an encyclopedia, and a collective portrait of a people who have long been stigmatized by others' misperceptions. Brooks's book manages to validate and consolidate the vast experience of blackness without sacrificing the artistic intensity of good poetry.

PLOT SUMMARY

A Street in Bronzeville, 1945

The forty poems in this section are mostly individual portraits of people who live in Bronzeville, Brooks's name for a neighborhood on Chicago's South Side. In poems like "The Murder" and "Patent Leather," Brooks rejects romantic notions of struggle and triumph, while avoiding the tricky territory of labeling and classification. "Matthew Cole" gives readers a spare portrait of a sixty-six-year-old man growing old alone in a tenement flat: "He never will be done / With dust and his ceiling that / Is everlasting sad." The characters portrayed in the poems

GWENDOLYN BROOKS

Gwendolyn Brooks was born June 7, 1917, in Topeka, Kansas, to Keziah and David Brooks. Her six-decades-long writing career began when she wrote her first poem at age seven; by sixteen, she had already amassed a portfolio of seventy-five published poems. In 1945, she published her first of collection of poetry, *A Street in Bronzeville*, to great critical acclaim.

Over the years, Brooks's style changed, as did the lives of those she represented in her poetry. Critics locate an important shift around the time her fourth book of poetry, *In the Mecca* (1968), was published. The American political climate was transforming during this period, reacting to the impact of the civil rights and black power movements. Brooks reacted by abandoning the traditional poetic language and forms that characterize her earlier work, favoring instead the more improvisational sounds and rhythms of urban black language.

Her accomplishments include twenty-one books of poetry, more than seventy honorary degrees, a lifetime achievement award from the National Endowment for the Arts, the National Book Foundation Award for Distinguished Contribution to American Letters, and induction into the National Women's Hall of Fame. Brooks was the first African American to win a Pulitzer Prize, which she received for her 1949 book of poetry, *Annie Allen*. She died December 3, 2000.

are realistic, entirely believable in their words, behavior, and experiences. The poet suggests a reverence for all of these perspectives, from the very young and hopeful to the old and resigned.

These poems adopt various perspectives on life in Bronzeville, a world that includes overcrowded apartment buildings, unfaithful and abusive spouses, abortion, neglect, and widespread poverty. Brooks steers readers away from purely emotional responses, focusing them on moments that expose what is really at stake for her characters. Bronzeville is not

Gwendolyn Brooks The Library of Congress

The section is organized into four parts. "Memorial to Ed Bland" begins the section, followed by "Notes from the Childhood and the Girlhood," in which the speaker observes how poverty erodes children's innocence. In this realm, everything to which one might look forward is already decaying and spoiled. The following section, "The Anniad," shows that even love is temporary for Annie Allen, whose affair with a soldier leaves her asking, "Oh mother, mother, where is happiness?" In poems like "The Sonnet-Ballad," Brooks suggests that Annie's fleeting love is typical of her life, in which sources of joy are uncertain and fragile.

The final section of *Annie Allen*, "The Womanhood," contains tightly structured poems. Brooks can thus delve into concepts such as love, loss, redemption, and faith, while remaining firmly anchored in forms and language that both demand attention and resist sentimentality. As a whole, the *Annie Allen* portion of *Blacks* does not offer solutions to the practical or philosophical problems threatening the central character. Instead, the reader must try to accept the often unforgiving, painful world that Annie inhabits.

represented in a fixed way; it evolves and responds to various stimuli in the community. Bronzeville and its inhabitants spring to life in these poems, some of which are sonnets (a fourteen-line poem with a specific rhyme scheme). Among complex discussions of beauty and identity, the characters' voices remain open, accessible, and even familiar to readers.

Annie Allen, 1949

In 1950, Gwendolyn Brooks won the Pulitzer Prize for *Annie Allen*. Most of the pieces in this part of *Blacks* follow familiar rhyme schemes and poetic forms, demonstrating the style often associated with Brooks's earlier work. Overall, the effect is nostalgic, recalling the musicality of childhood nursery rhymes. However, the subject matter is far from idyllic, as Brooks describes a youth spent on the fringes of society. These *Annie Allen* poems read like a *bildungsroman*—the story of a young person's journey from innocence into experience. For example, in the poem "The Ballad of the Light-Eyed Little Girl," a young girl deals with the death of a pet: "Sweet Sally took a cardboard box, / And in went pigeon poor. / Whom she had starved to death but not / For lack of love, be sure."

Maud Martha, 1953

The novel *Maud Martha* is Brooks's only long prose work, in which she uses the autobiographical character to explore her own experiences. Maud Martha reappears in several poems in *Blacks*, as well. The novel is a series of scenes tracing Maud Martha Brown's complicated transition from childhood into maturity; it is not a single storyline with a central climax and resolution. Brooks's story exposes the emotional and psychological impact of global and local events, on the black community in general and on the Brown family in particular.

Set in the early 1950s, *Maud Martha* relates the experiences of the title character, a dark-skinned black woman barely escaping poverty on Chicago's South Side. Despite these challenging circumstances, Maud Martha's story presents a balanced view of African American daily life at the time. As a child, she confronts racial prejudice both inside and outside her community. She begins to consider herself less attractive than other black girls who have lighter skin color and "better hair," like her sister Helen. Part of Maud Martha's evolution is in learning to assert and define her own identity in the face of prevailing ideals of physical beauty. Other scenes in the novel focus on different aspects of the human experience, including economic woes and social strife, as well as family, parenting, and suffering.

The Bean Eaters, 1960

Many of Brooks's best-known works are part of *The Bean Eaters*. The thirty-five poems in this section of *Blacks* return to Bronzeville, examining its atmosphere of poverty and the attitudes that grow out of deprivation and hardship. One political poem, "The Chicago *Defender* Sends a Man to Little Rock," deals with the controversial decision to desegregate public schools. Another, "A Bronzeville Mother Loiters in Mississippi. Meanwhile, a Mississippi Mother Burns Bacon," addresses the grievous acts of racially motivated violence typical of that period.

The Bean Eaters marks the beginning of a shift in Brooks's poetic style. Turning from the strict forms and structures of her earlier work, Brooks can comment openly on racial issues affecting America's political climate. Published in the midst of the civil rights movement, *The Bean Eaters* vividly depicts the dire circumstances in which the black community found itself. Many of these poems offer a grimly detailed picture of life on society's edges, including "The Ballad of Rudolph Reed":

> I am not hungry for bread.
> But hungry hungry for a house
> Where at night a man in bed
> May never hear the plaster
> Stir as if in pain.
> May never hear the roaches
> Falling like fat rain.

The poem's narrator relates the story of a black man who strives to provide a home for his family, but loses his life while protecting his dignity. Poems in *The Bean Eaters* acknowledge the widespread violence often associated with racism, criticizing those who seem to be ambivalent. They also offer several disturbing examples of prejudice inside and outside of the black community.

1963

The five poems in this section are more abstract than others in the collection. The verbal complexity of "Riders to the Blood-Red Wrath" at times threatens to overwhelm the emotional impact of lines like, "They do not see how deftly I endure. / Deep down the whirlwind of good rage I store." But, unlike "The Empty Woman" (which follows it), "Riders to the Blood-Red

Wrath" reads more like a personal declaration of purpose, with a tone that is consistently determined and enraged. The majority of Brooks's poetry seeks to capture an individual's particular experience, but this poem's scope includes the entirety of African history, including slavery and parallel references to historical oppression around the world.

In The Mecca, 1968

Published the same year that she succeeded Carl Sandburg as poet laureate of Illinois, *In The Mecca* (1968) was nominated for the National Book Award for poetry. It is still considered to be one of Brooks's greatest works. The thirty-page title poem uses playful irony and Biblical themes to evoke the often-dreadful conditions of humanity, relating a mother's frenzied quest for her daughter, who has gone missing in a Chicago apartment building called the Mecca. This section of *Blacks* exhibits the definitive transition in Brooks's form and subject matter, moving away from what many consider to be a more literary framework toward a more informal one. She uses shorter free verse lines (unrhymed and without fixed rhythm), innovative word patterns, and disjointed rhyme to frame her social concerns.

Fourteen poems from *In the Mecca* are included in *Blacks*, divided into two sections: *In the Mecca* and *After the Mecca*. The latter includes poetic dedications to figures like Malcolm X, Medgar Evers, and the "Chicago Picasso," a large sculpture given to the city by the renowned artist Pablo Picasso in 1967.

Primer for Blacks

The only poem from *Primer for Blacks* (1980) included in *Blacks* is "To Those of My Sisters Who Kept Their Naturals." It is a poem of validation and camaraderie addressed to black women who have made the somewhat controversial (and certainly political) decision to keep their hair natural: "You have not hailed the hot-comb recently. / You never worshipped Marilyn Monroe. / You say: Farrah's hair is hers. / You have not wanted to be white."

Brooks writes to black women who do not use chemical products like lye, alkaline, or heated appliances (hot-combs, hair irons, etc.) to change their hair's natural texture. When Americans and white Europeans held slaves, it was not uncommon for slave-owners to give preferential treatment to slaves who had some

European physical traits, such as straighter hair. This practice laid the foundation for an identity crisis among those of African descent. In 1905, Madame C. J. Walker's hair softening products were embraced by mainstream black consumers, making it common practice for black women to straighten their naturally kinky or curly hair—a practice that is still widespread today. Black women tried to change themselves to satisfy a white society's ideal of beauty. Many hoped they would thus become more acceptable or appealing to the white majority, as well as to those within their own communities.

In the 1960s and early 1970s, the "black is beautiful" movement proposed a distinctive black ideal. In this social context, it became increasingly difficult for educated black women like Brooks to continue shaping and judging themselves according to white notions of beauty. By including this poem in the collection, Brooks expresses solidarity with her self-proclaimed "sisters," who are reclaiming what Brooks refers to as their "Afrikan" identities by resisting the dominant white culture.

Beckonings

Brooks's collection *Beckonings* (1975) was published by Broadside Press, a now-renowned black press in Chicago. *Blacks* includes two poems from *Beckonings*: "Horses Graze" and "A Black Wedding Song." The latter takes the form of an epithalamium, a poetic ode to a bride and groom.

In "A Black Wedding Song," Brooks again deliberately targets a specific, external black audience. The speaker addresses the reader directly, "Strong hand in strong hand, stride to / the Assault that is promised you"—calling for black unity in the face of turmoil.

To Disembark

To Disembark (1981) was originally published by Third World Press, another esteemed independent black publishing house. This section is made up of three subsections—"Riot," "Family Pictures," and "To the Diaspora." The first two sections contain selections from Brooks's books by those names, while the third draws from a later poem.

Riot (1969), a long three-part poem published as a book, is a collage of images and voices emerging from urban centers in crisis. In this piece, Brooks delves into the chaos and violence of a race riot with explosive images and language, suggesting that rioting and other militant responses to localized oppression may be warranted and necessary. *Riot* was originally published by Broadside Press in Chicago, amid the real tumult of the 1968 Chicago riots following the assassination of Dr. Martin Luther King Jr.

Family Pictures (1970) includes six poems. "The Life of Lincoln West," which appears in *Blacks*, is a long poem detailing Lincoln West's birth and troubled childhood. He is depicted as being unusually ugly, having an appearance that sets him apart from others, including his own parents. The poem is narrated by an outside observer, allowing the reader to see how Lincoln's ugliness leads to his neglect and isolation. It seems that nearly everyone finds him repugnant; the few who can stand him care for him only out of pity or from a sense of obligation. The climax occurs when a white man at a movie theater comments loudly to his companion about Lincoln, saying:

> THERE! That's the kind I've been wanting
> to show you! One of the best
> examples of the specie. Not like
> those diluted Negroes you see so much of on
> the streets these days, but the
> real thing.
> Black, ugly, and odd. You
> can see the savagery. The blunt
> blankness. That is the realthing.

The cold, anthropological tone of these remarks offend Lincoln's mother, but surprisingly, Lincoln finds them comforting. Later, when he is mistreated or otherwise made aware of how people see him, Lincoln thinks of the man's words and reminds himself that he is "the real thing."

"Young Heroes" I, II, and III are poetic odes to people Brooks admired, including Keorapetse Kgositsile, a poet and early South African nationalist. The emphasis in these pieces is outside the narrative realm—instead of continuity, the reader finds emotion and rhetorical language. These poems are followed by "Young Afrikans," a tribute to the "furious" flowers who commit themselves to "chimeful / poemhood," and "Paul Robeson" an ode to "The major Voice"—a famous actor, singer, and civil rights activist.

The section concludes with "Speech to the Young. Speech to the Progress-Toward," a poem that calls the reader to act: "Live not for battles won. / Live not for the-end-of-the-song. / Live in the along."

To the Diaspora, the third part of *To Disembark*, includes three poems related to the theme of the African diaspora. The most controversial of the three is "Music For Martyrs," dedicated to Stephen Biko, a noted South African anti-apartheid activist in the 1960s who died in police custody in 1977 at the age of 30. "Music for Martyrs" is a classic lament, a song or poem expressing grief. It begins, "I feel a regret, Steve Biko. / I am sorry, Steve Biko. / Biko the Emerger / laid low." The poem's overall tone is melancholy, tinged with a pervasive mild sarcasm. Brooks suggests that America's support for the anti-apartheid movement arrived too late, made up of no more than "shapely American memorials" and "organized nothings," things too meager to save Biko from the South African government that killed him.

The other poems in this section are "A Welcome Song For Laini Nzinga" and "To Black Women."

The Near-Johannesburg Boy and Other Poems

The last section of *Blacks* includes five poems from the collection *The Near-Johannesburg Boy and Other Poems* (1986): "Whitney Young," "Tornado at Talladega," "The Near-Johannesburg Boy," "The Good Man," and "Infirm." These poems address the apartheid regime that governed South Africa from 1948 to 1990 and black South Africans' efforts to resist that oppression. From the image of the "wise, arch, and precise" civil rights activist Whitney to the "Fist-and-the-Fury" of Father in "The Near-Johannesburg Boy," readers confront the history of resistance and violence that gripped South Africa under apartheid. Both Whitney and Father are remembered in death for their courage and pride. These poems speak to a community on the move in the struggle for freedom, one that can survive to overcome South Africa's corrupt and racist regime.

THEMES

Identity, Racism, and Double Consciousness

Gwendolyn Brooks's collection *Blacks* presents a sampling of her wide-ranging work made up of poems and prose written during a period stretching from the 1940s through the mid-1980s. The lives of people in the black community are her primary subject matter, a topic that requires Brooks to document and comment on slavery, segregation, and social stigmas in terms of their lasting effects on black awareness and self understanding. Brooks's work thus illustrates the important idea of double consciousness.

The term "double consciousness" was coined in 1897 by W. E. B. DuBois, an African American civil rights activist and scholar, who wrote in *The Souls of Black Folk*:

> After the Egyptian and Indian, the Greek and Roman, the Teuton and Mongolian, the Negro is a sort of seventh son, born with a veil, and gifted with second-sight in this American world,—a world which yields him no true self-consciousness, but only lets him see himself through the revelation of the other world.

Prior to the trans-Atlantic slave trade, many blacks would have identified themselves by tribal or ethnic affiliations, rather than by the color of their skin. Arriving in America from Africa, blacks immediately became *colored* by interacting with a society that was predominantly white, in which black people were recognizably different from what was considered "normal." The double consciousness that DuBois discusses works in three distinct ways. First, blacks must constantly check themselves against pre-existing stereotypes and evaluate whether or not their behavior confirms these damaging representations. Second, the American racism that has historically set blacks apart from whites (slavery, segregation, etc.) continues to shape blacks' awareness of themselves as separate. Finally, and perhaps most significantly, African Americans identify culturally and physically with both their "African-ness" (as experienced in their physical difference from whites) and their "American-ness" (as experienced in their post-slavery incorporation, rather than absorption, into American society).

Many of the poems included in *Blacks* reflect an awareness of double consciousness. In "I Love those Little Booths at Benvenuti's," Brooks reveals the speaker's sense of stereotypes that shape white perceptions of blacks as well as shaping blacks themselves. At Benvenuti's, "The colored people will not 'clown.' / [....] / Handling their steel and crockery with no clatter, / Laugh punily, rise, go firmly out of the door." The poem examines the speaker's awareness of herself as it is altered by her desire to "hide ... while observing tropical truths." This play on perspectives—"us" versus "them"—is characteristic of Brooks's work and recurs throughout the text.

Brooks also exposes double consciousness and its corresponding effect on identity in the three-part poem *Riot*. The poem opens with a quotation from Martin Luther King, Jr.: "A riot is the language of the unheard." An omniscient narrator relates the events that lead to the death of the central subject, John Cabot. Seeing the group of " 'Negroes' ... Poor[,] sweaty and unpretty...coming toward him," John Cabot begins to itch "beneath the nourished white / that told his story of glory to the World." In a moment of hysteria, the narrator captures Cabot's reaction, quoting his panicked cries of "Don't let It touch me! the blackness! Lord!" and, "Lord! / Forgive these nigguhs that know not what they do." In *Riot* and elsewhere in her work, Brooks looks beyond the confines of her own life to explore the duplicity and multiplicity of the black experience.

Outsider Status

Brooks creates an insulated world in *Maud Martha*, one that focuses on the black experience and makes few references to whites. In this way, Brooks heightens the reader's own double consciousness as either an outsider or an insider relative to the black community described in the novel. In a chapter called "We're the Only Colored People Here," Maud Martha and her husband go to the World Playhouse, an upscale theater in Chicago. Maud Martha narrates the events, relating how she, "the Negro woman" is seen by the whites around her:

> The people in the lobby tried to avoid looking curiously at two shy Negroes wanting desperately not to seem shy. The white women looked at the Negro woman in her outfit with which no special fault could be found, but which made them think, somehow, of close rooms, and wee, close lives. They looked at her hair. They liked to see a dark colored girl with long, long hair. They were always slightly surprised, but agreeably so, when they did. They supposed it was the hair that had got her that yellowish, good-looking Negro man.

In this passage, Maud Martha's physical appearance becomes the focal point. As she experiences being "the Negro woman" as opposed to merely "a woman" or "a human being," she relates the ways that her presence affects those observing her. Maud Martha's description of what transpires is her own view

in her own words—it is not presented as objective or absolutely true. Even though she speaks from only her own perspective—as we all do—she has a narrative authority that lends credibility to her interpretation of her experience. Her reality is double-sided: she is at once an insider and an outsider.

Social Class

Most of Brooks's work raises the issue of class, both directly and indirectly. In particular, *In The Mecca* employs many interwoven voices and images to paint a picture of lower class blacks surrounded by urban decay in Chicago's South Side. In John Lowney's essay "'A Material Collapse that is Construction': History and Counter-Memory in Gwendolyn Brooks's *In the Mecca*," quotes a 1950 *Harper's* magazine article calling the Mecca "one of the most remarkable Negro slum exhibits in the world." The poem focuses on the lives of Mecca residents, but their abject poverty stands in sharp contrast to the building's lavish design.

HISTORICAL OVERVIEW

Civil Rights Movement

The civil rights movement occurred during the 1950s, 1960s, and 1970s, as black community leaders and their supporters made headway in a crusade to eliminate legalized racial discrimination. Two milestones that sparked the civil rights movement were the *Brown v. Board of Education* (1954) decision that integrated public schools, and Rosa Parks's 1955 arrest for refusing to yield her seat to a white passenger on a bus in Montgomery, Alabama. Her actions led to the Montgomery Bus Boycott and the subsequent desegregation of that system. At this time, many black writers began to write about the struggle for equal rights. Brooks's poetry increasingly conveyed her responses to political events during this time. Emmett Till, a black teenager from Chicago, was lynched in 1955 for supposedly flirting with a white woman while visiting Mississippi. "The Last Quatrain of the Ballad of Emmett Till" reflects a mother's loss when her child dies in appalling racially motivated violence; more broadly, the poem calls attention to the many racist, violent acts threatening to divide the country then. Brooks's piece added yet another voice to the political firestorm in America. Because of poems like this one, the literary community began to view Brooks as a militant black voice, one whose political philosophies increasingly resembled those of Malcolm X, Medgar Evers, and Bobby Seale, prominent figures of black power and resistance.

Apartheid in South Africa

In the 1980s, after achieving significant legal victories at home, many Americans began to focus on issues of racial discrimination elsewhere, particularly in South Africa. Apartheid, an Afrikaans term that means "separateness," was an elaborate social and political system enforced by South Africa's white minority government beginning in 1948. Under apartheid, races were separated from each other by law and convention, and the ruling minority denied many civil rights to the black majority. The government moved blacks to settlements outside cities, usually poorly constructed slums lacking jobs, social services, and educational opportunities. Many blacks thus had to find work in nearby cities, but a black person leaving settlements or entering white areas had to carry an identifying pass, a sort of internal passport. Government-sanctioned oppression and brutality were commonplace, and riots in places like Sharpeville (1960) and Soweto (1976) left hundreds of black citizens dead. Activists who called for an end to apartheid were often jailed with no trial and no prospect of release. Nelson Mandela, who would later become South Africa's first black president, spent twenty-seven years imprisoned at Robben Island for his involvement in the anti-apartheid movement.

Brooks speaks to her audience in the voice of a black South African boy in the poem "The Near Johannesburg Boy," which appears in the last section of *Blacks*. After watching how people close to him suffer under the oppression of apartheid, he decides to join a protest march to Johannesburg—a city where, as Brooks explains in an epigraph, "He is not allowed to live" because of the color of his skin. The poem ends with the determination: "we shall forge with the Fist-and-the-Fury: / we shall flail in the Hot Time: / we shall / we shall."

South Africa's brutal policy of apartheid came to an end in the early 1990s under the leadership of President F. W. de Klerk. In February 1990, de Klerk freed political prisoners who had been held for opposing the oppressive apartheid system, including Mandela, who was elected president of South Africa four years later.

CRITICAL OVERVIEW

Gwendolyn Brooks emerged on the literary scene in 1945 with her first book, *A Street in Bronzeville*. In his article, "Gwendolyn Brooks's 'A Street in Bronzeville'," the Harlem Renaissance and the Mythologies of Black Women" Gary Smith quotes a *New York Times* review that discusses Brooks's style:

> If the idiom is colloquial, the language is universal. Brooks commands both the colloquial and more austere rhythms. She can vary manner and tone. In form, she demonstrates a wide range: quatrains, free verse, ballads, and sonnets— all appropriately controlled. The longer line suits her better than the short, but she is not verbose. In some of the sonnets, she uses an abruptness of address that is highly individual.

Smith goes on to suggest that although critics of the period were quick to recognize Brooks's stylistic successes, not many went beyond the formal aspects of her technique to examine the social commentary in her work. In the 1940s, Brooks's work moved closer to an emerging style known as urban realism, emphasizing political and social awareness. As William L. Andrews notes in *Encyclopedia Britannica's Guide to Black History*, "Brooks's tribute to the vitality and rigours of black urban life" was significantly affected by this particular "decade of creative experimentation."

In 1950, Brooks received a Pulitzer Prize for *Annie Allen*, which established her as an esteemed poet. Smith notes that the American political climate generally produced reviews of Brooks's work that were at least somewhat favorable, if not entirely complimentary. Given the widespread view that race relations have improved since the 1950s, one might expect that by 1987, when Brooks published *Blacks*, critical analysis of her work would be plentiful and positive. However, a review of the book in *Black American Literature Forum* by Houston A. Baker Jr. indicates that the book was received "with less than exultant fanfare."

Critical response may have been influenced by Harper & Row's publication of a similar compendium entitled *The World of Gwendolyn Brooks* (1971). Baker notes that unlike *The World of Gwendolyn Brooks*, *Blacks* was published by Brooks's own imprint, The David Company, without the marketing and fanfare associated with large, international presses. The use of a small press was part of Brooks's continuing tradition of supporting black publishers, an effort that began with *In The Mecca*, published by Broadside Press, a small, Detroit-based company operated by African American poet Dudley Randall.

In her essay, "Whose Canon? Gwendolyn Brooks: Founder at the Center of the 'Margins,'" Kathryne Lindberg addresses another potential reason for Brooks's less-than-exuberant critical reception. Lindberg quotes from a 1969 *Contemporary Literature* interview by George Stavros, in which Brooks answers charges of having "abandoned lyric simplicity for an angrier, more polemical (purposely controversial) voice" in her later work: "No, I have not abandoned beauty, or lyricism, and I don't consider myself a polemical poet. I'm a black poet, and I write about what I see, what interests me, and I'm seeing new things."

Lindberg goes on to explain that beyond the stylistic shifts in her work, Brooks's own existence as a politically engaged, black, female artist would have had an observable effect on the analysis offered by her "white, mostly male, academic" critics. Lindberg argues "There is no reason to assume that a particular political commitment must turn one toward or away from artistic experiment or accomplishment." Interpretive questions still arise today about whether Brooks abandoned her focus on poetic artistry after *Annie Allen*, but critics' varied responses to her work have done little to hinder her lasting impact on American literature.

CRITICISM

Allison Cummings

In the following excerpt, literary critic Cummings offers an overview of the stylistic evolution of Brooks's poetry.

Critics, white and black, argue over the racial politics of Brooks's early and later work. In the first stage of her career, Gwendolyn Brooks's poetry was praised by a largely white critical establishment for its formal virtuosity, its verbal complexity, and its "transcendence" of racial themes. In the sixties and seventies, however, many African American critics admired and focused on Brooks's welcome treatment of racial themes, violence, militancy, and the new Black Aesthetic. These critical viewpoints are

MEDIA ADAPTATIONS

A recording of Gwendolyn Brooks reading her poetry is included in *Poetry Speaks: Hear Great Poets Read Their Work from Tennyson to Plath*. This three-CD set includes a book edited by Elise Paschen and Rebekah Presson Mosby, and is available from Sourcebooks Mediafusion.

The *Gwendolyn Brooks CD Poetry Collection* is an audio collection of Brooks reading her own work. It is available from HarperAudio.

much less segregated now, though as late as 2003, in a critical edition devoted mainly to her later work, Harold Bloom admitted his preference for Brooks's early work, its "wry turn upon the universal" and "imaginatively rich ... enigmas."

In its second stage, Brooks's poetry was praised by many critics for its political engagement, though more radical poets and critics found it insufficiently revolutionary. Houston Baker finds that Brooks's earlier poems negotiate and "equal the best in the black and white American literary traditions," though the "white" tradition (reflected by "the syllabi of most American literature courses") regards her as a "black writer." Meanwhile, some spokesmen for the Black Arts movement found her work rather pale: Baker notes that Amiri Baraka calls Brooks's work characteristic of "Negro literature," which is to say, not revolutionary or black enough. In an essay tracing the changes between Brooks' early and later poetry, John Callahan calls Brooks' "newish voice" an "evolution" rather than a revolution, noting that her later work, especially from *In the Mecca* (1968) to *Primer for Blacks* (1980), is less distant, more direct, "chiefly oral," and more apt to "celebrate and, therefore, intensify the integrity of African American life quite apart from the crises of white America." George Kent argues that, after 1967, "Brooks's poetry became far more attentive to blacks as an audience than it had previously." Brooks also more often used European poetic forms, such as sonnets and ballads, as well as allusions and complex diction, in her poetry before 1967 than after. Most of Brooks's critics accept her announced change after 1967 as a given, though they differ in their interpretation of the shift: some say her work moved from a private to a public realm, from white to black audiences, from apolitical to political, or from emotional distance to openness.

The Black Arts movement strongly influenced Brooks's thinking and rhetoric about her work, even if it left ambiguous marks on her work itself. After her legendary radicalization at the Fisk Writers Conference of 1967 and her involvement in the Black Arts movement, Brooks expressed a wish to speak to, for, and about black readers and thereby to forge an audience called to awareness of racial identity and politics. Her statements about her intended audience drew their focus from black cultural nationalism and have influenced numerous writers after her. Within the Black Arts movement, many spokespeople—Amiri Baraka, Larry Neal, Ron Karenga—called for a recognizably "black" voice to hail and forge a newly positioned, newly politicized black audience for art. As Karenga formulated it, black art must be unifying, collective, speaking for, about, and to the people: "Any art that does not discuss and contribute to the revolution is invalid." Gwendolyn Brooks heard the call to "the New Black, the Tall-Walker" at Fisk, and, inspired by the new aesthetic, left Harper & Row in 1968 for Dudley Randall's Broadside Press, founded in Detroit in 1965. Thereafter, she directed her work more specifically toward black readers: "I want to write poems that will be non-compromising ... [and] meaningful to ... Black people. . . . True black writers speak as blacks about blacks to blacks. . . . The new Black is understood by no white, not the wise, the Schooled, the Kind White." Brooks referred to her poetry of the forties and fifties as "high poetincense; the language-flowers were thickly sweet. Those flowers whined and begged white folks to pick them, to find them lovable." After Fisk, she viewed her work as "Independent fire!" In her autobiography, she announced her aim "to write poems that will somehow successfully 'call' all black people: black people in taverns, black people in alleys, black people in gutters, schools, offices, factories, prisons, the consulate."

The notion of "calling" to an audience, which will unify itself politically and spiritually as it hears, is useful for conceiving of the generational shift from Brooks's era to the present. In this call, African American artists hoped to interpolate audiences into the ideology of Black Power. The call that Brooks heard enabled her to recognize her "essential African" heritage, and recognizing that heritage gave her a new, deeper sense of "black fellow feeling." She felt immediately at home in her new self-conception, perhaps because the new self was comforting in its coherence, collectivity, and currency. However, followers of the Black Aesthetic became subject to certain political goals and intentions. After her "conversion," some critics judged Brooks's art according to its fulfillment of revolutionary ends, ends that might have encouraged her to unify her hitherto ventriloquial voice and project it as one steady chord, or to subordinate her previous focus on gender to one on race.

In sum, there are discernible shifts in Brooks's form from her early to late work: after 1967 she less often used complex diction, traditional forms and rhyme, and more often used personal pronouns in poems that speak more directly to her audiences. However, it is worth noting that Brooks's publicly announced awakening after Fisk encourages readers to discern more radical shifts than her work necessarily displays. The role of critics in her makeover is key; critics may have emphasized the changes in her work to recuperate a sufficiently politicized Brooks for her literary descendants. Critics who wanted to define and preserve a more militant province for the Black Arts movement regarded her work's changes as minimal. And later, in the 1980s and '90s, feminist critics regarded Brooks's poetry, early and late, as a major milestone in women's poetry. No doubt Brooks's dependable, if too brief, presence in American literature anthologies is due to multiple factors: her importance as the first African American Pulitzer winner and her role in American literary history, including decades of public activity and lecturing, and her poems' accessibility and (teachable) focus on race, gender, and class.

Source: Allison Cummings, "Public Subjects: Race and the Critical Reception of Gwendolyn Brooks, Erica Hunt, and Harryette Mullen," in *Frontiers: A Journal of Women's Studies*, Vol. 26, No. 2, June 2005, pp. 7–13.

Houston A. Baker

In the following excerpt, Baker offers an overview of Brooks's poetry and a favorable evaluation of Blacks.

When a compendium of her poetry entitled *The World of Gwendolyn Brooks* appeared in the 1970s, the Poet Laureate of Illinois seemed fitly rewarded for a life of creative labor. The collection represented more than three decades. And its very name seemed proper and patently personal—a tribute to the genius behind its assembled offerings. "The world of Gwendolyn Brooks," one thought. "Yes, that is certainly appropriate for a Pulitzer Prize winner, a Poet Laureate, a guardian, model, and mentor in the world of American and Afro-American letters."

Yet, in 1987, with less than exultant fanfare, "the world of Gwendolyn Brooks" gave way to the unadorned, firmly bound, and privately published compendium *BLACKS*. Issued under her own publishing imprimatur, The David Company, the new collection bears strikingly large gold letters on its cover which spell *BLACKS*. Beneath, and in smaller type, the poet's name appears.

From the proper "world" of Gwendolyn Brooks, we move to the common denomination BLACKS. A reading of *BLACKS* reveals the striking appropriateness of the retitling.

The poet's uniqueness resides most decisively in her clear rejection of glorifying ideologies of the common man. Her people have neither the blues temperateness of Sterling Brown's strong men getting stronger, nor the *joie de vivre* of Langston Hughes's black urbanites, who want to dig and be dug in return. They are not proponents or exemplars of obtainable egalitarian goals. They are not blessed with a consciousness of mission—a sense of manifest destiny or a surety of predestined roles in the unfolding of a mighty national enterprise. They live always at the limits of a bitterly tested tolerance.

Implicit in the poet's portrayals, in fact, is a grammar of dissent. Frontal irony and subtle antagonism are directed against all romantic ideologies of progress and metaphysical salvation. Race, class, gender, and nationality are the grounds of divisiveness and conflict that put such ideologies to shame. Skin color as a sign of race in America, for example, can cause unappeasable anguish. Maud Martha thinks: " . . . it's my color that makes h[er husband] mad. . . . What I am inside, what is really me, he likes

okay. But he keeps looking at my color, which is like a wall. He has to jump over it in order to meet and touch what I've got for him." Class causes white women who are putative "lovers of the poor" to grow sick with fear and disgust. Philanthropically entering narrow halls of poverty, they are overcome by sights, sounds, and smells of the lower class. Possibilities for heroism are few in a world overdetermined by race, class, gender, and nationality. The bleakness of this universe is in part a function of Brooks's modernism. Commencing her career during "The Great War," she seems to have absorbed a healthy dose of the artistic malaise that prompted somber reveries of a Godless and irreversible universe of atomic fission. But her grammar of dissent is not entirely a by-product of the era in which she began her career.

Her antagonism to glorifying ideologies is also a product of a distinctive artistic credo—a signal aesthetics. Her creative orientation is designed, in fact, to match a world that guarantees the "commonness" of blacks through its restrictive codes of race, class, nationality, and gender. Adornment, embellishment, flamboyance, and proclamations of heroism are as anomalous in such a world as (to summon the poet's own image) "a rose in a whiskey glass." Stability, sanity, physical and mental development, and day-to-day safety survival depend upon an almost brutal refusal of self-deception and artistic idealism.

Brooks's own poetical naming often *situates* itself within a common order rather than employing the vocabularies of such an order for names. Her polysyllabic verse with its taut syntax and her grammatical substitutions of adjectives and adverbs for nouns often make her poems anything but idiomatic. Her grammatical acrobatics produce memorability and subversion. It is difficult to forget a "thaumaturgic lass," a vaudevillean of "magnificent, heirloom, and deft," or a hipster whose title is bestowed by "inamoratas, with an approbation." Subversion results from the appropriation of the full weight and heft of the King's English to portray lives of common subjects.

A notion of the ever altering thingness of the commonplace—a shiftiness that requires and is a function of ceaseless naming—is the truly distinguishing notion of Gwendolyn Brooks's art. Her poetical portraits alter each time we call their names. They assume a different thingness each time she, as a brilliant and accomplished public reader, sets them eloquently before us. Their alteration, however, is not merely a result of our willed and continuous naming. An elusive and always expanding space called "context" also causes them to shift—to change in unaccountable ways "behind our backs."

For example, the lackluster and whimpering populace of Bronzeville that was "not brave at all" in the 1940s transformed itself, quite miraculously, in the United States during the 1960s and assumed the common name BLACKS. Thunderstruck as she was by this behind-the-back evolution of her bean eaters and garbagemen dignified as any diplomat, Brooks maintained her aesthetics of two decades' standing. She assumed that her task was to provide a common ground and denomination for these new BLACKS.

When BLACKS became bold, heroic rioters jerking the times out of joint, Brooks energetically relinquished her direct and implicit condemnations of nationalistic grandeur. She became a namer of the militant struggle that not so long ago comprised a common ground and cause for BLACKS in the United States. She came to know in her own life what she had always claimed in her aesthetics: Common denomination can sometimes be a matter of dramatic alterations. The job for the poet facing this continuing drama of transformation is to:

> Live not for battles won.
> Live not for the-end-of-song.
> Live in the along.

To live in "the along" is to inhabit the everyday. It is to confront race, class, national, and gender restrictions with a common lexicon. For Brooks it is to do exactly what she has done in offering a newly retitled volume of her work; it is to provide and share in the common denomination of BLACKS.

Source: Houston A. Baker Jr., "A Review of *Blacks*," in *Black American Literature Forum*, Vol. 24, No. 3, Fall 1990, pp. 567–73.

SOURCES

Andrews, William L., "Encyclopedia Britannica's Guide to Black History: African American Literature Overview," *Encyclopedia Britannica*, www.britannica. com/ Blackhistory (December 12, 2005).

Baker, Houston A. Jr., "A Review of *Blacks*," in *Black American Literature Forum*, Vol. 24, No. 3, Fall, 1990, pp. 567–73.

Brooks, Gwendolyn, *Blacks*, Third World Press, 1987.

DuBois, W. E. B., *The Souls of Black Folk*, Bantam, 1989.

Lindberg, Kathryne V., "Whose Canon? Gwendolyn Brooks: Founder at the Center of the 'Margins,'" in *Gendered Modernisms: American Women Poets and Their Readers*, edited by Margaret Dickie and Thomas Travisano, University of Pennsylvania Press, 1986, pp. 283–311.

Lowney, John, "'A Material Collapse that is Construction': History and Counter-Memory in Gwendolyn Brooks's 'In the Mecca,'" *Find Articles*, www.findarticles. com (December 8, 2005).

Smith, Gary, "Gwendolyn Brooks's 'A Street in Bronzeville,' the Harlem Renaissance and the Mythologies of Black Women," in *Melus*, Vol. 10, No. 3, Fall 1983, pp. 33–46.

Bury My Heart at Wounded Knee: An Indian History of the American West

DEE BROWN

1970

When Dee Brown's history of the American West, *Bury My Heart at Wounded Knee*, was first published in 1970, it was unlike anything readers had seen before. For a century, legends and stories about the Old West had told of events from a strictly white perspective. According to popular belief, heroic men such as General George Custer bravely battled savage Indians to open up the American landscape and spread the light of civilization from coast to coast. It was seen as the "manifest destiny" of white Americans to take control of the land. In the history that was written by the victors, the Indians were cast not only as treacherous and violent, but also as an outright threat to freedom and progress.

Brown's exhaustively researched history shattered those myths. Events once seen as sources of pride for Americans, such as Custer's last stand at Little Bighorn and the "battle" at Wounded Knee, were suddenly recast as the shameful consequences of decades of mistreatment of American Indians. To support these views, Brown pored over countless historical documents, including official government reports and personal eyewitness narratives; a surprising amount of the book's text consists of direct quotes by both American Indian chiefs and white government officials. In their own words, they reveal how the government repeatedly violated treaties and instigated violent conflicts with tribe members who played no part in attacks against whites.

Bury My Heart at Wounded Knee was the first historical account of the expansion of the American West to be told from an American Indian point of view. It is not, however, a one-sided account. Brown relies on facts to reconstruct the events he describes, which are seldom as clear-cut as some would like to believe. In many cases, he tells of senseless killings of settlers by American Indian warriors, including the Santee slaughter of traders and soldiers near Fort Ridgely in 1862 and the killing of hated government agent Nathan Meeker and his white workmen on a Ute reservation in 1879. Brown also tells of white men such as General William Tecumseh Sherman and General George Crook who, despite spending many years battling Indians across the West, also fought bravely for the reasonable treatment of tribes like the Navahos and the Poncas.

Far from being a comprehensive history of relations between whites and American Indians, *Bury My Heart at Wounded Knee* focuses on the thirty-year period from 1860 to 1890, often referred to as the final three decades of the "Indian Wars." Each chapter of the book is devoted to the ongoing saga of a different tribe or group of tribes. Because of this limited scope, some well-known tribes such as the Hopi and the Pawnee are mentioned only in passing if at all. Brown instead focuses on those Western tribes whose relations with whites were particularly troubled.

The book has proved steadily successful since its initial publication, selling over five million copies worldwide. In 2001, Owl Books released a thirtieth anniversary edition featuring a new preface by the author. *Bury My Heart at Wounded Knee* has become required reading for many American history courses and continues to capture the imagination of readers who want to learn more about American Indian culture. As Brown notes in his preface to the 2001 edition:

> Small though the comparative number of Indians is, almost all other Americans seem to have an earnest fascination for their history, their arts and literature, their attitude toward the natural world, and their philosophy of human existence.

PLOT SUMMARY

Chapter 1: "Their Manners are Decorous and Praiseworthy"

The first chapter of *Bury My Heart at Wounded Knee* provides historical background about

> 'THE GREAT SPIRIT RAISED BOTH THE WHITE MAN AND THE INDIAN,' RED CLOUD SAID. 'I THINK HE RAISED THE INDIAN FIRST. HE RAISED ME IN THIS LAND AND IT BELONGS TO ME. THE WHITE MAN WAS RAISED OVER THE GREAT WATERS, AND HIS LAND IS OVER THERE. SINCE THEY CROSSED THE SEA, I HAVE GIVEN THEM ROOM. THERE ARE NOW WHITE PEOPLE ALL ABOUT ME. I HAVE BUT A SMALL SPOT OF LAND LEFT. THE GREAT SPIRIT TOLD ME TO KEEP IT.'"

relations between Native Americans and whites prior to 1860. The chapter subtitle is taken from a letter written by Christopher Columbus to King Ferdinand and Queen Isabella of Spain, in which the explorer praises the Native Americans he has encountered as peaceable, sweet, and gentle. Columbus then kidnaps ten members of his host tribe, the Tainos, and takes them back to Spain so they may "be introduced to the white man's ways."

Over a century later, after hundreds of thousands of Native Americans have already been killed by Spaniards throughout the Caribbean, the first English settlers land in Virginia and Massachusetts. Like Columbus, the settlers are generally welcomed without hostility. Over the next two hundred years, though, the white settlers become so numerous that eastern Native American tribes can no longer remain on their traditional lands. In the 1830s, the surviving tribes are relocated west of the Mississippi River to a "permanent Indian frontier" established by the United States government. There, they are promised that whites will not disturb them. It does not take long before this promise is broken. The period from 1860 to 1890 sees the virtual extermination of Native Americans throughout this "permanent" territory.

Chapter 2: The Long Walk of the Navahos

The Navaho people occupy land later known as New Mexico. They form an uneasy friendship with the white soldiers who inhabit the string of

BIOGRAPHY

DEE BROWN

Dorris Alexander Brown, known throughout his life as "Dee," was born on February 28, 1908, near Alberta, Louisiana. His father died when he was five, and his mother moved the family to Arkansas shortly thereafter. His great-grandfather was an acquaintance of Davy Crockett, and Brown was fascinated by family anecdotes about the legendary man. He was also intrigued by real-life Native Americans he met as a youth; he found that they were not at all like the Indian savages depicted in the movies he saw.

While in college studying history, Brown began working in the campus library. This led to a career first as a government librarian and ultimately as a librarian and professor of library science at the University of Illinois. While working as a librarian, Brown's interest in history led him to write both fiction and nonfiction in his spare time. His first book, *Wave High the Banner* (1942), was a novel based on the life of Davy Crockett.

Subsequent books dealt almost exclusively with the Old West, with many delving into the untold stories of Native American tribes and their histories. Though he wrote or contributed to over twenty-five books—two of which won awards from the Western Writers of America—his crowning achievement is generally considered *Bury My Heart at Wounded Knee*.

Brown, who continued writing into his nineties, died in 2002 at the age of ninety-four.

Crazy Horse The Library of Congress

forts being built throughout their lands in the early 1860s. They trade with the soldiers and even engage in horse racing competitions at Fort Fauntleroy. In 1861, amid accusations of cheating after one race, soldiers inexplicably launch an attack on Navahos outside the fort, killing women and children.

Soon after, General James Carleton enters the New Mexico territory and demands that the

Navahos abandon their homeland. They are to relocate to reserved Indian land at Bosque Redondo, where other tribes such as the Mescalero Apaches have already been sent by force. Carleton enlists frontiersman Kit Carson to burn the Navahos' crops and take their livestock so they can be more easily forced from their land. He does so, destroying even the tribe's most prized achievement: meticulously cultivated peach orchards, over five thousand trees strong. Most of the Navahos surrender and make the long walk from their ancestral lands to the reservation at Bosque Redondo. A few rebellious chiefs like Manuelito elude capture for two years, but all eventually end up at the Bosque.

After spending years suffering in the reservation's poor conditions—infertile land, undrinkable water, and widespread disease—the Navahos are visited by General William Tecumseh Sherman, who promises to return them to their homeland. Sherman is mostly known for his merciless war tactics against both Confederates and Indians, but he often fights for the rights of Indians confined on inhospitable reservation lands. In 1868, the Navahos sign a new treaty with the whites; although they lose much of their most fertile land, they are allowed to return home. They are, as Brown puts it, "the least unfortunate of all the western Indians."

Chapter 3: Little Crow's War

By 1862, the Santee Sioux in the northern part of Indian Territory are squeezed into a narrow stretch of land alongside the Minnesota River. They have lost most of their land through unfavorable treaties, and due to the costs of fighting the Civil War, the government fails to pay money promised to the tribe. Their hunting grounds depleted, the Santees seek provisions from the government-run agency warehouses in their territory. One of the traders there tells the Santee they should "eat grass or their own dung."

Soon after, four hungry young Santee men foolishly kill five white settlers to prove their bravery. Knowing the whites will seek vengeance, the tribe, led by warrior chief Little Crow, decides to attack one of the government agencies first. Twenty whites are killed; the trader who suggested that the Santees eat grass is found dead, his mouth stuffed full of grass. The Santees also attack a nearby fort and town, but are soon overwhelmed by white forces. Most surrender, believing they will all be spared.

However, over three hundred of the Santees are tried and sentenced to death for the murders of whites. Eventually, President Lincoln commutes all but thirty-nine of the death sentences. It is later discovered that two of the men executed were not on the list of those condemned.

The last of the free Santee chiefs, Little Crow, is shot down in 1863 by white Minnesota settlers for a bounty. The surviving Santees are relocated to a reservation in Dakota territory in 1863; at least one out of every five Santees is dead by the end of their first winter there.

Chapter 4: War Comes to the Cheyennes

The Cheyenne and Arapaho tribes, living in what would come to be called Colorado Territory, are tragic victims of miscommunication. In the 1850s, they sign land treaties written in English, and are told years later that the documents do not contain stipulations they were told would be included. In 1864, one of the Cheyenne chiefs, Lean Bear, rides toward a large group of white soldiers by himself to speak to the officer in charge. As he approaches, the soldiers open fire, killing him. The soldiers continue firing on other Cheyennes, who are then forced to fight back. Because of this, the colonel in charge of the area orders officers to "kill Cheyennes whenever and wherever found."

Later, when many Cheyennes and Arapahos have already surrendered weapons and relocated their camp to an area near one of the soldiers' forts, they are attacked by the colonel's forces one morning at sunrise. Chief Black Kettle raises a U.S. flag and a white flag of surrender on a pole in the camp and tells the women and children to gather around it for protection. The soldiers ignore the plea for truce and murder the Indians indiscriminately, mutilating the bodies afterward. Almost one hundred and fifty Indians are killed, most of them women and children. This event soon comes to be known as the Sand Creek Massacre.

Chapter 5: Powder River Invasion

The tribes of the Powder River country (now part of northeastern Wyoming) include the Sioux and the Northern Cheyennes. In 1865, during their summer medicine ceremonies, they hear news of white soldiers approaching their land from four different directions. They dismiss this as rumor, and even ignore Cheyenne warrior Little Horse's report that he saw the soldiers approaching an Arapaho camp. Little Horse and his family move out of the camp, and the next morning soldiers attack it.

Two other columns of soldiers make their way through Powder River country as well, but they face massive resistance from many Sioux and Cheyenne tribes. These soldiers lose their battle, but the Indians know that more will soon come.

Chapter 6: Red Cloud's War

As the Indians of the Powder River country fight to drive the whites from their land, treaty commissioners make their way toward the disputed territory. They want to meet with the warrior chiefs, especially Red Cloud of the Oglala Sioux, to arrange peace treaties that would allow white settlers safe travel through the Powder River country to Montana and Idaho. While many of the Indians favor peace, the whites' roads traverse important hunting grounds that cannot be relinquished. The government presses forward without a treaty; the Indians fight back, routing an entire company of soldiers in a battle that the whites call the Fetterman Massacre. After hearing of this and other failed attempts to stop the fighting, government officials in Washington decide to remove their soldiers from the Powder River country so they can secure peace with the Indians.

A peace treaty is signed in 1868, and Red Cloud emerges as a hero for his people. However, over the course of the next twenty years, the terms of the treaty are disputed, reinterpreted, and ultimately ignored by the very government that issued them.

Chapter 7: "The Only Good Indian Is a Dead Indian"

By 1866, most of the southern plains have been cleared of Indians. Cheyenne chief Black Kettle, after surviving the Sand Creek massacre, has moved many of his remaining people to lands south of the Arkansas River as directed by the government. Some warriors refuse to leave the plains, though, and General Philip Sheridan is put in charge of all the forts in Kansas. Sheridan begins an indiscriminate reign of terror across the region, attacking even Black Kettle's peaceful camp just as other soldiers had done at Sand Creek; this time, Black Kettle does not survive. Soldiers kill one hundred and three Indians at Black Kettle's camp, only eleven of those being warriors. Sheridan's merciless tactics drive many groups to surrender. When a Comanche leader surrenders some of his tribe, he assures Sheridan that he is a "good Indian." Sheridan replies, "The only good Indians I ever saw were dead."

Chapter 8: The Rise and Fall of Donehogawa

Though he is known to whites by the name Ely Samuel Parker, Hasanoanda—later called Donehogawa, Keeper of the Western Door of the Long House of the Iroquois—is a full-blooded Seneca Iroquois. He changed his name as a young man in an attempt to be taken seriously by white people. Although he faces much discrimination, Parker works hard to become a successful civil engineer, and becomes friends with Ulysses S. Grant before the Civil War catapults Grant to national attention. During the war, Grant helps Parker win his right to fight for the Union. After the war, as a Brigadier General, Parker travels west to survey the treatment of Indians by the government. When Grant is

elected president, he appoints Parker as his Commissioner of Indian Affairs.

Parker is given control of a bureau rife with corruption, assigned the thankless job of trying to secure fair treatment of Indians even as the government whittles away Indian territories to accommodate the westward spread of white settlers and industrialists. He is resented by many politicians, both for his straitlaced behavior and his Indian ancestry. In 1870, he is attacked for failing to follow proper procedures when providing rations to Indian reservations, even though such action was necessary to prevent widespread starvation. Worried about tarnishing the image of his friend the president, he resigns as Commissioner of Indian Affairs after just two years of service.

Chapter 9: Cochise and the Apache Guerrillas

Cochise is the leader of the Chiricahua Apaches in an area that later became parts of Arizona and New Mexico. At first, the Apaches welcome white Americans to their region, but then a soldier wrongly arrests members of Cochise's family for stealing cattle. Two years later, in 1863, the Apache war chief Mangas Colorado is lured by soldiers waving a flag of truce; he is then taken prisoner, tortured, and killed at Fort McLean. In 1871, a band of unarmed Aravaipas living peacefully near a military camp are slaughtered in retaliation for a raid they did not commit.

After this final incident, which even President Grant calls "purely murder," government agents attempt to forge a peace with the Indian tribes of the southwest. Cochise eventually meets with them, and agrees to keep peace as long as his people can remain on a portion of their own lands instead of being relocated. Cochise dies of an unknown condition not long after. Other tribes in the region, including the Aravaipas, are less fortunate than the Chiricahuas; they are routinely relocated and arrested without cause.

Chapter 10: The Ordeal of Captain Jack

Kintpuash, chief of the Modoc tribe in northern California, is called Captain Jack by the local white settlers; many of the Modocs are given nicknames by the friendly whites who share their land. As the number of white settlers increase, however, tensions grow; Captain Jack is convinced to sign a treaty relocating the

Modocs north to a reservation in Oregon. However, without promised government provisions, and in conflict with the Klamath Indians on whose land they have been placed, the Modocs soon return to their former home. Soldiers are brought in to remove them, and although Captain Jack agrees to leave, the confrontation turns violent when the soldiers attempt to disarm the entire band. The Modocs flee to a nearby region of lava beds. There, trapped by soldiers, a group of Modoc warriors goad Captain Jack into killing the white leader, General Canby, during a truce council. Later, after Captain Jack surrenders his people, these same Modoc warriors testify against him at his trial for murder. He is found guilty and hanged.

Chapter 11: The War to Save the Buffalo

By 1869, General Sheridan's merciless tactics against the Plains Indians (described in Chapter 7) have resulted in the surrender of most tribes, including the Cheyennes and Arapahos. The Kiowas, along with some remaining Comanches, defy Sheridan's order to surrender; after all, they have signed—and abide by—a treaty that allows them to remain where they are. Commander George Custer is given the task of forcing their surrender. He meets with Kiowa leaders for a peaceful council, and then suddenly arrests the two most powerful chiefs, Satanta and Lone Wolf, though they have done nothing in violation of their treaty. General Sheridan proclaims that the two will be executed if the Kiowa people do not surrender themselves at Fort Cobb. Most of the tribe surrenders, and the two leaders are relocated with their people to a reservation.

Soon, in need of food beyond what they can grow on their reservation, a band of warriors slips across the border into Texas to hunt. They find and attack a wagon train, killing seven men, and when they return to the reservation, the chiefs responsible for the attack are charged with murder. Chiefs Satanta and Big Tree are sentenced to life imprisonment, but Lone Wolf convinces authorities that peace is not possible unless the other two chiefs are freed.

Peace does not last long. As whites continue to steal Indian horses and hunt the Plains buffalo nearly to extinction, Lone Wolf leaves the reservations and joins his band of Kiowas with the Kwahadi tribe in an attempt to live free among the last great buffalo herd at Palo Duro Canyon in Texas. They are captured, along with other

bands of Kiowas who have left the reservation without permission; unable to decide which Kiowas should be held responsible, government authorities order one of the less rebellious chiefs, Kicking Bird, to choose twenty-six of his own tribe for imprisonment in Florida. He makes the difficult selections—which include both Lone Wolf and Satanta—and two days after the prisoners are taken, Kicking Bird dies without explanation.

Chapter 12: The War for the Black Hills

In 1868, the U.S. government grants permanent ownership of the Black Hills in South Dakota to the Indians. Soon after, gold is discovered in the Black Hills, and the government is powerless to stop the rush of white settlers who violate the Indians' rights by entering their territory without permission. General George Custer leads troops into the territory, though they do little to keep white prospectors out. In September of 1875, government agents meet with Indian leaders to try to arrange for the sale or lease of the Black Hills. The Indians refuse. Within six months, soldiers are dispatched to clear the land of all "hostile" Indians, even though they are in their own territory.

This leads to a clash between Indian forces, including those of Oglala chief Crazy Horse and Hunkpapa chief Sitting Bull, and white soldiers led by General Custer. Custer and his soldiers are utterly destroyed in a battle near the Little Bighorn River in Montana Territory. This resounding defeat of military forces—the most decisive and devastating victory ever achieved by Plains Indians—has its price: after hearing of the massacre, the U.S. government demands that the Indians surrender both the Powder River country and the Black Hills. The Indians, they argue, have broken their treaty; the fact that the government broke the treaty first—by sending troops into Indian territory without permission—is ignored.

As soldiers pursue the remaining bands of Sioux across the northern plains, Sitting Bull leads his people into Canada, where he feels they will be safer. Crazy Horse eludes soldiers until 1877; with his Oglala people starving, and the government promising to allow them to return to their Powder River country soon, he surrenders. Months later, he is arrested after he makes comments about leaving the reservation to return to the Powder River country. As Crazy

Horse is led to a barred cell, a scuffle ensues and a soldier stabs him with a bayonet, killing him. Soon after, the remaining Sioux are marched to a new reservation far from their home. Crazy Horse's parents escape the march to join Sitting Bull in Canada. On the way, they stop at a creek called Wounded Knee, where they bury their son's heart and bones.

Chapter 13: The Flight of the Nez Percés

Prior to the great westward push of white settlers, the Nez Percé tribe inhabits an area that covers parts of Washington, Oregon, and Idaho. Throughout the early and mid 1800s, the Nez Percés pride themselves on their friendly relationship with whites. As more and more settlers move into Nez Percé territory, however, white commissioners present the Indians with a treaty that will reduce their land to a fraction of its former size. One chief, Old Joseph, refuses to sign. Though he dies soon after, his son, Young Joseph, is equally committed to preserving his tribe's homeland in the Wallowa Valley. When government agents demand that he and his tribe relocate to a reservation, he appeals to President Grant, who relents and signs an executive order that protects the Wallowa Valley from white settlement.

Local whites, eager to open up the Wallowa Valley for their own use, falsely accuse the Nez Percés of stealing cattle and horses from settlers. Two years after Grant gave protection to the Wallowa Valley, he reverses himself and declares it open for white settlement. The Nez Percés are told to report to the Lapwai reservation in 1877, and military forces are called in when they refuse.

Outnumbered and overwhelmed, Chief Joseph leads his people on the march to Lapwai. Along the way, after several Nez Percé warriors slip away and kill eleven whites as revenge for stolen livestock, Chief Joseph decides that the tribe must flee to the north or they will die at the hands of white soldiers. They make their way toward Canada, hoping to evade American soldiers just as Sitting Bull did. The tribe is overtaken just miles from the Canadian border. After five days and many Nez Percé casualties, Chief Joseph agrees to surrender his people. However, a small group of warriors escape and make their way on foot to the Canadian border where Sitting Bull's Sioux take them in.

Most of the Nez Percé, including Chief Joseph, are never allowed to go to Lapwai as

promised, held as prisoners of war far from Wallowa Valley. Chief Joseph spends many years petitioning the government to free his people, with no success. He dies in 1904. Brown notes that "the agency physician reported the cause of death as 'a broken heart.'"

Chapter 14: Cheyenne Exodus

In 1877, several bands of Northern Cheyennes surrender along with the Oglala Sioux chief Crazy Horse. The Northern Cheyennes expect to be placed on a reservation with the Sioux and object when they are told they will be relocated far south to a reservation containing Southern Cheyennes. The Northern Cheyennes agree to visit and inspect the reservation lands and then decide whether they will go. Once there, they find the conditions deplorable and request to go back; they are told they must stay until the president decides differently. The Northern Cheyennes fare poorly in the hot summer weather, and many become ill with malaria.

Chief Little Wolf of the Northern Cheyennes leads his people off the reservation and starts northward, hoping to return to their ancestral lands without incident. As they make their way, the tribe is attacked and splinters into two groups. Little Wolf's band meets with a sympathetic commander named Lieutenant Clark, who agrees to let the Cheyennes stay at his fort until a northern reservation can be established. The two groups of Northern Cheyennes are finally brought back together at a reservation on Tongue River, but only after suffering great losses.

Chapter 15: Standing Bear Becomes a Person

In 1868, a "bureaucratic blunder in Washington" leads to trouble for the peaceful, agrarian Ponca tribe. The borders for their land, located in Nebraska, were already determined by treaty ten years earlier. However, when government officials craft a treaty for a rival tribe north of the Poncas—the Sioux (discussed in Chapter 6)—they inadvertently include the Ponca territory as part of the Sioux treaty. For seven years, the Poncas are harassed by Sioux who threaten to drive them off the newly established Sioux territory. Eventually, the government gives the Poncas some money as repayment for their trouble.

Soon after, though, the Poncas—who have never fought with white soldiers or even resisted white encroachment on their land—are told that they will be relocated to Indian Territory. Several Ponca chiefs, including White Eagle and Standing Bear, are taken by train through Indian Territory to evaluate the land. They are told by government agent Edward Kemble that they will then be taken to the president, where they can tell him anything good or bad about the land they were shown. When the chiefs express disappointment at the Indian Territory land and refuse to accept it, Kemble abandons them far from home. Without money or horses, the wintertime journey back home takes them over a month on foot.

Kemble returns to the Ponca camp with troops and forces the Poncas to relocate to Indian Territory farther south. Like the Northern Cheyennes (discussed in Chapter 14), many become ill in the hostile southern climate. Nearly one-fourth of the tribe's population is wiped out within a year.

The following year, Chief Standing Bear's eldest son dies. Determined to honor his son's final request, Standing Bear leads a large party north to bury his son at their ancestral Ponca homelands. They reach Omaha, where General Crook—a longtime Indian-fighter who is becoming increasingly sympathetic to their plight—promises to help them return to their homelands. Crook relates the story of the Poncas to the press and helps orchestrate *Standing Bear v. Crook*, a court proceeding against himself. Lawyers for the Poncas assert that Standing Bear is a person in the eyes of the law and demand that Crook show cause for holding them as prisoners. The judge rules in favor of the Poncas, and they are freed; the government grants them several hundred acres of land from their former territory.

Unfortunately, the majority of Poncas are still held on the southern Indian Territory reservation and are not allowed to leave. Big Snake, Standing Bear's brother, attempts to make his way home with thirty other Poncas and is "accidentally" killed by soldiers as they try to arrest him.

Chapter 16: "The Utes Must Go!"

The Utes are Rocky Mountain Indians who see the white man as their ally; in fact, in the early 1860s, many Utes help white frontiersman Kit Carson subdue their longtime enemies, the Navahos (discussed in Chapter 2). By 1873, however, the discovery of gold in the Rocky Mountains has brought many miners into Ute territory, and the government is unwilling to remove them. Instead, the government strikes a deal with head Ute chief Ouray the Arrow to buy a large section of the Utes' Rocky Mountain territory. Knowing there is nothing else they can do, Ouray and the other chiefs accept.

In 1878, the government appoints Nathan Meeker as a new agent for the Ute reservation. Meeker plans to destroy the Utes' supply of ponies in order to force them to settle down and grow crops like white men do. When he orders the plowing of an important horse pasture, one of the chiefs, Canalla Johnson, argues with him and grabs him by the shoulder. Meeker exaggerates the incident and requests that soldiers be sent to the reservation; meanwhile, the local white communities are being worked into an anti-Ute frenzy with false news reports of Indian attacks.

The company of two hundred cavalrymen march onto Ute land after promising one of the chiefs that they would wait at the border. Two Ute leaders approach the men for a council, and someone—it could have been a white or a Ute—fires a shot that initiates an intense battle. News of the fighting spreads, and Utes at Meeker's agency kill him and his white workers and take the three white women captive. The women are ultimately released, and the Utes, now painted as murderous savages by the Colorado press and politicians, are forced to relocate to a Utah reservation.

Chapter 17: The Last of the Apache Chiefs

In 1876, two years after the death of Cochise (discussed in Chapter 9), the time of the reservation on Chiricahua Apache land comes to an end. The government closes the reservation and forces the Chiricahuas to relocate to another reservation at San Carlos. Half of the Chiricahuas comply, while the other half flee to Mexico under the leadership of an Apache named Geronimo. After stealing horses and cattle from Mexicans, Geronimo and his band return to New Mexico to sell the animals for supplies. They take shelter near a Mimbres Indian reservation; when that reservation is shut down, Geronimo and the Mimbres are taken to San Carlos. Four years later, believing Army agents are about to arrest "all leaders who had ever been hostile," Geronimo and several other Apaches return to Mexico and join up with other escaped Mimbres warriors.

In 1882, the Army calls on General Crook (discussed in Chapter 15) to restore order to the San Carlos reservation. Crook makes quick improvements to the reservation and brings Geronimo and hundreds of other fugitive Apaches back to San Carlos. Things are peaceful until 1885, when Geronimo and a number of others again flee to Mexico, reportedly because they hear rumors of impending arrests. Crook is reprimanded for failing to bring the Indians back peacefully and ultimately resigns. After being pursued by both the American and Mexican armies, Geronimo and his last few followers surrender to General Miles in 1886 and are shipped off to a dismal reservation in Florida. Hearing the news, the Kiowas and Comanches—once enemies of the Chiricahuas— offer Geronimo and his people a place at Fort Sill on their reservation. Geronimo, "the last of the Apache chiefs," dies there in 1909.

Chapter 18: Dance of the Ghosts

In 1881, Sitting Bull and his people, who have fled to Canada to escape conflict with American soldiers and settlers, return to the United States under the promise of a pardon and reserved land with other Sioux. The government reneges on part of its promise and holds Sitting Bull as a prisoner. This does nothing to diminish his popularity among both Indians and whites, and after he is released from prison, Buffalo Bill Cody asks government agents to allow Sitting Bull to join his Wild West show. Sitting Bull is a huge success, but he returns to his reservation in 1887 when he suspects government agents are trying to take advantage of his absences to take more of his people's land. Indeed, in 1889, the government convinces the other Sioux chiefs to sell off a large portion of the Great Sioux Reservation despite Sitting Bull's opposition.

In the winter of 1890, a religious craze known as the Ghost Dance movement sweeps through Indian reservations across the country. The movement—a mix of Christianity and Native American beliefs—asserts that Christ has returned to Earth as an Indian, and that the white men will be wiped from the land by spring. The Indians must perform Ghost Dance

ceremonies to protect themselves during this great cleansing. The Sioux agent, James McLaughlin, condemns the ceremonies and orders the arrest of Sitting Bull, who he believes is behind them. During his arrest, a conflict breaks out and Sitting Bull is killed.

Chapter 19: Wounded Knee

After the death of Sitting Bull, Minneconjou chief Big Foot leads his people away from their reservation, hoping to find another reservation where they will be better protected. Soldiers catch up to the band and force them to camp at Wounded Knee Creek. The next morning, the soldiers take the Indians' guns, axes, and knives; after giving up nearly all the weapons peacefully, a single Minneconjou protests the loss of his gun. As the gun is taken from him, shots ring out and chaos ensues. At the end of the slaughter, Brown notes, "One estimate placed the final total of dead at very nearly three hundred of the original 350 men, women, and children." For many, this massacre marks the closing of the American frontier.

THEMES

Ethnocentrism

Ethnocentrism is the judging of other cultures based on the standards of one's own culture, usually under the belief that one's own culture is ideal or superior. When dealing with American Indians, the attitudes and behaviors of white Americans as shown in *Bury My Heart at Wounded Knee* are largely shaped by ethnocentrism.

In the book, white Americans believe that the Indian way of life—in itself a faulty conception, since tribes in different regions had vastly different cultures—is inherently less civilized than their own society. Nathan Meeker, an agent for the Ute territory in Colorado, is typical of the white people who misinterpret Indian culture by measuring it against white American culture. Meeker believes that the Indians oppose farming because they are lazy; in truth, they see no need to farm because the land naturally provides everything they desire. He does not understand why the Utes want to be paid to work their own farmland, even though he pays white workers who also help with the labor. Ironically, many Indian tribes such as the Navahos and

The Trail of Tears, *painting by Robert Lindneux, 1838* The Granger Collection, New York

Poncas are excellent farmers before they are forced from their land by white soldiers; these same tribes are later told that they should give up their savage lifestyles and take up agriculture.

Perhaps the most fundamental misunderstanding that results from ethnocentrism in *Bury My Heart at Wounded Knee* has to do with the concept of land ownership. For white Americans, it is understood that all land is owned by specific individuals, and that ownership of that land can be transferred from owner to owner. Indians see the land as belonging to all, and therefore do not immediately understand the notion that they can be removed from their ancestral lands just because the government has given them money or provisions. After some tribes are confined to reservations, white agents attempt to eliminate tribe-owned land by encouraging individual land ownership, which they see as a civilized trait.

Relocation

The story of nearly every American Indian tribe is a story of relocation. Before the influence of whites in an area, local tribes naturally settled on the most fertile pieces of land available, places

where they could most easily sustain themselves. As the United States adds large amounts of territory to its domain, white settlers and lawmakers are not content to leave these prime lands in the hands of Indian tribes. Rather than honor long-established boundaries for tribal lands, the government instead "renegotiates" with Indian tribes for their removal to more distant—and almost always less fertile—lands. Some tribes are moved repeatedly, each time to progressively worse land.

Several Indian tribes are also relocated for other reasons. The Utes, for example, are moved after gold is discovered in their part of the Rocky Mountains. Likewise, the Black Hills, sacred to many northern Plains Indian tribes, are seized when gold is discovered there. Some tribes are moved far from their ancestral lands simply because it is more convenient for the government to operate a single large reservation than several smaller ones.

The majority of the bloody conflicts described in *Bury My Heart at Wounded Knee* are the result of these forced relocations. Often they occur when a band of Indians refuses to be relocated; just as often, though, they occur after a group of Indians submits to a reservation, finds the conditions inhospitable, and returns to ancestral lands in an attempt to continue life as it was before white settlers.

Communication Barriers

Problems arising from the communication barriers between Indians and whites are perhaps the most pervasive of all the problems described in *Bury My Heart at Wounded Knee*. In many cases, Indian chiefs like Red Cloud discover later that treaties they have signed do not include provisions they had agreed to. Because nearly all the chiefs require interpreters when dealing with white agents, it is entirely possible that some of these provisions were "lost in translation"—though such a consistent pattern suggests deliberate deception. Whatever the reason, such differing perceptions about treaty terms account for the source of much of the conflict between Indians and whites.

Poor communication also often leads to violence. When Cheyenne chief Lean Bear peacefully approaches a group of soldiers, at least one of the soldiers seems to misinterpret this as an impending attack and shoots him dead. This spurs a violent battle resulting in many deaths for both Cheyennes and whites. At Wounded Knee in 1890, the entire band of Big Foot's Sioux is peacefully disarmed with the exception of a Minneconjou warrior named Black Coyote. According to one witness, Black Coyote is deaf; he is willing to give up his weapon, but white soldiers misunderstand his intentions. In the end, hundreds of Indians are killed because of this misunderstanding.

The communication barrier between whites and Indians is also apparent in an incident involving Sitting Bull, who at the time has become a famous figure, well-regarded by the American public. Sitting Bull agrees to speak at a ceremony marking the completion of a transcontinental railroad across the northern part of the country. His speech, given in his native Sioux, consists of various insults and complaints about white people, who he describes as "thieves and liars." The Army translator who must convey the speech to the English-speaking public is put on the spot; rather than translate Sitting Bull's statement of hatred for white people, he improvises a warm, "Indian"-sounding speech that receives a standing ovation. Even though he is the most well-known and beloved Indian in the country, Sitting Bull's true words are not heard.

Assimilation

Assimilation occurs when a minority population adopts the behaviors and beliefs of the majority population in which they live. While most Indian tribes in the book initially welcome white settlers to their land, few Indians are willing to assimilate fully into the culture of white America.

When Chief Joseph of the Nez Percés refuses to allow white men to build schools on his lands, he explains that schools will also bring churches and that churches "will teach us to quarrel about God." Still, many Indians accept and even embrace the less quarrelsome aspects of Christianity. When many Poncas die during their relocation to Indian Territory in 1877, they receive Christian burials at the request of tribe members. Ultimately, Indian tribes across the country even adopt a new religious movement— the Ghost Dance movement—that borrows heavily from Christian tradition.

Though whites often attempt to "civilize" Indians in the book, very little effort is made to incorporate them into American society. In fact, as pressure builds to remove Indian tribes from coveted lands, the Indians themselves are demonized to such an extent that assimilation into the mainstream becomes all but impossible. For example, the relatively peaceful Utes are depicted in the Colorado press as bloodthirsty savages. They are blamed not only for acts they do not commit, but also for acts that have not been committed by anyone, such as the alleged burning of a former Indian agent's house.

The depiction of a successfully assimilated Indian is that of Donehogawa, also known as Ely Parker. Parker works as an engineer, serves in the Army during the Civil War, and eventually becomes President Grant's Commissioner of Indian Affairs. Still, even with his great successes, he is ultimately driven out of politics by opponents who paint him as nothing more than an untrustworthy savage.

HISTORICAL OVERVIEW

American Indians and the Westward Expansion of the United States

From its outset, the United States was a westward-expanding nation. The colonies along the East Coast had been populated with white settlers long before the United States became a country in its own right, often at the expense of East Coast Indian tribes. Any successful growth of the new nation meant moving west. President George Washington and Secretary of War Henry Knox sought a peaceful solution to the inevitable conflicts that arose when whites encroached upon lands occupied by Indians. In "No Idle Past: Uses of History in the 1830 Indian Removal Debates," Jason Meyers notes, "President George Washington recognized Indian sovereignty and promised Native Americans economic assistance, education, and protection." Washington also established the framework of peacefully obtaining land from Indian tribes by negotiating treaties between tribe leaders and the government.

This model was followed with success until 1830, when the government focus changed from negotiation with Indians to flat-out removal. Entire Indian tribes were relocated to more distant lands not yet occupied by white settlers—in this case, lands west of the Mississippi River. However, as the population of the United States continued to grow, soon those lands immediately west of the Mississippi were appropriated by whites, and Indian tribes were relocated yet again. This pattern was repeated throughout the nineteenth century as white settlers continued to spread across newly acquired territories, eventually reaching the West Coast.

For many Americans, this displacement of Indians was justified by the notion of "manifest destiny." This term, coined by New York journalist John O'Sullivan, suggested that the divine right and duty of Americans was to spread democracy and civilization across the land. Indians were seen as neither democratic nor civilized and were therefore an obstacle to the growth of the country.

By 1890, nearly all Indian tribes in the United States were confined to reservation lands that were repeatedly reduced in size as the government's resource needs grew. In 1924, the American Indian Citizenship Act granted American citizenship to all Indians without the need for their consent. This was characteristic of an officially sanctioned attempt to assimilate Indians into American society. Although assimilation has occurred to varying degrees with different tribes, the second half of the twentieth century saw a resurgence of interest in American Indian heritage and preservation that continues to this day.

The American Indian Movement

At the same time Brown was writing *Bury My Heart at Wounded Knee*, Native Americans across the country were actively organizing to promote the renewal of tribal heritage and awareness of the government's mistreatment of Native American people. The most influential organization was the American Indian Movement (AIM), launched in Minnesota in 1968. Originally intended to focus on local issues, the success of the organization defied tribal lines and became a nationwide phenomenon within a year, causing the group to focus instead on broader topics like reeducation and Native American civil rights.

Among the group's most notable actions was the occupation of Alcatraz Island in 1969. AIM members argued their right to be there due to a 1868 treaty that allowed Indians to occupy any federal land that was not currently in use. After eighteen months of occupation, federal troops forced the group off the island. In 1973, AIM occupied the Pine Ridge Reservation near Wounded Knee. The group objected to the federally imposed tribal government currently in charge on the reservation. During the seventy-one-day protest, federal agents killed two AIM members. Ultimately, despite the best efforts of AIM, the existing tribal government remained in place. Two years later, two federal agents in an unmarked car ventured onto Indian property near local AIM headquarters and were shot dead. This incident resulted in the conviction of one AIM member, Leonard Peltier; as of 2006, Peltier is serving two consecutive life sentences for the deaths of the federal agents. Many human rights groups have criticized the investigation and trial that resulted in Peltier's conviction and are attempting to secure a retrial or parole. Amnesty International has initiated a petition for clemency seeking to release Peltier through a presidential pardon.

The American Indian Movement continues to play an active role in protecting the rights of Indians and serves as a watchdog monitoring negative media portrayals of American Indians.

CRITICAL OVERVIEW

Critical response to the initial publication of *Bury My Heart at Wounded Knee* was overwhelmingly positive. This may be at least partly explained by the book's revelatory qualities: it presented information that was both little known and contradictory to the general public's ideas about the West. In a review from *The Washington Post* quoted on the back cover of the thirtieth anniversary edition, William McPherson calls the book both "shattering" and "appalling." In "Savages," Helen McNeil, writing for *New Statesman*, describes it as "deliberately revisionist," suggesting that Brown's goal is to force readers to challenge their own notions about Old West history. McNeil also notes that the book is "amazingly myth-free" and avoids stereotypes in its depiction of well-known Indians such as Crazy Horse and Geronimo.

Brown has also been acknowledged for the extensive documentation used to support his portrayal of events, as well as his use of a novelistic narrative style to engage the reader. McNeil describes the book as a "scholarly and passionate chronicle," and Douglas Martin, in an obituary for the author in the *New York Times* titled "Dee Brown, 94, Author who Revised Image of West," notes that the book is characterized by "meticulous research and masterly storytelling."

The most common criticisms of *Bury My Heart at Wounded Knee* have little to do with the book's literary or historical merits, but instead focus on its subject matter. As McNeil notes in *New Statesman*, "Brown's panorama is almost too broad and uniformly tragic." An obituary for the author in *The Economist* notes the book's success despite the fact that it "is not what publishers call a page-turner." McNeil also notes that Brown's perspective on the subject might seem presumptuous to some, considering the fact that he is white, but she points out that "a history of slavery written by a white 'from the Negro viewpoint' would hardly be so well received."

Bury My Heart at Wounded Knee has continued to enjoy strong sales, as evidenced by the release of a thirtieth anniversary edition of the book that remains in print as of 2006. It is considered by many to be the most comprehensive survey of nineteenth-century relations between Native Americans and whites ever written and a compelling introductory book for readers who want to learn about different Native American tribes and their cultures.

MEDIA ADAPTATIONS

An audio recording of *Bury My Heart at Wounded Knee* was released on audio cassette in 1992 by Books on Tape. It is currently unavailable.

CRITICISM

Donald Fixico

In the following excerpt, Fixico examines the impact of Bury my Heart at Wounded Knee *on Native American studies and the depiction of Native Americans in literature.*

In 1971 Dee Brown wrote *Bury My Heart at Wounded Knee*—a book that stunned America, persuading a generation to listen to the voice of Native Americans. Society learned about the Indian as a victim in the American West.

The full impact involved the emergence of an academic Indian voice in the following years. Native Americans had always expressed their concerns and opinions about issues ranging from legal status, to living conditions, to past mistreatment at the hands of the United States government. But the Indian voice was not widely heard, at least by the dominant society, until the 1960s during the Civil Rights protests and the concurrent rise of American Indian activism. During the late 1960s and at the start of the next decade, *Bury My Heart at Wounded Knee* opened the door for the Native American voice and launched a generation of American Indian studies in academia.

While many enthralled readers turned the pages of *Bury My Heart*, their consciences acknowledged this mistreatment of the American Indian. Guilt seized them. Scholars, however, remained doubtful about Brown's work. The late historian Wilcomb Washburn noted:

> While Brown's work, from the scholarly point of view, leaves something to be desired, its impact has been phenomenal in raising the consciousness of white Americans about the past history of Indians and whites in America.

Bury My Heart awakened scholars and writers, and especially Native Americans. Native scholars began writing about the feelings of Indian people and about their opinions. Indians felt the frustration of urban alienation and the influence of Red Power activists, and they began to put pen to paper.

In addition to Dee Brown's work, two other important books about Indians appeared during these years—Vine Deloria, Jr.'s *Custer Died for Your Sins: An Indian Manifesto* (1968) and N. Scott Momaday's *House Made of Dawn* (1966). The latter won the Pulitzer Prize, the only work written by a Native American to be recognized.

A part of this scholarly current to study American Indians derived especially from the political movements of Black Power, Brown Power, and Red Power. Civil Rights for minorities and equal rights for women expressed during political protests and activism caused society and institutions of higher learning to reconsider the status and past written histories of ethnic groups and women. Thus, the 1960s represented pivotal changes in American society, as people contemplated their own lives and the values of the mainstream society and the dominant culture that had stressed the importance of education, economics, religion, and individualism.

Until the 1960s, mainstream society had refused to listen to, or to learn from, Native Americans. Naturally, this provoked the title of Vine Deloria, Jr.'s book, *We Talk: You Listen: New Tribes, New Turf*. From an Indian point of view, Deloria predicted in 1972:

> American society is unconsciously going Indian. Moods, attitudes, and values are changing. People are becoming more aware of their isolation even while they continue to worship the rugged individualist who needs no one. The self-sufficient man is casting about for a community to call his own. The glittering generalities and mythologies of American society no longer satisfy the need and desire to belong.

On the heels of *We Talk: You Listen* came Deloria's *God Is Red* (1974), in which he pointed out that Native Americans identify with place rather than time as do white men, and that Indians galvanize toward group identity rather than individuality. Undoubtedly, Americans were looking for security in various ways and forms, even looking to Native Americans because of their traditional values of communalism and environmental relationship with the earth. As a result of the self-examining society

of the 1960s, people began to ask questions about their inner selves, wondering who they were, and they researched their roots. They needed something with which to identify, and to bring balance to their lives. Many looked toward history for answers, as the rugged individualist American began to break down.

Timing proved to be germane to the powerful influence of *Bury My Heart at Wounded Knee*. It was the link to the past, and a model by which people could re-examine that past. Although the revelation of America's mistreatment of Native Americans was shocking, it was not unique; 90 years earlier, Helen Hunt Jackson's, *A Century of Dishonor* had been published—an exposé that had alerted the public to the plight of the American Indian. However, it was as a result of Dee Brown's book in 1971 that journalists, writers, and scholars began to offer new ideas and theories, and they introduced new ways to look at their subjects in a broader context with open minds.

Until the 1960s, the dominant society had maintained strict control over learning, forcing Western linear teaching into the minds of Indian students at boarding schools and missionary schools, while public schools berated the ways of Native Americans and presented them as inferior to white ways. The Native American perspective was ignored until the unleashing in the 1960s.

The emotions that *Bury My Heart at Wounded Knee* brought forth in readers made for a precedent-setting work. Dee Brown described the feelings and emotions of Native Americans in such a way as no historians had successfully done—he humanized them.

And as *Bury My Heart at Wounded Knee* was appearing in January 1971, other interests were developing simultaneously in Indian activism and Native American militancy. Indian activists protested that colleges and universities offered very little about American Indians—or incorrect information—in their college courses. Non-Indians, too, began to embrace the opportunity to study Native Americans to see the courses they had to offer. This interest in Indian curriculum was not new, but was rather a renaissance of Native American issues, which led to a genre of literature with increasing demands. Writings and scholarship was changing, and new sources and inspiration were pursued.

Because of the emergence of Native American studies programs, the momentum carried throughout the 1970s. Even history as an academic discipline began to re-examine its basic approach. In an article entitled "American Historians and the Idea of National Character: Some Problems and Prospects," David Stannard wrote about the American search for "National Character" as a means for writing history, and that historians were looking toward the behavioral sciences in their analyses. Yet, although new ideas about writing history entered the discipline, the old habit of disregarding Native Americans and other minorities still prevailed.

In the early 1970s, the discipline as practiced by mainstream historians refused to make Native Americans a true part of American history. In 1970, Jeanette Henry reprimanded the history profession and American society for denying Native Americans a proper place in the written history of this country:

> Every dominant political class in any society attempts to control the ideology of the people most particularly though the learning process in the schools: It is not to be wondered at that "this" American society does the same. The school boards and curriculum commissions which control the adoption and purchase of textbooks usually adopt books to support the dominant political class. So too do the professors in universities, [*and*] departments of various disciplines.

In the 1970s, people learned that American Indians have always lived in their own way, in spite of federal policies designed to force them to assimilate into the dominant society. The current 547 federally recognized Native American tribes and other Indian communities exist according to their particular identity and heritage; and this need for freedom of expression involves culture, political concerns, religion, and intellectualism. Although American Indians have sought self-determination since the 1960s, a dominant control of the media, including textbook companies, the film industry, and a majority of publications, suppressed the advancement of Indian people and their communities throughout Indian country.

A "natural sovereignty" for Indian people has meant that all native communities possessed a heritage of freedom. A native identity is based on desired segregation from other peoples and their natural right to pursue their own way of life. This is done on reservations throughout Indian country and in urban Indian areas in most major cities where Native Americans survived the relocation program of the 1950s and 1960s. Currently, more than two-thirds of the total Indian population of just over two million live in urban areas; thus Indian country consists of reservations and urban Indian communities.

A history of struggle is common to all nations, and American Indian tribal nations have certainly had this experience. Their struggle has been one against European imperialism and the United States. The invasion of these foreign nations has defeated and suppressed the Native American, and, in some cases, annihilated Indian people.

Euroamerican colonization has a history of going beyond building homesteads and clearing the land for crops; this colonization experience has been one of deliberate destruction of Native Americans and their culture. Attempts at co-existence did not work out, and the Indian nations fell before the Euroamerican colonization after patriotic resistance in every region of the country.

Aside from attempts of genocide, the survival of Native Americans, even against overwhelming odds, compelled the United States to assimilate Indian people into the ideological "melting pot" of white values. Simultaneously, in order to accomplish this assimilation or desegregation, the United States government and its military sought to suppress the native intellectualism of Indian people. With biased scientific evidence in the late 1800s, and in an attempt to justify the American experience with Frederick Jackson Turner's "frontier thesis," America sought to subordinate Native Americans. An insecure American culture believed it necessary to deem Native American knowledge and native intellectualism to be inferior. Undoubtedly, this was intellectual racism on the part of America, which has not been fully addressed.

American Indian intellectualism has always existed, but it has not always been acknowledged. Unfortunately, the most brilliant Indian individuals were called to lead their people in war against the United States—those such as Tecumseh, Sitting Bull, and Chief Joseph in the 19th century. In post-modern America, Indian intellectualism should be allowed to be expressed; however, conservative academic attitudes have suppressed or ignored the opportunity for Native American thoughts and ideas. Should not American Indian intellectuals have the same right as others to offer their ideas, philosophies, and theories? Should not American Indian people have the same opportunities to obtain a college education and have the same opportunities to succeed as other Americans? Many years ago, before the first Native American Studies Program, the Lakota sage Luther Standing Bear challenged white society: "Why not a school of Indian thought, built on the Indian pattern and conducted by Indian instructors?"

The late 1960s and early 1970s represented a drastic change in the study of Native Americans, beginning with listening to the Indian voice of *Bury My Heart at Wounded Knee*—a voice that was varied, coming as it did from a myriad of Indian people who were outraged at the federal government, angry at the dominant society, and frustrated with their own people, or themselves. Dee Brown's work enabled this voice to be heard and gave it a sense of direction.

Source: Donald Fixico, "*Bury My Heart at Wounded Knee* and the Indian Voice in Native Studies," in *Journal of the West*, Vol. 39, No. 1, January 2000, pp. 7–9, 10, 11, 12, 14.

SOURCES

Brown, Dee, *Bury My Heart at Wounded Knee: An Indian History of the American West*, Owl Books, 2001, originally published in 1971.

"Dee Brown," in *The Economist*, December 21, 2002, Vol. 365, No. 8304.

Martin, Douglas, "Dee Brown, 94, Author who Revised Image of West," in *New York Times*, December 14, 2002, p. B18.

McNeil, Helen, "Savages," in *New Statesman*, October 1, 1971, Vol. 82, No. 2115, pp. 444–45.

Meyers, Jason, "No Idle Past: Uses of History in the 1830 Indian Removal Debates," in *The Historian*, Fall 2000, Vol. 63, No. 1, p. 53.

Ceremony

LESLIE MARMON SILKO

1977

Leslie Marmon Silko's novel *Ceremony* (1977) is a literary landmark. One of the first contemporary female Native American novelists, Silko was at the forefront of the explosion of Native American literature that took place in the 1970s and 1980s. *Ceremony* deals with the struggles of Indian men returning from World War II, where for a time they were considered "Americans" rather than "Indians." Back in the peacetime United States, however, they once again face prejudice and exclusion from white society. Tayo, the main character, is a Laguna Pueblo Indian of mixed ancestry. He returns home from the Pacific battlefields, but the cousin he vowed to protect during the war does not. Tayo had cursed the endless rain, which he blamed for his cousin's death during their forced march to the Japanese prisoner of war camp. He returns home a broken man, only to find that his curse was all too effective: rain not only disappeared from the island of his captivity, but a severe drought has come to the land of the Laguna Pueblo people. Awash in grief and guilt, Tayo must grapple with questions of identity and ethnicity, both in and out of the Pueblo tribe.

Tayo's quest for healing and identity through various ceremonies is the thrust of the novel. Discussing her reasons for writing *Ceremony* with Thomas Irmer of the online literary magazine *Alt-X*, Silko says that the novel is the story about how human beings can "get out of balance and out of harmony with our natural

surroundings and ... with one another." When this happens, she says, "it is quite difficult and painful but necessary to make a kind of ceremony to find our way back." Tayo's participation in such a ceremony not only helps him restore the rain to his homeland, but it also helps him restore his place in his family and his identity as a Laguna Indian.

As the son of a Laguna mother and white father, Tayo faces many kinds of prejudices. Fellow Indians shun him for being the product of his mother's liaison with a white man, calling him a "half-breed." His closest family members treat him differently because of his lighter eyes and skin. Out in the white world, unless he wears the uniform of the U.S. Marines, he is rejected because he is an Indian. Because of his mixed heritage, he is not fully at home in the Indian world or the white one. He embraces the power he gets from the military, but he can not bring himself to kill any Japanese soldiers because he sees his family in their faces.

The novel also explores the issue of Indian land seized by whites for profit. Throughout the story, characters discuss the disposition of Indian land. Areas around Gallup and Albuquerque, New Mexico, that had formerly belonged to Native Americans have been taken by white people and urbanized, changing the landscape almost beyond recognition. The open-pit uranium mines poison the water and air all over Pueblo lands. White ranchers and farmers put up miles of fencing to cordon off land that used to belong to the Lagunas. White people have changed even the names of places. The novel details the ongoing effect of white domination over Indians and how the interplay between whites and Indians has made both the land and people spiritually sick.

Because stories are important to the survival and well-being of Indian culture, the book itself becomes representative of the healing ceremony. By breaking the novel into irregular chunks of poetry and prose, Silko challenges the reader to accept a new kind of hybrid narrative, one that bridges the traditional storytelling form of the poem with the more western prose form. Moreover, by linking the poem that begins the novel to the poem at the end, the entire text can be seen as having a circular structure, which Silko says mirrors Native American concepts of time. The opening poem tells of the importance

> SEE THESE DUMB INDIANS THOUGHT THESE GOOD TIMES WOULD LAST…. THEY WERE AMERICA THE BEAUTIFUL TOO, THIS WAS THE LAND OF THE FREE JUST LIKE TEACHERS SAID IN SCHOOL…. [THEN THE] WAR WAS OVER, THE UNIFORM WAS GONE. ALL OF A SUDDEN, THAT MAN AT THE STORE WAITS ON YOU LAST, MAKES YOU WAIT UNTIL ALL OF THE WHITE PEOPLE BOUGHT WHAT THEY WANTED. AND THE WHITE LADY AT THE BUS DEPOT, SHE'S REAL CAREFUL NOW NOT TO TOUCH YOUR HAND WHEN SHE COUNTS OUT YOUR CHANGE. YOU WATCH IT SLIDE ACROSS THE COUNTER AT YOU, AND YOU KNOW."

of storytelling to Native Americans and its ability to heal and empower:

> I will tell you something about stories,
> [he said]
> They aren't just for entertainment.
> Don't be fooled.... You don't have anything
> if you don't have the stories.

PLOT SUMMARY

Ceremony opens with a poem about importance of stories to the Indians. The male speaker in the poem says that stories "are all we have, you see, / all we have to fight off / illness and death." A female speaker responds that the only way she knows to cure an illness is through a ceremony.

Tayo is tossing and turning in bed, watching the morning light come in through a small window. He is haunted by his war experience and thinks about the Japanese soldiers he saw in combat that reminded him of his uncle, his mother's brother Josiah. Traumatized and shaken by his time in the Philippines as a prisoner of war, he was treated for "battle fatigue" at a veterans' hospital in Los Angeles. He has returned home to the Laguna Pueblo but is far from feeling whole. The Japanese in the Philippines had captured him and his cousin Rocky. Rocky was badly hurt and was carried

BIOGRAPHY

LESLIE MARMON SILKO

Leslie Marmon Silko was born in Albuquerque, New Mexico, on March 5, 1948, to Virginia and Lee Howard Marmon. Her father managed the Marmon Trading Post in Laguna Pueblo, about fifty miles west of Albuquerque. Silko is of mixed ancestry: Mexican, Laguna Pueblo Indian, and white. She attended Indian school in the pueblo (permanent settlement of the Pueblo people) and later went to school in Albuquerque. She graduated magna cum laude from the University of New Mexico in 1969.

Her first published work was the short story "Tony's Story" (1969), and her first book was a collection of poems called *Laguna Women Poems* (1974). *Ceremony*, her first novel, was published in 1977. The novels *Storyteller* (1981), *Almanac of the Dead* (1991), and *Gardens in the Dunes* (1999) followed. She has published collections of essays, letters, and two histories, in addition to her poetry and fiction. In 1981, she was named a MacArthur Fellow for her continued creative work—an honor bestowed upon other literary luminaries such as Thomas Pynchon and Sandra Cisneros.

Silko has lived in New Mexico and Alaska, and as of 2006, resides in Arizona with her husband and two children.

on the difficult, muddy march to the prison camp during the monsoon. A Japanese soldier noticed the hindrance to their progress and killed the wounded man. Tayo cursed the rain for contributing to Rocky's death. At home, he discovers the land has been transformed by a drought. He immediately feels responsible, as if he "prayed the rain away." Where there once had been fertile grazing land, there is now desert. Likewise, where there once had been an intact family, Rocky is gone, Josiah is dead, and Tayo is a broken man.

Tayo thinks about his time in the hospital after the war, when he felt "invisible" and broke into tears at the mere thought of Rocky. At the train station in Los Angeles on his way back to the Laguna Pueblo, Tayo fainted. A Japanese family called for help, and Tayo wondered why they were not in internment camps as they were during the war. The man who helped him explained that times have changed. When Tayo looked at the little Japanese boy, he saw Rocky's face and wondered if people have the ability to move backward and forward in time.

Harley, one of Tayo's friends who also fought in the war, comes to visit. Tayo is amazed to find that "it [doesn't] seem as if the war [has] changed Harley" at all, as he is still fun loving and full of laughter. Harley convinces Tayo to saddle up one of his uncle's old burros and come with him to a bar in the nearby town. Harley makes a reference to the time that Tayo almost killed their friend Emo when they had just returned from the war. The two set off on their donkeys, and Tayo thinks about how his family wishes he had died instead of Rocky. When he had first returned, his grandmother suggested taking him to an Indian doctor because the "white doctors haven't helped [him] at all." Auntie protested, worried what the others would think about taking someone who is "not a full blood" to see an Indian doctor. Grandmother won, and brought Ku'oosh to treat Tayo. The Indian doctor told him that some things are no longer curable since the white man came, and he was "afraid of what will happen to all of us if you and the others don't get well." Tayo drank the tea that Ku'oosh left for him, which stemmed his frequent vomiting and helped him sleep.

Several weeks before Harley's current visit, they had gone to a nearby bar with fellow Laguna veterans Emo, Leroy, and Pinkie. As they drank, they exchanged war stories about how white women did not ignore them while they were in uniform and about the freedoms they experienced as soldiers. Tayo pointed out that they were back to being discriminated against now that their uniforms were gone. He saw that his friends were only interested in reliving the good times and bringing back "that feeling they belonged to America the way they felt during the war."

As Tayo sways on the donkey behind Harley, his mind goes back to that moment

Navajo Code Talkers in the field Corbis

when a Japanese soldier crushed Rocky's head with the butt of his rifle. The guilt and pain from seeing Rocky die haunted Tayo's return from the war. Rocky was the talented athlete and favored one in the family, the one who was likely to succeed in the white man's world. He believed in book learning and in his own individual potential. Tayo, on the other hand, was always more connected to Indian ways, with little desire to succeed outside of his family and home.

Harley and Tayo stop to rest shaded from the hot sun. Tayo ventures over to a spring that he used to visit with Josiah, where Josiah told Tayo that the "earth keeps us going." Tayo immerses himself in the cool water, thinking about his connection to the earth. After their rest, Harley and Tayo tie the burros to a windmill near the road and hitchhike to the bar. As he drinks, Tayo thinks back to the time when Rocky killed a deer on a hunt. While Tayo followed traditional practices of covering the

animal's head while it was skinned, Rocky laughed at him. Tayo knew that Rocky "deliberately avoided the old-time ways" in preparation for a life off the reservation.

Harley brings Tayo out of his memories by giving him another beer. Tayo jokingly tells him that he will not stab him with a broken bottle like he did to Emo on the night when all of the veterans were out drinking. Harley tells him they were worried about him that night and asserts that Tayo was not crazy, just drunk. Tayo thinks, "They all had explanations; the police, the doctors at the psychiatric ward, even Auntie and old Grandma; they blamed liquor and they blamed the war."

On the night of the fight when the veterans were all drinking together, Emo was talking about how the white men had taken everything from the Indians and left them with nothing. Tayo was sitting silently, and Emo baited him, saying, "He thinks he's something all right. Because he's part white. Don't you, half-breed?" Tayo knew that Emo hated him because he was part white and tried to ignore him. Emo continued to tell stories about his experiences with white women as a soldier. As he talked, he tossed a tobacco pouch up and down, which rattled. It was full of teeth he had taken from Japanese soldiers as souvenirs. Tayo reached the boiling point, screaming "Killer!" at Emo and lunging at him with a broken beer bottle. He stabbed Emo in the stomach.

Before the war, Rocky and Tayo had talked with an Army recruiter, who told them, "Anyone can fight for America ... even you boys." Rocky had been interested in signing up and asked the recruiter if he and his "brother" could fight together. Tayo was touched because it was the first time Rocky had ever referred to him as his brother, even though they had been raised together since they were four years old. Auntie, his mother's sister, had always treated Tayo differently and made sure he knew that she did not love him as much as her own son. Rocky's decision to enlist was not well received by his family, especially his mother, so Tayo told Auntie that he would bring Rocky back from the war safe.

After the boys' decision to enlist, Josiah decided to invest in cattle, despite the difficulty of keeping animals in near-desert conditions. They did not buy any of the more popular breeds of cattle, opting instead for a tougher Mexican breed, one they hoped would be able to survive in a land where there is very little grass and almost no water. When Tayo, Rocky, Josiah, and Auntie's husband Robert released the cattle to graze, the animals fled, heading south and disappeared into the hills. The men caught them and branded them but realized that fences would not hold them. Josiah had been convinced to buy the cows by his lover who lived above Lalo's bar. The woman, called the Night Swan, was Mexican and therefore an outcast in the Indian community. Auntie was embarrassed that Josiah was seeing her, so he tried to keep it a secret. When rains kept Josiah away, he asked Tayo to tell her he would not be coming. While there, Tayo and the Night Swan made love, drawn to each other because of their outsider status and light-colored eyes. She told him that people always blame those who look different so "they don't have to think about what has happened inside themselves."

After his night out with Harley, Tayo tells Robert that he is feeling better and would like to help out around the farm. He acknowledges to himself, however, that "Maybe there would always be those shadows over his shoulder and out of the corner of each eye .... Maybe there was nothing anyone could do for him." Robert tells him that everyone thinks he better get help soon, and Tayo agrees to do whatever is called for. He and Robert travel to Gallup, where Tayo recalls his early childhood living in a gully with his mother in a cardboard shelter. The gully was where all of the Indians in Gallup who had no money lived: "Reservation people were the first ones to get laid off because white people in Gallup already knew they wouldn't ask any questions or get angry; they just walked away." Tayo lived among them until his mother dropped him off to stay with her family. He never saw her alive again.

Robert takes Tayo to Old Betonie's place (called a hogan) located near the gully shantytown. Betonie is another healer, and he tells Tayo that he chooses to live where he does because "this hogan was here first. Built long before the white people ever came. It is that town down there which is out of place. Not this old medicine man." Tayo notices that Betonie has light eyes like him, and Betonie reveals that his grandmother was Mexican. Betonie, whose hogan is full of artifacts and evidence of Indian rituals, asks Tayo if anyone has taught him about these things. Tayo decides to trust the old man.

Old Betonie begins the healing process. He tells Tayo stories, some of which Tayo believes and some of which he does not. Tayo, in turn, tells Betonie his story: about the war, about Rocky, and about his guilt over Josiah's death because he was not there to help him retrieve the cattle. When he confesses that he could not kill the Japanese because they looked like him, Betonie tells him, "You saw who they were. Thirty thousand years ago they were not strangers. You saw what the evil had done: you saw the witchery ranging as wide as this world." Tayo begins to see that his "sickness [is] only a part of something larger, and his cure [will] be found in something great and inclusive of everything."

Betonie surprises Tayo by telling him that ceremonies evolve: "[A]fter the white people came, elements in this world began to shift; and it became necessary to create new ceremonies." Betonie explains that the source of Tayo's pain, and the suffering of all Indians, is the witchery that caused Indians to "invent" white people. But blaming white people for problems in the world, Betonie says, is missing the point: "white people are only tools that the witchery manipulates." A long creation myth, in verse, follows Tayo's visit to Betonie. Early the next morning, Tayo, Betonie, and Betonie's helper head into the mountains to perform a ceremony. They paint a traditional scene in the sand, and as Betonie is chanting, he cuts Tayo across the top of the head as part of the beginning of the Scalp Ceremony. As the ceremony proceeds and Tayo moves through each of the five hoops that have been set up, blood runs down his head and neck. He is given tea and told to sleep. In his dreams, he sees the cattle that Josiah had bought and which had run away. Betonie has a vision about stars, a woman, a mountain, and cattle. Tayo realizes his mission: the recovery of his family's cattle. He tries to pay Betonie for the ceremony, but Betonie refuses, telling him that the ceremony is far from over: "This has been going on for a long long time now. It's up to you. Don't let them stop you. Don't let them finish off this world."

Tayo hitchhikes a ride with a trucker, and in San Fidel he stops to buy a candy bar. The red-headed man at the counter refuses to serve Tayo, but Tayo feels as if he is the one who is in control: "He want[s] to laugh at the station man who [does] not even know that his existence and the existence of all white people [has] been conceived by witchery." He decides to walk and makes his way down the road. A truck stops behind him, and he sees Harley hanging out of the window with a bottle of liquor. Harley talks him into getting into the truck with him, their veteran friend Leroy, and a girl named Helen Jean. As they speed down the road, Tayo wishes he were still walking. Leroy tells Tayo that he has bought this new truck with no money down and payments on the first of the month—if they can find him. Harley laughs and adds, "They owed it to us—we traded it for some of the land they stole from us!" Tayo tells him to pull over once they are near Laguna, but they do not let him out. Leroy guns the car down a bumpy road, and Tayo takes a swig from the liquor bottle. He loses himself in the sensation of the bumpy ride and warm liquor and wishes that the truck ride will never stop.

The group stops at the Y bar for more drinks. Tayo notices Helen Jean getting looks from a group of Mexicans, and knows that she will not stick around with Leroy and Harley. When she leaves with one of the Mexicans, Leroy and Harley are too busy drinking to notice. After Helen Jean leaves, a white man kicks Tayo out of the bar after Leroy and Harley have gotten into a fight. Tayo puts them in the truck and drives them away. He thinks about how Indian veterans get drunk and try to "silence their grief with war stories about their courage, defending the land they had already lost."

Several weeks later, Tayo rides his horse up an old path into the mountains. The narrative is interrupted with a lengthy poem about Kaup'a'ta, the Gambler, who stole everything from the Indians, including the rain clouds. He offers Indians a gamble to win fancy things from him, but he killed them when they lose. Kaup'a'ta torments the Indians for three years until the Sun Man learns how to beat him at his own game, and is able to release the rain clouds: "Then he opened the doors of the four rooms / and he called to the storm clouds: / 'My children,' he said / 'I have found you!'"

Tayo comes across a woman at a small farm at the foot of the mountain. She offers to feed him, and as Tayo follows her into the house, he notices the design woven into the blanket she is wearing over her shoulders: "patterns of storm clouds in white and gray; black lightning scattered through brown wind." He looks out the window at the stars and sees the constellation that Betonie had drawn in the sand during his ceremony, which led him to begin his search for the cattle. He and the woman make love, and he leaves to go up the mountain in the morning. As he goes higher up the mountain, he notes that almost all of it has been taken over and fenced by white ranchers or the government. Floyd Lee, a white rancher who employs rangers to patrol the fence, has built a particularly long and sturdy fence at the crest of the mountain. It is on Lee's side of the fence that Tayo spies the cattle in the distance. He thinks about how he hesitates to call the cattle stolen, filled instead with a "crazy desire" to assume that Lee perhaps bought them from the real thief. Tayo catches himself believing the lie that "they had wanted him to learn: only brown-skinned people were thieves; white people didn't steal, because they always had the money to buy whatever they wanted." He realizes that as long as people believed that lie—both white and Indian—there would never be a resolution to the problem.

Under the cover of darkness, Tayo cuts a hole in the fence to go after the cattle, large enough to run them through when he returns. He is afraid of being caught because he thinks "they'd send him back to the crazy house for sure." He sees that he is following many of the Indian traditions that Rocky and his teachers and his doctors had dismissed as useless superstitions and that doing so is crazy. He falls asleep under a tree and wakes to the sound of a mountain lion prowling nearby. Tayo kneels in honor and whispers to the cat, which pauses before moving on. Tayo takes it as a sign and follows the animal's path toward him, which leads him to the cattle. As the sky lightens, he is able to wrangle the cattle through the open hole in the fence, but his horse stumbles and he is injured. When he comes to, two of Lee's patrolmen are watching him. They disagree on what to do with him but abandon him when they find mountain lion tracks and decide to hunt the big cat. Exhausted and hurt, Tayo falls asleep. When he wakes, he stumbles down the mountain as snow falls.

Tayo meets a hunter coming down the mountain. He accompanies the man back to the woman's farm at the foot of the mountain, where the hunter and the woman live together. There, he finds his horse and his cattle in a corral, waiting for him. Tayo tells her he will come back soon with a truck for the cattle.

When Tayo returns with Robert and a truck, he finds the hut abandoned. Looking around the room, Tayo sees an old warrior shield on the wall. When he examines it closer, he sees the constellation that Betonie had told him to watch for. Robert notes that someone has fed and taken good care of the cattle. After a few months, Grandma remarks that Tayo has recovered. Over the winter months, Tayo is haunted by dreams of the woman. During a dream of her, Tayo is awakened by the sound of rain. He believes he will see her again.

In May, Tayo goes to care for the cattle on the family's ranch. Feeling closer to nature, Tayo is reassured that mountains will always be mountains, no matter who thinks they own them. Therefore, the mountain could not be lost to them, even to Rocky and Josiah, as it

was a part of them: "As far as he could see, in all directions, the world was alive." When Tayo looks up, he sees the woman. She is camping at the nearby springs. She tells him to call her Ts'eh and teaches him about the roots and plants she collects, and how she uses them in small ceremonies. They fall in love as they spend the entire summer together.

When Robert comes at the end of the summer, he finds it odd that Tayo is choosing to sleep outside and is acting strangely. He says that some of the people at Laguna think Tayo is ill again. Emo is spreading rumors that Tayo has gone crazy living alone in the desert and is a danger to society. Robert suggests that Tayo come back to Laguna for a while and set everyone straight. Talking with Ts'eh, Tayo starts to realize just how lost he had been in the veteran's hospital in Los Angeles, where "the thick white skin . . . had enclosed him, silencing the sensations of living, the love as well as the grief." He now feels freer and healthier than he ever has. Ts'eh asks him how far he is willing to go to stop the destroyers like Emo and the others. They see a faded and neglected painting of A'moo'ooh, the she-elk, on the side of a cliff and stay all day to honor her. Upset and afraid for him, Ts'eh warns Tayo that Emo has caused white police officers to look for him, thinking he has gone crazy. If Tayo hides himself, they will soon tire of the search, but Emo will not. Ts'eh warns Tayo that Emo will be a difficult and dangerous foe to overcome. She tells him she must go and reminds him to "remember everything."

Tayo travels off the road to avoid being discovered, until he flags down Leroy and Harley, who are driving by. They are drunk, celebrating the anniversary of the day they enlisted in the military. Tayo begins to feel estranged and suspicious, as Leroy and Harley's story of what they have been doing does not match with the direction they have just come. It is more like they have been following him. He decides to hang out with Leroy and Harley for a while so that people will think that he is just "another drunk Indian, that's all." Later, he wakes up sweating, alone in the truck, which is parked somewhere in the desert. As he looks for Leroy and Harley, it is suddenly clear to him that they are no longer his friends and have turned against him. He tries to hotwire the truck but does not know how, so he grabs a screwdriver and starts running.

The final elements of Tayo's ceremony come together as he finds himself in an abandoned uranium mine on the outskirts of town. He realizes that he is only three hundred miles from Trinity Site, where the U.S. government tested the first atomic bomb in the New Mexico desert in 1945. As he wanders into the mine, he feels that the pattern of the ceremony is finally complete: the old stories, war stories, and the white man's stories are merging into "the story that [is] still being told." Tayo realizes that he had never been crazy but had been merely seeing the world without boundaries, distance, or time.

Hearing a car coming near the mine, Tayo takes cover behind some boulders. He recognizes that the car is Emo's. Leroy, Emo, and Pinkie get out of the car and make a fire. Tayo watches them and thinks of them as "destroyers" whose destruction would eventually leave "the people more vulnerable to the lies; the young people would leave, to go towns like Albuquerque and Gallup where bitterness would overwhelm them, and they would lose their hope and finally themselves in drinking." He sees evidence of witchery in their behavior. They pull Harley from the trunk of the car and begin to slowly torture him for his failure to bring Tayo to Emo. Clutching the screwdriver, Tayo prepares to kill Emo. A gust of wind makes the fire flare up and distracts the tormentors from their victim long enough for Tayo to reconsider. He stays behind the boulder, realizing that he too would have been a pawn of the witchery if he killed Emo. He would have been taken away to hospital, just one more Indian that could not cope: "The white people would shake their heads, more proud than sad that it took a white man to survive in their world and that these Indians couldn't seem to make it." Emo and the others put Harley's body into the trunk and drive away.

Exhausted, Tayo makes his way home to Laguna and tells Ku'oosh and the other elders about his ceremony. Overjoyed that he has seen A'moo'ooh, they are sure that their misfortune is over. He learns that Leroy and Pinkie have been killed as well, and Emo has been exiled from Laguna and has gone to California. When Grandma hears of their fate, she says, "It seems like I already heard these stories before . . . only thing is, the names sound different." The novel ends with a poem about how the darkness is dead for now: "Sunrise, / accept this offering, / Sunrise."

THEMES

Race and Identity

Ceremony presents a tale from within a marginalized culture. For centuries, interactions between whites and Native Americans often lead to destruction. Indians have been subject to racism, exile, and even genocide at the hands of white men since they arrived in North America. Ancestral homelands were essentially stolen from the Indians, whom the government removed to specially designated areas known as reservations. Relegated to largely inhospitable land where farming and ranching are difficult, today's Native Americans continue to feel the effects of racism. Many felt treated as equals for the first time when they joined the military to fight in World War II and had a difficult time relinquishing that status after coming home. Like the young Laguna men in *Ceremony*, once the war was over and the uniforms were taken off, they were no longer soldiers and once again invisible to the white culture.

For Tayo, however, with his hazel eyes and lighter skin, things are more complicated. He straddles the line between white and Indian cultures, neither of which fully accepts him. Indians refer to him as a "half-breed," while to white men he is merely an Indian. He has always identified with the traditional Indian way of life, and while most of the young men on the reservation made their plans to leave, Tayo wanted to stay and learn Indian traditions. This racial conflict goes back to his mother. As a student at an Indian school taught by whites, Tayo's mother had learned to be ashamed of the "deplorable ways of the Indian people." She left the reservation, became a prostitute, and gave birth to Tayo, whose father was a white man. This situation was not unusual, and Silko makes the point that "what happened to the girl did not happen to her alone, it happened to all of them." A mixture of racism, oppression, and shame have combined to create an identity crisis among the Laguna Pueblo Indians. Rather than live in an oppressed environment, many of the young Lagunas begin to seek out elements of the white world that are unavailable to Indians on the reservation.

As Tayo begins to search for a way to cure his illness, he discovers it is tied to the land, which had been stolen from the Indians and subsequently abused by the whites. The crux of

General view of the Laguna Pueblo, New Mexico, National Archives and Records Administration

the problem between Indians and white men, as Tayo sees it, is that Indians seem to have forgotten what has been taken from them. After spending an afternoon with Leroy, Harley, and Helen Jean, Tayo is furious at them because "the white things they admired and desired so much—the bright city lights and loud music, the soft sweet food and the cars—all these things had been stolen, torn out of Indian land."

Old Betonie, the medicine man, does not allow Tayo to take the easy way out. He does not let Tayo blame white people exclusively for Indian troubles: "They want us to believe that all evil resides with white people. Then we will look no further to see what is really happening.... But white people are only tools that the witchery manipulates." Tayo learns that this same witchery causes Indians to harm themselves: they begin to believe the lie what whites are always in the right and Indians are always in the wrong. Betonie makes the important point that harmony in the world does not fall cleanly down racial lines, and he tells Tayo, "you don't write off all the white people, just like you don't trust all the Indians."

As his identity and understanding of the world come full circle, Tayo is determined to avoid actions that would lead others to misidentify him. He resists killing Emo because he believes white people will see him as just "a drunk Indian war veteran settling an old feud," and the Indians on the reservation will blame the war, liquor, and the military. No one would understand his proactive decision as a part of a ceremony. His knowledge about the world and himself leads him to find a new identity and a new path in life.

Culture Clash

There are two distinct cultures at work in the Laguna Pueblo, and their clash becomes part of the witchery that is destroying the world. The older generation of Lagunas abide by traditional customs. For example, when Tayo's illness does not lift, old Grandma suggests that they take him to see a medicine man. When the first visit does not appear to work, Robert and Tayo go to see Betonie, who initiates Tayo into a ceremony that he says has been ongoing for many years.

At odds with the traditional aspects of the Laguna Pueblo is the younger generation of men and women who are seeking escape from the restrictions of reservation life. Rocky, Tayo's cousin, looks forward to leaving the reservation, whether to go to college or into the military. As Tayo notes when he and Rocky hunt, kill, and dress a deer, "Rocky deliberately avoid[s] the old-time ways." He stops caring what the elders and other villagers think about him, especially after he enlists: "He was already planning where he would go after high school; he was already talking about the places he would live, and the reservation wasn't one of them." Rocky is like Tayo's fellow veterans in his desire to be away from traditional reservation life and embrace the white world. Harley, Leroy, and Emo spend most of their time after the war at bars and in towns like Gallup and Albuquerque. When they discover that Tayo does not share their desire to get away, they become suspicious. After Tayo has been living on the ranch, sleeping outside, and embracing traditional ways, Emo begins to spread rumors that Tayo thinks he is a Japanese soldier living in a cave. Emo cannot understand why Tayo has chosen to embrace the traditional Laguna culture and its attendant ceremonies and therefore dismisses him as crazy. Emo has no way to know that his life is spared at the mine by Tayo's reverence for these same traditions.

The character of Betonie offers a middle ground between the conflicting cultures at the Laguna Pueblo. He engages in traditional rituals and ceremonies, but acknowledges the need for these ceremonies to change in order to accommodate present realities. With the novel *Ceremony*, Silko herself appears to be searching for a way forward for humanity and for a way to alter the traditional so that it can continue to be relevant in a much-changed world. The book argues for the importance of traditional rituals and identity, but also the importance of changing to move with the times.

Social Class

Serving in the U.S. military during World War II leads Tayo and his friends to expect that they can somehow climb to respectability within white culture. However, when the war ends and they return to civilian life, they lose their status as American soldiers and return to their former status as suspicious and impoverished Indians. This degradation is at the heart of Emo's troubles. He looks back on his time in the Army with pride and cannot bring himself to accept his return to his lower status.

Indians that leave the reservation are treated as second-class citizens by employers and residents of larger towns like Gallup. Surveying the shantytown of Indians north of the city, Tayo notes that Indians are "educated only enough to know they [want] to leave the reservation." Their lack of education and the prevailing racial prejudice toward Indians lock them into a lower-class status. They are given only menial jobs with low salaries and are the first ones to be fired when cuts are needed. With no housing options in town, they are forced to live in cardboard homes in a dry creek bed, where they are rounded up periodically before tourist festivals because they are an eyesore. Poverty and prejudice combine to create a cycle of dependence and despair.

A central part of Tayo's healing ceremony is to seek and return his family's cattle, which have been stolen by a white rancher. At least part of Tayo's recovery is his assertion of economic self-reliance. But this assertion comes with some difficulty. He encounters two white patrolmen, whose job it is to "shoot a coyote or catch a Mexican," who accuse him of stealing their cattle and trespassing on their land. They decide Tayo is too much trouble, however, and let him go, saying: "Yeah, we taught him a lesson . . . . These godd— Indians got to learn whose property this is!" Eventually, Tayo returns home with the cattle and is able to equalize, at least temporarily, the class balance between his family, who are small-time ranchers in the desert, and the powerful and wealthy white ranchers.

HISTORICAL OVERVIEW

Pueblo Indians

Archaeological evidence indicates that people have been in and around the Pueblo area, which spans large portions of New Mexico and Arizona, since about 3000 B.C. and perhaps much longer than that. The indigenous people in this area of North America lived in agrarian communities clustered around adobe dwellings. Each community, called *pueblo*, or town, by the Spanish settlers who arrived in the area in the late 1500s, governed itself and had its own distinct language and culture. The Pueblo peoples had frequently violent encounters with the first

Spanish settlers, most notably in the Pueblo Revolt of 1680, which succeeded in expelling the Spanish from Pueblo land for over a decade. In general, the Pueblo peoples have successfully asserted their national sovereignty within the boundaries of what was first Spanish territory and later the United States.

Modern Pueblo Indians have had a somewhat different relationship with the U.S. government than other tribes, as they are the only American Indians who have continued to occupy much of the same land that their ancestors held when white settlers first arrived. The various Pueblo tribes maintain self-government and tribal sovereignty, as do other American Indian tribes, but their land is not a reservation in the traditional sense because the government did not "reserve" it for them in lieu of their original land. Some historians believe the Pueblos would not have been so lucky if it had not been for the fact that the Spanish controlled the area first and had explicitly granted them land rights. When the United States later acquired the land, it maintained this special designation, though portions of the land were lost in intervening years.

Today, there are more than twenty federally recognized pueblos in existence, including Leslie Marmon Silko's Laguna Pueblo home, fifty miles west of Albuquerque. With a population of just under eight thousand, Laguna is the largest of the pueblos. It contains six major villages: Laguna, Paguate, Encinal, Mesita, Seama, and Paraje. Other prominent pueblos include Taos, Acoma, Zuni, and Hopi.

Native American Soldiers in World War II

Thousands of Native Americans enlisted or were drafted into every branch in the military during World War II. Nearly fifty thousand American Indians saw combat, and many were honored with medals for their performance. According to the U.S. Department of Defense's "Native Americans in World War II," a full 10 percent of the Native American population in America participated in the war. Another forty thousand left the reservations to work in military, industrial, or agricultural positions for the war effort. Many saw the war as an opportunity to prove their loyalty to the United States, just as another marginalized group, the Japanese Americans, did by fighting for their country. Several Indian

nations, including the Apache, Chippewa, and Sioux, declared war directly on Germany.

Native American soldiers fought mainly in the Pacific Theater, but they also saw action in Europe and the Aleutian Islands. On Guadalcanal in 1942, the U.S. Marines began using Navajo as a code language. The Japanese were never able to decipher it, just as the Germans had been unable to break the Choctaw code used during World War I. One of the most decorated units in World War II was the 45th Infantry Division, also known as the "Thunderbirds." Made up of Indians from Arizona, New Mexico, Oklahoma, and Colorado, the Thunderbirds fought for over five hundred days in Europe and were among the units that liberated the concentration camp Dachau. The Thunderbirds received a total of eight Congressional Medals of Honor.

As Silko writes in *Ceremony*, military service provided Indians opportunities and equality that they had not experienced before. Native American soldiers fought alongside and on equal footing with white soldiers. Because of the freedom and acceptance they experienced as soldiers, many chose to remain in white communities after the war. Those who did not, as is evident in *Ceremony*, often struggled with their reduced post-war status.

Though the inclusion of Native Americans in the war effort appeared to be a step toward acceptance, they remained disadvantaged in dealings with the government. According to the U.S. Department of Defense, "The federal government designated some Indian lands and even tribes themselves as essential natural resources, appropriating tribal minerals, lumber, and lands for the war effort."

Uranium and the Pueblo People

The climax of *Ceremony* takes place in an abandoned uranium mine near the Laguna Pueblo. One of the main sources of income for Pueblo Indians during Silko's youth was working in such mines. Various corporations set up uranium mines to fuel atomic weapons that the United States developed during World War II and afterward. This work was not without consequences. In addition to the mineworkers and people who transported uranium, those that breathed the air or drank the water nearby experienced severe health problems due to radiation contamination. Over one thousand uranium mines were dug on Navajo lands, mostly by underpaid Indian labor. One of the largest open-pit mines was at Mount Taylor, a landmark that figures prominently in *Ceremony*: the Jackpile mine, opened by a small corporation named Anaconda (later to be acquired by Atlantic Richfield). Acoma and Laguna Pueblos sit in the shadow of Mount Taylor, and the Pueblo people consider it sacred. Although never proven, locals blamed their many deaths from cancer and other illnesses on these mines. While Silko wrote *Ceremony*, the uranium mine was still operating and people were still becoming sick. The community rose up in protest by 1977, the year of the novel's publication, and by 1982, the mine had closed and become the subject of a joint federal-tribal land restoration project.

CRITICAL OVERVIEW

In their introduction to *Leslie Marmon Silko: A Collection of Critical Essays*, Louise Barnett and James Thorson write that the publication of *Ceremony* in 1977 "established Leslie Marmon Silko as a notable new talent in contemporary American literature." Indeed, the critical reception for Silko's novel *Ceremony* has been broadly positive since the book was published. Janet Wiehe writes in *Library Journal* that Silko "writes with insight and great sympathy for her characters." Writing in *American Indian Quarterly*, Peter G. Beidler calls *Ceremony* "a magnificent novel.... It conveys a loving respect for the problems faced by American Indians and a mature and sensitive feeling for some solutions to those problems."

By 1990, critics had accepted *Ceremony* as one of the few central texts in Native American literature, and it was beginning to be taught in American literature courses around the country. Paula Gunn Allen recognized the problems facing teachers of Silko's difficult text and published a kind of how-to guide titled "Special Problems in Teaching Leslie Marmon Silko's *Ceremony*" in *American Indian Quarterly*. By the mid-1990s, study of *Ceremony* had entered the mainstream American literary establishment. Articles on the novel appeared in a variety of scholarly publications including *World Literature Today*, *Critique*, and *Melus*, where critics used the novel to explore ideas of gender,

Cows grazing in a field © *by Alvis Uptis. Reproduced by permission*

property, nation, healing, mental illness, environmentalism, class, authorship, and the craft of writing, among other subjects.

The height of critical attention to *Ceremony* has come since 1999. In that year, a collection titled *Leslie Marmon Silko: A Collection of Critical Essays* was published by The University of New Mexico Press. In his preface, Robert Franklin Gish, a long-time advocate for Native American Literature, states,

> *Ceremony* was everything that a book could be, everything that literature was supposed to be, the realization of all the adages and quips, all the epigrams and sayings that I had heard and had quoted to students.

This volume, while indispensable for anyone who wishes to study Silko's career, does not devote much space to *Ceremony*. Instead, it focuses on her later works, which have received less critical attention.

A new critical edition of the novel appeared in 2002. *Leslie Marmon Silko's* Ceremony: *A Casebook* was published as part of the Casebooks in Criticism series by Oxford University Press. The collection includes essays by noted scholars such as Beidler, Allen, and Catherine Rainwater

MEDIA ADAPTATIONS

An unabridged audio version of *Ceremony* was released on audiocassette by Audio Editions in 2000. It is narrated by Adam Henderson.

on topics ranging from the novel's structural issues to the significance of animals. Scholarly attention regarding *Ceremony* remains intense and consistent. In 2004, another book useful for students investigating Silko's novel was published: *Understanding* Ceremony: *A Student Casebook to Issues, Sources, and Historical Documents*, by Lynn Domina. The book contains essays that discuss themes and contexts of the novel.

CRITICISM

Thomas E. Benediktsson

In the following excerpt, Benediktsson discusses Silko's Ceremony *as a work that violates, or "ruptures," expectations of realism that a reader might have. Silko tells Tayo's story with a circular, non-linear structure that transcends the bounds of straight realism.*

In this essay I would like to examine some "ruptures" in the realism of two postcolonial novels, each of which attempts to find alternatives to the Western rationalism, pragmatism, and linearity that support realism's codes. In the first, Leslie Silko's *Ceremony*, Tayo, half white and half Pueblo Indian, is a young World War II veteran who, as a prisoner of war, cursed the jungle monsoon that he felt was causing his stepbrother's death. Having returned to the reservation after a time in a veteran's hospital, Tayo is convinced that his curse caused the drought that is now afflicting his reservation. Suffering from this guilt and from other forms of distress, Tayo learns that his illness is part of a larger pattern of evil—the "witchery" brought about by those who seek

the world's destruction. Tayo is healed by a series of Pueblo and Navaho purification ceremonies and by a personal ceremony he performs for himself. During his quest he has an encounter with a mysterious young woman named Ts'eh, later identified as Spider Woman, a supernatural figure from Pueblo legend.

From the beginning of *Ceremony*, Silko introduces textual elements that disrupt the linearity of her narrative. By far the greater part of the novel is told from the point of view of Tayo. At first, the narrative moves freely and confusingly, juxtaposing incidents in Tayo's life which are separated widely in time:

> ... he got no rest as long as the memories were tangled with the present, tangled up like colored threads from old Grandma's wicker sewing basket when he was a child ... He could feel it inside his skull—the tension of little threads being pulled and how it was with tangled things, things tied together, and as he tried to pull them apart and rewind them into their places, they snagged and tangled even more.

The reader's task to "untangle" these threads of experience is rather difficult in the opening fifty page of the novel. Before long, however, through iteration a temporal pattern emerges, and the reader can reconstruct the linear narrative of Tayo's life. What seems at first to be ruptures in realism are actually representations of the flow of consciousness of a disturbed man. As Tayo begins to heal, the narrative attains more linearity until the last eighty pages are told in straightforward chronological order. Thus realism, understood as the mimetic representation of linear experience, is not threatened.

A second disruptive element, however, is not so easily reconciled. From the beginning the "realistic" prose narrative—the novel—is interrupted by free-verse texts of Pueblo myths and stories. Thematically and tropologically, the stories bear complex intertextual relations to the novel, which by the end is understood as a part of a much greater web of meaning, encompassing all Pueblo cultural experience. Edith Swan has discussed the intricate structural relationships between Silko's novel and Pueblo and Navaho ceremonies.

The text of the novel enfolds and incorporates the texts of the stories. By the end, however, in a kind of chiasmus, the stories have incorporated the novel. The stories inscribe and circumscribe Tayo's own story, until the ceremonies by which he is healed serve a kind of hermeneutic: he can read his own life as a Pueblo story. Just as the limited claims of realism have become subsumed into the much greater claims of Pueblo storytelling tradition, Silko's role as novelist has been subsumed into the role of the Pueblo story teller—naming the world, defending the people, helping fight off illness and death. In the process, the linear flow of meaning that dominates mimetic representation has been supplanted by a kind of "spider web" of meaning in which the interrelationships among the stories revise time and space, just as Thought Woman tells her stories in a timeless realm.

The key moment in *Ceremony* that proclaims the storyteller's victory the moment when the world of Pueblo myth enters the text of the novel itself, not as an intertextual referent but as a third and irrevocable disruption of realism. In his relationship with Ts'eh, Tayo has an encounter with divinity. Ts'eh's love restores him to health, and she warns him of the plot against his life by the veteran Emo, agent of the witchery that now no longer seems merely figurative. The last stage of Tayo's ceremony occurs when, the site of the uranium mine that supplied the ore for the Manhattan Protect, he successfully resists the urge to kill Emo. In his victory over the witchery, Tayo has been healed with the help of incarnate divinity. In the process the realist novel, itself a manifestation of the hegemony of the white world over the Pueblo and therefore a symptom of the malaise from which Tayo has suffered, has been transformed.

Source: Thomas E. Benediktsson, "The Reawakening of the Gods: Realism and the Supernatural in Silko and Humle," in *Critique: Studies in Contemporary Fiction*, Vol. 33, No. 2, Winter 1992, pp. 121–126.

Dennis Cutchins

In the following excerpt, Cutchins reads Silko's Ceremony *as a "nativist restructuring" of Indian history. As such, it offers Tayo, Laguna Pueblos, and all readers of the novel the chance to reinterpret history in a way that could lead to the revitalization of Native American culture.*

Leslie Marmon Silko's (mixed-blood Laguna Pueblo) *Ceremony* is a powerful novel that tells the story of Tayo, a mixed-blood Pueblo war veteran who returns to Laguna mentally crippled by his wartime experiences. As Tayo struggles to

overcome the alienation his military service has created, he must also face the shame of his own mixed heritage. His suffering eventually leads him off the pueblo to a Navajo healer, Betonie, who helps Tayo create a new historical paradigm based on Navajo and Laguna mythology. Betonie's fictional re-vision of history is, perhaps, the novel's most important accomplishment. Through Betonie, Silko creates an alternative understanding of history that empowers both the Native American characters in the novel and Native American readers of the novel. *Ceremony* becomes, at least potentially, a powerful tool for the revitalization of culture.

What I will term Silko's nativistic restructuring of history offers Tayo the chance to enter and revitalize Laguna culture, and simultaneously to interpret and reject mainstream white culture. It also provides Silko and her readers the means to do the same thing outside the novel. Scholarship that ignores *Ceremony*'s historical impact, or that limits interpretation to an intracultural reading of the novel, strictly as a Laguna Pueblo artifact, is unlikely to recognize the powerful cultural and political tool Silko has offered to all Native Americans. The nativistic reading of Ceremony proposed here, though problematic in some ways, does situate the novel historically and politically and highlights aspects of the work that are obscured when it is read as an intracultural or ahistorical document.

Ceremony, popular in college classrooms, has received extensive critical treatment. Much of the criticism has focused on its mythic, ahistorical qualities. Paula Gunn Allen's (Laguna Pueblo/Sioux) comments on the novel in *A Literary History of the American West* are somewhat typical in suggesting that *Ceremony*, along with other Native American novels, is "achronistic," in that it functions "without regard to chronology." This is true, in the strict sense that Silko's narrative is not chronologically ordered. Allen, however, suggests a broader meaning for this term when she argues that *Ceremony* is ritually structured, and that its "internal rules of order have more to do with the interaction of thoughts, spirits, arcane forces and tradition than with external elements such as personality, politics or history." Certainly Silko is concerned with spirits, arcane forces, and tradition, but she is also deeply concerned with politics and history, and these aspects of the novel should not be neglected by scholars.

James Ruppert's analysis of *Ceremony*, and particularly his understanding of the role Betonie plays in the novel, illustrate the problems inherent in an ahistorical or achronistic reading of this text. In his 1995 *Mediation in Contemporary Native American Fiction* he approaches *Ceremony* as a novel of "mediation," and argues, in short, that it serves as a kind of space between cultures where both white and Native American readers can begin to understand and cope with cultural differences. He suggests, further, that it represents a kind of "Bakhtinian dialogism" since it includes aspects of mainstream Western, Laguna, and Navajo cultures. Ruppert's use of dialogism, however, indicates a real weakness in his approach to this particular novel. In "Discourse in the Novel," only a few pages from passages Ruppert quotes in support of his theory, Bakhtin explains how novels are radically different from other, earlier, literary forms. They establish "the fundamental liberation of cultural-semantic and emotional intentions from the hegemony of a single and unitary language, and consequently the simultaneous loss of a feeling for language as myth, that is, as an absolute form of thought." Novels, at least as far as Bakhtin is concerned, should include a multiplicity of voices or "languages," as *Ceremony* does, but they should also avoid the tendency to totalize or mythologize. For Bakhtin, mythological language is antithetical to the idea of a novel since it tends to destroy dialog. Simply put, how can one argue with a myth?

In *Ceremony*, on the other hand, Silko is openly mythic in both her approach and her intention. The novel incorporates mythic elements as part of the storyline, but it also begins to serve as a new myth illustrating the way mixed-blood Native Americans may harmonize their lives. Ruppert candidly acknowledges the "mythic" nature of much Native American literature:

> Much of the work of contemporary Native writers incorporates an overriding metanarrative and often mythic structure through which the narrative, the characters, and the readers find meaning. It seems that much of the work is characterized by a historical vision, a sense of social responsibility and a belief in the efficacy of the word—qualities not to be found in postmodern literature. From Silko to Vizenor, this is literature with a purpose.

Source: Dennis Cutchins, "'So That the Nations May Become Genuine Indian': Nativism and Leslie Marmon Silko's *Ceremony*," in *Journal of American Culture*, Vol. 22, No. 4, Winter 1999, pp. 79–83.

Karen Piper

In the following excerpt, Piper discusses Betonie's statement, "Things which don't shift and grow are dead things. They are the things the witchery people want," arguing that Silko guarantees that the reader does not become a complacent, or dead, receiver of narrative by telling Tayo's story in a challenging, non-chronological way.

Silko writes in *Ceremony*, "Witches crawl into skins of dead animals, but they can do nothing but play around with object and bodies." Witches are able to enclose themselves in static formations, magically separating themselves from life. Betonie says to Tayo, "Things which don't shift and grow are dead things. They are the things the witchery people want." Translating this into white culture, the witchery could be called the reified image, or that which is separated from its referent. It thus precludes growth or knowledge and, culturally, involves the erasure of a process-oriented people and the establishment of reified structures of meaning.

Betonie claims in *Ceremony* that the witchery does not come from the white people, but rather they themselves are manifestations of this witchcraft. Therefore the cure must be "inclusive of everything"—or, as Silko explains, "A great deal of the story is believed to be inside the listener, and the storyteller's role is to draw the story out of the listeners." *Ceremony* does not allow the reader to sit back passively and absorb the narrative; indeed, the narrative offers itself as a cure for which the reader is in need. Just as the traditional author is the active but separate individual, so the traditional reader is the passive but separate individual—and the means to separation is that third term, narrative. This is why Silko claimed in an oral presentation that Laguna people are generally suspect of writing, because it separates the speaker from the listener. The reader, in this sense, could be called the "dead object" that absorbs narration—he or she is the private subject that sits in a room and reads about something other than real life. The cure, then, is affected by the reincorporation of the private subject into the narrative.

Ceremony further requires that the reader take an active role through its non-chronological narration; it presents itself as a spatial and chronological enigma in need of understanding or ordering. The landscape of *Ceremony* is a teeming space of tangles, flows, and webs. It is non-linear and fragmented and fluctuates between native legend and modern novel. For this reason it is difficult even to summarize the plot of *Ceremony*. Ostensibly, a Laguna Indian has returned from World War II with "shell shock" problems, an illness that he attempts to cure throughout the narrative. Tayo is sent to white doctors, a medicine man, a woman healer, and so on. On his journeys he crosses many territorial boundaries that signify shifts in Indian identity. At the same time he struggles with friends also returned from the war (Emo, Leroy, and Pinkie) who are suffering under their own illness: alcoholism. In the dramatic conclusion these friends torture Emo, and Tayo refuses to participate. This refusal has been called a "hopeful" ending for a peaceful Indian future. However, I would suggest that Indian nonviolence is far from the moral of *Ceremony*. Instead, the narrative uses the ultimate signifier of violence—nuclear holocaust—to invoke a new global community, thus weaving even this destructive element back in the narrative. Violence is not something that can be avoided or put in the past, but rather something for which one must find a name to include in the narrative.*Ceremony* thus describes two narratives that spread throughout the world: the story and the bomb. The question, then, is which one will win.

Source: Karen Piper, "Police Zones: Territory and Identity in Leslie Marmon Silko's *Ceremony*," in *The American Indian Quarterly*, Vol. 21, No. 3, Summer 1998, pp. 483–89.

SOURCES

Barnett, Louise K., and James L. Thorson, eds., *Leslie Marmon Silko: A Collection of Critical Essays*, University of New Mexico Press, 2001, p. xx.

Beidler, Peter G., Review of *Ceremony*, in *American Indian Quarterly*, Vol. 3, No. 4, Fall 1978, pp. 357–58.

Irmer, Thomas, An Interview with Leslie Marmon Silko, *Altx Online Magazine*, www.altx.com/interviews/silko.html (December 7, 2005).

"Native Americans in World War II," *The United States Department of Defense*, www.defenselink.mil/specials/nativeamerican01/wwii.html (January 17, 2006).

Silko, Leslie Marmon, *Ceremony*, Penguin, 1986, originally published in 1977.

Wiehe, Janet, Review of *Ceremony*, in *Library Journal*, Vol. 102, No. 2, 1977, p. 220.

The Color Purple

ALICE WALKER

1982

Although she is an accomplished writer of novels, short stories, essays, and poems, Alice Walker is best known for her award-winning novel *The Color Purple*. It is a story of physical and spiritual survival set in a black community in the rural South of the early twentieth century. While some of the characters must fight the racism and discrimination of the outside world, almost all of them must fight for their individual identities and worth within the black community as well. In turns heartbreaking and triumphant, hopeless and hopeful, *The Color Purple* examines the struggle and rewards of being true to oneself in an atmosphere of oppression and loss.

The Color Purple is an epistolary novel (a book written as a series of letters), telling the story of Celie, a damaged young woman who is able to transform herself despite considerable opposition and to find ultimate happiness and fulfillment. The ninety letters that compose the book fall into two categories: letters written by Celie to God and letters exchanged between Celie and her sister, Nettie. Thematically, the majority of Walker's work—including *The Color Purple*—explores the many challenges that African Americans have faced throughout history, while remaining centered on the preservation of black culture, spirituality, and heritage. More specifically, she focuses on the often-harrowing experiences of black women, who encounter internalized racism, sexism, and violence within their own communities. In her

book of essays *In Search of Our Mothers' Gardens: Womanist Prose* (1983), Walker describes herself as a "womanist"—a term referring to a black feminist, or one who "[a]ppreciates and prefers women's culture, women's emotional flexibility, ... and women's strength" and is "[c]ommitted to survival and wholeness of entire people, male *and* female."

In *The Color Purple*, Walker's commitment to nurturing wide-ranging and versatile images of black people is revealed in her use of nonstandard diction. Celie, the protagonist of the novel, communicates in a manner that is consistent with her life as a poor, uneducated black woman in rural America near the turn of the century. The novel has none of the indicators usually provided by an omniscient narrator; instead, the reader must piece together seemingly disparate bits of information from the letters in the novel in order to build a larger picture. For example, it is not uncommon for long, unspecified periods of time to pass between the letters. In fact, the novel, which spans approximately forty years, relies heavily on the details Celie provides and her descriptions of the other characters as indicators of time shifts and change.

In 1983, *The Color Purple* won both the Pulitzer Prize and the National Book Award and received widespread critical acclaim. Two years later, it was adapted into an Academy Award–nominated motion picture by director Steven Spielberg. In 2005, it was adapted as a Broadway musical, produced by Oprah Winfrey, who co-starred in the 1985 movie. Because of its sexually explicit subject matter, *The Color Purple* is sometimes associated with controversy. It is among the American Library Association's "100 Most Frequently Challenged Books" of the 1990s for middle school and high school readers. Nonetheless, readers over the years have found Walker's characters, themes, and subject matter to be moving and unforgettable.

PLOT SUMMARY

Chapters 1–3

Fourteen-year-old Celie begins writing to God after she is raped repeatedly by the man she knows as her father and is pregnant with his child. He tells her, "You better not never tell nobody but God. It'd kill your mammy." In the

> SOFIA AND THE PRIZEFIGHTER DON'T SAY NOTHING. WAIT FOR HER TO PASS. MAYOR WAIT TOO, STAND BACK AND TAP HIS FOOT, WATCH HER WITH A LITTLE SMILE. NOW MILLIE, HE SAY. ALWAYS GOING ON OVER COLORED. MISS MILLIE FINGER THE CHILDREN SOME MORE, FINALLY LOOK AT SOFIA.... SHE SAY TO SOFIA, ALL YOUR CHILDREN SO CLEAN, SHE SAY, WOULD YOU LIKE TO WORK FOR ME, BE MY MAID?"

first few letters, she tells God how her Pa (who is often referred to simply as "He") took her baby away from her as soon as it was born and how she assumes that her child is now dead. Celie describes the circumstances surrounding her mother's death and the birth and abduction of her second child, a son, who she suspects has been sold to a couple in Monticello. The third letter ends with Celie's hope that her Pa will get remarried soon, as he has been recently eyeing her little sister, Nettie, suggesting that he might begin raping her as well.

Chapters 4–8

Celie explains how Pa has brought home a teenaged girl, Mary Ellen, to be his new wife. Mary Ellen's presence temporarily halts Pa's sexual advances toward Celie, and in a letter to God, she mentions, "[Pa] be on [Mary Ellen] all the time." Celie's younger sister, Nettie, is being courted by a widower, who is referred to as Mr. _____. Meanwhile, Celie continues to suffer, especially after Mary Ellen falls ill and the job of gratifying Pa's sexual demands returns to her. She stoically endures these rapes in order to protect her "new mammy" from harm and her sister from incest. She advises Nettie to marry Mr. _____, "an try to have one good year out your life" before getting pregnant. Celie mentions that she has stopped menstruating and realizes that she will no longer be able to bear children.

When Mr. _____ proposes to Nettie, Pa refuses to allow the union. Claiming among other reasons that the scandal of Mr. _____ wife's murder makes Mr. _____ an undesirable candidate for Nettie, Pa offers Celie's hand

BIOGRAPHY

ALICE WALKER

Alice Walker was born February 9, 1944, in the farming community of Eatonton, Georgia, to sharecroppers Willie Lee and Minnie Grant Walker. Her writing career began in 1967, when she published a short story titled "To Hell With Dying." Also in this year, she married civil rights attorney Melvyn Leventhal and lived with him in Mississippi, where they became the state's first legally married interracial couple. Her first book of poetry, *Once*, was published the following year.

Walker's first novel, *The Third Life of Grange Copeland*, was published in 1970, a year after she gave birth to her daughter Rebecca. In 1972, Walker left Mississippi and moved to Cambridge, Massachusetts, where she developed a course on African American women writers at Wellesley College—one of the first such courses in the country.

Among her many achievements, Walker is credited with the "discovery" of Zora Neale Hurston's contributions to American literature. In 1973, when Walker traveled to Hurston's hometown in Eatonville, Florida, she provided a gravestone displaying the epitaph, "a genius of the South," for what had been Hurston's unmarked grave. In 1975, Walker published an article titled "In Search of Zora Neale Hurston," which delivered the Harlem Renaissance writer from relative obscurity. Since that time, Walker has published more than twenty-five books of fiction, non-fiction, and poetry. As of 2006, she lives in California, where she continues to write.

Alice Walker Roger Ressmeyer/Corbis

Chapters 9–21

For Celie, life with Mr. _____ is no better than with Pa. In addition to caring for his four children, she must cook and clean the house, as well as help him on the farm. Mr. _____ frequently beats her. Celie's seemingly endless list of household duties is interrupted only by her worry about her sister, who is now unprotected, and thoughts of Shug Avery.

One day in town, Celie sees a girl she believes to be her daughter with the wife of a local minister. When she inquires about the child, the woman, who is later identified as Corrine, tells Celie that the girl, Olivia, will be seven years old in November or December.

Nettie joins Celie and Mr. _____ after running away from home when Pa begins to threaten her with incest. The sisters take refuge in the closeness of their bond while Mr. _____, who is still attracted to Nettie from their courtship, tries to pursue her. When his advances are rebuffed, Mr. _____ decides that Nettie must leave the farm immediately. Celie advises Nettie to seek help from the minister, whose wife she had previously met in town. The sisters part sadly, promising to exchange letters. Silently, Mr. _____

in her stead. After months of deliberation, Mr. _____ accepts Pa's offer and the men discuss the arrangements. With Mary Ellen's assistance, Celie acquires a photo of Shug Avery, a glamorous blues singer who is rumored to be Mr. _____'s mistress. Celie says Shug is "The most beautiful woman ... mama ... bout ten thousand times more prettier than me." This marks the beginning of Celie's fascination with Shug.

vows to prevent any further communication between them.

After hearing no word from Nettie, Celie begins to believe that her sister might be dead. A visit from Mr. _____'s two sisters offers some relief in the form of a new dress for Celie and some encouraging words. But when Shug Avery comes to town, Mr. _____ stops working on the farm, leaving all the work to Celie and his eldest son, Harpo. The brunt of the labor falls upon Celie when Harpo's new love interest, Sofia Butler, becomes pregnant and the couple makes plans to marry. Mr. _____ opposes the marriage, but after their child is born Harpo marries Sofia anyway, and the three of them live together on the farm. Headstrong Sofia disregards Harpo's demands upon her and when he asks for advice, both Celie and Mr. _____ advise him to beat her into submission. When Sofia confronts Celie about her betrayal, the women share their past experiences of abuse and forge a close bond of sisterhood.

Chapters 22–36

Shug Avery is sick and Mr. _____ decides to take her in against his father's advice. Not surprisingly, the burden of her care falls to Celie, who hears Shug call Mr. _____ "Albert." Celie, though, continues to refer to him as Mr. _____ until the very last letter in the novel. When bathing Shug, Celie reacts to the sight of her naked body, saying, "I thought I had turned into a man." Celie steadily nurses Shug back to health and the women grow closer despite the fact that Albert and Shug have resumed their sexual relationship.

Subsequent letters detail the erosion of Sofia and Harpo's marriage. Three children later, Harpo is still trying to find a way to control his wife. After unsuccessfully attempting to dominate Sofia physically, Harpo tries to gain weight in order to subdue his wife, who is built like an "amazon." Eventually, Sofia and the children leave Harpo. After Sofia's departure, Harpo opens a juke joint and Shug begins to perform again. When Shug tells Celie of her impending departure, Celie confides to her that Mr. _____ has been abusive. Shug promises not to leave the farm until Mr. _____ stops beating her. As the months pass, Shug helps Celie to explore her body and her sexuality as they share increasingly intimate moments.

Chapters 37–42

Celie relates the story of how Sofia ended up in jail for "sassing the mayor's wife" and punching the mayor. When the mayor's wife, Miss Millie, asked Sofia to come and work for her as her maid, Sofia replied, "Hell no." She was beaten almost to death and imprisoned as a consequence for refusing a white woman's request. When Celie visits Sofia in jail and sees the extent of her injuries, she does not know how Sofia could still be alive: "They crack her skull, they crack her ribs. They tear her nose loose on one side. They blind her in one eye. She swole from head to foot." The reaction of the mayor and Miss Millie to what is perceived as Sofia's insolence is accentuated by the fact that Sofia is black and poor, while they are rich and white.

In an effort to relieve Sofia of the unbearable conditions in jail, Squeak, the woman Harpo has taken up with since Sofia left him, conspires with other members of the family to manipulate the prison warden into releasing Sofia to the custody of the mayor and his wife. Before everyone can celebrate Squeak's return from her trip into town, she describes how the warden, who is Squeak's white uncle, raped and beat her during their brief encounter. Eventually, their plan to free Sofia succeeds and after three years in jail, her sentence is commuted. Sofia is allowed to serve the rest of her twelve year sentence as Miss Millie's live-in maid.

Chapters 43–48

Celie writes to God about the changes in Sofia's personality after she is released from jail. Sofia openly expresses her newfound resentment of whites, and Celie remarks, "Sofia would make a dog laugh, talking about those people she work for. They have the nerve to try to make us think slavery fell through because of us." After relating an episode involving Sofia's failed attempt to visit with her family after five years away from them, Celie quotes Sofia, who says, "White folks is a miracle of affliction."

When Shug visits with her new husband, Grady, Celie and Mr. _____ commiserate. Celie shares more of the details surrounding her Pa's sexual abuse and confesses to Shug that sex with Mr. _____ has been unfulfilling. Shug tells Celie that because she has never experienced sexual pleasure, she is still a virgin, despite her marriage. Shug kisses Celie, and the two women make love. In retrospect, Celie writes, "It feel like heaven is what it feel like, not like sleeping with Mr. _____ at all."

Chapter 49

The turning point of the novel occurs in this chapter, when Celie finally receives a letter from Nettie from Africa. Mr. _____ has been hiding letters from Nettie since the sisters first parted. This realization makes Celie so angry, she has murderous thoughts about Mr. _____.

Chapters 50–68

With Shug's help, Celie finds and reads all of the correspondence that Mr. _____ has been keeping from her over the years. The letters from Nettie fill in the gaps Celie missed in her sister's life. While Celie was afraid her sister was dead, Nettie had actually become a missionary in Africa after following Celie's advice to seek help from the minister, Samuel, and his wife, Corrine, whom Celie had once met. Nettie explains that Mr. _____'s decision to make her leave the farm came after he attempted to rape her. Nettie's preparation for the trip to Africa is described, as well as how Celie's children came to be in Nettie's care. She reassures her sister that both Adam and Olivia are now safe with her in Africa.

Nettie's letters about the landscape and the people of Africa reveal parallels between the isolated sphere of the Olinka tribe that she lives with, and Celie's world back on the farm. Just as Sofia, Harpo, Squeak, Shug, and Mr. _____ have become Celie's family in her sister's absence, Corrine, Samuel, Olivia, Adam, and Tashi, a member of the Olinka tribe, become Nettie's family. Nettie's letters about them familiarize Celie with the world beyond her reach. Through Nettie's letters, Celie confronts ideas of colonization, female circumcision, and indigenous religious traditions. Each letter shares more information on daily life in the Olinka village.

Five years after Nettie begins her missionary work with the Olinka, a road is built through the village, all but completely destroying the Olinka way of life. A forced relocation results in the Olinka having to pay the rubber company to use the same water, supplies, and land that was once their own. Meanwhile, stories of Adam and Olivia's friendship with Tashi reveal the various cultural differences, as well as the corresponding patriarchal (ruled by men) nature of African and American societies. After noticing how similar Adam and Olivia look to Nettie, Corrine becomes withdrawn and sick, which worsens as she worries that Samuel was unfaithful to her. Corrine dies peacefully after Nettie reveals to her that Adam and Olivia are in fact Celie's children, not her own.

Nettie tells Celie that the man they called Pa is not their real father, but their stepfather. At this point, Celie stops writing to God, saying, "My children not my sister and brother. Pa not pa. You must be sleep." Instead, she begins addressing her letters exclusively to Nettie. After Shug learns of the letters and the information in them, she tells Celie to pack her things because she wants Celie to move to Tennessee with her and Grady.

Chapters 69–82

After discovering that Pa (Fonso) is not her biological father, Celie goes to visit him. Fonso confirms Nettie's story and recounts the events that led to her biological father's death. Celie learns that her father was lynched by white townsmen for having property and a successful business of his own. Fonso tells Celie,

> The trouble with our people is as soon as they got out of slavery they didn't want to give the white man nothing else. But the fact is, you got to give 'em something. Either your money, your land, your woman or your ass.

After Celie's visit with Fonso, Shug restores Celie's confidence by telling her that the two of them are family now. Shug and Celie discuss Celie's decision to stop writing to God. Shug tells Celie to relinquish her image of God as a white-haired, blue-eyed, white man and to begin to look at God in a more inclusive way. Shug tells Celie to try and appreciate life and all of God's creations, saying, "I think it pisses God off if you walk by the color purple in a field somewhere and don't notice it."

Sofia is released on parole six months early, and the family arranges a gathering to celebrate her return. In the midst of dinner, Shug announces that Celie will be returning to Memphis with her. When Mr. _____ objects, Celie asserts years of pent-up anger, saying, "You a lowdown dog. . . . You took my sister Nettie away from me . . . [a]nd she was the only person love me in the world." Squeak decides to go with Shug and Celie, and then the party is interrupted by Eleanor Jane, the mayor's daughter. Because Sofia is on parole, she must "act nice" and accompany Eleanor Jane back to the mayor's house to help with some problems there. Sofia tells Squeak that she will look after Suzie Q, Harpo and Squeak's daughter, while Squeak is in Memphis.

In Memphis, Celie writes to Nettie about her new life. When Shug is on tour, Celie begins to sew pants and soon opens her own business, Folkspants, Unlimited. She continues to receive letters from Nettie in Africa, who has married the widowed Samuel. Nettie tells Celie about their struggles to aid the Olinka people, who are being forced further and further from their land. Meanwhile, back on the farm, Mr. _____ has had a dramatic change of heart and is working hard in the fields, cleaning his own house, and even taking care of his children. Celie writes to Nettie to tell her that she has received word that Fonso has died, leaving the sisters a sizeable inheritance due to them from their biological father, including a house and a dry-goods store.

Chapters 83–85

Celie goes home to look at the house she has inherited. When Shug confesses to Celie that she has fallen in love with a young man, Celie takes up residence alone in her new house and devotes herself fully to her pants business. Mr. _____ breaks his years-long vow to prevent Nettie and Celie's correspondence and gives Celie a telegram saying that the ship carrying her sister, brother-in-law, and the children, was sunk off the coast of Gibraltar. All are assumed drowned. The same day, all the letters that Celie wrote to Nettie over the years come back unopened.

Chapters 86–89

In her last two letters to Celie, Nettie describes the ever-increasing hardships of the Olinkas, who are dying from malaria as a result of the sudden change in diet and lifestyle brought on by the rubber plantation. She also summarizes the dramatic events leading to Tashi and Adam's marriage. She tells Celie that she looks forward to returning home in a few weeks.

In Celie's last two letters to Nettie, she talks about the radical changes in Mr. _____'s personality. Since her return from Memphis, the two of them have come to terms with their past difficulties and reconciled. Mr. _____ even suggests that they get back together. Celie also relates the end of Shug's love affair with the young man and her subsequent return to Celie. Shug moves into Celie's house, while Sofia renegotiates her relationship with her former employers so she can work in Celie's store.

Chapter 90

In her last letter, which is addressed, "Dear God. Dear stars, dear trees, dear sky, dear peoples. Dear Everything. Dear God," Celie gives thanks for her sister and children's return after being separated for more than thirty years. The telegram she had received about their death was wrong. As Shug, Albert (Mr. _____), and Celie sit on the porch of Celie's house one evening, they see a car arriving, and wonder who it could be. Celie nearly faints when she realizes it is her sister and her family. Everyone reunites to celebrate each other at the family reunion on the Fourth of July, and the book ends with Celie expressing her incredible gratitude, happiness, and feeling of youth.

THEMES

Race and God

Critics have often focused on Walker's unapologetic portrayal of the black experience as seen through Celie's narrative. Yet one of the most overlooked themes in *The Color Purple* is Walker's exploration of God and spirituality. The first forty-nine chapters of the novel are letters from Celie to God. As Celie's only confidant, God allows Celie to share the experiences that define her troubled existence. God is a character in the novel, whose absence or presence signifies major changes in Celie's character. After discovering that the man she thought was her father is actually her stepfather, Celie writes to God, "My daddy lynch. My mama crazy. All my little half-brothers and sisters no kin to me. My children not my sister and brother. Pa not pa. You must be sleep." From this point to the penultimate (second-to-last) chapter in the novel, Celie addresses her letters to her sister, Nettie, who is a missionary in Africa.

The transition between God as confidant and God as the remote "white man" who must be sleeping occurs when Celie must confront her notion of God in terms of his physical appearance and apparent race. Celie tells Shug that "the God I been praying and writing to is a man. And act just like all the other mens I know. Trifling, forgitful and lowdown." Shug, who helps Celie

Whoopi Goldberg and Margaret Avery in a scene from the film The Color Purple *The Kobal Collection*

negotiate this exploration, tells her that "this old white man is the same God she used to see when she prayed." She encourages Celie to look beyond the limitations of God's "blue eyes" and "white lashes" to see that "God love everything you love—and a mess of stuff you don't." This advice comes at a time when Celie is ready to give herself permission to go against the establishment—thereby developing into a more resolute and independent character.

Nettie's experience as a missionary in Africa contributes to the discussion when Celie notes, "Nettie say somewhere in the bible it say Jesus' hair was like lamb's wool," to which Shug responds, "The last thing niggers want to think about they God is that his hair kinky." With this exchange, Walker moves beyond more traditional concepts of God and Jesus, toward a more inclusive God, to whom Celie addresses her final letter. It seems that Walker is also suggesting that, like a mirror, the dominant physical representation of the Christian God reflects the white artist's view of himself.

This questioning of God's appearance, and the apparent manufacture of the popular image of God as a grandfatherly icon by white society,

is further complicated by the Olinka creation myth that Nettie shares with Celie. Celie tells Mr. _____ that according to the Olinka, Adam and Eve were not really the first humans as the familiar story goes, but the first *white* humans to survive to adulthood. She notes that to the Olinka, "naked" is the same word as "white" and those naked children (albinos) that were born to Olinka women were often discarded. This suggests that Adam and Eve's whiteness is derived from their original blackness. This inversion of the Judeo-Christian creation myth asserts the primacy of blackness, as opposed to the traditional notion of the primacy of whiteness.

When Celie begins to make peace with the men in her life who have so hurt her, she opens up a place for God to return. When he does, his nature has developed into a more complex concept. At the end of the novel, Celie writes, "Dear God. Dear stars, dear trees, dear sky, dear peoples. Dear Everything. Dear God," acknowledging the fullness she feels now that she is surrounded by the family that she had once lost. In this moment, the reader sees that Celie's spiritual connection with God has deepened far beyond the outpouring of secrets that "would kill [her] mammy."

Concepts of Beauty

The idea of beauty is a powerful one in *The Color Purple*. As Celie comes to see her own worth and beauty, she is able to love herself and consequently declare her independence from Mr. _____. In comparison to Nettie, Mr. _____ says of Celie, "She ugly. Don't even look like she kin to Nettie. But she'll make the better wife. She ain't smart either.... But she can work like a man." By the age of twenty, Celie, affected deeply by her environment, perceives herself similarly. Celie's evolution is only complete after she learns how to re-envision herself beyond Mr. _____'s estimation of her: "You black, you pore, you ugly, you a woman.... [Y]ou nothing at all." By the novel's conclusion, Celie has gone beyond her physicality to define herself, her life, and her experiences.

Celie establishes a self-deprecating tone early in *The Color Purple*. When she describes herself in relation to Shug, she comes out "ten thousand times" less attractive than the blues singer she idolizes and describes as "[t]he most beautiful woman I ever saw." Celie's view of Shug stands in contrast to the mainstream aesthetic bias toward lighter skin and Euro-centric features: "Under all that powder her face black as Harpo. She got a long pointed nose and big fleshy mouth. Lips look like black plum. Eyes big, glossy. Feverish. And mean." These descriptions of Shug resonate with the reader precisely because they avoid the exaggerations one might expect from a lover and are deliberately candid.

Celie's idea of beauty is linked both to her sexual naiveté as well as to mainstream beauty ideals. Only on occasion does Celie describe Shug in a manner that leans toward objectification. For example, when Celie describes Shug as "wearing a long white gown" with "her thin black hand stretching out of it to hold the white cigarette," it is clear that the emphasis is on the contrast between the whiteness of the gown and the blackness of Shug's hand, which Celie regards as "just right." These idealized notions are complicated by Celie's frank depictions of Shug: "She got the nottiest, shortest, kinkiest hair I ever saw, and I loves every strand of it." Celie thinks Shug is the epitome of beauty, despite other's reactions to Shug as being "black as tar, ... nappy headed ... [with] legs like baseball bats." In this way, Celie's

descriptions of Shug enhance the authority and believability of these two characters. By suggesting, with less-than-"ideal" descriptions, that Celie and Shug's relationship exists beyond the realm of idealized beauty, Walker is able to infuse the text with the authority it needs for Celie's voice to go beyond tragedy into triumph.

Independence

After years of oppression, abuse, and mistreatment at the hands of men, Celie makes a extraordinary bid for freedom and independence. Upon learning that her sister Nettie is not only alive but has been writing to her all these years, Celie's anger toward Mr. _____ becomes a motivating force. Combined with Shug's encouragement and love, Celie finds that she possesses a proactive spirit that had been dormant most of her life. When Celie announces that she is leaving for Memphis with Shug, Grady, and Squeak, Mr. _____ tries to hobble her self-confidence: "[W]hat you got? You ugly. You skinny. You shape funny. You too scared to open your mouth to people. All you fit to do in Memphis is be Shug's maid." In response to Mr. _____'s tirade, Celie calmly confronts him about Nettie's letters, showing a bravery Mr. _____ has never seen. She curses Mr. _____, telling him that for every hardship he has given her, he will suffer the same. As she drives away from Mr. _____'s house for the last time, Celie states her victory: "I'm pore, I'm black, I may be ugly and can't cook.... But I'm here."

Once Celie has escaped the abuse of her life with Mr. _____, she is able to achieve more than she had previously thought possible. One day, to keep her idle hands busy, Celie begins making pants that turn out to be popular among her friends and Shug's band. Shug suggests that Celie start selling them at a profit as a way to make a living. This endeavor becomes Folkspants, Unlimited, which Celie runs out of the dry goods store she and Nettie inherit from their biological father. She also inherits a house, so that she no longer has to depend on a man or even Shug in order to live—a tremendous accomplishment for any woman, black or white, at the time. For the first time in her life, Celie is free, and she writes to Nettie: "I am so happy. I got love, I got work, I got money, friends and time."

HISTORICAL OVERVIEW

Jim Crow Laws

The Color Purple is set in Georgia over a period of forty years, including the era of legalized Jim Crow racism and white terror attacks on African Americans in the South. Jim Crow laws (named after a blackface minstrel character) came about in the wake of *Plessy v. Ferguson* (1896), which created "separate but equal" facilities for blacks and whites in many Southern states. These laws were only struck down through the efforts of civil rights activists, who made significant inroads to fighting legal racism and segregation during the 1950s and 1960s.

Civil War historian Ronald Davis recalls in his article, "From Terror to Triumph: Historical Overview," that Jim Crow laws worked to deprive "African Americans of their civil rights by defining blacks as inferior to whites, as members of a caste of subordinate people." These laws affected every facet of life in the South, including education, religion, public transportation, and the use of other public and private facilities including bathrooms and restaurants. For Southern blacks, the former Confederate states were marred by hopeless violence and terror that saw "the imposition of a legal color line in race relations, and a variety of laws that blatantly discriminated against blacks" (quoted in Davis). This is evident in *The Color Purple* when Sophia receives a heavy sentence for "insulting" a white woman by refusing to become her maid. She is beaten by a white mob and thrown in jail, an experience that would never have happened if Sophia had been white.

Not only were public and private institutions under the governance of these "separate but equal" laws, but even personal relationships and marriage were legislated at this time. In many Southern states, blacks and whites were not legally allowed to marry. (Alice Walker and Melvyn Leventhal became the first legally married interracial couple in Mississippi when they wed in 1967). During the Jim Crow era, African Americans were also restricted in their economic mobility, being relegated to mostly lower- and working-class jobs like sharecropping. The penalty for violating any of these laws, which existed only to sustain the racial inequality that originated during the time of slavery, was sometimes death at the hands of angry lynch mobs of racist whites. Such a fate befell Celie's biological father, because he refused to pay off white men to compensate for his business's success. As Davis notes,

> It is impossible to know ... how many of the nearly 4000 (recorded) African Americans lynched (mutilated and burned alive) from 1882 to 1968, were men and women who had challenged Jim Crow by some overt act of defiance. Studies by Ida B. Wells-Barnett, the great anti-lynching crusader in the early twentieth-century, suggest that most of the lynch victims were random subjects of white rage.

Resisting Jim Crow Legislation

African Americans resisted the circumstances under Jim Crow legislation in a variety of ways. Davis recalls that "many southern blacks resisted Jim Crow by hoping for the day when they could escape the Jim Crow South—much as their ancestors had used the Underground Railroad to escape slavery by going to the North." Monica Maria Tetzlaff writes in her review of *Remembering Jim Crow: African Americans Tell About Life in the Segregated South* for the *Journal of Southern History* that Southern blacks often "protected one another, hiding men in danger of being lynched and laboring on the farms of families with too few able-bodied hands to make their crops." To provide a quality education for their children, communities often "pooled their resources to provide for black teachers who would teach longer than the four or five months allotted to them by whites in power."

For the most part, blacks were made to bear these conditions and often resorted to what Davis refers to as "accommodationist and appeasement tactics ... in which blacks assumed positions and the appearances of non-confrontation." Celie's stepfather, Fonso, gives Celie useful advice to this effect when he warns:

> I know how [white people] is. The key to all of 'em is money. The trouble with our people is as soon as they got out of slavery they didn't want to give the white man nothing else. But the fact is, you got to give 'em something. Either your money, your land, your woman or your ass. So what I did was just right off offer to give 'em money.

When Celie inherits her father's store, even though she hires Sofia, she keeps the white clerk who worked there before as a security measure against the Jim Crow acts of violence that led to her biological father's death by a white mob lynching.

Sofia, who responds "Hell no" when a white woman offers her a job as a maid, is Walker's example of Jim Crow resistance. This "insubordination" was punished by three years of hard labor and nine more of involuntary servitude to the mayor and his wife. African Americans mounted other forms of resistance against Jim Crow policies. This resistance, in whatever form, was often met with harsh violence from whites. Davis recalls that a friend of the great anti-lynching activist Ida B. Wells-Barnett—like Celie's father in the novel—was murdered for the crime of "owning a prosperous grocery store."

In *The Color Purple*, incidents like the rape and battery of Squeak, Celie's father's lynching, and the brutality of Sofia's twelve-year prison sentence are all examples of the living conditions for blacks during the time of Jim Crow. With the advances of black organizations like the National Association for the Advancement of Colored Peoples (NAACP), by the 1960s and 1970s, prominent black leaders had emerged. These leaders and their supporters were able to effect change, thereby achieving victories in law and on the level of public policy. Jim Crow was all but defeated as the problem of racial discrimination in the United States garnered worldwide attention and the civil rights movement was named.

CRITICAL OVERVIEW

Anyone looking for criticism on *The Color Purple* will soon realize that in many ways, the book has been overshadowed in the public arena by Steven Spielberg's 1985 film adaptation. When the book was originally published in 1982, its reception was, for the most part, laudatory. Mel Watkins, in "Some Letters Went to God," calls the book "No mean accomplishment," and "a striking and consummately well-written novel." Critics were quick to give Walker credit for taking on such an ambitious project. Yet, the sensitivity of the subject matter, combined with the epistolary and dialectical style of the novel, spawned more debate as to whether or not the overall project was successful.

The *New York Times*'s editor's choice for "The Best Books of 1982" excluded *The Color Purple*, saying that "Everyone . . . agreed that its first 75 pages contained probably the best fiction written this year but that the quality was not sustained." Watkins also suggests in his review that "If there is a weakness in this novel—besides the somewhat pallid portraits of the males—it is Netti's [*sic*] correspondence from Africa," which strikes him as "lackluster and intrusive." This hesitance to proclaim the book an all-around success is echoed by others, with many critics pointing to Walker's often unflattering portrayals of black males as the most problematic issue.

The novel's subject matter has also been a source of debate and even censorship. According to Andrea Glick and Renee Olson in "Lacking Policy, WV School Board Orders Books Off the Shelves," in the 1990s, *The Color Purple* came under fire when schools in Pennsylvania, West Virginia, and California challenged its appropriateness for school reading lists, citing themes of incest, lesbianism, and domestic abuse as reasons for its removal from school library collections. Since that time, *The Color Purple* has been challenged in several other states and continues to be controversial in school districts across the country.

In her article "Writing a Rationale for a Controversial Common Reading Book: Alice Walker's *The Color Purple*," Pepper Worthington pinpoints four issues that might explain the book's frequent censorship. These include: the subject matter (including rape, incest, lesbianism, drugs, and murder); specific words (like the word "nigger," used to articulate the oppressive nature of black experience); the narrator's overall use (or misuse) of grammar; and the epistolary motif of the novel (which may strike readers as dated). Worthington also adds that "the seedbed of censorship is a hidden, dreadful fear that the lurking unloveliness inside the human spirit may explode," as it does in *The Color Purple*, and that the only way teachers can illuminate the issue is by examining the "*genuine motives*" within "the entire issue of censorship." For the years 1990 to 2000, the American Library Association lists *The Color Purple* as the eighteenth most-challenged book in school classrooms and libraries.

Walker herself addresses many of the concerns and controversies that emerged from the publication of *The Color Purple* and the subsequent Spielberg adaptation in her book *The Same River Twice* (1996). She also writes extensively about the banning of her work, specifically the two short stories "Roselily" and "Am I Blue," in her book *Banned* (1996). *Banned*

MEDIA ADAPTATIONS

The film adaptation of *The Color Purple* (1985), written for the screen by Menno Meyjes and directed by Steven Spielberg, was nominated for eleven Academy Awards. It stars Whoopi Goldberg, Oprah Winfrey, and Danny Glover, and is available on VHS and DVD from Warner Brothers Home Video.

A Broadway musical based on the *The Color Purple* opened in December 2005. The musical is directed by Gary Griffin with music and lyrics by Brenda Russell, Allee Willis, and Stephen Bray. It is produced by Oprah Winfrey. An audio CD version of the original cast recording is available from Angel Records.

includes the aforementioned short stories and an excerpt from *The Color Purple*, as well as commentary about what Patricia Holt refers to in the introduction as, "the bizarre configurations of censorship that have forced Walker to respond to political attack." Nonetheless, many have cited Walker's 1983 Pulitzer Prize and National Book Award for *The Color Purple* as proof of the book's lasting triumph.

Regardless of past or present controversy, *The Color Purple* continues to be one of the defining examples of contemporary American literature and is further distinguished as a great work of feminist prose by critics and readers alike.

CRITICISM

Linda Selzer

In the following excerpt, Selzer discusses Walker's confrontation of race relations and class distinctions through the underlying text in The Color Purple.

An important juncture in Alice Walker's *The Color Purple* is reached when Celie first

recovers the missing letters from her long-lost sister Nettie.

Saturday morning Shug put Nettie letter in my lap. Little fat queen of England stamps on it, plus stamps that got peanuts, coconuts, rubber trees and say Africa. I don't know where England at. Don't know where Africa at either. So I still don't know where Nettie at.

What matters about not knowing "where Africa at"—according to Celie—is not knowing "where Nettie at." By clarifying Celie's characteristic angle of vision, this passage highlights the intensely personal perspective that Walker brings to her tale of sexual oppression—a perspective that accounts in large part for the emotional power of the text.

But Walker's privileging of the domestic perspective of her narrators has also been judged to have other effects on the text. Indeed, critics from various aesthetic and political camps have commented on what they perceive as a tension between public and private discourse in the novel. Thus, in analyzing Celie's representation of national identity, Lauren Berlant identifies a separation of "aesthetic" and "political" discourses in the novel and concludes that Celie's narrative ultimately emphasizes "individual essence in false opposition to institutional history." Revealing a very different political agenda in his attacks on the novel's womanist stance, George Stade also points to a tension between personal and public elements in the text when he criticizes the novel's "narcissism" and its "championing of domesticity over the public world of masculine power plays." Finally, in praising Walker's handling of sexual oppression, Elliott Butler-Evans argues that Celie's personal letters serve precisely as a "textual strategy by which the larger African-American history, focused on racial conflict and struggle, can be marginalized by its absence from the narration."

By counterposing personal and public discourse in the novel, these critics could be said to have problematized the narrative's domestic perspective by suggesting that Walker's chosen treatment of the constricted viewpoint of an uneducated country woman—a woman who admits that she doesn't even know "where Africa at"—may also constrict the novel's ability to analyze issues of "race" and class. Thus Butler-Evans finds that Celie's "private life preempts the exploration of the public lives of blacks," while Berlant argues that Celie's family-oriented point of view and modes of expression can displace race and class analyses to the point that the "nonbiological abstraction of class relations virtually disappears." And in a strongly worded rejection of the novel as "revolutionary literature," bell hooks charges that the focus upon Celie's sexual oppression ultimately deemphasizes the "collective plight of black people" and "invalidates ... the racial agenda" of the slave narrative tradition that it draws upon ("Writing"). In short, to many readers of *The Color Purple,* the text's ability to expose sexual oppression seems to come *at the expense of* its ability to analyze issues of race and class.

But it seems to me that an examination of the representation of race in the novel leads to another conclusion: Walker's mastery of the epistolary form is revealed precisely by her ability to maintain the integrity of Celie's and Nettie's domestic perspectives even as she simultaneously undertakes an extended critique of race relations, and especially of racial integration. In particular, Walker's domestic novel engages issues of race and class through two important narrative strategies: the development of an embedded narrative line that offers a post-colonial perspective on the action, and the use of "family relations"—or kinship—as a carefully elaborated textual trope for race relations. These strategies enable Walker to foreground the personal histories of her narrators while placing those histories firmly within a wider context of race and class.

Both the novel's so-called "restriction of focus to Celie's consciousness" (Butler-Evans) and one way in which Walker's narratology complicates that perspective are illustrated by the passage quoted above. Celie's difficulty interpreting the envelope sent by Nettie at first only seems to support the claim that her domestic perspective "erases" race and class concerns from the narrative. But if this short passage delineates Celie's particular angle of vision, it also introduces textual features that invite readers to resituate her narration within a larger discourse of race and class. For where Celie sees only a "fat little queen of England," readers who recognize Queen Victoria immediately historicize the passage. And if the juxtaposition of the two stamps on the envelope—England's showcasing royalty, Africa's complete with

rubber trees—suggests to Celie nothing but her own ignorance, to other readers the two images serve as a clear reminder of imperialism. Thus Africa, mentioned by name for the first time in this passage, enters the novel already situated within the context of colonialism. Importantly, Walker remains true to Celie's character even as she recontextualizes the young woman's perspective, because the features of the envelope Celie focuses upon are entirely natural ones for her to notice, even though they are politically charged in ways that other features would not be (for example, Celie might have been struck by more purely personal—and more conventional—details, such as the familiar shape of her sister's handwriting). Embedded throughout *The Color Purple,* narrative features with clear political and historical associations like these complicate the novel's point of view by inviting a post-colonial perspective on the action and by creating a layered narrative line that is used for different technical effects and thematic purposes. That Celie herself is not always aware of the full political implications of her narration (although she becomes increasingly so as the novel progresses) no more erases the critique of race and class from the text than Huck's naïveté in *Huckleberry Finn* constricts that work's social criticism to the boy's opinions. This individual letter from Nettie thus provides readers with a textual analogue for the novel's larger epistolary form, illustrating one way in which the novel's domestic perspective is clearly "stamped" with signs of race and class.

But it is not only through such narrative indirection and recontextualization that the novel engages issues of race and class. Walker's domestic narrative undertakes a sustained analysis of race through the careful development of family relationships—or kinship—as an extended textual trope for race relations. Any attempt to oppose political and personal discourses in the novel collapses when one recognizes that the narrative adopts the discourse of family relations both to establish a "domestic ideal" for racial integration and to problematize that ideal through the analysis of specific integrated family groupings in Africa and America.

An historical appropriation of domestic discourse for political ends, descriptions of the black mammy were used by apologists for slavery to argue that the plantation system benefited the people whom it enslaved by incorporating supposedly inferior blacks into productive white families. And Sophia explicitly ties her employers to such plantation definitions of racial difference: "They have the nerve to try to make us think slavery fell through because of us. . . . Like us didn't have sense enough to handle it. All the time breaking hoe handles and letting the mules loose in the wheat." But through Sophia's experience in the mayor's household, the narrative demonstrates that it is Miss Millie, the mayor's wife, who is actually incompetent—who must be taught to drive by Sophia, for example, and who even then can't manage a short trip by herself. Thus, when she suddenly decides to drive Sophia home for a visit, Miss Millie stalls the car and ruins the transmission, the mistress unable to master driving in reverse. Too afraid of black men to allow one of Sophia's relatives to drive her back home alone, Miss Millie reveals her childlike dependence upon Sophia, who must cut short her first visit with her children in five years to ride home with the distraught white woman. Sophia's position as domestic within the mayor's household thus enables Walker to subvert the discourse of plantation kinship by suggesting that it actually supports a group of people who are themselves incompetent or, in Sophia words, "backward, . . . clumsy, and unlucky."

Predicated on this plantation model of integration, relations between whites and blacks throughout the American South reveal a false kinship not unlike that of Doris Baines and the Akwee. But in this instance the false kinship is doubly perverse because it conceals an elaborate network of actual kinship connections. Thus Miss Eleanor Jane's husband feels free to humor Sophia by referring to the importance of black mammies in the community—". . . everybody around here raise by colored. That's how come we turn out so well"—while other white men refuse to recognize the children they father with black women. As Celie says of Mr.____'s son Bub, he "look so much like the Sheriff, he and Mr.____ almost on family terms"; that is, "just so long as Mr.____ know he colored." Like the apologists for slavery, then, the Southern whites in *The Color Purple* keep alive a counterfeit definition of family while denying the real ties that bind them to African Americans.

In fact, the underlying system of kinship that exists in the American South has more to do with white uncles than black mammies, as is clear from the scene in which Sophia's family and friends consider various stratagems for winning her release from prison. By asking, "Who the warden's black kinfolks?", Mr.—— reveals that kinship relations between whites and blacks are so extensive in the community that it may be assumed that *someone* will be related by blood to the warden. That someone, of course, is Squeak. Hopeful that she will be able to gain Sophia's release from the warden on the basis of their kinship, the others dress Squeak up "like she a white woman" with instructions to make the warden "see the Hodges in you." In spite of the fact that the warden does recognize Squeak as kin "the minute [she] walk[s] through the door"—or perhaps *because* he recognizes her—the warden rapes Squeak, denying their kinship in the very act of perverting it. As Squeak herself recounts, "He say if he was my uncle he wouldn't do it to me." Both an intensely personal and highly political act, Squeak's rape exposes the denial of kinship at the heart of race relations in the South and underscores the individual and institutional power of whites to control the terms of kinship—and whatever power those definitions convey—for their own interests.

In subverting the plantation model of kinship in general and the role of mammy that it assigns to black women in particular, then, Sophia's position as an unwilling domestic in the mayor's household underscores the importance of the personal point of view to the novel's political critique of race relations. Indeed, the personal point of view of *The Color Purple* is central to its political message: It is precisely the African American woman's *subjectivity* that gives the lie to cultural attempts to reduce her—like Sophia—to the role of the contented worker in a privileged white society.

Finally, it is not surprising that, in elaborating her domestic trope for race relations, Walker is able to foreground the personal experience of her narrators while simultaneously offering an extended critique of racial integration. As Walker's integrated families remind us, the black family has seldom existed as a private, middle-class space protected from the interference of the state; therefore, the African American household is particularly inscribed with social meanings available for narration. Rather than opposing public and private spheres, Walker's narrative underscores their interpenetration. If her narrative does reveal an opposition, it is not between public and private discourse but between the universalist ethos of the Olinka ideal for race relations and the historical experience of African Americans as reflected in the narrative's analysis of specific integrated family groupings. For if the Olinka ideal questions the true nature of kinship in the novel's integrated families, these families also serve to criticize the Olinka myth for tracing the origins of racial discrimination back to some imaginary sin of black people, rather than to real, historical discrimination by whites.

It may be, however, that the growing sense of racial separatism at the conclusion to the *The Color Purple* is not necessarily at odds with the Olinka ideal for race relations. Past discrimination itself may dictate that improved relations between the races must begin with the destruction of false relations—the discovery of kinship among the disenfranchised the necessary first step, perhaps, toward recognizing all others as part of the same family. Like the Olinka Adam myth, the conclusion to Walker's novel raises the question of the future of race relations, but also like that myth, the novel offers no certain predictions. One thing is certain, however. Critics who believe that *The Color Purple* sacrifices its ability to critique the public world of blacks in favor of dramatizing the personal experience of its narrators not only run the risk of reducing the narrative's technical complexity, but also of overlooking the work's sustained critique of racial integration levied from *within* the domestic sphere. Through its embedded narrative line and carefully elaborated kinship trope for race relations, *The Color Purple* offers a critique of race

that explores the possibility of treating all people as "one mother's children"—while remaining unremittingly sensitive to the distance that often separates even the best of human ideals from real historical conditions.

Source: Linda Selzer, "Race and Domesticity in *The Color Purple*," in *African American Review*, Vol. 29, No. 1, Spring 1995, pp. 67–82.

SOURCES

Davis, Ronald, "From Terror to Triumph: Historical Overview," *The History of Jim Crow*, www.jimcrowhistory.org/history/overview.htm (December 1, 2005).

Glick, Andrea and Renee Olson, "Lacking Policy, WV School Board Orders Books Off the Shelves," in *School Library Journal*, Vol. 44, No. 1, Jan 1998, pp. 13–15.

Holt, Patricia, Introduction to *Banned*, by Alice Walker, Aunt Lute Books, 1996, p. 1.

Tetzlaff, Monica Maria, Review of *Remembering Jim Crow: African Americans Tell About Life in the Segregated South*, in *Journal of Southern History*, Vol. 69, August 2003, pp. 733–35.

"The Best Books of 1982," in *New York Times*, December 5, 1982, p. BR3.

Walker, Alice, *In Search of Our Mother's Gardens: Womanist Prose*, Pocket Books, 1982, p. xi.

———, *The Color Purple*, Pocket Books, 1982.

Watkins, Mel, "Some Letters Went to God," in *New York Times*, July 25, 1982, p BR7.

Worthington, Pepper, "Writing a Rationale for a Controversial Common Reading Book: Alice Walker's *The Color Purple*," in *The English Journal*, Vol. 74, No. 1, Jan 1985, pp. 48–52.

Cry, the Beloved Country

ALAN PATON

1948

South African Alan Paton was forty-three years old when he began writing his first and most famous novel, *Cry, the Beloved Country*. He wrote it by hand while on a tour to several countries, which he paid for himself, to study prison reform. As luck would have it, one of the couples that he stayed with had connections to Max Perkins, a famous editor at the Scribner's publishing company. Scribner's published the novel in 1948, and it received immediate acclaim, though Paton had no literary reputation and the history of South Africa was virtually unknown in the United States. Influenced by the works of John Steinbeck and Knut Hamsun, Paton chose to tell his story in a direct, uncomplicated style and to focus nearly as much attention on the land as he did on the characters. Like Steinbeck's and Hamsun's novels, Paton's *Cry, the Beloved Country* demonstrates the ability of people to endure tremendous, nearly overwhelming, loss and tragedy, and to gain insight from their losses.

The story is very simple. An elderly Christian Zulu priest, Stephen Kumalo, receives word that his younger sister is ill in Johannesburg, so he takes the opportunity to discover the whereabouts of his missing son, Absalom, who had traveled to the city a couple of years earlier and stopped writing to his parents. When he gets to Johannesburg, the priest discovers that his sister had been a prostitute, his brother an influential but corrupt political figure in the pro-Africa movement, and his son a petty criminal who

spent time in a reformatory. Before Kumalo has a chance to rescue his son, Absalom murders a white man during a botched burglary. This white man was famous for working on behalf of blacks in South Africa and was the son of a prominent white farmer, James Jarvis, from Kumalo's home district of Ndothseni. The second half of the novel focuses on the ways that Kumalo and Jarvis come to terms with their respective losses. In the process, Paton demonstrates that these are not just personal tragedies, but the results of a social system gone horribly wrong.

Among the novel's strengths is Paton's ability to remain true to human nature and not to retreat into unwarranted sentiment. For instance, Absalom Kumalo remains weak and cowardly. He is unable to justify his actions other than to say that he was frightened and repents the murder only because it means that he will be executed. Similarly, Gertrude Kumalo, the sister who becomes a prostitute, abandons her child while hinting that she does so to become a nun, though it is far more likely that she will return to her old life. John Kumalo, Stephen's brother, offers no help with Absalom's trial, and indeed gets a lawyer to protect only his own son, who had participated in the burglary. To that end, John Kumalo's principal interest is his own power and prestige, which he will never risk, not even for his family. Stephen Kumalo is not a perfect man either, lashing out in anger against his brother John and his own son's pregnant girlfriend.

The novel has three main thematic levels. The first involves the various ways that people can be easily corrupted and the degree of difficulty inherent in resisting or overcoming such corruption. The second involves South African politics, a lifelong concern for Paton. Essentially, Paton rejected notions popular among whites in South Africa that the races were better off segregated, that blacks were inferior morally and intellectually to whites, and that blacks were naturally inclined toward crime. The third involves religious belief. Paton was brought up in the strict Christadelphian church, but in adulthood joined the more liberal Society of Christians and Jews. *Cry, the Beloved Country* reflects Paton's belief in the redemptive power of faith and the ability of a true faith to help one overcome tremendous personal tragedy. In this respect, *Cry, the Beloved Country* echoes such novels as Graham Greene's *Heart of the Matter* and Willa Cather's *Death Comes for the*

"CRY, THE BELOVED COUNTRY, FOR THE UNBORN CHILD THAT IS THE INHERITOR OF OUR FEAR. LET HIM NOT LOVE THE EARTH TOO DEEPLY. LET HIM NOT LAUGH TOO GLADLY WHEN THE WATER RUNS THROUGH HIS FINGERS, NOR STAND TOO SILENT WHEN THE SETTING SUN MAKES RED THE VELD WITH FIRE. LET HIM NOT BE TOO MOVED WHEN THE BIRDS OF HIS LAND ARE SINGING, NOR GIVE TOO MUCH OF HIS HEART TO A MOUNTAIN OR A VALLEY. FOR FEAR WILL ROB HIM OF ALL IF HE GIVES TOO MUCH.'"

Archbishop, which also depict men undergoing crises of faith. *Cry, the Beloved Country* remains the most famous South African novel ever written. Paton's ability to present suffering and redemption plainly yet beautifully makes this a timeless human story of caution and hope.

PLOT SUMMARY

Book I

Cry, the Beloved Country begins with a description of the land near Ixopo, which is split into two contrasting terrains. One consists of rolling grass hills, "lovely beyond any singing of it." In the valley, however, the land is hard and the grass burned. "It is not kept, or guarded, or cared for, it no longer keeps men, guards men, cares for men."

The story itself gets underway when Reverend Stephen Kumalo receives a letter from a Johannesburg minister, Theophilus Msimangu. Seeing the envelope reminds Kumalo of the family he has in Johannesburg: his brother John, a carpenter; his sister Gertrude, twenty-five years his junior; and his son Absalom, who has not returned since going to Johannesburg to find Gertrude. Kumalo has no knowledge of the whereabouts or fortunes of any of them. The letter itself tells him only that his sister is sick and that he should travel immediately to Johannesburg. Kumalo and his wife debate

BIOGRAPHY

ALAN PATON

Alan Paton was born in 1903 in Pietermaritz burg, Natal, a province on the east coast of South Africa. He attended the University of Natal, graduating with degrees in science and education. While attending the university, Paton began writing poetry and dramas, published mostly in student magazines. In 1925, he became the assistant master at the Ixopo High School. Three years later, he joined the staff of Pietermaritzburg College. He was appointed principal of the Diepkloof Reformatory in 1935.

After the 1948 publication of his first novel, *Cry, the Beloved Country*, Paton retired from government service. He became a well-known writer and lecturer, and was a founder of the Liberal Party of South Africa, which opposed apartheid and the white nationalism of the ruling government. The Liberal Party clashed with the government run by the conservative Afrikaner Nationalist Party and was outlawed and forced to disband in 1968 because it contained both black and white members. Paton continued to write and lecture against apartheid until his death in 1988 (some sources wrongly give the year as 1992).

---

about what money he should take with him on his trip to Johannesburg. He takes the money meant to send Absalom to school, because, "When people go to Johannesburg, they do not come back." He also takes the money that he had been saving to buy his wife a stove.

The two-day trip to Johannesburg is quite uncomfortable, in part because he must travel in the car for non-Europeans. In recounting the journey, the author shows how little Kumalo knows of life outside his home district of Ndotsheni. He does not understand how gold mines work, for instance. He mistakes a minor town for Johannesburg. To him, the noise, high

buildings, and multitudinous streets of urban life are only a confusion. When Kumalo arrives in Johannesburg, he does not understand street crossings and nearly gets run over by a bus. A young man helps him find his way to the bus station, but tricks Kumalo out of money by offering to buy what turns out to be an unnecessary ticket. An old man finally helps Kumalo find the church of Reverend Msimangu in the Sophiatown suburb.

At Msimangu's church, Kumalo dines with other Anglican priests, and they discuss the sickness of the land and the high crime rate in the cities. Finally, when Kumalo is alone, Msimangu reveals the real reason for the letter. Gertrude, it turns out, is not physically ill, but morally so, having become a prostitute and having spent some time in prison. She has a child, and Msimangu believes that while Gertrude may not be savable, the child needs someone to take him away from the dangers of Johannesburg. Kumalo inquires about his son and brother, and though Msimangu knows nothing about the son, he does tell Kumalo that his brother has now become a major political figure in Johannesburg, but has rejected Christianity. Msimangu arranges for Kumalo to stay with a Christian woman, Mrs. Lithebe.

The next day, the two priests go to see Gertrude. Kumalo's arrival frightens her. When he talks to her, she is evasive at first. However, when he offers to take her back to Ndotsheni, she falls to the floor begging to be taken from Johannesburg. Kumalo arranges for Gertrude and her son to stay with Mrs. Lithebe while he searches for Absalom. Gertrude herself knows nothing of Absalom other than that he spent much time with his cousin, the son of John Kumalo.

The following day, Kumalo and Msimangu visit John Kumalo. John has grown fat and acts like a chief. At first, he does not recognize his older brother. During the conversation, John automatically lapses into political rhetoric and posturing. His voice becomes like that of a bull or lion. Msimangu clearly does not like John, and repeatedly baits him about his lax moral standards. When Kumalo asks about the whereabouts of Absalom, John becomes cautious and provides only an address for a place where Absalom once worked. Unfortunately, the people there cannot say much about Absalom and provide only an address where he once lived. The woman who owns the house will say nothing about Absalom, but looks at Kumalo with pity. She gives another address for Absalom. Msimangu, noting the woman's strange look, has a private word with her, and she reveals that she did not like Absalom's friends.

When the two priests go to the new address in Alexandra, they discover that there is a boycott of the buses organized by the black leadership. They walk for several miles before a white man gives them a ride to Alexandra in his car. When they find the owner of the house where Absalom stayed, she is defensive and fearful. Once more, Msimangu is able to get more detailed information through one-on-one confrontation. He discovers that Absalom and his cousin had been thieves and had left the previous year because they were afraid of being discovered. She says that Absalom was friendly with a taxi driver. This driver, too, is afraid to discuss Absalom, saying only that he had gone to the Orlando shantytown.

When the two priests go to Shanty Town, they discover that Absalom had been taken by police to the local reformatory. At the reformatory, they learn that Absalom had been released the previous month for good behavior and had a job and a pregnant girlfriend. A young administrator from the reformatory takes them to where Absalom lives. They talk to his girlfriend, but discover that Absalom has disappeared. The futility of the long search and the corruption and degradation revealed in the process anger Msimangu, who makes a frustrated outburst. After Kumalo shows concern for Absalom's girlfriend, Msimangu tells him, "were your back as broad as heaven, and your purse full of gold, and did your compassion reach from here to hell itself, there is nothing you can do." Back at the mission house, the two read in the newspaper that a local white man and crusader for black rights, Arthur Jarvis, has been murdered in his home, most probably by three native youths. The following day, the priests learn that the police are now actively seeking Absalom in connection with the crime.

A day later, the young administrator from the reformatory tells Kumalo that Absalom has been arrested for murdering Arthur Jarvis and that his cousin is an accomplice. Kumalo visits his brother John to tell him of these events. The two of them go together to the prison. Stephen meets with his son, but can get very little out of him. Absalom readily admits that he killed Jarvis, but claims that it was an accident because he was afraid. Absalom appears to be weak and cowardly, unable to give a satisfactory or meaningful account of his lapse into crime. To compound matters further, John sees a way to get out of his own dilemma with his son because the only proof that his son was at the scene is Absalom's word. John's self-interested abandonment of his brother and nephew sinks Stephen into a depression so deep that he wonders if God has abandoned him. A white priest, Father Vincent, manages to give him some comfort and to help Kumalo find a lawyer for his son.

The following morning, Kumalo travels alone to visit Absalom's girlfriend. While there, his rage gets the better of him. He grills her quite severely and feels an overwhelming "wish to hurt her," but immediately repents, feeling ashamed of his cruelty. He offers to take her back with him to Ndotsheni if she agrees to marry Absalom. She is eager for the chance to escape Johannesburg and readily assents to marrying Absalom. He arranges for her to stay with Mrs. Lithebe. Book I ends when Father Vincent finds a lawyer for Absalom who will take the case without charge, "for God."

Book II

Book II returns the reader to Ixopo and goes back a few days in time. The narrative focus switches to James Jarvis, a white farmer who has not given much thought to the political and racial matters of South Africa, and so accepts the standard ideas of the criminal nature and untrustworthiness of blacks. The action begins when police captain Van Jaarsveld goes out to Jarvis's farm to inform him that his son, Arthur, had been murdered in Johannesburg. Jarvis and his bereft wife take an airplane, not a train, to Johannesburg to claim the body of their son. They are met at the airport by John Harrison, their son's brother-in-law, who takes them to his parents' house. John Harrison admired Arthur and agreed with much of his politics. However, Jarvis reveals that he often strongly disagreed with his son's views on the "native question." Harrison's father and Jarvis discuss Arthur's life. Harrison tells Jarvis of how people liked and admired Arthur, that he had learned to speak Afrikaans, and that he might have run for political office. Listening to this account, Jarvis feels as though he were hearing a story about a stranger.

The next day, Jarvis visits his son's house and discovers a life and viewpoint that he never really knew existed. He is fascinated by his son's large book collection, especially the books about Abraham Lincoln. He is equally fascinated by all the offers for memberships and meeting attendances that Arthur received. Jarvis reads the last few pages of writing that Arthur had been working on before his death, a speech about the ways that white destruction of the tribal system had been the main cause of black crime—"Our natives today produce criminals and prostitutes and drunkards, not because it is their nature to do so, but because their simple system of order and tradition and convention has been destroyed"—then spends some time reading the speeches of Abraham Lincoln.

After Arthur's funeral, James and Mr. Harrison discuss the "native problem" in South Africa. Harrison believes himself to be fair with natives, but thinks that the natives are getting "out of hand." Worst of all, as far as Harrison is concerned, they have started trades unions. After the conversation, the younger Harrison points out to Jarvis that when the elder Harrison talks of Afrikaners, he really means those in the Nationalist Party, whose major platform is the separation of the races. The following morning, Jarvis reads his son's manuscript in order to understand his son. The manuscript passages outline the basic rationale for liberal politics in South Africa. Arthur writes that white South Africans are often hypocritical in their Christianity and that it is both illogical and anti-Christian to believe that God created the white race for the purpose of dominating the black one. After reading the manuscript, Jarvis gives it to his wife to read.

Jarvis attends the trial of Absalom Kumalo, which Stephen Kumalo is also attending. The narrative focuses mainly on the examination of Absalom by the prosecutor. Once more, Absalom openly admits that he killed Arthur, and once more claims that he did so because he was scared. However, he is evasive, as he had been with his father, in his answers as to why he carried a loaded gun and why he entered into any plan to burglarize a house. During a break in the trial, Jarvis returns to his son's house, where he finds another of his son's essays. This one strikes Jarvis personally because in it Arthur discusses his upbringing. Arthur states that from his parents he learned about honor, charity, and

generosity, but about South Africa he learned "nothing at all." More than any of Arthur's other works, this one shocks Jarvis.

On a day of court adjournment, the Jarvises spend some time with the family of one of Margaret Jarvis's nieces, Barbara Smith. It so happens that the Smith family had been employers of a girl that Kumalo had agreed to look for when he left Ndotsheni. When Kumalo goes to the house, Jarvis answers the door. While Kumalo instantly recognizes Jarvis, Jarvis does not recognize Kumalo. Terrified by this unexpected encounter, Kumalo trembles and finds it difficult to stand. Kumalo manages to inquire about the girl, but she had already left the Smiths' employ. Only after this exchange does Jarvis recognize Kumalo. It takes Kumalo several minutes to admit that his son has killed Jarvis's son. Surprisingly, Jarvis is not angry at Kumalo and instead asks whether he remembers when Arthur was young and used to ride horses in the valley. Kumalo replies that he remembers, and that there was a "brightness" in the boy.

Jarvis and Kumalo, unbeknownst to each other, both attend a rally held by John Kumalo. As before, Kumalo is impressed by his brother's magnificent speaking voice. Msimangu is typically less impressed, saying that they should "thank God he is corrupt.... For if he were not corrupt, he could plunge this country into bloodshed." Jarvis, too, is disturbed by John Kumalo's speech, seeing in it a danger to the social order. The police keep an eye on John Kumalo, noting how carefully he treads the line of legality in his speeches.

At Mrs. Lithebe's house, things are not going well. While the pregnant girl is willing, obedient, and eager to start a new life, Gertrude continues in her old habits, flirting with men and consorting with the wrong sorts of people. However, Gertrude seems to have been impressed by the testimony of a black nun and tells Mrs. Lithebe in secret that she plans to become a nun in order that she may control her desire for men. Gertrude also tells this to the pregnant girl, asking that she take care of Gertrude's son and that she keep the decision secret from Kumalo, thus hinting that she is not being entirely truthful.

The judge's verdict is that Absalom is guilty and shall be hanged, but that there is not enough evidence to convict his two accomplices. After the verdict, Father Vincent arranges to marry Absalom to his girlfriend so that she may officially become part of the Kumalo family. Kumalo makes a final visit to his brother. John is not at all repentant about his selfishness in getting his obviously guilty son freed of the charges against him. John's attitude angers Kumalo, who retaliates by suggesting that he knows of a spy in John's political organization. When Kumalo reveals that this story is in fact a lie used to get John to see how he had hurt his brother, John is furious and kicks Stephen out of his shop, slamming the door behind him. Later that night, Mrs. Lithebe holds a farewell party for the Kumalos. After the party, Msimangu tells Kumalo that he is retiring from the mission to live alone in contemplation. He gives Kumalo a gift of money from the church, which, though not a significant sum, is more money than Kumalo has ever seen. Deeply moved, Kumalo repents how he behaved toward his brother. The next morning, when they are to leave Johannesburg, Kumalo discovers that Gertrude has vanished.

Book III

When Kumalo returns to Ndotsheni with Gertrude's son and Absalom's pregnant wife, he is warmly and respectfully greeted by the people of his community. They had not liked the priest that the bishop had sent to replace him while he was away. He discovers that Jarvis had returned a few days earlier and that Margaret Jarvis is very ill. Kumalo returns to his work as a priest beginning with a sermon asking for forgiveness. In particular, he prays for rain because there has been a long drought in the valley. However, Kumalo is also resolved that he should work harder for the benefit of the people in Ndotsheni. He visits the chief and tries to convince him to devise a plan that would keep more of the tribe in the valley. Though rather self-important and not very bright, the chief does understand the problem, but he sees little that he can do to fix it.

After visiting the chief, Kumalo is surprised to find the son of the slain Arthur Jarvis riding a horse outside of the church. The boy seems unaware of Kumalo's connection to him and asks to see the church, curious to know the differences between it and his own. The boy is eager to learn the Zulu language and takes an informal lesson from Kumalo before riding home. During this lesson, Kumalo tells the boy about the dying

children of the valley who have no milk. Later that night, Kumalo is surprised to find that his friend has brought down a wagonload of milk from Jarvis's house. The boy had told Jarvis of conditions in the valley, and Jarvis had decided to supply milk to the sick children until the drought is over.

A few days later, Jarvis and the local magistrate travel to Ndotsheni to survey a plot of land. The chief also shows up and tries to assert his importance by helping, but clearly does not understand what is happening. After the survey is over, all except Jarvis leave, though a large storm is on its way. Jarvis, instead, goes to talk to Kumalo. The rain arrives, and the church roof is so leaky that neither can find a dry spot inside. The two sit in silence for a while, then Jarvis asks whether Absalom will be executed in fifteen days. After hearing that there is no mercy, Jarvis stares at the church altar saying, "When it comes to this fifteenth day, he said, I shall remember," and leaves.

A few days later, the Jarvis boy returns to Kumalo's church to learn more Zulu. After the boy leaves, Kumalo is met by a young black man, Napoleon Letsitsi, whom Jarvis had hired to reorganize the farming habits of the natives so that the valley could be self-sustaining. A few days later, during a confirmation rite, the locals learn that Margaret Jarvis has died. Kumalo sends a letter of condolence to Jarvis. The bishop of Kumalo's church arrives to tell Kumalo that the church has decided to replace him and that he and his family should move to a nearby town where they are not known. At the same time, a letter arrives from Jarvis thanking Kumalo for his condolences. Since such a letter from a white man to a black man is so unusual in South Africa, the bishop asks for the story behind it and is so impressed that he decides to keep Kumalo in his position.

The novel ends when Kumalo travels alone up a nearby mountain to await the execution of his son. On the way he meets Jarvis, who, proud man that he is, refuses Kumalo's thanks for his good works in the valley. Jarvis declares that he is no saint, but that he had been a man in darkness before meeting Kumalo. Jarvis reveals that he is going to move away, but will often return to Ndotsheni to make sure that the farming reforms are carried through. After they part, Kumalo spends the day praying alone on the mountain. Kumalo realizes that though some

Richard Harris and James Earl Jones in a scene from the film Cry, the Beloved Country *The Kobal Collection.*
Reproduced by permission

good was done in his homeland, South Africa, and all of Africa, is a land in fear, and that total reconciliation of all its peoples will happen many years after both he and Jarvis are dead.

THEMES

Corruption and Inequality

One of the major concerns in *Cry, the Beloved Country* is the way that modernity, particularly a type of modernity that relies on the subservience of one group of people to another, is morally corrupting. The reader's first cue to this is when Kumalo's wife declares that those who go to Johannesburg do not return. The impression is further cemented when the first person whom Kumalo meets in Johannesburg robs him. The effect of the city on Kumalo's own family is profound. His sister has become a prostitute, his son a thief and murderer, and his brother a political iconoclast in love with power. Scattered

throughout the book are discussions and newspaper stories about the crime problem in Johannesburg, especially the crimes committed by blacks against whites.

Some critics have seen this depiction as a tacit agreement by Paton that blacks are the source of crime. However, Paton was merely demonstrating the way things really were. For instance, it is highly unlikely that South African newspapers, published by whites, would print stories other than those of black crimes against whites. Pronouncements about the criminal nature of blacks are placed entirely in the mouths of insensitive white characters. Finally, there are the writings and beliefs of Arthur Jarvis, who represents the conscience of the novel. Jarvis declares that there are two causes of corruption in South Africa: the destruction of the tribal lifestyle, and the modern industrial system that relies upon subjugation of uprooted tribal blacks. Paton demonstrates that such corruption runs deep. Absalom Kumalo seems controlled almost entirely by social forces and lacks the learning or vocabulary to express the reasons for his criminality, particularly when he has several opportunities to leave it behind. The depth and pervasiveness of this corruption in the black community of Johannesburg disheartens Msimangu so much that he gives up his mission. Ultimately, the voice of Arthur Jarvis explains what is to be done about this trouble. He writes that going back to old tribal ways is impossible—though the "old tribal system was ... a moral system"—so the only way out is to build a new social system based on morality.

Politics of Oppression

South African politics pervade *Cry, the Beloved Country*. In 1946, South Africa was not yet a country as such, but a confederation of states and districts run by different ethnic groups— descendants of English colonists, descendants of Dutch colonists (known as Afrikaners or Boers), and natives. The native states were similar to Native American nations in the United States, with little power, influence, or say over their own affairs. One of the strongest political movements of the day was represented by the Afrikaner Nationalist Party, whose ideas are voiced mainly by Mr. Harrison, who thinks the situation with black native South Africans has "got[ten] beyond us." The nationalists believed that only a separation of the races could keep South Africa stable. They argued that the existing system of social inequality was both economically justified and ordained by God, who had created whites specifically to rule over "uncivilized" blacks. Nationalists believed that giving blacks equal economic and political status with whites would ruin the economy for everyone, and that blacks were therefore much better off with the system as it existed. Mr. Harrison makes this argument in reference to the natives' attempts to unionize. He believes that their strikes will close down the gold mines, and "where will South Africa be then? And where would the natives be themselves? They'd die by the thousands of starvation."

Cry, the Beloved Country also shows the backlash against the prevailing nationalist mood in South Africa. One instance is the inclusion of the bus boycott in Johannesburg. This was a historical event, a reaction against plans to raise bus fares in order to limit the numbers of blacks entering Johannesburg. Another is the growing labor movements in the city, represented

by John Kumalo's group. Though Paton is clearly wary of the anti-Christian stance and incendiary rhetoric of many within this movement, he demonstrates that such a movement is an inevitable response to the oppression. Through the words of Msimangu in response to one of John Kumalo's speeches, Paton sounds a clear warning to those who would ignore or attempt to quash the labor movement, the fear that "one day when they are turned to loving, they will find we are turned to hating."

Christianity as Social Policy

There is no doubt that *Cry, the Beloved Country* is a Christian novel. The style is often similar to that of the King James Bible, and several passages are references to the Bible. All of the moral characters, with the exception of James Jarvis, are devout Christians. However, Paton's is not a smug Christianity; rather, he puts faith to the test. In particular, the main Christian characters, Kumalo and Msimangu, must go through severe crises of faith. Kumalo, for instance, must face the fact that he cannot save, in the Christian sense, his family members who have fallen into sin. Toward the middle of the novel, Kumalo nearly collapses in despair at the inability of his faith to make much of a difference. Msimangu is similarly affected. Seeing the effects of economic and political oppression on the morality of blacks living in Johannesburg causes him to make several angry and despairing remarks and finally drives him to give up his missionary post in order to live in isolated religious contemplation. What redeems faith in the novel are the numerous small acts of individual courage and charity that run throughout, mostly from whites who have no personal gain in such actions. Msimangu is confounded, for instance, that a white man is willing to risk arrest by giving rides to black men during the bus boycott. Jarvis's intellectual awakening and desire to continue some of the work his son had done is the most important example of the countervailing force of charity. There are no miracles, just individual people who see that a society holds together only when its people help each other.

Paton is aware of those, like John Kumalo, who would say that the church has been powerless in improving black people's conditions. Some people see Christianity as a white imposition on natives, another tool to destroy the tribal way of life. Arthur Jarvis, in his writings, recognizes this contradiction in the history of Christianity in South Africa: that the intention to do good may have caused harm. He notes, however, that the tribes cannot be rebuilt along the old models, and that the only truly Christian thing to do is to build a society based on the concept that faith and circumstance bring the races together, because, "whether we be fearful or no, we shall never, because we are a Christian people, be able to evade the moral issues."

HISTORICAL OVERVIEW

Pre–Twentieth Century South Africa
The first European settlements in southernmost Africa were established in the seventeenth century and served mainly as ports for European sailors on the trade route to India or the Far East. The original Dutch settlers and their descendants ("Boers") had established an agrarian lifestyle, in contrast with later, more educated and urban British colonists. The Boers retreated from the coast to distance themselves from the British, but clashed with the native peoples they encountered farther inland. When diamonds were discovered in the area in 1869, followed by gold in 1886, the English claimed the riches, coerced blacks into working the mines by demanding they pay "hut taxes" and denied the Boers a share in the economic boon. A series of wars toward the end of the nineteenth century led to agreement about British sovereignty, but with continuing resentment about the cultural, political, and economic domination of the Boers.

Black Townships around Johannesburg
In order to pay their hut taxes, many black South Africans had to leave their homes and work for white employers. While some black workers could find housing when they worked in the mines or as household servants, most had nowhere to live in Johannesburg. The solution to this problem was designated "locations" for blacks, coloreds (mixed race), and Asians. For black workers, most of these areas were compounds, barracks-style encampments with fences and gates for "security." Sanitation in most of the locations was extremely poor, and in 1904, a large population was moved farther away from the city center, provided with some corrugated iron huts, or left to build their own homes. This settlement, known as Kliptown, lasted until the 1970s, and became the basic pattern for later townships such as Alexandra, Newclare (called Claremont in *Cry, the Beloved Country*), and Soweto.

By the 1920s, many male workers started bringing their families into the townships. The leadership of Johannesburg was particularly slow and lax in dealing with the problems caused by overcrowding and poor infrastructure in its townships. As a result, by 1939 there were only 6,700 hostel accommodations and 8,900 houses to accommodate 244,000 native workers and families. During World War II, many white men left South Africa to fight in the war and black workers from the townships were brought in to fill the gaps. The result was an increasingly politicized and organized black labor movement, like that led by John Kumalo in *Cry, the Beloved Country*. Additionally, because of the massive influx of natives looking for work, there simply was not enough housing space. New arrivals from tribal lands had to create squatter communities on unused parcels; these included Pimville, Orlando, Sophiatown, and Alexandra. Chapter 9 of *Cry, the Beloved Country* is devoted entirely to describing the creation of these shantytowns.

The Union of South Africa and Apartheid
The Union of South Africa was formed in 1910 as a British territory where only whites could hold public office. The South African National Party, representing Boers and favorable to the British, took power. Later, the more separatist National Party formed to advocate independence from Britain and to champion the interests of white non-English South Africans ("Afrikaners"). Soon, laws to officially disenfranchise the majority black population proliferated. Eight percent of the country's land was set aside for the seventy-five percent of its population who were black, while the minority white population laid claim to ninety percent of the land. In 1948, the National Party gained power on a pro-apartheid platform, advocating the strict separation of the races. Instituted in the early 1950s, the system grew more oppressive and extreme for forty years, until resistance and international condemnation brought about its end in the early 1990s.

CRITICAL OVERVIEW

First published in the United States in 1948, *Cry, the Beloved Country* had become a popular success within a year. Reviews in America, and later in England, praised the novel for its simplicity of presentation and its powerful portrayals. In the

Military personnel walk around bodies after the Sharpeville Massacre, 1964 Hulton-Deutsch Collection / Corbis

foreword, Charles Scribner Jr. calls the novel "a cultural force of great power and influence." English reviews tended to focus much more on the novel's political dimensions, especially since the English publication came after the Afrikaner Nationalist Party took control of South Africa's government and promptly passed the laws that came to be known collectively as apartheid. Reception of the novel in South Africa was naturally quite different. Afrikaner reviewers virtually ignored it, and black South Africans had mixed views of the novel. Some welcomed it as a realistic account of South Africa's problems, while others felt that the solution posed in the book relied too heavily on charity from whites. Many were skeptical of its Christian themes, believing Christianity to be a tool of white oppression.

In his 1987 introduction to *Cry, the Beloved Country,* Edward Callan describes its enduring power, which he says may derive

> from an effect of history that affords present-day readers a perspective on the novel in some ways comparable to that of audiences in the Greek tragic theater who know the outcome of the fateful struggle unfolding before them. Such foreknowledge quickens the emotions of pity and terror that Aristotle thought proper to tragedy.

Since the end of apartheid in 1993, South African critics have warmed toward the novel, in particular because it helped bring world attention to South Africa's racial oppression. At the world premiere of the 1995 film adaptation, then-President of South Africa Nelson Mandela called the book "a monument to the future," and referred to Alan Paton as "one of South Africa's leading humanists."

Talk show host Oprah Winfrey chose *Cry, the Beloved Country* as one of her Book Club selections in the fall of 2003, catapulting the book onto the bestsellers list. On Winfrey's website, *Cry, the Beloved Country* is called "a timeless, universal story of love and home, compassion and endurance." Modern academic criticism of *Cry, the Beloved Country* often confronts the tensions created in Paton's solutions to South Africa's racial crisis. In short, scholars tend to see a kind of white paternalism in Paton's particular brand of liberalism. In "Stranger Fictions: Trajectories in the Liberal Novel," South African English professor Tony Morphet, for instance, claims that the common bond forged between Kumalo and Jarvis at the novel's conclusion "*moves backward.*" He goes on to note that "It is a return to the premodern forms of relation,

MEDIA ADAPTATIONS

The 1951 film adaptation of *Cry, the Beloved Country* was produced in England and directed by Zoltan Korda. It stars Canada Lee as Stephen Kumalo, Charles Carson as James Jarvis, and Sidney Poitier as Msimangu. It is currently unavailable.

The 1995 film adaptation, produced in South Africa, stars James Earl Jones as Stephen Kumalo and Richard Harris as James Jarvis. It is available on VHS and DVD from Miramax.

A musical tragedy version of the novel, called *Lost in the Stars*, was written by Maxwell Anderson, with music by Kurt Weill. There are two CDs of the musical, one of the original 1949 cast on the Decca label, and a 1993 version on the MusicMasters label.

The musical *Lost in the Stars* was filmed in 1974 by the American Film Theatre. It is available on VHS by Kino Video.

An unabridged audio version of *Cry, the Beloved Country* is available on CD from Blackstone Audiobooks. It is narrated by Frederick Davidson.

not only in the sense that it is a return to the rural out of the urban, but also in the sense that it predicates the relations between the men—and hence the races—on the foundation of irrational faith." Despite such criticism, *Cry, the Beloved Country* retains a high stature in world literature, both inside and outside of South Africa.

CRITICISM

Patrick Colm Hogan
In the following excerpt, Hogan examines the ways that Paton addresses racism and discriminatory issues between blacks and whites in South Africa in Cry, the Beloved Country.

As it is a novel of South Africa, the ideological concerns to which Paton addresses himself are centrally concerns about race: the condition of blacks, the relations between the white minority and the black majority, etc. But it is within a largely racist problematic that Paton defines his critique of South African racism.

First of all, racist (and sexist) ideology is always based on an affirmation of difference. Though much recent theory obscures this fact, the first function of ideology justifying oppression is to establish a firm distinction between the oppressor and the oppressed. Nazis did not rationalize the Holocaust by claiming that Aryans and Jews were the same, nor did American slaveholders defend slavery by asserting that blacks and whites share a universal humanity. Fascists, slaveholders, colonialists, patriarchs all seek to justify their domination by reference to deep and abiding differences that radically separate people on the basis of skin color, sex, national or class origin, etc., and that effectively dehumanize members of the oppressed group.

However, not all dehumanization is the same. While there are many variations on this theme, there are three particularly common motifs. Members of an oppressed group are most frequently portrayed as subhuman/animal, prehuman/juvenile, or posthuman/aged. Each of these types carries with it a cluster of properties defining members of the oppressed group in terms of their sexuality and instinctual life, intellectual capacities, morality, social formations, verbal abilities, stature, color, and miscellaneous physical attributes. In addition, each is typically associated with a range of images and metaphors which are appropriate to the putative bestiality, juvenility, or senility of the oppressed group. The juvenile category is most relevant to *Cry, the Beloved Country*.

The juvenile stereotype is first of all the assimilation of members of the oppressed group to children, with the correlate assimilation of the oppressing group to adults. It separates these groups by stage of development, knowledge, maturity—but not, as with the bestial stereotype by species. There are two common subtypes of the juvenile stereotype: the adolescent and the puerile. The puerile is asexual or presexual, rowdy perhaps but neither instinct-driven nor moral, playful rather than violent or rational, innocuously anarchic, chattering, small, cute. Members of a puerile group need basic education and the firm, loving guidance of the dominant, "parental" group. This is a common patriarchal characterization of women, and a standard characterization of colonial natives during times of peaceable relations. The adolescent, in contrast, is sexually irresponsible, overpowered by instinct, morally confused, violent, prone to delinquency, rough and deceptive in speech. This shares with the bestial stereotype a characterization of the oppressed group as sexual, violently criminal, and anarchic, but the degree is less in each case and the origin of these tendencies is in upbringing, not biological nature; thus the appropriate response to delinquency is a social equivalent of reform school and severe, rather than affectionate, parenting.

Both of these stereotypes were common in the ideology of "the white man's burden," and they remain common today in liberal views of black South Africans and black Americans. It is important to emphasize that a consistent practice based on such stereotypes can be part of a critique—a specifically liberal critique—of a dominant ideology which views members of the oppressed group as subhuman, rather than merely prehuman. Arguing that whites can and should educate and elevate blacks opposes the idea that blacks are innately inferior, that the appropriate treatment of blacks is punishment rather than (ideologically sound) education, etc. Advocating gallantry towards "ladies" involves, when sincere, active opposition to rape, harassment, and physical abuse. However, at the same time, child stereotypes remain solidly within the problematic which defines and justifies oppression; they reaffirm the superiority of white people and white culture or men and male culture, the absolute necessity of white or male domination—at least until that indefinite point in the future when the childlike blacks and women have matured. Thus they provide an interesting case of ideological critique aimed at the dominant ideology.

Who are the good characters in the novel? After discussion, we find that they are of two sorts: (1) Blacks who have devoted their lives to Christ, and (2) whites who help blacks, prominently including the director of a reformatory for black adolescents. We can see immediately how the latter group functions to critique one form of racist ideology, by holding up benevolent whites as figures to be emulated. This is

consistent with Paton's genuine criticism of the common treatment of blacks as animals—of which students can usually give many textual examples. But something else is already implied by the fact that the good black characters are virtually all devout Christians: the cultural superiority of Europe over Africa.

What are some examples of this in the novel? Father Msimangu explains that he cannot "hate a white man" because "It was a white man who brought my father out of darkness." Another character, told that he has "a love for truth" explains that "It was the white man who taught me." Indeed, the association of Africans with darkness and Europeans with light is ubiquitous in the book. A particularly striking case is at the white-run school for the blind. Speaking of this school, Father Msimangu tells Father Kumalo, "It will lift your spirits to see what the white people are doing for our blind." And later, Father Kumalo thinks, "those who spoke English and those who spoke Afrikaans came together to open the eyes of black men that were blind"—his words having both literal and metaphoric resonance. Even the native languages receive their only genuine value from Christianity, as when Father Kumalo finds "the Zulu tongue . . . lifted and transfigured" through a translation of the Bible.

Thus whites have light, vision, truth, knowledge, and they can guide blacks—help them, educate them. But what of black leaders? Who are the black leaders in the book? First of all, there are the priests. In addition, there are examples of tribal leadership and secular political leadership. Father Kumalo's brother John is the primary instance of a black secular leader. He is corrupt and deceitful, and betrays his brother and nephew at the first opportunity. Moreover, if he were not corrupt, Father Msimangu explains, he would be worse; he would not solve problems, but "plunge this country into bloodshed." The tribal chief, on the other hand, is an ignorant fool, who tries to take over the direction of land development from whites, but quickly shows that he has no knowledge, no understanding, no capacities. Thus black leaders fall into four categories: (1) those who are corrupt, (2) those who provoke senseless violence, (3) those who are incompetent, (4) those who are devout Christians. Moreover, even members of this last group are able to lead only by deferring to whites: by accepting European religion, by rejoicing in the help offered by whites to blacks ("Kumalo's face wore the smile, the strange smile not known in other countries, of a black man when he sees one of his people helped in public by a white man," by standing aside as the whites work out land development plans (unlike the tribal chief), by encouraging ordinary blacks to collaborate with the police, etc. Indeed, the narrator and the black characters are quite explicit in granting only whites adequate intelligence for leadership. For example, Kumalo is good and sympathetic, but painfully simple. And Father Msimangu speaks of four leaders, one European, one of mixed European and African descent, and two African: "Professor Hoernle ... he was the great fighter for us ... he had Tomlinson's brains, and your brother's voice, and Dubula's heart, all in one man." Africans may have deep feelings, or deep voices, but only the Europeans and those with European blood (i.e., Tomlinson,) have "brains." (Though ultimately of the same general category as Kumalo—a black man filled with Christian love, who can act for the good if led by whites—Dubula is a secular activist and thus a partial exception to the preceding schema. He is worth discussing in class, but I leave him aside here due to constraints of space.)

And what of ordinary blacks in this book—what are they like? They are murderers, thieves, bootleggers, and prostitutes. And the novel repeatedly tells us that these crimes—not the casual brutalization of black men and women nor the denial of political and economic rights to the overwhelming majority of the population—are the big problems in South Africa; they are, after all, the problems of Kumalo's own family, and, more importantly, they are crimes which affect whites. The narrator informs us about one region where "most of the assaults reported were by natives against Europeans." As Father Msimangu laments, today "children break the law, and old white people are robbed and beaten," and as Father Kumalo refects, on the edge of despair, "His son had gone astray ... But that he should kill a man, a white man!" And what is the cause of these problems? Again, it is not political oppression and economic exploitation. Rather it is the lack of an adequate familial structure in which a strong moral tradition can be handed down—and specifically the failure of Europeans to provide such a system, their failure to accept parental responsibilities.

Depending on the class, we might conclude by discussing the reception of the novel. Why would *The New Republic* refer to this as "one of the best novels of our time," and why would it be such a best seller, a novel still required reading in some American high schools? Ideally, I would eventually lead this into a discussion of the function of liberalism and paternalism, not only in South Africa, but in the United States as well, where the debate over minorities tends to be defined within quite comparable parameters. Even when we find the ideological complicity of Paton's paternalistic critique—its strict adherence to a racist problematic—quite obvious, many of us may still fail to recognize a similar complicity in writings on race by prominent white American liberals. While it is valuable to help students understand the operation and critique of dominant ideology in any context, it is most valuable when they can apply and extend that understanding within the context of their own society.

Source: Patrick Colm Hogan, "Paternalism, Ideology, and Ideological Critique: Teaching *Cry, the Beloved Country*," in *College Literature*, Vol. 19, No. 3, October–February 1992, pp. 206–210.

SOURCES

Callan, Edward, Introduction, in *Cry, The Beloved Country*, by Alan Paton, Scribner, 2003.

Hogan, Patrick Colm, "Paternalism, Ideology, and Ideological Critique: Teaching *Cry, the Beloved Country*," in *College Literature*, Vol. 20, No. 1, 1993, pp. 206–11.

Mandela, Nelson, Speech at the World Premiere of *Cry, the Beloved Country*, *OBS Online Archives*, archives. obs-us.com/obs/english/films/mx/cry/speech4m.hmtl (October 23, 1995).

Morphet, Tony, "Stranger Fictions: Trajectories in the Liberal Novel," *World Literature Today*, Vol. 70, 1996, p. 54.

"Oprah's Book Club Selection: Alan Paton's *Cry, the Beloved Country*, *The Oprah Winfrey Website*, www.oprah.com/obc_classic/obc_main.jhtml (October 1, 2003).

Paton, Alan, *Cry, The Beloved Country*, Scribner, 2003; originally published in 1948.

Scribner, Charles, Jr., Foreword, in *Cry, The Beloved Country*, by Alan Paton, Scribner, 2003.

The Diary of a Young Girl

The Diary of a Young Girl, by Anne Frank, is an actual diary kept by a young Jewish girl while she was in hiding from Nazi forces with her family and others in Holland during World War II. The book covers everything from mundane details of the group's daily life in hiding to passionate expressions of Anne's first feelings of romantic love. Her diary ends just days before she and her family are discovered by the Gestapo and subsequently relocated to concentration camps throughout German-occupied Europe.

Although Anne died before the end of the war, she had aspirations of becoming a famous journalist. As she wrote in her diary, "I want to go on living even after my death!" In March of 1944, Anne heard a Dutch news broadcast that mentioned the importance of preserving wartime documents such as letters and diaries for possible future publication. Excited by this prospect, she set to work editing and improving her diary in the hope that it might someday be published. She even chose a name for her book: *Het Achterhuis*, which loosely translates as "The Secret Annex." This was the Dutch term for the type of apartment where Anne and seven others lived in hiding for over two years.

Of the eight people who lived in hiding in the Secret Annex, Anne's father, Otto, was the only one to survive the war. He prepared a typed manuscript of Anne's diary, which was published as *Het Achterhuis* in Holland in 1947.

ANNE FRANK

1947

IT'S REALLY A WONDER THAT I HAVEN'T DROPPED ALL MY IDEALS, BECAUSE THEY SEEM SO ABSURD AND IMPOSSIBLE TO CARRY OUT. YET I KEEP THEM, BECAUSE IN SPITE OF EVERYTHING I STILL BELIEVE THAT PEOPLE ARE REALLY GOOD AT HEART. I SIMPLY CAN'T BUILD UP MY HOPES ON A FOUNDATION CONSISTING OF CONFUSION, MISERY, AND DEATH."

BIOGRAPHY

ANNE FRANK

Anne Frank was born in Frankfurt, Germany, on June 12, 1929, the younger of two daughters, to Otto and Edith Frank, both Jews from successful families. When Adolf Hitler rose to power in Germany in 1933, Otto and Edith moved their family to Holland in an attempt to avoid the harsh anti-Semitism spreading throughout their home country.

In July of 1942, Anne's sister Margot received a notice to report for relocation to a Jewish labor camp in Germany. Otto and Edith, who had been preparing for just such an event, abandoned their home and moved the family into a secret apartment at the back of the office building where Otto once worked. With the help of sympathetic Dutch friends, the Franks remained in this hidden apartment for over two years, along with four other Jews hiding from the Germans.

Shortly before going into hiding, Anne received a diary as a present for her thirteenth birthday. Over the next two years, she wrote extensively of her experiences in hiding, as well as her own emotional and physical transformation into adulthood. In August of 1944, Anne and the others in the secret apartment were discovered by the Gestapo and were sent to concentration camps. Anne died at the Bergen-Belsen concentration camp in March of 1945, just days after her sister Margot.

The book became a huge success throughout Europe and the United States; the American version, published in 1952 and containing an introduction by Eleanor Roosevelt, is still in print by Bantam Books. After Otto's death in 1980, a definitive version of the diary was published with previously omitted material. As Ruud van der Rol and Rian Verhoeven note in *Anne Frank: Beyond the Diary*:

> People throughout the world have read Anne's diary and, because it captured so well the feeling and experiences of one of the war's many victims, have made Anne Frank a symbol of the millions of Jews who perished in the Second World War. Moreover, Anne has become a symbol for all people who are persecuted today for their background, the color of their skin, or their beliefs.

In 1957, the Amsterdam building that housed Anne's Secret Annex was saved from demolition by a group of conscientious citizens that included Otto Frank. The building was renamed the Anne Frank House and was opened to the public in 1960. It contains exhibits dedicated to Anne's life and to the promotion of tolerance and racial harmony. In 2004 alone, the Anne Frank House received nearly one million visitors.

The Diary of a Young Girl is a rare book: beloved by both young and old readers, it is one of the most purely human accounts of war ever published. It remains an important part of many school curricula dealing with racism and intolerance, and will likely endure as a stirring monument to the incalculable losses of the Holocaust. As Ernst Schnabel writes in *Anne Frank, A Portrait in Courage*:

> Her voice was preserved out of the millions that were silenced, this voice no louder than a child's whisper.... It has outlasted the shouts of murderers and has soared above the voices of time.

PLOT SUMMARY

The Diary of a Young Girl is autobiographical, and the "characters" mentioned are all actual people who lived in Amsterdam during the

Anne Frank The Library of Congress

early 1940s (though many of their names are altered in the published version). The diary begins on June 14, 1942, and ends on August 1, 1944. Anne did not write in her diary every day; there are often gaps of several days or even weeks between entries. Likewise, some of the entries are brief, while others are quite long.

June–September 1942

The Diary of a Young Girl begins just two days after Anne's thirteenth birthday. She has received a number of gifts, the most significant being the journal in which she is now writing. She is excited by the opportunity to express herself, but feels conflicted:

> It's an odd idea for someone like me to keep a diary; not only because I have never done so before, but because it seems to me that neither I—nor for that matter anyone else—will be interested in the unbosomings of a thirteen-year-old schoolgirl.

Anne decides to declare her diary as a new friend to whom she can reveal her innermost feelings; she names her new friend Kitty. Anne then briefly tells Kitty her family history. Her sister was born in 1926, and she was born in 1929. In 1933, the family moved to Holland, where her father served as the partner in a local

business. Although the Germans have since occupied Holland and placed numerous restrictions on Jews like the Franks—including segregated schools and shops, and the mandatory wearing of large yellow stars to distinguish them from non-Jews—as of June 1942, everything is all right for the Franks.

In less than a month, however, the SS—the elite branch of Nazis responsible for the concentration camps—send a call-up notice for Anne's sister Margot. Knowing that people called up are almost certainly doomed to the concentration camps, the family decides to enact a plan that has long been in the works. They already have a hiding place waiting for them: the back half of the office building where her father worked has a "Secret Annex," accessible only through a doorway hidden behind a movable bookcase. Anne discovers that her parents have been preparing this small three-level apartment for months, knowing that the day would come when they would need to go into hiding. Another family, the Van Daans, plan to join them in the apartment.

Early in the morning, in heavy rain, the Franks make their way on foot from their home to the Secret Annex. Anne describes the trip saying, "We got sympathetic looks from people on their way to work. You could see by their faces how sorry they were they couldn't offer us a lift; the gaudy yellow star spoke for itself." Once they arrive at their hiding place, the Franks must take care not to make noises during the day that the workers in the front half of the building might hear. Only some of the office workers—like Mr. Frank's former business partners, Mr. Kraler and Mr. Koophuis—know about the secret hiding place. The family is never allowed to leave the building under any circumstances.

Mr. and Mrs. Van Daan arrive on July 13, along with their fifteen-year-old son Peter, whom Anne describes as "a rather soft, shy, gawky youth; can't expect much from his company." Anne also finds out that her parents have left behind evidence suggesting the Frank family has fled to Switzerland—to prevent the Nazis from searching for them—and that even many of their friends believe it. Anne starts to develop conflicts with some of the people in the Secret Annex—specifically, her mother and Mrs. Van Daan.

October 1942–March 1943

Anne begins to enjoy Peter's company from time to time, but only when he is able to overcome his shyness. Elli, one of Mr. Frank's former employees in the front half of the building, sends away for a correspondence course in shorthand for the three children in the Secret Annex to study while they are confined.

The residents of the Secret Annex hear news from the outside world; as Anne sums it up, "Our many Jewish friends are being taken away by the dozen." Anne and the others harbor no delusions about what happens to those who are taken away: "We assume that most of them are murdered. The English radio speaks of their being gassed."

The Franks and Van Daans listen to an English radio station to hear news of Allied victories against the Germans. They know that every victory is a small step toward their own freedom. The families also decide that there is enough room in the Secret Annex to invite one other person to stay there. After some discussion of who is most deserving, they invite a dentist named Dussel to join them.

When Dussel arrives, he brings the news that German soldiers are searching the city house by house for hidden Jews. Anne is grateful for her family's secure hiding place, but feels guilty: "I get frightened when I think of close friends who have now been delivered into the hands of the cruelest brutes that walk the earth. And all because they are Jews!"

Anne has to share her bedroom with Dussel, and she quickly tires of his constant complaining about nearly everything she does. Other conditions in the Secret Annex are becoming unpleasant as well: electricity must be rationed, and Peter is badly bitten when he accidentally touches a rat in the attic. Still, by peeking carefully out the window when she can, Anne notices that the wartime conditions outside the Secret Annex are not much better.

April–November 1943

As Allied bombs fall on the German-occupied city, destroying government and military buildings, Anne celebrates her fourteenth birthday. She receives a poem written for her by her father, as well as some sweets that the other residents have saved up. One morning about a month later, the residents of the Secret Annex are stunned to find that someone has broken into the office building where they live. Although the burglars did not discover their hiding place, they did steal some cash and food coupons.

The air raids and bombings continue unabated, making Anne and her cohorts anxious and keeping them awake. In July, they are thrilled when they learn that Mussolini, the Fascist leader of Italy, has resigned. The Axis forces are weakened as Italy descends into internal chaos and ultimately withdraws from the war. Tensions run high in the house due to their inescapable conditions. The residents always seem to be fighting with each other, with allegiances shifting every day. As Anne puts it, "Quite honestly, sometimes I forget who we are quarreling with and with whom we've made it up."

By October, the Van Daans have run out of money with which to purchase food and other supplies. Mrs. Van Daan sells her expensive fur coat, believing she will be able to save the money to buy nice clothes after the war; she is upset when she finds out the money will instead be spent on food.

In November, Anne discovers that her fountain pen—given to her by her grandmother when she was nine, and with which she has written so much in her diary—has disappeared. She searches to no avail; her father suggests that it might have accidentally been thrown in the stove fire along with some floor sweepings and moldy beans. When her father checks the stove ashes the next morning, he finds the pen's metal clip among them. Anne is upset by her loss, but remarks, "I have one consolation, although a slender one: my fountain pen has been cremated, just what I want later!"

Lying in bed one night, Anne suddenly has a vision of Lies Goosens, one of her best friends from school before she went into hiding. In her vision, Lies wears tattered clothes and is in great distress. The girl implores Anne to help her. Anne feels strongly that Lies, wherever she is, does indeed need help, but Anne is not in a position to offer any. She vows to keep Lies in her prayers.

December 1943–February 1944

Trapped in the cramped, isolated world of the Secret Annex, Anne finds herself longing more and more for the simple freedom of being outdoors. She is happy about her body's maturation and her coming womanhood. She continues growing taller, has recently begun her period, and finds she is increasingly interested in spending time with Peter. She makes it quite clear that her feelings are not romantic: "If the Van Daans had had a daughter instead of a son, I should have tried to make friends with her too."

As the months pass without any major developments in the war, many of the residents of the Secret Annex grow more weary of each other. They have all heard each other's stories many times over and long for fresh company. Anne appreciates that living with others has taught her much; however, she notes, "I think it's all to the good to have learned a bit about human beings, but now I think I've learned enough."

Like any teenager, Anne's emotions change drastically over days and weeks. On February 3, while everyone else in the Secret Annex is excited by the prospect of a liberating British invasion of the country, Anne's words express dark feelings: "I have now reached the stage that I don't care much whether I live or die." Three weeks later, as her emotions for Peter become stronger and more romantic, her thoughts are quite different. She describes her new habit of sitting with Peter each morning, staring out the attic window at their view of the city: "'As long as this exists,' I thought, 'and I may live to see it, this sunshine, the cloudless skies, while this lasts, I cannot be unhappy.'"

March–April 1944

March begins with another burglary in the building. This time, the burglar appears to have had a key to the main lock, which makes the residents suspicious that one of the building workers might be behind the break-in. In addition, the thief may have heard the Secret Annex residents—a worrisome thought, since anyone willing to steal might also be willing to tell German troops about a possible Jewish hiding place.

Anne's relationship with Peter continues to blossom. They spend a great deal of time talking together in the attic, though some of the adults disapprove of such conduct. Anne records, sheepishly, "I believe I'm pretty near to being in love with him." As happy as she is, she feels bad for her sister, who has no one like Peter to share her feelings with. Anne's infatuation with Peter is clear as she writes of his "dearness" and her "longing for a kiss."

After hearing a Dutch Minister of Parliament on the radio suggest collecting personal letters and diaries for publication after the war, Anne starts to ponder the possibility of her own diary being published. She feels that

> it would seem quite funny ten years after the war if we Jews were to tell how we lived and what we ate and talked about here. Although I tell you a lot, still, even so, you only know very little of our lives.

The regular visitors to the Secret Annex, like Elli, tell Anne and the others how the Dutch population is in chaos amidst the continuing German occupation and Allied bombings. Many of the Dutch men have been sent away to Germany; citizens must wait in line for meager rations of food, and even young children have turned to stealing. Elsewhere in Europe, the Allied forces are making progress on the Russian front, and have nearly pushed the Germans back to Poland. Still, Anne cannot help but feel that "the end of the war is so terribly far away, so unreal, like a fairy tale."

Anne confides to "Kitty" that one day she would like to become a professional writer. In addition to maintaining her diary, she also enjoys writing stories. She explains her desire to capture her thoughts and ideas on paper: "I want to go on living even after my death!" She considers sending one of her stories to a newspaper under a pseudonym, just to see if they would publish it.

In April, yet another burglary rattles the security of the Secret Annex. This time, the men catch the burglars in the act of tearing a hole in the door and scare them off. Before they can repair the hole, however, a couple comes by to investigate the break-in. Worried that the couple has called the police—especially after they hear additional noises on the other side of their hidden doorway—the residents stay as quiet as possible all through the night. The next day, they discover that a night watchman had seen the hole in the door and called the police to investigate the building. Fortunately, the police never made it past the bookcase that hides the doorway to the Secret Annex.

Less than a week later, Anne experiences her first kiss with Peter. She is torn by the thought that she has given her affections too freely. She knows her sister would not kiss a boy without a promise of engagement first, and Anne believes her mother never had such contact with a boy before she met Anne's father. Still, she feels that their unusual circumstances—as well as her highly developed sense of independence—make her situation different from the average four-teen-year-old girl's.

May 1944

Anne discusses with Peter whether or not she should tell her father about their relationship. She decides to tell her father, who is surprised; he had thought that Anne and Peter were merely friends. He asks Anne not to visit Peter so often, but instead Anne writes him a letter declaring her independence from her family. This hurts her father, who has never treated her with anything but kindness. Anne feels terribly guilty even after he forgives her and promises herself she will be a better person in the future.

Anne continues with her writing, finishing a story about a fairy named Ellen for her father's birthday. She announces to Kitty that she plans on writing a book about her experiences after the war is over, based heavily on her diary entries. She will call the book *Het Achterhuis*, or "The Secret Annex."

Throughout May, the residents of the Secret Annex anxiously await an Allied invasion of mainland Europe. However, Anne does not share the prevailing belief that the British (and other Allies) owe it to the Dutch to rush to protect them. The British and Americans, she understands, are not fighting to protect the Dutch but ultimately to protect themselves.

The man who supplies the residents of the Secret Annex with their vegetables is arrested for harboring Jews in his home. This rattles Anne and the rest of the residents, since they could just as easily end up in the same position. It also means that they must make do with fewer vege-tables than they have grown accustomed to. Anne's mother announces that they will elimi-nate breakfast entirely, and they will eat nothing but porridge and bread each day for lunch.

The growing hardship and threat of capture that weighs upon the residents of the Secret Annex is increasingly nerve-racking. "I hope something will happen soon now," Anne writes, "shooting if need be—nothing can crush us *more* than this restlessness." After nearly two years in hiding, she longs for any sort of resolution to their precarious situation. "Let the end come, even if it is hard; then at least we shall know

whether we are finally going to win through or go under."

June–August 1944

On June 6, they finally receive the long-awaited news: D-Day has arrived, and the Allied inva-sion of Western Europe has begun. Although the war is not over, Anne and the other residents of the Secret Annex allow themselves hope. "We have been oppressed by those terrible Germans for so long, they have had their knives so at our throats, that the thought of friends and delivery fills us with confidence!" They all hope for an end to the war within the year, and Anne even considers the possibility that she may be able to attend school again in the fall.

Anne celebrates her fifteenth birthday on June 13. Although the residents of the Secret Annex and their caretakers have little to give, Anne receives many presents, most notably books and food. While these gifts are wonderful, one of Anne's greatest desires remains unful-filled: to once again enjoy nature and the outside world. "Alas, it has had to be that I am only able—except on a few rare occasions—to look at nature through dirty net curtains hanging before very dusty windows."

Throughout July, the atmosphere in the Secret Annex lightens. The residents receive a large supply of strawberries and green peas to supplement their usual food, of which they pre-serve as much as they can for future meals. Anne is elated by the news that Hitler has narrowly escaped an assassination attempt by one of his own generals. Afterward, Hitler proclaims that any soldier or officer known to be involved in the plot may be shot by another soldier without the need for a trial. Anne predicts that this will lead to rampant insubordination within the German army, as soldiers make false claims against any officers they dislike.

Anne's final entry, on August 1, discusses her divided personality. When she is around others, she feels the need to appear lighthearted and cheerful; however, when she is alone, she cannot help but wrestle with more serious thoughts and emotions. She does not feel able to share this side of her character with anyone, including Peter. Being around others prevents her from fully expressing her true nature. With the last words in her diary, she cannot help but wonder about "what I could be, if ... there weren't any other people living in the world."

The doorway leading to the attic where Anne Frank was in hiding Getty Images

THEMES

Anti-Semitism

The driving theme behind *The Diary of a Young Girl* is anti-Semitism—prejudice or discrimination against Jews. Even before they are forced into hiding, the Franks and the others endure discrimination and oppression because of their Jewish heritage. One of the cornerstones of the German Nazi Party was its vehement anti-Semitism. Although the Frank family leaves Germany for Holland long before the war, Germany ultimately occupies Holland and enacts anti-Jewish laws there. Early in her diary, Anne lists some of these laws:

> Jews must wear a yellow star, Jews must hand in their bicycles, Jews are banned from trams and Jews are forbidden to drive. Jews are only allowed to do their shopping between three and five o'clock and then only in shops which bear the placard "Jewish shop." Jews must be indoors by eight o'clock and cannot even sit in their own gardens after that hour. Jews are forbidden to visit theaters, cinemas, and other places of entertainment. Jews may not take part in public sports. Swimming baths, tennis courts, hockey fields, and other sports grounds

are all prohibited to them. Jews may not visit Christians. Jews must go to Jewish schools, and many more restrictions of a similar kind.

This is only the beginning; soon Jews are called up to report to "labor camps" from which few will ever return. It is when Anne's sister Margot receives a call-up notice that the family ultimately goes into hiding. At first, Anne describes the non-Jewish Dutch people as sympathetic to the plight of the Jews. As they walk to the Secret Annex, Anne notes that the Dutch people they pass appear to want to help them, but they know they cannot. In addition, they rely upon several Dutch sympathizers like Miep and Elli to remain alive while in hiding. She remarks on their second-class status in April 1944, saying, "Sometime this terrible war will be over. Surely the time will come when we are people again, and not just Jews."

By the next month, however, Anne writes of a trend: "We hear that there is anti-Semitism now in circles that never thought of it before." There is a rumor that German Jews who have relocated to Holland—like the Franks—will be forced by the Dutch government to return to Germany after the war. Anne cannot understand why the Dutch would suddenly feel this way about Jews, whom she calls "the most oppressed, the unhappiest, perhaps the most pitiful of all peoples in the whole world." Anne dearly loves Holland and wants to become a Dutch citizen; she hopes "that this hatred of Jews will be a passing thing."

Genocide

Genocide—the systematic extermination on a group of people, usually based on their race or ethnicity—is a key theme in *The Diary of a Young Girl*. Those in the Secret Annex are hiding for their lives. Anne and the others have their suspicions about what is happening to all the Jews who are taken away, but they have little concrete information. "We assume that most of them are murdered," Anne writes. "The English radio speaks of their being gassed." When Dussel arrives in the Secret Annex, he tells them of Germans who methodically search neighborhoods for Jews. "Countless friends and acquaintances have gone to a terrible fate," Anne writes. Looking out the window in the evening, she sees these "hunters" rounding up their prey: "No one is spared—old people, babies, expectant mothers, the sick—each and all join in the march of death."

At first, Anne feels safe and secure in the Secret Annex, saying, "We wouldn't have to worry about all this misery were it not that we are so anxious about all those dear to us whom we can no longer help." Less than a month before her arrest, Anne understands the direness of her situation but has not fully abandoned hope:

> I see the world gradually being turned into a wilderness, I hear the ever approaching thunder, which will destroy us too, I can feel the sufferings of millions and yet, if I look up into the heavens, I think that it will all come right, that this cruelty too will end, and that peace and tranquility will return again.

Class

While class is mentioned only briefly in *Anne Frank: Diary of a Young Girl,* it serves to underscore the extent of the Nazi agenda toward Jews. After writing nearly two years' worth of diary entries, Anne finally takes a moment to describe her family's background: her grandparents on both sides had been extremely wealthy until after World War I, when inflation reduced their fortunes considerably. Still, her father "had a real little rich boy's upbringing." Thanks to her father's success in the business world, Anne and her family appear to have enjoyed a comfortable lifestyle prior to 1940.

Once the Germans occupy Holland, however, social status for Jews becomes virtually meaningless. Even the most successful Jews are sent to concentration camps. Still, those Jews with enough money to plan ahead—such as the Franks—are often able to survive much longer than those with no financial resources. As Anne puts it, "Yes, we are luckier than millions of people. It is quiet and safe here, and we are, so to speak, living on capital." Even this accumulated wealth only goes so far during food shortages and inflation, and status symbols—such as Mrs. Van Daan's fur coat—must be given up for next to nothing, just to keep food on the table.

When Miep tells Anne and the others about an extravagant engagement party she recently attended, Anne writes that "we gathered round her, as if we'd never heard about delicious food or smart people in our lives before!" While wealthy non-Jewish families still enjoy an opulent lifestyle, once-wealthy Jews live in hiding, eating rotten potatoes and porridge, fearful of even looking out a window. As Anne puts it,

"The world is a queer place!" Anne's experience and testament illustrate that any sense of security from one's social status is, at best, an illusion.

HISTORICAL OVERVIEW

Nazi Germany and the Final Solution

The Treaty of Versailles ended World War I in 1918, assigning the blame unambiguously to Germany. In addition to dealing with its own heavy losses during the war, Germany's surrender was accepted only after its leaders agreed to accept full responsibility for the war and agreed to pay war reparations to several other countries. These payments not only worsened Germany's already poor economic situation, but also caused resentment among many German citizens. When the Great Depression developed in the late 1920s and early 1930s, many Germans turned in desperation to a political party that promised change: the National Socialist, or Nazi, Party.

The Nazi Party was founded on fierce German nationalism, the idea of expanding Germany's territory, and an inherent distrust of foreigners and people of "inferior" breeding. Among those labeled inferior were Jews, blacks, and gypsies. Jews in particular were singled out for somehow causing many of the problems that plagued Germany at the time. When Hitler and the Nazi Party gained control of the German government in 1933, the rights of Jews were almost immediately restricted. These restrictions became even more extreme as the years passed. When German troops launched invasions of neighboring countries such as the Netherlands and Poland, they occupied these territories and instituted the same restrictions against Jews that existed in Germany. Ultimately, millions of Jews within German-occupied territory had been taken into custody and imprisoned in concentration camps.

By 1941, the Nazis sought a "final solution of the Jewish question." Although some plans were discussed for removing the Jews from German territory—one plan even mentioned Madagascar as a possible new Jewish homeland—Nazi officials decided that the most economical and effective solution was to eliminate them. They began building "extermination camps" at several locations throughout German-occupied Poland, which were engineered to murder as many Jews as possible as efficiently as possible. The most infamous of these was Auschwitz II, also known as Birkenau, where some one million Jews were killed within three years. Roughly six million Jews lost their lives through genocide sponsored by the German government by the end of World War II in 1945.

Jews in the Netherlands Before and During World War II

Anne Frank's family relocated from Germany to the Netherlands (commonly called Holland) in 1933, just as Hitler and the Nazi Party gained power in Germany. Since the Netherlands bordered Germany to the west and had a long-established tradition of offering refuge to persecuted groups, many German Jews fled to the Netherlands between 1933 and 1940. In fact, all the residents of the Secret Annex—the Franks, the Van Daans, and Dussel—were German.

In 1940, Germany invaded the Netherlands and seized control of the country's government. Jews who had relocated to the Netherlands to escape Nazi persecution suddenly found that they had not fled far enough. In June of 1942, the Germans announced that all Dutch Jews would be relocated to concentration camps. According to Ruud van der Rol and Rian Verhoeven, writing in *Anne Frank: Beyond the Diary*, the Netherlands contained about one hundred forty thousand Jews at the start of World War II. Approximately twenty-five thousand of these Jews went into hiding to avoid forced relocation at the hands of the Germans, and over a third were ultimately discovered—just like the residents of the Secret Annex.

The Fate of the Residents of the Secret Annex

One of the most-asked questions by readers of *Anne Frank: Diary of a Young Girl* is, "What exactly happened to Anne and the other people hiding in the Secret Annex?" The Secret Annex was raided by the German Gestapo on August 4, 1944, just three days after Anne's final diary entry. The eight residents were sent to Westerbork, a Nazi concentration camp in Holland. Two of the Dutch people implicated in the concealment of the Secret Annex residents—Mr. Kraler and Mr. Koophuis—were arrested, and Kraler ultimately spent eight months working in a labor camp.

The following month, the Franks, Van Daans, and Dussel were all taken to Auschwitz. From there the prisoners were divided by gender, and Otto Frank never saw his daughters or wife again. In October of 1944, Anne, Margot, and Mrs. Van Daan were transferred to the Bergen-Belsen concentration camp in Germany while Anne's parents remained in Auschwitz. Otto Frank later reported seeing Mr. Van Daan being led off to the gas chamber at Auschwitz; Mr. Dussel was transferred to another concentration camp at Neuengamme, Germany, where he died. Anne's mother, Edith, reportedly died at Auschwitz in January of 1945. At around the same time, Peter Van Daan was transferred from Auschwitz to another camp in Austria, where he died in May of 1945—three months after the prisoners of Auschwitz, including Otto Frank, had been liberated by Russian troops.

Mrs. Van Daan was transferred from Bergen-Belsen to another camp at Theresienstadt, where she died sometime in the spring of 1945. At Bergen-Belsen, disease and cold weather took their toll on both Anne and Margot. Amazingly, while at Bergen-Belsen, Anne encountered her old school friend Lies Goosens—the very girl who had haunted Anne's dreams, pleading for help. In *Anne Frank: Beyond the Diary,* an eye-witness described the condition of the Frank girls at Bergen-Belsen: "They looked terrible. . . . [I]t was clear that they had typhus. You could really see both of them dying." Margot died in March of 1945, from disease and malnutrition. A few days later, Anne also died. Less than one month later, the Bergen-Belsen concentration camp was liberated by British troops.

Otto Frank was the only resident of the Secret Annex to escape the German concentration camps alive. He returned to Amsterdam at the end of the war, where he was reunited with Miep and Elli. They gave him all the documents the Gestapo had left scattered about the Secret Annex after their raid, including Anne's diary.

CRITICAL OVERVIEW

After Otto reclaimed Anne's diary after the war, he circulated copies of portions of it for friends and others to read. An article about Anne's diary appeared in the Dutch newspaper *Het Parool* in 1946 and generated enough interest that the complete diary was published—with some edits—under the title *Het Achterhuis* (*The Secret Annex*) in 1947. Though the first printing consisted of only fifteen hundred copies, the book became hugely popular. It was published in Germany and France in 1950, translated into English for British and American publication in 1952, and received an overwhelmingly positive response from both critics and readers.

In an extensive 1952 review for the *New York Times,* novelist Meyer Levin writes, "Anne Frank's diary is too tenderly intimate a book to be frozen with the label 'classic,' and yet no lesser designation serves." Levin calls Anne "a born writer," and declares the book "a warm and stirring confession, to be read over and over for insight and enjoyment." Though the diary was never meant to be a finished piece of literature, Levin notes that the events as documented by Anne provide "the tension of a well-constructed novel." The reviewer also offers a prediction about the author herself: "Surely she will be widely loved, for this wise and wonderful young girl brings back a poignant delight in the infinite human spirit."

Other reviewers are equally complimentary right from the start. An uncredited writer for *Time* calls the book "one of the most moving stories that anyone, anywhere, has managed to tell about World War II." J. D. Casgrain, writing for *Catholic World,* calls Anne's writing "as rich as her character" and "beautiful and womanly." Antonia White, in *New Statesman & Nation,* praises one of the book's frequently overlooked qualities, calling it "a remarkable study in the psychology of a small group of people forced to live together in almost unbearable proximity."

Despite its popularity and the overwhelming praise it has received, *Anne Frank: Diary of a Young Girl* is not without controversy. Most notably, it became known that Otto Frank omitted many passages from the diary's first publication. These passages were considered especially harsh toward Anne's mother. In addition, some of Anne's descriptions of her blossoming sexuality were excised either by Otto or of the publishing house.

In an essay for the journal *Judiasm* in 1960, Henry Pommer declares "the quality of both her death and her life have given Anne Frank an extraordinary status in our culture." He goes on to lament the overshadowing of her skill by her circumstance: "Her self-consciousness and skill as an author receive only implicit

MEDIA ADAPTATIONS

An abridged audio adaptation of the book was released on audiocassette by Audio Partners in 1992. This version is read by Julie Harris.

An unabridged audio adaptation of the novel was released on audio CD by Recorded Books in 2000. This version is read by Susan Adams, and is currently unavailable.

An abridged audio adaptation of another translation of Anne's diary, touted as "the definitive edition" due to the inclusion of some passages left out of the original version, was released by Bantam Doubleday Dell Audio in 1999. This version, read by Winona Ryder, is currently available as an audio download through audible.com.

The Diary of a Young Girl was adapted into a play by Frances Goodrich and Albert Hackett in 1955. The play was first performed at the Cort Theater in New York, and earned its creators the Pulitzer Prize for Drama as well as the Critics Circle Prize. A paperback version of the stage play was published by Dramatists Play Service in 1998.

A filmed adaptation of the 1955 stage play was released by Twentieth Century Fox in 1959. The film, directed by George Stevens, earned ten Academy Award nominations and won three, the most notable being a Best Supporting Actress Oscar for Shelley Winters, who portrayed Mrs. Van Daan. The film is currently available in VHS and DVD format from Twentieth Century Fox.

Anne Frank: Diary of a Young Girl has been adapted at least twice for American television: first in 1967, and again in 1980. Both are based at least in part upon the 1955 stage play. The 1967 version was directed by Alex Segal, and stars Diana Davila as Anne and Max von Sydow as Otto Frank. The 1980 version was directed by Boris Sagal, and stars Melissa Gilbert as Anne and Maximilian Schell as Otto. Neither version is currently available. Additional television adaptations have also been produced, but these were either not made specifically for American audiences, or they draw upon other source materials in addition to Anne's diary.

acknowledgement if we regard her diary as no more than an educative historical document or an intimate disclosure of adolescence."

According to Random House, over twenty-four million copies of the original version of the book and its translations have been sold worldwide. The book has been publicly praised by Nelson Mandela and John F. Kennedy, among many others. As Richard Covington asserts in his 2001 article "Forever Young" in *Smithsonian*, "for many Americans, the diary was their literary introduction to the Holocaust." Across the United States, it has been adopted as a cornerstone of school curricula dealing with issues of race, prejudice, war and genocide, and continues to touch readers today just as it has for over fifty years.

CRITICISM

Judith Goldstein

In the following excerpt, Goldstein argues that Anne Frank's experience of hiding—and subsequently being discovered by the Nazis—should not be taken as a representative example of the fate of all Jews in the Netherlands during World War II.

For millions of people, Anne Frank's history has come to symbolize one of Europe's deadliest conflagrations—a time when one nation set fire to its democratic government, ravaged countries all over the continent, destroyed Jewish life in Eastern Europe, and irreparably damaged Jewish existence in many Western European countries, as well. The outlines of Anne Frank's history are clear: the escape with her family from Germany and resettlement in 1933 in Amsterdam, where her father Otto Frank had a business; German occupation of the Netherlands in May, 1940; and the family's flight in 1942 into hiding in the attic above Otto Frank's office. Then betrayal and capture in August 1944; imprisonment in Westerbork, a transit camp; deportation to Auschwitz in September 1944; and death in Bergen-Belsen a few weeks before liberation in March 1945. Otto Frank's return as the sole surviving member of the family led to publication, in the early 1950s, of the diary found by Miep Gies after the police arrested the Franks and to posthumous fame for Anne and her family.

An aura of sweet optimism and faith surrounds the *Diary*. Unfortunately, the sentiments are misapplied. Cynthia Ozick's critique is closer to the truth. She described the *Diary* as a "chronicle of trepidation, turmoil, alarm.... Betrayal and arrest always threaten. Anxiety and immobility rule. It is a story of fear." People know that Anne, her sister, and her mother were exterminated, but for many readers Anne's story ends with the hope that "people are really good at heart." These words, I believe, are the key to understanding the conversion of her diary and persona into a redemptive myth.

Despite the evolution of Europe's postwar secular spirit, the myth derives much of its force from a deeply ingrained Christian template. Anne's story converges on elements of Christian belief and symbolism: a hidden child, a virgin, a betrayal, the Holocaust as Hell, a form of resurrection through words. The redemptive tale seems tragically simple, but the real history is complex and convoluted. It is part of a national tragedy in a country of contradictions. The German occupation exacerbated passive political and social habits that affected the individual and collective life of the Dutch. The Anne Frank legend has further blurred the history of Dutch Jews and the Dutch nation during the War. A sorting out is long overdue.

In Rembrandt's time, the Jewish population was 10,000. Two centuries later, it was 140,000. By 1940, many Jews had attained high levels of prosperity, recognition, and acceptance in Dutch life, although not to the degree characteristic of German Jews before the rise of Hitler. Forty percent of the Jewish population lived in small villages, towns, or cities such as the Hague. The other 60 percent lived in Amsterdam. A large number of them were poor. Through the 1930s, Dutch Jews focused on internal issues of assimilation, integration, and the well-being of the Jewish community despite the fact that Nazi rule in Germany compelled thousands of Jews, such as Otto Frank, to seek refuge in the Netherlands.

It didn't take long for the Germans to differentiate Jews from other Dutch citizens through anti-Jewish decrees and administrative acts: first, prohibition against Jewish civil servants and teachers; then, in 1941, violent assaults against Jews in the Jewish Quarter in Amsterdam. The Germans insisted that the Jews form a Jewish Council to make their community respond to increasingly punitive German demands. Jews were separated from the rest of Dutch society when their rights to property, education, work, and mobility were taken away. Jews were not allowed to use trams or bicycles, enter parks or swimming pools, go to movie houses, or use beaches. Children's schools were segregated, universities were closed to Jewish professors and students, and Jewish musicians and actors were no longer allowed to perform. Shopping was only allowed in narrow time slots. These were the same kinds of restrictions that the Germans imposed upon their own Jews in the 1930s.

Resistance flared in the spring of 1942, when every Dutch Jew was ordered to buy and wear a yellow star with "Jew" written on it. Many Dutch non-Jews wore the yellow star or a yellow flower in solidarity. It made a strong impression on Miep Gies, protector of the Frank family. "The yellow stars and yellow flowers those first few days were so common," she wrote in her book *Anne Frank Remembered*, "that our River Quarter was known as the Milky Way.... A surge of pride and solidarity swelled briefly until the Germans started cracking heads and making arrests. A threat was delivered to the population at large: anyone assisting Jews in any way would be sent to prison and possibly executed."

Life for Jews in the Netherlands ground down to a devastating pattern of anxiety and violent roundups for Jews, their protectors, and those in the resistance movement. Unlike the Jews in Denmark who could escape to Sweden, the Dutch Jews had nowhere to go. Some, such as the Franks, withdrew into hiding. They were totally dependent on their Dutch protectors who resisted the Germans by housing, feeding, clothing, and caring for Jews. Of the 140,000 Jews in the Netherlands in 1940, about 20,000 went into hiding. Approximately 7,000 of them were discovered. They shared the fate of the majority of Dutch Jews: removal to the Westerbork camp and then deportation to Sobibor and Auschwitz in the East. By the time the process was complete, 110,000 Dutch Jews had been killed.

The German occupation sorely challenged traditional Dutch attitudes, built upon a seemingly strong façade of tolerance and compromise. The political and social acceptance of differences obscured the fateful gulf between tolerance, on the one hand, and disinterest and disengagement, on the other. In regard to national cohesion and separate ethnic, religious, and political identities, the war tested the viability of the so-called Dutch pillar society, based upon separate realms of allegiance among Protestant, Catholic, Socialist, and Liberal groups. With insidious understanding of these affiliations and, above all else, the Dutch yearning for order, the Germans surgically removed the Jews from Dutch life. And so the Jews disappeared from the realm of moral concern.

The German defeat finally came to the northern part of the country on May 4, 1945. When the Germans finally surrendered, the Dutch celebrated in the streets for days. The Queen returned. "People who had been in hiding came out onto the streets," Miep Gies wrote. "Jews came out of hiding places, rubbing eyes that were unused to sunlight, their faces yellow and pinched and distrustful. Church bells rang everywhere; streamers flew.... To wake up and go through a whole day without any sense of danger was amazing."

And then came the questions and the counting—a new kind of reckoning amid the decay of civilized life. Miep Gies recounted that she and her husband Henk

> and everyone else began waiting to see just who would be coming home to us. Shocking, unimaginable accounts circulated of the liberation of the German concentration camps. Pictures were printed in the first free newspaper; eyewitness information, too. Through the occupation we'd heard rumors of gassings, murder, brutality, poor living conditions in these camps, but none of us could have imagined such atrocities. The facts had far surpassed even our most pessimistic imaginings.... I needed to do everything I could to keep my optimism about our friends. It would have been unbearable to think otherwise.

Their friends included nine Jews who had been hiding above the offices where Gies had worked for Otto Frank's firm. Day after day she asked returning Jews if they had seen any of the Frank family. In June, Otto Frank returned to the Netherlands from Auschwitz with the news that his wife had died there. He was unsure about what had happened to his two children, Margot and Anne. Months later he got word from a nurse in Rotterdam that the daughters had not survived their imprisonment in Auschwitz and Bergen-Belsen. The finality of all the deaths mixed into the tortured lives of those who survived. "I heard it said," Gies wrote in her book, "that where the Jews had looked like everyone else before [the war], after what they had endured, those who returned looked different. But people hardly noticed because everyone had been through so much misery that no one had much interest in the suffering of others." Despite the fact that Dutch Jewry lost nearly 75 percent of its population—the highest number of deaths in any Western European country under occupation—despite the fact that the Dutch Jews had lost everything, the few who came back were expected to make do with what they found, or did not find, of their former lives.

The survivors were told to be quiet—to keep their nightmares and losses to themselves. A once thriving Jewish Dutch world of family, community, institutions, and property was gone. The Dutch constructed effective bureaucratic remedies to bury Jewish claims to emotional and full financial restitution. Many survivors retreated into silence as European countries began to rebuild, to cleanse themselves, and to adjust to the development of the Iron Curtain.

The world thinks that the Franks were emblematic of what happened to the Jews in the Netherlands. From Anne's story, the international public has gained the impression that whole Jewish families could go into hiding together; that most could remain in one place for a few years; that numerous Christian friends or employees could sustain and succor them in hiding; and that the unfortunate hidden Jews were the ones betrayed by some unknown informer. And there was the final impression: that after the war Dutch Jews would be welcomed back to the country in which they had lived.

In the Netherlands, as in all European countries, there were extremes of valor and decency along with villainy, greed, brutality, and cowardice. In the large middle ground there were bystanders who lived with fear and indifference to the threatened minority. At Yad Vashem in Israel and the U.S. Holocaust Memorial Museum in Washington, thousands upon thousands of Dutch are honored as Righteous Gentiles, including Miep Gies. Risking their lives, they had to resist not only the Germans but their fellow citizens as well. Yet Dutch collaborators or Nazis—as well as rogues just desperate for money—hunted Jews down and turned them over to the authorities. In the official report on the Franks, the record simply states that someone was given the pitifully small amount of sixty guilders—seven guilders for each person he turned over in the Frank hideout.

The history of Otto Frank and his family was unique in many ways. Most of the Dutch were too afraid of German terror and punishment to aid those in hiding and most couldn't be sure that their neighbors could be trusted. Most Jewish families were broken up, as children were sent away by themselves into hiding and people had to move from place to place to escape detection. Many Amsterdam Jewish families were too poor to pay for places to hide, although a considerable number of Dutch protected Jews without initially asking for payment. And then, after the war, most Dutch Jews came back to a society that was largely indifferent or cruelly hostile to what the Jews had suffered. Otto Frank's welcome was an exception. Miep Gies and her husband, who had protected and aided the Franks in hiding, received him warmly, brought him into their family for seven years, and helped him to rebuild his life.

These exceptions never impinge on the myths. In the service of the redemptive legend of Anne Frank, there is a pattern of pilgrimage to 263 Prinsengracht in Amsterdam. People go to Anne Frank's house to have contact with a consecrated space of suffering. The Dutch are somewhat appalled that the Anne Frank House is such an attraction for tourists—especially for Americans who pay homage to Holocaust remembrance. Nonetheless, this flood of attention is a convenience and a distraction for the Dutch—as well as a lucrative source of income. Tourists don't dig deeper into the history, and the Dutch don't push the matter. Few of the visitors explore what happened to the rest of Dutch Jewry and to the Dutch themselves. There are 800,000 visitors annually at the Anne Frank House, but only 19,000 visit the Hollandse Schouwburg, the former theatre—now a museum and a monument—where the Germans processed many Dutch Jews for deportation.

There is a clear irony here. The 1950s public, including the Dutch, welcomed Anne Frank's miraculously preserved diary. But had she herself returned, few in the Netherlands would have wanted to learn about her suffering. Testimony was not in style. After enduring the occupation and the impoverishment of both the economy and public morale, the Dutch didn't want to hear about the orderly disappearance of 110,000 Jews between 1942 and 1944.

There is, however, one place in Amsterdam, and maybe others as well, where the myth of Anne Frank does not flourish. This is in the social hall of the Liberal Jewish Synagogue. After attending a service in the sanctuary, one goes into an adjoining room to eat and socialize. On the central wall is a picture of Anne Frank at age twelve—one that we have all seen numerous times. There is no written explanation on the wall—no attempt at identification, just a remembrance. The Franks were members of the original Liberal Jewish Synagogue.

No one in the congregation needs any explanation for what happened to her. In this place, there are no misconceptions concerning the symbolic and the real Anne. The burden of living with that past is hard enough. Living in today's somber shadows of Dutch tolerance, indifference, national victimization, and the Anne Frank myth may be almost as hard.

Source: Judith Goldstein, "Anne Frank: The Redemptive Myth," in *Partisan Review*, Vol. 70, No. 1, Winter 2003, pp. 16–23.

SOURCES

"Anne Frank Museum Amsterdam," The Official Anne Frank House Website, www.annefrank.org (April 26, 2006).

Casgrain, J. D., Review of *Anne Frank: The Diary of a Young Girl,* in *Catholic World,* August 1952, issue 175, p. 395, as quoted in *Review Digest: Forty-eighth Annual Cumulation,* The H. W. Wilson Company, 1953, p. 302.

Covington, Richard, "Forever Young," *Smithsonian,* Vol. 32, No. 7, October 2001, pp. 70–76.

Frank, Anne, *Anne Frank: The Diary of a Young Girl,* translated by B. M. Mooyaart-Doubleday, Bantam Books, 1993, originally published in 1952.

Frank, Anne, *The Diary of Anne Frank: The Revised Critical Edition,* translated by Arnold J. Pomerans and B. M. Mooyaart-Doubleday, Doubleday, 2003.

Levin, Meyer, "The Child Behind the Secret Door: An Adolescent Girl's Own Story of How She Hid for Two Years During the Nazi Terror," in *New York Times,* June 15, 1952, Section 7, pp. 1, 22.

"Lost Child (review of *The Diary of a Young Girl*)," in *Time,* June 16, 1952, p. 102.

Pommer, Henry F., "The Legend and Art of Anne Frank," in *Judaism,* Vol. 9, No. 1, Winter 1960, pp. 37–46.

Schnabel, Ernst, *Anne Frank: A Portrait in Courage,* Harcourt, 1958, as quoted in Afterword of *Anne Frank: The Diary of a Young Girl,* Bantam Books, 1993, p. 283.

Van der Rol, Ruud, and Rian Verhoeven, *Anne Frank: Beyond the Diary,* Viking, 1993, pp. 56, 101, 104.

White, Antonia, review of *Anne Frank: The Diary of a Young Girl,* in *New Statesman & Nation,* May 17, 1952, issue 43, p. 592, as quoted in *Book Review Digest: Forty-eighth Annual Cumulation,* The H. W. Wilson Company, 1953, p. 302.

"Everything that Rises Must Converge"

FLANNERY O'CONNOR

1961

Flannery O'Connor's short story "Everything that Rises Must Converge" was originally published in 1961 in *New World Writing*. By the time of its publication, O'Connor was already an acclaimed Southern writer known for fiction that often employed violence and the grotesque to convey a message. The violent episodes in her fiction provide opportunities for characters to receive spiritual redemption, though they do not always obtain it. As a practicing Catholic, O'Connor believed it was necessary to use violence and depravity in her stories in order to, as Patricia S. Yaeger notes in the "Flannery O'Connor" entry in *Modern American Women Writers*, "make modern perversions visible to a nonreligious audience accustomed to seeing perversions as 'natural.'"

O'Connor has become synonymous with the literary use of the grotesque. A grotesque is a character or situation whose features and attributes have been heightened or distorted, as in a caricature drawing. Grotesques allow O'Connor's readers to encounter extreme situations with heightened consequences so that they might discover a new perspective. Though O'Connor hated to be labeled merely as a Catholic writer—she believed her themes and subject matter to go beyond religion—she readily acknowledged her faith's influence on her writing. As Nancy K. Butterworth writes in the *Dictionary of Literary Biography*, "The core

THE FURTHER IRONY OF ALL THIS WAS THAT IN SPITE OF HER, HE HAD TURNED OUT SO WELL. IN SPITE OF GOING TO ONLY A THIRD-RATE COLLEGE, HE HAD, ON HIS OWN INITIATIVE, COME OUT WITH A FIRST-RATE EDUCATION; IN SPITE OF GROWING UP DOMINATED BY A SMALL MIND, HE HAD ENDED UP WITH A LARGE ONE; IN SPITE OF ALL HER FOOLISH VIEWS, HE WAS FREE OF PREJUDICE AND UNAFRAID TO FACE FACTS.''

concern of her fiction is the fallen state of modern humanity unaware of its need for redemption.''

Most, if not all, of O'Connor's stories, including "Everything that Rises Must Converge," are set in the South. Born in Savannah and raised in Milledgeville, the pre–Civil War capital of Georgia, O'Connor spent the majority of her life near her hometown. Her experiences as a Southerner, a woman, a member of a historically wealthy family, and a Catholic in a Protestant region deeply influenced her writing. Her mother, Regina Cline O'Connor, was from a wealthy Georgia family concerned with traditional Southern appearances. She took great pains to maintain her family's reputation for gentility and class and was occasionally scandalized by the subject matter of O'Connor's stories. She was not alone, as many of O'Connor's readers and critics were baffled and even offended by the bizarre violence and inhumanity present in her fiction.

"Everything that Rises Must Converge" is a story about race, class, and identity set in an early 1960s Southern city. Young college graduate Julian accompanies his mother to her classes at the Y because she refuses to ride integrated buses alone. While they are on the bus, their views on class, race, entitlement, obligation, and power are tested against each other and the environment they live in. Julian confronts the world with a modern, integrationist point of view, while his mother dwells on the past and refuses to address the changing times. The routine bus ride becomes a moral showdown between Julian and his mother, and the outcome

BIOGRAPHY

FLANNERY O'CONNOR

Mary Flannery O'Connor was born March 25, 1925, in Savannah, Georgia, to an old-money family of high social standing. The O'Connors lived in Savannah for thirteen years before moving to Milledgeville, Georgia, where O'Connor would spend most of her life. As a child, O'Connor enjoyed writing and often wrote stories for and about her family. Her family attended a Catholic church, and her religion would influence her life and writings.

O'Connor attended Georgia State College for Women in Milledgeville, and in 1945, was awarded a prestigious fellowship to the Writers' Workshop at the University of Iowa. Her Southern upbringing and the idea that decorum, race, class, or family history could define a person were frequent themes in her writing, as was humanity's need for spiritual redemption. She received her master's degree in 1947. In 1950, O'Connor fell ill with lupus, the disease that killed her father when she was sixteen. She died while in a coma brought on by lupus on August 3, 1964.

O'Connor's writing includes two novels, *Wise Blood* (1952) and *The Violent Shall Bear it Away* (1960), and two short story collections, *A Good Man is Hard to Find* (1955) and *Everything that Rises Must Converge* (1965). *The Complete Stories of Flannery O'Connor* (1971), assembled by her publisher after her death, won the National Book Award.

leaves no clear winner. As O'Connor's friend Robert Fitzgerald writes in his 1965 introduction to the story collection *Everything that Rises Must Converge*, "'Rising' and 'convergence' in these stories, as the title story at once makes clear, are shown in classes, generations, and colors." As Julian and his mother battle over the issue of race, their argument escalates into an attack on the mother's perceptions of class and stature. However, Julian's moral high ground is shaky at best, and his motives suspect, as he attempts to show his mother his superior culture and breeding. By the end of the story, it is clear that Julian's mother's idea of identity based on class, history, and social obligation are outdated and useless in an evolving world. O'Connor herself saw no value in holding on to the past, but neither was she a vocal integrationist or participant in the civil rights movement. She has simultaneously been lauded for depicting relatively liberal characters in her stories and criticized for seemingly holding to Southern prejudices and discrimination. The reoccurring use of the slur "nigger" in her fiction has troubled even her staunchest supporters.

"Everything that Rises Must Converge" won the 1963 first prize O. Henry Award for short stories. O'Connor had previously won a first prize O. Henry for the short story "Greenleaf" (1957) and would win another posthumously (after death) in 1965 for "Revelation." All three of these award-winning stories are included in the collection *Everything that Rises Must Converge* (1965) and also *The Complete Stories of Flannery O'Connor* (1971), a collection published by Farrar, Straus and Giroux. *The Complete Stories of Flannery O'Connor* won the National Book Award in 1971.

Flannery O'Connor AP Images

PLOT SUMMARY

Julian's mother goes to the Y every Wednesday night for weight loss classes. Her doctor told her she must lose twenty pounds due to high blood pressure. She does not like to ride the buses at night since they have been integrated, so she insists that Julian accompany her. He is easily annoyed by his mother, but she tells him he owes it to her for all the things she has done for him through the years. Begrudgingly, he goes with her. Julian's mother, a widow, supports Julian, who is just out of college and hoping to be a writer. As they walk through their neighborhood to the bus stop, Julian notes that it is no longer the fashionable neighborhood it was forty years ago, though his mother does not seem to notice this. His mother makes a comment about their small home, and Julian tells her that when he finally starts making money, they will have a large place in the country. Neither Julian nor his mother believes that is likely to happen anytime soon.

Julian's mother is wearing a new purple and green hat that she just bought, but she is unsure if she truly likes it. Julian thinks she looks ridiculous, but says nothing. His mother decides at the last minute to take off the hat, return it, and use the money to pay the electric bill. Julian demands that she keep it on. His mother mumbles on about how the world has become a "mess," and that the "bottom rail is on the top." She tells him that she knows who she is, referring mostly to her bloodline, and despite the changing times and neighborhood, she is still the same person. To underscore her claim, she recounts what she considers to be their family's prestigious history: "'You remain what you are,' she said. 'Your great-grandfather had a plantation and two hundred slaves.'" When Julian reminds her that slavery has long since been abolished, she says that blacks "were better off when they were [slaves]." Julian is used to this conversation, as it is a recurring one. He notes that it always ends the same way: his mother thinks that blacks should "rise, yes, but on their own side of the fence."

To change the subject, Julian's mother talks about her family's old plantation house that has long since fallen into ruin and been sold out of the family. Julian pictures it in its heyday, as in his mother's stories, and believes that he would have appreciated it more than she ever could. His mother circles back around to talking about race, this time telling him, "I've always had a great respect for my colored friends.... I'd do anything in the world for them." To pay for what he considers his mother's sins in regard to race, Julian makes it a point to sit next to a black person anytime he rides the bus alone. As Julian and his mother wait at the bus stop, his irritation with her grows. He defiantly takes off his tie and shoves it in his pocket, and his mother accuses him of "deliberately embarrass[ing]" her. She manages to shame him into putting the tie back on, but after doing so, he tells her that "True culture is in the mind, the *mind.*" She counters that it is in the heart and is a result of who a person is, again alluding to one's family pedigree.

Once on the bus, Julian's mother tries to start conversation with anyone who is willing. After surveying the half-full bus and noting that there are only white passengers on board, she proclaims that they have the bus to themselves. Julian cringes. Several of the other passengers make similar statements. Julian's mother tells anyone who is listening that Julian wants to be a writer, but is selling typewriters to make ends meet. Julian reads a newspaper to ignore his mother. She tells him that struggling is fun, and he is resentful that she not only considers struggling fun, but that she thinks she has won the struggle because he went to college. He believes that he has been successful despite his mother and that "in spite of all her foolish views, he [is] free of prejudice and unafraid to face facts."

At the next stop, a black man dressed in a suit and carrying a briefcase boards the bus and sits near one of the women that Julian's mother had been talking with earlier. She elbows Julian and whispers to him, "Now you see why I won't ride on these buses by myself." The woman changes seats as soon as the black man sits down next to her, and Julian's mother gives her an approving look for doing so. Julian crosses the aisle and sits next to the black man, feeling as if "he [has] openly declared war" on his mother. He wonders if the man noticed the changing of seats and wishes he could strike up a conversation with him. He asks the man for a light, and the man gives Julian a packet of matches, but Julian does not have any cigarettes on him and there is a "No Smoking" sign on the bus. He returns the matches to the man, who is annoyed. Julian's mother stares at Julian, and she appears to be getting ill before his eyes. The man refuses to allow Julian to start a conversation and remains hidden behind his newspaper. Julian toys with the idea of making his mother get off the bus and walk to the Y alone so that she does not think that she can always depend on him.

Julian begins to fantasize about ways to teach his mother a lesson: bringing a black person home for dinner, or making black friends, though "of the better types" like lawyers or doctors. All of his attempts to do so in the past had been failures, as none of the black people he meets seem to have any interest in befriending him. He imagines participating in sit-ins, or bringing a black doctor to treat his mother. For the ultimate lesson, he imagines marrying a black woman. He thinks this last idea might be too much for his mother's blood pressure to handle. At the next stop, a black woman and her child board the bus. The woman is wearing the same green and purple hat that Julian's mother has on. The woman sits next to Julian, and her young son sits next to Julian's mother; "she and the woman had, in a sense, swapped sons." Julian rejoices in the two women wearing the same hat, as he feels it teaches his mother a lesson about her presumptions about class and her feeling of entitlement. He immediately sees, however, that his mother does not see the event as a lesson, but rather "as if the woman were a monkey that had stolen her hat." The woman's son becomes enamored with Julian's mother and begins to play little games to get her attention. The boy's mother grabs him up like "she [is] snatching him from contagion."

At the next stop, the man reading the newspaper gets off the bus and the woman moves over one seat so that her son is sitting between her and Julian. The child plays peek-a-boo with Julian's mother, for which his mother roundly disciplines him. As they approach the next stop, both Julian and the woman pull the cord to get off. Julian is worried that his mother will give the woman money, a "gesture [that] would be as natural to her as breathing." His mother searches her purse for a nickel, but can only find a penny. Julian begs her not to do it. His mother runs after the woman and her son, offering the penny. Furious, the woman yells that her son does not take anyone's pennies and knocks Julian's mother to the ground. Julian tells her that she got what she deserved. He helps her off the ground and she looks at him as if "trying to determine his identity." She tells him she is going home, and begins to walk. He tells her that that woman is her "black double," wearing the same hat as her, and that her old ways of thinking and acting are obsolete in these modern times. His mother walks ahead as if unhearing. He tells her she is acting like a child, and then he stops walking and insists they wait for a bus to take them home. When he grabs her arm to stop her, she tells him to get her (deceased) grandfather or her childhood servant, Caroline, to come get her. She is disoriented, believing she is in the past. She collapses to the ground. Julian runs for help as his mother dies in the street.

THEMES

Social Class

Class plays an integral role in Julian and his mother's relationship in "Everything that Rises Must Converge." Julian's mother defines herself by the past fortunes of her family, the Chestnys, though that fortune is long gone. She still considers herself a member of the upper-class, genteel society that holds to old Southern customs. Even without money, she clings to her right to be a part of that elite group. Julian's mother takes pride in being one of the only ones in her class at the Y who comes dressed "in hat and gloves and who [has] a son who [has] been to college." Julian notes that "[a]ll of her life had been a struggle to act like a Chestny without the Chestny goods, and to give him everything she thought a Chestny ought to have." She insists throughout the story that her history allows her to know who she truly is, a fact that remains constant in spite of her reduced financial status. Julian argues that class and distinction are purely mental, the result of an education and an open mind. However, it is Julian who cherishes the image of the Chestny mansion, long since fallen into disrepair and sold away. He believes himself alone to be fully able to appreciate the history and significance of the home because of his education. He considers himself of a higher class, at least intellectually, than his mother, and therefore more deserving of fine things.

Julian's mother also uses her class status as a form of protection, a way of separating "us" from "them." Patricia S. Yaeger notes in the "Flannery O'Connor" entry in *Modern American Women Writers* that Julian's mother, like many of O'Connor's female characters, is "preoccupied

with rules separating and sanctioning the divisions between the South's races . . . and classes." Race and class collide when a black woman boards the bus wearing the same hat as Julian's mother, a hat that Julian considers "a banner of her imaginary dignity." Julian's mother had debated whether or not to even keep the hat in the first place because of its cost. She considered returning it and using the money to pay bills instead. Julian delights at his mother's discomfort in seeing the black woman in the same hat, but his mother is determined to show her breeding and "culture" by behaving in a way that demonstrates—to both Julian and the woman—that she remains socially superior. When she offers the woman's son a penny, she shows that she has money enough to give away to those she considers beneath her. Her concept of class division is leveled, literally and figuratively, when the woman knocks her to the ground.

Fear and Racism

The plot of "Everything that Rises Must Converge" is based on Julian's mother's fear of black people on the bus. As a woman whose grandfather had owned slaves and whose family formerly enjoyed a privileged life, she is unable to conceive of blacks and whites sharing the same place in society. She finds the recently integrated buses and social advances of blacks a "mess," and "simply not realistic. They should rise, yes, but on their own side of the fence." Julian's mother's racism is a product of her class and of the time period. She is an old woman set in her ways and resistant to change. Julian, however, having just come out of college, views the situation differently. He has come of age in the civil rights era and embraces it in a way the older generation cannot or will not. Julian is afraid that he will be associated with the likes of his mother, so he goes out of his way to befriend black people that he encounters, always choosing a seat next to them on the bus or trying to strike up conversation. He wishes to talk with the black man who gets on the bus with him and his mother, but the man refuses to look up from his newspaper, and there is "no way for Julian to convey his sympathy" over the reactions of his mother and the others on the bus.

In some ways, Julian uses race as a weapon in the silent war he has declared on his mother. He imagines her discomfort, fear, and rage at the thought of him making black friends, bringing them home to dinner, or participating in civil

A plantation house in Convent, Louisiana Getty Images

rights sit-ins. He considers the ultimate shocker: marrying a black woman. Though he thinks the last idea might push his mother's blood pressure too high, he relishes the idea of her having to face her racism and fears. The idea of convergence—coming together and merging, which, as the title of the story indicates, must occur as people rise—between black and whites, rich and poor, is not only distasteful to Julian's mother, but beyond her comprehension.

To prove to her son that she will not be bested by his behavior on the bus, Julian's mother, firmly asserting her belief in the superiority of her race and class, offers a penny to the boy in an act of condescension masked in light-hearted goodwill. Julian tries to stop her, but his mother chases after the woman and her son to give the boy a shiny penny. The boy's mother swings at Julian's mother and yells, "He don't take nobody's pennies!" Julian tells his mother that she has gotten what she deserves, and that her "old manners are obsolete." Unable to recognize her son or understand the time in which she is living, Julian's mother collapses in a stroke.

Romanticized Past

For nearly a century after the Civil War, many whites in the South romanticized the times before war. Many clung to the old ways, manners, and social structures of the antebellum (pre-war) years, and glorified the past. O'Connor was not one of them, though she was familiar with the phenomenon. After her father died, O'Connor and her mother moved into her maternal grandfather's house in Milledgeville. The home was part of the city's garden tour, and O'Connor was, in essence, living in an artifact of preserved history.

Julian's mother's memories of her family's plantation sustain her, even as she condemns the integrated world as a mess: "I don't know how we've let it get in this fix." She continually talks of her family's long-gone wealth, expansive plantation, and gentility, and daydreams back to her childhood days at her grandfather's house. Julian tells her that she cannot continue to identify herself with her family's former wealth and social station because "Knowing who you are is good for one generation only.

You haven't the foggiest idea where you stand now or who you are.'' She disagrees and tells him she knows exactly who she is because of her family history. This changes, however, when a black woman knocks Julian's mother to the ground after she offers a penny to her son. Dazed, Julian's mother begins to walk home and Julian reprimands her: "From now on you've got to live in a new world and face a few realities for a change.'' She stares at him as if she does not recognize him, then instructs him to tell her long-dead grandfather to come get her. Julian's mother retreats into the past, into a world that she can understand and recognize. She calls for Caroline, her childhood servant, a black woman whom she knew how to control. Julian's mother cannot live in an integrated, changing world where her past means nothing, and therefore she dies on the street. As Yaeger writes, "O'Connor's characters are most at risk when they try to recapture the past, when they pay homage to faded plantation glories. . . . [She] finds the persistence of these Southern values fatal.''

HISTORICAL OVERVIEW

The Montgomery Bus Boycott

On December 1, 1955, a black seamstress named Rosa Parks was arrested in Montgomery, Alabama, when she refused to give up her seat on the bus to a white man. The event, though not the first of its kind in the segregated South, sparked a boycott that would eventually lead to the Supreme Court's decision one year later to desegregate the buses.

In response to Parks's arrest, Jo Ann Robinson, the president of the Women's Political Council, and the young Reverend Dr. Martin Luther King Jr. called for a boycott of Montgomery public buses on the following Monday, December 5. The black community in Montgomery refused to ride the buses until they were desegregated. Ridership plummeted, and the city lost nearly three-quarters of a million dollars in revenue from its empty buses. For almost a year, blacks carpooled, walked, and rode bicycles instead of taking the bus. On November 13, 1956, the U.S. Supreme Court found the racially segregated seating on all Alabama buses to be illegal and demanded their integration. This decision eventually trickled into neighboring Southern states, until the

practice of segregation—in all public areas, not only buses—was struck down throughout the country. The Supreme Court decision was a major victory for the civil rights movement, which would continue to gain momentum throughout the 1950s and 1960s.

Racial Tension in the South

Racial tension and oppression have long been aspects of life in the South. The Civil War, fought largely over the issue of slavery, did not alleviate these issues. Rather, the events that followed the war heightened tensions between black and white Americans. After slavery was abolished in 1865, Northern investors (known derisively as carpetbaggers) and federal troops descended on the southern states to rebuild and govern the region, a period known as Reconstruction. During this time, African Americans enjoyed a level of social, economic, and political freedom greater than they had ever known. In 1870, the Fifteenth Amendment to the Constitution allowed black men the right to vote, and many owned businesses and property. Reconstruction ended in 1877 with the withdrawal of federal troops from the South and the emergence of oppressive, racist governments there. The Supreme Court case of *Plessy v. Ferguson* (1896) allowed for a "separate but equal" status for blacks which, in the South, paved the way for legislated segregation in the form of Jim Crow laws.

Jim Crow laws not only restricted African Americans' access to public facilities, including drinking fountains, restrooms, parks, transportation, schools, and hospitals, but also created harsh restrictions on their ability to exercise their legal right to vote. As Yaeger notes, "The white Southerners of [O'Connor's] era struggled to enforce sharp demarcations between genders, between classes, and, most brutally, between races." Though *Brown v. Board of Education* (1954) nullified the "separate but equal" doctrine of *Plessy v. Ferguson* and called for desegregated schools, many places refused to comply. Federal troops were called upon to enforce school integrations in Arkansas, Mississippi, and Alabama. In the early 1960s, civil rights advocates—Southerners and non-Southerners, black and white—worked in the South to support integration and voting rights. Local resistance, led by the white supremacist organization the Ku Klux Klan, was often violent. Several sensational murders and bombings drew the nation's attention to the region's plight, which bolstered support for a fair, legal remedy. The Civil Rights Act of 1964, signed into law just one month before O'Connor died, outlawed racial discrimination in public life.

Southern Literary Renaissance

The Southern literary renaissance began in the 1920s and continued through the 1960s, when Southern writers turned away from romanticizing the past and lamenting the loss of the Civil War, and began to write about modern experiences in the South. This turning point in Southern literature began after World War I, an event that altered artistic expression the world over and ushered in the modernist movement. Modernist writers tried to look at the world from a new perspective, as they found traditional views and values inadequate in the aftermath of the immense war.

Three generations removed from slavery and the Civil War, Southern writers in the 1920s and 1930s began to explore the war and its repercussions with a cool rationalism that was impossible earlier. These Southern writers began to examine the idea of history itself and how past events continued to affect individuals and society as whole. They also examined slavery and racism more critically than their literary forebears had dared to do. In the idiosyncratic, family-centered, and tradition-bound atmosphere of the South, writers also addressed the ways people could celebrate their individuality in a conservative, conformist society.

Other writers of the Southern literary renaissance include William Faulkner (*The Sound and the Fury*), Eudora Welty (*The Optimist's Daughter*), Walker Percy (*The Moviegoer*), Carson McCullers (*The Heart is a Lonely Hunter*), Katherine Anne Porter (*Flowering Judas and Other Stories*), and Harper Lee (*To Kill a Mockingbird*).

CRITICAL OVERVIEW

Though Flannery O'Connor is now considered one of the best American writers of the twentieth century, critics and readers in her own time had mixed feelings about her work. As Nancy K. Butterworth writes in "Flannery O'Connor," "Many readers have been disturbed by her bizarre characters and pervasive use of violence; others have been confused by her confounding

of traditional regional, religious, and literary categories." After the publication of O'Connor's first novel, *Wise Blood* (1952), Butterworth notes that the book was greeted by "unsympathetic criticism reflecting almost total incomprehension of her intent." Reviews improved with the publication of *A Good Man is Hard to Find* (1955), as critics, readers, and fellow writers began to appreciate O'Connor's skill. In his introduction to *The Complete Stories of Flannery O'Connor*, her publisher Robert Giroux quotes O'Connor's fan and fellow writer Thomas Merton, who would not compare her with great modern writers, but with "someone like Sophocles. . . . I write her name with honor, for all the truth and all the craft with which she shows man's fall and his dishonor." Poet Elizabeth Bishop calls O'Connor's writing "clear, hard, vivid, and full of bits of description, phrases, and an odd insight that contains more real poetry than a dozen books of poems" (quoted in Giroux). Nearly fifty years later, *Washington Post* reviewer Jonathon Yardley, in a commemorative review of *The Habit of Being* titled "The Writer Who Was Full of Grace," calls O'Connor "one of the greatest American writers."

"Everything that Rises Must Converge" was initially published in *New World Writing* in 1961, for which O'Connor won an O. Henry Award First Prize. The honor, which recognizes the best American short story published in a magazine, was the fifth of six O. Henry Awards—the second of three first prize awards—that she received. The story was republished as the title story in a posthumous 1965 collection, which was roundly praised for its unique voice and accomplished writing technique. Giroux deems her last works "as nearly perfect as stories can be." Even critics who found fault with the stories or with O'Connor's writing style admired the work. In the *New York Review of Books*, Irving Howe's review titled "Flannery O'Connor's Stories" acknowledges that "Everything that Rises Must Converge" is "unquestionably effective." Yet, he continues, it is "lacking in that resonance Miss O'Connor clearly hoped it might have." Nevertheless, Howe calls the writing in the collection "firm, economical, complex: we are engaged with an intelligence, not merely a talent."

"Everything that Rises Must Converge" was reviewed twice by the *New York Times* in May 1965: once in the book review section, and once in the recurring "Books of the Times" feature.

Two men ride in the first seat behind the driver of a city bus in Montgomery, Alabama, 1956 AP Images

In the "Books of the Times" article, "The Wonderful Stories of Flannery O'Connor," Charles Poore hails O'Connor as a "wonderfully gifted" writer whose stories in *Everything that Rises Must Converge* "[show] us how finely her promise was fulfilled." Richard Poirier's "If You Know Who You Are You Can Go Anywhere" appeared three days after Poore's review. Poirier notes O'Connor's abilities as a comic writer, but also writes that her "major limitation is that the direction of her stories tends to be nearly always the same," a habit that "is more bothersomely apparent in this collection" than in her previous work. However, he says, her "repetitiousness is an indication of how serious a writer she is."

Critical praise continued when, in 1988, the Library of America issued O'Connor's *Collected Works*, which includes short stories, letters, essays, and her novels. In Doris Grumbach's review for National Public Radio, she raves that

"Her perfectly formed prose burns with the passion she perceived in every human being, especially those with a vision, no matter how askew, of God and transcendence" (quoted on Library of America website). A review of the collection in *The New Yorker* states that "No other major American writer of our century has constructed a fictional world so energetically and forthrightly charged by religious investigation" (quoted on Library of America website). The *Washington Post* writes that "her vision was universal" (quoted on Library of America website). In "Flannery O'Connor: Collected Works" for the *National Review*, Chilton Williamson Jr. calls O'Connor "consistently one of the finest literary artists to appear in this (or any) country in this century."

Some reviews have questioned O'Connor's stand on integration and other race issues. Though some argue that O'Connor's race sensibilities were a product of time and geography, others insist that her opinions were a personal decision, not merely a society-wide mentality. In "Flannery O'Connor's Racial Morals and Manners," Ralph C. Wood argues that "O'Connor's liberal use of the word 'nigger' discloses an illiberal numbness to the evils that blacks suffered in the segregated South." Patricia S. Yaeger, in "Flannery O'Connor," notes:

> Although she was a resolute integrationist who recognized the plight of Southern blacks, O'Connor also accepted the most painful Southern conventions.... Although O'Connor satirizes this world in her fiction, in public she would not take a stand.

O'Connor continues to be appreciated as one of America's greatest writers of the twentieth century, and she is regularly mentioned alongside Nobel Prize–winning author William Faulkner in discussions of great Southern writers. That O'Connor's writing continues to reverberate to readers in the twenty-first century is a testament to her skill and the messages her writing convey.

CRITICISM

Charles T. Rubin and Leslie G. Rubin

In the following excerpt, Rubin and Rubin argue that O'Connor's characters in the collection Everything that Rises Must Converge *are struggling against the changing political and social nature of the South in the 1950s and 1960s*

More than a matter of regional interest, the focus on the South in Flannery O'Connor's last work, the collection of short stories *Everything Than Rises Must Converge*, is her reflection on a change of regime that was reaching a culmination in the period during which the stories were written, roughly from 1956 to her death in 1964. Each story shows interactions among characters formed by or struggling against ideas, expectations, or institutions that, in their egalitarianism or materialism or progressivism, challenge old Southern ways and assumptions. While examining these confrontations, O'Connor raises questions about the Old South and about the new American regime that reach far beyond the Mason-Dixon line.

O'Connor's characters are explicitly, if quietly, presented as living in the wake of World War II, the GI Bill, postwar prosperity for some, the space race, and the Civil Rights movement. We suggest that their personal spiritual struggles are formed at least in part by that context. The social and political settings also present competing moral visions that are arguably unique, at least in their conjunction, to the South of the mid-twentieth century. By placing her stories in the South that she knew, O'Connor was fortunate in being able to deal dramatically with conflicts among various strands of modernity and Christianity and between old and new understandings of democracy.

That the results of challenging the old ways are nearly uniformly violent and "grotesque" should not mislead one into thinking that O'Connor is herself merely a partisan of the old ways. She is an equal-opportunity exposer of false-hood and pretension. Her stories seem to be efforts to sort out what of the old should be abandoned, and what either needs to be saved or is unfortunately destined to be lost in light of what in the new is most problematic. The old, aristocratic, spiritually rich South has lessons that the modern, democratic, secular North ignores at its peril.

To the extent, at least, of offering useful correctives, O'Connor can be read as a friend of postwar, American liberal democracy and its inexorable reformation of the South and itself. It must be immediately acknowledged, however, that her friendship is of a distanced or perhaps more precisely Augustinian character. Although the broad context of her stories reflects a concern for the requirements of "well-ordered concord of civic obedience and rule," she jealously guarded her position as a "captive and stranger" in the earthly city, and her ultimate concern with the shape and destiny of human souls transcends any particular place and time.

There is no novelty in suggesting that there can be some tension within this kind of critical friendship, but there is some in finding it in O'Connor's stories. It is not wrong to see those stories as primarily complex, spiritual parables—unless so doing reduces the context and setting for the dramas to mere accident or to the idiosyncrasy of simply writing what one knows. That error is part of what makes it easy for some to dismiss the stories as merely grotesque, as caricatures without any connection to the world beyond Southern landscapes and accents. Even if one's concern is (appropriately) with the spiritual teaching of the stories, that teaching loses some of its power to speak to the reader unless it presents a world that is in some way recognizable. Indeed, the power of the spiritual critique of business as usual depends on an accurate representation of what business usually is.

It is not, therefore, difficult to see why someone with O'Connor's otherworldly concerns about the tendencies of an increasingly secular, materialistic, and egalitarian regime should be willing to take those tendencies seriously. It is less clear why this regime should take the corrective suggested by her stories seriously, given the divergence of underlying premises. Leaving aside the vexed question of the place of religion within American founding principles, we show that the stories suggest in particularly dramatic ways the inherent limitations of the new ways and the points at which they founder on the rocks of unpleasant but undeniable realities.

We begin with short summaries of the stories in *Everything That Rises Must Converge* to show the pervasiveness of both the spiritual and political themes. Then we look more closely at a few key topics related to the changing Southern regime to investigate how O'Connor combines them with her spiritual concerns.

The first story, "*Everything That Rises Must Converge,*" is steeped in the social transformation brought about by the regime changes of the Civil Rights era. As Julian's mother (she is not given a name) puts it, "The bottom rail is on the top." She goes on to repeat to Julian her regularly expressed opinion, obviously tied to the title: "'They were better off when they were [slaves],' she said. . . . 'It's ridiculous. It's simply not realistic. They should rise, yes, but on their own side of the fence.'" A like-minded stranger provides us with a more specific sign of the change, when she notes that on a bus ride the previous day, "They were thick as fleas—up front and all through." Julian, like a number of other O'Connor characters, has received a collegiate education in the new doctrines of racial equality, while his mother lives with the new, integrated transportation arrangements. His training makes him go out of his way to make overtures (even, perhaps, particularly pointless ones) to black people; her training makes her both nostalgic for her black nanny and apprehensive about riding the bus downtown alone. The crux of the plot, when Julian's mother is struck by a black woman, suffers a seizure, and dies, turns

essentially on the new political society of the South—a world in which white women may no longer give pennies to "cute ... little Negroes" without arousing wrath.

The discovery that Julian's overweight mother and the "large" black woman wear the same hat both heightens Julian's pleasure in pointing out his mother's political incorrectness and reveals O'Connor's critical distance from her characters. The convergence of the rising classes is embodied in identical, ridiculous hats. Although Julian's mother is generally the object of our sympathy, her hat is ugly, and her imagined social position as a descendent of the former ruling class is untenable. Her widowhood and her devotion to her only son have reduced her to the hard-working class. She has more in common with the black woman across the aisle from her than she will admit. The gravamen of the story's climax rests on Julian, however. He wants his mother to learn a lesson about her true place in the new world and about the new respect due to the "Negroes." The intellectually satisfying yet brutal way in which it is delivered kills her.

It is not easy to characterize O'Connor's attitude toward the egalitarian civil rights initiatives of the 1950s and early 1960s. There is no doubt that she shows characters dealing with the social consequences of a change in political rules. As if from outside, the United States as a whole has imposed a new way of thinking about social and political relationships on the small towns and countryside of the South.

O'Connor shows sympathetically the resentments that arise as a result of self-righteous outside interference, on the one hand, and an equality that rises only to "mind your own business," on the other. Julian's mother is innocent in her inability to understand the "symbolic significance" of the identical hats or the patronizing attitude that prompts her to give the little boy a penny—even Julian glimpses that innocence before "principle rescued him." O'Connor pulls no punches with regard to the black characters' attitude about their new situation: The "large Negro" man, "well dressed and carr[ying] a briefcase," ignores or does not notice Julian's gesture of moving to the seat near him, appears annoyed when Julian uselessly asks for a match, and refuses "to come out from behind his paper." The "large, gaily dressed, sullen-looking colored woman" who sits next to Julian is described as brimming with resentment:

> Her face was set not only to meet opposition but to seek it out. The downward tilt of her large lower lip was like a warning sign: DON'T TAMPER WITH ME.... [She] muttered something unintelligible to herself. He was conscious of a kind of bristling next to him, a muted growling like that of an angry cat.... The woman was rumbling like a volcano about to become active.

And when Julian's mother suggests that the woman's son likes her, "the woman stood up and yanked the little boy off the seat as if she were snatching him from contagion." When Julian's mother persists, playing peek-a-boo with the boy, the child's mother "slapped his hand down. 'Quit yo' foolishness,' she said, 'before I knock the living Jesus out of you!'" To say the least, neither Julian nor the reader is surprised when the woman hits Julian's mother for giving her son a penny.

The abstract egalitarianism that the young bring back from their forays North seems inextricably bound up with a distortion of human feeling—a wish to be left alone. Julian is proud that "he was not dominated by his mother." The patent falsity of this conclusion, which is based on his contempt for her willingness to sacrifice herself for his advancement, does not diminish his certainty in it. In contrast, Julian sees himself as a martyr, forced to accompany his mother downtown on the bus because of her prejudices toward blacks.

The South that O'Connor portrays is a world of ironies and distorted meanings. "Northern" demands for equality produce a desire to be left alone rather than a sense of common humanity. The ties that remain to bind people together in the new South are those of lazy dependency (sons living off their mothers) or the decaying remnants of outright subjugation. Scientific knowledge and technology, usually seen as liberating extensions of human capacity, are shown to narrow and limit our ability to understand the world around us. Efforts to control the unruly and unpleasant aspects of the world regularly lead to disaster rather than to commodious self-preservation.

These reversals account for a good deal of what is commonly labeled "grotesque" in O'Connor's fiction. The justice behind this label is that the events on which she focuses surely do not occur everyday. Can these situations then be dismissed as figments of a Southern writer's imagination? Such things do happen in real life, and the death and betrayal that she describes are a stock element in various genres of contemporary fiction. For the most part we approach such events, whether real or imagined, thoughtlessly, and when we do think about them it is likely to be with conveniently available categories. O'Connor's stories work if she can shake us out of that thoughtlessness or complacency and suggest the need for, and the parameters of, some new vision to go along with the terrible events.

We have suggested that O'Connor's is a vision that entails substantial doubts, doubts neither original nor unique to her, about the transformation and modernization of the South as well as about its traditional ways. Following up on the implications of that vision would produce a withdrawal from much of the common enthusiasms of the new regime and a general lowering of expectations about the prospects for human justice. And yet in another sense, such an outlook might actually strengthen one's attachment to the regime; at least it might be seen as strengthening it within reason. For on these terms, could one not be more forgiving of a nation that strives for equality but fails to reach abstract goals of perfect equality? Could one not be attached more to the here and now, rather than looking always toward a worldly future of more, better, and faster? It would not have to be a dismissal of the regime to point out the isolating effects of a certain understanding of equality; it could be a due regard for genuine civic concord. It is not only out of technophobia that one can suggest the limits of the belief that "you have to *have* certain things before you could *know* certain things" particularly when the "things" in question are pig parlors and black farm workers. Whether Flannery O'Connor can be seen as a friend of the new American regime depends finally on whether it is possible to hate the sin but love the sinner.

Source: Charles T. Rubin and Leslie G. Rubin, "Flannery O'Connor's Religious Vision of Regime Change," in *Perspectives on Political Science*, Vol. 31, No. 4, Fall 2002, pp. 213–14, 219, 221.

SOURCES

Butterworth, Nancy K., "Flannery O'Connor," in *Dictionary of Literary Biography*, Vol. 152: *American Novelists Since World War II, Fourth Series*, edited by James Giles and Wanda Giles, The Gale Group, 1995, pp. 158–181.

Fitzgerald, Robert, Introduction, in *Everything that Rises Must Converge*, by Flannery O'Connor, Farrar, Straus and Giroux, 1996, p. xxx; originally published in 1965.

Giroux, Robert, Introduction, in *The Complete Stories of Flannery O'Connor*, by Flannery O'Connor, Farrar, Straus and Giroux, 1971, pp. xv, xvi.

Grumbach, Doris, Review of *Flannery O'Connor's Collected Works*, The Library of America, www.loa.org (November 30, 2005), originally aired on National Public Radio, November 11, 1988.

Howe, Irving, "Flannery O'Connor's Stories," in *New York Review of Books*, September 30, 1965, pp. 16–17.

O'Connor, Flannery, "Everything that Rises Must Converge," in *Everything that Rises Must Converge*, Farrar, Straus and Giroux, 1996; originally published in 1965.

Poirier, Richard, "If You Know Who You Are You Can Go Anywhere," in *New York Times*, May 30, 1965, p. BR6.

Poore, Charles, "The Wonderful Stories of Flannery O'Connor," in *New York Times*, May 27, 1965, p. 35.

Review of *Flannery O'Connor's Collected Works*, The Library of America, www.loa.org (November 30, 2005), originally published in *The New Yorker*, November 7, 1988.

Review of *Flannery O'Connor's Collected Works*, The Library of America, www.loa.org (November 30, 2005), originally published in the *Washington Post*, September 4, 1988.

Williamson, Chilton, Jr., "Flannery O'Connor: Collected Works," in the *National Review*, Vol. 40, No. 2, October 28, 1988, pp. 44–46.

Wood, Ralph C., "Flannery O'Connor's Racial Morals and Manners," in *The Christian Century*, Vol. 111, No. 33, November 16, 1994, pp. 1076–81.

Yaeger, Patricia S., "Flannery O'Connor," in *Modern American Women Writers*, Charles Scribner's Sons, 1991, pp. 375–88.

Yardley, Jonathon, "The Writer Who Was Full of Grace," in the *Washington Post*, July 6, 2005, p. C01.

Farewell to Manzanar: A True Story of Japanese American Experience during and after the World War II Internment

Farewell to Manzanar: A True Story of Japanese American Experience during and after the World War II Internment, the memoir that Jeanne Wakatsuki Houston coauthored with her husband, James D. Houston, in 1973 and dedicated to her deceased parents and brother, presents a vivid sequence of episodes illustrating the disastrous effects of racial prejudice on law-abiding, patriotic Japanese Americans during World War II. Beginning with the announcement of the Japanese attack on Pearl Harbor on December 7, 1941, Jeanne (the narrator) shares a flood of painful memories and reflections about her own family and her Japanese American neighbors in Southern California. Jeanne recalls the frightening events leading up to her family's forced evacuation to Manzanar Internment Camp when she was only seven years old. She also shares her impressions of her father's imprisonment at Fort Lincoln, near Bismarck, North Dakota (for suspicion as an enemy spy), her brother's meeting with Japanese relatives in Hiroshima after the bombing of that city, and her own challenges as a young Japanese American girl living in the 1940s and 1950s. But the central action of her story takes place at Manzanar, near the Sierra Nevada Mountains, 225 miles north of Long Beach, California.

As scene after tragic scene of daily life unfolds at the internment camp, readers gain insight into the tremendous physical, economic, and psychological challenges faced by internees.

JAMES D. HOUSTON
JEANNE
WAKATSUKI HOUSTON
1973

Jeanne reflects upon the most serious consequences of these wartime challenges: a disintegration of family unity and a loss of personal identity. As a result of his internment, the once-proud Ko Wakatsuki, Jeanne's father, is transformed from a multitalented, hardworking patriarch of a large family to a broken man, ultimately dependent upon his wife to pay all of their bills. Meanwhile, Ko's son Woody is transformed from an obedient child into an independent young man who risks his father's rejection in order to join the military so that he might prove his loyalty to the same nation that imprisoned him. Equally transformed, Jeanne's mother abandons the role of submissive housewife to become the family breadwinner. For young Jeanne, the Manzanar experience introduces her to a strange new world of personalities far beyond that of her nuclear family. Throughout her years at Manzanar, Jeanne is confronted by a variety of sometimes attractive, sometimes repellent, sometimes frightening—but always fascinating—strangers of different cultural and ethnic backgrounds. These encounters surely spark her future interest in the professions of journalism and sociology.

Unfortunately, racial discrimination and injustice toward Japanese Americans does not end after World War II and the closing of the internment camps. Jeanne must combat many instances of prejudice against Asian Americans. This discrimination is particularly painful for Jeanne during her years in high school. Unlike her father, who withdraws completely from the world, Jeanne tries to fit in with her white classmates by participating in as many popular activities and clubs as possible. Simultaneously, she attempts to appease her father by taking up traditional "Japanese" activities such as *odori* dancing. Toward the end of her memoir, Jeanne acknowledges her sense of not belonging in either world.

Jeanne keeps her story of Manzanar and its aftermath secret for thirty years, due to her sense of personal shame at the racial discrimination that she and her family endured. Yet, in the last chapter of the book, the author returns to the long-abandoned Manzanar Internment Camp with her husband and three children. She finally allows herself to recall, and to share with James and their children, some of the experiences that she and her family members had survived decades earlier. Today, teachers throughout the United States consider Jeanne's memoir a valuable tool that can teach lessons about the necessity for

> IT WAS THE CHARGE OF DISLOYALTY. FOR A MAN RAISED IN JAPAN, THERE WAS NO GREATER DISGRACE. AND IT WAS THE HUMILIATION. IT BROUGHT HIM FACE TO FACE WITH HIS OWN VULNERABILITY, HIS OWN POWERLESSNESS. HE HAD NO RIGHTS, NO HOME, NO CONTROL OVER HIS OWN LIFE. THIS KIND OF EMASCULATION WAS SUFFERED, IN ONE FORM OR ANOTHER, BY ALL THE MEN INTERNED AT MANZANAR."

human justice and interracial harmony. As part of California's curriculum on history and civil rights, every school and each of the fifteen hundred public libraries in the state now have a copy of *Farewell to Manzanar*, along with a copy of the 1976 film adaptation of the book.

By 2003, the publishers had sold more than one and a half million copies of the book in more than sixty editions. The book has earned widespread praise, including recognition from United States Senator Daniel K. Inouye, a veteran of the famous Japanese American 442nd Regimental Combat Team. Senator Inouye noted that *Farewell to Manzanar* made "vividly clear . . . the psychological distress and fear within a Japanese American child and the crude isolation of a racial group." Readers learn about the devastating consequences of racial mistrust and misunderstanding that can affect every part of human life during an international conflict—from an internee's diet and simple need for personal privacy to the loss of dignity that results when an immigrant is forced to choose between allegiance to two warring "homelands" and is suddenly labeled as "disloyal."

Today, Jeanne continues to write and lecture about her experiences at Manzanar. Speaking with an interviewer from the *San Francisco Chronicle* in 2003, she admitted that "[s]ometimes, we may feel like we're 'up to here with it' about camp. . . . Then you meet someone who doesn't know about the internment, and it makes you wonder, 'Who's going to write about it?'" It was not until 1998 that the U.S. government formally apologized for the internment of 120,000 Japanese Americans during World War II.

BIOGRAPHY

JEANNE WAKATSUKI HOUSTON AND JAMES D. HOUSTON

Jeanne Wakatsuki Houston was born in California on September 26, 1934. Her family was sent to Manzanar Internment Camp in April 1942, but Jeanne remained silent about her experiences for thirty years until her nephew urged her to share her memories. Houston's original intent was to write a memoir for her family, but her husband and coauthor, James D. Houston, urged her to share her story with all Americans. She has also written a fictional account of three generations of Japanese American women living at Manzanar; this unique novel, *The Legend of Fire Horse Woman*, is structured in the form of a five-act Japanese Kabuki drama.

The Houstons met as college students studying journalism. Facing job discrimination against Asian women journalists in the 1950s, however, Jeanne turned her attention to sociology, becoming a social worker and juvenile probation officer. Jeanne was the first in her family to graduate from college—including study in France at the Sorbonne and the University of Paris—and the first in her Japanese family to marry a white person. James Houston is the author of several historical novels, short stories, and nonfiction works. The authors live in Santa Cruz, California.

PLOT SUMMARY

Part 1
Chapter 1: "What is Pearl Harbor?"– Chapter 4: A Common Master Plan
The first of many brief episodes in this memoir begins on December 7, 1941, with seven-year-old Jeanne's astonishment as she watches the small sardine fishing fleet (which includes her father, Ko Wakatsuki, and two oldest brothers, Bill and Woody) abruptly turn around and return to the harbor on a bright, sunny morning in good weather. As the fleet's anxious wives and daughters wait on shore, one of the women's male coworkers from the local cannery shouts out the news of the attack on Pearl Harbor. Like Ko, who had lived in America for decades, all Japanese Americans in California—law-abiding first-generation immigrants (*Issei*) (who were forbidden citizenship) and their native-born American children (*Nisei*)—come under suspicion by the FBI for potential collaboration with the enemy in Japan. Two FBI men soon arrest her "Papa":

> About all he had left at this point was his tremendous dignity.... Ten children and a lot of hard luck had worn him down, had worn away most of the arrogance he cane to this country with. But he still had dignity, and he would not let those deputies push him out the door. He led them.

After Ko's arrest and imprisonment at Fort Lincoln near Bismarck, North Dakota, Jeanne's mother attempts to keep the family together at all costs. She moves her children and her nearly blind mother from their Ocean Park neighborhood, where the Wakatsuki family were the only Japanese Americans, to Terminal Island. Jeanne's brother, Woody, and their married sister are already living there in a community of Japanese immigrants, most of whom speak only their native Kyushu dialect, "a rough fisherman's language, full of oaths and insults." Jeanne, on the other hand, "had never spoken anything but English, and the other kids in the second grade despised me for it." Equally difficult for young Jeanne is her terror of Asian people. "This was partly Papa's fault. One of his threats to keep us younger kids in line was 'I'm going to sell you to the Chinaman.'"

Because Terminal Island is so close to Long Beach Naval Station, the Japanese American community there is evicted, in accordance with President Roosevelt's Executive Order 9066, which protected military rights over the rights of ordinary citizens. "Even though most of us were American-born, it was dangerous having that many Orientals so close to the Long Beach Naval Station."

Secondhand dealers take advantage of the vulnerability of Japanese Americans, "offering humiliating prices for goods and furniture they knew many of us would have to sell sooner or

"High School Recess period, Manzanar Relocation Center, California," photograph by Ansel Adams, 1943 The Library of Congress

later." In contrast to such predators, the American Friends Service (a Quaker organization) help Jeanne's family relocate for the second time in two months, this time to a "minority ghetto, in downtown Los Angeles, now inhabited briefly by a few hundred Terminal Island refugees." The Wakasukis are desperately aware of the inevitability of being sent inland to an internment camp. Issei refugees remind one another of a traditional Japanese phrase used to describe the endurance of great trials, "*Shikata ga nai*, meaning "It cannot be helped. . . . It must be done."

Along with other Japanese Americans, Jeanne and her family endure increasing hostility from whites. Stories of racial violence began to spread:

> Public attitudes toward the Japanese in California were shifting rapidly. In the first few months of the Pacific war, America was on the run. Tolerance had turned to distrust and irrational fear. The hundred-year-old tradition of anti-Orientalism on the west coast soon resurfaced, more vicious than ever.

Thus, Jeanne feels relief and a sense of adventure when the government orders their evacuation to Manzanar. Although many families are separated during the forced evacuation, Jeanne's mother once again keeps her family together, on the same bus, leading to the same barracks in the overcrowded, underprepared internment camp. Except for Ko and Jeanne's married sister who live in another barracks with her husband and six total strangers, the twelve remaining members of the Wakatsuki family now live together at Manzanar. Bill (with wife Tomi) and Woody (with wife Chizu and their baby daughter) share one unit of the barracks; Granny, Lillian (age fourteen), Ray (age thirteen), May (age eleven), Kiyo (age ten), Jeanne (age seven), and Mama share the other unit. The internees, including newly married couples, have lost all of their privacy, along with most of their possessions. Their new homes consist of little more than a pair of adjoining one-room drafty, tarpapered shacks (in the six-unit barracks) with gaps in the floorboards and walls, straw mattresses, an insufficient number of army blankets, no kitchen table, and no indoor plumbing.

Woody helps to alleviate these desperate circumstances with a combination of optimism, innovation, and hard work in his determination to make the barracks livable. Meanwhile, Jeanne's mischievous brothers, Kiyo and Ray, provide a regular source of humor. Nevertheless, the internees suffer in many ways. Physically, they become sick with diarrhea from spoiled food and typhoid inoculations; psychologically, they are shamed by the public latrines. "Like so many of the women there, Mama never did get used to the latrines. It was a humiliation she just learned to endure: "*shikata ga nai*, this cannot be helped."

Chapter 5: Almost a Family–Chapter 8: Inu

Soon after their arrival at Manzanar, refugee family members begin to drift apart, losing their most precious possession: connection with one another. Although Jeanne relays that "mealtime had always been the center of our family scene," the Manzanar "mess hall system" (where Jeanne's mother works as a dietician) makes family meals an impossibility. Now, as families no longer eat meals together and as the traditional roles of the breadwinning family patriarchs are lost, family units quickly disintegrate, even after the fathers return from North Dakota. Writing her memoir thirty years later, Jeanne realizes that "[w]hatever dignity or feeling of filial strength we may have known before December 1941 was lost, and we did not recover it until many years after the war, not until after Papa died."

While Jeanne's nuclear family is beginning to dissolve, she discovers a wider world, filled with the strange faces, costumes, and behavior. In good weather, the refugees spend as much time as possible outside. "[We] only went 'home' at night, when [we] finally had to: 10,000 people on an endless promenade inside the square mile of barbed wire that was the wall around our city." This crowd includes "a half-black" woman "with light mulatto skin" who always wore an "Aunt Jemima scarf" to conceal her hair, "passing as a Japanese in order to remain with her husband"; another elegant woman with a "long aristocratic face" that "was always a ghastly white" because she followed the old tradition of powdering it with

rice flour; and a pair of nurses, each with a bleached face, a sharp widow's peak, and no lips—two faces so strange that Jeanne describes the nurses as "a pair of reptilian kabuki creatures." The internees also include a pair of Japanese Maryknoll nuns in black robes with white hoods and Father Steinbeck, "one of the few Caucasians to live among us inside the compound and eat in our mess halls. He was greatly admired for this, and many internees converted to Catholicism before the camp was closed." Fascinated by stories of saints and martyrs, young Jeanne yearns to convert, but is forbidden to do so by Ko, who has finally been allowed to return to his family.

After nine months in prison, Ko looks ten years older when he steps off the bus at Manzanar. The great-great-grandson of a samurai warrior in Hiroshima, Ko has pride in his ancestor's former power and wealth. But Ko is ashamed of the gradual erosion of his father's estate that results in his father's new occupation managing a teahouse in Hiroshima. "For Papa, at seventeen, it made no difference that times were hard; the idea of a teahouse was an insult to the family name." In 1904, this "insult" leads to Ko's immigration to Hawaii, and soon after to Idaho, where he works for five years for a wealthy attorney who had paid his passage. Ko's patron helps him enter the University of Idaho to study law. He quits school, however, to elope with Jeanne's mother, the daughter of a Japanese immigrant to Washington. Jeanne's maternal grandparents are suspicious of Ko, especially since he seems to lead "a perilously fast life," borrows money from them, and is insulted when Granny once loans him five dollars. "'It's not enough,' he said.... 'If that's all you've got, I'd rather have nothing!' And he threw the bill into the fire."

Despite his attitude of entitlement—and his ability to learn new skills in a wide variety of jobs, ranging from translating government documents to lumberjacking, dentistry, fishing, and farming—Ko experiences a continual series of disappointments: "he never quite finished anything he set out to do. Something always stopped him: bad luck, a racial barrier, a law, his own vanity or arrogance or fear of losing face." In spite of Ko's many failures, "[w]hatever he did had flourish." Aware that her Papa "was a poser, a braggart, and a tyrant" on the verge of becoming an alcoholic on homemade rice wine, Jeanne imagines his honest responses to an interview at the Fort Lincoln prison camp, where he is asked to choose sides between the Japanese and the American enemies: *"When your mother and father are having a fight, do you want them to kill each other? Or do you just want them to stop fighting?"* Because Ko returns from Fort Lincoln earlier than most of the Issei men, their wives gossip about him, calling him an *inu* ("dog"). They accuse Ko of acting as an informer against their husbands in his job as interpreter for the War Department. In response to their insinuations, Ko "exiled himself like a leper, and he drank," becoming increasingly violent with his wife and children.

Chapter 9: The Mess Hall Bells–Chapter 11: Yes Yes No No

Ko does not discuss his experiences at Fort Lincoln. Although he had suffered physical hardships there, his much deeper pain is emotional:

> It was the charge of disloyalty. For a man raised in Japan, there was no greater disgrace. And it was the humiliation. It brought him face to face with his own vulnerability, his own powerlessness. He had no rights, no home, no control over his own life.

While Ko retreats into drunken silence at Manzanar, punctuated by angry outbursts at his family, other frustrated men imprisoned in the camp begin to riot. Led by Joe Kurihara, a veteran of World War I, this riot, which takes place in December, a year after the Japanese attack on Pearl Harbor, results in the death of two young men. Jeanne recalls the tolling of the bells, signifying the internees' mourning. Toward the end of this month of grief, a new director of Manzanar gives each family a Christmas tree as a gesture of good will, along with "a promise of better treatment and better times to come." Instead, in February of 1943, the government mandates a Loyalty Oath; internees must swear their allegiance to the United States and willingness to serve in military combat.

Woody is eager to prove his loyalty by joining the Army, even though this means leaving his wife and children behind and confronting his father's disapproval. Ko is furiously indignant over the Loyalty Oath; yet, he realizes that "disloyal" Japanese Americans who signed "no" will be taken to Tule Lake for possible exile to Japan. The refugees have no choice but to agree with the Loyalty Oath.

Part 2: Chapter 12: Manzanar, U.S.A.– Chapter 21: The Girl of My Dreams

As more Japanese Americans leave Manzanar to join the military, the camp becomes less crowded; the living conditions of those who remain behind become more comfortable. Thanks to Mama's quick thinking and her job at the camp hospital, the Wakasukis double their living quarters in early 1943. Papa and his neighbors begin to decorate their barracks and plant gardens:

> The fact that America had accused us, or excluded us, or imprisoned us, or whatever it might be called, did not change the kind of world we wanted. Most of us were born in this country; we had no other models. Those parks and gardens lent it an oriental character, but in most ways it was a totally equipped American small town, complete with schools, churches, [and] Boy Scouts.

Young Manzanar refugees form softball and football leagues, glee clubs and dance bands. Ten-year-old Jeanne joins the baton club at Manzanar because she is "desperate to be 'accepted.'" She continues this activity later in high school because "baton twirling was one trick I could perform that was thoroughly, unmistakably American." Although Jeanne also attempts to learn traditional Japanese *odori* dancing from an elderly *geisha*, she is more fascinated by the Japanese ballet teacher, until Jeanne notices the teacher's bloody toes and other wounds. "Ballet seemed then some terrible misuse of the body, and she was so anxious to please us, her very need to hold on to whatever she had been scared me away." Also enchanted by the ceremony and costumes of the Catholic confirmation ritual, Jeanne begs Ko to allow her to be baptized and confirmed as soon as the Maryknoll nuns would allow. Ko's refusal leaves Jeanne with a feeling of "total separateness." Ko is gravely concerned about his pregnant daughter, Eleanor, and shows momentary tenderness toward Mama upon learning of Eleanor's successful delivery of a healthy son.

Soon after Eleanor gives birth, she moves to Reno, Nevada, to stay with friends while her soldier husband fights in Germany. The internment camp population steadily decreases. Woody is drafted in 1944 and Jeanne's older siblings move to New Jersey the next year. The east coast is "3,000 miles away, with no history of anti-Orientalism, in fact no Oriental history at all. So few people of Asian ancestry had settled there, it was like heading for a neutral country." Sadly, Ko's children know that their father will never join them in New Jersey.

> He was too old to start over, too afraid of rejection in an unknown part of the world, too stubborn and too tired to travel that far, and finally too proud to do piecework on an assembly line.... The truth was, at this point Papa did not know which way to turn.

Resisting still another move, Ko waits until the camp officially closes and he is forced to leave. Rather than take advantage of the government's offer of a free bus ride back to the internees' former homes, Ko purchases a beat-up old car so that he and his family can "leave in style, and by our own volition." Ko makes three separate trips to move his large family and their meager belongings back to Boyle Heights— only to discover that his two fishing boats and all of their family furnishings had been stolen while the Wakasukis were at Manzanar. To support the family, Jeanne's mother returns to her job at the cannery while Ko stays home sketching blueprints for a housing cooperative that never materializes; family pride will not allow the unemployed Ko to "accept anything like a cannery job."

With her family resettled in Boyle Heights, Jeanne enters sixth grade. On her first day, she reads a lesson aloud, perfectly, only to be shocked at her classmate's response.

> "Gee, I didn't know you could speak English." ... I smiled and sat down, suddenly aware of what being of Japanese ancestry was going to be like. I wouldn't be faced with physical attack, or with overt shows of hatred. Rather, I would be seen as someone foreign, or as someone other than American, or perhaps not be seen at all.

Jeanne is determined to prove that she belongs, but she "lived with this double impulse: the urge to disappear and the desperate desire to be acceptable." Refused membership in the Girl Scouts because of her ethnic background, Jeanne becomes the lead majorette in the Boy Scout band. While Jeanne is "striving to become Miss America of 1947," however, Ko is "wishing I'd be Miss Hiroshima of 1904." Father and daughter find a compromise to this dilemma: "You want to be the carnival queen? ... I'll make a deal with you. You can be the queen if you start odori lessons at the Buddhist church as soon as school is out." Jeanne keeps her bargain, attending ten lessons, until her teacher sends her away. She wins the award of carnival queen, despite the teachers who try to sabotage the election results. Still, the carnival ceremony turns into a devastating embarrassment for Jeanne, who feels that she does not belong there any more than she belongs in the Japanese dancing class.

Part 3: Chapter 22: Ten Thousand Voices
In the last brief chapter of her memoir, Jeanne observes:

> As I came to understand what Manzanar had meant, it gradually filled me with shame for being a person guilty of something enormous enough to deserve that kind of treatment. In order to please my accusers, I tried, for the first few years after our release, to become someone acceptable. I both succeeded and failed.

The first in her family to marry a white person, Jeanne recognizes that she must finally reveal the secret of her Manzanar experiences, sharing her story with her husband and children. Thus, thirty years after she entered the internment camp, she returns with James and their three children. Walking over the dusty remains of the deserted landscape, Jeanne relives scenes from the past, accepting the fact that Manzanar had become "[m]uch more than a remembered place, it had become a state of mind. Now, having seen it, I no longer wanted to lose it or to have those years erased."

THEMES

Racial Profiling
Regardless of the number of years *Isseis* had lived as law-abiding residents in the United States since emigrating from Japan, they were still classified as "aliens." In what is now called "racial profiling," Japanese Americans like Ko Wakatsuki who lived along the West Coast of California were forced to leave their jobs, homes, vehicles, and most of their other precious possessions, including family pets. Even the *Nisei* children of these immigrants were forced into the internment camps, although they had been born and raised in America, holding the American citizenship that was denied their parents until 1952. Unlike most German and Italian immigrants, who were not sent to internment camps, the physical characteristics of Asian Americans were immediately recognizable, making them easy to identify.

The authors emphasize that before the war, "traditionally racist organizations like the

A grocery store, owned by interned Japanese Americans, with a sign indicating it had been sold National Archives and Records Administration

American Legion and The Native Sons of The Golden West . . . had been agitating against the west-coast Japanese for decades." Later groups, with names such as San Diego's "No Japs Incorporated," Sacramento's "Home Front Commandoes," and the "Pacific Coast Japanese Problem League" in Los Angeles were established to keep the internees from returning to their homes after the war ended. Thus, Jeanne and the rest of the Wakatsuki family members remaining at Manzanar in 1945 were afraid to return home to Boyle Heights. Listening to the stories about

violence, Jeanne felt as anxious "as if Ku Klux Klansmen lurked outside the window." She began to fear the appearance of "a row of Burma-Shave signs saying JAPS GO BACK WHERE YOU CAME FROM" as she and her sisters wondered aloud why people hated them.

Ethnic Stereotypes

After an entree of Vienna sausage and canned green beans, the Wakatsuki's first meal at Manzanar, prepared by whites, includes over-cooked rice, which was topped by canned apricots as a "good desert. Among the Japanese of course, rice is never eaten with sweet foods, only with salty or savory foods. Few of us could eat such a mixture." However, according to strict rules of Japanese etiquette, which were not suspended because of internment, "no one dared protest. It would have been impolite."

Seven-year-old Jeanne feels "horrified" upon seeing "the apricot syrup seeping through my little mound of rice" at Manzanar, but she had been absolutely terrified two years earlier, as "the only Oriental" in her kindergarten class. Because Ko had often tried to control his children with the threat, "I'm going to sell you to the Chinaman," Jeanne experiences such an uncontrollable fear of unfamiliar Asian faces that she assumes a white classmate with "very slanted eyes" is in fact the dreaded "Chinaman." Her terror increases upon moving to Terminal Island, where she encounters children who only speak Japanese. These children, who were "a little proud of their nickname, *yo-go-re*" (which Jeanne translates as roughneck), "would swagger and pick on outsiders and persecute anyone who didn't speak as they did." Although the children never attack Jeanne or her brother Kiyo, she assumes the worst, based upon "their fearful looks, and the noises they would make, like miniature Samurai, in a language we couldn't understand."

Years later, Jeanne becomes the victim of her sixth-grade classmate's stereotyping, related to language and appearance.

> "Gee, I didn't know you could speak English."... I smiled and sat down, suddenly aware of what being of Japanese ancestry was going to be like. I wouldn't be faced with physical attack, or with overt shows of hatred. Rather, I would be seen as someone foreign, or as someone other than American, or perhaps not be seen at all.

Social Stigma

Several of Jeanne's examples in *Farewell to Manzanar* suggest that invisibility could serve as an ultimate fortress of power and self-protection against racism and social stigma. For example, Mrs. Wakatsuki, raised in a culture that values privacy and hygiene, with a social stigma against dirtiness, feels tremendous shame and embarrassment at Manzanar's deplorable toilet conditions. Therefore, she and other female internees use large cardboard boxes to create walls of temporary invisibility. Ko gradually retreats into a realm of invisibility within the confines of his small barracks room in order to cope with a different source of humiliation: the stigma of being a suspected traitor.

The humiliation suffered by Ko Wakatsuki and other *Issei* forced to live at internment camps was surely more painful than any physical sacrifices that they had to make for the nation that would not grant them citizenship. Making matters a thousand times worse, Ko (along with other men who were allowed an early release from imprisonment or given any other special privilege) must deal with mistrust on both sides of the racial barrier. Neighbors of Asian descent suspect Ko of serving as a spy for the American military at the same time that the military suspects him of collaborating with the Japanese enemy. Thus, the proud descendant of samurai warriors hears himself being labeled as "inu" (dog). He hides at home while his wife works as a dietician, earning the highest wage of any internee at Manzanar. Returning home after the war to discover that all of their warehoused possessions and his two fishing boats have been stolen, Ko can not find employment worthy of his talents. "And if he did, Mama's shame would be even greater than his.... So she went to work with as much pride as she could muster."

As a young Nisei, born and raised in American culture, and wanting to assimilate, Jeanne Wakatsuki "lived with this double impulse: the urge to disappear and the desperate desire to be acceptable." For over twenty-five years, the author can not allow herself to share with anyone, even her husband and children, her sense of humiliation caused by racial prejudice and the Manzanar experience. Indeed, she tries to suppress all memories of the shame that resulted from prejudice against her and her family. Toward the end of her memoir, Houston admits,

> As I came to understand what Manzanar had meant, it gradually filled me with shame for being a person guilty of something enormous enough to deserve that kind of treatment. In order to please my accusers, I tried, for the first few years after our release, to become someone acceptable. I both succeeded and failed.

HISTORICAL OVERVIEW

Discrimination Against Japanese Immigrants Before World War II

The *Encyclopedia of Japanese American History* reports that America's first Japanese immigrants came to Hawaii in 1868 as contract laborers, to work on sugar plantations. Their immigration marked the beginning of a series of interracial conflicts based upon economic motives. In 1900, President McKinley's "Organic Act" incorporated Hawaii as an official American Territory, resulting in the prohibition of contract labor and subsequent strikes by more than eight thousand workers. Anti-Japanese citizens in San Francisco formed the Asiatic Exclusion League in 1905. Two years later, President Theodore Roosevelt outlawed the immigration of additional Japanese laborers from Hawaii and Mexico. For the next several decades, Japanese immigrant workers fought racial discrimination with a series of labor strikes; by early 1920, more than two-thirds of the work force (8,300 Japanese and Filipino workers) went on strike. In 1938, fifty strikers were wounded in the infamous "Hilo Massacre." The Alien Land Law of 1920 and other federal legislation reinforced the discrimination against early Japanese immigrants. The Supreme Court Ozawa ruling (1922) prohibited Japanese American citizenship, and President Calvin Coolidge's immigration law (1924) prohibited further Japanese immigration.

The World War II Era

Each episode in *Farewell to Manzanar* reflects the experiences of many Japanese American internees, whose own oral histories describe challenges similar to those the Wakatsukis endured. President Franklin D. Roosevelt's Fair Employment Practices Committee, created in June of 1941 to protect the rights of African Americans working for the federal government, did nothing to help immigrants from Asia, who were still denied citizenship or the right to own land in the United States. In the months preceding the attack on Pearl Harbor, Japanese Americans were subjected to increasing acts of suppression and hostility. Their financial assets were frozen on July 25, 1941. A month later, Representative John Dingell of Michigan suggested the arrest of Japanese Americans in Hawaii. Other state leaders echoed this suggestion.

Idaho's attorney general argued that "all Japanese should be put in concentration camps.... [W]e want to keep this a white man's country." The Army Chief of the Western Defense Command, John L. DeWitt, claimed that "The Japanese race is an enemy race.... [The] very fact that no sabotage has taken place

to date [was a] disturbing and confirming indication that such action will be taken." By November 1941, the FBI began to arrest Japanese American community leaders in California; within a month, over a thousand Issei were in custody, with no formal charges against them. Then, on February 19, 1942, Executive Order 9066 gave official permission for military authorities to evacuate Japanese Americans from the West Coast; residents of Terminal Island were the first to be removed a few days later. For the next several months, Japanese Americans from on the West Coast, from California to Washington, were sent to internment camps scattered throughout the United States (at Manzanar and Tule Lake, California; Amache, Colorado; Minidoka, Idaho; Topaz, Utah; Heart Mountain, Wyoming; Rohwer and Jerome, Arkansas; and Gila River and Poston, Arizona). The Tule Lake camp became the "segregation center" for anyone who refused to sign "yes" to a loyalty oath. Only a few Japanese Americans, such as Minoru Yasui, Gordon Hirabayashi, and Fred Korematsu officially challenged the constitutionality of the evacuation.

Like Woody Wakatsuki, many Nisei went directly from their internment camps into the military, joining the all-Nisei 442 Regimental Combat Team, which combined forces with the 100th Infantry Battalion of Hawaiian Nisei. Harry H. L. Kitano's *Japanese Americans: The Evolution of a Subculture* reports that these two battalions

> suffered more than 9,000 casualties, had more than 600 killed in action, and become known as the most decorated unit in American military history. There was also a significant contribution by Nisei in the Pacific against Japanese of their own ancestry.

With the exception of the members of the "Heart Mountain Fair Play Committee," formed in 1944, few Nisei resisted the draft. These Heart Mountain protesters loyally agreed to serve in the military, but demanded full civil rights for their interned families before they would take the physical examination required for military service.

Conscientious Objectors and Other Internees

Although it is not widely known, not all of the refugees at the internment camp were Japanese American. Seiichi Higashide, the author of *Adios* to Tears: Memoirs of a Japanese-Peruvian Internee in U.S. Concentration Camps*, was an immigrant to Peru from Hokkaido. Higashide and other Japanese-Peruvians were deported to the Crystal City, Texas Internment Camp as part of a hostage exchange program with the Japanese government. Americans of Italian and German ancestry were also imprisoned on the suspicion of their divided loyalties. Lawrence Distasi's *Una Storia Segreta: The Secret History of Italian American Evacuation and Internment During World War II* reports that ten thousand Italian immigrants were forced to relocate from their homes on the West Coast and "[a]bout 250 individuals were interned for up to two years in military camps." John Christgau's *Enemies: World War II Alien Internment* includes the story of German prisoners at the Fort Lincoln Internment Camp in North Dakota, where Ko Wakatsuki was sent at the beginning of the war. In a 2001 interview printed in the *San Francisco Chronicle*, Tak Hoshiaki remembers the conscientious objectors (mostly Quakers, Mennonites, and Jehovah's Witnesses) who were sent to the internment camps along with the Nisei. "We got to be pretty close friends.... We used to have little seminars and readings. I remember reading *War and Peace*." Jeanne Wakatsuki frequently refers to Quaker volunteers in her memoir; she later expressed appreciation for the "mountain of books" they had been donated to the camp. Dr. Yoshiye Togasaki, a specialist in communicable diseases who had graduated from Johns Hopkins Medical School in 1935, volunteered to establish the medical unit at Manzanar, fighting tuberculosis and typhoid. In her chapter of *And Justice for All: An Oral History of the Japanese American Detention Camps*, Dr. Togasaki praised the Quaker volunteers who helped her, in contrast to whites who called her a traitor because she was Japanese. "The Quakers were great, though. A Quaker doctor came to me and said, 'Togi, if there's anything we can do, let me know.'"

Direct Effects of Internment

Many refugees suffered from lifelong illnesses due to poor conditions at the internment camps. According to *Children of the Camps,* a PBS documentary, "Health studies have shown a two times greater incidence of heart disease and premature death among former internees, compared to non-interned Japanese Americans." Roger Daniels explains in *Prisoners Without Trial: Japanese Americans in World War II* that the military had outlawed "the shipment of household goods to camp, so people had to sell, give away, or discard what they could not carry. Those with cars and trucks were not allowed to drive themselves to camp."

According to *Japanese American Internment Camps: At Issue in History*, families who had once lived in middle-class homes "were housed in converted horse stalls among other places." At the mercy of extremely low salaries, the fenced-in refugees often could not afford to purchase even the most basic supplies from a catalog to improve their living conditions.

> The WRA directed camps to be self-sufficient in labor, but paid internees lower wages than were paid U.S. army privates. This meant that all Japanese internees, including professionals, such as doctors and educators, made a fraction of what WRA personnel and other outside employees of the camps were paid.

The average salary for these camp jobs was sixteen to nineteen dollars a month. "Many Japanese families were ruined economically," according to Harry H. L. Kitano, author of *Japanese Americans: The Evolution of a Subculture*. Audrie Girdner and Anne Loftis report, in *The Great Betrayal: The Evacuation of Japanese Americans During World War II* that "in publicity releases the unheard-of low wage rates were often cited with pride rather than apologies, as an example of the sacrifice evacuees were making like soldiers in the service of their country." Nevertheless, white employees who did similar jobs were paid much higher salaries. Although the Japanese American Evacuation Claims Act of 1948 awarded $28 million in damages, *Japanese American Internment Camps: At Issue in History* reports that "the Federal Reserve Bank of San Francisco estimated wartime property losses of Japanese Americans to reach $400 million."

In 1988, President Ronald Reagan signed House Resolution 442, which authorized payments of $20,000 to each of the sixty thousand surviving internees. This law, named in honor of the Japanese American 442nd Regimental Combat Team, also established a $1.25 billion education fund. Upon signing the law, President Reagan spoke of Congressman Norman Mineta, whose family had been sent to live at Santa Anita Racetrack before being relocated to Heart Mountain Internment Camp; then, President Regan added,

The Yonemitsu family in the living room of their house at the Manzanar Relocation Center, photograph by Ansel Adams, 1943 The Library of Congress

no payment can make up for those lost years. So, what is most important in this bill has less to do with property than with honor. For here we admit a wrong; here we reaffirm our commitment as a nation to equal justice under the law.

CRITICAL OVERVIEW

Literary critics and historians have consistently praised *Farewell to Manzanar* since the book first appeared in 1973. Soon after its publication, a critic for the *New Yorker* magazine observed that the author told the painful story of her family's internment and her father's subsequent disgrace "with great dignity." In the *Saturday Review,* Dorothy Rabinowitz noted that "Houston and her husband have recorded a tale of many complexities in a straightforward manner, a tale remarkably lacking in either self-pity or solemnity." A 1974 *New York Times Book Review* recommended the memoir as "a dramatic, telling account of one of the most

reprehensible events in the history of America's treatment of its minorities."

A 1998 article in "Asian-American Literary Traditions" by Jeffrey Paul Chan and Marilyn C. Alquilozo of San Francisco State University places Jeanne Wakatsuki Houston "among the most widely read contemporary Japanese American voices." These reviewers categorize *Farewell to Manzanar* as "one of the finest literary products of the relocation camp experience." In their 1998 essay "Japanese and Japanese American Youth in Literature," Connie S. Zitlow and Lois Stover point to *Farewell to Manzanar* as "a particularly outstanding example of young adult literature that is very appropriate for high school classrooms." More than twenty-five years after the novel first appeared, the *Los Angeles Times* emphasized the fact that *Farewell to Manzanar* offered important lessons, as an "accessible and unsentimental work" that "shed light on a subject that had been largely ignored in popular histories."

Eric Waggoner's 2001 doctoral dissertation, "Living Protest: Resistance and Testimony in Twentieth-Century American Autobiography," argues that the book's "central character is, in one compelling view, not Jeanne herself but the Wakatsuki family in sum, whose internal and inter-generational clashes serve as simulacra for the damages caused by the internment." Dr. Waggoner emphasizes the important role of "family narratives" as a mean of educating "middle class America" about the traditional values and concerns of Asian Americans, as well as their World War II internment experiences. In "American Uses of Japanese American Memory: How Internment Narratives are 'Put into Discourse,'" Professor Brian Lain of the University of North Texas highlights the personal, nonpolitical side of Houston's memoir. Professor Lain quotes the 1973 *Publishers Weekly* article by Barbara Bannon, who perceived *Farewell to Manzanar* as "a sober and moving personal account." He also refers to another review, in 1975, from *Booklist*: "it is written, 'not as political history, but as the story of one person's life-altering experience.'" Traise Yamamoto observed in her 1999 essay, "Masking in Nisei Women's Autobiography," that Jeanne Wakatsuki Houston and other Nisei women writers had to balance "historical motive and cultural reticence" in their revealing stories about personal and family shame. According to Yamamoto, Houston "had everything to lose and little to gain by revealing the private self."

Whether *Farewell to Manzanar* is viewed as a personal memoir, a family narrative, or a historical document, all readers are touched by Houston's poignant story. Historians and educators are unanimous in their agreement of the book's importance. In 2002, *Publishers Weekly* announced that the book had been chosen for a new statewide reading program in Missouri (called "ReadMOre") "because the issue of ethnic profiling during time of war seemed especially timely." To teach lessons of racial tolerance and respect for ethnic diversity, California provided ten thousand copies of the memoir and its 1976 film adaptation to schools and libraries throughout the state in 2003.

Theresa Kulbaga and Wendy Hesford included *A Farewell to Manzanar* in their 2005 *New Dictionary of the History of Ideas* as "one of the most famous internment narratives" whose "narrator describes the racialization process by

MEDIA ADAPTATIONS

Farewell to Manzanar was adapted as a film for television, produced and directed by John Korty in 1976 and distributed by National Broadcasting Company (NBC). It is currently unavailable.

---

which Japanese immigrants and citizens were reconstructed as enemies of the state solely on the basis of their ethnicity and without regard to their citizenship status or national loyalties."

CRITICISM

Traise Yamamoto

In the following excerpt, Yamamoto describes the risks that second-generation Japanese American autobiographers have taken in telling their stories and revealing family secrets.

However, we should also recognize that Japanese American autobiography exists between two impulses: historical motive and cultural reticence. On the one hand, Nisei autobiographies are the written record of a community betrayed by the dark side of democracy—majority rule or, in this case, majority racist hysteria. On the other hand, the autobiographical form is fundamentally at odds with the Nisei tendency to downplay the individual self, a behavioral adaptation largely shaped by the desire to "fit in" and thus avoid racist discrimination. The result is an autobiographical tradition grounded in the desire to witness, not in the introspective impulses of self-contemplation. And yet, as Jeanne Wakatsuki Houston writes in the foreword to *Farewell to Manzanar*:

> It became [clear] that any book [I] wrote would have to include a good deal more than day-to-day life inside the compound. To tell what I knew and felt about it would mean telling something about our family before the war, and the years that followed the war, and about my father's past, as well as my own way

of seeing things now. Writing it has been a way of coming to terms with the impact those years have had on my entire life.

While these narratives function as records of "day-to-day" life in the camps, they are also the statement of a subject whose constitution is intimately tied to the fact of the internment. To write about the internment is to write about an event whose very basis was the denial of subjectivity, and it is thus an act of writing the self—and by extension the community of interned Japanese Americans—as subject. Because much of their narrative is addressed to a potentially defensive and hostile white American audience, Nisei autobiographers are selective in their use of personal detail and guarded in their criticisms of white America. If as Sidonie Smith writes, the female autobiographer "can speak with authority only insofar as she tells a story that her audience will read" Nisei women who assume autobiographical authority must be even more careful to present their stories in "acceptable" terms. However strongly they might feel about their experiences of the camps, there is also a reluctance to speak about those experiences and feelings, a guardedness about the act of revelation. Already marginalized and delegitimized by race, gender and, often, class as they critiqued, however subtly, an audience whom they were largely addressing, these writers had everything to lose and little to gain by revealing the private self.

Source: Traise Yamamoto, "Masking in Nisei Women's Autobiography," in *Masking Selves, Making Subjects: Japanese American Women, Identity, and the Body*, University of California Press, 1999, pp. 105–106.

SOURCES

Chan, Jeffrey P., and Marilyn C Alquilozo, *Asian-American Literary Traditions*, www2.tcu.edu/depts/prs/amwest/html/wl1119.html (March 15, 2006).

Children of the Camps: The Japanese American WWII Internment Camp Experience, www.pbs.org/childofcamp (March 14, 2006).

Christgau, John, *Enemies: World War II Alien Internment*, Authors Choice Press, April 2001.

Daniels, Roger, ed., *Prisoners Without Trial: Japanese Americans in World War II*, Hill and Wang, 1993, p. 55.

Dudley, William, ed., *Japanese American Internment Camps: At Issue in History*, Greenhaven Press, 2002, pp. 15–20.

Gilbert, Sandra, and Lawrence Distasi, eds., *Una Storia Segreta: The Secret History of Italian American Evacuation and Internment During World War II*. Heyday Books, 2001.

Girdner, Audrie, and Anne Loftis, *The Great Betrayal: The Evacuation of the Japanese Americans During World War II*, Macmillan, 1969, p. 170.

Higashide, Seiichi, *Adios to Tears: Memoirs of a Japanese-Peruvian Internee in U.S. Concentration Camps*, University of Washington Press, 2000.

Houston, Jeanne Wakatsuki and James D. Houston, *Farewell to Manzanar: A True Story of Japanese American Experience During and After the World War II Internment*, Dell Laurel-Leaf, 1973.

Kitano, Harry H. L., *Japanese Americans: The Evolution of a Subculture*, Prentice Hall, 1969, pp. 32–45.

Lain, Brian, "American Uses of Japanese American Memory: How Internment Narratives are 'Put into Discourse,'" www.comm.unt.edu/faculty/american_uses_of_japanese_americ.htm (March 15, 2006).

Nakao, Annie "A Unique Tale of WWII Resistance: Japanese American Internees Refused Draft," *San Francisco Chronicle*, October 26, 2001, p. A21.

———, "'Farewell to Manzanar' Author Returns to Internment Days in First Novel," in the *San Francisco Chronicle*, December 14, 2003, p. E1.

Niiya, Brian, ed., *Encyclopedia of Japanese American History: An A to Z Reference From 1868 to the Present*, Checkmark Books, 2000, pp. 29–58.

Rabinowitz, Dorothy, Review of *Farewell to Manzanar*, in *Saturday Review*, November 6, 1973.

Reagan, Ronald, "Remarks on Signing the Bill Providing Restitution for the Wartime Internment of Japanese American Civilians, August 10, 1988," history.wisc.edu/archdeacon/404tja/redress.html (March 15, 2006).

Review of *Farewell to Manzanar*, in *New Yorker*, November 5, 1973, p. 186.

Review of *Farewell to Manzanar*, in *New York Times Book Review*, January 13, 1974, p. 31.

Singh, Ajay, "The Lessons of History," *Los Angeles Times*, November 6, 2001, p. E1.

Tateishi, John, ed., *And Justice for All: An Oral History of the Japanese American Detention Camps*, Random House, 1984, pp. 222–25.

Waggoner, Eric Garner, "Living Protest: Resistance and Testimony in Twentieth-Century American Autobiography," Ph.D. diss., Arizona State University, 2001.

Yamamoto, Traise, "Masking in Nisei Women's Autobiography" in *Masking Selves, Making Subjects: Japanese American Women, Identity, and the Body*, University of California Press, 1999. pp. 105–106.

Zitlow, Connie S., and Lois Stover, "Japanese and Japanese American Youth in Literature" in the *Alan Review*, Vol. 25, No. 3, Spring 1998, scholar.lib.vt.edu/ejournals/ALAN/spring98/zitlow.html (October 31, 2005).

Flowers for Algernon

DANIEL KEYES

1966

Flowers for Algernon, Daniel Keyes's best-known novel, has remained in print continuously since it was first published in the 1960s. Constructed from first-person "progress reports," the novel chronicles the transformation of protagonist Charlie Gordon from a mentally retarded adult into an intellectual genius. Charlie is the first person to undergo an experimental surgery that produces such a change. However, his increased intellectual capacity is only temporary, as the scientists first learn from Algernon, a lab mouse who has also had the surgery.

During the months of Charlie's transformation, he remembers much about his past, in which he was often used and abused because of his disability. Yet the intelligent Charlie suffers from loneliness and an inability to relate to much of the world. He also feels that the scientists who help him look at him only as the subject of an experiment, not as a person. Throughout the story, Keyes explores the depths of Charlie's revelations about himself and the world around him, showing that intellectual intelligence does not always equal personal happiness.

Keyes's inspiration for *Flowers for Algernon* came from several sources gathered over many years. While a college student, he came up with the idea of a surgery that could make someone smarter and the consequences that might follow. When Keyes was working as an editor and writer for pulp magazines and comic books in the early

1950s, this idea resurfaced and continued to germinate. However, the story never gelled and he did not want to publish it in comic book form because he thought the idea had significant potential.

Keyes eventually took a job as an English teacher and was the instructor for a class for slower students. One of Keyes's male students asked if he could be moved into a normal class if he did well and was smarter by the end of semester. Before his student asked him this question, it had never occurred to Keyes that someone who was mentally challenged might have this desire. Keyes spent extra time working with the student and helped him learn to read, but the student lost the new skill when he had to leave school for a matter of weeks due to a family situation. This incident provided Keyes with the final element he needed for his story.

Keyes, however, did not turn this idea into a novel right away. He originally wrote *Flowers for Algernon* as a short story published in 1959 in the *Magazine of Fantasy and Science Fiction*. It won the Hugo Award at the World Science Fiction Convention. After the story was made into a successful television special and included in several anthologies, Keyes decided to expand it into novel form so that he could address issues from Charlie's childhood. Though Keyes initially received several rejections from publishers because of the novel's "down" ending, he eventually found a publisher. The novel won the Nebula Award from the Science Fiction Writers of America in 1966.

As with the short-story version, the novel *Flowers for Algernon* was originally seen primarily as a work of science fiction. The concept asks a "what if" question and explores how a possible path of scientific progress could create ethical quandaries. Because the novel also explores what it means to be human, addressing both social and philosophical questions about the self as well as including a few romantic moments, it has transcended the science fiction genre and is generally regarded as a work of popular fiction. In *Censored Books: Critical Viewpoints*, Robert Small Jr. writes that the novel has "achieved literary success in an unusual variety of forms, and may well be the best known work of science fiction to the general public, that is, to non-science fiction fans."

The novel was popular from the time it was first published, with many critics noting *Flowers*

> YOU'VE BOASTED TIME AND AGAIN THAT I WAS NOTHING BEFORE THE EXPERIMENT, AND I KNOW WHY. BECAUSE IF I WAS NOTHING, THEN YOU WERE RESPONSIBLE FOR CREATING ME, AND THAT MAKES YOU MY LORD AND MASTER. YOU RESENT THE FACT THAT I DON'T SHOW MY GRATITUDE EVERY HOUR OF THE DAY. WELL, BELIEVE OR NOT, I AM GRATEFUL. BUT WHAT YOU DID FOR ME—WONDERFUL AS IT IS—DOESN'T GIVE YOU THE RIGHT TO TREAT ME LIKE AN EXPERIMENTAL ANIMAL. I'M AN INDIVIDUAL NOW, AND SO WAS CHARLIE BEFORE HE EVER WALKED INTO THAT LAB."

for Algernon as a positive, thought-provoking portrayal of the mentally handicapped. Critics also have stated that the first-person point of view allows readers to fully understand and relate to Charlie, thus giving the book its power. In addition, reviewers have commented positively on the compelling plot and interesting questions the novel poses about science, the desire for personal growth, and self-awareness. After its first publication, *Flowers for Algernon* went on to be published in at least forty countries and has sold several million copies. Other works by Keyes include *The Touch* (1968), *The Minds of Billy Milligan* (1981), and a memoir about Keyes's experiences writing *Flowers for Algernon* titled *Algernon, Charlie, and I: A Writer's Journey* (1999).

PLOT SUMMARY

Progris Riport 1 Martch 3

Flowers for Algernon opens with Charlie Gordon's first progress report. It is part of the first-person journal entries he states he is writing at the behest of Dr. Strauss and Professor Nemur: "I tolld dr Strauss and perfesser Nemur I cant rite good but he says it dont matter he says i shud rite just like I talk." With poor grammar and many misspellings, Charlie explains that he is thirty-two years old and works in a bakery.

BIOGRAPHY

DANIEL KEYES

Born August 9, 1927, in Brooklyn, New York, Daniel Keyes was the son of working-class parents. Keyes's mother pushed him to improve himself through education, and both parents pressured him to become a doctor. However, Keyes enjoyed reading and storytelling and wanted to write from an early age. Keyes attended college and earned a degree in psychology. Though his parents wanted him to have this education, the changes he underwent in college affected his relationship with them, a tension that found its way into *Flowers for Algernon*.

Instead of becoming a psychologist, Keyes worked as a writer and editor of pulp magazines and comic books. He drew on his psychology background and longtime interest in the workings of the human mind in his writings. One particularly fruitful method he learned was free association, a concept he used to create fictional situations in his work.

While Keyes had some of the ideas for his famous novel in late 1940s and early 1950s, it was not until the late 1950s that he was able to find his inspiration for Charlie and produce the story. After publishing the novel version of *Flowers for Algernon* in 1966, Keyes spent twenty-six years as a college creative writing teacher and wrote several more works of fiction and nonfiction that deal with topics of the mind. As of 2006, he lives with his wife in Boca Raton, Florida.

Charlie claims that he wants to be smart and uses his free time to go to Miss Kinnian's class at a center for "retarded adults." Charlie is being considered for something that will make him more intelligent.

Progris Riport 2—Martch 4

Charlie takes a test for Nemur during his lunch hour, but is afraid he has failed it. The administrator, Burt, gives Charlie a Rorschach test, in which Burt shows him pictures of spilled ink on cards and asks him what he sees. As hard as he tries, Charlie can only see the blots, not pictures: "I tryed hard but I still coudnt find the picturs I only saw the ink."

3d Progris Report

Charlie is still being considered for the experiment. Strauss and Nemur ask him why he is so interested in becoming smarter. Charlie has wanted to be smart his whole life and his mother also wanted him to learn. Charlie is unconcerned about the potential hazards that may result from the surgery. However, Strauss and Nemur need permission from his family, and Charlie has not seen his mother, father, or sister for many years.

Progris Report 4

Charlie describes the tests that he undergoes. After these tests are completed, Burt takes Charlie to the lab where the animals are kept. There, Charlie meets Algernon, a mouse who has undergone the same procedure to be performed on Charlie. Charlie and Algernon compete in doing mazes. Algernon wins every time.

Progris Report 5 Mar 6

Charlie is happy because the scientists have found his sister Norma and she has given her permission for the surgery. Charlie will now undergo the surgery to increase his intelligence, though Nemur has some concerns about using Charlie.

Progris Riport 6th Mar 8

Charlie is excited by the prospect of learning to read and write as well as fit in with other people: "Ill be abel to reed better and spell the werds good and know lots of things and be like other pepul." Nemur tells him if the change is permanent for him, others will benefit and he will be famous. However, he is not allowed to tell his coworkers at the bakery what kind of surgery he is having.

Progress Report 7 March 11

Charlie writes that the surgery did not hurt. He believes that being smarter will bring him lots of friends and he will never be lonely. Among his postsurgical visitors is Miss Kinnian. He tells her that he is disappointed that he did not immediately become smarter.

Progress Report 8

Charlie is out of the hospital. He works with the scientists and Burt on puzzles and games, but is frustrated by his lack of progress. He especially hates losing to Algernon. Miss Kinnian continues to help him learn. When Charlie returns to work at the bakery, he is happy to see his friends again, though his surgery remains a secret. Mr. Donner, the bakery owner, promises Charlie that he will always have a job at the bakery.

A few days later, Charlie reports he has stopped going to the lab because he is not smarter yet. The scientists bring a special kind of television set to his room that he is to watch before he goes to sleep and while he is sleeping. One of the phrases emanating from the television is "remember," and Charlie's previously poor memory starts to improve. Charlie also has to go to therapy sessions with Dr. Strauss. Soon, Charlie finally beats Algernon in a maze race. He also starts to read better and improve his spelling.

Progress Report 9

Charlie's growing intelligence is starting to show in his more complex grammar and better spelling. He reports that he now works on the dough mixer at the bakery. His coworkers are amazed that Charlie can do this better than the man who unexpectedly quit.

Charlie finishes reading the novel *Robinson Crusoe*. Miss Kinnian continues to be impressed by his progress and helps him further his education about people, writing, and reading. A few days later, Charlie skips work after going to a party with some of his friends from the bakery. They had slipped alcohol in Charlie's drink and made him dance with a woman who rubbed herself against him. While his work friends laughed at him, Charlie felt shame.

By the end of this report, Charlie's writing is impeccable. He notes that he is retaining what he is learning and is ready to learn foreign languages. Charlie is reading many novels, but is not yet allowed to read any psychology. Through free association and what he remembers from his dreams, Charlie is able to recall an incident from when he was eleven years old and gave a female classmate a present. When he asked a classmate to write a valentine to a Harriet, the girl he liked, the boy who did it wrote a dirty note instead. Harriet's brother

beat him up. During a session with Burt, Charlie has to take a Rorschach test again. This time Charlie sees pictures, but remains distrustful of the process.

Progress Report 10

While Charlie's suggestions for improving production at the bakery are accepted, he also sees that his coworkers are becoming frightened of him. He feels more alone at work, writing, "Nobody at the place talks to me any more, or kids around the way they used to. It makes the job kind of lonely." Charlie remembers a time when he was less intelligent and made fun of, yet more accepted. As Charlie becomes more intelligent, he wants to ask his teacher, Miss Kinnian, out on a date. He also starts to hang around the university, carrying books and conversing with students, to both combat his loneliness and stretch his intellectual muscles. Charlie reads more and more. While his intellectual capacity increases, Charlie also remembers a number of incidents from his childhood. Before his younger sister was born, Charlie's mother, Rose, desperately wanted to believe her son was normal and tried to force him to learn when he could not. She insisted, "He's normal! He's normal! He'll grow up like other people. Better than others." She beat him for any mistakes.

Progress Report 11

Charlie describes his date with Alice Kinnian. Alice notices that Charlie's intellectual capacity has increased tremendously and he is developing insights about the world around him. She is supportive, but concerned about what will happen to him. It becomes apparent that Charlie also has much emotional growth to experience as well, though he assures Alice, "My feeling for you won't change because I'm becoming intelligent. I'll only love you more." However, his attraction to Alice and other women is affected by his childhood experiences, including being physically harmed for trying on his sister's clothes and looking at her after she took a bath.

Charlie continues to work at the bakery. He now realizes that one of his coworkers, Gimpy, has been cheating Mr. Donner. Charlie feels guilty about the situation. He finally turns to Alice for advice, who tells him that he must decide what to do. They also discuss their relationship, with Charlie insisting he wants to continue to see her outside of the lab. Charlie admits to himself that he is love with her. The next day,

Charlie indirectly confronts Gimpy about his activities and seems to convince him to stop the thievery.

Outside of work, Charlie spends much of his time at the university's library studying a variety of subjects on a very advanced level. He is now focusing on ancient languages and history as well as calculus variations. What was intellectually interesting to him only a few weeks ago now seems too simple for him. The more intelligent Charlie becomes, the more he realizes people he thought were so smart, like professors, really only know information about one area.

Charlie and Alice go on another date. When he and Alice are about to become physically closer, he thinks he sees a teenage boy watching them nearby. He also feels physically sick. After the date is over, Charlie starts to believe that it was a hallucination and an indication of his sexual immaturity.

Charlie is fired from his job at the bakery, in part because he has become too smart for it and also because of his coworkers' fears of him. Charlie feels even more isolated and avoids going to the lab for a few days. He eventually turns to Alice for comfort. Though panic still overwhelms him when he is close to her, he understands why it is happening.

Progress Report 12

Charlie is now earning a salary from the foundation that supports the scientists' research. He is preparing for a psychological convention at which the scientists will present their findings about him and Algernon. Charlie is still upset about being fired from the bakery and remembers other emotionally turbulent events from his childhood. Distressed by a memory, Charlie seeks out Alice to talk, but she is frustrated by her inability to communicate with him because of his high intelligence level: "I wanted you to be intelligent, I wanted to help you and share with you—and now you've shut me out of your life." She feels inferior to him, and he sees they now have nothing in common.

Charlie goes out to Central Park one evening and meets a woman. Charlie wants to prove to himself that he can be "normal" with women and not let panic overcome him. Just before they leave together to get a hotel room, the woman reveals that she is five months pregnant. Charlie thinks back to his mother's pregnancy with his sister, when she was pushing him away to protect the coming baby. Charlie reacts violently to the memory and scares the woman, who shouts for help. Charlie waits in the bushes, feeling as though he deserved to be caught and beaten for his actions: "Shadows out of the past clutch at my legs and drag me down."

Progress Report 13

Charlie is on an airplane on his way to the convention. He continues to remember more about his childhood. Charlie recalls the time his mother insisted on taking him to yet another doctor who promised to make him normal. Reflecting on his past, Charlie comes to understand that his quest to become smart is connected with his mother's desire to improve him as a small child. Though his mother gave up that idea when her daughter was born, Charlie still wants to show her that he can be intelligent and earn her love.

At the convention, Charlie is stunned to learn that the scientists have only limited knowledge of certain areas. Charlie believes that the scientists are frauds. After a conversation with Burt, Charlie comes to understand that only he is a genius. When Nemur and Strauss's presentation is at hand, Charlie resents that the scientists, especially Nemur, do not look at him as a person, but only an experiment. Charlie becomes concerned when he learns during Burt's talk that Algernon has recently exhibited some erratic behaviors. Increasingly disturbed by the presentation, Charlie decides to release Algernon from his cage. As everyone looks for the valuable mouse, Charlie takes it to his room, where he plans their escape: "we'll take off—just you and me—a couple of man-made geniuses on the run." Charles decides to return home to see his parents.

Progress Report 14

Back in New York, Charlie reads about the search for Algernon and him in the newspaper. His sister is interviewed in one article and says she was told he was sent to a state hospital seventeen years earlier and had died there. This article jogs more memories of his childhood. Charlie remembers being a teenager when his mother, worried he would have a negative effect on Norma, wanted to send him to the Warren State Home, though his father disagreed. Returning to the present, Charlie withdraws all his money from the bank and moves into a furnished apartment. Algernon is still with him, and Charlie builds a three-dimensional maze so the mouse continues to be intellectually stimulated. Charlie also becomes friendly with his neighbor, Faye. She is a painter who loves to dance and lives a freewheeling life.

Charlie decides to visit his father, Matt, who runs a barbershop. Though Matt gives Charlie a haircut and shave, Charlie cannot work up enough courage to tell Matt that he is his son, and Matt does not recognize him. Charlie remembers the night his mother insisted that he be sent away to the home. Rose threatened to kill Charlie—"He's better off dead. He'll never be able to live a normal life"—unless Matt took him away for Norma's sake, which he did.

At home, Charlie continues to work with Algernon. The mouse is still acting erratically at times. Faye buys a female mouse to keep Algernon company. A few days later, Faye and Charlie kiss and spend the night together after drinking. Charlie does not remember anything. Faye tells him that they did not have sex and Charlie had acted odd, like a frightened child.

Not wanting to be alone, Charlie visits Alice. He tells her he has come to the conclusion that he still has the emotional wiring of the mentally challenged Charlie. He accepts that this Charlie is with him. This emotional block prevents him from having a physical relationship with Alice. He then tries to become physically involved with Alice by thinking of her as Faye, but still the old Charlie makes him panic. When Charlie gets home, he makes love to Faye, aware that the old Charlie is watching. He and Faye become involved. He starts going out dancing and drinking with her at night, while doing his intellectual work doing the day. Charlie worries he might only have limited time to do his research as Algernon has grown more unpredictable, has bitten both Faye and his mouse companion, and has lost some of his intellectual ability.

Progress Report 15

Charlie returns to his work at the lab only after contacting the foundation himself and negotiating his own work arrangements. Granted his own study of the project, Charlie brings Algernon back. While the scientists are welcoming, some seem unsure whether Charlie can contribute anything. When Burt shows him around the lab, Charlie learns that if he regresses, he will be sent to the Warren State Home. Charlie spends a few days reading all he can about every facet of psychology.

Progress Report 16

Charlie goes to visit the Warren State Home and gets a thorough tour from the head psychologist. Charlie finds a general lack of hope, but the dedication of those who work there and touches of human affection impress him. At the lab, Algernon's condition worsens considerably. Charlie has not gone out dancing with Faye as much, as he focuses his attention on work, but he still drinks and has sex with her. One night, when Alice visits because of concerns about what Algernon's state means for Charlie, Alice and Faye meet. Charlie tells Alice that he has not told Faye the truth about him and that he is still in love with Alice.

Because Charlie feels pressure to get work done, he has a cot placed in the lab. He knows that he only has a few weeks to finish his research and is very clear-minded and energetic about reaching his goals. Algernon does not move much and often becomes frustrated to the point of hurting himself when he runs mazes. Charlie wants to find out why Algernon has regressed and focuses much attention on this matter. It helps that Faye has found a new boyfriend.

Charlie goes to a cocktail party where all the scientists are in attendance. He gets into a shouting match with Nemur, who believes Charlie is ungrateful and has compromised much of the work the scientists have done. Charlie tells him that he has only been treated as an experiment and not a human being, just as he has always been, even before the surgery.

After stepping away from the situation, Charlie believes there was truth to what Nemur had said in that he had become arrogant and unable to relate to people. After the party, Charlie has an insight into a problem with the experiment. He does lab work to confirm his idea and writes a report explaining that the surgery he and Algernon had lacks any practical value. Charlie concludes that the intelligence gained by such procedures depreciates at a rate that is proportional to how long it took to increase. Other scientists confirm Charlie's data and conclusion. Charlie worries about his decline and does not blame the scientists for what is happening to him. As Charlie's condition starts to worsen, Algernon dies. Charlie buries him in his backyard and puts flowers on his grave.

Some days later, Charlie decides to visit his mother. He finds his mother, Rose, suffering from senility. Norma still lives with her and is quite happy to see her long-lost brother. While he appreciates the unexpected affirmations that Norma gives him, Charlie is happy that in a moment of clarity his mother knows who he is and that he has become the smart boy she always wanted him to be. The happy scene is broken when Norma hugs Charlie, and Rose grabs a knife and tells him not to touch his sister because he has sexual thoughts about her. Norma removes the knife from Rose's hands and both feel a little ashamed. When Charlie leaves, he cries as he walks to his car.

Progress Report 17

Charlie spends much of his time in his apartment. During a therapy session with Strauss, Charlie feels physically sick and angry toward the doctor. He describes how his mental sensations are changing and he feels like he is shrinking: "I can't feel my body any more. I'm numb. I have the feeling that Charlie is close by." A few days later, Charlie is in the psychology lab and takes a long time to do a maze. He also cannot complete a Rorschach test. He grows frustrated at his regression and never returns to the lab.

At home, Charlie tries to read a book he could read a few months ago, but cannot. Alice shows up. She wants to spend time with him while he is still intelligent. They make love. Alice continues to stay with him and take care of him until he sends her away. As the days progress, Charlie becomes more irritable and his motor skills decline. He realizes that all his language skills are gone. Charlie checks out books from the library, and though he cannot read most of them, he tries to hold on to his intelligence as best he can. For days, he stays inside his apartment, avoiding the scientists and Alice, allowing only the landlady to bring him meals.

The last few entries in his report are short and full of spelling and grammar errors. Dr. Strauss and Alice give the landlady money for rent and food for Charlie, but Charlie will not allow Alice to visit nor does he want to take their money. Charlie returns to the bakery and gets his old job back from Donner. When a new employee tries to hurt him, one of his old coworkers, Joe, stands up for him.

By force of habit, Charlie goes back to the adult center school. Miss Kinnian is upset by his presence: "She started to cry and run out of the room and everybody looked at me and I saw alot

of them wasnt the same pepul who use to be in my class." Only then does Charlie remember some of what has happened to him. He decides that he must check himself into the Warren State Home. Charlie writes that he will continue his pursuit of intelligence and asks that someone put flowers on Algernon's grave.

THEMES

Prejudice

One of the primary themes of *Flowers for Algernon* is the poor treatment of and social disregard for the mentally handicapped. As Charlie grows more intelligent and his memory of his past improves, he remembers a number of acts of prejudice against him. Many of these incidents occurred within his family. His mother, Rose, cannot accept that her son is mentally retarded. When Charlie was small, she tried to force him to learn, and she beat him when he failed because she wanted him to be "normal." Because of his handicap, Charlie could not control his bodily functions at times. This led Rose to inflict even more physical harm on Charlie, because she believed he should be capable of controlling himself. She took him to many doctors, trying to find a cure for a condition that could not be cured. Her husband, Matt, tried to intercede, but Rose was fervent in her desire to have a normal son.

The situation with his family only grew worse as Charlie grew older, reflecting the social stigmas a mentally challenged person can face. After the birth of his sister, Rose rejected Charlie when it became clear that Norma was normal. Rose feared that Charlie would reflect poorly on Norma socially, and that Norma would not be able to have friends over. More deeply, Rose feared that Charlie would act out sexually against his sister and/or one of her friends, although there is no evidence that Charlie ever had such an inclination. Eventually, Rose insisted that Charlie must be sent away, no matter what effect the move would have on her son. Matt reluctantly took him out of the home.

Charlie's work situation is also problematic. Charlie remembers that his coworkers once invited presurgery Charlie to a party, got him drunk, and made him dance with a woman who rubbed herself against him. They laughed at Charlie's confused and nervous reaction. As his

A custodian pushes a broom through an empty hallway The Terry Wild Studio. Reproduced by permission

act. He yells at the customers: "Shut up! Leave him alone! He can't understand. He can't help what he is ... but for God's sake, have some respect! *He's a human being!*" After he leaves, Charlie notes that it is strange that "people of honest feelings and sensibility, who would not take advantage of a man born without arms or legs or eyes ... think nothing of abusing a man born with low intelligence."

As Charlie's own emotional intelligence continues to grow, he becomes no less intolerant of society's actions and attitudes toward the mentally challenged. However, his understanding and empathy for people's limitations also increases, and he sees that not everyone acts in prejudice. At the beginning of Progress Report 16, he visits the Warren State Home, where he had been placed briefly as a child and will voluntarily go again when his condition worsens. During the tour, Charlie observes people trying to help the mentally handicapped and give what they can in sometimes trying circumstances. As Charlie is coming to terms with his own past and future when leaving the home's campus, he notes that "The feeling of cold grayness was everywhere around me—a sense of resignation." However, he also thinks about those who work there, that he "wished [he] knew how they had found their way here to work and dedicate themselves to these silent minds."

intelligence increases, he realizes that he was the butt of other jokes by his coworkers as well. The intelligent Charlie also remembers that the mentally challenged Charlie did not know any better and regarded these people as his friends, but he now feels shame and discomfort at the way he was treated.

As Charlie's intelligence increases, he becomes more aware of acts of prejudice against the mentally handicapped in society. After walking around the city at night on one occasion, Charlie goes into a diner and witnesses a mentally challenged dishwasher become the focal point of a crowd's laughter and an employer's wrath. The teen-aged boy drops some dishes while clearing a table. Charlie notes, "The whistles and catcalls from the customers ... confused him." The boy's boss calls him a "dope" and an "idiot," while ordering him to clean up the mess. As he does so, the boy continues to be heckled by a few customers. Charlie is ashamed that he initially shares their amusement and decides to

Loneliness and Isolation

Related to the prejudice against the mentally handicapped is the sense of loneliness and isolation Charlie feels, which permeates *Flowers for Algernon*. One of the reasons that Charlie wants to have this operation in the first place is to meet other people. In his sixth progress report, written before the operation, Charlie notes, "I just want to be smart like other pepul so I can have lots of frends who like me."

In nearly all the incidents Charlie remembers from his childhood, he is beaten, taken advantage of, or pushed aside—acts that isolated him. Recalling one traumatic incident from his childhood, Charlie reflects that "I guess I was pretty dumb because I believed what people told me. I shouldn't have trusted ... anyone." Because of these incidents, young Charlie does not even go to school and becomes further withdrawn from the outside world. He spends all his time at home until his mother insists he be sent away.

Yet, it is only after the operation, when his intelligence has increased, that Charlie truly feels and completely understands the depths of his loneliness and isolation. The intelligent Charlie can remember what happened to him as a child, something the mentally challenged Charlie could not. The intelligent Charlie also comprehends what his coworkers and customers at the bakery did to him, increasing these feelings of isolation. Worse yet, Charlie does not gain social and emotional understanding as quickly as he does intellectual ability. In a few short months, Charlie goes from being a mentally retarded individual to being an intellectual genius, but he remains the same emotionally. The smarter he becomes, the more unable he is to relate to people he cares about, such as Alice and Faye, and others in his professional circle, like the scientists who performed the surgery and students he meets at the university. After a tense scene between Alice and Charlie chronicled in Progress Report 12, Charlie writes, "I am just as far away from Alice with an I.Q. of 185 as I was when I had an I.Q. of 70." He also becomes intolerant of the ignorance of others.

Charlie comes to realize that he had more friends when he was mentally challenged: "When I was retarded I had lots of friends. Now I have no one.... I don't have any real friends. Not like I used to have in the bakery." He was nice to everyone and wore a smile on his face. Though his coworkers made fun of him, they also generally watched out for him. This sense of protection is evident when Charlie's condition deteriorates and he returns to working at the bakery. A new employee, Meyer Klaus, physically harms Charlie until Joe Carp, who has worked there longer, steps in. Charlie reports that Gimpy told him, "We all want you to remember that you got frends here and dont you ever forget it." Hearing this, Charlie writes, "That makes me feel good. Its good to have friends."

Being Human vs. Being an Experiment

As Charlie develops an ever increasing self-awareness after the operation, he comes to realize that he is a human being with intricate feelings and emotions. Keyes contrasts this emerging sense of self with how the scientists, primarily Professor Nemur, view Charlie: as an experimental subject. While everyone related to the study is generally kind to him by all appearances, it is only after Charlie's intelligence begins to grow that he sees they are primarily concerned with him as an experiment. Like his coworkers in the bakery, the scientists care about Charlie, but also use him for their own purposes.

When Charlie reaches the heights of his genius, his resentment over the way the scientists see him comes to a boiling point. This occurs at the psychology convention where the scientists are presenting their findings related to Charlie and Algernon. Charlie realizes that he is now more intelligent than the men who have experimented on him and shows it, much to Nemur's chagrin, at a preconvention cocktail party. Just before the scientists are to present their work to their peers, Charlie writes, "If only Nemur would look at me as a human being." His antipathy increases as the presentations take place, ending with Charlie kidnapping Algernon and making his way back to New York on his own.

When Charlie negotiates his return to the lab, he forces the scientists to see him as more than an experiment by insisting that he be allowed to work on the study himself, independently. Even after Charlie makes contributions to the study, incidents at a cocktail party given by Nemur's wife show how little has changed. Nemur confronts Charlie, accuses him of jeopardizing the study through his actions, and calls him "arrogant, self-centered [and] antisocial." While Charlie later admits that his focus on himself has been to his detriment, he also accuses Nemur of only wanting "someone who could be made intelligent but still be kept in a cage and displayed when necessary to reap the honors you seek." Charlie may have learned life lessons the hard way, but he never forgets he is human, something Nemur and the other scientists often seem to overlook.

HISTORICAL OVERVIEW

Treatment of the Mentally Challenged in the 1950s and 1960s

Throughout the 1950s and 1960s, the mentally retarded and their plight began to reach the attention of mainstream America. It was not even until the late 1950s and early 1960s that a comprehensive definition of mental retardation was produced by the American Association on Mental Deficiency, with five classifications of mental retardation following soon after. For example, Charlie was in the "borderline" range of mental retardation, which is defined as having an IQ of 67–83. Scientists also worked on discovering what caused different forms of mental retardation, and better ways of defining the various types of mental handicaps. In 1954, Congress passed the Cooperative Research and Education Act, which gave funds to such scientists for mental retardation research.

As researchers came up with other tests to define and better understand the mentally handicapped, one test in particular was controversial: the Rorschach Test. The test was developed in Germany by Dr. Rorschach to, among other things, distinguish "normal" people from the mentally challenged. Charlie himself takes this test in the novel, though at first he is unable to see anything in the inkblots. Similarly, the Thematic Apperception Test, developed by H. A. Murray, was also used on Charlie. This test, which consisted of twenty pictures, was used to explore the intellectual functions of the mentally retarded. Though both tests were regularly given to the mentally handicapped and revealed information about their personality and feelings, it was determined such tests could not adequately assess intelligence.

In the United States in this period, people who were mentally handicapped in any way, including the mentally retarded and the mentally ill, were often institutionalized. Many state-run institutions resembled prisons or warehouses, where patients were merely kept alive. There was often little or no therapy (depending on the state and institutional philosophy), no stimulation, and minimal education at best. While there was a reform movement in the late 1950s and early 1960s, its effects were not felt fully until the 1970s. Until the end of the 1960s, mentally retarded Americans had to be residents at a state mental hospital in order to receive any government support. By 1969, there were about two hundred thousand such patients in American mental hospitals.

This attitude toward the care of the mentally challenged shifted philosophically, especially in the late 1960s and early 1970s. Though not all states embraced the change, experts believed that many mentally challenged people would be better served by living in a small-group setting, often with assistance, rather than in a mental hospital. Counseling, therapy, and education were also seen as more effective on a smaller, community-oriented scale. Those who lived at home could be served as out outpatients by clinics, workshops, day care centers, and community programs. This small-group setting was

regarded as making mentally retarded people happier and better-served socially and emotionally.

Groups like the National Association for Retarded Citizens (later known as the Association for Retarded Citizens of the United States) also formed during this period to raise awareness about the mentally handicapped, support the mentally retarded and their families, develop related programs, encourage research, and promote legislation. Special education curricula were also under development, though only about twenty percent of the mildly mentally handicapped population was receiving attention through such programs in 1963. Special education curricula for all but the moderately and most severely mentally retarded become more widespread and better developed as the 1960s progressed.

While this change was taking place, mentally handicapped Americans were still suffering from many inhumane practices. For example, lobotomies were commonly conducted on the mentally retarded from the late 1930s through the early 1970s; about fifty thousand Americans in total underwent this procedure. Most of these operations took place before 1960. The operation was conducted with the intention to better manage and control, if not help, the mentally challenged. Many doctors, including psychiatrists, were encouraged by professional bodies to perform such operations until the 1960s.

However, about one-third of those who underwent a lobotomy felt no effect. One-third also saw their condition worsen, suffered extensive brain damage, or died during the surgery. One of the most famous cases involving a mentally retarded person suffering brain damage after a lobotomy was Rosemary Kennedy, the sister of President John F. Kennedy. After the surgery in 1941 and her regression, she was placed in an institution where she lived until her death in 2005. Other "cures" for mental retardation that had mixed or poor results included electric shock, various drugs treatments, and vitamin therapies.

CRITICAL OVERVIEW

As with the earlier short story version, the novel form of *Flowers for Algernon* was immensely popular with readers and critics alike. The reviews in 1966 were generally positive, with many noting that the format of the novel was particularly effective. While the critic in *Publishers Weekly* notes "the poignant journal," the book as a whole is also called a "weird but absorbing story." Mark R. Hillegas of the *Saturday Review* comments in "Other Worlds to Conjure" that "the author offers compassionate insight into the situation of the mentally retarded," while also noting, "At times the novel is profoundly moving."

Not all the initial reviews were entirely complimentary. Eliot Freemont-Smith of the *New York Times* tempers his praise in "The Message and the Maze." He calls *Flowers for Algernon* "predictable," but also finds the novel "affecting." Of Keyes, Freemont-Smith writes, "He has taken the obvious, treated it in a most obvious fashion, and succeeded in creating a tale that is convincing, suspenseful and touching—all in modest degree, but it is enough."

One area that a number of critics have touched on since the late 1960s is that *Flowers for Algernon* is a work of science fiction. Many have found it to be an effective illustration of the genre. Reviewing the original publication of the novel, a critic writing in the *Times Literary Supplement* comments in a review titled "Making Up a Mind" that *Flowers for Algernon* is:

> a good example of that kind of science fiction which uses a persuasive hypothesis to explore emotional and moral issues. By doing more justice than is common to the complexity of the central character's responses it gives body to its speculations.

Nearly ten years after the novel was published, Robert Scholes touches on its kind of science fiction in "Structural Fabulation." Scholes notes something many critics touched on since its original publication: though the book is science fiction, it is not so overtly a part of the genre that it cannot go beyond it. He writes:

> Daniel Keyes's *Flowers for Algernon* might be called minimal SF [science fiction]. It establishes only one discontinuity between its world and our own, and this discontinuity requires no appreciable reorientation of our assumptions about man, nature, or society. Yet this break with the normal lifts the whole story out of our familiar experimental situation. It is the thing which enables everything else in the novel, and it is thus crucial to the generation of this narrative and to its affect on readers.

For many years, *Flowers for Algernon* has remained a popular text used in American middle and high school as part of the English curriculum. Though the book is recommended by such bodies as the National Council for Teachers and American Library Association, its use has been controversial at times. *Flowers for Algernon* has been removed from some curricula due to the pressure of parents upset over the sexual content. Others have objected to perceived blasphemous elements found in the story.

Despite such incidents, the novel remains popular in the United States and around the world. *Flowers for Algernon* was published in Japanese in 1978, and in an early 1999 survey was named the most memorable book by a survey of readers in Japan. The novel is also regularly featured in book clubs and reading groups.

Critics continue to note its power years after its publication. Summarizing the book's long-standing appeal, Robert Small, in the section devoted to *Flowers for Algernon* in *Censored Books: Critical Viewpoints*, writes that the book "gives its readers profound insights into people, retarded, average, brilliant, kind and cruel, and it does so with stylistic brilliance and control. Perhaps most important, it creates one of those rare truly round fictional characters." Small argues that the book's success has made it perhaps "the best known work of science fiction to the general public, that is, to non-science fiction fans." Its crossover appeal speaks to Keyes's unforgettable character and the accessible themes of the story.

CRITICISM

Patrice Cassedy

In the following essay, Cassedy examines Flowers for Algernon *as a work of science fiction which focuses on the dubious benefits of increased intelligence while reflecting certain medical and psychological beliefs of the era in which the book was written.*

Flowers for Algernon is a work of science fiction. Science fiction is a relatively new form of fiction that, as scholars have written, "can be most broadly defined as a literary response to the rise of modern science." Science has always attempted to expand human knowledge, and

MEDIA ADAPTATIONS

Flowers for Algernon was adapted by Stirling Silliphant for a film called *Charly*. It was directed by Ralph Nelson and released by Cinerama in 1968. Actor Cliff Robertson won an Academy Award and National Board of Review Award for his portrayal of the title character. Silliphant won a Golden Globe Award for best screenplay. It is available on DVD from Metro-Goldwyn-Mayer.

David Rogers adapted *Flowers for Algernon* into a two-act play published by Dramatic Publishing in 1969.

A musical version of *Flowers for Algernon*, entitled *Charlie and Algernon*, was first performed at the Citadel Theater in Alberta, Canada, in 1978. A recording of the musical featuring the 1979 London cast is available on CD and cassette from Original Cast Record.

Flowers for Algernon was released in an abridged version on audiocassette by Parrot Audio Books in 1995. It is narrated by the author. This audiocassette is out of production.

Flowers for Algernon was released in an abridged version on audiocassette by Recorded Books in 1998. It is narrated by Jeff Woodman.

John Pielmeier adapted *Flowers for Algernon* for a television movie directed by Jeff Bleckner. It aired on CBS in 2000 and starred Matthew Modine as Charlie. It is currently unavailable.

---

science fiction has often used the quest for knowledge as a key theme. *Flowers for Algernon* is a work that follows this theme, but instead of visualizing the potential rewards of the quest, Keyes's novel considers the possible tragic costs. Keyes's work is not the first to ponder the negative consequences of scientific advances. In fact, according to one writer, in science fiction the thirst for knowledge is "often shown as ambiguous, unsettling, even paradoxical." As a novel written from this perspective, *Flowers for Algernon* joins other works of science

fiction that question whether the benefits of greater knowledge are worth the price paid for them.

Science Fiction Supermen

Because of its subject matter, *Flowers for Algernon* can be classified as intelligence or superman science fiction. This type of science fiction deals with characters that are abnormally intelligent. The first example of such a work is *The Hampdenshire Wonder*, by J. D. Beresford. Written in 1911, it draws a conclusion similar to that of *Flowers for Algernon*, namely that super intelligence does not necessarily bring about well-being. Born a supergenius, the child in *The Hampdenshire Wonder* becomes so brilliant that he develops contempt for books, which, he believes, express a human wisdom that is beneath his newfound intellect. He soon finds that he can no longer communicate with anyone. His father abandons him. Devastated and lonely, he commits suicide at the age of seven.

Other superman fiction followed. The man born a supergenius in Olaf Stapledon's *Odd John*, published in 1935, also despairs and finally commits suicide. His story is similar to Charlie's in that he educates himself with amazing speed and finds he is intellectually above other humans. But he is different from Charlie in one important way. Charlie is emotionally immature, yet remains moral. As critic John J. Pierce explains, Stapledon's hero "comes to see himself as beyond the norms of human morality as well as beyond human intelligence—incest, robbery, even murder are justified in the name of his survival and awakening."

The hero of Stanley G. Weinbaum's 1939 novel *The New Adam* also commits suicide because, according to critic John J. Pierce, the man finds that brilliance does not bring him happiness. To illustrate this point, Pierce quotes from the novel: "With the growth of intellect, happiness becomes an elusive quantity, so that doubtless the Superman, when he arrives, will be of all creatures the most unhappy."

America After World War II

Although *Flowers for Algernon* is part of a legacy of science fiction dealing with increasing intellect, the tale is also a product of its times. Keyes published the short story "*Flowers for Algernon*" in 1959 and the novel in 1966, in an era when Americans were experiencing the power of science to dramatically improve the quality of life. Medical advances were occurring at an astonishing rate, changing lives in dramatic ways. Jonas Salk developed a polio vaccine. A kidney was successfully transplanted from one human to another. Procedures to implant artificial heart valves were developed. Science was capable of prolonging life, and many scientists were seen as miracle workers.

In 1953, researchers James Watson and Francis Crick, building on recent work of colleagues, created a model of the double-helix structure of DNA. This accomplishment led to rapid advances in the field of biotechnology, specifically in the field of genetic engineering, which science writer Frauds Leone suggests "holds more promise for the future and peoples' well-being" than any other field of genetics. Discoveries that followed from the modeling of DNA led to the identification and treatment of genetic diseases as well as the production of such beneficial substances as insulin and human growth hormone.

But at the time *Flowers for Algernon* was conceived, the United States was also experiencing the frightening power of scientific advances. Less than fifteen years before Keyes published the short story version of the novel, American atomic bombs exploded in the Japanese cities of Hiroshima and Nagasaki, killing more than two hundred thousand people. Scientists working in the United States had created the nuclear threat, but in 1962 that threat was turned on Americans in a location closer to home than ever before. That year the U.S. military discovered that Soviet ships had placed missiles on Cuba, off the coast of Florida, well within range of Washington, D.C., and American strategic military bases. Historian Martin Walker describes the episode like this: "The next thirteen days were the most dangerous period of the Cold War [the rivalry for world influence between the Americans and the Soviet Communists]. A nuclear exchange was so close that both White House and [Soviet] Kremlin officials frankly expected the bombs to fall." While the Soviets finally backed down, few Americans alive in 1962 have forgotten their fear that they were about to die in a nuclear war.

In the field of medicine, the race to improve the quality of life was also exhibiting a dark side. In 1961, the drug thalidomide, released in Europe to treat nausea in pregnant women, was found to cause catastrophic birth defects. Thousands of babies were born malformed.

While *Flowers for Algernon* does not incorporate these world events specifically, the novel can be seen as a cautionary tale that reflects society's ambivalence about the benefits of modern science. Keyes's attitude can be seen most obviously in the structure of the novel. Instead of writing about a scientific experiment that succeeded and brought happiness to its subject, Keyes penned a tragedy that shows the dark side of science, a subject on the minds of Americans of his generation.

Psychological Advances

Just as twentieth-century scientific advances altered the treatment of physical illnesses and conditions, advances in the field of psychology changed the way psychological problems and conditions were treated. Two significant psychological developments figure prominently in *Flowers for Algernon*. One is the widespread acceptance of psychological classification methods that include intelligence and personality tests. The other is a method of therapy called psychoanalysis, commonly used to treat psychological problems.

The psychological events of the twentieth century are portrayed skillfully by Keyes, who studied psychology in college and in graduate school. In the novel, Charlie is frequently referred to as a "moron," a term that was medically accepted when *Flowers for Algernon* was written. Use of the term by the medical community began in 1910 at a meeting of the American Association for the Study of the Feebleminded. Meeting attendees adopted a classification system based on an adult's mental age: idiots had mental ages less than two, imbeciles three to seven, and morons eight to twelve. While the term was originally medical in nature, it was "later used to perpetuate negative stereotypes about people with mental retardation" and is no longer considered an appropriate term in everyday conversation. It is also no longer used as a psychological classification. However, when *Flowers for Algernon* was written, the term "moron" not only was used popularly to ridicule a person of lower intelligence but was still an accepted classification of the mentally challenged.

More complex classification methods followed. Intelligence quotient (IQ) tests were first introduced in 1916 to the United States through the publication of revisions to a French test called the Binet-Simon test. By the time *Flowers for Algernon* was written, other IQ tests had been introduced. The tests were administered widely throughout the United States to classify the mental ages of many citizens, not only the mentally challenged.

Keyes also drew on other psychological tools popular at the time. Early in the novel, Burt Seldon administers a Rorschach test in which Charlie must look at abstract inkblots and report what he sees. Hermann Rorschach first publicized that test in 1921 for use in assessing personality traits and psychological conflicts. In the novel, Charlie cannot, at first, imagine any scenes in the inkblots, but after the surgery, he can interpret the images. This change is viewed by the scientists as an indication that Charlie's intelligence is increasing.

While IQ tests and the Rorschach test are used to compare Charlie's intellect and personality before and after the surgery, his personal psychological growth results, in large part, from therapy sessions he undergoes with Dr. Strauss. Dr. Strauss uses a kind of therapy called psychoanalysis that was developed by Sigmund Freud, an Austrian physician born in 1856. In Freud's method, the doctor (a psychoanalyst) encourages the patient to "say everything that comes to mind." Through this technique, called free association, the patient becomes aware of previously unrecognized childhood feelings and memories that influence behavior, self-esteem, and relationships. Charlie explains this process of reaching the unconscious part of the mind in an early progress report:

> I had a nightmare last night, and this morning, after I woke up, I free-associated the way Dr. Strauss told me to do when I remember my dreams. Think about the dream and just let my mind wander until other thoughts come up in my mind. I keep on doing that until my mind goes blank. Dr. Strauss says that it means I've reached a point where my subconscious [unconscious] is trying to block my conscious from remembering. It's a wall between the present and the past. Sometimes the wall stays up and sometimes it breaks down and I can remember what's behind it.

The Rights of the Mentally Challenged

Charlie's psychoanalysis leads him to many important insights. One such insight is that the mentally challenged deserve to be treated with dignity. Society as a whole was coming to this same conclusion around the time that *Flowers for Algernon* was written. Followers of the nineteenth-century evolutionary theories of Charles Darwin had insisted that the mentally challenged be separated from society.

As a recent author on the subject explained, "According to some people's views, allowing individuals with mental retardation to mix freely with other members of society interfered with the process of natural selection." The mentally challenged were routinely institutionalized, often in facilities that did little to promote their well-being. Those who lived with their families were kept home from school or placed in regular classes where they could not compete.

The notion that the mentally handicapped could benefit from individualized instruction, geared to an individual's level of development, and that a stimulating environment could raise IQ, were discussed by theorists in the first several decades of the twentieth century. Still, until the 1940s and 1950s, when parents of the mentally challenged organized and established the National Association for Retarded Children (today called the Arc of the United States), few improvements were made. As a result of the association's efforts, Americans became increasingly aware of the needs and problems of the mentally retarded. In 1961, President Kennedy established the President's Panel on Mental Retardation, which recommended the expansion of services to the mentally retarded. By 1975, legislation now called the Individuals with Disabilities Education Act or IDEA, passed. If Keyes had written his book after enactment of that law, he might have dealt with its requirement that mentally retarded students like Charlie be provided a public education appropriate to their individual needs.

Science Fiction Reflects the Times

Keyes used the events of his time to add depth to the novel *Flowers For Algernon*. When Charlie's story is finished, the reader is left to wonder at the mixed blessings of our modern scientific age, and to ask how mentally challenged individuals should be treated.

Source: Patrice Cassedy, "Science Fiction in the Time of Change," in *Understanding "Flowers for Algernon,"* Lucent Books, 2001, pp. 28–34.

SOURCES

Fremont-Smith, Eliot, "The Message and the Maze," in *New York Times*, March 7, 1966, p. 25.

Hillegas, Mark R., "Other Worlds to Conjure," in the *Saturday Review*, Vol. 49, No. 13, March 26, 1966, pp. 33–34.

Keyes, Daniel, *Flowers for Algernon*, Harcourt, Brace & World, 1959, 1966.

"Making Up a Mind," in the *Times Literary Supplement*, No. 3360, July 21, 1966, p. 629.

Review of *Flowers for Algernon*, in *Publishers Weekly*, Vol. 189, No. 9, p. 91.

Scholes, Robert, "Structural Fabulation," in *Structural Fabulation: An Essay on Fiction of the Future*, University of Notre Dame Press, 1975, pp. 45–76.

Small, Robert, Jr., "*Flowers for Algernon* by Daniel Keyes," in *Censored Books: Critical Viewpoints*, edited by Nicholas J. Karolides et al., Scarecrow Press, 1993, pp. 249–55.

"A Good Day"

PRIMO LEVI

1947

As a chapter in Primo Levi's 1947 Holocaust memoir *Survival in Auschwitz*, "A Good Day" offers an intimate, first-hand account of life in World War II concentration camps. The attempt by Nazi Germany to exterminate Europe's Jewish population in the 1930s and 1940s stands as one of history's most notorious episodes of racism and hatred. Millions died in camps created for the express purpose of genocide, and the majority of those murdered were of Jewish descent. It would be easy to simply acknowledge that the events occurred and avoid the details of what happened to these people, for they are appalling and brutal. However, for those who survived, the urge to bear witness—to make humanity confront what was allowed to happen and in doing so perhaps prevent such inhumanity from occurring again—often struggles against the instinct never to revisit such a debasing experience. Levi had the misfortune of being one of thousands of Italian Jews transported to the Auschwitz camp in Poland. He was one of the few to survive, return to his native land, and resume his life as before.

In this brief chapter, many of the major themes of Levi's book are expressed strongly, much of it based on the corruption of human achievement in the service of inhumane goals. The very hierarchy of the camp embodies such corruption. Far from being an undifferentiated mass, a number of factors lead to different levels of status among the prisoners, such as their

reason for imprisonment, their ethnicity, and their length of imprisonment at the camp. Language also plays a part in the hierarchy. The gathering of prisoners from across Europe has created a cacophony of voices, creating a "Tower of Babel" at the Buna factory's Carbide Tower, where Levi works as slave labor during his time in Auschwitz. Moreover, the official language of the camps—German—is used to further alienate, humiliate, and confuse the prisoners, as many did not speak or understand it. As someone who deeply appreciates the virtues of work and craftsmanship, Levi sees how the slavery of the camps perverts those values. "A Good Day" examines how existence in the face of these dehumanizing conditions affects a person's mental state. As Levi writes in the preface of Simon & Schuster's 1996 edition, his aim in writing *Survival in Auschwitz* was to "furnish documentation for a quiet study of certain aspects of the human mind."

Though trained as a chemist, Levi balances a reporter's eye for capturing details of camp life with a poet's sensitivity to the toll the parade of injuries takes on the human spirit. Vivid images of harsh life in the Lager (camp) are often balanced by a philosophical perspective on the realities of human nature that is equally unforgiving. Levi explains the very notion of a "good" day in a situation as horrible as Auschwitz, asserting that humans can never be completely happy or unhappy, as they allow themselves only to consider the most immediate cause of such emotions. In the story, the promise of coming warm weather after a harsh winter allows the prisoners to stop thinking about the unrelenting cold, only to find themselves focused on their constant hunger. Then, by a stroke of good luck, even hunger is staved off for a few hours with an unexpected extra ration of soup. With these constant causes of unhappiness and discomfort momentarily alleviated, Levi describes how the men can briefly be unhappy—since one unhappiness is always replaced with another—like free men and concentrate on the troubles that have nothing to do with the camp. A "good" day is relative.

Amid this undeniable bleakness, Levi also describes small signs of hope—from the boast of the Greek Felicio that he will be home next year, to the painful dreams of home and food, to the reprieve gained on this one day—which prove the natural resilience of the human spirit. Levi

> AT SUNSET, THE SIREN OF THE *FEIERABEND* SOUNDS, THE END OF WORK; AND AS WE ARE ALL SATIATED, AT LEAST FOR A FEW HOURS, NO QUARRELS ARISE, WE FEEL GOOD, THE KAPO FEELS NO URGE TO HIT US, AND WE ARE ABLE TO THINK OF OUR MOTHERS AND WIVES, WHICH USUALLY DOES NOT HAPPEN. FOR A FEW HOURS WE CAN BE UNHAPPY IN THE MANNER OF FREE MEN."

wisely recounts these moments as well; as a result, his work is not only a powerful account of the a great abomination, but also a clear-eyed testament to the virtues necessary to defy such evil. As he warns in his preface, "The story of the death camps should be understood by everyone as a sinister alarm-signal."

PLOT SUMMARY

"A Good Day" opens with Primo Levi's observation that by nature people must believe in some purpose in life. For those in the camps, their sole purpose is to survive until spring, nothing more. As they stand in the freezing wind during roll call, they watch the horizon for signs of the coming spring, such as longer daylight and warmer weather. They are waiting for the weather to improve and the cold to "call a truce," so that they have one less enemy in their lives. On this day, the sun is warm and clears away the mist; fellow prisoner Ziegler observes, "The worst is over." Levi notices a group of Greek Jews, who have been at the camp for three years, chanting among themselves. One of them, Felicio, greets Levi and shouts, "*L'année prochaine à la maison! ... à la maison par la Cheminée!*" ("Home by next year! ... At home by the fireplace!") Felicio and the other Greeks return to their singing.

When the fog clears, the prisoners can see the area surrounding the camp. They see mountains, a church steeple in the city of Auschwitz, the factory where the prisoners work, and

BIOGRAPHY

PRIMO LEVI

Primo Michele Levi was born July 31, 1919, in the Italian city of Turin. After graduating from the University of Turin with a degree in chemistry, he joined the Italian resistance during World War II. He was captured by the Fascist militia in December 1943, placed in an internment camp in Italy, and sent to Auschwitz soon after. He survived at the camp for a year until it was liberated by Allied forces in January 1945. Afterward, he returned home to his life in Turin.

Levi wrote two memoirs of his experiences in the camps and his journey home, *If This is a Man* and *The Truce*; when published in the United States, these works were later renamed *Survival in Auschwitz* and *The Reawakening*, respectively. Levi worked at the SIVA chemical factory as a research chemist for most of his life, even as his writing came to worldwide renown. He wrote essays, poetry, short stories, a novel (*If Not Now, When?*), and further memoirs such as *The Periodic Table*. Levi retired from SIVA in 1977 to pursue a full-time writing career.

Said to be suffering from depression at the time, Levi fell over a banister down three flights of stairs and died on April 11, 1987. His death was ruled a suicide by the Italian government, but many believe it was an accident.

Birkenau, the nearby extermination camp. The sight of Birkenau causes their chests to tighten, for though they know their wives, sisters, and mothers "finished there," and though they will probably do so as well, they are "not used to seeing it." The prisoners notice that the meadows by the road are green, but the Buna is not. The grayness of the factory stands in contrast to the signs of spring in nature. The Buna is a factory where synthetic rubber is supposed to be manufactured (but never is). Over forty thousand foreigners from all over Europe work there. The prisoners live in different Lagers (camps) surrounding the Buna. Levi's own Lager (*Judenlager*, or "Jew Camp") provides ten thousand of the workers and functions as "the slaves of the slaves," the bottom of the hierarchy. His Kommando—the group of workers from his hut—helped build the Carbide Tower rising from the middle of the Buna. They refer to the edifice as a Tower of Babel, after the biblical story in which God thwarts a plan to build a tower into Heaven by confusing the workers' languages until they could neither understand nor be understood: "in it we hate the insane dream of grandeur of our masters, their contempt for God and men, for us men."

Today is a good day, though, as they need not worry so much about the cold and now find themselves thinking of their hunger instead: "If it was not for the hunger!," they think. Levi believes that this is human nature: one focuses on the most immediate source of unhappiness, and when that disappears one looks to the next most immediate source. With this perspective, one can never be completely unhappy, nor can one be completely happy.

Hunger is the very way of life in the camps, and the prisoners are "living hunger." Levi and his co-workers stop to watch a steam shovel seemingly gobble up mouthfuls of earth as it digs and deposits dirt. They cannot watch it without thinking of their own hunger. Sigi, a seventeen-year-old laborer, speaks of his mother's cooking back home in Vienna, which leads to Béla discussing the food he remembers from Hungary. Despite the torment of such thoughts, Levi remembers the spaghetti he ate the day before he was shipped north from an Italian sorting camp to Auschwitz. He agonizes over having not finished the meal: "if we had only known!" The newest arrival in their work detail, Fischer, eats the portion of bread he saved from morning; the more experienced prisoners, who have been deprived of adequate food for much longer, cannot imagine saving any food for later. They even create justifications for their voracious habits, telling themselves that stale bread is not as nutritious as fresh bread, and that food eaten piecemeal is not digested as well.

At midday, Levi's Kommando is greeted with more good news back at their hut. Along with their usual sparse meal rations, there are eleven extra gallons of soup obtained by

Primo Levi The Library of Congress

Templer, their Kommando's official organizer. Each person will receive six extra pints of soup that day: two pints at lunch, and in the afternoon they will take turns coming in from the Buna to have the final four pints. This means both extra food and a five-minute break to eat the afternoon portion: "What more could one want?" As they take their breaks in the afternoon, the Kapo of their hut asks in German who still has to eat, using the word *fressen*, which describes animals eating, instead of *essen* for humans eating. Levi considers this a correct word choice, given their wildly enthusiastic consumption. Meister Nogalla, the Polish civilian superintendent of their Kommando, turns a blind eye to the five-minute soup absences. Levi thinks that if it were not for social convention, perhaps he would even share in the soup. When it is Templer's turn to eat, it is agreed by all that he will take ten pints from the bottom of the pot, which holds the richest portion of the soup. Before he does so, he takes advantage of his ability to empty his bowels at will, enabling him to eat more whenever the opportunity affords itself.

At the end of the day, the men of Levi's hut do not worry about the cold and for a few hours do not feel hunger. The Kapo does not want to hit them, and they are able to think of their mothers and wives. Thus, for a brief time, they find themselves "unhappy in the manner of free men."

THEMES

Genocide

"A Good Day" takes place in the Auschwitz concentration camp during its final year of operation before being liberated at the end of World War II. While there had been many attempts to destroy entire ethnic or racial groups before World War II and have been several since, the Holocaust remains the most emblematic and terrible example of genocide in the popular imagination. The reason is that it was carried out through careful planning by the Nazi government of Germany, contributing a previously unseen breadth, efficiency, and cold-blooded rationality to the goal of exterminating the Jews of Europe. As a prisoner of Auschwitz, Levi witnessed the daily horrors of Hitler's "Final Solution of the Jewish Question" and the dehumanizing effects it had on prisoners, causing them to become like animals in order to survive. As Jonathan Druker describes in

Children stand behind a barbed wire fence in a still from a postwar Soviet film at Auschwitz, Poland
USHMM Photo Archives

"The Shadowed Violence of Culture: Fascism and the Figure of Ulysses in Primo Levi's *Survival in Auschwitz*," the very rational administration of Nazi Germany's irrational plans created a philosophical tension for intellectuals such as Levi. Druker highlights Levi's

> memoir's embrace of scientific method and knowledge, as expressions of human dignity, and its rejection of the social Darwinism used to justify the creation of Auschwitz. The dilemma for the rational humanist is that Darwin's potent theory, a credit to the powers of the human mind, actually dethrones humans, transforming them into animals subject to exploitation and even natural selection.

In "A Good Day," Levi and his fellow prisoners take for granted that they will die in an extermination camp like Birkenau. They know that "the insane dream of grandeur of our masters" leaves no doubt that their fate is to become victims of genocide. Genocide is the terminal logic of those who wish to actively enforce a rule of "survival of the fittest" based on racial

ideology. This was, in effect, what made the Holocaust—and especially camps such as Auschwitz—so horrifying. Nazi Germany not only promoted a mandate of racial mass murder, but did so with a system of rules and protocols that took into account the most efficient means to exterminate the Jews and other "undesirables" without acknowledging the humanity of those it destroyed. The Kapo uses the German word for "eating" (*fressen*) that refers to animals when talking about the prisoners, and Levi does not disagree. They are no longer humans in the camp, and when he compares the prisoners to the machinery at the Buna, he writes that while they are the only things that are alive there, the machines are more alive than the prisoners. Throughout *Survival at Auschwitz*, Levi returns time and again to the notion of "usefulness" as a way to avoid the selections by which prisoners were sent to the gas chambers. This was built into the very rationale of camps such as Auschwitz: as long as one could provide some kind of benefit to the camp or to the larger project of supporting the war, one could escape death and instead function as a laborer. In short, the only alternative to death in Auschwitz was slavery.

Class and Ethnicity

Just as in society outside the camp, a class system developed in Auschwitz based partially on ethnicity but also on seniority. The prisoners of the camp are known by the tattooed numbers on their arms. A higher number indicates a recent arrival and the likelihood that the prisoner is ignorant of camp ways. For example, when Fischer, the newest arrival in Levi's Kommando, saves part of his bread past breakfast to eat later, Levi notes that "none of us old ones are able to preserve our bread for an hour." There are various theories as to why that is, but most of the men agree that the safest place to keep bread from being stolen is in one's stomach. Further, blocks of numbers differentiate ethnic groups— Jews from non-Jews, as well as different nationalities of Jews—and Levi casually recounts the stereotypes for certain groups. He takes special note of the "Greeks, those admirable and terrible Jews of Salonica, tenacious, thieving, wise, ferocious and united, so determined to live, such pitiless opponents in the struggle for life." This is a vivid portrait of one of the hardiest groups in the camp, a description that balances negative connotations of opportunism with a positive struggle to live. The Greeks have been in the camp for three years, a nearly unheard-of tenure. It is worth noting that the only character who dares to imagine aloud a future outside of the camps is the Greek Felicio.

Such a class system was officially ratified in part by the Kapo system, first established in Dachau, where prisoners were given responsibility for fellow prisoners. Kapos were often Poles and political prisoners rather than foreign Jews. The Kapo has the ability to enforce rules, which Levi indicates was often done arbitrarily. For example, part of their "good day," after the promise of warmer weather and extra soup rations, is that "the Kapo feels no urge to hit us." These internal social systems gave a way for prisoners to differentiate those who could survive camp life and those who would perish quickly, what Levi calls "the drowned and the saved."

Another effective way to enforce racism and social hierarchy is to use language to make people of other races and ethnicities stand apart. German was the official language of the camps, which many of the prisoners did not speak, as they came from all over Europe. In "A Good Day," Levi recounts the casual way that *fressen*—the German term for how animals eat—replaces *essen*, the term for how humans eat. Levi himself accepts this term, thus acknowledging the debasement of his life as a camp prisoner and his lower status as a Jew in comparison to Germans.

The nature of the camps made language even more problematic: the wide range of ethnicities and nationalities meant that communication was often difficult. One not only needed to learn German, but also the languages of other ethnic groups present as well in order to work together. Levi refers to his work camp and their building of the Carbide Tower as a modern Tower of Babel. This speaks to the biblical story about how God punished an attempt to build a tower that reached Heaven, giving the people different languages so they could no longer communicate. The Carbide Tower is a monument to a very human evil, not to any god, but the curse of incomprehension remained the same for this act of hubris, "erected in defiance of heaven like a stone oath."

Resilience

Perhaps the most striking aspect of "A Good Day" is its emphasis on the positive: what Levi describes is a *good* day. He does not allow for absolutes in human emotion, but instead he finds that the unknown quality of any experience is what causes both grief and hope. In only focusing on the most immediate causes of one's emotional states, one is constantly surprised by the further complexities of the situation. This limited vision is not only the cause of man's basic discontent, but also a key to enduring in a place as sinister as Auschwitz—"our means of surviving in the camp." Levi argues that the inability to realize the "complex nature of the state of unhappiness" leads a person to discover that after the most immediate cause of suffering is removed, "you are grievously amazed to see that another one lies behind."

In this way, when the problem of cold weather seems solved by the coming of spring, it gives way to the problem of hunger, which is itself solved on this day. Without those two constant sources of unhappiness burdening their every thought, the prisoners are free to think about other things besides their survival. In this manner, the men are not happy, but they are able to enjoy the more mundane unhappiness experienced by free men—something they had not likely experienced since being taken away to Auschwitz. This does not mean Levi and his fellow prisoners accept their fate, but rather that hope is a crucial part of surviving such horrors. In its own way, being allowed to assume the mantle of unhappy free men is to struggle against the bleakness of their camp lives—not to openly acknowledge hope (something only the bold Greek Felicio dares), but to remember there is something beyond the Lager and that they were once a part of it.

HISTORICAL OVERVIEW

World War II

Many issues have been considered as the cause of World War II (1939–1945). Among the most often cited include the treatment of Germany after World War I, as well as the rise of nationalism in aggressor countries Germany, Japan, and Italy (later known as the Axis Powers) and their desire for more territory. World War II began officially on September 9, 1939, with Germany's invasion of Poland. Until that point, countries such as Great Britain had been applying the policy of appeasement—attempting to settle disputes through compromise rather than military action—toward Germany as it appeared to be ramping up for war. The United States initially remained neutral, though close ties to Great Britain made America sympathetic to the Allied Forces, which also included the Soviet Union and France. The Japanese bombing of Pearl Harbor on December 7, 1941, brought the United States into the war on both the European and Pacific fronts, as Germany joined Japan in its declaration of war against America.

Levi's role in the war was tied specifically to his Italian nationality. When Italy's Fascist dictator Benito Mussolini was removed from power in 1943 after the Americans landed in Sicily, the new prime minister, Field Marshal Pietro Badoglio, negotiated a cease-fire with the Allies. However, German forces struck from the north, freed Mussolini, and split Italy in half: the south was protected by the Allies, but

the north fell under Hitler's control. The majority of Italian Jews lived in the north. Many were placed in local internment camps, and some were shipped further north to concentration camps such as Auschwitz. Levi had sought to join the anti-Fascist partisans in 1943 but was caught and sent to Auschwitz.

The tide of the war turned on June 6, 1944, with the Allied invasion of Normandy, France. Caught by surprise, Hitler's forces were never able to fully recover. The sweeping Allied reclamation of Europe took a very personal form for Levi, as he was there when Auschwitz was liberated by Soviet forces on January 24, 1945. In April 1945, Soviet troops captured Berlin. On May 7, 1945, the Allies celebrated V-E (Victory in Europe) Day, which ended the war in Europe. Following the United States' devastating nuclear bombings of Hiroshima and Nagasaki, Japan, in August 1945, victory on the Pacific front was finalized with Japan's surrender on September 2, 1945.

The Holocaust

Under Adolf Hitler, Germany's National Socialist regime, also known as the Nazi Party, emphasized the anti-Semitism prevalent in Germany as well as other parts of Europe in the 1930s and 1940s. The anti-Semitic riots on *Kristallnacht*—"The Night of Broken Glass," on November 9, 1938—is often considered the start of the Holocaust. From there, pogroms (officially encouraged massacres) took place that terrorized Jews; anti-Semitic laws stripped Jews of their rights; and ghettos were established where Jews were forced to live. Germany at first claimed that the deportation of Jews from Germany was a "resettlement" project and suggested that Jews were to be shipped to the island of Madagascar. But as time passed, the pretenses dropped, and the ideological demand for racial purity and the presence of "undesirable" populations using valuable German resources made the "Jewish Problem" central to the Nazi agenda.

Initially, Jews were placed in internment camps, concentration camps, and slave labor camps. These were not death camps—whose specific aim was the mass extermination of the Jews—but were instead used for incarceration and forced labor. Because of unsanitary conditions, limited nutrition, and brutal work schedules, many prisoners died of starvation, disease, and exhaustion. In January 1942, the Wannsee

Conference ratified what would be known as the "Final Solution," Hitler's plan to systematically exterminate all Jews in Europe. From then on, Jews were sent to extermination camps. Jews from across Nazi-controlled Europe were rounded up and transported, often in overflowing railroad cattle cars, to the camps. They were immediately divided by age, gender, and health. Those considered "unfit" were immediately shot or sent to the gas chamber. Those who survived the selection were stripped of all of their belongings—including gold fillings, eye glasses, wedding rings, and anything of value—and were given a tattoo on their forearm with an ID number. Living conditions were squalid. Prisoners were forced to share cramped sleeping quarters, often infested with lice and vermin. Food allotments for one day usually consisted of a slice of bread and a cup of thin soup. Many of the camps were located in areas of Poland that receive heavy winter snow, and prisoners were forced to work in brutally cold conditions without proper clothing in winter, as is illustrated in "A Good Day."

There were six known extermination camps in operation between 1941 and 1945: Belzec, Sobibor, Chelmno, Majdanek, Treblinka, and Auschwitz-Birkenau. Auschwitz began as a concentration camp like Dachau and Buchenwald, handling political prisoners and putting them to work to further German ends. It became an extermination camp with the addition of the Birkenau crematorium in 1943. More Jews were killed in Auschwitz than in any other extermination camp. As Laurence Rees observes in *Auschwitz: A New History*, Auschwitz became a model example of combining Germany's "twin goals of work and murder." The crematoria and gas chambers became the central focus of the camp. Prisoners were farmed out to nearby sub-camps, and, as Rees writes, "when they were deemed no longer fit to work after months of appalling mistreatment, they could be transported a few miles to the extermination facilities of Auschwitz-Birkenau."

While the exact number killed during the Holocaust has never been definitive, popular estimates hold that roughly six million people were killed as a result of this monstrous policy. Much contemporary debate about the Holocaust has been centered on how much ordinary German citizens knew about the extermination of the Jews, and why they did nothing to stop it. Jews claim it was impossible that the Germans did not know what was going on, yet many Germans claim that they knew nothing of the slaughter being carried out in the camps.

Italian Jews

Jewish people have a long history in Italy, dating back to the Roman Empire. Their importance and contributions to many aspects of Italian culture had been recognized, though such recognition was also often tinged with racism and resentment. While anti-Semitism was quite common, it was worsened by decrees from Pope Innocent III at the start of the thirteenth century, paving the way for many more such anti-Semitic decrees from the Vatican that would persist for centuries. Despite such oppression, Italy was considered a relatively benevolent refuge for Jews, compared to other parts of Europe. As Primo Levi's biographer Ian Thomson points out in *Primo Levi: A Life*, "Like most northern Italian Jews, the Levis claimed descent from the Sephardim (after *Sefarad*, Hebrew for 'Spain') who had fled anti-Semitic Castile in the fifteenth century." The Levis were among many Jewish families who assimilated into Italian culture and played a role in the nation's development. In the early twentieth century, this included supporting the rise of Fascism and of Benito Mussolini. Thomson notes that most of the 130,000 Jews living in Italy in the 1920s supported Mussolini because "the Fascist Party seemed to endorse the Jews' patriotic, middle-class aspirations."

The ties between Mussolini's Italy and Hitler's Nazi Germany led to growing anti-Semitic feelings in Italy, with accusations from the Fascist party and the general Italian media exploding in 1937 and 1938. In September 1938, the Fascists began to implement racial laws, similar to those in Germany, with wide restrictions on the activities of Jewish people. After the armistice with the Allies in 1943, Italian Jews started being transported to camps in Poland and elsewhere.

Language and Bearing Witness

Survivors of the Holocaust fall roughly into two broad categories: those who cannot or will not speak of what happened to them, and those who are compelled to speak not only for themselves, but for those who no longer have a voice. The latter feel the need to bear witness to what happened, and are compelled, as Levi states in his preface, by the "need to tell our story to 'the rest,' to make 'the rest' participate in it.'' Language, therefore, is part of Levi's salvation. As Daniel R. Schwarz observes in *Imagining the Holocaust*, "In the camps, language had been reductive, destructive, and persecuting, but [Levi's] narrating and witnessing language has the capacity to be vital.'' In "Primo Levi and the Language of Witness," Michael Tager adds,

> Levi's struggle to develop a style suitable to his material helps explain his fascination with language itself, both as a creator and reflection of our identities and politics.... Linguistic patterns disclose political concepts and relationships that enable him better to understand his experiences. Sensitivity to such patterns also helps him construct a powerful language for his witness.

Literary accounts of the Holocaust and the racial oppression of Nazi Germany began to appear shortly after the war, including *The Pianist* (1945) by Wladyslaw Szpilman (originally published as *Death of a City* in Poland), *The Diary of a Young Girl* (1947) by Anne Frank, and *Night* (1958) by Elie Wiesel. In later years, survivors and descendants of both Germans and Jews began to weigh in on the Holocaust in both fiction and nonfiction. Notable books include *The Tin Drum* (1959) by Günter Grass; the collection *Auschwitz and After* (1965) by Charlotte Delbo; *The Painted Bird* (1965) by Jerzy Kosinski; *This Way for the Gas, Ladies and Gentlemen* (1967) by Tadeusz Borowski; *The Shawl* (1980) by Cynthia Ozich; and *Schindler's List* (1982) by Thomas Keneally.

CRITICAL OVERVIEW

When first published in Italy under the title *Se qesto e un uomo* (*If This Is a Man*, published in America as *Survival in Auschwitz*) in 1947, Levi's book received little attention from readers or critics. Sales were poor for the first printing of two thousand copies, six hundred of which were damaged by a warehouse flood. One of the concerns that initially dogged Levi was whether he was simply a witness to the Holocaust whose account had factual significance but little aesthetic merit, or whether he was indeed a writer of literary value. Levi did not see why the roles were mutually exclusive. At the time, only two reviewers paid special attention to Levi's unique accomplishment: Italo Calvino, himself a promising new writer at the time, and the critic Arrigo Cajumi. Biographer Ian Thomson, in

Primo Levi: A Life, quotes Cajumi's *La Stampa* review of November 26, 1947, in which he calls Levi a "born writer" who "arrives naturally at art." According to Thomson, Cajumi was also the only critic at the time to pick up on the "survival of the fittest" undertone present in the book.

Many believed that it would take years, even decades, before people could face the horrors of the Holocaust and read such an unvarnished account of what took place. Later reactions to Elie Wiesel's original manuscript for *Night* seem to bear this out. Levi's own book was long forgotten by the Italian public when the author secured a contract for a new edition in 1955; that edition finally debuted in 1958, with significant changes made to the manuscript. The initial run was again two thousand copies, and it went through two reprints of the same size in the years that followed. The English version was first published in 1960 to strong critical praises but weak sales.

The success of *Survival in Auschwitz* was quite gradual, as recognition for Levi's other works led to greater recognition of his first major book. The immediate Italian success of *La Tregua* (*The Truce*) in 1963 boosted sales of *If This Is a Man*. *The Truce*—later re-titled *The Reawakening* in English—is the sequel to Levi's Auschwitz account, covering his trek back to Turin, Italy, after being liberated from Auschwitz.

With a subject as powerful and significant as the Holocaust, controversy is unavoidable. The very existence of the Holocaust has been called into question, and Levi was active in denouncing revisionists who denied the genocide or its universal human relevance. Other, narrower criticisms also surfaced. Thomson recounts that in 1985, author Fernanda Eberstadt took issue with the style of writing in *Survival in Auschwitz*, contending it "was marred by 'psuedo-scientific prose' and 'hackneyed social psychology'" and that this approach did not properly address the specific anti-Semitic aims of the Nazi's Final Solution. Levi responded personally to these points, as well as to more personal attacks by Eberstadt on whether his anti-Fascist activities were opportunistic in nature and reflected a lack of Jewish consciousness.

Modern critical assessments of Levi agree on his contribution to Holocaust literature. In Jonathan Druker's "The Shadowed Violence of Culture: Fascism and the Figure of Ulysses in

Primo Levi's *Survival in Auschwitz*," he calls Levi an "indispensable author ... one of the most authoritative, most cited Holocaust witnesses." In a *New York Times* review of the stage production *Primo* titled "Crystallizing Legacy of Auschwitz Survivor," reviewer Ben Brantley calls *Survival in Auschwitz* "one of the essential books of the 20th century." One of the most common praises of Levi's work is how his combination of journalistic detail and aesthetic allusions combine to create a powerfully unique account of a uniquely powerful world event. In "Primo Levi—174517," George Jochnowitz calls *Survival in Auschwitz* "a lacerating book" that has a devastating impact "even though one knows about what happened at Auschwitz." Despite the horrors it recounts, Jochnowitz notes that the memoir is "written without expressing the anger and grief he felt. The book is awful fact after awful fact." A review of *Survival in Auschwitz; and, The Reawakening: Two Memoirs* by *Publishers Weekly* in 1985 calls *Survival in Auschwitz* "remarkable and truthful," and like Jochnowitz, notes that Levi writes "as witness rather than judge."

Levi's training as a chemist is a key part of his analytical perspective. This training has also made him aware of the wonder implicit in all human interaction, even at the worst of times. In *Imagining the Holocaust*, Daniel Schwarz suggests that Levi's books are among the most effective Holocaust literature because "they reveal his stance of presumed objectivity, which he attributes to his scientific temperament. Yet, he observes human behavior not as part of general rules but of wondrous particulars to be observed."

Levi's literary stature has grown over the years, ensuring that his memories of the Holocaust will remain valuable to future generations—an inspiring literary feat of historical witness.

CRITICISM

Susan L. Boone

In the following excerpt, Boone stresses the struggle by Levi between the shame Holocaust survivors felt and the equally strong urge to pay witness to the events so that the rest of the world can properly recognize its significance.

MEDIA ADAPTATIONS

Primo, a play based on *Survival at Auschwitz*, was adapted by Antony Sher and directed by Richard Wilson. It was staged at the Music Box Theater in New York City in the summer of 2005. A filmed version of the play is available on DVD through Kultur Films International.

A film adaptation of Levi's other autobiography, *The Reawakening*, was produced in 1997 under the title *The Truce*. Directed by Francesco Rosi, the film stars John Turturro as Primo Levi. It is available on DVD from Miramax.

Levi saw himself first and foremost as witness, and set about fulfilling his duty to write the story of Auschwitz on behalf of all those who perished (the true witnesses) and for those who survived and could not or would not tell. It is part of the pain of telling to recognize that the story must be reduced to what is hearable, that it must be simplified. Confusion may result if we do not remain aware that it is a reductive process which has its costs.

From the teller's side Levi knew the grievous distance between the experience of "down there" and its story. And as time went on he saw the gap widen between the world's perception of Auschwitz and its lived reality. The simplification which is merely and painfully essential in order to tell becomes abundant and convenient to the hearing. Levi felt our hearing was much too indulgent, readers took too many liberties in order "to understand."

In his "Afterword" to the combined edition of *Survival in Auschwitz* and *The Reawakening*, published in 1986, Levi turned from the goal of understanding altogether: "Perhaps one cannot, what is more one must not, understand what happened, because to understand is almost to justify.... If understanding is impossible, knowing is imperative, because what happened could happen again. Conscience can be seduced and obscured again—even our consciences." The date, 1986, is important. A year before his death and 40 years after Auschwitz, he was warning us about the seduction of power and prestige, about the oversimplification of inherently unpalatable facts in order to contain, and possibly disarm, their charge against us. He reviewed it for us chapter by chapter in *The Drowned and the Saved*. He was speaking to his readers—now, about our world and our prospects—now; although he refers back to the Lager, he "lingers more willingly on the state of affairs such as it is now." It is unnerving—his topic is the contemporary human situation and we are perilously close to the categories of Auschwitz. He is pointing "here," and reminding us of "down there." And if shame is a reigning theme in Levi's writing, the absence of shame in both of these realms is his greater concern.

In Levi's accounts, shame is the immediate response to a recognition of degraded humanity: he describes it on the faces of his liberators, a shame that the Germans never knew; and he describes it in the prisoner's transition to freedom. "Coming out of the darkness, one suffered because of the reacquired consciousness of having been diminished." Levi recognizes that for the prisoners, "on a rational plane, there should not have been much to be ashamed of, but shame persisted nevertheless." It was the failure of human solidarity—the "I do not know who my neighbor is . . ."—that produced the overwhelming sense of being "oppressed by shame." Forty years later, the burden of shame is still evident, expressed now by Levi in relation to Genesis 1:2: "the anguish inscribed in every one of the 'tohubohu' of a deserted and empty universe crushed under the spirit of God but from which the spirit of man is absent: not yet born or already extinguished."

As a chemist, Levi knew the value of catalysis and had a special fondness for the impurities in matter which give rise to reactions. In *The Periodic Table* he proudly declares: "I am the impurity that makes the zinc react." He was himself a catalyst to change, encouraging in his readers an awakened availability to enter into and undergo transformation. He did not want his witness to be a solitary, self-referential broadcast. And he acknowledges, first in *Survival in Auschwitz* and then elsewhere, the prisoners' fear that they would not be believed in the free world. This thwarted telling, the theme of regular nightmares, is juxtaposed, in *Survival in Auschwitz* to another dream, about the nearness and tangibility of food which at the very moment of tasting is forestalled: "every time

a different circumstance intervenes to prevent the consummation of the act." It remains a question in some minds as to whether Levi considered his witness to be a consummated act, or one never quite fulfilled, and where exactly his readers might figure in that question.

His witness, in any event, was a call to awaken, perhaps never put harshly enough to his reader: " 'Getup': the illusory barrier of the warm blankets, the thin amor of sleep, the nightly evasion with its very torments drops to pieces around us, and we find ourselves mercilessly awake, exposed to insult, atrociously naked and vulnerable."

Reveille in the camps brought prisoners face-to-face with their fragility and shame, and Levi's testimony becomes a verbal echo of that exposure. "Illusory barrier," "thin armor," and "nightly evasion" may also refer to the reader's post Holocaust defenses, and Levi wants to illuminate their flimsy nature. His witness ends with a vehemence that readers might have grasped as imperative from the first. "Wstawach"—"it happened, therefore it can happen again."

Source: Susan L. Boone, "Unvarnished Truth: The Chemistry of Shame in Primo Levi," in *Judaism: A Quarterly Journal of Jewish Life and Thought*, Vol. 48, No. 1, Winter 1999, p. 72.

SOURCES

Brantley, Ben, "Crystallizing Legacy of Auschwitz Survivor," *New York Times*, www.nytimes.com (July 12, 2005).

Druker, Jonathan, "The Shadowed Violence of Culture: Fascism and the Figure of Ulysses in Primo Levi's *Survival in Auschwitz*," in *Clio*, Vol. 33, No. 2, Winter 2004, pp. 143–61.

Jochnowitz, George, "Primo Levi—174517," in *Midstream*, Vol. 50, No. 3, April 2004, pp. 43–44.

Levi, Primo, *Survival in Auschwitz: The Nazi Assault on Humanity*, translated by Stuart Woolf, Simon & Schuster, 1996; originally published in 1947.

Rees, Laurence, *Auschwitz: A New History*, Public Affairs, 2005, p. 170.

Schwarz, Daniel R., *Imagining the Holocaust*, St. Martin's Griffin, 1999, pp. 76, 98.

Tager, Michael, "Primo Levi and the Language of Witness," in *Criticism*, Vol. 35, No. 2, Spring 1993, pp. 265–88.

Thomson, Ian, *Primo Levi: A Life*, Henry Holt, 2002, pp. 6, 27, 79, 238, 449.

Heart of Darkness

JOSEPH CONRAD

1902

Joseph Conrad's short novel *Heart of Darkness* is widely considered one of the richest examples of the use of symbolism in modern literature. Though the story is a mere fraction of a normal novel's length, Conrad's dense, layered prose can make for a slow and potentially frustrating—though ultimately rewarding—reading experience. The main story is centered on a riverboat pilot named Marlow who signs on to work for a Belgian company making inroads into the African Congo. Once he reaches Africa, Marlow's piloting job transforms into a quest to locate a mysterious company employee named Kurtz who has all but vanished into the African jungle. Marlow's journey is a nightmarish trip through a land he does not understand, where his European cohorts operate without the influence of laws or "civilized" society.

Heart of Darkness is a frame tale, a structure that was quite popular in the last half of the nineteenth century. A frame tale features a story within a story: the narrator of the frame tale meets a character who proceeds to tell a story, usually based on personal experience, to the narrator. The narrator of the frame tale is essentially an observer who interacts with the storyteller only before and after the "story within a story" is told, thus creating a "frame" around the bulk of the narrative. This structure was used by many of the greats of the period, including Edgar Allan Poe, Mark Twain, and Samuel Taylor Coleridge. The frame tale technique is

especially useful when the narrator and the storyteller hold contrasting views on the main subject of the tale. In *Heart of Darkness*, the unnamed narrator expresses nothing but pride at his nation's success at spreading civilization across the world. This is in stark contrast to Marlow's views at the end of the tale.

An experienced seaman, Conrad loosely based *Heart of Darkness* on his own experiences working as a steamboat pilot in the Belgian Congo in the 1890s. The book is now generally recognized as a bitter indictment of the European imperialism that took place, mostly in Africa, at the close of the nineteenth century. However, some modern critics see the book in a less favorable light. Nigerian author Chinua Achebe has referred to *Heart of Darkness* as "an offensive and deplorable book" and to Conrad himself as "a thoroughgoing racist." Some critics acknowledge that the book reflects racist views; however, they argue that these views do not belong to Conrad himself but to his fictional creation Marlow. In any case, even Achebe agrees that "Conrad saw and condemned the evil of imperial exploitation" of Africa, and he did it before such a sentiment was popular throughout Europe.

The novella was originally printed in three parts in *Blackwood's Magazine* in 1899 and was first published as a standalone work in 1902. The author's abundant use of the symbolic—particularly the frequent use of "light" and "dark" to convey ever-shifting meanings—has prompted over a century of lively critical analysis and has kept the book high on reading lists in high schools and colleges across the United States. Conrad wrote several other notable novels, novellas, and short stories, including *Lord Jim* (1900), another nautical tale in which Marlow serves as narrator. *Heart of Darkness* secured Conrad's place as one of the masters of modern literature.

PLOT SUMMARY

Part I

Heart of Darkness opens aboard the ship *Nellie* on the Thames River in London at dusk. Five longtime friends have gathered on the boat, though only one is mentioned by name: Marlow. The other men are referred to by their current occupation, such as the Lawyer and the Accountant. All were once seamen, but Marlow

> THEY WERE CONQUERORS, AND FOR THAT YOU WANT ONLY BRUTE FORCE—NOTHING TO BOAST OF, WHEN YOU HAVE IT, SINCE YOUR STRENGTH IS JUST AN ACCIDENT ARISING FROM THE WEAKNESS OF OTHERS. THEY GRABBED WHAT THEY COULD GET FOR THE SAKE OF WHAT WAS TO BE GOT. IT WAS JUST ROBBERY WITH VIOLENCE, AGGRAVATED MURDER ON A GREAT SCALE, AND MEN GOING AT IT BLIND—AS IS VERY PROPER FOR THOSE WHO TACKLE A DARKNESS. THE CONQUEST OF THE EARTH, WHICH MOSTLY MEANS THE TAKING IT AWAY FROM THOSE WHO HAVE A DIFFERENT COMPLEXION OR SLIGHTLY FLATTER NOSES THAN OURSELVES, IS NOT A PRETTY THING WHEN YOU LOOK INTO IT TOO MUCH."

is the only one who remains a sailor. Like all sailors, Marlow shows a "propensity to spin yarns." At dusk, as the sun falls into a patch of brooding clouds in the west, the unnamed narrator ponders the centuries of great ships and great men the river has seen during the glorious expansion of the British Empire.

Suddenly, Marlow begins to speak of the region's earlier, darker history. He imagines how desolate and wild the region must have seemed to the first Romans who claimed the land as part of their empire two thousand years before. Although the area now holds the most important city in England—and arguably all Europe—Marlow is quick to point out that they "live in the flicker," implying that darkness can return at any time. Marlow then tells of his own experience with darkness—similar to the first Romans, but in Africa. Since his story makes up the bulk of the rest of the book, Marlow acts as a narrator to the reader and to his friends aboard the *Nellie*.

Having recently returned from several years in the Pacific and Indian Oceans, Marlow tries to keep himself busy in London. He becomes restless, though, and calls upon his relatives in

BIOGRAPHY

JOSEPH CONRAD

Though renowned as an English author, Joseph Conrad was actually born Jozef Teodor Konrad Korzeniowski in the Ukraine in 1857. By the time Conrad was twelve, both of his parents had died of tuberculosis. He spent the rest of his youth under the care of his uncle Tadeusz in Switzerland. Conrad then went to France to become a merchant seaman. He eventually continued on to England, where he found greater success and ultimately became a British citizen in 1886.

In 1890, Conrad took a job piloting a boat in the Congo for a Belgian company, much like the character Marlow in *Heart of Darkness*. After a few short months of declining health, Conrad decided to return to England, where he spent several weeks hospitalized, recovering from his African excursion. During this time, Conrad concentrated his efforts on writing. His first novel, *Almayer's Folly*, was published in 1895 and received generally favorable reviews. Several books later, Conrad was vaulted into the most esteemed echelons of living writers with the publication of *Lord Jim* (1900).

Conrad continued writing for twenty years after the publication of *Heart of Darkness*, achieving financial success only in the last decade of his life. He died of a heart attack on August 3, 1924 and was buried in Canterbury Cemetery.

Joseph Conrad The Library of Congress

continental Europe to help him secure a position piloting a boat along the Congo River in Africa. His family's influence, and the fact that a Belgian company has just lost a boat captain in the Congo due to an argument with a native chief, lands Marlow an immediate appointment. Marlow travels to Belgium to sign the employment contract, noting that the city from which the Company operates looks to him like "a whited sepulchre," or burial vault. The contract is signed, and a French doctor examines Marlow to affirm his health for the trip. He bids farewell to his aunt and heads to Africa aboard a French steamer.

Long before reaching his port, Marlow encounters the African coastline, made seemingly impenetrable by "a colossal jungle, so dark green as to be almost black," and extending as far as he can see. The steamer passes numerous ragged outposts, as well as a warship firing its cannons into the dense jungle for what appears to be no reason. A member of the crew informs Marlow that there is "a camp of natives—he called them enemies!—hidden out of sight somewhere."

Marlow finally reaches the mouth of the Congo River after a month of travel. He boards another vessel and continues up the river, since he is to be stationed more than two hundred miles from the coast. The captain of the boat, a Swede, tells Marlow of a recent passenger who had hanged himself for no known reason. Marlow is deposited thirty miles upriver at one of the Company's stations to await further passage. The station is a "scene of inhabited devastation," riddled with broken-down machines and apparently pointless excavations. Marlow sees a group of black men chained together—judged by the colonists to be criminals—carrying baskets of dirt. Marlow ducks into a stand of trees for shade and finds himself among a group of black men on the verge of death, each too ill or weak to continue working. He offers one a biscuit from his pocket and then leaves the men to their suffering.

Continuing on, Marlow encounters the Company's chief accountant, an astonishingly well-dressed man who is to be the first to mention a name Marlow will come to know well: Kurtz. The accountant comments that Marlow is bound to meet the fellow Company agent when he travels upriver. According to the accountant, Kurtz is not only "a very remarkable person," but also brings in more ivory for the Company than all other traders put together.

Ten days later, Marlow leaves camp with a large caravan to begin the two-hundred-mile, two-week trek to the Central Station. When he arrives, Marlow is told the boat he was meant to pilot has sunk. It is now his job to reclaim the boat and fix it. The general manager of the station, an anxious man who seems concerned about Kurtz's well-being at an outpost farther inland, asks Marlow how long it will take to repair the ship and head on. Marlow estimates that it will take a few months and quickly sets to work.

Marlow notices that, other than himself, none of the employees at the camp appears to do anything productive. They spend their time talking about ivory and devising plots and schemes against each other that are never enacted. Marlow becomes acquainted with another Company agent, a brick-maker who has not made any bricks because of the absence of some key component never specified. The brick-maker is very interested in Marlow and his connections back in Europe, but Marlow is interested only in repairing his ship and learning about Kurtz. The brick-maker tells Marlow that Kurtz is "a prodigy" and accuses Marlow of being from the same "gang" as Kurtz—a gang that is destined to assume control of the Central Station in due time.

After beginning his work on the boat, Marlow realizes he will need rivets ordered to finish his repairs. There are no rivets to be found in Central Station, yet he had seen piles and cases of them back at the station he had only recently

left. Marlow muses, "Three carriers could have brought all that was wanted to set that steamboat afloat." Marlow asks the brick-maker, who maintains a close relationship with the general manager, to make sure he gets rivets. In the meantime, the general manager's uncle emerges from the jungle. He is the leader of the Eldorado Exploring Expedition, a secretive group whose only goal seems to be to "tear treasure out of the bowels of the land"—in Marlow's view, a calling no higher than "burglars breaking into a safe."

Part II

One night, as Marlow falls in and out of sleep on the deck of his sidelined steamer, he hears two men below him in conversation. It is the general manager and his uncle, discussing Kurtz in less than glowing terms. The manager dislikes Kurtz for his brazen lack of respect, and fears Kurtz is plotting to take over his position. The uncle tells the manager that Kurtz—or another unnamed "pestilential fellow" thought to be in the district with Kurtz—should be hanged to serve as an example. The manager speaks contemptuously of Kurtz's notion that the stations should not only be for trade, but also for "humanising, improving, instructing." Marlow leaps to his feet and startles the two men, who then try to slip away coolly. A few days later, the uncle departs camp with the Eldorado Exploring Expedition. Much later, Marlow hears news that all of the expedition's donkeys have died. He reports dryly, "I know nothing as to the fate of the less valuable animals," meaning the uncle and his fellow explorers.

Marlow finishes repairing his boat; accompanied by the manager, a few pilgrims from the Central Station, and a crew of natives, he sails up the Congo toward Kurtz's camp. Marlow compares journeying upriver to "travelling back to the earliest beginnings of the world," a place of stillness but not peace. Marlow describes it as "the stillness of an implacable force brooding over an inscrutable intention." The journey takes two months, though Marlow keeps busy with the many challenges of navigating an unfamiliar river. His crew of natives, referred to as cannibals though they are never seen to eat people, prove to be hard workers. Marlow is especially fond of the fireman, who looks after the boiler that provides the boat's steam power. Marlow calls him "an improved specimen," but also compares the man to "a dog in a parody of breeches and a feather hat, walking on his hind legs."

Fifty miles from Kurtz and his Inner Station, the boat reaches a hut with a stack of cut wood intended for them and a note warning the travelers to approach the station with caution. In the hut, Marlow finds a well-worn book devoted to various trivial matters of seamanship. He finds notes in the margins left by the previous owner, apparently written in some kind of code. He takes the book with him to serve as a diversion from the gloom of the enveloping jungle.

A few days later, with the boat within ten miles of the Inner Station, they become trapped in blinding fog and must stop. While waiting for the fog to lift, they hear a human cry from somewhere nearby. The pilgrims on board fear an attack by the local natives, but Marlow thinks the impenetrable fog will protect them. The fog eventually lifts and they continue, approaching within a mile and a half of Kurtz's Inner Station. There, the river is split by a shallow sandbank that forces Marlow to steer the boat close to shore.

At that moment, a flurry of arrows rain down upon the boat from the shore. The pilgrims blindly fire back with their guns. The native helmsman of the boat, also trying to return fire, is hit with a spear. Marlow blows the boat's steam whistle, and the attackers flee. The helmsman dies, leaving a pool of blood in the pilothouse that soaks Marlow's shoes. Marlow removes his shoes and tosses them into the river. The surprise attack leaves Marlow convinced that in a region of such violence, Kurtz must be dead. This thought fills Marlow with loneliness, even though he has never met the man. Marlow puts on dry slippers, pulls the dead helmsman's body out of the pilothouse, and throws him overboard to prevent the cannibals from eating him.

At last, they reach the Inner Station. On the shore, a young Russian man dressed in colorfully patched clothing, "like a harlequin," greets them. He already knows of the attack on the boat but tells them that everything is fine now. The manager and the pilgrims go to meet Kurtz. Marlow stays behind with the Russian and learns that he was the one who left the stack of wood at the hut downriver. Marlow shows him the book he took from the hut, and the Russian thanks him for returning it. Marlow realizes that the notes in the margin are not written in code, but in Russian. Marlow also learns from the

Russian why his boat was attacked: the natives do not want the white men to take Kurtz away from them.

Part III

The Russian tells Marlow how he came to meet Kurtz and how Kurtz immediately captured his devotion. He also mentions that Kurtz enlisted the local tribe to help him acquire ivory—not through trade, but through violence. Kurtz, for all his lofty ideas, seems obsessed with obtaining ivory. Once, he even threatened to kill the Russian over a small piece of ivory the man received as a gift from a local chief. Even after this, the Russian remains as close to Kurtz as anyone can; he even cared for the man when he became ill. This time, however, Kurtz's illness is grave enough to demand more serious treatment.

Through his binoculars, Marlow surveys the hilltop house where Kurtz rests. He is shocked to find the surrounding fence posts topped by the decapitated heads of natives. The Russian defends Kurtz, claiming that these are the heads of rebels. Marlow notes, "Those rebellious heads looked very subdued to me on their sticks." Kurtz is brought from the house on a makeshift stretcher. Tribesmen swarm out from the jungle, surrounding the stretcher and its carriers. Kurtz sits up and shouts something that Marlow cannot hear, and the natives clear out. The men carrying Kurtz place him in a small cabin on the boat. Suddenly, an exquisitely decorated native woman appears on the shore next to the steamer; she stares intently at the men on board, then walks away. The Russian says that if she had tried to board the ship he would have tried to shoot her and that she was acquainted with Kurtz.

Inside Kurtz's cabin, Marlow hears Kurtz arguing with the manager. Kurtz insists that the manager has not come to save him but to save the ivory. He also insists that he is not so ill that he should be removed from his station. The manager steps out of the cabin and complains to Marlow that Kurtz has ruined the region for the Company, doing far more harm than good.

The Russian tells Marlow that he trusts him to look after Kurtz and will take his leave. He also informs Marlow that it was Kurtz who ordered the natives to attack the steamboat as they approached. Kurtz had hoped to scare the manager and his men and send them back to Central Station thinking he must already be dead. Marlow gives the Russian gun cartridges, tobacco, and a pair of shoes, and the colorfully dressed man disappears into the night.

After midnight, Marlow is awakened by drumming and a burst of ritualistic cries. He checks Kurtz's cabin and discovers him missing. Marlow goes ashore and heads toward the drumming in search of Kurtz. Just thirty yards from the closest native fire, he catches up to Kurtz, crawling toward it like a man under the spell of great magic. Kurtz warns him to go away. Marlow first threatens Kurtz and then flatters him in an attempt to get him back to the boat. Kurtz speaks of his grand plans and the manager's attempts to ruin him, but much to Marlow's relief, Kurtz returns to the boat.

The steamer departs at noon the next day, and a thousand natives line the shore to watch the "splashing, thumping, fierce river-demon beating the water with its terrible tail and breathing black smoke into the air" as it carries Kurtz away. Kurtz is moved into the pilothouse, which is better ventilated than his previous cabin. The native woman appears along the shore, and the entire tribe lets loose a chorus of cries. The pilgrims aboard the ship ready their guns, so Marlow blasts the steam whistle to disperse the natives before the pilgrims can start trouble.

Traveling with the river's current, their pace away from Kurtz's camp is twice as fast as it was on their trip there, but Kurtz's condition quickly worsens. The ship breaks down and must stop for repairs. Kurtz, sensing his end might be near, gives Marlow his personal papers and a photograph of his intended bride back in Europe. One night, when Marlow checks in on him, Kurtz tells him he is waiting to die. Marlow dismisses the remark, but Kurtz, seemingly lost in some vision, softly cries, "The horror! The horror!" Marlow leaves him alone and joins the other pilgrims in the mess-room for dinner. Soon after, the manager's assistant enters and informs them that Kurtz is dead. The pilgrims rush to see, but Marlow stays in the mess-room. The pilgrims bury Kurtz the next day in a muddy hole.

Marlow keeps Kurtz's documents with him all the way back to Europe, despite the manager's attempts to confiscate them as property of the Company. He meets with several people, including Kurtz's cousin—to whom he gives some of Kurtz's family letters—and a journalist who considers himself one of Kurtz's colleagues.

The journalist remarks that Kurtz would have made a great leader for an extremist political party. When Marlow asks which party, the journalist responds, "Any party." Marlow gives the man one of Kurtz's reports intended for publication, and the journalist departs, satisfied.

The last of Kurtz's belongings are meant for his fiancée, and Marlow visits her to deliver them. Although by this time it has been a full year since Kurtz's death, she still wears black and appears to be in mourning. The two discuss Kurtz's best qualities, and his intended bride calls his death a loss to all the world. The woman begs Marlow to tell her Kurtz's last words. Knowing she seeks comfort more than truth, Marlow lies and says, "The last word he pronounced was—your name." The woman breaks down, claiming that she knew this all along.

Marlow ends his tale. The narrator looks out over the Thames, which, under a dark and foreboding sky, appears to flow "into the heart of an immense darkness."

THEMES

Imperialism and Oppression

Heart of Darkness directly addresses the issue of imperialism, or the practice of taking control of other lands and people to extend the territory under a nation's rule. In the novel, Marlow's employer—known only as the Company—seems to operate with the approval of the Belgian rulers. The agents of the Company enslave and murder the native people of the Congo and seize control of any area they see fit. Imperialism is sometimes justified with the argument that civilized nations are morally obligated to look after "savage" nations and show them how to improve themselves. This idea is often referred to as the White Man's Burden, after a Rudyard Kipling poem of the same title. The poem, published in the United States in 1899, was meant to rally Americans to support their government's takeover of the Philippines. In the name of progress, these less-industrialized countries are often robbed of their natural resources, and their citizens are oppressed or enslaved.

On his way to the mouth of the Congo, Marlow encounters a gunship firing into the jungle in an attempt to subdue a native tribe, referred to for some unknown reason as "ene-mies." Once he reaches the Congo, Marlow sees a group of native men conscripted as prisoners to do the menial work the Company agents require. Some natives are treated as "employees," and paid with bits of wire and other useless decorative items. Often, though, the natives are simply seen as an impediment to progress and are killed.

In *Heart of Darkness*, it is clear that the main reason for the Company's presence in the Congo is to obtain ivory. The agents at the Central Station spend their days plotting ways to get it, and envy Kurtz not just for his cleverness, but also for his ability to retrieve more ivory than anyone else in the region. For all his notions of lifting up the native people through education, Kurtz seems more obsessed with finding ivory than with any of his other grand plans.

Although Marlow often implies that the natives are in many ways inferior to the white men of the Company, he also seems to disapprove of the despicable treatment of the native people. When he sails away from the Inner Station with Kurtz, for example, he blasts his steam whistle in an attempt to keep the white pilgrims aboard from shooting the natives on the shore.

Dehumanization

Throughout the novel, Marlow describes the native people of the Congo in ways that make them seem less than human. At the first Company station, he sees black people moving about "like ants." The men of a chain gang have rags around their waists "and the short ends behind waggled to and fro like tails;" these same men also have joints "like knots in a rope." The dying men he encounters at the station are nothing more than "black shapes" and "bundles of acute angles." He often describes groups of natives by collectively referring to a specific body part: the whites of their eyeballs, the flaring of their nostrils, the whirling of their limbs. The natives who attack the steamboat as the pilgrims near the Inner Station are seen only as "naked breasts, arms, legs, glaring eyes." The effect is to cause the reader to never picture the natives as fully human.

Some critics argue that Marlow's descriptions are meant to reflect his ultimate inability to understand the native people as his peers. Although he clearly acknowledges that they are indeed human, he quickly notes that "that was the worst of it—this suspicion of their not being inhuman." It takes a true man, he argues, to even admit to feeling a "remote kinship" with the natives. Viewing them as peers is simply not conceivable. This was a fairly common feeling in nineteenth-century Europe. In the words of philanthropist Albert Schweitzer, as quoted by author Chinua Achebe in "An Image of Africa: Racism in Conrad's *Heart of Darkness*": "The African is indeed my brother but my junior brother."

Prejudice

In *Heart of Darkness*, Marlow makes many assumptions about the native people of the Congo. Although he admits their basic humanness, he often ascribes to them superstitions that he does not know exist. He describes his fireman as believing an evil spirit lurks inside the boiler of the ship; later, he begins to wonder if that description, meant to illustrate a native's lack of scientific understanding, might not be accurate after all. Marlow also takes for granted the fact that native workers are good only so far as they have been instructed—but even this is unnatural, and he muses that the fireman "ought to have been clapping his hands and stamping his feet on the bank" with the other natives. His prejudices extend beyond Africa, however: when he finds a book on seamanship with unreadable notes in the margins, he assumes them to be the ciphers of a madman—never even considering the possibility that they might just be written in another alphabet, like the one used by Russians.

HISTORICAL OVERVIEW

Imperialism in Africa

Heart of Darkness was published at the height of Britain's second great push to expand its worldwide colonies, popularly known as the "New Imperialism." One of the main targets of European colonial growth during this period was Africa. Until the mid-nineteenth century, all but the northernmost and southernmost parts of the continent had remained free of foreign interest due to its harsh and mysterious environment. However, the explorations of David Livingstone affirmed Africa's potential wealth of resources and the real possibility of obtaining that wealth.

The nations of Europe moved to stake their own claims, with England and France ignoring much of central Africa in favor of mineral-rich southern areas and important trade ports in the north. This left King Léopold II of Belgium to claim nearly one million square miles of the Congo as part of his domain. A conference was held in Berlin in 1884–1885 so that European countries could lay down ground rules for dividing up the great continent of Africa with a minimum of conflict among them.

These African territories were plagued by decades of abuse and exploitation on the part of their occupying nations. As European public opinion turned against the notion of imperialism, many of these territories were eventually allowed to form their own independent governments. Today, most African countries—even those who have broken free from colonial rule—are still defined by those boundaries set forth by the empires of Europe. The loss of resources and other damages inflicted upon Africa by colonial rule have been responsible, at least in part, for the continent's relatively slow economic development.

The Congo Free State

When the nations of Europe met in Berlin in 1884–1885 to discuss the colonization of Africa, King Léopold II of Belgium was granted private control of the region he had already "bought" through trade with tribal chiefs. As privately held land, the area—which was seventy-five times larger than Belgium itself—was not under the direct control of the Belgian government. This was allowed because Léopold was believed to be a humanitarian, and he promised to hand control of the territory over to its own people as soon as they demonstrated the ability to govern themselves. The area was named the Congo Free State.

Léopold offered leases that allowed different companies to control certain markets in an area. One lease, for example, would allow a company exclusive rights to all ivory within a specified region. The lack of an official government and the institution of a commission system of payment for district officials that was tied directly to profits meant that company agents could use whatever means necessary to extract riches from a region, including slavery, torture, and murder. It was not uncommon for agents who had not met profit goals to provide baskets of severed hands of Congolese natives in an attempt to make up for the shortfall.

This situation continued into the first years of the twentieth century, with the true nature of the atrocities finally coming to light in Europe at about the same time *Heart of Darkness* was published in book form. With public opinion against him, Léopold turned over control of the Congo Free State to the Belgian government. Belgium maintained control of the region for over fifty years, until it gained independent rule in 1960. The ensuing decades saw numerous internal conflicts, culminating in the current Transitional Government of the Democratic Republic of the Congo, which is attempting to establish a truly democratic, constitution-based government for the region.

CRITICAL OVERVIEW

Heart of Darkness was first published in book form in 1902 as one-third of a story collection titled *Youth*. The critical response to the book was uniformly favorable, with many considering the book one of Joseph Conrad's finest works. Most critics recognized *Heart of Darkness* as the standout piece of the book. Edward Garnett, in a review for *Academy and Literature* titled "Mr. Conrad's New Book," refers to the story as "the high-water mark of the author's talent," and a "psychological masterpiece." Hugh Clifford, in "The Art of Mr. Joseph Conrad" for *The Spectator*, also notes that the story seems "to represent Mr. Conrad at his very best." An unsigned reviewer for *Athenaeum* also singles out *Heart of Darkness* as "a big and thoughtful conception." Clifford also offers general praise for the author, stating that his talent "is surely not far removed from genius," while an unsigned reviewer for the *Manchester Guardian* refers to Conrad as "one of the greatest of sea-writers."

Some of these reviews by the author's contemporaries, viewed with modern eyes, provide insight into the culture in which Conrad lived and wrote. For example, despite the story's seemingly clear condemnation of the horrors that accompany imperialism, the aforementioned reviewer for the *Manchester Guardian* warns the reader, "It must not be supposed that Mr. Conrad makes attack upon colonisation, expansion, even upon Imperialism." In addition, despite modern views of Conrad's treatment of native Congolese people in the story, Garnett's review in *Academy and Literature* notes "no prejudice one way or the other" on the part of the author. However, seventy-five years later, Chinua Achebe, the Nigerian author of *Things Fall Apart*, writes in "An Image of Africa: Racism in Conrad's *Heart of Darkness* that Conrad's "obvious racism" has not been addressed by past reviews and needs to be confronted: "the question is whether a novel which celebrates this dehumanization, which depersonalizes a portion of the human race, can be called a great work of art. My answer is: No, it cannot."

While *Heart of Darkness* was frequently singled out as the jewel of the *Youth* collection, many reviewers also felt that its grimness and harsh subject matter might put off some readers. While Garnett lavishes his highest praise on *Heart of Darkness*, he acknowledges that the other two stories in the collection "will be more popular." The reviewer for the *Manchester Guardian* makes this comment about the story: "Even to those who are most impressed an excitement so sustained and prolonged, in which we are braced to encounter so much that menaces and appals [sic], must be something of a strain."

An unsigned reviewer for *The Monthly Review* shares similar feelings, but applies them to the whole collection by calling *Youth* a "most depressing book." The anonymous reviewer for the *Times Literary Supplement* (London) concludes a brief review of the stories by asserting, "'The End of the Tether,' the last of the three, is the longest and best." Though his first assertion may be factual (the story "The End of the Tether" is indeed the longest), history has shown his final claim to be an opinion squarely in the minority.

CRITICISM

Chinua Achebe

In the following essay excerpt, Nigerian author Chinua Achebe asserts that Conrad's Heart of Darkness, *due to the objectionable attitude it conveys about black people, is an offensive book not worthy of its "classic" status among literary scholars or readers.*

Heart of Darkness projects the image of Africa as "the other world," the antithesis of Europe and therefore of civilization, a place where man's vaunted intelligence and refinement

MEDIA ADAPTATIONS

Two electronic versions of the book, compatible with Adobe Acrobat Reader and Microsoft Reader, were released by Amazon Press in 2000. Both are available from www.amazon.com.

An unabridged audio version of the book was released on CD by Tantor Media in 2002. It is narrated by Scott Brick.

An unabridged audio version of the book, narrated by Richard Thomas, was released by Dove Audio in 1993. This version is currently available as a digital download through www.audible.com.

Director Francis Ford Coppola updated the story and locale of *Heart of Darkness* for his 1979 movie masterpiece, *Apocalypse Now*. Coppola's film is set in Southeast Asia during the Vietnam War, but follows the basic plot of the book closely. It stars Marlon Brando as Colonel Kurtz and Martin Sheen as Captain Willard. It is available on DVD and VHS from Paramount Home Entertainment.

A direct film adaptation of the novel was made for television in 1994 by director Nicholas Roeg. The movie stars John Malkovich and Tim Roth and was released on VHS from Turner Home Entertainment.

are finally mocked by triumphant bestiality. The book opens on the River Thames, tranquil, resting peacefully "at the decline of day after ages of good service done to the race that peopled its banks." But the actual story will take place on the River Congo, the very antithesis of the Thames. The River Congo is quite decidedly not a River Emeritus. It has rendered no service and enjoys no old-age pension. We are told that "going up that river was like travelling back to the earliest beginning of the world."

Is Conrad saying then that these two rivers are very different, one good, the other bad? Yes, but that is not the real point. It is not the differentness that worries Conrad but the lurking hint of kinship, of common ancestry. For the Thames too "has been one of the dark places of the earth." It conquered its darkness, of course, and is now in daylight and at peace. But if it were to visit its primordial relative, the Congo, it would run the terrible risk of hearing grotesque echoes of its own forgotten darkness, and falling victim to an avenging recrudescence of the mindless frenzy of the first beginnings.

The most interesting and revealing passages in *Heart of Darkness* are, however, about people.

It is clearly not part of Conrad's purpose to confer language on the "rudimentary souls" of Africa. In place of speech they made "a violent babble of uncouth sounds." They "exchanged short grunting phrases" even among themselves. But most of the time they were too busy with their frenzy. There are two occasions in the book, however, when Conrad departs somewhat from his practice and confers speech, even English speech, on the savages. The first occurs when cannibalism gets the better of them:

> "Catch 'im," he snapped, with a bloodshot widening of his eyes and a flash of sharp white teeth—"catch 'im. Give 'im to us." "To you, eh?" I asked; "what would you do with them?" "Eat 'im!" he said curtly.

The other occasion was the famous announcement: "Mistah Kurtz—he dead."

At first sight these instances might be mistaken for unexpected acts of generosity from Conrad. In reality they constitute some of his best assaults. In the case of the cannibals the incomprehensible grunts that had thus far served them for speech suddenly proved inadequate for Conrad's purpose of letting the European glimpse the unspeakable craving in their hearts. Weighing the necessity for consistency in the portrayal of the dumb brutes against the sensational advantages of securing their conviction by clear, unambiguous evidence issuing out of their own mouths, Conrad chose the latter. As for the announcement of Mr. Kurtz's death by the "insolent black head in the doorway," what better or more appropriate *finis* could be written to the horror story of that wayward child of civilization who wilfully had given his soul to the powers of darkness and "taken a high seat amongst the devils of the land" than the proclamation of his physical death by the forces he had joined?

It might be contended, of course, that the attitude to the African in *Heart of Darkness* is not Conrad's but that of his fictional narrator, Marlow, and that far from endorsing it Conrad might indeed be holding it up to irony and criticism. Certainly, Conrad appears to go to considerable pains to set up layers of insulation between himself and the moral universe of his story. He has, for example, a narrator behind a narrator. The primary narrator is Marlow, but his account is given to us through the filter of a second, shadowy person. But if Conrad's intention is to draw a cordon sanitaire between himself and the moral and psychological *malaise* of his narrator, his care seems to me totally wasted because he neglects to hint, clearly and adequately, at an alternative frame of reference by which we may judge the actions and opinions of his characters. It would not have been beyond Conrad's power to make that provision if he had thought it necessary. Conrad seems to me to approve of Marlow, with only minor reservations—a fact reinforced by the similarities between their two careers.

Marlow comes through to us not only as a witness of truth, but one holding those advanced and humane views appropriate to the English liberal tradition which required all Englishmen of decency to be deeply shocked by atrocities in Bulgaria or the Congo of King Leopold of the Belgians or wherever.

Thus, Marlow is able to toss out such bleeding-heart sentiments as these:

> They were all dying slowly—it was very clear. They were not enemies, they were not criminals, they were nothing earthly now—nothing but black shadows of disease and starvation, lying confusedly in the greenish gloom. Brought from all the recesses of the coast in all the legality of time contracts, lost in uncongenial surroundings, fed on unfamiliar food, they sickened, became inefficient, and were then allowed to crawl away and rest.

The kind of liberalism espoused here by Marlow/Conrad touched all the best minds of the age in England, Europe and America. It took different forms in the minds of different people but almost always managed to sidestep the ultimate question of equality between white people and black people.

When Marlow's African helmsman falls down with a spear in his heart he gives his white master one final disquieting look:

And the intimate profundity of that look he gave me when he received his hurt remains to this day in my memory—like a claim of distant kinship affirmed in a supreme moment.

It is important to note that Conrad, careful as ever with his words, is concerned not so much about "distant kinship" as about someone *laying a claim* on it. The black man lays a claim on the white man which is well-nigh intolerable. It is the laying of this claim which frightens and at the same time fascinates Conrad, "the thought of their humanity—like yours ... Ugly."

The point of my observations should be quite clear by now, namely that Joseph Conrad was a thoroughgoing racist. That this simple truth is glossed over in criticisms of his work is due to the fact that white racism against Africa is such a normal way of thinking that its manifestations go completely unremarked. Students of *Heart of Darkness* will often tell you that Conrad is concerned not so much with Africa as with the deterioration of one European mind caused by solitude and sickness. They will point out to you that Conrad is, if anything, less charitable to the Europeans in the story than he is to the natives, that the point of the story is to ridicule Europe's civilizing mission in Africa. A Conrad student informed me in Scotland that Africa is merely a setting for the disintegration of the mind of Mr. Kurtz.

Which is partly the point. Africa as setting and backdrop which eliminates the African as human factor. Africa as a metaphysical battlefield devoid of all recognizable humanity, into which the wandering European enters at his peril. Can nobody see the preposterous and perverse arrogance in thus reducing Africa to the role of props for the break-up of one petty European mind? But that is not even the point. The real question is the dehumanization of Africa and Africans which this age-long attitude has fostered and continues to foster in the world. And the question is whether a novel which celebrates this dehumanization, which depersonalizes a portion of the human race, can be called a great work of art. My answer is: No, it cannot. I do not doubt Conrad's great talents. Even *Heart of Darkness* has its memorably good passages and moments:

> The reaches opened before us and closed behind, as if the forest had stepped leisurely across the water to bar the way for our return.

Its exploration of the minds of the European characters is often penetrating and full of insight. But all that has been more than fully discussed in the last fifty years. His obvious racism has, however, not been addressed. And it is high time it was!

Whatever Conrad's problems were, you might say he is now safely dead. Quite true. Unfortunately, his heart of darkness plagues us still. Which is why an offensive and deplorable book can be described by a serious scholar as "among the half-dozen greatest short novels in the English language." And why it is today perhaps the most commonly prescribed novel in twentieth-century literature courses in English departments of American universities.

There are two probable grounds on which what I have said so far may be contested. The first is that it is no concern of fiction to please people about whom it is written. I will go along with that. But I am not talking about pleasing people. I am talking about a book which parades in the most vulgar fashion prejudices and insults from which a section of mankind has suffered untold agonies and atrocities in the past and continues to do so in many ways and many places today. I am talking about a story in which the very humanity of black people is called in question.

Secondly, I may be challenged on the grounds of actuality. Conrad, after all, did sail down the Congo in 1890 when my own father was still a babe in arms. How could I stand up more than fifty years after his death and purport to contradict him? My answer is that as a sensible man I will not accept just any traveller's tales solely on the grounds that I have not made the journey myself. I will not trust the evidence even of a man's very eyes when I suspect them to be as jaundiced as Conrad's. And we also happen to know that Conrad was, in the words of his biographer, Bernard C. Meyer, "notoriously inaccurate in the rendering of his own history."

As I said earlier Conrad did not originate the image of Africa which we find in his book. It was and is the dominant image of Africa in the Western imagination and Conrad merely brought the peculiar gifts of his own mind to bear on it. For reasons which can certainly use close psychological inquiry, the West seems to suffer deep anxieties about the precariousness of its civilization and to have a need for constant reassurance by comparison with Africa. If Europe, advancing in civilization, could cast a backward glance periodically at Africa trapped in primordial barbarity it could say with faith and feeling: There go I but for the grace of God. Africa is to Europe as the picture is to Dorian Gray—a carrier on to whom the master unloads his physical and moral deformities so that he may go forward, erect and immaculate. Consequently, Africa is something to be avoided just as the picture has to be hidden away to safeguard the man's jeopardous integrity. Keep away from Africa, or else! Mr. Kurtz of *Heart of Darkness* should have heeded that warning and the prowling horror in his heart would have kept its place, chained to its lair. But he foolishly exposed himself to the wild irresistible allure of the jungle and lo! the darkness found him out.

In my original conception of this essay I had thought to conclude it nicely on an appropriately positive note in which I would suggest from my privileged position in African and Western cultures some advantages the West might derive from Africa once it rid its mind of old prejudices and began to look at Africa not through a haze of distortions and cheap mystifications but quite simply as a continent of people—not angels, but not rudimentary souls either—just people, often highly gifted people and often strikingly successful in their enterprise with life and society. But as I thought more about the stereotype image, about its grip and pervasiveness, about the wilful tenacity with which the West holds it to its heart; when I thought of the West's television and cinema and newspapers, about books read in its schools and out of school, of churches preaching to empty pews about the need to send help to the heathen in Africa, I realized that no easy optimism was possible. And there was in any case something totally wrong in offering bribes to the West in return for its good opinion of Africa. Ultimately the abandonment of unwholesome thoughts must be its own and only reward. Although I have used the word "wilful" a few times here to characterize the West's view of Africa, it may well be that what is happening at this stage is more akin to reflex action than calculated malice. Which does not make the situation more but less hopeful.

Although the work of redressing which needs to be done may appear too daunting, I believe it is not one day too soon to begin.

Conrad saw and condemned the evil of imperial exploitation but was strangely unaware of the racism on which it sharpened its iron tooth. But the victims of racist slander who for centuries have had to live with the inhumanity it makes them heir to have always known better than any casual visitor, even when he comes loaded with the gifts of a Conrad.

Source: Chinua Achebe, "An Image of Africa: Racism in Conrad's *Heart of Darkness*," in *Hopes and Impediments: Selected Essays*, 1989.

SOURCES

Achebe, Chinua, "An Image of Africa: Racism in Conrad's *Heart of Darkness*," in *Hopes and Impediments: Selected Essays*, Doubleday, 1989, pp. 1–20.

Clifford, Hugh, "The Art of Mr. Joseph Conrad," in *Heart of Darkness*, by Joseph Conrad, edited by D.C.R.A. Goonetilleke, Broadview Press, 1999, pp. 164–68, originally published in *The Spectator*, November 29, 1902, pp. 827–828.

Conrad, Joseph, *Heart of Darkness*, from Vol. 2 of the *Norton Anthology of English Literature*, 6th edition, edited by M. H. Abrams, W. W. Norton, 1993, pp. 1759–1817.

Garnett, Edward, "Mr. Conrad's New Book," in *Heart of Darkness*, by Joseph Conrad, edited by D.C.R.A. Goonetilleke, Broadview Press, 1999, pp. 163–64, originally published in *Academy and Literature*, December 6, 1902, pp. 606–607.

"Mr. Conrad's New Book," in *Heart of Darkness*, by Joseph Conrad, edited by D.C.R.A. Goonetilleke, Broadview Press, 1999, pp. 168–69, originally published in the *Manchester Guardian*, December 10, 1902, p. 3.

Review of *Youth*, in *Heart of Darkness*, edited by D.C.R.A. Goonetilleke, Broadview Press, 1999, pp. 170–71; originally published in *Athenaeum*, December 20, 1902, p. 824.

Review of *Youth*, in *Heart of Darkness*, by Joseph Conrad, edited by D.C.R.A. Goonetilleke, Broadview Press, 1999, p. 173, originally published in *The Monthly Review*, April 7, 1903, pp. 21–22.

Review of *Youth*, in *Heart of Darkness*, by Joseph Conrad, edited by D.C.R.A. Goonetilleke, Broadview Press, 1999, pp. 169–70, originally published in the *Times Literary Supplement* (London), No. 48, December 12, 1902, p. 372.

The House on Mango Street

SANDRA CISNEROS

1984

The House on Mango Street by Sandra Cisneros resists classification, with reviewers and critics alike labeling it differently. At one hundred and ten pages, it is about the length of a novella, or short novel, but its pages have more white space than text, and headings frequently divide them. This suggests a collection of stories, though some entries are shorter than one page. Cisneros's use of language causes more questions of classification: it is not only insightful and moving, but evocative and poetic. Maybe, indeed, it is a book of prose poetry.

Ultimately, it fills each of these classifications at different times. Each of the forty-four vignettes (short literary sketches) can stand alone, sentences are often more like verse, and stories combine to give the larger perspective of a novel. In "Do You Know Me?: I Wrote *The House on Mango Street*," Cisneros has this to say about the book's structure:

> I recall I wanted to write stories that were a cross between poetry and fiction. . . . I wanted to write a collection which could be read at any random point without having any knowledge of what came before or after. Or, that could be read in a series to tell one big story. I wanted stories like poems, compact and lyrical and ending with a reverberation.

The House on Mango Street is the story of Esperanza and her neighborhood on Mango Street. As Esperanza struggles to break free from the cycle of poverty, marriage, motherhood,

and broken dreams she sees on her street, she must also come to terms with her place in the community and the responsibilities she has toward it as a member. The source of the book's inspiration has practically become part of its story. When Cisneros was a graduate student in the University of Iowa Writer's Workshop, one of her classes was discussing the idea of physical space, based on writings by French philosopher and poet Gaston Bachelard. In his book *Poetics of Space*, Bachelard suggests that space deeply affects, even inspires, a person. Cisneros's classmates seemed to agree, but she felt at odds with the whole concept. In her introduction to the Knopf 1994 tenth anniversary edition of *The House on Mango Street*, she writes of her reaction: "What was this guy talking about when he mentioned the familiar and comforting 'house of memory'? It was obvious he never had to clean one or pay the landlord rent for one like ours."

Growing up, Cisneros and her family shuttled between Chicago and Mexico, where her father's family lived. Because of this constant moving, she lived between two worlds, both of which were short on friends and space. When her family finally bought a house in Chicago, it fell short of what Cisneros had imagined a house would provide. It was small and, in her words, "ugly," and situated on an impoverished street. It held the promise of familiarity and long-lasting friendships, but could not satisfy Cisneros's yearning for something more comfortable and secure.

In her graduate class, Cisneros did not relate to the descriptions of fellow students' homes or share the sense of pride or affection they seemed to have for them. When the class was assigned to write about their memory of "space," Cisneros set out to distinguish her past life in the Chicago barrio from the experiences of her classmates in affluent white neighborhoods. She credits this episode with the discovery of her writing voice. A few years later, after completing the program, Cisneros elaborated on the original assignment, producing *The House on Mango Street*. The year after it was published it won the Before Columbus Foundation's American Book Award and was soon a regular on classroom reading lists. Cisneros continued writing with financial support from National Endowment for the Arts grants and invitations to teach from universities around the country. But like Esperanza, the

> " I KNEW THEN I HAD TO HAVE A HOUSE. A REAL HOUSE. ONE I COULD POINT TO. BUT THIS ISN'T IT. THE HOUSE ON MANGO STREET ISN'T IT."

book's narrator, she did not forget where she came from and made frequent trips back to her home in Chicago.

The House on Mango Street is available in a tenth anniversary edition, published in 1994 by Knopf, that includes an introduction by the author. Cisneros's other books include *Woman Hollering Creek* (1991), a collection of short stories; *My Wicked Wicked Ways* (1992), a collection of poetry; *Loose Woman* (1994), a collection of poetry; *Hairs/Pelitos* (1997), a children's book; and *Caramelo* (2002), a novel.

PLOT SUMMARY

Chapter 1: The House on Mango Street

Esperanza, the first-person narrator, begins by explaining that her family "didn't always live on Mango Street." She lists the names of previous streets to make the point that the family, which includes two sons and two daughters, has spent a lot of time moving. The new house is different because they own it; still, she says "it's not the house we'd thought we'd get." The house of their fantasies was white with trees and a big yard. The house on Mango Street is "small and red" with a few small trees by the curb and no front yard. For Esperanza, it disappoints in every way. The chapter ends with her describing an encounter with a nun from her school outside the family's previous home. The nun could not believe she lived in an apartment above a laundromat. Her embarrassment at the nun's reaction made Esperanza long for "a real house."

Chapter 2: Hairs

In one of the shortest vignettes in the book, Esperanza describes the different kind of hair each person in her family has. She focuses most on her mother's hair, which she has the strongest associations with. Not only is it "curly and

BIOGRAPHY

SANDRA CISNEROS

Sandra Cisneros was born December 20, 1954, the only daughter among seven children. For years her family moved between poor Chicago neighborhoods and Mexico City, where her paternal grandmother lived. When Cisneros was eleven, the family moved into its own home, an experience that inspired *The House on Mango Street.*

Cisneros wrote poetry as a child, but it was not until high school that she concentrated on it seriously. Later, her creative writing professor at Loyola University urged her to pursue writing in graduate school. She graduated with an English degree in 1976 and then began a master's degree at the acclaimed University of Iowa writing program. While she felt out of place as the only Latina student, she has said it was there that she found her writing voice, partly by distinguishing it from the writing of her white, affluent classmates. With the publication of *The House on Mango Street*, she became the first Mexican American woman writer to find mainstream literary success.

Since then, Cisneros has published an array of books, including a children's picture book, several poetry collections, and a novel. In 1995, she won a MacArthur Foundation Fellowship. As of 2006, she lives in San Antonio, Texas.

Sandra Cisneros Dana Tynan. AP Images

pretty," it is part of what makes her mother so safe and comforting.

Chapter 3: Boys & Girls

This brief chapter describes the divisions between Esperanza's brothers and sisters. The boys and girls do not play together; her own brothers only talk to her inside the house where no one else can see. Her brothers are each other's best friends, but her younger sister Nenny is too young to share secrets with. Instead, Esperanza feels responsible for her. She dreams of a day when she will have a best friend to tell secrets to.

Chapter 4: My Name

It is not until this chapter that the reader learns Esperanza's name. First she describes what it means, both in English and Spanish. In English it means *hope,* but its Spanish meaning is much more complicated. She was named after her great-grandmother, a woman who was forced into marriage and spent her life looking out a window. Esperanza wonders, "[W]as she sorry because she couldn't be all the things she wanted to be?" Esperanza distinguishes between inheriting the name and inheriting the life. She does not want to spend her life at a window.

Chapter 5: Cathy Queen of Cats

Identified by her houseful of cats and where she lives on the street in relation to other neighbors, Cathy introduces Esperanza to the rules, and some of the gossip, of Mango Street. She claims to be a distant relative of the queen of France. Cathy agrees to be Esperanza's friend, but then breaks the news that she is moving because "the neighborhood is getting bad." Esperanza is aware that families like Cathy's are moving "a little farther away every time people like us keep moving in."

Chapter 6: Our Good Day

Esperanza meets a pair of sisters, Rachel and Lucy, who say they will be her "friends forever" if she gives them five dollars. They are trying to raise enough money to buy a bicycle and need five more dollars. Cathy tells Esperanza not to talk to them, but Esperanza likes them and is desperate for friends. Using three dollars of her own and sneaking two from Nenny, Esperanza gets the five dollars and the three of them buy the bike. They ride it together—Lucy on the pedals, Esperanza on the seat, and Rachel on the handlebars—around the neighborhood.

Chapter 7: Laughter

Even though Nenny and Esperanza do not look alike, they laugh the same, and their common experiences have given them a similar understanding of things. Esperanza considers this sisterly bond in relation to her new friendships.

Chapter 8: Gil's Furniture Bought & Sold

The local junk store is full of refrigerators, couches, and televisions. It is dark and dusty and the owner, a quiet black man, is barely visible. Nenny asks him questions about merchandise, but Esperanza does not speak unless she buys something. He shows Nenny a music box, and Esperanza excitedly expects to see a girl's pretty box "with a ballerina inside." Instead, it is an old wood box with a brass record that plays music "like drops of water." Esperanza is moved by the music, but hides this from her sister; she acts as if Nenny is stupid for wanting to buy the box. The man tells Nenny it is not for sale.

Chapter 9: Meme Ortiz

Meme, whose real name is Juan, moves into Cathy's old house. He is clumsy like his sheepdog that has two names, one in Spanish and one in English. The best part of the house, which is wooden with crooked steps, is the tree in the backyard. From the branches kids can see neighboring roofs and lost balls. Esperanza can see her house from a distance, "its feet tucked under like a cat."

Chapter 10: Louie, His Cousin & His Other Cousin

Louie lives in a basement apartment downstairs from Meme. He is Esperanza's brother's friend. Marin, an older girl cousin from Puerto Rico, lives with them. She wears makeup and sings in the doorway while she babysits Louie's younger sisters. Esperanza only saw Louie's other cousin once, but, she says, "it was important." She recounts how a group was playing in the alley near Louie's house when a yellow Cadillac drove up and honked. The cousin took everyone for a ride in the car until they heard sirens. He told the children to get out, then took off in the Cadillac. He crashed nearby, and the police arrested him.

Chapter 11: Marin

Marin has a boyfriend in Puerto Rico. They plan to get married when she goes back. Louie's parents are sending her back because she is "too much trouble," and Esperanza regrets this. Marin is older and knows things Esperanza and the others do not. She sits out front with her radio and smokes cigarettes. Marin says the most important thing about sitting outside is to see and be seen by boys. Esperanza imagines Marin in the future, "singing the same song somewhere . . . waiting for a car to stop, a star to fall, someone to change her life."

Chapter 12: Those Who Don't

The chapter title refers to people who do not know better than to be scared of Esperanza's neighborhood. They arrive there "by mistake" and think they will be attacked. The people who live in the neighborhood know better than to be afraid. They see beyond the surface. For them it is the opposite. They feel safe around other brown-skinned people, but are nervous themselves when they enter "a neighborhood of another color."

Chapter 13: There Was an Old Woman She Had So Many Children She Didn't Know What to Do

Rose Vargas is known for her many misbehaved children. She is single and tired and still grieving over the man who left her. The kids are in the trees and the street, with the threat of injury, even death, always lingering nearby. At first, the neighbors look after the kids and watch out for them, but eventually they give up because nothing changes. The children's injuries go unnoticed, even Angel's, "who learned to fly and dropped from the sky like a sugar donut, just like a falling star."

Chapter 14: Alicia Who Sees Mice

While Alicia makes tortillas and cleans the house, she sees mice run and hide. Her father dismisses her fear. Alicia's mother is dead and she is the oldest daughter. She is expected to be the woman of the house. Alicia attends college "because she doesn't want to spend her whole life in a factory or behind a rolling pin."

Chapter 15: Darius & the Clouds

Esperanza appreciates the sky. It is a comfort to her and the neighborhood. There is not enough of it to ease all of the sadness in the neighborhood, but they appreciate it anyway. Darius, a kid who is usually a pest, points out a cloud. He says the cloud is God and Esperanza decides it is a wise comment.

Chapter 16: And Some More

Esperanza and Nenny are hanging out with Rachel and Lucy. The conversation begins with Esperanza boasting that she knows Eskimos have many names for snow. This leads to discussion of how many names there are for clouds, including metaphors for the way clouds look. Esperanza compares a cloud to Rachel's face, and the conversation devolves into the girls flinging insults at each other. Nenny does not participate and continues giving clouds people names like "Jean, Geranium and Joe," despite the heated exchange going on with the others.

Chapter 17: The Family of Little Feet

This chapter begins with a kind of fairy tale of a family distinguished by their feet. The family becomes real when the mother offers the girls— Esperanza, Rachel, and Lucy—a sack full of shoes. There are three pairs and as the girls try them on, Esperanza becomes aware of how much she has grown. Attached to her foot is a "long long leg." She notices the others' legs too. Rachel walks in the high heels best and teaches the others how to behave in them. Men on the corner watch, and Mr. Benny at the store tells them shoes like that are dangerous. A bum offers Rachel a dollar if she will kiss him. They run away and Lucy hides the shoes under a basket. One day, her mother throws them away.

Chapter 18: A Rice Sandwich

Esperanza wants to eat lunch at school in the canteen. That is where the kids whose mothers are not home, or who live far from the school, eat instead of going home for lunch. She talks her mother into making her a sandwich and sending her to school with a note. A nun immediately notices that she is not a regular canteen student

and calls her out. Esperanza brings the note to the Sister Superior, who berates her for not being able to go home for lunch when she lives so close. She is allowed to stay this once, but must continue going home for lunch otherwise. She cries as she eats her rice sandwich in the canteen, and other kids stare.

Chapter 19: Chanclas

Esperanza's mother buys new clothes for the children to wear to their cousin's baptism party, but forgets to buy Esperanza shoes. The party is in a church basement where people are dancing and laughing and eating tamales. Esperanza feels dumb in her new pink dress and her old brown saddle shoes. Then Uncle Nacho pulls her onto the dance floor. She gradually forgets the shoes and dances while people watch and clap.

Chapter 20: Hips

The girls jump rope and discuss hips. Esperanza is anticipating her body's changes and wants to compare notes. Rachel says hips are for holding a baby. Lucy says they are needed for dancing. Nenny thinks that without them one could turn into a man. Esperanza feels like an expert because she understands hips from a more scientific perspective: "It's the bones that let you know which skeleton was a man's when it was a man and which was a woman's." She thinks to be ready for them, and they need to practice. The older girls begin to move to the rhythm of the jump rope. They take turns chanting a rhyme about hips. Then Nenny jumps in singing the same old childhood songs. Esperanza tries to redirect her, but Nenny does not listen. Esperanza realizes she is in a different world from Nenny now.

Chapter 21: The First Job

Esperanza wants to work to help pay for her Catholic school, but does not expect to get the job she does. Aunt Lala, who works at Peter Pan Photo Finishers, finds Esperanza a job. She has to wear white gloves and match negatives to prints. Unsure of what to do on the first day, she stands until she sees other people sit down. She eats lunch in a bathroom stall and goes back to work early. On her break, she goes to the coatroom. An older man offers to be her friend and then tells her it is his birthday and asks for a kiss. As she goes to kiss his cheek, he grabs her face and kisses her on the mouth.

Chapter 22: Papa Who Wakes Up Tired in the Dark

Esperanza's father wakes her up and tells her that her grandfather, *abuelito,* is dead. For the first time she sees her Papa cry. He has told her first because she is the oldest. She will have to tell the others. She thinks about what she would do if Papa died, then she holds him while he cries.

Chapter 23: Born Bad

Esperanza feels guilty about Aunt Lupe. Once her aunt was pretty and a good swimmer, but then she got sick and became an invalid. Esperanza tries to understand how her aunt could have been once healthy, like in the pictures she has seen, and suddenly become so sick. Esperanza and Nenny go to visit Aunt Lupe sometimes, and Aunt Lupe listens to their stories and Esperanza's poetry. Rachel, Lucy, and Esperanza have a game where they imitate people, and one day they imitate Aunt Lupe. They did not know it would be the day Aunt Lupe died. Now Esperanza's mother prays for her and tells her she was born on an evil day.

Chapter 24: Elenita, Cards, Palm, Water

Elenita is a fortune-teller, or "witch woman." She works in her kitchen where her holy candles and other religious objects are. Esperanza goes to get her tarot cards read. Elenita claims spirits are in the room and Esperanza pretends to sense them. Esperanza asks specifically about a house, and Elenita tells her she sees "a home in the heart." Esperanza is disappointed by this. She pays her five dollars and leaves.

Chapter 25: Geraldo No Last Name

Geraldo is the victim of a hit-and-run accident and is dead. Marin dances with him the night he dies. He only tells her his first name. She is the last person to see him alive, so she has to tell her story to the hospital and the police. She does not understand why, though. She did not know him. She tells them he did not speak English, "just another wetback." Esperanza considers the fact that his family, "the ones he left behind" in his native country, will never know he has died.

Chapter 26: Edna's Ruthie

Edna owns the building next door and Ruthie is her adult daughter. Ruthie plays with the girls and walks her dog named Bobo and laughs to herself. Esperanza appreciates Ruthie's insights, the way Ruthie will suddenly notice something.

Edna's friends invite Ruthie to go play bingo with them. Ruthie hesitates while they wait in the car for fifteen minutes. Then they leave without her. Esperanza thinks Ruthie is very talented and does not understand why she lives with her mother.

Chapter 27: The Earl of Tennessee

Earl lives in the basement apartment of Edna's building. He works nights and keeps his blinds closed during the day. He is a jukebox repairman and has boxes of 45 rpm records. He also has a Southern accent. Supposedly, he has a wife somewhere and all of the neighbors have different accounts of her. The only thing they agree on is her visits. Earl rushes her into the apartment and locks the door, but they do not stay long.

Chapter 28: Sire

Sire is a boy who lives in the neighborhood. He stares at Esperanza as she walks past his house and she looks back just to prove to herself that she is not scared. Then he gets a girlfriend named Lois. Esperanza sees Lois at the store and notices her pink toenails and her "big girl hands." She hears them laughing at night and watches them together. Her mother warns her about girls like Lois. Esperanza imagines what it would be like to sit outside at night with a boy.

Chapter 29: Four Skinny Trees

Esperanza sees a connection between herself and the four skinny trees that grow near her house. They are skinny like her, but they are strong, with deep roots in the soil. They keep growing and living, and they inspire her: "Four who grew despite concrete. Four who reach and do not forget to reach. Four whose only reason is to be and be."

Chapter 30: No Speak English

The man who lives across the street saved his money to bring his Mamacita over from their country. Mamacita is a large lady who does not leave the apartment. Esperanza thinks this is because she does not speak English, though others think it is because she does not want to walk the three flights of stairs. The neighbors hear her fighting with her son. She tells him in Spanish that she is sad and wants to go home. He tells her they are home and commands, "Speak English."

Chapter 31: Rafaela Who Drinks Coconut & Papaya Juice on Tuesdays

Rafaela's husband locks her inside the apartment when he plays dominoes on Tuesday night. She calls to the girls out the window and throws down a dollar for them to get her juice at the store. Then she sends down a shopping bag on a clothesline when they return. The juice, always coconut or papaya, is not sweet enough, not as sweet as freedom.

Chapter 32: Sally

Esperanza admires her classmate Sally, who wears "nylons the color of smoke" and paints her eyes like Cleopatra. Sally's father does not trust her beauty and does not allow her to go out. Boys tell stories of Sally, but Esperanza does not believe them. She wonders why Sally rubs off her makeup and walks quickly home after school. She imagines Sally someday walking away from Mango Street, free of the "nosy neighbors," free of the whispering. Sally does not belong on Mango Street; she only wants to love and Mango Street thinks that is crazy.

Chapter 33: Minerva Writes Poems

Minerva is not much older than Esperanza but she already has two children. She cries because her husband left. After the kids are asleep, she writes poems on paper that she folds into small pieces. When her husband comes, they fight. Minerva says she is through, but then the husband says he is sorry and she lets him come back. She is bruised when Esperanza next sees her, but Esperanza knows there is nothing she can do to help her.

Chapter 34: Bums in the Attic

Esperanza's family goes out on Sundays to look at the houses on a hill where her Papa works in the gardens. She does not go with them anymore. She is ashamed of the family "staring out the window like the hungry." People who live on hills forget the people who live on the ground. She knows she will own a house someday, but she will not forget who she is or where she came from. She will even allow "passing bums" to stay in her attic, because she knows "how it is to be without a house."

Chapter 35: Beautiful & Cruel

Esperanza thinks she is ugly and does not expect a man to choose her. Nenny has pretty eyes, so she has the privilege of choosing the way in which she will leave her parents. Esperanza does not want to wait for a husband, but she also does not want to get pregnant. She has decided not to be like the other girls "who lay their necks on the threshold waiting for the ball and chain." She wants to be "beautiful and cruel," like the women with "red red lips" in movies. She does not want to give her power away.

Chapter 36: A Smart Cookie

Esperanza's mother has regrets. She says, "I could've been somebody." She sings to opera records, embroiders flowers, and knows how to fix a television. She points to her friends, one whose husband died and one whose husband left, as examples of how a person is on her own. She quit school, even though she was smart, because she did not have nice clothes. This disgusts her.

Chapter 37: What Sally Said

Sally has bruises on her face. She tells the school that she fell, but she tells Esperanza that her father does not hit her hard. She goes to stay with Esperanza's family but her father begs her to come home. He says it was the last time, so Sally goes. Then one day, he sees her talking to a boy and he goes crazy. She does not come to school the next day.

Chapter 38: The Monkey Garden

The kids are afraid of the garden with the monkey because he screams and bares his teeth whenever they try to enter. When he and his owners move, the neighborhood kids take it over. It is full of flowers and fruit trees, but then it grows wild and dead cars begin appearing. Esperanza plays in the garden with the kids while Sally stays by the curb talking to a boy and his friends. They take Sally's keys and will not give them back unless she kisses them. Esperanza wants to defend Sally, but Sally tells her to go home. Esperanza feels stupid. She hides at the other end of the garden and tries to will her heart to stop beating. The garden feels foreign to her after this.

Chapter 39: Red Clowns

At the carnival, Sally tells Esperanza to wait by the red clowns. Sally leaves with a boy but she says she will come back. Esperanza waits a long time but Sally never comes back. Boys harass Esperanza while she waits, and she calls out for Sally, but Sally does not answer. A boy grabs her and presses his mouth to hers. Esperanza believes Sally lied about what it is like to be with a boy.

Chapter 40: Linoleum Roses

Sally marries a marshmallow salesman she met at a school bazaar. She is not yet in eighth grade. Esperanza suspects Sally has married to escape her father. Her husband will not let her talk on the phone or look out the window. No one can visit her unless he is at work. She comforts herself by looking at all the things they own.

Chapter 41: The Three Sisters

Rachel and Lucy's baby sister dies and many people come to visit, including three aunts. They are interested in Esperanza. They look at her hands and tell her she will go far. They tell her to make a wish and then tell her it will come true. Finally, one of them tells her that when she leaves, she "must remember to come back for the others." The aunts remind Esperanza that she will be a part of Mango Street, no matter where she goes. Esperanza feels as if the aunt reads her mind, and she feels guilty for making a "selfish wish."

Chapter 42: Alicia & I Talking on Edna's Steps

Alicia gives Esperanza a purse from her hometown with "Guadalajara" stitched on it, and Esperanza feels jealous that Alicia has a home. Alicia tells Esperanza that Mango Street is her home, but Esperanza shakes her head and says she does not belong on Mango Street. Alicia tells her that whether she likes it or not, it is her home.

Chapter 43: A House of My Own

Esperanza envisions the house she will someday have, with a porch and a pillow and "pretty purple petunias." It will be "a space for myself to go, clean as paper before the poem."

Chapter 44: Mango Says Goodbye Sometimes

Esperanza likes to tell stories. When she writes about the Mango Street house, it frees her from some of the pain she feels from living there. She acknowledges that one day she will say goodbye to the house, but that she will come back "for the ones who cannot get out."

THEMES

Gender

Gender plays an interesting role in the lives of the residents on Mango Street. The boys and men of Mango Street are often introduced in relation to the girls and women of Mango Street. Women fear them, desire them, and are victims of them. As Esperanza matures, she becomes more aware of this dynamic, both in her own life and in her neighbors' lives. It begins when she, Rachel, and Lucy walk down the street in their hand-me-down high-heel shoes, imitating grown-up ladies. Men call out to them and the girls become conscious of their budding sexuality. Rachel tries out this power by speaking to a bum. When he offers her a dollar for a kiss, the other girls sense the danger: he is capable of taking more than a kiss. They do not wear the high heels again, suddenly aware of the risks men pose.

There are abundant examples of these risks throughout the story. Sally's father, disturbed by her sexuality, threatens her with a loss of beauty, and even death, with regular beatings. Sally does not equate boys with her father. She is thrilled by their attention and sees them as a way out of her father's house. In reality, they only offer a change. When she marries before eighth grade, she goes from being a subordinate daughter to being a subordinate wife, "afraid to go outside without [her husband's] permission." Many of the women on Mango Street see marriage as a way of escaping, but it often ends up as just another oppressive situation. Locked inside the apartment on Tuesday nights by her husband, Rafaela throws down a dollar to the neighborhood girls so they can buy her juice. Marin expects to escape by returning to her boyfriend in Puerto Rico, but while she lives on Mango Street, she is forced to stay home and babysit. Both Rosa Vargas and Minerva spend their time crying over the men that have deserted them, leaving them without money or support. Esperanza's own great-grandmother, her namesake, did not find freedom in marriage, either: her husband "threw a sack over her head and carried her off. Just like that, as if she were a fancy chandelier." From that point on, she stares out the window, watching life go by. Esperanza does not want to end up like these girls and does not want to "grow up tame" waiting for a man to rescue her.

Regardless of Esperanza's vision and will to be different from the likes of Sally and the others, she cannot prevent herself from becoming a victim of sexual assault. At her first job, an older male employee tells Esperanza they can be friends, and she naively believes him. But when he asks for a birthday kiss and Esperanza offers him a peck on the cheek, "he grabs [her] face with both hands and kisses [her] hard on the mouth and doesn't let go." In another instance, Esperanza is waiting for Sally at the carnival when she is approached by a group of men. One of them grabs her arm and presses his mouth to hers. Clearly traumatized, she does not describe what else he did, but she implies that he did not stop there. She is upset that Sally did not answer her calls for help, but the more experienced Sally was probably also with a man.

Esperanza's determination to leave Mango Street and the stifled lives she sees there makes her different from most of the women in her neighborhood. But even as a young girl, she knows she must return to Mango Street to help those who cannot help themselves.

Poverty

Mango Street is a working-class neighborhood with predominantly Latino immigrant residents. Because of education and language barriers, many live a life of poverty, looked down upon by the rest of the community. Esperanza is aware that the neighborhood is not a "good" one by society's standards and is embarrassed about the small, rundown house her family buys. She tells the reader "it's not the house we'd thought we'd get." Esperanza is aware of the prejudices and assumptions that others have about people who live on Mango Street. When she tries to eat lunch at school one day, the nun tells her she lives too close by. She takes Esperanza to the window and points "to a row of ugly three-flats, the ones even the raggedy men are ashamed to go into," and asks if that is where Esperanza lives. Esperanza says yes, even though it is not her house. This is the second time she had been made to feel ashamed of her living conditions by a nun at school. Before the family moves to Mango Street, a nun sees Esperanza playing out in front of a recently robbed laundromat that the family lives above. She tells the nun that she lives upstairs, and the nun responds, "You live *there*?" Her reaction and "the way she said it made [Esperanza] feel like nothing. *There*. I lived *there*."

Many residents dream of leaving the poverty of Mango Street behind and of being accepted by mainstream society. Marin talks of looking for a job downtown, not locally, "because that's where the best jobs are ... and you can meet someone in the subway who might marry you and take you to live in a big house far away." Alicia studies so that she can leave the world of cooking and cleaning behind. And Esperanza dreams of the day she will own her own house somewhere else and will let bums stay in the attic because she knows "how it is to be without a house."

Community

The residents of Mango Street are connected by their shared existence in a Chicago barrio. There is no hierarchy based on material possessions; no single house stands out as better than any other. Poverty puts the residents on the same level, and they assume a kind of resigned unity as a result. The children are especially connected. They witness each other's family dramas, play in each other's yards, and share an understanding of the neighborhood adults.

People who live on Mango Street are also connected by language and skin color. They are Mexican, Puerto Rican, and first-generation Americans, and they are linked by the experience of immigration, of learning English, and of being outsiders in America. Strangers to Mango Street are fearful of them, just as Mango Street residents are fearful of strange neighborhoods. As Esperanza understands it, "All brown all around, we are safe."

As many of the residents of Mango Street are immigrants with families living back home in Mexico, the neighbors become like extended family to one another. For example, Rosa Vargas has too many children to handle on her own, and so the neighborhood assumes some of the responsibility for watching over the children. However, after the children seem to prove themselves incorrigible, Esperanza writes that the neighbors got "tired of being worried about kids who aren't even [theirs]." When Sally's father beats her, Esperanza's family takes her in. Lucy, Rachel, and Esperanza imagine themselves as sisters in their fairy tale about the family with little feet.

Even though Esperanza is desperate to leave Mango Street and says, "I don't ever want to come from here," she knows she will be part of the community forever. One of the aunts at Rachel and Lucy's sister's funerals tells her plainly, "You will always be Mango Street. You can't erase what you know. You can't forget who you are." By the end of the book, Esperanza realizes her place within the community and its importance to her as an individual. She comes to understand the "home in the heart" that the fortune-teller said was her destiny.

Hope for the Future

As Esperanza settles into her life on Mango Street, she gradually begins to find both symbolic and real reasons to hope. The sky and clouds offer her relief from the neighborhood's sadness, as well as the promise of a faraway place. At night, she listens to the elm trees along the front curb. They may be skinny and misplaced, but Esperanza understands that their secret roots are strong and persistent. They inspire her to "keep, keep, keep," and signal the connection between growing roots and growing up. Esperanza must first grow roots on Mango Street before she can find a home somewhere else.

One neighbor, Alicia, serves as an example of someone who has a life beyond Mango Street. In spite of her cooking and cleaning obligations at home, she manages to attend the university "because she doesn't want to spend her whole life in a factory or behind a rolling pin." Near the book's end, Rachel and Lucy's aunts arrive from out of town. Esperanza immediately senses they are alien to Mango Street, and they bring an entirely new perspective. They see Esperanza's desire to leave Mango Street written on her face. The aunt "with marble hands" validates this desire just by acknowledging it. She only insists that Esperanza remembers "to come back for the others." This exchange marks a shift in Esperanza. Suddenly, because she understands it is okay for her to leave, she knows without question that she will. Her hope for her own future allows her to become an agent of hope to the rest of Mango Street's marginalized residents, those who cannot leave. She promises to return on their behalf and perhaps become an inspiration to them, just as Alicia is an inspiration to Esperanza.

HISTORICAL OVERVIEW

Chicana Literature

Sandra Cisneros's work is part of a blossoming of Chicana literature that occurred in the 1980s in the United States. Defined as literature by American women descended from Mexico,

writers in this category also include Lorna Dee Cervantes, Denise Chavez, Gloria Anzaldua, Ana Castillo, and Cherrie Moraga. Chicana writers are united by their Mexican heritage, but more importantly, by racism, poverty, and gender marginalization, all of which help account for their late entry into the publishing world. The defining moment for their male counterparts came a decade earlier when Tomás Rivera, Rudolfo Anaya, and Rolando Hinojosa were all published. But, as Cisneros points out in an interview with Reed Dasenbrock in *Interviews with Writers of the Post-Colonial World*, Chicanas were still figuring out they did not "have to go the route that society puts on [them]."

University and independent presses took notice of these new female writers. One such publisher, the Arte Publico Press in Houston, which specializes in Latino literature, published *The House on Mango Street*. When the book won the Before Columbus Foundation's American Book Award, Cisneros became the first Chicana writer to garner mainstream attention, prompting a surge of interest in Chicana literature as a whole. Literature by other Latin American women gain attention at the same time.

Since the 1980s, many Latina and Latino writers have gained national prominence, most notably Cuban American Oscar Hijuelos, who won the Pulitzer Prize in 1990 for his book *The Mambo Kings Play Songs of Love*. Cisneros is now considered among the most prominent of popular Latina writers, alongside Dominican American Julia Alvarez, Cuban American Christina Garcia, and Puerto Rican American Judith Ortiz Cofer.

Mexican Immigration

One of the first major waves of Mexican immigration to the United States occurred in the early twentieth century. At the start of the Mexican Revolution in 1910, many Mexicans fled north into the United States in order to avoid the political turmoil and dangers of the revolution. For the most part, these immigrants were elderly or sick, but when fighting escalated in 1914, many middle- and upper-class Mexicans also fled the country in search of peace. According to PBS's *Mexican Revolution and Immigration*, in the years between 1910 and 1920, over 890,000 legal Mexican immigrants came to the United States. Many were hired for jobs in construction, maintenance, and railroad work.

The number of Mexican immigrants entering the country continued to grow in the first half of the century. Because of the proximity between the United States and Mexico, many immigrants moved back and forth between the two countries, just as Esperanza's family does before settling down on Mango Street. As the Library of Congress's "American Memory: Mexican Immigration" records, Mexican immigrants left rural areas in droves and settled in cities such as Los Angeles, San Antonio, Chicago, and Detroit after the Depression. With this urban migration came increasing tension between whites and other ethnic and racial groups in the cities.

World War II led to an increased need for cheap labor, and the United States and Mexico partnered in a program that encouraged immigrants to come to the United States. These laborers were often treated poorly and paid unfairly for their work. The program was especially popular on farms, where a culture of underpaying Mexican workers for backbreaking labor began—and essentially continues to exist to this day. After the war, according to the "American Memory: Mexican Immigration," the U.S. government deported nearly four million immigrants back to Mexico.

Since that time, many Mexican immigrants have opted to come into the United States illegally in order to avoid the expense and bureaucracy involved in legal immigration. These immigrants cross the border in lightly patrolled areas of California, Arizona, New Mexico, and Texas. Many come ill prepared for the harsh desert crossing, and some immigrants die from these conditions every year. Those that do make it into the country are vulnerable to exploitation, as they are fearful of being turned in or deported. According to Samuel P. Huntington in "Reconsidering Immigration: Is Mexico a Special Case?," nearly two-thirds of all illegal immigrants in the United States are Mexican.

Mexicans and Mexican Americans have become an influential presence in the United States, accounting for three percent of the total population with over twenty million people. Some states, particularly those near the border, are home to large percentages of the Mexican and Mexican American population. The Center for Latin American, Caribbean, and Latino Studies cites the following 2000 census numbers: forty-one percent of the Mexican-origin population is found in California; 5.2 percent in Arizona; 24.6 percent in Texas; and 5.5 in Illinois. Though the census counted over twenty million Mexicans and Mexican Americans in the United States, the actual number is unknown due to the continuous influx of illegal immigrants to the country.

CRITICAL OVERVIEW

When *The House on Mango Street* was published in 1984, few reviews followed; the ones that did, mostly in newspapers in the same Southwest region as the publisher, did not give it a full page. Even then, as Maria Elena de Valdes notes in "The Critical Reception of Sandra Cisneros's *The House on Mango Street*," these "brief impressions of the book [were] often hampered by the lack of literary context in which the writers were reporting." This may have been in part because critics had not seen anything quite like *The House on Mango Street* before. Not only is the book written by a Mexican American woman, a rare perspective at the time, but its style and form are both hard to classify. As Robin Ganz notes in "Sandra Cisneros: Border Crossings and Beyond," Cisneros was "the first Chicana to enter the mainstream of literary culture."

Generally, though, the initial reception was positive. *Booklist* finds the writing style too cute at times, but quickly compensates for this admission by writing that the book "is refreshing and authentic, vivid in its metaphors, affectionate in its treatment of the young girl and others, exact in its observations, and full of vitality." In the end, it recommends the book highly.

More people took notice of the book after Cisneros won the American Book Award from the Before Columbus Foundation in 1985. De Valdes describes a review in *ViAztlán* in which Roy Gomez notes "[T]his novel brings home the emerging consciousness of the modern Chicana." Reviews continued as news of the book spread. Literary criticism also began to appear. Scholars explored subjects from patriarchy and violence to feminism and cultural consciousness. Soon, the book was appearing on reading lists in classrooms across the country, and preadolescents and college students alike were discussing Esperanza and her neighbors. When it was republished in 1991 by Vintage, another flurry

MEDIA ADAPTATIONS

The unabridged audio version of *The House on Mango Street* (2005) is available on CD by RH Audio. It is read by Sandra Cisneros.

of publicity followed. The *Los Angeles Times* calls it "poetic and perceptive," saying its writing style "bespeaks [Cisneros's] unusual talent."

Cisneros has published two collections of poetry, a collection of short stories, and a novel since her debut, but it is almost impossible to find mention of any of them without the reviewer first nodding to *The House on Mango Street*. By the time *Woman Hollering Creek* was published in 1991, Cisneros warranted a review in the *New York Times* by well-known writer Bebe Moore Campbell. Campbell calls *The House on Mango Street* "radiant." The success of the book and Cisneros's emergence as a major writer gives American literature a welcome new perspective.

CRITICISM

Jacqueline Doyle

In the following excerpt, Doyle compares Cisneros's The House on Mango Street *to the aims of Virginia Woolf's "A Room of One's Own" and explores how Cisneros has been able to give voice to the stories of Chicana women.*

"Books continue each other," Virginia Woolf told an audience of young women some sixty years ago, "in spite of our habit of judging them separately."

While feminists following Woolf's advice to "think back through our mothers" have expanded the literary canon in the past two decades, too many have ignored the questions of race, ethnicity, and class in women's literature. Adrienne Rich laments the "white solipsism" of white feminists—"not the consciously held *belief*

that one race is inherently superior to all others, but a tunnel-vision which simply does not see nonwhite experience or existence as precious or significant." Barbara Smith, Alice Walker, and Toni Morrison have angrily denounced the canon implicit in early studies of women's literature such as Moers's and Spacks's. To Spacks's tepid defense that she preferred to dwell on authors depicting "familiar experience" and a "familiar cultural setting," Walker counters: "Why only these? Because they are white, and middle class, and because to Spacks, female imagination is only that—a limitation that even white women must find restrictive."

Cisneros's *The House on Mango Street*, dedicated in two languages "A las Mujeres/To the Women," both continues Woolf's meditations and alters the legacy of *A Room of One's Own* in important ways. Her series of vignettes is about the maturing of a young Chicana and the development of a writer; it is about the women she grows up with; it is also about a sense of community, culture, and place. Esperanza, the young protagonist, yearns for "a space for myself to go, clean as paper before the poem," and for a house of her own:

> Not a flat. Not an apartment in back. Not a man's house. Not a daddy's. A house all my own. With my porch and my pillow, my pretty purple petunias. My books and my stories. My two shoes waiting beside the bed. Nobody to shake a stick at. Nobody's garbage to pick up after.

The dilapidated series of apartments and houses Esperanza inhabits with her mother, father, sister, and two brothers—particularly their dwelling on Mango Street—represents her poverty, but also the richness of her subject matter. "Like it or not you are Mango Street," her friend Alicia tells her, "and one day you'll come back too." "You must remember to come back," the three aged sisters tell her, "for the ones who cannot leave as easily as you." *A Room of One's Own* would seem to allow Esperanza this subject, even to encourage it. "All these infinitely obscure lives remain to be recorded," as Woolf told her young female audience. Pondering the shopgirl behind the counter, she commented, "I would as soon have her true history as the hundred and fiftieth life of Napoleon." But Woolf's class and ethnic biases might also deter Esperanza from achieving her own literary voice.

Cisneros's *The House on Mango Street* covertly transforms the terms of Woolf's vision, making room in the female literary tradition for a young working-class Chicana who "like[s] to tell stories": "I make a story for my life," Esperanza tells us, "for each step my brown shoe takes. I say, 'And so she trudged up the wooden stairs, her sad brown shoes taking her to the house she never liked.' " If Esperanza's name means "too many letters," means "sadness" in the life she knows in Spanish, it translates as "hope" in English. Thinking back through her mothers and their comadres and across through her sisters, she builds her house from the unfulfilled hopes and dreams around her. "I could've been somebody, you know?" sighs her mother. As Esperanza revises and lays claim to her matrilineal inheritance, so Cisneros in *Mango Street* offers a rich reconsideration of the contemporary feminist inheritance as well.

While Woolf expresses the hope that young women of the future will actually be "capable of earning over five hundred a year," and suggests that they limit child-bearing to "twos and threes" rather than "tens and twelves," she seems to overlook the obstacles to creative freedom that a job and motherhood might pose even for the woman privileged with an income and a room of her own. She sees little future for women without those privileges.

Cisneros has acknowledged the importance of Woolf's belief that a room of one's own is a necessary precondition for writing. Allowing her room of her own, Cisneros's mother enabled her daughter to create: "I'm here," Cisneros explained to an audience of young writers, "because my mother let me stay in my room reading and studying, perhaps because she didn't want me to inherit her sadness and her rolling pin." In "Living as a Writer," Cisneros again stresses that she has "always had a room of [her] own": "As Virginia Woolf has said, a woman writer needs money, leisure, and a room of her own."

Woolf stressed the importance of a female tradition for the woman writer: "we think back through our mothers if we are women." For both Alice Walker and Sandra Cisneros, these mothers include women outside the "tradition" as it is conventionally understood, women who, perhaps anonymously, "handed on the creative spark, the seed of the flower they themselves never hoped to see; or . . . a sealed letter they could not plainly read." Esperanza's mother—her encouragement, but also what she has not written, not expressed—is central to the community of female relationships informing her daughter's development as an artist. Esperanza's tribute to her mother, "A Smart Cookie," opens: "I could've been somebody, you know? my mother says and sighs." Her list of talents—"She can speak two languages. She can sing an opera. She knows how to fix a T.V."—is framed by her confinement in a city whose subway system she has never mastered, and extended in a list of unfulfilled desires: "Someday she would like to go to the ballet. Someday she would like to see a play." *The House on Mango Street* strikingly enacts what Rachel Blau DuPlessis sees as a "specific biographical drama that has entered and shaped *Künstlerromane* by women": "Such a narrative is engaged with a maternal figure and . . . is often compensatory for her losses. . . . The daughter becomes an artist to extend, reveal, and elaborate her mother's often thwarted talents." Esperanza's mother points to the girl's godmothers (her own *comadres*, or, literally translated, "comothers," powerful family figures in Chicano culture) as examples of the necessity "to take care all your own." In the extended filiations of her ethnic community Esperanza finds a network of maternal figures. She writes to celebrate all of their unfulfilled talents and dreams and to compensate for their losses.

Woolf specified gender and class as the two subject areas yet to be explored. The female writer of the future need no longer depict women exclusively in relation to men; she would be free to explore "relationships between women," particularly friendships, "those unrecorded gestures, those unsaid or half-said words, which form themselves, no more palpably than the shadows of moths on the ceiling, when women are alone, unlit by the capricious and coloured light of the other sex." Further, Woolf wrote, "[S]he will not need to limit herself any longer to the respectable houses of the upper middle classes." In lectures Cisneros has explained that her subject emerged in a "defensive and rebellious" reaction to her white middle-class fellow graduate students at the University of Iowa Writer's Workshop: "My intent was simply to chronicle, to write about something my classmates couldn't."

Poverty was the "ghost" she attempted to escape before she found her subject, Cisneros told an audience of young writers. "As a poor person growing up in a society where the class norm was superimposed on a t.v. screen, I couldn't understand why our home wasn't all green lawn and white wood like the ones in 'Leave It To Beaver' or 'Father Knows Best.'" The metaphor of the house emerged, Cisneros said, in a heated graduate seminar discussion of Gaston Bachelard's *Poetics of Space*: "What did I know except third-floor flats. Surely my classmates knew nothing about that. That's precisely what I chose to write: about third-floor flats, and fear of rats, and drunk husbands sending rocks through windows, anything as far from the poetic as possible."

The domestic realm arouses a variety of responses in contemporary women writers. Tillie Olsen has most vividly described the difficulty of making space in a woman's daily life for writing: "habits of years—response to others, distractibility, responsibility for daily matters—stay with you, mark you, become you." Esperanza boldly proclaims her intention to break these habits early: "I have begun my own quiet war. Simple. Sure. I am one who leaves the table like a man, without putting back the chair or picking up the plate." Gender roles, as well as class, condition Esperanza's response to women's confinement to the household. Olivares is largely correct in his central premise that "for Cisneros the inside, the here, can be confinement and a source of anguish and alienation." In story after story of the women in her community, Esperanza recognizes that a room—if not of one's own—can be stifling.

Her own grandmother, unhappily married, "looked out the window all her life, the way so many women sit their sadness on an elbow." Because Rafaela is beautiful, her husband locks her indoors on Tuesday nights while he plays dominoes; Rafaela is "still young," Esperanza explains, "but getting old from leaning out the window so much." Louie's cousin Marin "can't come out—gotta baby-sit with Louie's sisters—but she stands in the doorway a lot." "We never see Marin until her aunt comes home from work," Esperanza tells us, "and even then she can only stay out front." Across the street on the third floor, Mamacita, who speaks no English, "sits all day by the window and plays the Spanish radio shows and sings all the homesick songs about her country." Sally's father keeps her inside and beats her when he thinks of his sisters who ran away. Later Sally's husband won't let her talk on the phone or even look out the window:

> She sits at home because she is afraid to go outside without his permission. She looks at all the things they own: the towels and the toaster, the alarm clock and the drapes. She likes looking at the walls, at how neatly their corners meet, the linoleum roses on the floor, the ceiling smooth as wedding cake.

Princes are conspicuously absent or threatening in almost all of Esperanza's stories. Rosa Vargas's husband "left without even leaving a dollar for bologna or a note explaining how come." Minerva's "mother raised her kids alone and it looks like her daughters will go that way too." Edna's daughter Ruthie sleeps on a couch in her living room and "says she's just visiting and next weekend her husband's gonna come back to take her home. But the weekends come and go and Ruthie stays." Esperanza's god-mothers' husbands left or died. Minerva's husband, who "left and keeps leaving," throws a rock through the window when she "finally" puts him out. "Then he is sorry and she opens the door again. Same story. Next week she comes over black and blue and asks what can she do? Minerva. I don't know which way she'll go. There is nothing *I* can do." When Sally marries a marshmallow salesman out of state, she tells Esperanza she is in love, but Esperanza thinks "she did it to escape" her father's beatings. Trapped in her room with its linoleum roses and "ceiling smooth as wedding cake," Sally is imprisoned by the very prince who was to rescue her.

Indifferent to the prince's glass slipper, Esperanza seeks to develop an autonomous identity. She and Lucy and Rachel decisively abandon their high heels after a day of playing grownup princesses at the ball. In a related episode, Esperanza, dressed in new clothes for her cousin's baptism, is ashamed to dance because of her old and scuffed brown and white saddle shoes.

Esperanza reconciles herself to "ordinary shoes" as she will later reconcile herself to Mango Street. In both cases this reconciliation entails a new freedom, to dance, to imagine a house of her own with her "two shoes waiting beside the bed," a house "quiet as snow," "clean as paper before the poem." The blank page allows her the freedom to imagine new scripts for women's lives. "You can never have too much sky," she tells us.

Source: Jacqueline Doyle, "More Room of Her Own: Sandra Cisnero's *The House on Mango Street*," in *Melus*, Vol. 19, No. 4, Winter 1994, pp. 5–35.

SOURCES

"American Memory: Mexican Immigration," *Library of Congress*, memory.loc.gov/learn/features/immig/mexican (January 31, 2006).

Campbell, Bebe Moore, "Crossing Borders," in *New York Times*, May 26, 1991. p. A1.

Cisneros, Sandra, "Do You Know Me?: I Wrote *The House on Mango Street*," in the *Americas Review*, Vol. 15, No. 1, Spring 1987, pp. 77–79.

———, *The House on Mango Street*, Vintage Contemporaries, 1991, originally published in 1984.

Dasenbrock, Reed Way, "Sandra Cisneros," in *Interviews with Writers of the Post-Colonial World*, edited by Feroza Jussawalla and Reed Way Dasenbrock, University Press of Mississippi, 1992, pp. 298–306.

de Valdes, Maria Elena, "The Critical Reception of Sandra Cisneros's *The House on Mango Street*," in *Gender, Self, and Society: Proceedings of the IV International Conference on the Hispanic Cultures of the United States*, edited by Renate von Bardeleben, Peter Lang Publishing, 1993. pp. 287–95.

Ganz, Robin, "Sandra Cisneros: Border Crossings and Beyond," in *Melus*, Spring 1994, pp. 19–30.

Huntington, Samuel P., "Reconsidering Immigration: Is Mexico a Special Case?", *Center for Immigration Studies*, www.cis.org/articles/2000/ black1100.html (November 2000).

"Mexican Revolution and Immigration," *Public Broadcasting Service*, www.pbs.org/kpbs/theborder/history/timeline/14.html (January 31, 2006).

"Mexican-Origin Population of the U.S. in Percentages of Total Mexican-Origin Population, by State, Census 2000," *Center for Latin American, Caribbean, and Latino Studies*, web.gc.cuny.edu/lastudies/Mexican%20Population%20 by%20State,%20largest%20concentrations.pdf (January 31, 2006).

Review of *The House on Mango Street*, in *Booklist*, October 15, 1984, p. 281.

"I Have a Dream"

MARTIN LUTHERKING JR.

1963

Martin Luther King Jr. delivered his "I Have a Dream" speech on August 28, 1963, at the March on Washington for Jobs and Freedom. Many regard it as the greatest speech of the twentieth century and, more than that, one of the greatest speeches in history. Though King was one of several featured speakers that day, "I Have a Dream" became synonymous with the aims of the march and the entire civil rights movement. His dream represented the dream of millions of Americans demanding a free, equal, and just nation.

A scholar and a pastor, King was able to combine academic, political, and biblical elements in his "I Have a Dream" speech. He referenced the Bill of Rights, the Declaration of Independence, the Emancipation Proclamation, and the Bible. When delivering his address, he spoke with accessible language and used repetition to drive home important points; the phrase "I have a dream" is repeated nine times in the speech. Though King had a script in front of him, as the speech progressed and the crowd responded, he began to improvise his message. The "I have a dream" section of the speech is the most well-known portion of the address, and it was entirely extemporaneous. The power of this section is a testament to King's oratory skills and the conviction with which he spoke. Just as his namesake Martin Luther sparked the Protestant Reformation in the sixteenth century, King and his "I Have a Dream" speech emboldened his followers and changed history.

In the speech, King demands the same justice and equality for black Americans that is promised to all citizens in the Declaration of Independence. While he calls on fellow civil rights activists to persevere in the face of brutality, violence, and oppression, he also cautions against the use of violence. King believed in what Henry David Thoreau termed "civil disobedience," in which individuals use nonviolent means to achieve social change, and studied Mahatma Gandhi's peaceful protests for Indian independence in the 1930s and 1940s. "Again and again," he counsels the crowd, "we must rise to the majestic heights of meeting physical force with soul force."

Television played an important role in delivering King's speech to the masses. Recent events in the civil rights struggle had been televised, including police brutality in Birmingham, Alabama, earlier in 1963, and television had become an important catalyst for the civil rights movement. The March on Washington, including King's speech, was broadcast live throughout the country. This allowed leaders like King to reach a new demographic. As William G. Thomas III writes in "Television News and the Civil Rights Struggle":

> They had talked to the converted and they had talked to the irreconcilable, but it was the vast mass of Americans who either had no opinion of the matter or did not yet care that they needed to reach.

"I Have a Dream" comprises a large part of King's legacy. Portions of the speech are instantly recognizable and have become part of America's culture. King's dream became the nation's dream, and it did not die when he was assassinated in 1968. That year, his widow Coretta Scott King founded the King Center for Nonviolent Social Change in Atlanta, Georgia, as a way of furthering her husband's work for change. In 1986, King became the only twentieth-century figure whose birthday has been designated a public holiday, celebrated on the third Monday of January. However, it was not until 1993 that Martin Luther King Day was celebrated in all fifty states.

The text of "I Have a Dream" is widely available on the Internet and is collected in several anthologies and books, including *I Have a Dream: Writings and Speeches That Changed the World*, by Martin Luther King, and the *American Rhetoric* website at www.americanrhetoric.com.

BUT ONE HUNDRED YEARS LATER, THE NEGRO STILL IS NOT FREE. ONE HUNDRED YEARS LATER, THE LIFE OF THE NEGRO IS STILL SADLY CRIPPLED BY THE MANACLES OF SEGREGATION AND THE CHAINS OF DISCRIMINATION. ONE HUNDRED YEARS LATER, THE NEGRO LIVES ON A LONELY ISLAND OF POVERTY IN THE MIDST OF A VAST OCEAN OF MATERIAL PROSPERITY. ONE HUNDRED YEARS LATER, THE NEGRO IS STILL LANGUISHED IN THE CORNERS OF AMERICAN SOCIETY AND FINDS HIMSELF AN EXILE IN HIS OWN LAND."

PLOT SUMMARY

Martin Luther King Jr. greets the crowd assembled at the Lincoln Memorial by expressing his joy over the turnout for "the greatest demonstration for freedom in the history of our nation." He refers to Abraham Lincoln, in whose "symbolic shadow" the crowd is gathered. Lincoln was responsible for issuing the Emancipation Proclamation in 1863, thus freeing American slaves from "the long night of their captivity." However, King continues, black Americans are far from free one hundred years later. Segregation, discrimination, poverty, and marginalization remain realities for black Americans in the 1960s, and it is for the purpose of dramatizing this "shameful condition" that hundreds of thousands have gathered for the March on Washington.

He tells the crowd that they have come to the nation's capital to "cash a check" that was promised to all men by the Declaration of Independence. All Americans, regardless of color, are heirs to the promise of life, liberty, and the pursuit of happiness, yet he declares the government has defaulted on this promise for black Americans. He says that blacks have received instead a "bad check, a check which has come back marked 'insufficient funds.'" But the crowd gathered at the capital, King says, refuses to believe there are not enough funds or opportunity for all Americans, and thus they have

BIOGRAPHY

MARTIN LUTHER KING JR.

Martin Luther King Jr. was born January 15, 1929, in Atlanta, Georgia, to Martin Luther King Sr. and Alberta Williams King. His father was the pastor of Ebenezer Baptist Church in Atlanta and provided him with a middle-class upbringing that allowed for a more extensive education than was typically available to black children in the South. Though it was expected that King would follow in his father and maternal grandfather's footsteps and become a pastor, he was initially more interested in working for social change.

King attended Morehouse College in 1944 and, after a change of heart in 1948, entered Crozer Theological Seminary. From there, he attended Boston University, where he received his Ph.D. in 1955. Shortly after, he became the pastor of Dexter Avenue Baptist Church in Montgomery, Alabama, where he was instrumental in organizing the Montgomery bus boycott in 1955. He was named the president of Southern Christian Leadership Conference (SCLC) in 1957, a position that gave him even wider influence on the civil rights movement. King married Coretta Scott in 1953, and the couple had four children.

Throughout the 1950s and 1960s, King led nonviolent protests, demonstrations, and marches in support of civil rights across the South, and was a featured speaker at the 1963 March on Washington. He won the Nobel Peace Prize in 1964. On April 4, 1968, King was assassinated in Memphis, Tennessee.

Dr. Martin Luther King, Jr. The Library of Congress

come to demand "the riches of freedom and the security of justice."

King emphasizes the importance of making sweeping changes to the racial disparity found in America. He rejects the idea of gradual changes or taking excess time to consider the problem. He demands immediate action and encourages the rise of brotherhood and equality throughout the country in order to "make justice a reality for all of God's children." King insists that black Americans will continue to rise against institutionalized racism and injustice until these evils are eliminated. This is not a temporary letting off of steam or a momentary need for revolt, he warns: "[T]here will be neither rest nor tranquility in America until the Negro is granted his citizenship rights."

He implores lawful and peaceful demonstrations and acts of civil disobedience. He warns against falling into rage, bitterness, and hate, extolling the crowd to seek the "high plane of dignity and discipline." Peace and equality will not be possible through hatred, especially by blacks hating white people, as King notes that there are many whites in the crowd as well, and "they have come to realize that their freedom is inextricably bound to our freedom. We cannot walk alone." Those fighting for freedom must always seek progress and forward motion; they cannot stop and cannot turn back.

King turns his attention to those watching the civil rights movement from the outside, wondering when the civil rights activists will be satisfied.

To this question, he responds: "We can never be satisfied as long as the Negro is victim of the unspeakable horrors of police brutality." Alluding to the book of Amos in the Bible, King says they will not be satisfied until "justice rolls down like waters, and righteousness like a mighty stream."

He acknowledges that it has not been an easy struggle for many present in the crowd, who have endured brutality, violence, and jail time. He encourages them to continue their fight:

> Go back to Mississippi, go back to Alabama, go back to South Carolina, go back to Georgia, go back to Louisiana, go back to the slums and ghettos of our northern cities, knowing that somehow this situation can and will be changed.

Encouraging the crowd not to be disheartened or defeated, King tells them that he has a dream, "a dream deeply rooted in the American dream." He dreams of a day when the descendents of slaves and slaveholders in Georgia will sit down together; when Mississippi, "a state sweltering with the heat of oppression," will be a place of freedom to all; and when black and white children will hold hands and join together in the state of Alabama. King dreams of a day when his four children will live in a country "where they will not be judged by the color of their skin but by the content of their character." He dreams of a day when all the obstacles preventing equality and respect between black and whites in America have been leveled. It is with the faith in this dream that King resolves to return to the South and fight. This faith can unify the masses, and "we will be able to hew out of the mountain of despair a stone of hope." This faith will sustain those who fight, "knowing that we will be free one day."

On the day that this freedom is achieved, King believes that all Americans will be able to sing "My Country 'Tis of Thee" with new meaning. The words to this anthem must be true in order for America to be a great nation. King closes his speech by invoking freedom to ring from New York to California, but also from "Stone Mountain of Georgia ... Lookout Mountain of Tennessee ... [and] every hill and molehill of Mississippi." He assures that when this freedom is a reality,

> we will be able to speed up that day when all of God's children, black men and white men, Jews and Gentiles, Protestants and Catholics, will be able to join hands and sing in the words of the old Negro spiritual: "Free at last! Free at last! Thank God Almighty, we are free at last!"

THEMES

Equality

The purpose behind the 1963 March on Washington for Jobs and Freedom and King's speech was a demand for equality for all Americans, regardless of skin color. King speaks in front of the Lincoln Memorial one hundred years after Lincoln issued the Emancipation Proclamation. Though the Proclamation legally freed the slaves, King argues that "one hundred years later, the Negro still is not free" because of racism and discrimination. Segregation, Jim Crow laws, fear, and violence have kept black Americans from enjoying freedom and equality, and instead "the Negro is still languished in the corners of American society and finds himself an exile in his own land." America's persistence in this inequality based solely on race is keeping the country from truly being great, King insists. He encourages those fighting for equality and freedom to continue their fight in a peaceful manner, confident in the knowledge that this collective action has the power to change the nation. He tells the crowd not to despair over the struggle and not to give up: "I have a dream that one day this nation will rise up and live out the true meaning of its creed: 'We hold these truths to be self-evident, that all men are created equal.'" King is certain that this dream will some day lead to a country where equality is the birthright of every citizen of every color. Until then, he says, blacks and whites fighting for equality will continue their peaceful, determined fight: "This sweltering summer of the Negro's legitimate discontent will not pass until there is an invigorating autumn of freedom and equality."

Justice

King's demand for equality is a demand for justice. In a nation that prides itself on constitutional justice and freedom, the lack of both for black citizens denies them their quintessential American rights. King points to the Declaration of Independence's promise of the "Inalienable Rights" of "Life, Liberty, and the Pursuit of Happiness" for every man. He states that the government has written a "bad check" to black Americans with respect to those rights, and he is demanding full payment. He refuses to believe that "there are insufficient funds in the great vaults of opportunity of this nation." Therefore, black citizens' lack of access to these rights and opportunities constitutes an injustice, one that

The March on Washington, 1963 National Archives and Records Administration

must be immediately righted. Rejecting calls for gradualism or time to think, King insists, "Now is the time to make real the promises of democracy. Now is the time to rise from the dark and desolate valley of segregation to the sunlit path of racial justice."

On the theme of justice, King alludes to the Old Testament book of Amos, in which Israel's prosperity conceals corruption, asserting that "we will not be satisfied until justice rolls down like waters, and righteousness like a mighty stream." King dreams of the day when justice will come, allowing his children and future generations of black Americans to be judged on their individual merit, rather than physical characteristics. On that day, Americans of every color, creed, race, and gender will be able to sing "My country, 'tis of thee / sweet land of liberty" with the conviction that is it true for every citizen. King is adamant that the livelihood and future of the country depends on this: "[I]f America is to be a great nation, this must become true." Justice for every American is nothing short of the American dream itself, King argues, and his dream for this justice is therefore nothing less than a patriotic plea. He urges for

freedom to ring not only in the North, but in the South as well, and in every place in America.

Oppression

By 1963, the civil rights movement had been a force to be reckoned with for several years, after having slowly gathered steam for generations. As the movement grew, so did the violent response to it. Many in the crowd who heard King's speech, and even King himself, had been victims of violence and oppression, both at the hands of private citizens and public servants. In the opening paragraphs of King's speech, he refers to this brutality as a modern slavery: "the manacles of segregation and the chains of discrimination." Because of this subjugation, King explains, both black and white citizens fighting for racial equality will not cease until freedom has been won, no matter what the consequences might be: "The whirlwinds of revolt will continue" until justice has been achieved for all.

King's speech is peppered with references to the oppressive system that blacks are forced to live under, not only in the South, but in northern cities as well. He refers to the voting restrictions in Mississippi that make it nearly impossible for a black person to vote, and the "Negro in New York [who] believes he has nothing for which to vote." He also calls Mississippi a state "sweltering with the heat of oppression," and refers to Alabama with "its vicious racists, with its governor having his lips dripping with the words of 'interposition' and 'nullification.'"

Though he acknowledges the heavy price many have paid for their participation in the civil rights movement, King cautions against turning to violence. He refuses to embrace the same brutal, dehumanizing tactics that many white segregationists and racist politicians have employed in an effort to keep black Americans separate and unequal. King recognizes those who have been jailed, "veterans of creative suffering," and those who have been "battered by the storms of persecution and staggered by the winds of police brutality." Yet despite these hardships, King encourages those who have suffered this violence to return to the South and keep fighting, "knowing that somehow this situation can and will be changed."

Brotherhood

Throughout his speech, King repeatedly uses the term *we* to refer to those involved in the fight for civil rights. This rhetorical device has the effect of creating unity and suggests the brotherhood of those involved in the civil rights movement. By doing so, King connects individual suffering with the greater movement, creating the big picture of progress. In this way, civil rights proponents are forwarding the movement "until the bright day of justice emerges" each time one is threatened, beaten, or jailed.

The solidarity that King encourages is not just among black Americans, but among all Americans fighting for civil rights. As he looks out into the crowd, he acknowledges "our white brothers" who are a part of the movement and cautions against a rising black militancy that leads to a "distrust of all white people." "We cannot walk alone," King points out, and therefore "we must make the pledge that we shall always march ahead." As King relates his dream for a free America, he speaks on behalf of all black Americans, and indeed every American of every color. His dream is a future where color does not divide the nation, and where the freedoms promised in Lincoln's Emancipation Proclamation are realities. King has faith in this dream; it is why he fights and

why he will return to the South. But he knows this faith in the dream is not his alone, but that of the brotherhood of both white and black civil rights activists. "With this faith," he says, "we will be able to work together, to pray together, to struggle together, to go to jail together, to stand up for freedom together, knowing that we will be free one day."

HISTORICAL OVERVIEW

King and the Civil Rights Movement

Though black Americans had been struggling for equality and freedom since the rise of Jim Crow legislation at the end of the nineteenth century, the civil rights movement began in earnest with the use of civil disobedience, or the disregard for unjust laws. In 1955, African American Rosa Parks refused to yield her seat on a Montgomery, Alabama, bus to a white passenger. Her subsequent arrest led to a boycott of the Montgomery bus system, organized in part by Martin Luther King Jr. The boycott lasted for thirteen months and resulted in the integration of the bus system.

In the wake of the success in Montgomery, black leaders formed the Southern Christian Leadership Conference (SCLC) as a way to organize further social protests against segregation and racism in the South. King became a major figure and main spokesman for the SCLC as its president and traveled across the country giving speeches and participating in rallies. After a trip to India, King became increasingly interested in Gandhi's nonviolent protest tactics and encouraged civil rights supporters in the United States to embrace peaceful, passive resistance rather than violence.

In 1963, King traveled to Birmingham, Alabama, a stronghold in the segregationist South. He helped organize a protest against segregated lunch counters and downtown stores. Alabama police officers with attack dogs and billy clubs met these first protests. The city sought an injunction against King and his associates to prevent them from congregating in town; when King refused to follow the order, he was arrested and found guilty of contempt of court. When he was released, he organized a second march that included many women, students, and children. Under the direction of police commissioner Bull Connor, Birmingham police turned high-pressure fire hoses on the unarmed protesters and jailed nearly three thousand. In 1964, the year King won the Nobel Peace Prize, the Civil Rights Act was passed by Congress, banning discrimination in schools, public areas, and the workplace.

In 1965, King organized a voters march in Selma, Alabama, which was met with similar resistance. Six hundred civil rights marchers were attacked by police on the Edmund Pettus Bridge on March 7; only one-third of the marchers reached Selma. The day become known as "Bloody Sunday" and was televised nationwide. The event drew national attention and helped bring increasing awareness to the civil rights movement. Two marches followed. That year, President Johnson signed the Voting Rights Act into law, which prohibited discrimination, literacy tests, and poll taxes in voting places.

March on Washington

The concept for the March on Washington originated in the early 1940s. Angered at how black Americans failed to prosper from the New Deal programs during the Depression, A. Philip Randolph, a labor union president and civil rights activist, organized a march to demand change. He initially called for five thousand participants, but as news of the march grew and was published in black newspapers, the expected turnout grew to tens of thousands. In order to avoid the embarrassment that such a march could bring to his administration, President Franklin D. Roosevelt signed Executive Order 8802, which prohibited racial discrimination in certain lines of work. The march was cancelled.

The idea of a march resurfaced in the 1960s as the civil rights movement gathered momentum and began to see progress. The organizers of the march hoped that it would influence the civil rights legislation that was stalled in Congress. Randolph organized the march, with a goal of bringing one hundred thousand people to the nation's capital to demand freedom and equality. Organizations such as the SCLC and the NAACP (National Association for the Advancement of Colored People) lent their support to the march. On August 28, 1963, over two hundred thousand citizens, black and white, participated in the march of nearly a mile from the Washington Monument to the Lincoln Memorial. In "Backers Pleased with Washington Civil Rights March," Al Kuettner quotes Floyd McKissick,

the chairman of the board of the Congress of Racial Equality, as saying that the march marked "the end of the Negro protest and the beginning of the American protest." Kuettner also notes President Kennedy's reaction to the peaceful assembly; the president "could not help but be impressed with the 'deep fervor and the quiet dignity' of the gathering." Kennedy backed the Civil Rights Act that summer, and it became law in the 1964.

Though the 1963 March on Washington for Jobs and Freedom was overwhelmingly viewed as a success, there was quite a bit of opposition to it. President Kennedy himself was initially opposed to the march for fear that it would anger segregationists in Congress and permanently sink the Civil Rights Act. White supremacist groups such as the Ku Klux Klan feared the galvanizing power of the march. Some black groups also opposed it; Malcolm X and the Nation of Islam prohibited its members from participating, as they viewed the march as a whitewashing of the race issue in America. Thomas's "Television News and the Civil Rights Struggle" records that Virginia Congressman Thomas N. Downing called the March itself "orderly, well done, and well coordinated." Yet, many Southern lawmakers were derisive about the march's ultimate ability to make an impact; Congressman J. Vaughan Gary dismissed the march as nothing more than "a giant pep rally" (quoted in Thomas).

King's Assassination

On April 4, 1968, Martin Luther King Jr. was in Memphis, Tennessee, preparing for a demonstration on behalf of the predominantly black local sanitation workers' union. That evening, while on the balcony of the Lorraine Motel near downtown Memphis, King was shot in the throat by a sniper in a nearby building. He was rushed to the hospital and pronounced dead an hour later. Following the news of King's death, riots broke out in over sixty U.S. cities. President Johnson declared April 9, the day of King's funeral, a national day of mourning. Over three hundred thousand mourners attended the funeral.

The night before his assassination, King delivered a speech in Memphis that has come to be known as "I've Been to the Mountaintop." In it, he appears to presage his own death, though he is focused only on the victory to come:

A man stands under a "Colored Waiting Room" sign outside a bus station The Library of Congress

Like anybody, I would like to live a long life. Longevity has its place. But I'm not concerned about that now. I just want to do God's will. And He's allowed me to go up to the mountain. And I've looked over. And I've seen the Promised Land. I may not get there with you. But I want you to know tonight, that we, as a people, will get to the promised land!

James Earl Ray was apprehended two months after King's assassination and pleaded guilty to the murder. In 1969, he received a ninety-nine-year sentence. Until his death in 1998, the imprisoned Ray insisted that he was not involved with the murder and had never intended to plead guilty. His initial plea had eliminated the need for a trial, and Ray petitioned the court for an opportunity to try his case. King's son Dexter became an unexpected ally in Ray's cause, and the entire King family fought on Ray's behalf for an opportunity to try the case in open court. Ray maintained that his brother Johnny and a Canadian man using the alias "Raoul" were involved in the assassination and that he himself did not shoot King. The King family maintains that Ray was not involved in the assassination. The Lorraine Motel is today the site of the National Civil Rights Museum, where King's hotel room—preserved as it was on the night of his death—serves as the final exhibit.

CRITICAL OVERVIEW

The speech "I Have a Dream" by Martin Luther King Jr. closed the March on Washington for Jobs and Freedom and immediately came to symbolize the civil rights movement. By the time of the march, King's reputation was already nationally known; in a 1962 *New York Times* article titled "Spokesman for Negroes; Martin Luther King Jr.," King is noted as having "power and prestige approach[ing] the dimensions of Booker T. Washington." For many Americans, King was the face of the civil rights movement. His academic training and experience as a pastor helped him become a great orator. He drew on biblical, historical, political, and educational images and themes in his speeches, which allowed him to reach a wide audience. In "Voice Merging and Self-Making: The Epistemology of 'I Have a Dream,'" Keith Miller refers to this mix of influences, stating "No other liberal or radical in [the twentieth] century has approached King's success in defining the stock motifs of nationalism and Biblical religion as demands for massive social change."

Reaction to King's speech was immediate and overwhelming. The more than two hundred thousand march participants gathered at the Lincoln Memorial applauded wildly. According to "Marching for a Dream" in *Time* magazine, as President Kennedy listened to King's speech, he remarked that King was "damn good."

The true measure of King's speech was felt long after it was delivered, and many critics and historians use it as a meter to measure the progress made toward racial equality and justice. While some praise the strides made since 1963, many see various unfulfilled promises yet to be addressed. Peter Ling calls the speech "far more of an icon than a simple historical document" in "Martin Luther King's Half-Forgotten Dream." In Jerelyn Eddings's "'I Have a Dream'—30 Years Ago and Now," she notes the "emotional chord" that King's speech struck, and that the "magic of the moment was that it gave white America a new perspective on black America and pushed civil rights forward on the nation's agenda." However, writing thirty years later, she notes that the discrimination King spoke out against still exists, yet it is "more a matter of dark hearts than evil laws." Pamela Schaeffer agrees in "A Dream Dishonored After 30 Years." Quoting scholar Roger D. Hatch, Schaeffer writes that "some of King's most ardent ideals seem frozen in time," and that Hatch believes that "King's 1963 message has been twisted and exploited by opponents of civil rights."

In 2003, on the fortieth anniversary of the March on Washington and King's speech, thousands of black Americans gathered at the nation's capital to reflect on King's dream. In "Dr. Martin Luther King, Jr.'s Dream Remembered as Thousands Gather at Lincoln Memorial" in *Jet* magazine, King's son Martin Luther King III speaks of the enduring legacy of his father's words: "I do think people remember because they resonate so clearly. . . . Components of the dream have been realized, but the entire vision of freedom, justice and equality for all humankind has not." In the *Black Collegian*, Martin Luther King III further reflects on the impact of his father's speech in "'I Have a Dream': 40 Years Later," in which he remembers his father as "more than a dreamer" whose top priority was "redeeming the bad check that America had given African Americans."

Numerous books and texts have been devoted to studying King's rhetoric and impact on American and world history. It is often studied in history and speech curricula, as well as English courses. As Doug DuBrin notes in "'I Have a Dream' as a Work of Literature," King's speech "became one of the most influential and inspirational pieces of rhetoric in American

MEDIA ADAPTATIONS

Audio recordings of Martin Luther King's "I Have a Dream" speech are widely available on the Internet, including www.americanrhetoric.com/speeches/Ihaveadream.htm where it is available as an audio MP3.

Martin Luther King Jr.—I Have a Dream is a collection of archival footage and images including King's memorable speech, scenes of opposition that civil rights supporters faced in Alabama, King's death, and Robert Kennedy's eulogy. It is available on VHS and DVD from Mpi Home Video.

The Speeches Collection: Martin Luther King, Jr. is a collection of King's speeches, including "I Have a Dream" and "I've Been to the Mountaintop," among others. It is available on VHS from Mpi Home Video.

The 1978 television miniseries *King* follows King's rise in the civil rights movement, from his days as a pastor in Alabama to his assassination in Memphis. Starring Paul Winfield as King and Cicely Tyson as Coretta Scott King, the series is directed by Abby Mann. It is available on DVD from MGM.

history." In 2000, *USA Today* reported that "I Have a Dream" had been rated as the greatest political speech of the twentieth century, topping other notable entries such as John F. Kennedy's inaugural address, Franklin D. Roosevelt's "A Date that Will Live in Infamy," and Malcolm X's "The Ballot or the Bullet."

CRITICISM

Anne Wortham
In the following excerpt, Wortham argues that King's appeal to the masses in his "I Have a Dream" speech rather than the individual was a

critical mistake that negatively impacted future generations of black Americans.

Annually, throughout the month of February, known as Black History Month, Martin Luther King Jr.'s voice punctuates the airwaves like a public-service announcement, delivering his "I Have a Dream" speech at the 1963 March for Jobs and Freedom in Washington, D.C.

What listeners usually hear is the speech's rousing "Let freedom ring!" finale, which begins with King's invocation of the patriotic hymn "America" and ends with the vision of

> the day when all God's children—black men and white men, Jews and Gentiles, Protestants and Catholics—will be able to join hands and sing in the words of the old Negro spiritual, "Free at last! Free at last! Thank God Almighty, we are free at last!"

Although this climax receives the most airplay and seems to be most often included in film documentaries, it is the preceding "Dream" sequence that is most often quoted. King told a quarter of a million people at the Lincoln Memorial that "even though we face the difficulties of today and tomorrow, I still have a dream. It is a dream deeply rooted in the American dream."

The rhetorical flourish that followed, in which he wished that his children "will one day live in a nation where they will not be judged by the color of their skin but by the content of their character," was but an abbreviated portrayal of his vision of the Beloved Community.

King's dream was "no private vision, nothing esoteric," observes biographer William Robert Miller in *Martin Luther King, Jr: His Life, Martyrdom, and Meaning for the World* (1968). Rather, it was "a personalized translation of the American heritage taught to every schoolboy, forged anew in a context of the Negro experience."

The words of the speech, which invoked the patriotic symbolism of the Declaration of Independence, Gettysburg Address, and Emancipation Proclamation, "came right out of elementary school civics," Miller concludes. Indeed, as King stated in the Washington speech and asserted several years later, in the May 1968 issue of *Negro History Bulletin:*

> It is a dream of a land where men of all races, of all nationalities and of all creeds can live

together as brothers. The substance of the dream is expressed in these sublime words, words lifted to cosmic proportions: "We hold these truths to be self-evident—that all men are created with inalienable fights; that among these are life, liberty, and the pursuit of happiness. This is the dream."

But as Richard Lescher points out in *The Preacher King: Martin Luther King, Jr. and the Word That Moved America* (1995), King meant to convey more than a civics lesson; the speech was a rhetorical strategy that identified black aspirations with the traditional consensus ideals of America and "assured his hearers that history and universal moral law are aligned with the black quest for freedom."

As King stated in a 1967 *Playboy* article, "A Testament of Hope," he believed that blacks could provide "a new expression of The American Dream that need not be realized at the expense of other men around the world, but a dream of opportunity and life that can be shared with the rest of the world." His aim was to expand the dream and give blacks a central role in its fulfillment.

That the speech was more than rhetoric for King is clearly documented by Ira Zepp in his study *The Social Vision of Martin Luther King, Jr.* (1989).

As Zepp shows, through the use of a synthesis of biblical and civil-religious rhetoric, King expressed his preoccupation with the establishment of the Beloved Community—a completely integrated society, a community of love and justice, based on what he called the "solidarity of the human family" and the "inescapable network of mutuality" with which we are tied together. He believed the Beloved Community would be the ideal corporate expression of the Christian faith and was the only form of association that could foster an egalitarian approach to wealth and property.

King's abiding faith, as he said in the Washington speech, was that "the glory of the Lord shall be revealed," that God had the power to achieve His purpose among mankind within history. And it was with this faith that Americans

> will be able to transform the jangling discords of our nation into a beautiful symphony of brotherhood. With this faith, we will be able to work together, to play together, to struggle together, to go to jail together, to stand up for

freedom together, knowing that we will be free one day.

King saw his dream as rooted in the American dream. His dream is more properly seen, however, as a collection of conflicting premises borrowed from the American creed and its corollary, the American dream.

In his powerfully argued book, *American Exceptionalism* (1996), sociologist Seymour Martin Lipset quotes G.K. Chesterton, who observed that "America is the only nation in the world that is founded on a creed. That creed is set forth with dogmatic and even theological lucidity in the Declaration of Independence."

The two values at the core of the American creed are individualism and egalitarianism, or freedom and equality. As Lipset points out, "Americans believe strongly in both."

King's dream of the Beloved Community was partially grounded in a distorted version of the egalitarian element of the American creed, not in its individualism. Had he been an advocate of individualism, he would have possessed a conceptual basis for a far more inspiring dream speech, the thrust of which would have served both blacks and whites better than the speech he delivered.

For the country surely could have used a good dose of back-stiffening rational individualism rather than the sugarcoated collectivism that was ladled out that day. Such a speech would have had as its central feature not compulsory social egalitarianism in racial matters but the primacy of individual freedom, achievement, and equality of opportunity and their dependence on a competitive market economy.

Had King's dream been a more consistent reflection of the American dream, there would have been less talk about the table of brotherhood and more about the table of plenty. He would have done better by us to insist not on a Beloved Community (which can hardly be taken as an irreducible primary) connected by the most unrealistic quality of "disinterested love" but on a pluralistic community of achievers connected by the very real requirement of individual rights.

Harold Cruse points out in *Plural but Equal* (1989) that King was the first black leader in over seventy years who possessed the charisma, moral authority, and broad-enough community base to tell blacks in the wake of civil rights gains "how they might reorganize their lives to cope with the demands of freedom in a pluralistic society."

King came close to doing so, even to the extent of using the words of Booker T. Washington to say in *Where Do We Go From Here?* that "[the Negro] must not wait for the end of the segregation that lies at the basis of his own economic deprivation; he must act now to lift himself up by his own bootstraps." But, as Cruse demonstrates, in the end King foundered and dissipated his moral authority in the interests of the "brotherhood of man" and the redemption of America's soul.

The Martin Luther King who is lionized by intellectuals, theologians, the media, civic organizations, and professional black activists is not the potential bootstraps King but the "I have a dream" King. One wishes that if he could not have strategically delivered a bootstraps speech during the March on Washington, that he could have at least delivered a "civics lesson" which more accurately depicted the American creed and the American dream.

I truly believe that my life would be different and my country would be a better place had Martin Luther King been the kind of man who could insist on the whole of the American creed and merge his voice not only with Jefferson and Lincoln and Isaiah but with John Locke, Adam Smith, and Booker T. Washington. And not just these, but with the voices of ordinary blacks like my working-class, achievement-oriented father—a true yeoman of black progress—who, by the time of King's emergence as a black leader, had already taught me those commonsense sayings of Benjamin Franklin's Poor Richard (some of which can also be found in Saint Paul):

> God helps them that help themselves.
>
> Lost time is never found again.
>
> Never leave that till tomorrow which you can do today.
>
> If you would know the value of money, go and try to borrow some; for he that goes a borrowing goes a sorrowing.

Imagine hearing words like these punctuating the airwaves during Black History Month!

Source: Anne Wortham, "Martin Luther King's Flawed Dream," in *World and I*, Vol. 13, No. 6, June 1998, pp. 66–71.

Jerelyn Eddings

In the following article, Eddings traces the influence of King's speech at the March on Washington on the civil rights movement and modern racial and political climates

Few issues are as clear as the one that drew a quarter-million Americans to the Lincoln Memorial thirty years ago this August 28. "America has given the Negro people a bad check," the nation was told. It had promised equality but delivered second-class citizenship, a back-of-the-bus status because of race. Few orators could define the injustice as eloquently as Martin Luther King Jr., whose words on that sweltering day remain etched in the public consciousness: "I have a dream that my four little children will one day live in a nation where they will not be judged by the color of their skin but by the content of their character."

The March on Washington had been the dream of a black labor leader, A. Philip Randolph, who, like the NAACP's Roy Wilkins, was a potent figure in the civil-rights movement. But it was King who emerged as the symbol of the black people's struggle. His "I have a dream" speech struck such an emotional chord that recordings of it were made, sold, bootlegged, and resold within weeks of its delivery. The magic of the moment was that it gave white America a new perspective on black America and pushed civil rights forward on the nation's agenda.

When the march was planned by a coalition of civil-rights, union, and church leaders, nothing quite like it had ever been seen. Tens of thousands of blacks streamed into the nation's capital by car, bus, train, and foot, an invading army of the disenfranchised singing freedom songs and demanding rights. By their very numbers, they forced the world's greatest democracy to face an embarrassing question: How could America continue on a course that denied so many the simple amenities of a water fountain or a lunch counter? Or the most essential element of democracy—the vote?

Three decades later, we still wrestle with questions of black and white, but now they are confused by shades of gray. The gap persists between the quality of black life and white life. The black urban underclass has grown more entrenched. Bias remains. And the nation is jarred from time to time by sensational cases stemming from racial hate. But the clarity of the 1963 issue is gone: No longer do governors stand in schoolhouse doors. Nor do signs bar blacks from restaurants or theaters. It is illegal to deny African-Americans the vote. There are 7,500 black elected officials, including 338 mayors and 40 members of Congress, plus a large black middle class. And we are past the point when white America must look to one eloquent leader to answer the question "What does the Negro want?"

The change is reflected in the variety of causes on the wish list of this year's anniversary March on Washington. Health care reform. Job training. Religious freedom for American Indians. Statehood for the District of Columbia. Head Start for young people. Security for the disabled. And an end to racism.

The compelling issue of 1963—discrimination—today is more a matter of dark hearts than evil laws. And the legislative agenda of modern-day marchers is American, not black.

Source: Jerelyn Eddings, "*'I Have a Dream'* - 30 Years Ago and Now," in *U.S. News and World Report*, Vol. 115, No. 9, August 30, 1993, p. 10.

SOURCES

"Dr. Martin Luther King, Jr.'s Dream Remembered as Thousands Gather at Lincoln Memorial," in *Jet*, Vol. 104, No. 11, September 8, 2003, pp. 4–8.

DuBrin, Doug, "'I Have a Dream' as a Work of Literature," *PBS: NewsHour Extra*, www.pbs.org/newshour/extra/teachers/lessonplans/english/dream_english2_8-27.html (February 9, 2006).

Eddings, Jerelyn, "'I Have a Dream'—30 Years Ago and Now," in *U.S. News & World Report*, Vol. 115, No. 9, August 30, 1993, pp. 10–11.

King, Martin Luther, Jr., "I Have a Dream," *American Rhetoric*, www.americanrhetoric.com/speeches/Ihaveadream.htm (February 9, 2006), originally delivered August 28, 1963.

———, "I've Been to the Mountaintop," *American Rhetoric*, www.americanrhetoric.com/speeches/Ihaveadream.htm (February 9, 2006), originally delivered April 3, 1968.

King, Martin Luther, III, "'I Have a Dream' 40 Years Later," in the *Black Collegian*, Vol. 34, No. 2, February 2004, pp. 84–86.

"King's 'I Have a Dream' is Greatest Political Speech of the Century," in *Jet*, Vol. 97, No. 6, January 17, 2000, pp. 4–6.

Kuettner, Al, "Backers Pleased with Washington Civil Rights March," in *UPI's 20th Century Top Stories*, August 29, 1963.

Ling, Peter, "Martin Luther King's Half-Forgotten Dream," in *History Today*, Vol. 48, No. 4, April 1998, pp. 17–22.

"Marching for a Dream," in *Time's 80th Anniversary: 80 Days that Changed the World*, Vol. 161, No. 13, March 31, 2003, p. A45.

Miller, Keith, "Voice Merging and Self-Making: The Epistemology of 'I Have a Dream,'" in *Rhetoric Society Quarterly*, Vol. 19, No. 1, Winter 1989, pp. 23–31.

Schaeffer, Pamela, "A Dream Dishonored After 30 Years," in *National Catholic Reporter*, Vol. 35, No. 11, January 15, 1999, p. 5.

"Spokesman for Negroes; Martin Luther King Jr.," in *New York Times*, July 16, 1962, p. 35.

Thomas III, William G., "Television News and the Civil Rights Struggle," *Southern Spaces: An Internet Journal and Scholarly Forum*, www.southernspaces.org/contents/2004/thomas/4f.htm (November 3, 2004).